'A delight to read . . . Oliver Soden's vivid biography of this major figure in twentieth-century music brings Tippett very clearly to life'
Philip Pullman

'. . . year's stand-out biography'   *The Spectator* 'Book of the Year'

'E austively researched, lovingly detailed, epic in scale, revelling in ssip, stuffed with information, this book furnishes every event . . om birth to death, with comment, observation, quotation . . . [A iper-abundant, loving account. Its like will not come again'
Fiona Maddocks, *Observer*

'[/ narrative in which readers can effortlessly lose themselves . . . So n's biography paints an authoritative, intricate portrait of Tippett, pe providing a stunning, delicate and engrossing portrayal of the co poser as very much a child of his time'
Yvonne Sherratt, *Literary Review*

'A eautifully written, emotionally comprehensive account of one of ur finest twentieth-century composers'
Nicholas Kenyon, *Times Literary Supplement* Summer Books 2019

'Th t rarest of things: a genuine landmark publication . . . Essential rea ing'.   Tom Service, *Music Matters* on BBC Radio 3

'Ti ely as well as dashing is Oliver Soden's page-turner of a bic aphy whose irresistible brio drills deep into a psychologically co plex man . . . Soden's formidable research is able to contradict pre ous erroneous claims . . . un-put-downable, it crackles with a lif orce worthy of Tippett himself' Paul Riley, *BBC Music Magazine*

'[T]horoughly researched . . . [Soden] tells the story of this socially fertile life with skill'   Michael Henderson, *The Times*

Oliver Soden is a writer and broadcaster. *Michael Tippett: The Biography* was a Book of the Year in the *Observer*, *Times Literary Supplement* and *Spectator*, and was read by the author on BBC Radio 4. It was shortlisted for the Elizabeth Longford Prize and won a Somerset Maugham Award and the Royal Philharmonic Society Award for Storytelling. Soden's other books include *Jeoffry: The Poet's Cat* and an edition of John Barton's *Tantalus*. His essays and reviews have appeared in a wide variety of publications including the *Guardian*, *Literary Review* and *Art Newspaper*, and he is part of the production team behind BBC Radio 3's *Private Passions*. He grew up in Bath and Sussex, and lives in London.

Michael Tippett

The Biography

OLIVER SODEN

WEIDENFELD & NICOLSON

First published in Great Britain in 2019 by Weidenfeld & Nicolson
This paperback edition published in 2020 by Weidenfeld & Nicolson
an imprint of The Orion Publishing Group Ltd
Carmelite House, 50 Victoria Embankment
London EC4Y 0DZ

An Hachette UK Company

1 3 5 7 9 10 8 6 4 2

A CIP catalogue record for this book is .
available from the British Library.

ISBN (Mass Market Paperback) 978 1 4746 0603 5
ISBN (ebook) 978 1 4746 0604 2

For Yrja Thorsdottir

and for my parents,
Louise and Ian Soden

The essential in a biography, so I believe, is that the subject of the biography should have known himself.

Sylvia Townsend Warner, *Letters*, 1964

For the whole of my life my creative work has been determined by what is happening in the world outside, and by what is happening in the world inside – that is, inside me.

Michael Tippett, *Songs of Experience*, 1990

CONTENTS

LIST OF ILLUSTRATIONS

FIRST PLATE SECTION

WITHIN TEXT

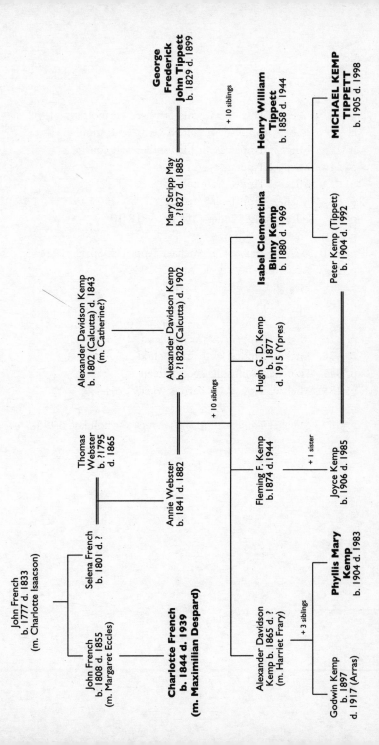

INTRODUCTION

In August 1944 Michael Tippett walked along a Surrey lane, holding in his arms an infant whose mother had been killed the night
before by a bomb. "Carrying baby Sheila down the road in the
morning sun", he wrote to a friend, was a "fantastic symbol of
vitality ever-renewed. She's a beautiful babe. It all adds up to what
Yeats called an 'experience' and will surfeit the biographers."[1] He
was reading W.B. Yeats's *Autobiographies* at the time, in which Yeats
considers that "experience", however painful, is the essential input
into a creative life.

Michael Tippett had more than enough experience to feed any
creative urge, and to surfeit any biographer. He lived to hear
himself acclaimed as one of the century's greatest composers; the
philosopher Isaiah Berlin called him "a major asset to our age,
morally as well as aesthetically".[2] Yet Tippett has suffered more
acutely than most the neglect that can initially afflict an artist's
posthumous reputation, and his certainty that he would be biog-
raphied seemed for a while unfounded. Here, finally, twenty-one
years after his death, is the first book-length account of his life. My
chief aim in writing it was to begin filling a yawning hole in the
study of twentieth-century culture, and to bring back into view a
man whose music was once described as "worthy of comparison
not only with Stravinsky, but, by God, with Beethoven himself".[3]

I have set out to tell the story of Michael Tippett's life, which
began on 2 January 1905 and ended on 8 January 1998, more fully

than it has been told before, clearing away the dead wood of myth and misconception. The mise-en-scène is the ninety-three years of the twentieth century through which he lived, his music by turns reflecting, correcting, forming, ignoring, and springing from the times in which it was composed. My hope is that the story may be read and enjoyed by anyone interested in the cultural history of the twentieth century, and be of interest to Tippett's admirers and detractors (of which there have been not a few). This book is a "life", not a "life-n-works". The works and their impact on the listener are omnipresent and the book's raison d'être, but discussion and description are contained within the narrative of Tippett's life. There is little to no technical or evaluative analysis of the music, and no extensive consideration of his published writings. I invite musicologists and performers to go on from here.

The biographying of Michael Tippett dates back to the late 1970s, when Ian Kemp, then a professor at Leeds University, sought and received permission to write Tippett's life story, and became the composer's close friend in the process. But the biographical portrait that emerged when Kemp's *Tippett: The Composer and his Music* was published in 1984 ran to only sixty pages, the rest of the book being devoted to musical analysis.* In 1991, when Tippett was eighty-six, his autobiography, *Those Twentieth Century Blues*, was published. The book, a valuable resource, was written by his partner, Meirion Bowen, using transcribed interviews and letters. Necessarily more chatty than precise, it prioritised anecdotes and reminiscence.[4] After Tippett's death the way was clear for Kemp or for Bowen to update their work or begin anew on a scholarly, albeit subjective,

---

* Ian Kemp, *Tippett: The Composer and his Music* (London: Ernst Eulenburg, 1984). I would direct to this book any reader seeking a dedicated study of Tippett's music. Introductory surveys are provided by David Matthews's *Michael Tippett: An Introductory Study* (London: Faber and Faber, 1980) and by the revised edition of Meirion Bowen's *Michael Tippett* (London: Robson Books, 1997). Of these, only Bowen's book covers the final two decades of Tippett's output, of which further study is eagerly awaited.

biography, but both men faced severe ill health.* In 2005 the *Selected Letters of Michael Tippett* was released, a volume which, arranged by correspondent rather than by date, made only more pressing the need for a chronological narrative. Not long afterwards, Dennis Marks, an arts director at the BBC and at English National Opera, was contracted to write Tippett's biography, but completed only preliminary notes before his premature death from cancer in 2015. News of the deaths of Tippett's friends and colleagues began to follow thick and fast, and with them died their memories. The need for an account of Tippett's life became urgent. With the generous help of Marks's widow and Tippett's publisher, Sally Groves, I inherited the project.

The enforced hiatus has allowed time for the dust to settle on Tippett's life before being blown off. All the previous accounts were published when their subject was alive and well to read the result. The Cold War was at its height and homosexuality only recently decriminalised. Many figures mentioned were still alive, and neither the darker reaches of Tippett's political involvement, nor the intricacies of his love affairs, could be easily detailed. Researching this book, I began to realise how many secrets Tippett had managed to keep. He had a hazy, selective memory, and could vividly recollect a piece of music heard sixty years ago, while just as easily managing to give somebody a vital manuscript and then to forget completely what he had done with it. He was appalling with dates, sometimes so appalling as to raise suspicion. Asked in one interview to clarify the year he became linked to Morley College (answer: 1932), he dithers for ages, suggests 1940, before giving up: "Oh this is hopeless." Then he yells for help: "IAN!" – this

---

* Author's note (April 2019): Ian Kemp died in 2011. With the generous assistance of his widow, Sian Edwards, I have been given full access to his extensive archive. Meirion "Bill" Bowen suffered a brain haemorrhage in 2004, from which he is much recovered, and he has generously shared his papers and memories with me. Some of his recollection is self-professedly hazy, and we agreed that, for a detailed and chronological account of his life with Tippett, I would necessarily rely on correspondence and on Bowen's published work.

to Ian Kemp, staying in another corner of the house. A television documentary catches him at a seminar responding to a question about his past with a wry smile: "Better ask my biographer!" The delivery of this line, so innocuous on paper, won him a round of applause, and Kemp, sitting next to him, duly filled in the detail.[5] How cultivated was this vagueness is hard to discern. It was as if Tippett's past life were separate from himself, and had become someone else's territory.

Over the past three years this territory has been mine for the writing. I shared the earth with my subject for only eight years. When I interviewed the soprano Jill Gomez, she asked me whether I had ever met Tippett. No, I replied, to the best of my knowledge I neither met nor saw him. "Oh," she said. "You would have adored him. You really would have adored him." Reading his letters in the British Library, I came suddenly across him, walking along with the baby in the wartime sunshine and writing the next day of an experience that would "surfeit the biographers". It was as if an actor behind the screen had looked directly down the lens, and as I travelled through the surfeit of experience that formed the life and music of Michael Tippett, he suddenly offered me a shiver of a ghostly handshake.

A NOTE ON SOURCES

A near-complete set of Tippett's working notebooks and music manuscripts is preserved at the British Library in London, but personal documents are an altogether different story. Tippett kept almost none of the letters sent to him, most ending up in the waste-paper basket, on the fire, or (during the paper shortages of the war years) returned to their sender with a reply scrawled on the back. He was rarely a diary keeper, and never of the "met T.S. Eliot, 2 p.m." variety. The domestic vicissitudes of his boyhood, and the eventually nomadic life of his parents, led to an almost complete lack of childhood memorabilia; the earliest of Michael Tippett's letters yet discovered was written when he was twenty-five. For many decades he had no inkling that he was on the cusp of a career successful enough to merit any interest in his personal life, and during the bomb attacks of the Second World War lost a great number of papers. Nor did he make copies of his outgoing mail. Thankfully some of his correspondents (by no means all) kept meticulous files, and many of his letters were either returned to him or deposited in archives.[6]

Not long after Tippett's death, the documents that remained the property of his estate were purchased by the co-executor of his will, and director of what was known as the Tippett Office, Nicholas Wright. At Wright's death in 2005 these passed into private hands, where they have remained, unseen and thought lost, until I discovered their whereabouts during research for this biography. Other material, including several taped interviews, is held by Meirion Bowen. To these, and to many other private collections hitherto unavailable to scholars, I have been given full access. Overall I have been able to read, in archives public and private, almost all of Tippett's letters known to survive: more than 2,000 lengthy epistles, and around 500 cards and notes. Only a fifth of these has been previously published. (To give a sense of scale, I should note that Benjamin Britten's surviving correspondence runs to more than 80,000 letters.) Factoring in the dense press coverage that Tippett's career received in its final three decades, the box upon box of papers generated by the Tippett Office, and the great number of radio and television broadcasts with which the composer was involved, I estimate that, scattered across the world, tens of thousands of documents and many hours of audio-visual material can now be said to form a sprawling and disparate "Tippett archive", of which this book may be said to be the result of a first rummage. It is to be hoped, as private collections are eventually transferred to public archives, that many more discoveries will emerge and find their way into print.

In the absence of a collected letters edition at the time of writing, I have tried to allow Michael Tippett, as far as is possible, to tell his story in his own words. I have smoothed his shorthand into more navigable prose, silently expanding contractions and abbreviations, and correcting his infrequent spelling mistakes. I have altered his punctuation only to remove ambiguity or to bring the use of quotation marks into line with the main narrative. Tippett's frequent use of the dash to divide sentences, and his emphatic underlining, remain untouched. Cuts are indicated by ellipses in square brackets: [. . .]. The all-but-complete lack of incoming correspondence has led to a number of strangely one-sided conversations, and I have tried to keep in mind that what now appear to be Tippett's garrulous monologues were once heated duets. The survival or disappearance of correspondence, in combination with Tippett's declining enthusiasm in old age for writing letters at all, has dictated the pace of the narrative. There remain swathes of Tippett's life in which it is possible to chart in only the vaguest terms what he was doing. Tracing his movements week by week is only occasionally an option; tracing them day by day mostly impossible, a task made doubly difficult by the fact that most of his letters are undated. Concert schedules and travel plans for his last decades survive in the papers of the Tippett Office, but I have mostly spared the reader such detailed timetabling, lest the narrative begin to resemble an itinerary.

To his closest friends he was Mike or, occasionally, Micky. At prep school he was Tippett Junior; for a short while in his twenties he was Michael Kemp. Dealing with three generations of Tippett men in early chapters led to the decision to use his first name, and the form of address stuck. (I hope he would forgive the familiarity.) By the time of his ninetieth birthday he was Sir Michael Tippett, OM. There was a rush of tributes, concerts, articles. He was interviewed for a Channel 4 documentary called *Tippett's Time*, white-haired, sometimes sharp, sometimes vague, alternating, like the very old and the very young, between giggling laughter and choking tears. His eyes are half blind, pale and piercing and frosted with cataract. His mind is full of half-remembered poetry and music, his voice fading away. He shows off his new toy, a child's cassette player, with a white plastic handle and large coloured buttons. Gleefully he presses "play", listens with helpless laughter to the tinny music that introduces the audiobook: John Mortimer's *Clinging to the Wreckage*.

"You see," he begins, "if you look back from ninety, it's a very long time. You see, I can't go back now. I can take myself back, as I am now. Or look back, whatever you like to say. But I can't go and be the child I was. No way, it's not possible, I'm here. And I'm looking towards some kind of end, somewhere or other. And the beginning? God knows."[7]

PART ONE

A CHILDHOOD, FAR AWAY AND LONG AGO

1905–1923

A Ringing of Bells

A bell rang in Trafalgar Square. On the morning of 27 January 1913, a Monday, Mrs Isabel Tippett went to a shop on the Haymarket and purchased, using her husband's account, a large number of dinner bells. That afternoon, as expected, the government rejected a proposed conciliatory Bill that would have allowed women the vote. A large crowd of protestors soon gathered outside the Houses of Parliament, and the streets swarmed with mounted policemen. Sylvia Pankhurst got herself into the Commons and threw a stone at a stained-glass window, but otherwise the crowds remained calm, and eventually dispersed.

Isabel Tippett had gone to Caxton Hall, Westminster, to attend one of the many suffragist meetings that had sprung up across the city. At twenty minutes past nine that evening, she joined a group of women who went quietly through a back entrance into the darkness of the street. They were driven in taxis up Whitehall, inching their way through another crowd that had since gathered. Nearly 3,000 people had descended on Trafalgar Square, which became a black sea of feathered hats and dark overcoats buttoned against the ubiquitous London fog. Statues and gas lamps and billboards – "To all MPs, Honour First!" – are the haziest of ghosts on the day's newsreel footage. The windows of government offices were barricaded, but by the time Isabel arrived, the crowds had once again started to melt away.

At ten o'clock the ladies split. Some headed for the steps of St

Martin-in-the-Fields, while others set up ladders against the plinth of Nelson's Column. Isabel distributed the bells. Up the ladders went three of the women, while the others scattered, ringing the bells fiercely from all over the square to attract attention. With this stereophonic chiming emanating from the lamp-lit gloom, the women initially outwitted and separated the policemen who had tried to intervene. Other officers reached the base of Nelson's Column, and an almost farcical chase ensued, with more and more women climbing up onto the plinth. Back-up policemen arrived and the women were pulled away. Many of the protestors were arrested. Isabel Tippett was imprisoned for two weeks within the red-brick turrets and battlements of Holloway Prison. Her husband and two sons waited at home in Suffolk for her release.

One month later, on 28 February, a suffragist newspaper printed the following article by Isabel's younger son:

MICHAEL, THE CHAMPION

Michael, aged 8, speaks in public unflinchingly thus: "Women want the vote. But why should they have the vote? Well, women pay their share of the taxes the same as men. They are humans. So why should they not have the same privileges as men? Some people say that the men are more clever than the women, and stronger and bigger. But you can just tell them that they are not right, for some women are even bigger than the men – like my mother – and cleverer too. I do not think that it is fair that the women should not have the vote, for the men have always had the vote. So I think the women should have a turn to have it. Anyhow, I will not give up standing for the women. And let my country have freedom for evermore. THE END."[1]

Ringing bells around Trafalgar Square to outwit the police was an appropriately musical idea of Isabel's, for "Michael, aged 8" grew up to become one of the most famous composers of the twentieth century. His little speech, written at the suggestion of – and maybe polished by – his mother, was his first published work. The country's division over female suffrage was not the only epoch-defining event in which Michael Tippett's life and work became swept up, as he and the century grew older.[2]

ONE

Henry and Isabel

Michael Tippett (right) with his brother and mother, c.1908

The death of Sir Michael Tippett, in January 1998, a few days after his ninety-third birthday, was an event of recent history. Tony Blair had been Prime Minister for eight months and the first *Harry Potter* book published. Internet traffic was growing by 100 per cent a year, and the Tippett Office even had an email address. But to look at a picture of Michael as a toddler, his arm around his mother's neck, is to look at a vanished world. At his birth, Queen Victoria had been dead for only four years. The changes and horrors of the twentieth century, which the toddler holding the gollywog doll would grow to experience and chronicle, could hardly be anticipated.

Climbing into even the nearest branches of the Tippett family tree takes us into ancient leaves. At the birth of Michael's father, Henry William Tippett, on 29 May 1858, Charles Dickens was giving his first professional tour of readings, Charles Darwin had just begun *On the Origin of Species*, and the House of Commons was soon to abandon work, unable to bear the stink from the Thames. A clamber upward to the birth of Michael's paternal grandfather, George Frederick John Tippett, on 12 August 1829, and George IV was on the throne, Lord Wellington was his Prime Minister, and Beethoven was not long dead.

George Tippett was to become the family's black sheep, and his background has been smudged into fable. In his grandson's account he was a Dick Whittington figure, who left his native Cornwall to make his fortune in London. Michael made much of this Cornish heritage, and in consequence numerous journalists emphasised his supposed ancestry and Celtic good looks. Had he lived to appear on the genealogy television series *Who Do You Think You Are?*, his would have been a gripping episode – but a picturesque trip to Cornwall would have led to not a few disappointments.

Family legend had it that George was a choirboy at Truro Cathedral (which was not then built), and had met Napoleon as a child (a chronological nonsense). George was actually born in Middlesex, and married his wife, Mary Stripp May, in Kensington.[1] George, whose background was reasonably humble, worked as a carpenter and a silversmith, but became considerably wealthy as a London property builder. By 1860, aged only thirty-one, he was building a number of large terraced houses in Prince's Square, in Leinster Square, and in Paddington, where he had set up his own home. Soon he was combining the roles of developer, builder, architect, and, most lucratively, landlord. Population growth and the Industrial Revolution resulted in property boom after property boom, and George Tippett was helping to create the much-needed plethora of middle-class London accommodation. He bought seventeen acres of land in Kensington, and his tall white-stucco houses with their pillared porches − thought to have been built to his own design − stand there still, in Colville Square and Powis Square, and on the Portobello Road. Over the next fifteen years George Tippett built over 250 houses, and the total capital invested by him in these properties has been estimated at £250,000 − nearly £20 million in today's money. He began to mix in the highest circles, and supposedly turned down a baronetcy, offered on the condition that he clear the debts of the Prince of Wales.

George amassed a large number of his own properties and an even larger number of children, both legitimate (eleven) and illegitimate (who knows?). His Handelian name − George Frederick − was not the only thing musical about him. His fellow congregation members at church meetings apparently fell silent in order to listen to his beautiful singing voice, and he was said to have covered for the odd indisposed tenor in concert performances. If talent stems from the gene pool, in George lies one source of his grandson's musicality.

Henry Tippett, George's second son, was born and raised in Paddington. By 1869 − a year in which George's rental income amounted to, in today's money, nearly £1 million − the whole household (which, including servants, numbered fifteen) had moved to 2 St Michael's Place, a six-storey townhouse in fashionable Brighton, by then an easy railway journey from London.[2] At the age of fourteen Henry was sent to Brighton College, a relatively new and atypical institution − corporal punishment was prohibited, there was no prefect system, and sports were voluntary. Henry went up to Oxford in 1876, and read Law at Oriel College, where he became friends with Cecil Rhodes. Upon his graduation, in 1879, he should have been free to live his adult life as he wished. But his older brother, another George, emigrated to South Africa, eventually to become chief engineer of the Cape railways, leaving Henry to help support the other eight children, the youngest of whom was not yet five.

Henry qualified as a solicitor's clerk but was never articled to a firm, instead working freelance as a lawyer and making property investments. He bought a stake in the Lyceum Theatre (then under the management of Henry Irving), and founded the City and West End Property Company. He had inherited the best parts of his father's entrepreneurial skill, and as his son Michael later said, "could charm the hind leg off a donkey".[3] He was soon reasonably wealthy in his own right, but as his success increased, his father's fortunes had been nose-diving.

The portions of North Kensington on which George Tippett's houses had been erected, sandwiched between a street market (on Portobello Road) and a slum (on Bolton Road), quickly became undesirable among the upper-middle classes for whom they had been designed. He had failed to foresee the coming change in demographic. The arrival of the Hammersmith and City Railway created a demand for much smaller houses, and George found it increasingly hard to let or remortgage the buildings, some of which were already being subdivided into flats, in order to raise the funds on which his livelihood, and the demands of his creditors, depended. The fall was quick and abrupt. By 1885, the year of his wife's death from cancer, George Tippett was bankrupt, his liabilities amounting to "not less than £867,309" (over £90 million today).[4] It was an *annus horribilis* for the family, social shame combining with private grief and the sheer hard work of keeping heads above water.

Henry had moved to Chiswick, where he continued to work as a lawyer. In October 1894 he purchased the London Mineral Estates Corporation, which came with the lease of a run-down copper mine on a farm in Snowdonia, North Wales.[5] He sold the corporation for a song to his father, and they acted as joint directors, which meant, in practice, that Henry oversaw much of the day-to-day running of the business. But it was not an instant success, and he turned to weird and wonderful schemes in order to raise funds. Intrepid and optimistic at thirty-six, he set out to find gold at the end of the rainbow. On 1 January 1895 he sailed from Liverpool on HMS *Britannia*, making a 7,300-mile, sixty-day trip to Rosario, Argentina, before travelling a further thousand miles on land into Paraguay.

There he purchased 8 million acres of forest and pampas, intending to dig for the buried treasure that had supposedly been hidden by Francisco Solano López, the country's former President.[6] The hunt continues to this day, a particular rush in 2013 causing a landslide. But Henry's acres yielded no riches.

Meanwhile, left to his own devices, George Tippett had fallen in with two men, Marcus Leon and James Blumenthal, who, as would later come to light, had a history of claiming money fraudulently from banks, using fictitious names on cheques and paperwork. Their presence in the story at least provides a tempting serpent, lest the blame for the scheme that would ruin him be laid solely at George's door. His actions suggest stupidity born of desperation rather than malicious criminality. Leon and Blumenthal, for a substantial fee, brokered a number of meetings with banks to which George applied for a loan. He supported his application with paperwork that purportedly listed large payments due on the Welsh mine's production of copper ore. The slight snag was that the mine produced no copper whatsoever, being in nothing like working order. Larger and larger sums were doled out by more and more banks, even as the value of the Tippetts' company dwindled and shrank. Having received a great deal of money via these false claims, George was then unable to meet the repayments. Henry returned to England, perhaps for damage control, but the London Mineral Estates Corporation was put into liquidation in 1897, which exposed the whole sorry scheme.

On 10 September 1898 George and Henry were arrested, and charged with having obtained the sum of £441 16s. from the Brown, Janson and Co. bank by false pretences. What must have been a miserable and anxious four months and Christmas followed, before father and son appeared together at the Old Bailey on 16 January 1899. The total amount of illegally acquired money was listed at almost £7,500 (nearing three-quarters of a million pounds today). George pleaded guilty, Henry not guilty, having been abroad when the fraudulent bills were shown to the bank. The jury believed Henry and he was discharged. Although the banks in question declined to prosecute, the Public Prosecutor forged ahead.

The jury found George Tippett guilty of obtaining credit from banks by false pretences. On 10 February he was sentenced to nine months' imprisonment, without hard labour, in Pentonville Prison. Pentonville, not quite a panopticon, nevertheless had isolation built into its architecture, with five wings radiating from a central hall. After half a year in this silent and unsanitary world, one of 500 prisoners trudging in serried ranks around the yard for exercise, mute and masked, George was released three months early, perhaps due to ill health, for on 21 July he died in Bromley, aged seventy.[7]

Henry was forty-one, and had watched, over the last years, his family's prosperity and security shrivel. He had been arrested and had appeared in court; his once-renowned father had been imprisoned, and was now dead – a loss made doubly painful by the fact that Henry was back in Paraguay when the news reached him. The scandal had been splashed across the London newspapers, and the family name was tainted. George became a sad embarrassment, and was wiped from the Tippett history. Some of his descendants still clung to the vague notion that his arrest was for bigamy rather than fraud, and it was even claimed that, at his funeral, another "wife" turned up with a large brood of his children. He had become a legend around whom myths clotted. A shadow had fallen across the Tippett family, and not until he was on his deathbed did Henry mention the story again.

All was not lost. Henry's affairs were separate from his father's, and he was still the majority shareholder in the City and West End Property Company. Not long after the coronation of the prince who had once asked George for a loan, Henry made for himself a new beginning. He had advanced money to a client who wanted to raise a mortgage on a hotel in France but who then defaulted on the repayments. Henry found himself, by odd but happy chance, the owner of the Hôtel Beau-Site, the second-largest hotel in Cannes, prime holiday destination of the upper classes who flocked to the

Riviera once the railway reached Nice.[8] It was an ideal opportunity to move away from London and its memories. He sold most, but not all, of his shares in the property company, and reinvested them in the Beau-Site. A manager remained responsible for the general running of the place, and Henry lived there during the winter. He saw potential to extend and improve, making the hotel famous for its food, and building a garden at the back. With the gravel produced from the necessary excavation into the surrounding rock he created hard tennis courts, and had them designed by a world-renowned player, William Renshaw. These were good enough for international championships, and soon the hotel was hosting not only leading tennis players but European royalty. It was in the glow of this success that Henry, now forty-four, decided to settle down in England, able essentially to retire on the hotel's income, having secured the future of most of his siblings. Staying with one of his sisters, he was introduced to a young nurse, red-haired, nearly six foot tall: Isabel Kemp.

Isabel, born on 6 September 1880, was twenty-two. Her great-grandfather, a captain of the East India Company based in Calcutta, had been lost at sea, leaving the Kemp finances wobbly. Her father, Alexander Davidson Kemp, was born in Calcutta in 1828; when he was six, the family was declared bankrupt.[9] Eventually he came to England to work his way up to a senior rank in the Exchequer and Audit Department of the Treasury. He made a financially expedient marriage to Annie Webster, who had been an art student and exhibited her still lifes at the Royal Academy – an unusual path for a woman in the 1860s. But almost incessant pregnancy put paid to all that. Isabel was born in a small village near the Essex town of Chigwell, and was almost the baby of the family, having just one younger sister and twelve older siblings. Youngest children are not always indulged, but as she grew older Isabel gave signs that she was well used to having her own way. In 1882, just days after Isabel's second birthday, her mother died in childbirth. Annie had borne fourteen children within nineteen years, and died at the age of forty-one; the single surviving picture of her shows an old woman with white hair.

Isabel Tippett's parents, Alexander Kemp and Annie Webster

The Kemps moved ten miles north, and Isabel spent her childhood brought up by nursemaids and governesses at Burnt House, a grand manor set into spacious grounds. Her father was aloof and distant, and towards the end of his life invested a great deal of money in an Australian gold mine and lost the lot. He had enough left over to save the family from destitution, but Isabel was now expected to carve out her own financial future, which meant making a good marriage. She was sent to India to trawl through the never-ending supply of military officers – but no luck. Her father died in 1901, and Isabel boarded in Portsmouth for a time with an older brother, before moving to London. She married Henry on 22 April 1903 at St Thomas's, Westminster.

Mr and Mrs Henry Tippett, with twenty-two years between them in age, bought a large house – known as "Sigers" – in what was then the rural village of Eastcote, Middlesex. It was a move to the countryside, bringing Henry some much-needed tranquillity now that his finances were secured by the hotel. Isabel was soon pregnant, and the Tippetts' first son, Peter, was born on 11 February 1904.

By April Isabel was pregnant again. On 1 January 1905 the bells rang in the new year. On 2 January, a day of "snow, sleet, or rain all day" in London, their second son was born in a nursing home at 51 Belgrave Road, Pimlico, and they called him Michael.[10]

TWO

A Suffolk Childhood

Birth was nearly the death of him. It had been a difficult pregnancy, and Michael immediately proved unable to digest milk, leading him to develop such a high fever that Isabel's ordained brother, William, was called to perform a baptism in the middle of the night, lest the baby should not see it through. A potent remedy of gravy laced with brandy alleviated the symptoms, and Michael regained strength. Following this health scare, Henry and Isabel had no further children.

The Eastcote house was large enough for the family, but the Tippetts soon decided to move to Suffolk. Ostensibly the sticks-upping was owing to Eastcote's damp soil, blamed for a downturn in Isabel's health, but the Tippett court case was still in recent memory, and Henry may have wished to set up home at a safe distance from London, from which a Suffolk-bound train took some four hours. The Tippetts' house-hunting brought them to Wetherden, a tiny village (pre-war population 400) halfway between Bury St Edmunds and Stowmarket. It was about thirty-five miles inland from the Suffolk coast, and nearly two miles' walk from the nearest station, at Elmswell. Along the Stowmarket Road was scattered a handful of Elizabethan farmhouses, and one of these – St Briavels Cottage (pronounced "Brevels") – was thought suitable. Henry designed an extension that would add a drawing room and master bedroom, and the family remained in Eastcote until the works were completed, in the first months of 1907.[1]

It was a large L-shaped property of grey brick, its rooms numerous but small, with low-beamed ceilings. The front of the building faced directly onto the Stowmarket Road, while an acre of garden, with two large barns, a pond, and a small farmyard with sheds and pigsties, wrapped around the other three sides. At that time Wetherden had no electricity, no gas, no mains water or drainage, and no telephone service. The house was lit with candles and paraffin lamps, and warmed by fires in each room. Water was pumped by hand into the attic cistern from a well in the garden and heated over the kitchen stove every morning, although Henry shared the age's belief that in the cold bath lay the basis of hygiene and rectitude, and insisted his boys should shiver in one each day.

This was the decade before the First World War, etched into history as a period of languid hot summers, the world maps on classroom walls still splodged with Empire pink. But bar two hot years (1906 and 1911), Edwardian weather was unusually bad, "characterised by hammering hail and rain-swollen clouds".[2] Golden summers of cricket matches and pre-war harmony are mainly the stuff of fiction. The culture and philosophy of Victorian Britain were fast being abandoned in a rush of change and social unrest. Nevertheless, Michael's early childhood, fairly typical of a prosperous Edwardian family living in the countryside, would seem to paint a temporarily idyllic picture, as in Dylan Thomas's "Fern Hill", of his being "young and easy under the apple boughs | About the lilting house and happy as the grass was green". The boys played together in the garden and orchard, and in the barns, which were their exclusive domain. There were apple trees to be climbed, currants to be picked, tadpoles to be caught in jam jars from a pond large enough to fall into. The Tippetts were not the only prosperous family in the village, but they were the only residents who could stretch to the considerable expense of a motor car. Henry purchased a De Dion-Bouton, which Michael could visualise quite clearly almost a century later, remembering its "particular ring" and propensity to "break down on the slightest incline, and my dad got under the car, fiddled around, and we went and played in the ditches on either side".[3]

Michael Tippett (left?) with his brother and cousin

The roads were otherwise free of traffic, and the boys could walk unaccompanied around the village, fishing in the small stream that ran through Wetherden, riding the horses during harvest, and playing with the family dogs, Crispin and Piper. There were trips to nearby towns and, very occasionally, to London. In his fifth spring Michael saw Halley's Comet, as it brushed the earth with its tail.

Jessie Brand, the seventeen-year-old daughter of teachers at the local school, was employed as the boys' governess and slept in the corridor that joined their communicating rooms. There was a cook, Kate Sore (the daughter of a farm worker in a neighbouring village), and a parlour maid, Cassie Sore (the daughter of a local miller). The Sores were not sisters but may have been cousins, and likely joined the household when in their early teens.[4] And Alfred Dodson came occasionally from the village to work in the garden, to drive the family to Stowmarket, and to court Jessie Brand, whom he later married. The house's layout was such that staff could not be tucked away in an attic room or in a distant wing; instead the core household of seven cohabited around the upstairs landing and shared the single bathroom (though the maids used a privy during the day). By modern standards it was a cramped life, and the house was frequently filled to the brim with friends and relations, three couples in the house and the barns employed for overspill.[5] (The boys had more than twenty aunts and uncles, and the cousins on their mother's side alone numbered thirty-one.) Henry and Isabel were something of a first couple in the social life of the villagers, loaning the house for entertainments, serving on parish councils and attending meetings, helping to organise jumble sales and harvest festivals at the church. Twice the whole family holidayed at the Hôtel Beau-Site, with Jessie in tow, but otherwise life played itself out in the Suffolk countryside.

When Michael turned five or so, Henry decided that both boys should be circumcised, wanting to spare them the potentially hereditary physical problems that had led him voluntarily to undergo the operation himself as an adult. Michael's first operation was botched, and a second was called for. But it was done without anaesthetic. The blood, and the pain, and the shock at someone slicing so coolly into the childhood idyll, caused him lasting distress. His brother's memories are the more potent, the violence exacerbated in its occurring, as in a Greek tragedy, off-stage: "I can remember the doctor and an assistant arriving, Michael being carried upstairs by Father while I sat with Mother in Father's study. A little later I heard Michael screaming. I did not know, of course, what the operation was, or, in fact, that it was an operation which caused the screaming; all I felt was that the men upstairs were hurting Michael and they shouldn't be doing it."[6]

The family's intellectual views and pursuits, and the way in which the children were encouraged to share and participate in them, were untypical of the time. Henry Tippett had settled, despite the strains of his former life, into an easy and kind-hearted man. He had, in his younger son's words, "an inner sort of vitality", and was a peacemaker with whom Michael often sided in family rows.[7] Henry read widely, and developed fiercely held views. He broke away from his God-fearing upbringing and became a religious sceptic, going so far as to rename the family home from "St

Briavels" to "Rosemary Cottage", rather than let it be associated with a Christian saint. He was not politically active, but espoused the laissez-faire economics that had allowed his own business transactions to function free from government interference, and joined the National Liberal Club, a gentlemen's club established by Gladstone that was said to have an almost Bohemian character. He made an annual trip alone to check all was well at Cannes, but otherwise, with his income emanating steadily from the hotel, his other business interests did not fill the days. When asked what their father did, the boys' reply became a part of family lore: "He reads *The Times* all day and sleeps in Mummy's bed all night."[8] Henry was no distant Edwardian patriarch whose children were occasionally permitted to visit the study before bedtime. He spent much of his time devising elaborate games, even getting the local carpenter and blacksmith to erect a swing, seesaw, and roundabout in the garden. For the boys he had an aura of mystery: rifling through the barns one day, they discovered a black trunk full of unintelligible papers, though they could make out "Paraguay" and "Señor Henry Tippett". That their father had travelled the world in search of buried treasure was thrilling.

And then there was Isabel, any portrait of whom is reliant on Michael's often wounded recollections. She had never known her mother, and motherhood did not come naturally to her. Gregarious, overbearing, and extrovert, she was determined to get her own way, and thought herself firmly on the right side of the neat divisions she made of life. Her appearance, already striking on account of her height, became eccentric: she wore startlingly bright colours – and no hat. As the *East Anglian Daily Times* described, with cryptic unhelpfulness, she "attracted attention by her flowing but abbreviated costume [. . .] – somewhere between the robe of Portia and that of a nurse".[9] In the boys' earliest childhood she was taken up almost entirely with raising them, but began to itch for a creative and a political life. She was initially quite a devout Christian, which accounts for the baptism of the children, but her husband's agnosticism proved contagious, and she worshipped instead at the altar of one of her mother's cousins, the suffragist Charlotte Despard.

Despard, a widow, lived in Battersea but was a frequent visitor to Rosemary Cottage, and Michael remembered her as an "especially kind aunt".[10] She had briefly been a member of Emmeline Pankhurst's radical institution, the Women's Social and Political Union, and was twice imprisoned in Holloway. But in 1907, unhappy with the WSPU's knotty internal politics and increasingly violent protests, she and two others had formed the Women's Freedom League, which advocated civil disobedience and peaceful demonstration. Isabel devoted herself with passion to the WFL and its cause, becoming one of a small army of Despardites who shared their heroine's Utopian vision. Mrs Despard wore a trademark mantilla of black lace that Isabel soon emulated. Mrs Despard was a member of the Labour Party; so was Isabel. Mrs Despard was vice-president of the London Vegetarian Society; Isabel became a missionary vegetarian. Mrs Despard was a novelist, so Isabel tried her hand at novel-writing, and in 1908 published her first book, *Flower of the World*, in which a young girl of eighteen marries a fifty-year-old man, and ructions ensue. If Henry found the plot close to the bone, it didn't stop him financing publication. Soon Isabel was writing at a rate of knots, churning out almost a novel a year between 1908 and 1915. These are geographically wide-ranging (one is set in Rome, another in Calcutta) and resolutely move away from the ornately written Victorian triple-decker to explore, in dialogue-heavy and relatively simple prose, various philosophies and ideals pertaining to the Edwardian woman or artist. The influence of George Bernard Shaw, to whose work Isabel was devoted, is palpable. As Michael later said tersely of his mother's books, "they were what they were".[11] But in general they were well received and reached quite a wide audience, the *Daily Mail* believing that *The Power of the Petticoat* confirmed "the impression, left by its predecessors, that Mrs. Tippett is a writer of considerable power".[12]

The Tippett household as listed in the 1911 census shows Jessie Brand and the Sore girls, and the two boys, Peter and Michael, left in the care of a sixty-five-year-old "Mrs Tippett", presumably an aunt. On census night (2 April) women from the WFL took over the Ipswich Old Museum Rooms, which were next door to their headquarters in Arcade Street, in order actively to refuse the filling-in of their census forms. Isabel had been a key organiser of this campaign, and she returned her own form without listing her own or Henry's details, instead scrawling across it "No votes for women no information from women". Twice. Many husbands, including Henry, went along in case protection was needed. Henry's liberal-ism led him not only to tolerate but to support Isabel's suffragist activities, and while he was never a member of the Men's League for Women's Suffrage, he put the family car at Isabel's disposal, financed her literary projects, and once made a donation to the Ipswich branch of the WFL large enough to open a shop.[13]

On 16 June 1911 the suffragettes agreed a truce for the corona-tion, and 40,000 women walked through the streets of London to celebrate the crowning of George V, with Isabel leading the Ipswich and Hadleigh groups. Conciliation Bills, which would have extend-ed the vote to property-owning women, continually failed to make progress through the Lords and backbenchers. There were many protests in Trafalgar Square, which Isabel often joined. She spent the summer of 1912 with Charlotte Despard, touring rural Suffolk in a caravan while spreading the WFL's message despite constant and occasionally violent heckling. In December she was arrested. It was mandatory for dog owners to pay for a dog licence, a law that persisted in this country until 1987. As had many in the WFL, Isabel refused. She drove herself to the trial at Stowmarket, and attached to the car a banner proclaiming "Taxation Without Representation Is Tyranny". (Either the banner was very large or the writing very small.) A report in the WFL magazine – written by the woman Isabel called as witness for the defence, so to be read as the work of a passionate supporter – claimed that "the gentlemen on the bench appeared much more nervous than the defendant, who promptly pleaded 'Not guilty'". Isabel then harangued the court, arguing that as the government did not recognise women as persons it was illegal to prosecute them. This defence was thought so novel that the case was covered in national as well as local newspapers. The magistrates "were too perturbed to offer any opposition save an occasional feeble interjection", but Isabel was nevertheless found guilty, and ordered to pay ten shillings. She announced that she would not pay, and "mildly suggested that they should commit her to prison in default".[14] The court wouldn't hear of it, and dismissed the case, leaving Isabel to sail triumphant into a further protest in the market square that very afternoon.

Soon the boys were old enough for Isabel to involve them with her concerns. Topics such as religion and agnosticism were encouraged in conversation. Off they all went to the East End to help serve soup to the poor. Michael even ended up at a WFL meeting, and crawled under the table to crouch in a copse of skirted legs and buttoned boots, as the voices droned overhead. He and Peter were pressed into giving speeches on female suffrage to the household, and, when there was a major workers' strike in Stowmarket that plunged many local families into dire poverty, found themselves sharing Rosemary Cottage with four strikers' children whom Isabel had brought home.[15] She could be playful but was also a disciplinarian and insisted upon rigorous exercise routines for the mornings, followed by brisk and lengthy walks. On one occasion the boys were reprimanded for waving to their mother in the street when out walking with Jessie and were told they should have bowed formally. Her sartorial eccentricity led her to dress them in corduroy trousers, red smocks, black capes with pointed hoods, and pairs of elasticated shorts that bore an unfortunate resemblance to ladies' knickers. How the local children jeered. In the world of the small boy, such humiliations are difficult to forgive. Her nonconformist views, which made her such an oddity in the town, began to embarrass, as the consequences of her activism threatened to become severe.

Michael found refuge in the life of the mind. Home's routine settled into lessons with the governess. Religious studies were off the curriculum, but otherwise the boys were taught with all the structure of a school, and the year was divided into terms, with exams at the end of them. A retired schoolmaster, Mr Razor, came to teach French and Latin. Michael had a marked ear for languages

– he became fluent in French by the age of nine or so, helped by his father and the holidays at Cannes – and a facility for science and mathematics. Vague notions of becoming a scientist began to form. His reading and understanding quickly became precocious, and he inherited some of his mother's conviction and gift of the gab. "Oh," as he said later, "intellectuality began very early indeed."[16] The household books were eclectic and uncensored, and Michael cheerfully read his way through volumes such as *Marriage and the Sex War* and *The Montessori Method of Education*. Henry would read aloud to the boys, and after improving books had been got through, they could move on to entertainment. Historical romances were a favourite: Stanley Weyman; Tennyson's *Idylls of the King*; and Ford Madox Ford's time-travelling story, *Ladies Whose Bright Eyes*. Isabel could only be persuaded to read Oscar Wilde's *The Happy Prince*, which left them all in tears. The boys were allowed to thrive in their imaginative worlds, and amateur theatricals and writing were encouraged. They were separated for lessons between the two garden barns, and otherwise were dependent on each other's company. Wetherden was small, and play with the village children was forbidden. The maids, though young, could never become friends. Isabel was mainly distant, and when she was close, nagging and intense. A picture emerges of two boys often having to amuse themselves when studies were over. Michael withdrew into a world of books, clutching at intellectual stimulus without discrimination. The eclecticism of references and thoughts in his compositions has its base in these diffuse and all-embracing tastes that were formed, almost by necessity, in early life.

There was no more music than was typical for a middle-class household making its own entertainment half a century before the advent of television. The family had no gramophone, and the wireless was not yet a household fixture. There was a small upright piano in the hall at Rosemary Cottage, and Isabel could play well enough to accompany herself in a handful of parlour songs, by Roger Quilter and others, all performed in her gravelly contralto. Henry had inherited nothing of his father's musical talent, and Michael was exposed to no real family tradition of music-making, bar singing in the church during Isabel's short-lived religious phase, and hearing warbled hymns at bedtime from an aunt or two. Professional music there was almost none, the Suffolk musical world being non-existent, and London's concert scene far off. Perhaps one of his aunts saw a kernel of musicality that she decided should be nourished, for in 1913, when Michael was eight, she took him to hear the Russian bass Feodor Chaliapin, and shortly afterwards to the Queen's Hall, where Henry Wood conducted the pianist Benno Moiseiwitsch in Tchaikovsky's first piano concerto.[17] Moiseiwitsch was only fifteen years older than Michael – but Michael Tippett was no infant prodigy. He received piano lessons, first from a local farmer's wife named Mrs Foster, and then from a Mr Shand, organist at Bury St Edmunds. But although he took devotedly to the instrument he displayed no startling abilities. Long periods spent "improvising" at the piano produced little more than childish splashing. So when he suddenly announced to his parents that he wanted to be not a scientist but a composer, he wasn't taken very seriously. It was not a precocious technical aptitude for music that marked him out of the ordinary, but a heightened aural awareness, a pronounced receptivity towards music and sound. The acoustic of childhood resonated into his old age, when he had vivid recollections of the whistle of the cross-Channel steamer en route to Cannes, or the terrifying chug and shriek of the local trains.[18] Music could "go right in", and he was able, even at four years old, to find and appreciate beauty in one of his mother's songs. When music was played, he listened. "It's either genetic or some drive that takes you into the world of the ears rather than the world of the eyes [. . .] it's like a dam opening. Absolutely unbelievable."[19]

One morning, aged about six, Michael watched Cassie and Kate in the little orchard at the back of the house. One of them wanted to sing him a song, and did:

Ev'rybody's doin' it, Doin' it, doin' it
Ev'rybody's doin' it, Doin' it, doin' it
See that ragtime couple over there,
Watch them throw their shoulders in the air . . .

Irving Berlin's song, written in 1911, encapsulated the dance craze then sweeping America. What Michael wondered afterwards was how the girls had heard it. "I've no idea, because apparently nothing ever came into the village at all. [. . .] There wasn't radio, there weren't discs, so communications were very odd."[20] It was an injection of popular glamour into the sleepy Wetherden existence, and it stayed with Michael ever after. He remembered the moment vividly, clearly, deep into his eighties: "I can't sing it properly but I can remember it. I can see it, and hear it, I can almost hear exactly what they did, and from that moment music has remained, and as it were grown and grown."[21]

On 27 January 1913, with the country unaware of the impending gash in its history, came the Trafalgar Square demonstration, with the bell-ringing and the foggy chase around the plinth of Nelson's column. Mrs Despard's address blocked up the roads around the square with listeners, cheering and booing. Eventually she was arrested, and taken to Bow Street Police Station with a member of the Men's League called John Simpson, who was soon released. Isabel was taken to Cannon Row Station with a doctor who gave the false name of "Lady Crewe". All three women were released on bail, with a trial called for the following day. The next morning the taxi driver who took them to Bow Street Magistrate's Court refused to take payment and wished them luck. In court all three refused to plead, to give a defence, or to call witnesses. Mrs Despard delivered a passionate speech, vowing to continue her fight. Isabel, refusing to list her name and address, said of the police, "They were obstructing me in the execution of my duty." As was reported: "the magistrate opined that there was no 'statute' enjoining on her the ringing of bells and gathering of crowds; but she rejoined, with much good humour, that her actions were dictated by conscience, which was higher than statute!"[22]

"Lady Crewe" was given a ten-shilling fine or a week's imprisonment; Isabel and Mrs Despard a forty-shilling fine or a fortnight's imprisonment. All three refused to pay. A prison sentence in Hollo-way, even for a short time, was seen as a necessary rite of passage for the truly devoted, and Mrs Despard would present members of the WFL with a Holloway Badge. This was evidently not clear to the anonymous benefactors who paid suffragists' fines to get them off a prison sentence, and Mrs Despard was rather irritated to be released from Holloway on 29 January, her fine paid by a well-wisher. "Lady Crewe" was also released, but Henry Tippett was likely under stricter instructions, for Isabel served the full two weeks. Members of the WFL protested outside the prison "each evening at 7.30 p.m. until the release of our third prisoner!"[23]

By the time of Isabel's sentence, which lasted from 28 January to 11 February 1913, a stint in Holloway was not too rigorous for all but the most devoted, whose hunger strikes led to the horrors of force-feeding. The composer Ethel Smyth, who was imprisoned the year before for her part in a window-smashing, found that "during those two months in Holloway" (she often neglected to mention that her sentence was reduced to three weeks) "for the first and last time of my life I was in good society!" The authorities were keen to avoid hunger strikes, and were dealing with a huge influx of pris-oners; in consequence, they relaxed the rules. Suffragists were given a special wing and were allowed to wear their own clothes. Blind eyes were turned to smuggled-in provisions, warders neglected to notice that inmates had not returned to their cells, and enough material was found to hoist defiant banners in the prison yard, in which exercise usually descended into riotous games and there was much singing of Smyth's anthem "March of the Women".[24] Isabel may have found herself something of an outsider as a member of the WFL amid predominantly WSPU members, but it is unlikely that her time in prison was all that gruelling. On her release *The Vote* paid tribute to "Mrs Tippett, again in her proper sphere – the home".[25] She discovered that the dog Crispin, whose licence she had refused to pay, had died. A new puppy was promptly chris-tened "Holloway".

Isabel's prison sentence, long a possibility, was, when it finally came, an open cause of pride. But it would take the most blasé and comforting of attitudes towards prison for young children not to be scared at the prospect of a parent's incarceration. And it cannot have escaped Henry in his private thoughts that, however different the circumstances, the two people to whom he had been closest, father and wife, had served time in gaol. But the sentence did nothing to break Isabel's spirits. She attended a WFL meeting a week after her release, where the convenors extended their "thanks to her for her recent protest for the cause!"[26] By September she was back protesting in Trafalgar Square, and was soon accompanying fellow suffragists to prison gates for their sentence, or greeting others on their release. She may have travelled abroad for a demonstration, and stood as an independent candidate in a local election for the borough council against a Conservative government minister. It was not a successful campaign, despite her boys loyally flinging mud at the Conservative posters.

Isabel may have thought it a necessary evil to sacrifice family life on the altar of activism. She had written a handful of plays, and one, The Stuff that 'Eroes are Made Of, was performed in Chelsea Town Hall in 1913. It depicts, in a Cockney patois that even Dickens might have thought overdone ("Krikee, 'tis time I was hoff"), a young suffragist who refuses to give up her protest, and loses her loved one in consequence. While conscious of the misery of this ("I did love 'im so"), the play is certain about the rightness of the heroine's choice. "Mrs Tippett", wrote The Vote, "has done admirable propaganda work in her dramatic, yet touching, presentment of the sacrifice for the Cause."[27] To both children, such priorities and sacrifice created an almost impossible strain. "Your mother had suffragette leanings?" Roy Plomley tentatively asked Michael when interviewing him on Desert Island Discs. "She had leanings all right," came the sardonic reply. "She leaned on her children it seems to me, but that's another matter."[28] When younger the boys had worshipped Isabel: "In our eyes she could do no wrong and in any case we had been well indoctrinated by her into the iniquities of male domination."[29] But as they grew older it became harder and harder to live up to her demands or tolerate her frequent absences. "I never felt I had a mother sometimes," Michael later said, feeling that he had suffered most of all from her overweening do-goodism, the "mother-ish moral reasons which spoilt so much of childhood".[30]

Nineteen thirteen was the year before the storm, the year of Isabel's imprisonment, of Emily Wilding Davison's fatal attempt to pin a suffragette banner to a horse at the Epsom Derby, and of the premiere of Stravinsky's *The Rite of Spring* in Paris, amid scandal and riot. Far from enjoying a final period of calm, Britain was in a mess, the population divided into factions variously marginalised and deprived: servants, women, the poor, the unemployed. On one occasion the boys, though they realised what they had seen only later, witnessed the inhabitants of neighbouring cottages being carted off to the workhouse. There was a diphtheria scare in Suffolk that year, and Isabel took the boys away to escape a disease that was then decades away from a vaccination, and one of the leading causes of death among children. They stayed in Bedford, at the home of Harriet Kemp, the divorced but evidently not outcast wife of Isabel's brother Alexander. As the train pulled into Bedford Station Michael fell suddenly and violently ill with what was diagnosed as a heart murmur. No drastic treatment other than rest and monitoring was required, but the long convalescence led him to spend most of that year away from his family, left behind in Harriet's care for some six months. Michael struck up a close friendship with her daughter Phyllis, who was just a year his senior, and considered to be similarly precocious and maverick. The relationship between the cousins would deepen as they grew older. Finally he returned to Suffolk for what must have been a peculiarly solitary time, once Peter had been despatched to boarding school.

And then the war came.

THREE

The Great War

"It's a long way to Tipperary, it's a long way to go . . ."

"Pack up your troubles in your old kit-bag and smile, smile,
smile . . ."

"Turn the dark cloud inside out 'til the boys come
home . . ."

He was standing under a tree in the garden – decades later he
could pinpoint the place with accuracy – when he first heard that
the country was at war. It wasn't the Tippetts' style to keep the
developments of the adult world from their children, and it can't
have been long after 4 August 1914, when Asquith declared war on
the German Empire in response to its demands for military passage
through Belgium, that Michael first heard the news. He watched the
men of Wetherden depart for the front. "I remember the sense of
their light-hearted confidence, singing those songs [. . .]. I was so
young still that I could reduce the significance of the war to those
songs." They remained "written in my mind, etched in acid. And
they're always there."[1]

In a nine-year-old's world, the war may have taken up fewer
thoughts than did an imminent departure for a preparatory boarding
school 230 miles away. "I was very slow politically to know what
was going on and simply took things for granted."[2] But certain
facts, which he never spoke of in his lifetime, make clear that the

conflict had a greater impact on him than he would ever afterwards admit.

Family life was fraying, as the boys were only too aware. Their domestic set-up changed beyond recognition. Petrol was rationed, making Henry's beloved motorcar impractical to run, and it was eventually requisitioned for the war effort. In France, as in England, the government wished to prevent landlords from profiteering during years when demand for housing exceeded supply, and rent control on the Hôtel Beau-Site was introduced, a problem compounded by its being taken over to hospitalise war-wounded. The days of luxury holidays and tennis-filled summers were at an end. A mortgage had to be raised on Rosemary Cottage, and the household staff was regretfully dismissed. The maids left the house weeping. For Peter and Michael, a mainstay of childhood had been removed almost overnight.* The boys were now expected to help with the housework. Henry, never one to admit financial defeat, turned the garden into a vegetable allotment in order to raise money from the produce.

By September 1914 almost a quarter of a million men had voluntarily enlisted to join what became known as Kitchener's Army. That month Michael travelled to Swanage, in Dorset, to become a pupil at Brookfield House School. Home no longer felt like home, and departure to Brookfield meant that he never knew his parents in the same way again. "The point really that knocked me out was that I was sent quite early – nine years old – to boarding school and therefore I lost my parents." To lose them was partially to escape from them, but quitting the bosky Wetherden cocoon left him "heartbroken – and I never got [childhood] back".[3] In an interview filmed some seventy years after his schooldays, his hands slapped down in anger on the arms of his chair: "I think the problem for all parents who send their children away to school is they don't realise that to some children it breaks the family altogether. I never forgave

---

* Kate Sore married James Bennett in 1918 and died in Suffolk in 1968. Cassie Sore married Peachey Betts in 1919 and died in Ipswich in 1981.

my parents. Not inside, no, because they'd done me down. The whole family ended. Of course I remained with them and all the rest of it, but somehow the trust that you have is gone, so you're on your own."[4]

Little survives to narrate Michael's time at Brookfield, or to explain the choice of a school hundreds of miles away and situated on a coast vulnerable to invasion. It was daunting to continue life in another part of the country with only Peter a familiar figure, and in a new world of discipline, teachers, and other boys. A year's gap can create a chasm impossible to bridge in a playground world, and the relations between Tippett major and Tippett minor were not especially close. But Swanage has the whiff of holiday. The school was a five-minute walk from the sandy beach and the sea, and the town is set into Swanage Bay, which curves round into a vista of chalk cliffs over which the boys were occasionally permitted to roam, looking for wild orchids. At the school Michael became reasonably content. His parents encouraged both boys' independence, to the extent that they set up bank accounts for them, even requiring them to buy their own clothes (at last, a reprieve from the vestiary humiliations of boyhood). Brookfield's charismatic headmaster was much admired by the pupils; the rest of the male teachers had enlisted, and female replacements were employed. The curriculum was stripped to its bare essentials, which at that time included Greek and Latin, both great favourites for Michael. Music was dismissed as unpatriotic. While Michael's relatively secluded upbringing and recent heart trouble had led to a distinct lack of skill at team sports, always the key to schoolboy popularity, his intellectual precocity doesn't seem to have made him an outcast. A brief but fervent religious phase had succumbed to his parents' persuasive agnosticism, and the fact that, aged nine, he distributed among his friends a self-penned tract arguing against the existence of God, didn't make him, in the eyes of his teachers, a rebellious spirit to be quashed.

By the time of the first school holidays, at Christmas 1914, well over a million British soldiers had volunteered, and were either in training camps or on their way to Flanders' trenches. In rural villages, they slept in local farmhouses or under canvas in nearby fields. Many troops were billeted at Swanage in 1914 and 1915, and five large army camps built to the north of the town. Whether the Tippett boys were aware of them, or of the ninety-nine young men from Swanage who were killed, is unknown. Back at home in Suffolk, ninety-five men had departed Wetherden for war – around half of the village's male inhabitants. Some of the first bombs to be dropped on England were at King's Lynn, just a little further north. When the Military Service Bill was introduced, calling for the mandatory enlistment of single men aged eighteen to forty-one, Michael found himself too young by just five years. Conscription was eventually extended to married men and the upper age limit raised to fifty-six: his father escaped by the narrowest of margins. But the family did not survive intact.

On 24 April 1915 Isabel's brother Hugh was shot and killed at the second battle of Ypres. He had been living in Canada but made regular visits to England, and while the news, if it reached Swanage, may have been a distant and adult tragedy, Hugh was the brother closest in age to Isabel, and was Peter's godfather.[5]

The second family tragedy of the war was even closer to home. Two years almost to the day after the death of Uncle Hugh, Michael's cousin Godwin was killed at the Battle of Arras, on 23 April 1917. He was twenty years old. Michael had spent his long recuperation from a heart murmur staying with Godwin's family, and had become especially close to Godwin's sister Phyllis.

Then, early in 1918, the widow of Henry's older brother, George (who had emigrated to South Africa), visited Wetherden with her daughter, Mary. On 5 March Mary collapsed and died of a cerebral haemorrhage in one of the upstairs bedrooms of Rosemary Cottage, and was buried in the Wetherden churchyard.

These deaths cannot have escaped a bright and observant boy entering his early teens. But there is no record of Michael's ever mentioning them, as if he had purposefully suppressed the painful memories. Such was his method with later trauma.

Meanwhile the vegetable allotment had predictably not been the answer to the family's financial prayers, and Wetherden was suffering from food shortages. In 1917 Henry managed to purchase three tons of potato seed to help food production in the district.[6] Isabel was forced to get a job, and put her speaking prowess to use as a campaigner for the National Savings Movement, which had been recently founded as a means of financing the government's deficit. On her salary, and on the dwindling amounts brought in from Henry's property company, they got by for the remaining years of the war.

Popular support for the war effort, cheered on by propaganda films such as The Battle of the Somme, was remarkably consistent during hostilities, despite the unimaginable number killed or wounded and the first-hand evidence of regular dispatches from the battlefields. Pacifists were in a tiny minority, and while the Military Service Act made a small provision for conscientious objectors, it was worded ambiguously, and many were forced into the army or, on refusing to fight, into prison. But the branch of civil campaigners with which Isabel associated herself mainly supported pacifism, a cause to which her son would devote himself with a seemingly inherited ardour. Charlotte Despard refused to talk of the "enemy" in her speeches and campaigned on behalf of conscientious objectors, forming a new organisation: the Women's Suffrage National Aid Corps. Of this, Isabel became a devoted member. She resuscitated a former soup kitchen on Everett Street in Battersea, turning it into a vegetarian restaurant offering "Belgian soup", "jam puddings", and "lovely tomatoes with rice". Her children, when home for the holidays, were quickly set to work, and Michael remembered "ladling out soup at a halfpenny, pudding for a penny" at his mother's restaurant, which provided nearly 200 meals daily.[7] Maintenance became tricky, cutlery was stolen, and recruiting staff was a problem, but Isabel persevered, turning the restaurant into a care home for children and creating a milk depot for nursing mothers. She and Henry were indefatigable in their war efforts, donating money for a local hostel, setting up a Wetherden social club, and getting the boys to help with jumble sales and charity evenings to raise funds for the milk depot.[8]

In February 1918 the government faced a crisis. A general election was overdue, and millions of soldiers returning from the front line were still not entitled to vote. The Russian Revolution had made politicians nervous of similar events unfolding in Britain. The Representation of the People Act was passed: all men over twenty-one gained the vote, as did all women over thirty – if they were married to a property owner. Isabel, after all her years of campaigning, qualified, though there were another ten years to wait until females could vote on equal terms with men.

During Michael's final year at Brookfield House rationing was introduced. Typical school meals contained less and less meat, and more and more potato bread, served with a greasy scrape of margarine. A starch shortage made school uniforms, collars especially, more comfortable. A coal shortage brought cold winters. Many schools set boys to work on allotments, hoping that in the production of fruit and vegetables they would become at least partly self-sufficient. Michael left Brookfield in the summer of 1918, on the brink of his secondary education. A biography must circle round him, catching him in a sideways glance, filtering him through his recollections of himself. How tall he was, what he sounded like, whether he was friendly or aloof – all is conjecture. The small number of his childhood photographs shows first a confident toddler, even then beginning to develop the habit, so characteristic in later life, of arranging his limbs in variously angular and dramatic postures. Here he is at twelve, his face still rounded with youth and yet to develop its striking, high-cheekboned length.

At thirteen, life as he knew it ruptured.

Michael Tippett, aged twelve

Peter expressed a wish to go to naval college, and went. There remained the question of what to do about Michael's education, and how best to nourish this curious, precocious adolescent, happier in a library than on the sports field. Henry was content to engage a private tutor. Isabel, deeming her younger son fey and oversensitive, argued that the rigours of a public-school education would provide a necessary toughening. She won. Michael, who blamed his mother for so much, showed her little mercy when apportioning responsibility for the disaster that followed.

An uncle who lived in Scotland recommended Fettes College, in Edinburgh. The school was one of Scotland's most exclusive and expensive: a strange choice for a couple with liberal beliefs and strained financial resources. But Fettes offered bursaries, and in late September 1918 Michael became a foundationer. Somewhere among the crowds of troops, many of them hideously wounded, making the eight-and-a-half-hour journey between London and Edinburgh on the Special Scotch Express, was a thirteen-year-old boy, dangerously ill-equipped for the shock of being catapulted into the predatory world of the single-sex public school. He arrived at the cold and imposing cluster of spires and arches and gargoyles to find Fettes numbed by the war, which, for his first few months of term, raged on. The school had been founded in 1870, and by the time war was declared had 2,000 alumni. Of these, 1,094 joined up, representing the school on twenty-five different fronts. Two hundred and forty-six were killed, sixteen of them in Michael's first weeks, their names printed in the fatality lists of the school magazine and read out in chapel. The headmaster, William Heard, was already nearing seventy when war broke out and had stayed on to lead Fettes during the conflict. He was old, tired, and perilously unaware of day-to-day goings-on.[9]

The school was keen to maintain a world of enthusiastic rugger, of stiff-upper-lipped teenagers finding that "casualty lists were hardly more significant than cricket reports".[10] But life at Fettes was Spartan. Each boy's small cubicle in the dormitories contained a jug of cold water and a tin bath, fifteen-minute hot baths being permitted once a fortnight. Lighting was poor, especially when maintaining the blackout before the war's end, and the boys often had to strain to read. Desks and chairs were so uncomfortable they gave rise to what was known as the "Fettes stoop". The diet was meagre and meatless. Classes followed the English education system and were banded according to talent rather than age. Michael, his entrance exams evidently showing pronounced ability, was placed in the fifth form, finding himself up to two years younger than the majority of his classmates. And it was the treatment of younger boys at the hands of their seniors that was especially brutal. The older pupils knew that, upon leaving, they were to fight and most likely die. Each boy hollowed out a space in his study wall or on his desk, in which he hoped would be placed his name and the dates of his occupancy. These hollows were known in school parlance as "graves". The shadow of death made the atmosphere fatalistic, and fatalism fostered a savagery that made the life into which Michael was plunged a violent misery. The fagging system, through which prefects were served by younger boys on pain of often-severe corporal punishment, was in full force, and Michael was soon flogged by a prefect for misbehaving in the choir. One initiation ritual for new boys, passed off like most others as a character-building rite of passage, was known as "rabbiting". It involved being beaten with hockey sticks. These dormitory "games" were played with such fervour that, much later, one alumnus wondered "why we were not all killed".[11]

"No one who was at Fettes in 1918", a pupil remembered, "needs to be reminded of the Armistice, announced by a babel of sirens and whistles."[12] That afternoon the whole school went outside after lunch to cheer, and could hear Edinburgh's celebration. Above them aeroplanes swooped low over the city in victorious flight. In Suffolk Henry and Isabel hosted a reception in the Wetherden schoolroom:

> Mr Tippett explained that the effort was an expression of appreciative feeling from the people of Wetherden to the men who had been spared to return from war. Wetherden had done well, for there were ninety-five names on the Roll of Honour, fourteen [actually sixteen] of whom had made the great sacrifice. Words were inadequate to voice the feelings of the inhabitants of Wetherden; but they were deeply grateful to them, and extended the deepest sympathy to their sorrowing relatives. He thanked the men for all the hardships they had so patiently endured and the gallant work they had so nobly done.[13]

An estimated seventeen million people had been killed. The world had changed for ever, but for Michael the worst trauma was yet to come.

FOUR

No Longer a Virgin

A few weeks after Armistice Day all the boys at Fettes, in a rather grisly celebration ritual, were taken out in boats onto the Forth to cruise round the surrendered German ships. On 21 November George V visited Edinburgh and the school was given a holiday to greet him at Waverley Station. But these were special occurrences. Life carried on much as it had before, and the business of memorial and commemoration began. Food was still scarce, and military training continued unabated. The older pupils were told to hold themselves in readiness to be called up. The Spanish 'flu pandemic worsened, and the sanatorium became stuffed with boys. In December there was a general election, and Isabel, pushing forty, will have voted for the first time. Charlotte Despard stood for Parliament. That Christmas was the last the Tippett family spent together in Rosemary Cottage.

The details of what happened next at Fettes are obscure and shrouded in euphemism. That there was sexual experiment between pubescent boys pent up in the dormitories of a single-sex boarding school is not surprising. But the mainly unchecked persecution of the younger pupils had in some cases extended to sexual bullying. Among Michael's contemporaries was Selwyn Lloyd, later Chancellor of the Exchequer, who, as his biographer describes, "was a good-looking boy, and, together with others in his year, soon attracted the attentions of a group of senior boys".[1] Michael suffered similarly. The painter Wilfred Franks, to whom Michael

later became close, remembered hearing the following story about
Fettes: "The first-years at the school, they all had to wear kilts,
even if they were English or Dutch or anything else. Then they
got them in a room and felt under their kilts to make sure they
were not wearing anything. And they did this to Michael Tippett
and he was very offended and struck back and apparently he was
maimed. He would never say how he was maimed or where he was
maimed."² Michael reported all in his communications home, more
in the spirit of description than denunciation. On the receipt of
one letter, in July 1919, his parents travelled instantly to Scotland,
removed Michael from the school, and threatened to expose the
whole situation to the press unless the headmaster was removed.
The plans for Dr Heard's departure were likely already laid, and he
did indeed leave Fettes a month later.³

Michael spent the summer holidays in Corsica, staying with his
family at a hotel that was hosting a notorious local bandit. Left to
his own devices, he slept one memorable night on a mountainside
and watched the dawn mist lift from the island beneath. On his
return to England a letter awaited his parents from Alec Ashcroft,
headmaster elect at Fettes. Ashcroft is now credited with reform-
ing Heard's ancien régime, and in promising to rid the school of
Michael's tormentors he persuaded the Tippetts to send their son
back to Scotland after the summer holidays.

In the first week of September the whole family put on one of
Isabel's plays, The Magic Lamp, in the largest barn, with an extensive
cast of villagers. The pianist was one "M.K. Tippett".⁴ But this was a
rare show of family unity amid a crumbling home life. Not for the
first time, Henry was now on the brink of financial ruin. In England
taxes had risen considerably. Much of his capital was in France,
where military expenditure, inflation, and property reconstruction
had badly undermined the strength of the franc. He and Isabel
sold Rosemary Cottage and took up residence in France, where
life and their tax bill were cheaper. Michael was packed off back
to Fettes in late September. On 6 October the Wetherden Social
Club presented "Mrs Tippett [with a] silver travelling clock, on
her departure abroad".⁵ Henry and Isabel lived first at the Beau-Site

(now functioning as an hotel again), but even there life became financially impractical, and they began a nomadic existence, spending the next years drifting across Europe, from pensions to boarding houses to rented rooms. Michael now lacked any kind of domestic safeguard against the horrors of school. Life was lived from a trunk. Collections of toys and books and childhood memorabilia cannot have been dragged from hotel room to hotel room – a reason for their absence today. The majority of Henry's library was sold and the boys were allowed to choose one book each. Peter took Byron, and Michael a collected Shakespeare. Boyhood had been sold off. Michael left Wetherden, the village of his childhood, late in his fourteenth year, and six decades passed before he ever went back.

At Fettes a witch-hunt ensued. Michael's housemaster, J.S. Edwards, forced him and a few fellow sufferers to stand in front of the whole school, which then numbered 235 pupils, and to name every boy who had engaged in homosexual activity. Many of those he identified were then expelled. The situation was made more complex by the fact that Michael had begun an affair of sorts with another boy. In his autobiography he used two uncharacteristically coy phrases: "I was myself 'involved' with a boy" and "I was no longer a virgin".[6] The quotation marks encasing "involved" admit their own euphemism, but the word would seem to describe a consensual, even a reciprocal, relationship. "No longer a virgin" implies a physical intimacy that expressed itself in more than schoolboy fumbling. In France, where Henry and Isabel were now living, same-sex activity had been legal for over a century; the recent revolution in Russia had also decriminalised homosexuality. But in Britain, sodomy had been a capital felony until 1861. The Labouchere Amendment, enacted in 1885, meant that sexual activity of any kind between men was punishable with imprisonment. Oscar Wilde's widely publicised trial and two-year sentence were in recent memory. But the illegality of his love affair was less of a dilemma to Michael than the hypocrisy of which he thought himself guilty. Having accused others, he himself "wasn't innocent!"[7] His blossoming sexuality withered beneath his guilt, which was exacerbated by his mother's sending him a copy of Arthur

Trewby's *Healthy Boyhood*. This was a religious tract that preached the sinfulness of erections and nocturnal emissions, and warned that masturbation, all too easily enjoyed with friends, was the beginning of a slippery slope to disease, homosexuality and, ultimately, damnation. Inevitably Michael's fellow boarders discovered the book, with all the gleeful violence of which cooped-up teenagers can be capable.[8]

A grim victory was achieved by the fact that Michael, now in his second year, refused to exercise the unspoken prerogative that allows established pupils to bully new arrivals, and persuaded others to follow suit. That autumn, in a conscious effort to improve the school's cultural life, B.J.F. Picton, who had been an organ scholar at Oxford, was appointed as a permanent organist and music master. Michael played the piano in a newly formed college orchestra and sang in a rejuvenated choir. But he did not thrill to this injection of school music, and had nothing to do with literary or theatrical endeavours, all pursuits in which he later thrived. He was a boy keeping his head down, cowed by the forbidding atmosphere, the obligatory military training, and an apparently vengeful bullying that began to increase in intensity.

The winter of 1919 was bitterly cold. Dormitory baths froze solid. Michael and Peter joined their parents in France for Christmas, and travelling unsupervised made for a long and grim journey, crawling down through the ruins in which France found itself. Michael suffered acute seasickness on ferries, gulping for air on the wooden deck and longing "for some technical invention that would [. . .] let me cross the Channel without being seasick".[9]

There was no escape from his oppressors on his return to school. As he later said, "cubicle walls had been torn down, all that sort of thing".[10] He held on until April 1920, when he successfully sat exams for his School Certificate. Then, in desperation, he revealed to his mother in every detail the extent of his sexual life at Fettes, somehow knowing that to admit his sexual experiences as consensual, as well as coerced, would provoke the desired reaction. It could be expected that two liberally inclined thinkers would find their son's confessions far less worrying than the fact of his being bullied. Henry's own experience of public school had lacked the brutal regime and fagging system of Fettes, but he would have known well the atmosphere of a single-sex boarding school. Isabel had even published a book, Passing the Love of Women, which had "lightly touched on homosexuality".[11] But it was a sort of sexual puritanism that made her refuse to countenance her son's return to the school she had originally insisted upon. Michael did not go back to Fettes that summer, or ever again.[12] He did not list the school on his Who's Who entry, and did not visit, the famous composer, to present prizes on Speech Day or to open a new music department. His time there, like the more violent moments of the First World War, was simply wiped from accounts of his life and from his own memory: "for decades afterwards I had such amnesia about the whole experience that I hardly acknowledged the existence of Fettes".[13]

The school would "either make you or break you" was one pupil's summation.[14] In a curious way it did both to Michael. As he said, it was a "nasty story", and eventually he came to acknowledge that he had experienced "sadism, cruelty, bullying, everything".[15] It could have destroyed him, "but there was some toughness inside you see, which was not a physical toughness, I couldn't have gone and bashed somebody in, but there was some internal toughness. I can't tell you what it was [. . .] you were just trying to live through it."[16] But there is perhaps some truth in the old chestnut that the rigours of public-school life can be "character-building", for he would greet his more mature sexuality with a calm acceptance, and he soon became rebellious, eccentric, and resolute in his refusal to conform.

Henry Tippett, ever the peacemaker, travelled from France to search out a new school for his clever and difficult son.

FIVE

Four Horsemen

At Stamford School in Lincolnshire life improved. The school buildings lie at the heart of a picturesque market town of golden stone, a few miles north of Peterborough. Stamford was a more venerable and much cheaper institution than Fettes, with roughly the same number of pupils (200-ish), but far fewer boarders. The accommodation was nevertheless cramped and insufficient and the chapel was used as the main schoolroom.[1]

Stamford's regime, when Michael joined at the beginning of the summer term 1920, was in a way as arduous as at Fettes. Rugby ruled supreme, there was a four-mile daily run extended to ten miles for the boarders at weekends, and only on Sundays would hot water grace the large unheated dormitories. The school was free of sexual blackmail but had its fair share of initiation rituals, "accompanied", wrote the school's historian with understatement, "by fairly rough treatment".[2] The conductor Malcolm Sargent had been a pupil from 1907 to 1910, and on his first day was "mobbed and thumped and pinched by his seniors".[3] Michael, who joined his form halfway through the academic year, may have been spared such rites, though arriving at a new school later than most and finding friendship circles already formed is rarely easy. It was in his nature not to "fit in", and he soon didn't, in any number of ways. But Stamford would also be a formative and important community for him, about which he was always more affable in conversation than in his more negative official accounts.[4]

Once again he had been put a year ahead of himself and, aged only fifteen, joined the Lower Sixth Form to study towards the Higher School Certificate (the A-Level equivalent of the day). In Scotland he had excelled at Latin, but, scarred by Fettes and all things associated with it, he promptly enrolled for science subjects instead. In these he was only a beginner, and was made to sit, now a lanky teenager, in classes with the most junior boys. But he was a quick learner and got through most of his lessons with ease and success, seemingly emerging from his social shell. For the very first time he made a friend close enough to merit a mention in later reminiscence: he and Robert Woodbridge, a fellow boarder two years his junior, would spend holidays together in Lincoln-shire, speeding around the countryside on a two-seater motorbike, unleashed from school's limestone coop, with the fens spread out all around.

The entirety of Stamford's pre-war staff had been killed. A new English master joined the school at the same time as Michael: Henry Waldo Acomb, just down from Cambridge and not yet thirty. He went on to become a distinguished librarian of Durham Univer-sity, and when teaching at Stamford took Michael under his wing. One of his endeavours was a production of The Merchant of Venice in autumn 1920, in which he cast Michael as Portia. "The fair Portia", thought the school magazine, "spoke clearly and with feeling, and in the tragic portions of the play was indeed good. The trial scene speech was well delivered and like all her speeches, with good enunciation. But as a desirable young heiress, she was a little gauche."[5] Acomb broadened Michael's intellectual horizons, inspiring a love of all things Ancient Greek and an abiding passion for the works of the Victorian writer Samuel Butler. He was also, as Michael remembered, a "gifted amateur musician [who] sang and played me one day some of the English folk songs collected and arranged by Cecil Sharp, and some of Dowland's lute songs, then recently published. I can recall even now the profound impression this musical experience made on my totally untutored musical mind."[6] Another pupil, William Hare, remembered that Acomb "possessed a gramophone and a good collection of records", among them "some lovely spirituals". Much later, hearing that Michael had incorporated spirituals in his most famous work, *A Child of Our Time*, Hare found himself wondering, "were the seeds sown then?"[7]

Music, for the first time in Michael's life, was starting to take pride of place. In a handsome double-fronted house on Broad Street, five minutes' walk from the school, lived a tiny white-haired widow in her fifties, a piano teacher who rejoiced in the name of Frances Tinkler. Malcolm Sargent had been her star pupil, and now Michael found his own playing progressing under her tutelage. The house was a haven for him, its garden a riot of jasmine and honeysuckle, and its panelled drawing room housing a Bechstein grand on which sat a plaster bust of Beethoven.[8] It was a world away from the harsher side of school life. "Tinkie", as she was known behind her back, became Michael's confidante, "the sort of person to whom a schoolboy could take his troubles (as I often did) and be listened to understandingly and helpfully". She was one of the few supportive and constant women in his teenage years. "She helped. This on top of teaching me piano. She was a Mother Figure in the Freudian sense. But never sentimental."[9]

What troubles he had to take to Mrs Tinkler derived from his increasing rebelliousness. At first he went along with what the school asked of him, gritting his teeth through rugby and attending church services, but it didn't take him long to become more openly bolshie. He began to make a serious enemy of the headmaster, John Day, who, in an unhappy double challenge to Michael's growing convictions, was both an ordained Anglican minister and a commissioned army officer who led the school's mandatory Officer Training Corps. Michael instantly protested that he was a pacifist and could not take part, managing to obtain a letter from his parents in support of his stance. An easy opt-out from the arduous military training his pacifism may then have been, but here at fifteen is the first explicit sign of a conviction that would come to shape his life. The school grudgingly agreed, but ordered him instead to march with the junior cadets: "I remember parading around on the quadrangle outside the school, looking conspicuous among those younger lads, and the passers-by along St Paul's Street used to laugh at me."[10]

To friends that would listen he was entertaining and garrulous company, and some admired to the point of hero worship his scornful attitude to rules and regulations. A fellow boarder recalled that, as soon as Michael was made a house prefect, "he led a revolt [. . .] and erected a curtain across our study. Some trivial matter was at stake."[11] The teachers were maddened by Michael's open lack of religious belief, and by his refusal to play the piano for chapel services or to contribute to the collection. His liking for ritual and ceremony led him frequently to attend the local Catholic Mass, an apparent contradiction which enraged the headmaster. "I was very pig-headed and Canon Day tried to reform me with constant lecturing and with the aid of religious texts from eminent bishops, but all to no avail. I had my beliefs and I stuck to them."[12] More and more of his time he devoted to music, for which he became something of a school celebrity, winning the music prize two years running and accompanying house songs at the piano in the evenings. Soon he was practising every morning, and made sure his lessons clashed with the physical exercise classes.

On 26 July 1921 Henry Acomb decided to mount an ambitious concert at Stamford Town Hall, plumping out the school ensembles with local musicians. Michael and his friend William Hare were the star soloists in the Adagio from one of Bach's Concertos in C minor for two keyboards and strings. "Hare was much better than I was," Michael thought afterwards, "but despite that we played the concerto rather badly."[13] Malcolm Sargent, now twenty-six and a distinguished old boy, kept half an eye on music at Stamford. He attended the rehearsal and gave advice to both pianists, and Michael marvelled at "this slim, well-dressed figure. I was terribly frightened. Yet fascinated. He was so 'un-school'."[14]

A few months before the concert, Michael had gone with some friends to see *The Four Horsemen of the Apocalypse*. Rex Ingram's silent film became the top-selling of that year, beating even Chaplin's *The Kid*. The draw for the boys was Rudolph Valentino, who played Julio, an Argentinian artist killed by a shell in no man's land. At the end of the film Julio's father visits his son's grave, and a bearded stranger speaks via the ornate title cards that flash up between murky film footage of galloping horses. "Peace has come – but the Four Horsemen will still ravage humanity – stirring unrest in the world – until all hatred is dead and only love reigns in the heart of mankind." The screening was accompanied by a cinema pianist, who will have chosen the soundtrack, but it was not the famous tango sequence early in the film that hit Michael.

> All I remember is the violence and destruction of the war sequences. And what I never forgot was the extraordinary image of four horsemen flying across the screen at every moment of destruction, and the doom-laden sound of Beethoven's "Corio-lan" overture. These things combined to give me the sense that there were enormous forces beyond human control which could simply destroy the whole fabric of our civilization. At the end of the film came the first pictures I had ever seen of the Flanders graveyards: row upon row of little white crosses. This gave me the horrified understanding that so many thousands of young men whom I had seen marching lightheartedly away, had ended under the earth. I burst into tears (virtually) and went out.[15]

Soon afterwards there was talk of Michael's studying for the Oxbridge scholarship examinations but he refused. The reason: he wanted to be a composer. In accounts of his life, he was always keen to pinpoint the moment when certain ideas or compositions began to form in his head, and set great store by what he termed these moments of "Einfall" (Freud's term, roughly translated as "idea" or "invasion", to denote what comes spontaneously into the mind). Henry Acomb occasionally led school trips to concerts: they went to London to hear the Crimean virtuoso Leff Pouishnoff; to Peterborough for an all-Mozart programme; and, most vitally, on 10 February 1922, to a concert at De Montfort Hall in Leicester. Here Michael heard Malcolm Sargent conduct the orchestral version of Ravel's Mother Goose suite, and "made up my mind that I would become a composer".[16] He was ravished not by the swelling climax of the suite's finale, "The Fairy Garden", but by the loose meter and mysterious, plaintive melody of the "Tom Thumb" movement, the diminutive hero wandering in circles in the forest amid high, chirruping bird-calls. But these vocational light bulbs were not lit as neatly as Michael made out. He told Sargent's biographer that by the time of hearing the performance of Mother Goose, "already he had thought of making music his career".[17] Occasionally his story went that it was during Mrs Tinkler's lessons that he decided where his future lay. As a child he had shared compositional ambitions with his parents, and one cousin remembered a family holiday in Cannes: "even then as a teenager, Michael said he wanted to write music".[18] A steady stream of influence and inspiration had accrued at compound interest. Now he was on the verge of adulthood, and his musical ambitions had been moulded further by the force with which The Four Horsemen of the Apocalypse had struck him.

> I realized that although I was still a very young man and had a great deal to learn about the merely technical questions of music and was going to immerse myself in everything to do with the technique of my art, this was something which I simply could not forget: there was a necessity for art of our time in some way, when it had learned its own techniques, to be concerned with what was happening to this "apocalyptic" side of our present time.[19]

Michael's plans confused and worried his parents; Canon Day pooh-poohed the ambition and so, more considerately and sensibly, did Sargent, underlining the precariousness of the profession. For Christmas 1921, instead of going to France as usual, Michael stayed with his cousin Phyllis and her family, and in January the next year, under his own steam and without a word to the school, sat Common Entrance university exams at the now-disbanded London Matriculation Board.[20] He passed six or seven subjects, the particular triumph coming in Italian, which he had taught himself. He had arranged the whole enterprise not to secure himself higher education, but to prove a point. Returning to school, he decided to prove another point, and refused to attend house prayers for a whole two weeks. It was the last straw, and things with Canon Day came to a head. Michael's official account ran that Day wrote to his parents with what was, in effect, an order of expulsion: he "would not be allowed to return to the school after the summer term of 1922".[21] Perhaps this made a better story. School records make clear that Michael had successfully completed the two years of the Sixth Form by that stage, and had obtained his Higher School Certificate in Natural Sciences the year before – no mean feat for a pupil of sixteen (the exams were more usually sat at eighteen).[22] There was no reason for him to return. His name is calmly included in the school magazine's list of official leavers that year. The school had likely insisted that Michael no longer be allowed to board at the school for his final weeks or terms, during which, with his exams comfortably passed, he had little to do but make music. He left the boarding house for a room behind the local church. Canon Day's panic was such that he instantly put the whole street on which Michael lived out of bounds, an edict soon and frequently flouted.

On officially leaving school, Michael carried on lodging in the town and visiting Mrs Tinkler. Stamford was the second institution from which he had left under a cloud. Now seventeen and more self-possessed, he cared little, and stood firm amid the agonising rows caused by his adamant refusal to follow his father's path through Oxbridge and then into a lucrative law career. His parents had reason to fear for their son's financial security. The year before, the franc had depreciated to such an extent that Henry had been forced to sell the hotel in Cannes so as to live off the invested proceeds. His relationship with Isabel buckled under the strain of their nomadic life, continuing financial difficulties, and various health problems. They considered a divorce, but managed to keep things together. Isabel, denied the outlet of suffragist activities or a speaking job, turned again to writing novels.[23]

It may be that Michael Tippett played down his teenage musicality in order to make his later success appear the more remarkable, and to excuse his initial difficulty in achieving it. He would describe Mrs Tinkler's instruction as being of a "very primitive kind", or claim that he didn't know "one end of the piano from the other".[24] This was likely exaggeration, given that he and Mrs Tinkler began to work through Mozart's Piano Concerto No. 23. Ideas of taking on music professionally were not a total pipe dream, and he had come a long way from bashing about on the Wetherden upright. But Michael's precocity manifested itself in an all-embracing and rather messily powerful intellect that was now never to be structured by a university degree. His comprehension of harmony and music theory was so rudimentary that, when asked to name his favourite fugue from Bach's *Well-Tempered Clavier*, he was not able to say that the one he had chosen was in C minor. What was innate in him was not musical ability but the intense expression and engagement of the creative artist. Composition was a genuine, though vague, vocation, satisfying a powerful creative urge in a way that acting, writing, painting, even dancing (all of which he did to varying degrees of success) did not. The thoughts clotting in his brain about the political and social events through which he had lived could, he realised, be syphoned into artistic creation. At some point in 1922, as if determined to educate himself politically, he went to Brussels alone to attend an International Congress of Youth, organised by the Mouvement de la Jeunesse Suisse Romande, a Swiss youth movement still going today. The conference was convened in order to discuss methods in which funds could be raised to send child war victims to Swiss sanatoria, and Michael called his attendance his "first political act".[25]

Back in Stamford, he visited a local bookshop. With all the confidence of youth, and riding on the success of his tried-and-tested auto-didacticism, he believed wholeheartedly that, having decided he would be a composer, he would now teach himself to compose. "I thought if you could buy a book on woodwork you could buy a book on composition, and sure enough it's absolutely true."[26] He purchased Charles Villiers Stanford's *Musical Composition* and read the opening pages, which warned that there was "no short cut to mastery. The house cannot stand if it is built upon insecure foundations, and its security depends upon a knowledge of technique which involves the hardest and at times the driest drudgery. [. . .]

Technique is of no use without invention, invention is of no use without technique."[27] This was a solemn warning, but also stirring advice. Michael would spend some years trying to live up to it. The book enabled him to write some simple exercises, and Stanford's contrapuntal instruction was supplemented by some basic lessons from the organist at the local church, in return for bolstering the tenor line in the church choir. Malcolm Sargent was involved in local amateur music and dramatic societies, and Michael performed for him in a handful of productions. In this determined but rather haphazard existence he continued for nearly a year, living mainly off his own company.

Early in 1923 he joined his parents at their pension in Florence. The Tippetts had become friends with the expatriates living there, all in their different ways on the run: a Russian prince fleeing the revolution; the British novelist Norman Douglas, living in exile after a series of sexual scandals that had culminated in his assault of a sixteen-year-old boy. Douglas was living openly with another man, which didn't prevent Isabel's befriending the pair. She began to adapt Douglas's most famous novel, South Wind, for a London theatre and pushed hard but unsuccessfully for the script to be filmed.[28] Had Michael's parents not found themselves soon afterwards sitting near a professional musician on a train, his Lincolnshire routines would have continued for a longer time. Instead, the professional musician told Henry and Isabel of a Royal College of Music in London, into which their son could duly make investigations. Hugh Allen had taken over from Hubert Parry as the college's principal a few years before, and had greatly expanded it, seeking to modernise and improve the curriculum. Michael was granted a short interview with Allen in which enthusiasm, and some evidence of unharnessed ability, shone through his musical greenness. His parents agreed to pay the fees on condition that he worked towards a doctorate. On 30 April 1923, a few months after his eighteenth birthday, Michael Tippett became a student at the Royal College of Music.

A description of Michael at eighteen must rely on a handful of surviving photographs, which, as he grew into his long, slightly craggy, bone structure, variously captured his mercurial features in arrangements that run the gamut from gawky and weak-chinned to sculpted and handsome. In one he is beautiful, though these monochrome images do not show the bright-blue eyes on which people so often commented.

Michael Tippett, late teens

He was thin and, like his mother, he was tall, well over six foot, with fast-moving long legs and strikingly long-fingered hands. In reports of his life Michael whizzed speedily through childhood, but the events of his first eighteen years can be seen as forming and fostering so many of the traits, interests, and concerns that would define him as an older man and as a composer. He openly stated his debt to Henry "for the argumentative and philosophical side of my nature", but was much less eager to admit the intellectual inheritance from his mother: his atheism, his political activism, his pacifism, his rebelliousness, his interest in community and in amateur performance, his surety that through intellect and creativity the events of the world could and should be engaged with and challenged.[29] He even threw convention to the winds, as his mother had done before him, in matters of clothing. But he blamed his parents bitterly for the unhappinesses of childhood. In the operas that he grew up to write, parent figures are either absent, or ranting and negligent, even abusive. Orphans, changelings, wards – these are abundant. Both Michael and his brother recalled their childhood with a sense "of not being loved".[30]

The pre-war society in which he had been brought up could not be maintained, and the world of servants and Empire was replaced by housing shortages, the compensation of the war-wounded, the scourge of the Spanish 'flu, and political uncertainty, as Europe had its maps redrawn. Michael had seen poverty from the upper end of the social scale, but knew that riches were transient. He was from the provinces but was not provincial, and had become a fiercely independent person, in need of solitude. And in almost no aspect of life had he found himself conventional, accepted, at home, or at ease. Already his self-perception was of being the perennial outsider, looking in on a world that didn't accept him, and that he found hard to accept. But he had high hopes for his new life as a composition student, and of discovering what he recognised as a "huge ferment of artistic creation of the period and the general mood – in England at any rate – of frenetic gaiety".[31] To scratch away at the gaiety was to reveal a broken society dancing its way, drug-fuelled, into another abyss. But no matter for eighteen-year-old Michael Tippett. For the first time in his life an urban world beckoned, one of sex, politics, music. "I now knew that my life lay in artistic creation. I had no misgivings whatsoever."[32]

DIARY:

Suffolk – Lincolnshire – Edinburgh

An enchantingly bright and sunny day, the sort of day that makes sense of the flat Suffolk landscape: there is so much sky. The first step of my curious pursual of Michael Tippett is to visit his childhood home. I am driven from the tiny station at Elmswell to the house that shrugged off the name "Rosemary Cottage" soon after the Tippetts left, and is now called "Briavels House".

The family that lives there is kind and welcoming, and aware that Michael Tippett once grew up in their house – it has changed hands only a few times since – but not that they repeat history so uncannily. Where once Michael had played with his brother and the dogs, and with his cousin Cicely, now a young girl called, astonishingly, Cecily, runs around the lawn with her sister and the family dog. The house still lacks neighbours for half a mile around, is still set in fields that stretch to the horizon. A vestige of the Tippetts' lifestyle has been preserved in this distinctive and consistent countryside.

I stand in the kitchen and see the village's prominent Norman church clearly framed through the window. What an irony for religion-hating Henry. There are fireplaces in every room, and bells (push-button, not ropes) with which the maids could be summoned. Even the Tippetts' downstairs loo, of dark wood with a tall water tank behind, has survived. Upstairs, we work out the way the various rooms were allocated and on this sunny day some of the rooms at the back of the house are still quite dark – darker still in the Tippetts' candlelit Edwardian days. The bedrooms are grouped together upstairs; family and staff on top of one another. How much in the grain of everyday life the Sore girls and Jessie Brand must have been. What a wrench for the boys when they left so suddenly.

In the garden I see the well from which water was drawn, and the pond in which Peter and Michael caught tadpoles, falling in more often than not. Later, in the girls' bedrooms, I see vats of tadpoles. Beyond the garden is a field, and beyond the field a stream. We go into the barns, and one especially is much larger than I had imagined, now Grade-II listed; but the house, many of its original features having been blithely replaced by Henry with a frilly Edwardian frontage of white stucco, is not. I feel haunted not only by the ghost of Michael as a boy, but of Michael as an old man. In September 1974 he returned to Wetherden in the company of Ian Kemp and the composer David Matthews, who were both writing books about him. Matthews remembers the trip: "We asked to see the barn, where Tippett had often played with his brother, and were given a rusty key; we had to clear away many years' growth of ivy from the door before we were able to unlock it, and then an ancient interior was revealed by shafts of sunlight streaming through the dormer windows, the dilapidated timber looking as if it was just about to collapse. Tippett was very moved."[33] I am, too. Much of the timber has been restored.

We walk to St Mary's church. The road is tarmacked but empty, and it takes no stretch of the imagination at all to picture the area in 1915, or to think of the boys singing in the choir. There is an organ, put in to replace the manually pumped instrument that Michael would have known. And there is a memorial to the near-100 men of Wetherden who went to war – and to the sixteen who didn't come back. In the graveyard is a stone cross, nearly submerged in holly, but the words can be made out: "Mary Molly Tippett. Called home. March 5th 1918." Michael's cousin, who died of a brain haemorrhage at thirty-three in one of the upstairs bedrooms of the Tippetts' house.

But it is not until I am back at the house that I feel the prickle of history scurry up the back of my neck. I am caught short by the circular terracotta plaque, featuring a portrait of Rubens, that Henry, an admirer, had attached to the outside wall. This eccentric, personal, rather handsome touch, with its visible fixings so evident of the Edwardian hand that set it into the brickwork, and which stared down at Michael over a century ago, stares at me now, and continues staring as I say goodbye, and take the train back to London.

Months later, I visit both of Michael's secondary schools, travelling first to Stamford. Instantly I see that the honey-coloured stone of the market town would be a warm architectural embrace for one so recently isolated beneath Scottish baronial spires. The glimpses of him I find in magazines bespeak a boy at the heart of the school's life, annoyingly impish as he may have been, the lead in plays, the soloist in concerts. And he appears as a distinguished old boy, in touch with fellow alumni, judging house music competitions, and most of all continuing to pay visits to his beloved piano teacher Mrs Tinkler, whose golden house I find on the high street behind the market. Later I see a copy of *A Child of Our Time*, affectionately – or cheekily – inscribed to "Tinkie".

I arrive at Fettes College in midwinter, a day of ice and sunshine, Edinburgh hovering behind me as if beneath a sheet of glass. Today the city's buildings have crept to the edge of school grounds, but pictures from Michael's time make clear that the school was much more remote, surrounded by acres of hallowed sports field. His boarding house was in the main school building, and almost as soon as he arrived all leave was cancelled due to the Spanish 'flu. During the near-four-month term, there was little release from the cold stone walls. The school magazines are thick with casualty lists, and I find that the name M.K. Tippett leaps out of the page, mainly as a leading member of the chess club, but also as a singer in the choir, occasionally a soloist, listed among the trebles well into 1920, his voice unbroken months into his fifteenth year. An unusually delayed onset of puberty, even for the time. He was unmoored from his contemporaries in two directions: intellectually ahead of himself, physically behind himself. Flicking through school photographs, suddenly I find him, in a portrait of his boarding house, his already long legs struggling in vain to fold themselves into the compactness required of the new boys, crouched on the floor in the front row. Is it just my knowledge of what happened that makes me cast the tall sixth-formers, who are standing at the back in their striped blazers, as slightly menacing, and the housemaster, trim as his moustache, as exuding a certain efficient cruelty? But there is no doubting the sternness of the matron, with her scraped-back hair and terrifying eyebrows, her knees pushed into Michael's back. Michael himself, fourteen or fifteen years old, returns my gaze steadily, so different from his fellow pupils, looking at once younger and older. What was going on in that pained and passionate young mind?

Schoolhouse, Fettes College, 1918–19. Tippett is third from the right
on the front row.

PART TWO

WANDERER
1923–1934

SIX

Royal College of Music

London. 30 April 1923. To one side of the Prince Consort Road in Kensington a waterfall of shallow steps leading from the terracotta coliseum of the Albert Hall. To the other the fairy-tale towers and dark-red brick of the Royal College of Music. And perhaps, then as now, the odd vocal warm-up or a tangle of piano scales drifting through the windows, and students carrying scores and instruments as they walk along the road outside. Arriving at an institution partway through the academic year was becoming a habit for Michael. He enrolled at the college on the first day of the summer term, having to find his way among a year group already bonded into friendships, and au fait with the routines of student life. His parents were over from Europe but had their own distraction. The night before, Isabel's adaptation of Norman Douglas's novel *South Wind* had been premiered, to riotously damning reviews, at the (now defunct) Kingsway Theatre. The second performance was that very afternoon. His father put himself down as guarantor for Michael's fees: £12 12s. a term, not including extras. That done, Michael was left, as ever, to fend for himself.[1]

That first day Hugh Allen, a visionary and sympathetic principal under his balding and severe exterior, addressed the entire college, as was his custom at the beginning of term. His theme was the rush in which post-war London found itself. "It seems to young minds ridiculous that anything should take a long time doing, and nowadays to spend years over preparation seems impossible. We think that to have passed a milestone or two is to be at the end of the journey but there is no end to the journey by which we learn our job."[2] Michael, on the contrary, was in for the long haul, self-aware enough to realise his musical limitations, determined enough to overcome them. He had set himself an extraordinary and unexpected task, one that could take a lifetime if necessary: to respond to the age in which he was living via an artistic form for which he showed no outstanding aptitude. It is one of the most remarkable traits of the young Michael Tippett: the ability and willpower to separate his monumental ambition from the need to gauge his weaknesses and ignorance. It was a strange concatenation of hubris and humility, in that he had the absolute self-confidence openly to admit what was left to learn. There was no rush, and he had the London musical world on his doorstep.

The city was revelling in a determinedly hedonistic enjoyment of an existence that had recently proved so precarious. Michael was never quite a Bright Young Thing, partying away in the newly flourishing nightclubs as if in a novel by Evelyn Waugh. He couldn't really afford to, and his true quest was to satisfy a voracious appetite for culture. "You went over the top just to have fun – such idiocy young people got up to. And I didn't go in for that. I didn't want it."[3] Much of his intellectual geography had already been mapped, though its boundaries were soon to be extended. He was radical in outlook, European in sensibility, and the artistic banquet that post-war London offered was exactly what he needed. His mind was both sponge and filing cabinet: porous, capacious, and preternaturally retentive. He relished arriving in London for the spring, and realised his luck in becoming an adult just as the country had come through the long, destructive winter of the war and cultural shoots were pushing up through the snow. Six months before Michael joined the college, the British Broadcasting Company was established, making use of the wireless radios beginning to appear in a number of homes, the amazement of the age. That same month, a literary magazine called *The Criterion* had published T.S. Eliot's *The Waste Land*, which Michael soon devoured greedily.

The war cast long shadows, not only into London but into the

Royal College. Hugh Allen had led the conservatoire through a swift recovery from the losses, both human and financial, of the war years, and the class lists were augmented with demobilised students returned from the trenches. But the college had lost a great number of its students and staff. Thirty-eight names are on the war memorial that was erected in the entrance hall a few years into Michael's tenure. The list was inescapable, engraved in deathly marble under a fragment of the motto that Wilfred Owen called "the old lie: *Dulce et decorum est pro patria mori.*" There, six names down, is George Sainton Kaye Butterworth, now famous for his settings of A.E. Housman's poetry. Further down is Ernest Farrar, the college's star scholar, who was killed in 1918 after just two days at the front. Michael found among his new peers several "men who had lost their limbs, and of whom I was acutely aware".[4] On those who had survived the war uninjured, distress was engraved like an open wound.

He had taken temporary lodgings at 44 Queensborough Terrace, Bayswater, but then moved into a small house in Chiswick. Here he shared a single room with three others, one of whom was a trainee surgeon having a rampant affair with the landlady. The two others were fellow students, both organists: Ralph Downes, and an Australian named Claude Monteath who had lost an arm in the war.[5] Michael shared a bed with the latter, seemingly through cramped necessity rather than physical attraction. Nothing could have brought the injuries of war closer than to lie, night after night, with a shell-maimed body. From this rather eccentric set-up Michael could commute to Kensington on the District Railway, although he mainly preferred travelling round London on his bicycle, past motor car and omnibus (a perilous exercise for one who could get so lost in his thoughts).

Michael wasn't formally enrolled in any classes for the summer term of 1923.[6] Perhaps he was granted a settling-in period, to sort himself out domestically and throw himself into the extra-curricular activities on offer. All students had to sing in the choir, and Michael joined the college's dance group; that July he performed the role of "Mr James Formal, or Don Diego" in a ballet scored to a Purcell medley. The same month he took part in the traditional cricket match played annually between the Royal College and the Royal Academy of Music. Michael wasn't much keen on cricket, but he could run fast. The team assembled in their white flannels. Michael was batting with a student called Roberts and didn't achieve a single run. But he was distracted. His eye had alighted on a fellow pupil.

Herbert Sumsion, known as John, was twenty-four, six years older than Michael almost to the day. Those six years made all the difference, for Sumsion had fought in the Flanders trenches. He had been born and brought up in the cathedral city of Gloucester, and his involvement with the Three Choirs Festival, one of the primary breeding grounds for British composers, had given him a musical pedigree as comprehensive and rounded as Michael's was erratic. The day of the cricket match, 9 July 1923, was a watershed. The two sat together on the tram to the playing fields, and continued talking back at Sumsion's rooms until late into the night. A close friendship had developed, but for Michael it was something more. "Three days after our first encounter", he remembered, "I had to leave for Italy to visit my parents at a little hotel on Lake Garda, and John came to Victoria Station to see me off. On the train to Dover, not really aware of what was happening to me, I wrote him a love-letter. Once I had reached my parents, I wrote him letters almost daily. Without knowing it, my feelings were moving beyond public-schoolboy sex towards love and tenderness."[7]

In the clinging heat of the Italian summer Michael knew himself to be desirous of an illegal relationship, and eager to pursue innate feelings that had previously caused scandal and upset. This led to confusion and turmoil, but not shame or self-disgust, and there was no question of repression or falsification. These were his first steps in his remarkably determined and occasionally perilous journey to know himself, and to accept such knowledge. "I fell in love with a student, but it was a man. Now at eighteen years old I had this clear feeling that I lived by my instincts, and while that love experience developed into a sexual drive, I accepted it. It was myself."[8] Everything poured out into the daily letters to Sumsion.

For some reason Michael decided also to write to George Bernard Shaw, hoping that the great playwright might offer a solution to the "problem" of same-sex relations, but received only a noncommittal reply. Sumsion enjoyed Michael's company, and later in the summer they holidayed together in Polperro, Cornwall. This was Michael's first visit to the county he ever afterwards adored, tugged back to a place first discovered in the company of one he loved. He wrote to a friend years afterwards that he would "never forget the thrill of first crossing the Tamar".[9]

In private conversations Michael described the friendship with Sumsion as moving briefly onto a physical plain, characterised by "hugging and kissing in ecstasy but no sex", the "most genuine feeling ever had".[10] But soon the devotion got too much, Michael's desires went unrequited, and Sumsion, who was to marry four years later, broke off relations entirely. (In 1926 he took a job in America, returning two years later in order to become organist of Gloucester Cathedral.) This was to be the pattern for some time to come: a passion for a heterosexual or bisexual man that, even if reciprocated to some degree, was soon overwhelmed by Michael's almost overbearing capacity for love and conversation. It had been a short-lived and one-sided affair. "Love and heartbreak within a few months!"[11] wrote Michael mock-dramatically in his autobiography – but so it had been. He buried himself in music.

In 1904 the German writer Oscar Schmitz had coined his infamous phrase to describe the United Kingdom: "The Land Without Music". He was decades out of date. Victorian novels, art, and industry had thrived, but, despite the best intentions of composers such as Hubert Parry, nothing came out of England in the nineteenth century to match the achievements of, to name only three, Tchaikovsky, Brahms, or Wagner. The situation improved with the peak creative years of Edward Elgar and Frederick Delius, which began at the turn of the century, and a few decades later Michael found himself in a city leading a British musical resurgence. Hugh Allen, as the head of an institution that did much to mould the country's musical tastes, had appointed to the Royal College two prominent composers: Gustav Holst (fresh from the success of *The Planets*), and Ralph Vaughan Williams, who after *The Lark Ascending* and the *Fantasia on a Theme by Thomas Tallis* had become a leading voice of his generation. Vaughan Williams's creed was that ease of communication between composer and audience was paramount, and he believed in adhering to a pastoral tradition of folk-song, largely dismissing the musical developments exploding like fireworks around the world in the 1920s: the game-changing experiments of Schoenberg and others in the second Viennese school; the angular ballets of Bartók and Stravinsky; and the jazz records by Bessie Smith and others in America that influenced French composers such as Satie and Ravel. It was Michael's generation of Young Turks at the college, in a movement led by his contemporaries Constant Lambert and Elisabeth Lutyens, who fought hard against the folk-song fortress. And although Michael later remembered with affection "the exciting spectrum of English musical life" in the 1920s, as a student he was less forgiving, and thought himself hampered by a national fustiness that lagged behind developments on the Continent.[12]

When he returned to London in August 1923, he was largely ignorant of different musical schools, and of much else besides. In one of their discussions Sumsion had recommended the Henry Wood Promenade Concerts, a music festival that had been running for nearly thirty years. Unwittingly he unlocked a musical education for Michael that was of more importance than anything on offer from the Royal College. The early Proms seasons started late (8 p.m.), and had programmes that seem vast to modern attention spans, but also bitty: a typical concert could contain fifteen or even twenty short works. The festival continued well into October each year, and was held not at the Albert Hall but at the Queen's Hall in Langham Place. The venue was drab, but the acoustics were world-renowned and the atmosphere famously relaxed. Michael could afford the cheap entry into the arena of the hall, where the seats had been removed for standing space in which punters ate, drank, and smoked (though Michael's one attempt at smoking, in the hope of adding a pipe to his innately eccentric appearance, made him sick enough to put him off it for life).

At the Promenade Concerts of 1923 Michael Tippett drank music like a life-giving elixir. As a friend described, he "rarely missed a night at the Proms; and [. . .] was usually to be found on the same spot of the Queen's Hall floor, dressed in white flannels and laden with miniature scores".[13] There he lay, white and transported amid the fug of cigarettes, hearing music he could scarcely have imagined in Suffolk or Lincolnshire. He had caught the Proms at a moment when its core repertoire, in reaction to the new popularity of Americanised dance music, became heavy and reasonably narrow. German music could now be included without upset (some festivals had banned it completely during the war), and Wagner, programmed almost every other day in various bleeding chunks, ruled the roost. There was only a smattering of Baroque music, Elgar was the most frequently featured of living composers, and little of the Continental avant-garde made its way across the Channel – although Stravinsky's puppet-ballet *Petrushka* was given its Proms premiere on 16 October. And every Friday, just before the interval, Wood conducted the New Queen's Hall Orchestra in a Beethoven symphony and, occasionally, overture or concerto. Michael followed the symphonies avidly in his loaned scores, from the revolutionary innovation of the "Eroica" to the sweet especial rural scene of the "Pastoral". (He had to wait a while before experiencing the Ninth Symphony's "Ode to Joy", for Wood did not include the last movement in that year's performance.) The impact was cataclysmic: "Beethoven became my musical god and has remained so ever since."[14] What was it in Beethoven that captured him so? If the Beethovenian influence on Michael's own music is any answer, then the intensity of the symphonies' blazing affirmation of liberty and joy, achieved only through a fierce struggle in which the listener is almost demanded to participate, caught him in unrelenting hold.

Innumerable friendships have sprung up between concertgoers at the Proms, and it was in the 1923 season that Michael got to know Aubrey Russ, to whom he quickly became close. Aubrey Russ was thirty-two when he came across Michael Tippett, not yet twenty, poring over scores on the floor of the Queen's Hall arena. Russ had studied Classics at Jesus College, Oxford, graduating a few months into the war, during which he was decorated for his work in France with the Young Men's Christian Association.[15] He became a schoolteacher, first in Bath and then in Barbados, but was dismissed for making advances towards his pupils. When he met Michael he was working in his father's law firm and living in Herne Hill. He slotted easily into the role of older companion who, with his extensive record collection and library, could steer Michael's tastes and enthusiasms. He plied him with books and records, and so began Michael's lifelong exploration of Beethoven's string quartets, playing the Léner Quartet's recordings, on scratchy shellac discs, until they wore out. Russ very quickly intimated that he would like to start an affair, but on this point the younger man was clear: "I never reciprocated physically."[16] This is quite a tribute to Michael's resistance. Russ was adept at navigating his necessarily underground sexual life, which Michael once described as an "out and out town bugger life".[17] With this subterranean night-time world Michael at least began to flirt, likely with Russ as a guide. The white flannels in which he was often seen at the Proms were not just an eccentricity but a coded uniform worn by homosexuals at the Criterion Bar in Piccadilly Circus.[18]

Russ offered theatre tickets too, some for private performances in clubs that could escape the censure of the Lord Chamberlain, others for established classics. The Proms had provided the itinerary for Michael's belated voyage of musical discovery, but it was his eclectically receptive temperament that was the passport to other new worlds. In the world of London theatre he experienced the full canon of English drama, from Shakespeare and Restoration comedies to the contemporary plays of Noël Coward and George Bernard Shaw. These were essentially conservative in form and staging, and it was the foreign imports (Ibsen, Chekhov) that imprinted themselves on Michael's imagination. In May 1924 he was to see Sybil Thorndike in Ernst Toller's controversial *Man and the Masses*, which interwove balletic and cinematic dream sequences with realistic

scenes of political – and pacifist – protest. It was a few years before
the politics depicted in the play would really come to fire his
thinking, but his mind stowed everything away, and the residue of
this youthful theatregoing can be detected in his own works for the
stage, even those composed half a century later.

He made a further important friendship on the introduction of
Aubrey Russ, who, old boy of Oxford, had brokered a meeting,
sometime in 1924, with an undergraduate at Christ Church called
David Ayerst.[19] Ayerst is remembered today for writing a history
of the *Guardian* newspaper; footloose and professionally unhappy
in the early 1920s, he was a deeply serious and politically radical
figure, a member of a group of Oxford graduates that was to play a
significant role in shaping English left-wing thought in the 1930s.
He counted the future Labour leader Hugh Gaitskell among his
social circle, and would go on to give distinguished service in the
Department of Education and as an army colonel during the Second
World War. This soon-to-be military man and quiet Christian
struck up a firm friendship with Michael, the avowedly secular and
soon-to-be-pacifist musician. "We met only intermittently," Ayerst
remembered, "but, when we did [to quote William Cory] 'we tired
the sun with talking and sent him down the sky'. We argued, of
course we did. We have always argued. As young men we were
both eagerly exploring new ideas, playing snap so to speak, with
each other's latest enthusiasms."[20] There may have been a spark of
attraction between them. Ayerst was in crisis over his faith and sexuality. "Many of my closest friends were homosexual," he wrote.
"Was I? I came to think so."[21] But it was a short-lived conclusion.
His close friendship with Michael lasted for the rest of his life.

In the course of a few months, Michael's social and cultural life
had been transformed from his Lincolnshire existence. Cut loose
from his secluded rooms in Stamford, he found himself falling in
love, fending off an older man's advances, and drinking greedily
from all the plays, literature, and music that London could offer
him – a cultural glut that didn't abate for the entirety of his student
days. Once the Proms ended he took up residence in the upper
gallery of the Queen's Hall for the winter seasons, in which British

orchestras alternated with guest ensembles from Continental Europe, and Ravel came to conduct his own work two years running. With what openness Michael had thrown himself into this new world, and with what determination he had set about devoting his life and his learning to culture.

Came the autumn term of 1923 and the need to decide upon a course of study. The teaching at the Royal College did not really provide the guidance, pastoral or academic, that Michael needed, and there was no formal structure of tutorials. Everything revolved around composition classes, taught by Charles Wood. Wood, who was nearing seventy, had lost his son in the war, and was suffering from cancer, which led to frequent absence. He was a prolific composer, of six string quartets and numerous sacred vocal works, and offered a solid grounding rather than stimulating excitement. He could fill holes in Michael's technical knowledge, but despite Wood's devotion to Beethoven, the pupil found himself uninspired by his teacher, whose taught repertoire concentrated exclusively on a German tradition, from Bach to Wagner. Michael quickly came to the conclusion that the lessons were too narrow, and itched to move away from harmony and to explore counterpoint and word-setting. The handful of his first-year pieces that survive proves that he quickly grasped the rudiments of composition, but the music is basic and tentative.[22] His "second study" was piano, and his teacher, Aubyn Raymar, despite focusing on a wide repertoire (they even looked at some Bartók), could coax from his pupil no signs of a shift from proficiency to virtuosity. And then there was the "second conducting" class, which was led by a familiar face: Malcolm Sargent. The re-exposure to his old mentor from school filled Michael with nerves: "I was frightened, very frightened. The score in front of me would blur and disappear. But that soon passed."[23] Sargent, who did much to foster his college reputation as dapper and debonair, concentrated less on the nitty-gritty of conducting technique, and more on performing his own purposefully wayward versions of choral classics, which the students then had to wrestle into accuracy.

More helpful was Adrian Boult. Michael was never formally enrolled to be taught by Boult, a distinguished conductor, bald, moustachioed, and on the verge of being appointed to his first major orchestra. But many students were allowed to sit in on Boult's sessions with the senior ensembles, and Michael went so far as to ask whether he could perch literally at Boult's elbow to observe proceedings. He did this every week for years, standing close enough to read the score while presumably avoiding the jabs of Boult's trademark long baton. "I wasn't actually watching him conduct," Michael later admitted, "I was listening to the sound. I knew quite early I had an ear for texture."[24] He soon earned the nickname "Boult's darling", either in harmless jest or in accusation of being a teacher's pet. He wrote to Boult half a century later: "What I learnt, as a composer, through those four years of Fridays at your side is nobody's business."[25]

Many students spent only the shortest time possible in college, and the composers, more isolated than instrumentalists, grew frustrated by the lack of stimulating friendships and conversation. Michael had little in common with the majority of his fellows, whom he later dismissed, bar some honourable exceptions, as a "dreary lot".[26] In the end, the college didn't furnish him with a single enduringly close friend, and his social life continued to flourish in the outside world. He had remained friends with his closest cousin, Phyllis Kemp, who was now reading for a degree in Slavonic languages at London University and was a comfortingly familiar figure in this new city. She and Michael had always shared a special rapport and enjoyed each other's company, but he may have found it a substantial shock, especially given his own recent affairs of the heart, when she admitted that she was in love with him.

It was not through worry at their genetic close weave that Michael had to reject Phyllis's declaration of love. (A marriage between first cousins was not unheard of, and his brother eventually married their cousin Joyce.) Having been so recently troubled by an overarching love for a man, he was startled to be presented with the possibility of a heterosexual affair. He never dismissed such an option out of hand, and in later life he would actively try to engineer sexual encounters with women, his relations with whom often became so close that they shared all the intimacy of lovers, conducting affairs of the heart and mind. He once introduced himself to the composer David Matthews with the words, "The first thing you ought to know about me is that I'm bisexual", and while he was happy for Ian Kemp's Tippett study to narrate his various affairs, insisted that the word "homosexual" never be used, either in admission of his love for women or in mistrust of verbal umbrellas.[27] Sally Groves, his eventual publisher, was not alone in her sense that Michael "loved women, and he knew that gender wasn't really, at the end, the most important thing. I think he thought that the world of emotion and the world of love and joy was just beyond gender."[28] But despite a continual wish to exist in a world where "sexuality" might need no prefix, his explorations with women were more through curiosity than a physical urge. There could be no question of his becoming Phyllis's lover. She was not the only woman who would fall for Michael and be upset by his disinclination, his inability even, to reciprocate. While he was open about his preferences to a trustworthy close circle, he seemingly gave off no signs, even to the more worldly of his female friends, that their advances would be unwelcome. Phyllis had grown into a passionate and volatile young woman, and Michael's rejection upset her deeply, remaining a grievance for some while.

In Stephen Spender's autobiographical novel *The Temple* (written in 1929), a young man travels to Germany and discovers a culture both exhilarating and foreboding, more open in its attitudes than England, not least towards sexuality: "a paradise where there was no censorship and young Germans enjoyed extraordinary freedom in their lives".[29] Michael's own travels in Germany, which began in the summer holidays of 1924, were similar voyages of discovery.

He and a fellow student, the cellist Gethyn Wykeham-George, embarked on a walking tour of Bavaria. These were formative wanderings, and the trip was a progenitor not only of a decade's Teutonic rambling, but of a lifetime's need for travel, for the discovery of other vistas and the lives being lived within them, for familiar existence to be paused and returned to, with ears and mind refreshed.

Despite having fluent French and conversational Italian, Michael had realised that to speak German would be of considerable use to a musician, and wanted first-hand experience of the country. Germany could be reached by a four-hour ferry from Dover to Ostend, followed by a lengthy train journey across Belgium. It was rather a perilous trip, and the war had left German frontiers fluid and in dispute. There was at least one sticky situation with border guards. Only a few years earlier, Bavaria had tried violently to proclaim independence from the Weimar Republic. Michael and Gethyn ended up staying in a boarding house in Munich, where, just half a year previously, Adolf Hitler had brought the Nazi Party its first national exposure through the failed coup attempt of the Beer Hall Putsch. But the holiday was just the right kind of romantic musical expedition. The Weimar Republic was moving into its so-called Golden Age, and Germany was recovering from the years of hyperinflation in which wheelbarrows of marks were exchanged for a loaf of bread. Michael was in search of forest walks and opera houses, rather than the smoky nightclubs of mascaraed sexual ambivalence that came to define inter-war Berlin, a city he didn't visit until some time later. Instead he and Gethyn witnessed at first hand the violin-making trade in Mittenwald, and after pilgrimages to the castles of Wagner's eccentric patron, Ludwig II, they attended the four music-dramas of the Ring.

The planned route took them through the haunting Bavarian landscape, and as they pressed onward, often on foot, Michael began to construct his own intellectual route map. The dense forests and dramatic skies chimed with his travels into the imaginative worlds of Goethe and Schiller. Wandering and wondering, he revelled in the disconnectedness and spontaneity of which the twenty-first-century traveller knows little. Despite his wish that teaching at the Royal College would depart from its Germanic base, he was laying the foundations for his lifelong immersion in German culture. At the turn of the century the prevalence of German thought had been taken for granted. Michael's generation had entered adolescence just as England was rejecting everything Teutonic and Germany was mutating from apogee to anathema. Now, post-war, the balance could be temporarily redressed, and Michael earnestly imbibed Germany's language and literature, despite its being a tough task every morning to stumble untutored through the irregular verbs of a tongue that came to him with far less ease than the Romance languages in which he excelled.

When he got back to London he had to find new lodgings, and, on the introduction of his new friend David Ayerst, boarded for three months at Haileybury Boys Club, a charitable institution in Stepney. The club had been managed the previous decade by Clement Attlee, and was founded to help working-class children of the East End. Michael got involved with its general organisation and played games with the boys, many of whom were suffering the effects of severe poverty and living in slums. Finding the life too rowdy for work, he then returned briefly to the house in Chiswick, upsetting Aubrey Russ in the process, who was determined they should live together. Finally Michael and two other students took a basement flat in Redcliffe Gardens (just over a mile's walk from the Royal College).[30]

In the autumn term of 1924 his Suite for Strings in C major (the manuscript now lost) was played by some college musicians in an informal chamber concert, apparently the first ever performance of Michael Tippett's work beyond his own piano approximations. But this was a rarity, and Wood's lessons continued uninspiring. With his inveterate reliance on auto-didacticism, Michael took matters into his own hands, and, hoping to expand his knowledge of the repertoire, asked the registrar at the college whether there were a small amateur choir in need of a conductor. The absence of television and other forms of home entertainment often led to a far higher standard of amateur music-making than communities can invariably manage today, and it so happened that a close-knit group of talented amateur singers in Surrey was on the lookout for a choral conductor. Michael fitted the bill perfectly. He conducted a madrigal concert on 27 May 1925 that marked the beginning of a warm and enduring association with the musicians of Oxted, a town some twenty miles south of London. As a member of the choir recalled, most of the performers were "Michael's elders. Even so, nobody ever questioned his authority. He was an inspiring leader, and while he was distinctly temperamental, and often lost his temper with us, this made the rehearsals all the more eventful. Young and old, we were his devoted slaves."[31]

In the summer of 1925 Michael went again to Germany, this time to the south-west of the country, accompanied by Aubrey Russ. They visited Heidelberg and Rothenberg, before Michael went on alone, crossing right through France to join his parents in Biarritz. En route he was briefly mistaken for a German, to the angry consternation of the locals. The war was hard to forget, even then. When he reached his parents, he found further confirmation that the Tippett family had permanently dissolved. His father had changed the family name.[32] Why? Henry was perfectly capable of following whims, and claimed at the time that he was sick of the name being misspelled. But "Tippett" is not all that difficult to write correctly, give or take a p or a t. The name may have carried a taint of disgrace, but the Tippett trial was a quarter of a century ago. Perhaps it was a tax-avoidance scheme. Whatever the truth, the whole family took Isabel's maiden, and her sons' middle, name: Kemp. The change stuck with all but the youngest of the family, who speedily reverted, with typical independence and rebellion, to his former styling. He was now not even a family member in name only.

In May 1926 the General Council of the Trades Union Congress called a general strike that lasted nine days, in a failed attempt to force the British government to improve conditions for coal miners.

The post-war coal output had fallen badly, as had miners' pay, and the country as a whole was beginning the economic downturn that would lead to the next decade's depression. The nation's transport came to a standstill. The practical effect on Michael was more positive. The Royal Opera House at Covent Garden usually relied on Grenadier Guardsmen to act as supernumeraries in their large-scale productions, but they were out dealing with the strike, and the final scenes of Wagner's *Die Meistersinger* threatened to be very sparsely populated indeed. So students from the Royal College were invited to take part. Michael was used to helping out in musical crises (he had padded out the percussion section of the British Women's Symphony Orchestra on occasion) and eagerly volunteered for the opening night. The evening of 12 May, the final day of the strike, found him revelling in the chance to stand, in full medieval ceremonial dress, metres away from the legendary German soprano Lotte Lehmann and the conductor Robert Heger. Michael's journey through the classical canon was to continue from the balcony of the opera house just the next month, when he queued all night to attend one of Dame Nellie Melba's many "farewell" concerts.

The rest of that spring and summer was spent commuting between Kensington and Surrey, where, in addition to conducting the Oxted choir, Michael had been persuaded to take over (or may even have founded) an amateur orchestra. The recent opening of the local Barn Theatre, a tiny building on a residential street, with capacity for 246, allowed him to mount ambitious performances, and on 2 June his various ensembles joined forces with the local am-dram society to put on Harley Granville-Barker's and Laurence Housman's musical play *Prunella* (1906), which had an orchestral score by Joseph Moorat. "It is interesting to note", thought a local paper, that "the musical section of the Players appeared for the first time, under the able conductorship of Mr Michael Tippett." The orchestra apparently performed "with admirable quality and colour, but might have been a little quieter during some of the speaking parts".[33]

On 12 July Michael's teacher, Charles Wood, died of cancer. It is a shame that, at this point, Michael was not able to study with Gustav Holst, whom he admired greatly, but Holst was unavailable.

Studies with Vaughan Williams were then mooted, but Michael refused, perceiving at the college and in the country's wider musical life "an anti-intellectualism which disturbed and irritated me", and for which he rather blamed the Vaughan Williams school.[34] In fact Vaughan Williams actively and generously encouraged his pupils to find their own voices, and bemoaned teaching standards at the college just as much as Michael, who later grew to value him as a composer and as a friend. Eventually Michael ended up studying, for the summer term of 1926, with Reginald Owen Morris, a renowned teacher of counterpoint, called "R.O." even by his friends. Morris asked his students to imitate the music of the first "Golden Age" of British composers, such as Byrd, Gibbons, Tallis, Purcell, and other masters of Renaissance and Elizabethan polyphony.[35] Michael needed no encouragement, feeling that such figures were unjustifiably ignored. He had gone some way to acquainting himself with this repertoire through his work in Oxted, and had attended services at Westminster Cathedral specifically to hear it. Had the arrangement with Morris lasted, it is possible that Michael's compositional voice would have developed earlier and faster, and it was perhaps this sudden burst of contrapuntal inspiration that accounted for a small flourishing in his student career. He was awarded a Signor Foli scholarship for composition, to the value of £10, which was then doubled when another scholar dropped out. In July he was répétiteur for the college's four full-length performances of Wagner's *Parsifal* under Adrian Boult (no mean task), and the same month conducted a small college orchestra in incidental music for a production of *As You Like It*. But then R.O. Morris was offered a position at the Curtis Institute of Music in Philadelphia, and (taking Herbert Sumsion along as an assistant) he and his wife left for America in September 1926.

Michael was consequently enrolled for "2nd composition" lessons with Charles Kitson, alongside instruction in musical criticism from Henry Cope Colles (chief music critic of *The Times*). Kitson was a highly regarded organist saturated in the English choral tradition, but for Michael he was a disappointment. After the pleasure of a term's counterpoint with Morris, he found himself again splashing around in the waters of Germanic harmony. He thought the lessons were fatally dry, and it was not his style to make the best of a bad job. Kitson, notoriously pedantic, evidently took against his pupil. Only one of Michael's scores from this period survives. Enthused by a passion for the novels of H.G. Wells, he took a long and unwieldy chunk of prose from Wells's 1919 retelling of the Book of Job, The Undying Fire, and embarked upon a large-scale setting for full orchestra, with Wells's dialogue between Job and God divided between a baritone and chorus. He prefaced the score with a quotation from the novel: "There burns an undying fire in the hearts of men. By that fire I live. By that I know the God of my Salvation." The religiosity of the sentiment was untypical of Michael, but its strongly affirmative strain suited his passion and optimism very well. He managed the first chorus, a fugue in C major that grows and swells, but abandoned the enterprise on Job's first entry, having set less than a third of the text he had intended.[36]

More successful was a performance with his Oxted forces of Vaughan Williams's one-act opera The Shepherds of the Delectable Mountains (an adaptation of Bunyan's The Pilgrim's Progress), on 17 March 1927. The first half of the evening was taken up with the medieval Morality play Everyman, which Michael padded out with off-stage renditions of anthems by Orlando Gibbons. Vaughan Williams was persuaded to attend the performance, the opera's first amateur revival. The Times reviewer thought that "the most successful music of the evening was the singing of Orlando Gibbons's 'Hosanna to the Son of David' at the end of Everyman" and praised Michael for holding it all together, "not an easy thing, since the orchestra and chorus were under the stage, and it must have been difficult for the singers above to hear them".[37] The reviewer didn't know the half of it. Michael was conducting while sitting in a puddle of water on the floor of the makeshift and subterranean orchestra pit. The instrumentalists wore wellington boots, and the singers desperately tried to hear them via holes drilled through the stage floor for that express purpose.

Through Aubrey Russ, on one of their many excursions into London's theatrical scene, Michael met the man who became his first live-in lover: a jobbing actor-cum-theatre manager, four years his senior, called Roy Langford. Openly homosexual, Langford was connected to theatre orchestras that could be future sources of employment, and got friends in on the sly to performances and rehearsals at the two theatres he ran in Hammersmith and Wimbledon. Michael thought he was attractive and found his company enlivening. With Russ he had firmly resisted a sexual relationship, but a love affair with Langford became secure enough for Michael to move out of the Kensington flat and into Langford's large apartment in West Hampstead. As he said, "We all disregarded the law. We had to because it was our nature."[38] Such placidity would endure for nearly a decade before splintering into psychological crisis. At one point he and Langford were joined by Russ, and it would be easy to imagine a rather rackety ménage, eking out a financially impoverished but artistically rich existence. The reality was more mundane. Michael was focused on his studies and on conducting duties in Oxted, to which he would ride pillion on Langford's motorbike. He professed himself more interested in work and sleep than in a tempestuous sex life. Careful budgeting meant that they could get by without too much difficulty and the two lived together quite happily for some years.

Or so Michael remembered it. David Ayerst visited them in Hampstead, and was instantly and seriously disturbed. He wrote to a friend that he had

> stayed in the most evil household I have ever been in, where an actor aged about twenty-eight is sucking the vitality out of a poor musical genius of twenty-three. [. . .] I've never met a man more vampire-like than this actor in my life, and the events of that household, which also contains a young dull stockbroker and a middle-aged solicitor [Aubrey Russ], far surpass the madness of [a recent and unhappy holiday]. So I am not going to describe them here.[39]

In what it reveals, and in what it does not reveal, this letter is both unnerving and frustrating, and shines a disconcerting new beam on a personality that has so far seemed quite confident enough to stand up for itself. Ayerst, who was no prude, could bear to include no substantiating detail about the "evil household", and apparently never spoke again of the impression it gave him of the young and pliable composer held under the thumb of a nastily overbearing and manipulative older man. So little survives to narrate this first major love affair that it is impossible to say whether Michael was truly being preyed upon so ruthlessly. Aubrey Russ had left his teaching career under a dark cloud, and his behaviour would eventually land Michael in sticky situations, suggesting a strange and easily influenced judgement in the young composer when it came to friendships. It was not to be the last time that Michael, usually so clear-sighted in self-analysis, was blinkered from within the bounds of a relationship, while others could see quite clearly that figures to whom he was devoted were taking intense and questionable advantage. Michael, for his part, thought he had lived with Langford a "gay sensual life" (gay used not in its modern sense).[40] For him, Roy was "the chap with whom I lived as close as may be for some years – experimenting in sensuality, despite my virginal abhorrence of that time [. . .]. It's very curious, but there's definitely a mellowness, even fragrance, in this particular past and person, which seems only possible from having paid thus the debt to the Earth."[41] These are cryptically phrased memories. One reading of "virginal abhorrence" would be that Michael, still wounded deeply by the Fettes abuse, had developed an antipathy towards penetrative sex that resulted in his rarely going further than the foreplay of sensual experimentation. What is meant by a "debt to the Earth" is uncertain; it is the only phrase that hints at any awareness of a darker side to the relationship, whose true nature is probably caught somewhere in the gap between the external and internal viewpoints that have survived.

The difficulties, such as they were, in the life with Roy Langford may account for a bad judder in Michael's tenure at the Royal College. Approaching the end of his fourth year, he was a strange quandary for his teachers: half precocity, half plod, a quick learner but a slow developer. His musical knowledge grew almost weekly, his piano-playing had evidently improved, and a short burst of lessons was soon to make him a reasonably proficient string player (good enough to stand in for a violist at an Oxted concert). He was becoming a skilful conductor, of the Oxted players and of the college's second orchestra, which regularly performed under his baton.[42] But his compositions lagged behind, earthbound. So few of his early scores survive that evidence of their quality (or lack of it) must be read by other means.[43] He gained no commissions and his pieces rarely reached the college showcases of student work. At the end of 1927 he was awarded the £13 Dove prize "for general excellence, assiduity and industry", but this was notably *not* a composition prize. Most startling is a realignment in lessons earlier that year, when it was decided that Michael would focus more on his piano-playing than on composition. His piano lessons became his principal study, and Kitson's "junior composition" classes were demoted to mere "extras".

Proving as well as anything the chequered nature of Michael's formal musical education, the college records relate that Michael was then absent for the first two terms of 1928, a gap that coincided with an unplanned series of lengthy foreign adventures, and with a large-scale passion project in Oxted. Whether the hiatus were a necessary accident after being delayed abroad, or some form of sabbatical, the archives do not relate. A few years before, in Roy Langford's Hammersmith theatre, a wildly successful run of John Gay's *The Beggar's Opera* had spawned a surge in popularity of eighteenth-century ballad operas. Michael had come across a set of vocal parts for Charles Johnson's *The Village Opera* (1729), and set about nipping and tucking both text and music into something that could be mounted at Oxted, while writing a rather eccentrically orchestrated accompaniment that, all but entirely ignorant of eighteenth-century performance practice, included both piano and harpsichord.

It was while working on this project, staying with a friend at Oxted early in 1928, that he received an urgent telegram from his

cousin Phyllis. After graduating she had developed an interest in
the vernacular culture and healing rituals of the South Slav lands,
and relocated to Serbia – then known as the Kingdom of the Serbs,
Croats and Slovenes – to further her research. Suddenly she was
in trouble, and it is a mark of the closeness of their relationship,
despite the woes of her unrequited love for him, that Michael
dropped everything, drained a savings account, and arranged to
go to Belgrade. It was another opportunity to expand his linguistic
skills, and as he travelled through yet more disputed territories with
frontiers left ragged by the Treaty of Versailles, spending thirty-six
hours on an uncomfortable train carrying him first through Venice
and then through Trieste, he digested the basics of Serbo-Croat.
What followed was later recalled by Michael in good humour as
another picaresque adventure. On his arrival in Belgrade he found
that Phyllis had been diverting herself with a local worker who
had abandoned his wife and moved into Phyllis's apartment. Now
the lover had disappeared and Michael, tasked with retrieving him,
soon got comprehensively lost in the outskirts of Belgrade. Having
found a possible patch of hunting ground, he then took a train
that turned out to be going in the wrong direction. After several
frustrating encounters with unhelpful waitresses, truculent locals,
and swarms of bedbugs, all in his quest for the recalcitrant Serb, the
object of his search turned out in the meantime to have returned to
Phyllis's tiny apartment.

In truth, the story had had a much darker side. After the affair
with the married man, Phyllis had become pregnant, and the child
was stillborn. According to the law of the country at the time,
she could have been arrested and imprisoned for up to two years,
had the wife of her lover made a formal complaint. The story
became a national scandal, and it was vital to get Phyllis, who
had lost her passport, out of the country. Embassies Serbian and
British piled in; the Belgrade police were pushing for her arrest and
deportation. "Ever since her arrival here Miss Kemp's behaviour
and conduct have been most unfortunate and reprehensible", wrote
a vice-consul on 2 February 1928. The case was "serious", and
"there was a danger of proceedings being taken against her".[44] On

5 March Phyllis was issued a passport, but matters became grave when she developed typhus, probably brought on by less than sanitary living quarters. With remarkable resource and at his own expense, Michael somehow despatched the lover back to his wife, and arranged medical treatment for Phyllis. This left him alone in an insect-infested flat that had to be professionally disinfected; somehow, he ended up staying with a young diplomat from the British Consulate with whom, he tacitly implied later, he had a mild fling. Phyllis was being cared for in a convent infirmary but, when funds ran out, had to be transferred to a crumbling Belgrade state hospital, much against her will. She was admitted on the condition that Michael was also inoculated against typhus, with the inevitable result that he suffered a violent reaction to the injection. After an abortive attempt to transfer the two of them to a children's hospital run by English expatriates, he finally managed to contact a relation and beg that Phyllis be rescued. In the event she stayed in hospital for over a year.

But the curtain had yet to fall on his Balkan black comedy. It was a holiday of telegrams. One arrived from his parents, who were then in Italy, saying that his father had been bitten by a poisonous spider. Michael, barely recovered, secured a cheap berth on the *Orient Express* and sped to Padua, presumably expecting to find his father foaming at the mouth, only to discover that something had got lost in translation amid his mother's melodramatics and the vagaries of the Italian telegraph office. The offending insect was a wasp. Then things took a yet darker turn, with the arrival of the third telegram.

After a time in naval colleges at Osborne and Dartmouth, Michael's brother, Peter, had joined the Submarine Service. A crew had got into difficulty, and in what has been described as "a courageous and successful attempt to prevent a fatal accident" Peter's leg was crushed.[45] The operation to amputate was touch-and-go, and Henry and Isabel were told Peter would not survive. They left at once by the *Orient Express*, onto which Michael had literally pushed them after an altercation with the guard over lack of tickets. He was left to sort out his parents' things and bring everything back to London, but fraternal affection, such as it was, did not inspire a panicked rush. Instead he was not able to resist squeezing in a few days enjoying the local artwork; nor did he turn down a brief liaison with an importunate young man who propositioned him in the city streets. The candour with which he afterwards related these dalliances is as startling as the fact of his delay. After more missed trains and misplaced luggage, probably the consequence of his continual failure to understand European railway regulations, he finally returned to England, sometime around March 1928. Peter survived the amputation, and was invalided out of the naval life with a prosthetic leg and the rank of lieutenant commander.

Michael had got back in time to follow through his ambitions for The Village Opera. On 22 April his "realization" was performed in the Barn Theatre, with valuable contribution from a local troupe of Morris dancers. It was a considerable success, although The Times's special correspondent thought that Michael could have gone further in his judicious pruning: "The worst mistake was at the beginning, where the young lover had no fewer than nine love-songs." But the review also praised as the most successful a scene that was in fact a Tippett interpolation, "the elopement, where Mr. Michael Tippett [. . .] showed a real sense of how to handle a dramatic situation in music. The instrumentation in this scene was delightful. But on the whole the music and the performance had too little gaiety in it, and the slow tempi at which most things were taken did not make for lightness."[46]

The legend has arisen that Michael Tippett graduated from the Royal College of Music only on a second attempt, failing the first time round. What happened was more complex. He had promised his parents that he would expand his potential for employment by studying towards a doctorate. At the time, the college offered only Associate status. Needing to furnish himself with an under-graduate degree, Michael decided not to return to the college and instead was entered as an external candidate to sit exams at London University. His studies had been on hold for many months, and four years' training in composition and performance do not auto-matically lead to success in timed essays on the history and theory of music. A rough parallel might be a student from drama school suddenly having to sit undergraduate exams in literary theory. It is no surprise that Michael found himself "hopelessly at sea" in the exam hall, especially when denied the use of the piano to aid his answers. He did not have, and never acquired, perfect pitch. To work without the aid of a piano struck him as impossible and absurd, and he had recourse to one ever afterwards. Some of his later claims of ignorance must be taken with a pinch of salt: an exam question on Orlando Gibbons had apparently flummoxed him, because "not having heard any Gibbons, I said he was completely unimportant".[47] Given his triumphant incorporation of Gibbons into performances at Oxted the year before, either his memory deserted him completely or he was groping at an excuse after the event. More likely he was under-prepared, and over-reliant on his hitherto successful ability to get by on little more than innate wit. As it was, when the results were announced in summer 1928, he found that he had failed.

SEVEN

Macaroni-cheese and
Stewed Rhubarb

Michael frequently arrived at the junctions of his life secure in his long-term plans but with no immediate strategy. With no qualification to show for his many years at the Royal College of Music, he was lucky to find employment so quickly. A small Oxted boarding school was looking for a part-time music teacher, and a member of the choir suggested Michael.

Hazelwood Preparatory School is set into a hillside above a panoramic view of the Weald and the Ashdown Forest. Leaving the bustle of Hampstead and of Kensington a few times a week brought Michael much-needed relief from the pressures of exam resits. He spent his first term as a teacher, in autumn 1928, commuting to Oxted by train or motorbike from the Hampstead flat. He had returned to the college for a term of booster lessons from Charles Kitson in music theory, in which they went over past papers. London University finally awarded him a Bachelor of Music degree late in 1928, allowing him formally to depart from the Royal College on 8 December.

Hazelwood was a tiny institution of fewer than thirty boys, aged between eight and thirteen. Michael's responsibilities were to play the organ in chapel services and provide basic lessons in musical appreciation. The school was led by the charismatic headmaster Hugh Irving, who was an enthusiast for the latest musical crazes, playing Gracie Fields records to the students over dinner. Irving had a good eye: in spring that year he had appointed a twenty-year-old

English teacher called Arthur Hammond Harris, who promptly changed his name, partially on Michael's suggestion, to Christopher Fry. Within twenty-five years Fry's verse-dramas would make him one of the most successful playwrights in the West End, and his most famous title, *The Lady's Not for Burning*, was immortalised by Margaret Thatcher's quip, "You turn if you want to, the lady's . . ." But for now, these two soon-to-be renowned men of twentieth-century culture were teachers in a small primary school. Fry was living on-site at Hazelwood and became a close friend, serene and handsome, quiet and measured where Michael was bouncy and highly strung. The two were soon jointly organising school plays and became responsible for the artistic life of the place. After knowing each other for only a term, they decided to travel together for the Christmas holidays of 1928, going first to Bonn, so that Michael could pay his respects to Beethoven's birthplace, and then a little further north to Cologne.

Fry wrote up his memories of Hazelwood, beginning with Michael's missionary zeal for Samuel Butler:

We used to have extracts from Butler read aloud over the macaroni-cheese and stewed rhubarb. Michael's eager mind and freedom from stuffiness startled me a bit. On certain Sundays members of the staff delivered a short sermon in the school chapel. I dutifully wore my Sunday suit – my only suit – for the occasion, and used the lectern as a pulpit. Michael, on his sermon day, was happy in flannel trousers and gym shoes, and propped himself on the altar rails to give his address. [. . .] I remember the boys of the school challenging Tippett and me to have a sprinting race across the cricket-field. His legs were so much longer than mine, I was surprised that he beat me by only the shortest of heads, until I realised that he had deliberately been taking it easy so that I shouldn't seem to be a hopeless loser in the eyes of my pupils.[1]

Teaching was never really Michael's vocation, but he took easily enough to the lessons and the boys enjoyed being taken through a selection of his favourite records. One pupil, John Strange, remembered him as an inspiring and formative teacher, willing to take on a pastoral role as well as a musical one: "I was summoned to an interview [. . .] where with great delicacy and kindliness he introduced me to the biological facts of puberty." Michael was evidently an affable pillar of the Hazelwood community, though was able to maintain discipline, as Strange found to his cost:

> I suspect the noise we made [in singing lessons] must have placed Michael's genial forbearance under considerable strain. This geniality to which I refer seems to me in retrospect to have been a particularly admirable quality of Michael as a schoolmaster. He had a rather comic cackling laugh and there was a particular kindliness in his glance which made him approachable. At the same time he could be quite terrifying with those who played the fool. I can remember an occasion when he was conducting a singing class, as he often did, with us clustered around him at the upright piano. [. . .] My attention had wandered however on this occasion and I was with typical schoolboy ineptitude assing about with one of my companions. Suddenly Michael stopped in the middle of a bar and in a flat cold voice with a steely look in the eye quenched me.[2]

In the meantime, the relationship with Roy Langford had soured considerably. Michael later thought that he had turned against Roy "with almost disgust", though didn't record why.[3] The frequent commutes to Hazelwood, the intensity of the friendships he made there, and the stress of resitting his examinations may have put their life under strain. He looked back on his time with Langford through apparently rose-tinted spectacles, but may privately have come to perceive the life-sapping hold that had so disturbed David Ayerst. The best thing to do would be to move out of the capital, and settle permanently in Oxted.

Happily, the role of French teacher became vacant at Hazelwood, and Michael, with his easy and conversational French, was inevitably promoted. Early in 1929 he left London, a city he would never

live in again. Hazelwood had two cottages (known as Chestnut and
Oak) used as accommodation for staff. Michael moved into Chestnut, although the cottage was not a perk of the job, and he had
to pay rent and furnish the place himself. His domestic mainstay
was his bookcase, "a rather horrid pitch-pine colour like the pews
in a Victorian church",⁴ stuffed with the works of his intellectual
heroes, chief among them Samuel Butler, Goethe, George Bernard
Shaw, and James Frazer.* He had happily set up an independent life
for himself while his parents were hundreds of miles away, and his
brother a distant figure. A small allowance from his father bolstered
his £80 yearly salary, but even in today's money it would be a
tiny income, barely in five figures, and he invited Aubrey Russ to
share Chestnut Cottage with him and pay some of the rent. Unwise
it may have been to bring onto school grounds someone whose
own teaching career had ended in scandal but, at least for a while,
the set-up worked. Russ became a stalwart member of the Oxted
and Limpsfield Players and took the lead in a number of Michael's
ventures.

Settling into Chestnut Cottage, Michael was helped immensely
by his friendship with a local music enthusiast, thirteen years his
senior, called Evelyn Maude. Her son was a pupil at Hazelwood and
it had been on her recommendation that Michael found himself
there at all. But Evelyn gave him more than a good reference;
she swiftly became a soulmate to the young composer. She was a
skilled pianist who had considered performing professionally, and
had played for Michael at the Barn Theatre. After studying German
language and literature first in Berlin and then at Cambridge, she
married the successful and influential civil servant Sir John Maude.
They lived at The Copse, a large nearby house set in grounds extensive enough to require a full-time gardener, and Michael became

---

* James Frazer was a renowned anthropologist whose twelve-volume study of
mythology and religion, The Golden Bough, Tippett read in full. The volumes were
a great influence on Tippett's first opera, The Midsummer Marriage. His cousin Phyllis Kemp worked as Frazer's assistant from 1933 to 1934.

a frequent visitor. With their shared loves of music, literature, and German culture, it was inevitable that a deep bond would be forged between Michael and Evelyn. She developed a strong emotional and perhaps sexual attraction to him: their intense relationship provided a rich and fruitful outlet for this clever and cultured woman, otherwise existing within a life of domesticity and a rather distant marriage. But Michael was sadly, guiltily, unable to reciprocate. What he wanted from Evelyn was not a lover, but someone who could occupy the psychological space left vacant by his distant and difficult mother. Quickly accepting the nature of their relationship, Evelyn filled this role perfectly, becoming a constant mainstay and support in matters financial and otherwise. Michael went on to share with her his most intimate thoughts and feelings about every aspect of his life, including his love affairs, and she would open up new intellectual worlds for him.

Far from letting his compositional ambitions trickle away in favour of pursuing a comfortable teaching career, Michael had jumped at the chance of a part-time job in rural seclusion. Already the qualities that would mark his later years as a composer are evident: an absolute devotion to music and to composition, and the growing sense that a life approaching isolation was necessary for the focus required. He taught at Hazelwood every morning; the afternoons and weekends were his own. But he had little hope of becoming a full-time professional composer. The times were not easy for would-be musicians. London's musical scene was poorly funded and lacked such mainstays, now taken for granted, as the London Philharmonic, the BBC Orchestras, or even a permanent opera company. There were few opportunities for new commissions, but with intensive self-discipline Michael began to compose at a startling rate, producing a dozen major pieces in less than two years. "I knew that I was developing to find my own song very slowly," he said afterwards. "In those days you could live much more near the bone. You could live on a very small amount, you could have one decent suit and get on with it. And then I just lived, and wrote and wrote and wrote."[5] Never in his life would he be so prolific again.

There are hints in these unpublished and unrecorded pieces of the techniques he came to use in more mature works (a piano sonata contains syncopations and fanfares of octaves that are typical of the more developed piano writing that followed a decade later). A string quartet is clearly indebted to Beethoven, and sets of piano variations show him playing about with the hallmarks of both Beethoven and Bach, teetering between parody and homage. He was reprogramming his musical taste in the Surrey countryside, away from Kensington fashion, and his composition began to incorporate his new-found veneration of Handel, who had taken the place of Wagner in his affections. But the pieces occasionally wear such influences too heavily, or lose themselves in their ambition, as he watered down his musical gods rather than engaged with them in pointful dialogue. Most assured, and lying comfortably within the bounds of his talent as it then stood, is a delicate setting of a poem by Charlotte Mew that, although never published, would hold its own alongside Gerald Finzi or Roger Quilter in any compilation of English song.

Newly prolific and focused, Michael began to think about studying abroad and accordingly applied, in spring 1929, for the Mendelssohn scholarship, a prestigious award that funded a period of study at the Leipzig Conservatoire. He had found the Leipzig tradition, as transmitted by his teachers, stultifyingly narrow. That he applied to study there indicates a slight desperation at what to do next. Evidently the compositions he submitted to the board had at last started to show serious potential, for he found himself in the final shortlist of three but got no further. Then, on the last day of August 1929, a small but momentous thing occurred. Michael had somehow secured a tiny music commission. The Children's Theatre company, run by Joan Luxton and based in a theatre on Endell Street in the West End of London, opened a mixed programme of plays and dances. One of the items was a mime play by Margaret Carter called *Bolsters*, for the five scenes of which Michael was asked to write the music.[6] He produced five jaunty little piano trios, mainly arrangements of traditional tunes and nursery rhymes that were designed to illustrate the mimed action on stage, replete with a dawn announcement of cock crows. It was the first ever professional performance of Michael Tippett's music, but was not the only musical endeavour that competed with teaching at Hazelwood, and to his roster of amateur choirs he added, late in 1929, an operatic society linked to the Hackney Technical Institute, whose conductor had got cold feet during rehearsals of Holst's opera The Perfect Fool. Michael thought he might be able to make a success of it, and enjoyed the process, continuing to see the society through a handful of other productions. On 28 February 1930 the Oxted players put on James Elroy Flecker's Don Juan, for which he wrote the incidental music. But soon another concert began to take up most of his attention.

Prior to 1930 only two of Michael's pieces had been performed in Oxted: a piano sonata in C minor, and a setting for choir, string quartet, and orchestra of a poem by Christopher Fry called "The Gateway" that its author thought was "very creaking".[7] The Barn Theatre could now be the venue for an ambitious all-Tippett programme, for which, with Evelyn Maude generously footing the bill, a professional choir and orchestra were hired. Michael picked the best of his back catalogue as it then stood, and the date was set for 5 April 1930.* While the music proved a challenge for the performers and rehearsal time was tight, the concert was a considerable success, despite the double-bass player thinking a round of golf more important than the final run-through. It even made a splash beyond the immediate vicinity, and The Times and the Telegraph sent reviewers, who wrote the whole thing up rather

---

* The concert featured a concerto in D major for flutes, oboe, horns, and strings; settings of three poems by Charlotte Mew; a string quartet in F minor; piano variations on the Irish jig "Jockey to the Fair"; and a second outing for the setting of Christopher Fry's poem. The conductor was a friend from the Royal College, David Moule-Evans, who had beaten Michael to the Mendelssohn scholarship. Evidently there were no hard feelings.

positively. Frank Howes, junior reviewer of *The Times*, heard a
composer whose music remained tonal but was not old-fashioned,
who was plainly influenced by eighteenth-century structures and
techniques, and whose tunes had all the familiarity of folksong,
despite their being original. He occasionally wished that the music
would blossom more often into melody, and (most surprisingly
of all, given Michael's interest in counterpoint) thought that "one
other feature in which Mr Tippett is not in the fashion is that his
use of counterpoint is sparing". But the generously lengthy review
concluded that there "is no more searching test of the quality of a
man's music than the devotion of a whole concert exclusively to
it: Mr Tippett's music held the attention and came out of the test
well".[8] The *Telegraph* thought the concert an example of "the hidden
musical activities of this country that gives hope for the future, and
are so unwontedly stirring [. . .] though not all young musicians
have the remarkable gift of Michael Tippett".[9]

High praise indeed, much of which has to be taken on trust,
given that some of the scores performed seem to have been lost
for ever. Such a reaction from four distinguished ears complicates
the now-accepted view that Michael Tippett was a slow-developing
composer who never showed early promise or facility. The entire
programme, after all, was composed before he had turned twenty-
five. And yet, and yet. Hugh Allen, in a show of support to his
former student, had got himself to Oxted to hear the concert, and
was overheard saying, "immature, but very interesting". This struck
a chord, as had the *Telegraph*'s certainty that "Michael Tippett will
prefer to put all behind him and go on to fresh ideas". The feed-
back from the BBC, to whom Michael frequently sent manuscripts
in the hope of achieving performances and broadcasts, was dismissive. An assistant music director thought these early scores gave
"the impression of having been written by one who, possessed of
the slenderest musical ability, determined by hook or by crook to
compose something". Intemperate perhaps, and given the BBC's
response to later works such as *A Child of Our Time* ("sterile") or the
Concerto for Double String Orchestra ("dry, austere, unattractive"),
this early rejection is less a proof of Michael's inability than evidence

of a more general clash of taste.[10] Nevertheless, the concert was the first time Michael had ever heard much of his music outside of his own head. Can it only have been through absent-mindedness that his own name never appeared on the concert programme? Or did he suddenly feel that he didn't want to link his name with what he could already see were examples of juvenilia? He had easily developed an almost stubborn devotion to his art, but not yet a truly inventive mastery of its craft. He was able precisely to pinpoint inadequacies in his technique, and resolved not to go on composing good but somehow uninspired music, and to organise further and more sympathetic teaching.

By great good luck his favourite teacher from the Royal College, R.O. Morris, had just returned from Philadelphia. Michael applied to him for private tuition, but it quickly became evident that the lessons would be too expensive. Morris had the answer. Michael could re-enrol as a student, apply for a grant (which he got), and quickly absent himself from any other commitments. Thus began five terms of darting up to Kensington, when he had a gap in his Hazelwood timetable, for lessons in music theory with Morris, beginning in September 1930. That same month a seventeen-year-old student, on the first day of his studies at the college, wrote in his diary "Go directly after breakfast with Mummy to College. Make stupid mistake in ridiculously easy entrance exam. [. . .] Sir H. Allen's address. 1'o'clock."[11] But it was many years before Michael would be introduced to Benjamin Britten. Did they pass each other in a corridor, these two future titans of British music?

Before starting formally with Morris, Michael had departed for Germany over the summer vacation from Hazelwood, arriving in a country much changed from the one he had discovered the previous decade, battered by the Great Depression, and on the brink of a federal election in September that saw a dramatic rise in the Nazis' popularity. The six weeks he spent on his own in Germany that summer of 1930 made up the longest period of solitary travel he had yet experienced. Some years earlier, when on holiday in Italy, he had befriended two boys who were pupils at the famously progressive Odenwaldschule in south-west Germany. Michael had resolved to learn more about such attractive and alternative methods of European education and was now able to fulfil his long-term ambition of visiting the place, even finding the younger of the two boys still there. But he concluded that the pupils had so much say in the running of the school, in short were so wrapped up in adult responsibilities, that there was little time left to enjoy childhood.

The whole summer was an educational tour, and in addition to the Odenwaldschule, Michael went much further south to teach maths at an experimental and highly primitive school-cum-children's home: the Kinderheim Winkelhof, near the medieval town of Markdorf, where short walks away from the town centre are rewarded by Wagnerian vistas of snow-capped Swiss Alps afloat on the blue waters of Lake Constance.[12] The children in the Kinderheim had found themselves orphaned or abandoned in the eight months following the Armistice, during which the Allies had continued to control food importations into Germany, causing widespread famine and often fatal starvation. These were intense weeks, spent teaching mathematics to children orphaned, uprooted, and stateless, and seeing once again at first hand the hideous fallout not only of the war, but of the Allied treatment of the Central Powers. He added a third progressive institution to his roster of visits that summer, shadowing one of the Kinderheim orphans who had won a scholarship at Kurt Hahn's influential School of Salem Castle. But Michael found the place too redolent of his own schooldays. All three of the schools Michael had visited were run by Jews and were forced to relocate as the Nazis took control of Germany. Only once more before the Second World War would Michael travel to this country so dear to him.

One sure sign that he was now deep-rooted in his Oxted life is that he spent a great deal of his German holiday feeling homesick for Surrey. Returning to the Hazelwood routine was welcome, and he soon began his lessons with R.O. Morris. Morris had recently given up writing music entirely and discussion either of this decision, or of the compositions to which it put paid, was a sore point. Gerald Finzi, another admiring pupil, remembered Morris as a "strange fantastic creature", reserved but with a "fantastic humour", a "faun-like sensuousness", and a "tender devotion to cats".[13] In all these aspects a perfect teacher for Michael, Morris took his pupil apart and put him back together again. The lessons were rigid, and for well over a year they focused without deviation not on the sixteenth-century repertoire that was Morris's specialism and Michael's passion, but on technical analysis of a single subject from one of Bach's fugues. "For one and a half years", as Michael described, "I discovered all the possibilities of this one subject."[14] Bar some revisions of earlier pieces, and a fragment of a symphony aborted after 120 bars, Michael's own compositions slowed almost to a stop during the first year of lessons, although he worked hard with his Oxted ensembles, and in October 1930 conducted them in Charles Stanford's vast fairy-tale opera, *The Travelling Companion*. Six months later the mimed play *Bolsters* was revived in London for a children's revue, accompanied by the piano trios he had written for its first outing. But that appears to have been the final performance of his music before a period of silence that lasted for nearly three years.

In summer 1931 Michael returned to his beloved Cornwall, accompanied by Christopher Fry. The friendship had intensified. Afterwards, both men recalled their association with warm brevity, when reminiscence was necessarily tempered by Fry's subsequent marriage and fatherhood. But it is clear that the relationship was fervent and loving, and Michael referred to Christopher in private as someone "whom I had fallen in love with".[15] His love for Fry was never consummated: "Christopher didn't understand about sex. I had to tell him the facts of life on a bridge in Bonn."[16] But the love was reciprocated on an emotional level to such an extent that the pair decided they might set up a family together. Ian Kemp made notes of a conversation in which Michael stated that he and Fry "went on holiday to Cornwall together, [. . . and] took two cockney boys of seven or eight with them. This arose because the relationship with Fry became very deep and Tippett somehow wanted children. The solution was to adopt together, but this was stopped by Evelyn Maude who said only women can do that, but what you can do is take children on a holiday."[17]

The urge to become either an adoptive or a biological father soon became very great in Michael, and his wish to spend extra-curricular time with the boys in his charge is evidenced by his pupil John Strange, who remembered "arguing with [my parents] long and desperately when Michael invited another boy and myself to join him in a rambling holiday on the continent".[18] Any plans to adopt with Fry emerged from serious rebellion against the status quo, or apathetic disregard for societal norms, or just sheer unworldly ignorance of the law. Neither rebellion nor ignorance was a marked characteristic of Christopher Fry, and it may be that these airy domestic castles were mainly of Michael's building. As it was, the Cornish holiday was not a success. Michael, awash with the jealousy born of love, believed Fry was ignoring him and poisoning the boys against him. Things came to a head and there was a major argument. Fry, like Herbert Sumsion before him, had found himself in too deep, and was unable to reciprocate the intensity of Michael's feelings. Michael believed the fallout that followed to have been a violent physical reaction to the crisis.[19] By the time he returned to Oxted he was seriously ill. Double pneumonia was diagnosed, and he very nearly died of it.

Much of that term was spent in a sick-bed, with Aubrey Russ his most frequent visitor. John Strange thought that Russ had "a particularly strong devotion to Michael at this time and I recall when the latter was desperately ill with pneumonia in the Cottage Hospital round the corner from my house, Aubrey called at the house in a state of unrestrained agitation: it was the first time I had seen a grown man weep".[20] Eventually Michael moved into an empty dormitory at the top of the sanatorium. The room had a tiny balcony on which, when it was warm enough, Fry would spend the night, concern over Michael's recovery evidently eclipsing their quarrel. But one evening Aubrey Russ invited a male escort onto school grounds, and brought him into the dormitory. The encounter turned nasty, the escalating row soon reaching the sleeping English teacher outside. Fry reported all to Hazelwood's headmaster, who demanded that Russ leave school premises (a lenient reaction under the circumstances, and the police were not called). There was talk of Michael's dismissal, but in protest many parents threatened to remove their children from the school. Michael tied a tight and uncharacteristically enigmatic knot on his account of the story: "Christopher was the one who left."[21] Fry had ostensibly departed for a secretarial job, but may have felt continuing at Hazelwood to be untenable. Whatever the truth of the fracas, their friendship survived these heady times, and was of a longevity that implies neither blamed the other to any lasting degree. Meanwhile Michael's friendship with Aubrey Russ, whose actions could have put a number of people in serious legal jeopardy, continued without recrimination.

A few months later Michael moved away from school premises and, instead of joining Aubrey Russ in the town, set up home on his own. Local friends offered one half of a double cottage situated on their farm nearby. By October 1931 his notepaper was headed with his new address: Whitegates Cottage, Oxted, Surrey.[22] The cottage was small and sparsely furnished, and there was little space for any overnight visitors, who often found themselves camping out on the floor. David Ayerst's sister-in-law later remembered: "It was a cottage, two rooms down, a narrow staircase between, two rooms up. The bathroom was in the kitchen, a grand piano just fitted into the sitting room, where Michael did his composing. I was entranced by the whole outfit. There was a jar on the mantelpiece, hard-up friends took money out, well off friends put money in!!"[23] The cottage was on the fringes of the town, and Hurst Green Station was a mile's walk away down long tree-canopied lanes, muddy and unlit, that an icy night would make treacherous and impassable. It was a lonely life, with few neighbours nearby, and the events of the summer had lost him the domestic companionship of two close friends.

From Hurst Green Station it was not too long a journey to either Victoria or London Bridge, and as once he had been taken by sympathetic teachers to London concerts, now in his turn Michael led school trips from Hazelwood, and took his pupils to the Albert Hall to hear Handel's *Messiah*, most likely in one of Malcolm Sargent's Easter or Christmas performances with the Royal Choral Society. The concert would have been typical of the time, both in its cuts from the score and in the massed ranks of its forces: around 800 voices, slowly breasting the billowing waves of a large symphony orchestra. To Michael the sound was clogged, the score needlessly slashed, and the orchestration thick and at odds with the clarity of Handel's original instrumentation. It was decades before the revolutionary movement of historically informed Baroque performance, but there had been tentative calls in the 1920s and 1930s for less bloated presentations, and Thomas Beecham had produced, in 1928, a recording with smaller forces and surprisingly brisk tempi. But still, wrote Elizabeth Benn, a devoted member of Michael's choir, "there was no doubt that this version was a Beecham–Handel collaboration". Michael decided to schedule a year's worth of *Messiah* rehearsals, culminating in two performances, on 15 November and 2 December 1931, that, as Benn relates

> would be *Handel* only, performed as it had been written, without a single variation in tempo. There would be no lingering on high notes for the sopranos, and no pauses for effect or hurrying toward climaxes. [. . . Most performances at the time relegated] the beautiful duet "O death, where is thy sting?" and the glorious chorus "Let all the angels of God worship Him" and various recitatives to an appendix. These we restored to their proper places.[24]

Performances since have realised that to vary tempi is not to jeopardise Handel. Nor did Michael use a harpsichord in place of a piano or have access to period instruments. Nevertheless, in preceding by some years an avowedly "authentic" 1934 BBC broadcast and a 1935 concert in Worcester, these two Surrey performances have a claim to be among the first complete and even partially authentic mountings of Handel's great oratorio in the twentieth century. Elizabeth Benn had vivid memories of the concert, and of the brilliant soloists:

How Michael discovered their individual talents, we never knew. The soprano soloist was the daughter of the local chemist, the contralto was the postmistress, the tenor was an under-gardener from the Titsey estate, and the bass was a country solicitor [Aubrey Russ]. They all had glorious voices: the chemist's daughter later won a scholarship to the Royal Academy of Music. I can sincerely say that I never hear a professional tenor, however well-known, sing the "Comfort ye" without experiencing a nostalgic twinge for the Titsey under-gardener. [. . .] The final performances of the Messiah lifted us to heights that were real "mountain-top" moments – never to be forgotten.[25]

His eruption into student life had coincided with a period of dynamic prosperity, cultural and economic, but it was Michael Tippett's misfortune to arrive at musical maturity during the century's Great Depression. The roar of the 1920s curdled from exuberance to despair. On 20 September 1929 the London Stock Exchange had crashed. A month later came the Wall Street Crash. The 1920s had been no stranger to unemployment, but by the end of 1930 mass joblessness was the crisis of the decade.

Henry and Isabel Kemp, as Michael had learned to call his parents, withstood the downturn. It was not straitened finances but typical allegiance to social conscience that brought about their permanent return to England. Henry, now in his mid-seventies, had continued to invest in property, which was being speedily built and cheaply bought in a successful attempt to lift the country out of recession. With nearly a quarter of the workforce unemployed, the Kemps decided to provide what jobs they could, and, with their wealth revived after years of impecunious wanderings, were able to buy an exquisite Bath-stone manor house in the Somerset village of Timsbury, so as to hire a four-strong staff. But Michael's relationship with them remained badly tattered, and he was only an occasional visitor.

In Michael, who was not yet thirty, the economic situation

stirred not jaded despair but youthful fire in his determination to overcome social inequality, and in his mistrust of government. He was beginning to arrive at the far-left politics that would come to dominate the best part of a decade of his life. Christopher Fry remembered that he and Michael had cheered when, in May 1929, Ramsay MacDonald's Labour Party had won the majority of seats in a hung Parliament. Fry had turned twenty-one a few months before, and as a present Michael gave him a copy of H.G. Wells's *Men Like Gods*. The novel features a protagonist, Barnstaple, transported to a parallel universe called Utopia, ruled not by government but by the "Five Principles of Liberty": privacy, free movement, unlimited knowledge, truthfulness, and free discussion. In his loopy, erratic italics, Michael inscribed the flyleaf with a quotation from the tale within, choosing the moment when Barnstaple realises that he must leave Utopia and create its world on Earth:

He went to the parapet again and stood [staring] at the loveliness of this world he was to leave so soon . . . "We could do it." And suddenly it was borne in upon Mr. Barnstaple that he belonged now soul and body to the Revolution, to the Great Revolution that is afoot on Earth; that marches and will never desist nor rest again until old Earth is one city and Utopia set up therein. He knew clearly that this Revolution is life [. . .]. He stood up. He began walking to and fro. "We shall do it," he said.[26]

EIGHT

The Beggar's Opera

Even before his fame, Michael Tippett had an ability to fall into the path of the great and good of the age. David Ayerst, when an undergraduate at Christ Church, Oxford, had got to know a captivatingly intelligent fellow student who had since gone on to make a name for himself as a poet: Wystan Hugh Auden, blond, bohemian, his face yet to be cross-hatched with its tracery of cigarette-carved grooves. In the early 1930s Auden was teaching in a Scottish school, had already published his first volume of poetry, and was well on the way to becoming the golden boy of London's literary scene. Ayerst had been keen to broker a meeting between Auden and Michael, thinking he had found two kindred spirits, sexually, politically, and intellectually in sympathy. Accordingly, sometime in the first week of April 1932, Michael went to Woodgate, a village on the Somerset–Devon border, in order to meet Auden, who was staying with his friend William McElwee.[1] Auden read aloud from his long (and openly homosexual) poem The Orators, which was to be published a month later. Michael found his own work distinctly shallow by contrast and remained a lifelong admirer of Auden's writing. But the poet stayed an acquaintance, rather than a friend. It was a meeting that took place a few weeks later that truly transformed Michael's personal life.

David Ayerst had left Oxford for Manchester, and was working for the Manchester Guardian, a paper that suited his firmly socialist politics. His articles bristled with prophetic stories about conflict between

Jews and Arabs in Palestine, revolution in Spain, and the global shadow of economic crisis that had caused so many to lose faith in capitalism and flee to the farthest reaches of the political spectrum. A trip to Berlin had thrilled Ayerst with horror at the threat of Hitler and the danger of fascism, which had already gained control of Italy. In October 1932 Oswald Mosley formed the British Union of Fascists, to which members flocked in black-shirted droves. In response, Ayerst was soon involved in efforts to relieve the blight of unemployment in the north-east of England.

In East Cleveland, a coastal stretch of the North Riding of York-shire, nearly 100 ironstone mines had been built into the hillsides during the nineteenth century, producing almost half a million tons of iron annually. Workers flocked, and villages of small terraced cottages sprung up all across the north-east coast. But by the 1930s, iron was available more cheaply from abroad, and the depression forced closure after closure. David Ayerst found that unemployment rates of more than 90 per cent were common in almost every Cleveland village. Visits to dole offices entailed long walks, and the intrusion and complexity of the means test, through which a barely sufficient social security was apportioned, were considered cruel and unfair. There was a feeling that the National Government, a coalition formed mainly of Conservatives and opposed by a Labour Party who appeared to have no visible alternative plan, had aban-doned such villages to their fate. National newspapers printed grave unemployment statistics for some of the larger northern towns, and a few years later George Orwell would visit Yorkshire and Lancashire to chart, in The Road to Wigan Pier, the bleak conditions experienced by the unemployed. But the hopelessness and desperation of the Cleveland villagers, the vicious cycles of joblessness, poverty, shop closure, and near-starvation, went mainly unchronicled.

Enter the Pennymans.

Just outside Middlesbrough stands an eighteenth-century manor house, Ormesby Hall, which Major James Pennyman and his wife, Ruth, had inherited, along with most of the surrounding land and a highly developed social conscience. The Pennymans determined to find alternative sources of employment and food for the families of out-of-work miners. Major Pennyman leased various portions of local land and turned them into a smallholding on which miners could grow fruit and vegetables. What they didn't eat they could sell. Meanwhile Ruth, who had startlingly left-leaning politics and a love for community projects, be they amateur theatricals or land cultivation, formed various needlework clubs for the miners' wives. And so the Cleveland Unemployed Miners' Association was born.

Enter Rolf Gardiner.

It was through Gardiner, met in Germany a few years before, that David Ayerst came to hear of the scheme. Gardiner, who since his studies at Cambridge had become a disciple of D.H. Lawrence, was the leader of various youth groups set up to further his numerous passions, which ranged from forestry to organic farming, from Morris- and sword-dancing to mysticism and folk music. A man of means, he had been associated with German Youth Movements, and many of his interests lay too close for comfort to Nazi *völkisch* ideals, of which he was often an outspoken supporter. It did not take long for the seemingly innocent doctrines of the organisations he venerated, known as the *Wandervögel* – "wandering birds" – to shift emphasis into an ideology of nationalism and racial purity. Gardiner had brought a number of German students on a musical tour of Cleveland in 1931, and had seen in the workers on the Pennymans' smallholdings an irresistible example of a rural community returning to live, rigorous and healthy, off the land. Into the scheme he could add his own beloved activities (hiking, games, music, dance) and create an outdoor community akin to the movements in Germany that he so admired.

The Pennymans suggested that David Ayerst might join Rolf Gardiner in forming a work camp, the first of a planned series. A number of university students, some local but most from Germany and Scandinavia, was recruited by Gardiner to join the miners, and an ambitious schedule was drawn up: a five-hour dig in the morning, followed by an afternoon of social activity to be shared with the locals. Ayerst readily agreed, seeing an opportunity to enrich life for locals and visitors alike. He was spurred on by the captivating Ruth Pennyman, who was determined to add a cultural and spirit-raising dimension to her husband's drier and more bureaucratic plans. The first Cleveland work camp was held in April 1932, and, despite small attendance and initial difficulty in getting the miners to socialise with the student influx, was thought a success. A second camp was planned for September of the same year. It was much needed, for although the country was slowly lifting itself from the depression, the mines were dead for ever, and employment was gravely required for men who were otherwise waiting around in the forlorn hope that their former jobs would return. The first camp's musical activities had been led by Gardiner and a friend of his, neither of whom could attend the second camp (both were getting married).* A substitute musical director was needed.

Enter Michael Tippett.

Ayerst can't have taken long to alight on his young composer friend, who was a lover of outdoor exercise and in political sympathy with the scheme. Michael also had first-hand experience of German schools, which had given him a small taste of the ambience that Gardiner was trying to recreate in Cleveland. And, lest Michael not agree, Ayerst had the ideal bait.

Enter Wilfred Franks.

Three years younger than Michael, and almost a foot shorter, Wilfred was the middle child of a working-class and very musical family of twelve from the East End. He had left school at fourteen, rebellious, curious, and determined to be an artist. After scraping a living running errands at an art studio in London, he joined a hiking and woodwork movement called the Kindred of the Kibbo Kift, a pacifist group of strange mystical ceremonies. Through the Kibbo Kift he met fellow member Rolf Gardiner and followed him to Gore Farm, in Dorset. He became a strange sort of mascot for Gardiner and his pursuits, but soon resented the patronage. Eventually Gardiner arranged for him to enrol as an art student at the renowned Bauhaus school in Germany. Here Wilfred met

---

* Rolf Gardiner's younger son, born in 1943, is the conductor John Eliot Gardiner.

and learned from Paul Klee and Wassily Kandinsky, and became a talented artist in his own right. But natural restlessness, and his dismay at the growing popularity of the Nazis, led him to give up his studies. He wandered across Europe, selling his paintings and sculptures to pay his way, before finally ending up back in England, resolutely Marxist, avowedly atheist, more or less penniless, and unsure what to do next. He heard that Gardiner had started a camp in Cleveland, hitch-hiked there on the back of a lorry, and talked his way in by pretending to be a university student.[2]

The camp ended on 18 April 1932, and the very next day David Ayerst brought several students, Wilfred among them, back to his family home in Prestwich, where Michael was shortly to visit. David took Wilfred with him to meet Michael's train at London Road Station (now Manchester Piccadilly). It was evening. The days were getting longer. "When Michael saw Wilf on the platform," David remembered, "he was visibly stirred and disturbed. Before a word was spoken Wilf had moved to the vacant centre of Michael's life and filled it."[3]

What was it that Michael saw? Wilfred's beauty was Mercurial; he was a shape-shifter. David Ayerst remembered him as "short, black-haired, with large piercing brown eyes". One journalist later discovered a man whose "cloudy blue eyes [. . .] are piercing and intense, and although he is tiny, he seems to fill the whole room". Wilfred's grandson is adamant: "his eyes were green!"[4] So were his clothes, for he had continued to dress in the green uniform of the Kibbo Kift, designed as an environmental protest against Oswald Mosley's black-shirted supporters. As the steam cleared on the platform he swam into view clad in green shirt and green shorts. Michael was entranced.

Rolf Gardiner wrote reports of Wilfred's Cockney twang, his "semi-illiterate" letters, and habit of greeting strangers with the line "I don't know who you be."[5] In fact, although Wilfred lost over the years what had originally been a Cockney accent, his few surviving letters are misspelled but otherwise fluent and grammatical. Rolf Gardiner and Michael were tempted to romanticise Wilfred's class, and this use of him – as a totem onto whom his admirers' own concerns could be painted – was one of which Michael later professed himself guilty. His passion for Wilfred was intense and hot-blooded: "the deepest, most shattering experience of falling in love".[6] Like many who are almost defensively independent, Wilfred often needed looking after even as he disdained offers of help, a quality Michael appears always to have found attractive. There would be no question of his not going up to Cleveland later in the year.

Michael spent a happy time with David and Wilfred in Prestwich, where he also met Wilfred's sister, and doppelgänger, Evelyn Franks. Evelyn took an instant shine to Michael, and as his friendship with Wilfred developed, she watched from the sidelines, eventually, as Michael thought, "hoping that I would marry her".[7] But Michael had eyes only for her brother. A few days later, he, Wilfred, and David made their way east to Derbyshire. A twenty-year-old political activist called Benny Rothman, secretary of a subsidiary group from the Young Communist League, had organised a mass trespass of a moorland plateau in the Peak District, known as Kinder Scout, in order to highlight the fact that walkers in England and Wales were denied access to areas of open country. To Michael, a devoted and experienced walker, the belief that open country should be free to all, rather than privately owned by the wealthy for the pastime of shooting, was indicative of a larger class struggle in which he was fast becoming embroiled. The trespass, which rode a wave of publicity, wasn't a country stroll but a political protest. On the afternoon of 24 April 1932 Michael, Wilfred, and David joined a huge number of impassioned ramblers (the highest estimate was 800), who set off in good weather from the village of Hayfield in the direction of Kinder Scout, singing party anthems and watched by flocks of policemen. David reported what happened next in the *Manchester Guardian*:

As soon as we came to the top of the first steep bit we met the keepers. There followed a very brief parley, after which a fight started – nobody quite knew how. It was not an even struggle. There were only eight keepers, while from first to last forty or more ramblers took part in the scuffle. The keepers had sticks, while the ramblers fought mostly with their hands, though two keepers were disarmed and their sticks turned against them. Other ramblers took belts off and used them, while one spectator at least was hit by a stone.[8]

The spectator was Michael, whose face was cut by an errant flying missile. Despite the violence, the Mass Trespass of Kinder Scout went down in history as a success. It is still commemorated today as an act of civil disobedience responsible, at least in part, for a number of eventually implemented walkers' rights. For Michael, trudging along somewhere in the crowd, it was his first experience of mass protest and political violence, his first experience at close hand of the working-class solidarity that he was beginning to find so attractive, as he tried to sand away the privileged surface of his upbringing. In this he was typical of the artistic left wing, and through his politics he was rejecting middle-class life: "I can't take bourgeois standards seriously," he wrote. "I think because they are self-righteous, built on a slavery; economically and morally."[9] But it would take the experiences promised to Michael in the Cleveland work camps really to light the political fire.

Back in London, R.O. Morris had completed the extended and rigorous preamble of fugal instruction in Michael's lessons, and the shift from "theory" to "composition" arrived at precisely the same time, almost to the week, of meeting and falling for Wilfred, of the invitations north, and of the Kinder Scout protest.[10] To cast Wilfred as wandering muse, breaking Michael's nearly two-year compositional silence, may be too fanciful, but politics, love, and music were chronologically plaited. Michael began a string trio in B flat, which instantly shows that the demanding groundwork of his lessons had paid off. In combination with the remnants of an imitative Romanticism are the first signs of a rhythmic suppleness and invention that, made all the more individual in subsequent pieces, would be the hallmarks of a Tippettian style. Gradually Morris, who appears to have done much to slow Michael down as a composer, suggested a progression to larger canvases. At the end of July 1932 the lessons with Morris stopped, and he arranged for Michael instruction in orchestration with the composer Gordon Jacob. Jacob was renowned at the Royal College for his skill in instrumental balance and scoring; his own music was resolutely melodic, even conservative, and Michael thought he was learning little from these new lessons. He left unfinished a project to orchestrate the string trio into a symphony, but this second bout of training had made him, in his own words, "not a master, but someone who knew what mastery was".[11]

Michael had continued teaching at Hazelwood some way into the year – he is in the 1932 school photograph – but at some stage and for reasons ill defined, he left. Newly calibrated as a composer, newly alive politically, with the promise of the work camps to attend and of Wilfred to court, he may have felt the need to wipe clean his professional slate and to abandon the smart fee-paying school. He created a disciplined daily routine, settling down to composition after a brisk morning walk. A local couple provided one main meal, but otherwise he seems to have survived on coffee, porridge, and marmalade. It was several months before he set up for himself even a small number of paid jobs and he descended into a state approaching penury, which his unpaid work in Cleveland would do nothing to alleviate. He was reliant less on his parents, and more on dodging train fares and hoping for support from better-heeled friends such as the Maudes. (His political convictions, speeding leftwards, he somehow reconciled with such friendships, even though the Maudes were a fine example of the Establishment bourgeoisie.) It was a domestic life that by today's standards was almost startlingly basic. But he didn't much mind. There was always music.

There was also Wilfred, who had returned to London in the interim between the two 1932 camps, and was living with his family in a house to which Michael soon tracked him down. Wilfred overcame his initial suspicions, was soon a frequent visitor to Whitegates Cottage, and the two became intimate friends. "At bedtime", Michael remembered, "I showed him the spare bedroom, but he wanted to share mine with me. Pyjamas he would not tolerate, and we slept naked together many nights – chastely, to the amazement of David – until the inevitable happened."[12] By "the inevitable", Michael presumably meant that he and Wilfred had sex, or variations thereto, breaking in the process what he called his "four-year continence" since the split from Roy Langford. In old age Wilfred insisted that he and Michael "never had any kind of sexual relationship".[13] But Michael's correspondence leaves no room for doubt, portraying the affair as one of reciprocated passion, as in 1934: "I am by no means always the first to get an erection when we are together."[14] Michael was willing to take on a more passive role sexually, with which his ostensibly heterosexual partners could more comfortably fall in. "In sex", as he admitted, "there is always the very profound and apparently basic feminine reaction, that comes up from within. It does not disturb me to know myself tender towards a man's virility."[15]

But despite an evident mutual affection, Michael's physical infatuation with Wilfred was not reciprocated to the same degree. Soon Wilfred's initially laissez-faire sexuality gave way to protestations that same-sex relations couldn't possibly exist, although their affair remained intermittently physical. The consequent to-ing and fro-ing made for painful complications, with Michael exuding almost oppressive affection and persuasion, flicking uncomfortably between near-parental responsibility and seductive entreaty. Wilfred, for his part, was vividly aware of his own attraction and consequent sexual power, teasing Michael with protestations that beds must be shared but responding sexually with a wounding indifference that was followed by active recrimination. His post-coital refrain was "I only do this for your sake."[16] Michael attempted to tolerate what soon proved to be Wilfred's literal flightiness with something approaching good humour. He had a pronounced though hardly unique tendency to exist in a love affair as under intense enchantment, in which he was then held to the exclusion of all else. And complicating matters yet further was another relationship, of longer standing but equal intensity, that came to its long-promised fruition that summer of 1932.

Enter Francesca Allinson.

She was the woman to whom Michael was closest in his whole

life. Her real name was Enid, but everyone knew her as Francesca, "Fresca" for short. She was born, on 20 August 1902, into a remarkable family. Her German-Jewish mother, Anna Pulvermacher, was a portrait painter; her father, Thomas Allinson, a doctor who had treated Mahatma Gandhi, and whose then-unusual, now-proven methods led to his being struck off.* Francesca was fearsomely intellectual, very well read, very musical. David Ayerst found her "always captivating, whether she was being still and quiet or overflowing in liveliness. [. . .] She was indeed racy in speech, warm in affection, no beauty but a lovely person."[17] By contrast another friend found she had a "strange beauty [that] wasn't particularly photogenic".[18] With this in mind, the few surviving photographs of Francesca can build only the most tentative portrait. Physically she was petite and delicate; her attractiveness was a matter of expression as well as of features, her gaze intense, vividly alive even in monochrome stillness, her hair strikingly thick and wayward.

Francesca Allinson

---

* Thomas Allinson's mill in Bethnal Green, bought to prove his conviction that wholemeal bread was healthier than white, led not only to the family's wealth but to the Allinson loaves still stocked in supermarkets.

Photos do not show the physical attribute that Michael instantly noticed on their first meeting: she had an enlarged thyroid gland that resulted in a swelling, known as a "goitre", on her neck, just in front of the windpipe. Her voice, never recorded, may have developed the hoarse quality that can afflict sufferers. After schooling in London and some private tuition, she studied at London University where among her fellows was Michael's cousin Phyllis Kemp, who soon lodged at Francesca's family home, 22 Christchurch Avenue. Michael had paid a visit to the large red-brick house in Kilburn. He went downstairs to the kitchen. And there she was. "Something happened between us."[19] What, precisely, he didn't say. But there again is that flash of compulsive attraction coming upon him like a charm.

Thyroid trouble seems to have aborted Francesca's London degree; on recovering, she went up to Oxford to begin her studies afresh, reading English at Lady Margaret Hall, and this delayed the relationship with Michael coming to any kind of fruition, though it had been on her introduction that he had made his visit to the Kinderheim in Markdorf. Now, in the summer of 1932, Francesca, though privately wealthy, was making music her profession, editing scores and conducting the Tottenham branch of the London Labour Choral Union. In preparation for his role at the Cleveland work camp, Michael found himself needing to go to Germany. He was to take over as music director from the capable hands of Georg Götsch, one of the most prominent figures in the German Youth Movement and director of a music school in Frankfurt an der Oder. Rolf Gardiner insisted that Michael, in order to fill Götsch's large and popular shoes, should travel to the Frankfurt school for training. Wilfred Franks, surely the first choice of companion, was unavailable. Michael invited Francesca, who may have funded the trip. Neither was the sort to think an unmarried couple travelling alone through Europe verged on impropriety, and the only difficulty they encountered before they set off was cousin Phyllis, who had recently returned to England, her passion for Michael undimmed despite the unpleasant escapades in Serbia four years before. Wild with jealousy at his evident liking for Francesca, she saw in the

German holiday any number of opportunities for the relationship to be consummated. She swore Michael to celibacy – a promise he would find himself unwillingly having to keep.

Georg Götsch's music school in Frankfurt was a state-funded institution for the training of music teachers. The town was just a little way east from Berlin, where on 31 July, during the very weeks of Michael's and Francesca's visit, a hurried federal election saw the Nazis become the largest party in parliament. Francesca's fluent German helped Michael through the classes, which centred on Baroque choral music, although he found himself unsympathetic to the school's rather restrictive methods. At the end of the course, she and Michael decided to extend the holiday and go to Prague. They went south by train through a Europe that was still Versailles-carved, travelling down through Lower Silesia to reach the Karkonosze mountain range, in what was then Germany and is now Poland. Across the mountains they decided to walk, Francesca bravely trying to keep up with Michael's pace on an expedition half romantic, half primitive. They threw themselves on the mercy of mountain farmers, and slept together in barns like any married couple. Finally they crossed over into Czechoslovakia. On 19 August, Michael sent Evelyn Maude a postcard from the village of Vrchlabí: "We've come down from the hills and are running short of money. At any rate we shall be back on Friday in London [. . .]. We're making a last final burst."[20] For that final week, they went on by train to Prague and then Dresden, cities on the brink of unknowable destruction. Michael returned to England on 26 August to prepare for the Cleveland camp, while Francesca decided to stay on with German relatives.

It was perhaps on this holiday that they discovered their sexual incompatibility. Michael later confided that, when trying to make love to Francesca, "I just couldn't get an erection."[21] Later he wondered "why in certain cases when a man is tender to me I can respond and have satisfaction which seems impossible from and to a woman".[22] Francesca in her turn perceived a feminine side to Michael's sexuality that she found off-putting. The relationship was left to settle onto a non-physical plain and their love soon became, as Michael thought, "serene and passionless".[23] The word "serene" is studded repeatedly through his various memories of Francesca, as forty years later: "It was a serene relationship. Now, whether that was because in a way the elementary biological sexual thing was not present in that form made it possible, I don't know. I mean, I wasn't able to be biologically her lover. I don't know [if she wanted that]. I think so, yes."[24] Whether either was distressed as to their having no physical bond is hard to say, but their apparently unpossessive love for one another ran on a deep groove, and withstood the intense affairs that each pursued over the next decades. The situation, however, threatened to kill the possibility, just stirring in their minds, that they might have children together. At this stage there was apparently no notion of marriage, and Michael's passion for Wilfred loomed large. But bringing up a child together in domestic harmony, while attending independently to their own sexual needs, was one potentially desirable future.

On 4 September 1932 Michael took the five-hour train journey from King's Cross to Middlesbrough, and arrived at Ormesby Hall, where he stayed the night.[25] Here he met Ruth Pennyman, the cultural and political conscience behind her husband's land scheme. Although Michael and Wilfred were privately teasing when she professed herself "communist", thinking her nothing of the sort, they liked her very much. It wasn't long before she had taken her inevitable place in the line of mother figures to whom Michael could turn in a crisis.

The next day was the first of the camp, and he travelled from Ormesby to the town of Guisborough, where he joined Wilfred Franks and a group of miners, and walked the five miles to the campsites. Wilfred was cannily determined that the miners should not associate Michael with Rolf Gardiner and his contingent, and did much to smooth the passage of this smart-sounding stranger into the insular community. "Mike" (as Wilfred had christened Michael), "was a great person with everybody", and was soon trusted enough to become ambassadorial in uniting the various disparate groups of the community.[26] They arrived at a cluster of villages nestling on the edge of the North Yorkshire moors, just a few miles inland from the German Ocean, as the North Sea was then known. At the village of Margrove Park, which was no more than a square of tiny cottages arranged around a central patch of lawn, work had already begun on a nearby smallholding, and another field was being dug on a steep hillside along the mile's stretch of road that connects Margrove to the village of Boosbeck.

In 1932 Boosbeck was no more than a high street, with a small church, a pub, precious few shops, and a tiny station. Wilfred evocatively recalled the dilapidated cottages and the large families they housed. Frequent mining fatalities made orphans of a number of children, who were taken in by their neighbours to sleep, six on the mattress and the same again on the floor underneath the bed, in the tiny upstairs rooms. Meat was a once-weekly treat, Sunday lunches usually consisting of a lone pig's trotter, eked out by potatoes and resilience. The visitor to Boosbeck would be awoken every morning by the noise of possing, a traditional method of laundry using a stick and a tub. "It was like Voodoo," Wilfred thought: "On Monday morning they all vied with each other to be the first person to start possing, at six o'clock in the morning, and the first person to finish, of course, was the first person to start. The noise of these poss-tubs, 'vroom, vroom, vroom'. Every miner's cottage had a man or woman or child, possing hell-for-leather."[27]

Ruth Pennyman had offered Michael the use of Ormesby Hall as a domestic mainstay, but he was determined to live and rehearse among the miners. His later claim that he "joined in the digging of the land, living in a tent with the students" was strongly contradicted by Wilfred and by David, who both recalled Michael's finding a morning's digging a little too much like hard work.[28] Accordingly he devoted his energies exclusively to music rehearsals, and took a room in Boosbeck.

David Ayerst was only an intermittent visitor but witnessed with pleasure the way Michael exploded into the village. "Who would not fall", he wrote, "for this exuberantly friendly, untidy young man who wore a faded blue linen jacket, dressed in shorts, wore no socks and walked about in a pair of gym shoes with holes cut in the canvas to accommodate his big toes. He was like nothing else to be met with in Boosbeck [. . .], an irresistible Pied Piper wherever he might be."[29] Michael was an enticing and impassioned anachronism, and became quite the local celebrity. Those who remembered the rather rigid activities organised by Rolf Gardiner and Georg Götsch at the first work camp were in for a surprise. Michael threw the whole thing up in the air from the get-go, deciding that he would put on a production of John Gay's politically and socially resonant *The Beggar's Opera*, only slightly shortened, in the church hall. Determined to build some bridges between visitors and locals, he ruled that the cast was to be all-inclusive, made up of villagers, miners, and students. The whole thing was to be auditioned, learned, and performed within two weeks. Intrigue got the better of suspicion, and people flocked to audition for the lead roles: the highwayman Captain Macheath and the two girls Polly Peachum and Lucy Lockit whose affections he balances precariously; Polly's vengeful parents; and their faithful servant Filch. A local insurance agent landed the lead part of Macheath; Wilfred was to play Filch; and Michael had asked Francesca Allinson to join them in Boosbeck in time for performances and ready to play the part of Lucy.

A sixteen-year-old miner's daughter from the village, Marjorie Bradley, was encouraged to audition and suddenly found herself cast as the heroine, Polly. She remembered performing for Michael as one of the highlights of her youth, and marvelled at the activity that had suddenly descended on Boosbeck.

We learned it in three weeks [actually two] and had to go every day to people's houses to learn our singing parts, as we couldn't get into the church hall. Tippett was very quiet and gentle and had a great big scab on his knee where he'd been digging up on that rough land and he'd fallen on a rock. I'll never forget that for the time he wore his wavy hair quite long, just like you would expect of someone artistic. He was very engrossed in what he was doing, his music and that. I liked him very much. He wasn't one for airs and graces, he always seemed like one of us. I think he was a perfectionist because I remember making a mistake once and he nearly gave up on me. But it was really wonderful and we all enjoyed doing it. It was something different for us, something for us to do. One of the brightest spots in my teenage years.[30]

Ruth Pennyman provided most of the costumes, an injection of vivid colour into the monochrome villages. Marjorie Bradley remembered in detail the "apple-green crinoline and muslin cap" that she wore to play Polly, as "it was unusual to see such beautiful clothes". Michael rigged up a curtain in the church hall to create a makeshift orchestra pit. Ruth managed to cobble together the players, while Wilfred constructed the set. Francesca arrived too late for rehearsals but with her part dutifully learned, and the villagers immediately assumed that she and Michael were married. Marjorie Bradley noticed their physical closeness, and thought this "very nice lady, tall and slim" was clearly Michael's wife "because he was always with her".

The two performances of The Beggar's Opera, which came in the penultimate week of September, were a triumph. The production's success was proof not only of what Michael had achieved with a fortnight's rehearsal but of the sudden outlet of creative joy and entertainment that had arisen in the stricken community. The tickets were cheap, the hall was small, the seats were few, the audience large. It was the only time in Michael's whole career that police had to stop latecomers from overcrowding a performance. Wilfred remembered the show as a "a rip-roaring success", sure that "everybody loved it". Michael agreed: "It was a wonderful thing, taught me a hell of a lot. It was most extraordinary. Electric."[31]

When reports got back to the original founders of the work camps, Rolf Gardiner and Georg Götsch, they were less than happy, thinking the opera a frivolity that had moved too far from the scheme's original aims. Michael and David, though they were cautiously admiring of Götsch, had become suspicious of Gardiner and the increasingly disturbing implications of his principles. Quite quickly they distanced themselves from him and a rift opened up. Gardiner told Ruth Pennyman that the second camp had been all over the place: "The liberalist elements (Ayerst, Tippett etc) would not accept the imaginative discipline essential to the success of such a camp. [. . .] Far more important one psychologically successful night-choral than ten dozen productions of the *Beggars Opera*! The details, the form, a sort of reverence in approach [. . .] these are EVERYTHING."[32] Michael usually paid the things about which he was most serious the compliment of gleeful irreverence, and the two approaches were at loggerheads. David admitted that it was thought "the enemy had got hold of the machine", and that he and Michael came to regard Gardiner "as a rather bogus person".[33] But Michael was not yet finished with Boosbeck.

Whatever the complications in the emotional triangle of his life with Wilfred and Francesca, arrangements with the latter were evidently comfortable enough for him to go on holiday with the former. The pair left the work camp towards the end of September, flush with their success, to take a walking holiday across the Pennines and into the Lake District, just as the leaves were beginning to turn. Neither was very practical and the trip, during which they shared a small tent, furnished Michael with plenty of anecdotes about discomfort and disaster, featuring both flood and fire (the moral of the story was not to dry damp clothes on a gas holder). Instead of returning to Surrey, Wilfred decided to go back to Boosbeck where, supported by Ruth Pennyman, he spent the next year developing the camp's carpentry activities into a small furniture shop. And Michael returned to Oxted alone.

For all the joy of the music-making, Michael's time at Boosbeck was, in David Ayerst's description, "the first time really when he came in contact with working-class life in a disaster area".[34] This contact was a catalyst. Michael retained a vivid memory from the hiking holiday: "Sitting on the kerbside, we lunched on bread, cheese and apples. The apple cores we threw away were immediately seized by some small children nearby: these poor mites had sores on their faces and were obviously half-starved; coming from the well-fed South, I found it mortifying. The sight of these under-privileged, malnourished northern children haunted me for years afterwards."[35]

NINE

To Rob the Rich, to Feed the Poor

On 30 January 1933 *The Times*'s correspondent in Berlin wrote:

> President von Hindenburg received Herr Adolf Hitler, leader of
> the National Socialist German Workers' Party (Nazis) this morn-
> ing, and appointed him Chancellor of the Reich.[1]

Finally Michael had a paying job back at Oxted, a happy result of
his time at Boosbeck, where he had met a friend of Rolf Gardiner's
called Allan Collingridge, an influential activist in providing aid to
the unemployment crisis. Two months after *The Beggar's Opera* was
performed, Collingridge helped to found the London Council for
Voluntary Occupation during Unemployment, an organisation that
quickly set up an orchestra of unemployed players. Professional
musicians had suffered not only from the general blight of low
funding and joblessness, but from the dawn of the talkies. Gone
were the days when Michael could sit in the movie theatre and
watch the silent reels of *The Four Horsemen of the Apocalypse* accompanied by cinema musicians. In 1927 Al Jolson had ushered in the era
of sound film with *The Jazz Singer*, and players soon found themselves
replaced by built-in loudspeakers and pre-recorded soundtracks.
They flocked to the South London Orchestra, as it was christened,
and were in need of a conductor. Michael's fee was set at just under

£2 an hour, and weekly rehearsals began late in 1932. These were held at Morley College, an adult education college in Lambeth, south London, which soon became an important professional base for Michael. Wilfred Franks's father, Daniel, a talented violinist, played in the orchestra and helped with its administration.

Michael now had a well-honed and remarkable ability to communicate clearly and infectiously to the excited players under his wing. In later life his baton technique was hampered by poor eyesight, and became erratic and hard to follow, but as a younger man he was accounted by his concertmaster "a genuinely fine conductor".[2] He infiltrated popular repertoire with the odd contemporary piece of startling ambition – not least Stravinsky's Violin Concerto – and led the orchestra through years of success, the set-up continuing throughout the 1930s, and long after employment prospects had improved. Distinguished soloists were persuaded to perform, and news of the orchestra's achievements travelled quickly. Concerts were programmed thick and fast, not only at Morley College but at local schools and churches, the takings distributed equally among the players.

This new conducting job would need to be combined with others to keep Michael's head even slightly above water, and accordingly he applied to the Royal Arsenal Co-operative Society, based in Woolwich. Unusually for such enterprises, the RACS was directly affiliated to the Labour Party, and alongside housing developments and shops it ran an education branch that sponsored cricket clubs, reading rooms, orchestras, a Rolf-Gardiner-esque "woodcraft folk" – and two choirs, in Abbey Wood and in New Malden that, late in 1932, Michael was asked to conduct.[3] His professional life consequently became expensively peripatetic, as he criss-crossed south London.

Michael's first concert with the South London Orchestra was held at Morley College on 5 March 1933, a few weeks before he was due to join David, Wilfred, and Francesca on a camping holiday in Spain. They had formed a tight unit at Boosbeck the year before, and a strange quartet they made, lashed together by their passions and beliefs. It is a brave woman who decides to ferry camping gear across

Spain with three men, two of whom are in the throes of a somewhat tempestuous relationship, and it is unsurprising that at the last
minute Francesca pulled out. She had recently gone to Switzerland
for a long-overdue thyroidectomy, which her father had forbidden
during his lifetime. On 24 March she left for New York, for – in
Michael's words – "one of what she called her 'rutting seasons',
with a married man, I guess".[4] The three men were left to go on to
Spain without her. Michael went up to Manchester to fetch David's
recently acquired Morris Minor. Driving tests were introduced just
the next year, but in spring 1933 Michael was able to drive himself
and Wilfred down to Dover for the ferry after the most cursory of
lessons and the purchase of a five-shilling licence. David, delayed by
work, made his own way by train, in the process escaping the car's
maiden voyage with Michael at the wheel – a wise decision, as the
combination of risk-taking, bad eyesight, and a taste for speed made
Michael an exceptionally poor driver. The subsequent holiday, once
the ferry had taken them and the car over to Boulogne and they
began their trip down through France, was one of near-misses.

David Ayerst may already have felt a spare part, accompanying
Michael and Wilfred, but anyone with a taste for well-organised
travel would have found Michael the most exasperating of travel
companions, forever spending what little money he had on frippery
and leaving nothing for necessities; abandoning the car in a fit of
pique and going off alone for the nearest train station; getting in
trouble with the police for skinny-dipping; drinking unclean water
from wells and making himself ill. But the holiday, spent during
the warm but not sweltering Spanish spring, was a happy one, lived
from the car and a single tent, punctuated by mountain climbs and
sea-swimming. Ayerst took a photograph of Michael and Wilfred
somewhere in the Pyrenees, and thought they looked "for all the
world like Don Quixote and Sancho Panza".[5] What is most striking
about the picture is that while the car, swamped with camping
clobber, is an impossibly bygone remnant of a former age, the two
men themselves, their hair falling forward in unstyled floppiness,
their clothes chosen for coolness rather than fashion, look as unspe-
cific to their time as the mountains undulating behind them.

Wilfred Franks (left) and Michael Tippett in Spain, 1933

A reminder of the times came when they drove along the south-east coast of France and reached the Spanish border. The guards were asleep in the middle of the road and roused themselves enough to inspect the car's papers, which had been issued by the Royal Spanish Automobile Club. Two years previously the Spanish King had been overthrown and the Second Spanish Republic declared. Visitors or vehicles with "Royal" imprimatur were not welcome. Michael lost his temper and insisted on dumping all their luggage in the middle of the road before reluctantly following the guards' instruction that he and David should retrace their steps and hand over a great deal of cash to one of their "friends" in order to obtain a "valid" document. They laughed afterwards about the merry dance on which they had been led, especially given that they returned to find Wilfred happily drinking and smoking with the guards. But the republic they had entered with such difficulty was already seriously threatened by fascism: in just over six months the Spanish elections were won conclusively by parties of the far right, and the country buckled under violence and instability in the years that led to the Spanish Civil War.

When Michael got home, there was a telegram from Francesca.

"If I have children with a man will you accept marriage and fake fatherhood?"[6] Agonised conversations with his friends followed about whether this serious proposition would work. Eventually he responded, his letter now lost, but its contents were remembered by David Ayerst's brother-in-law, Bryan Fisher: "[Michael] wrote a long letter back saying that he would rather talk such a complicated matter over with her face to face but, if she wanted an answer now, he would have to say no – and he gave his reasons: he must be free legally to live his life and he could not father a child without being legally and emotionally responsible for it and the home where it lived."[7]

If he and Francesca were to have a child, Michael was determined to be the biological father. Setting up a family life would mean finding a way of withstanding the complications of Wilfred, and of Francesca's own relationships. She had money enough to ensure that Michael's slender means would not be a problem, but parenthood would distract from composition, or vice versa, and his priorities remained almost ruthlessly unwavering. For two liberal-minded people, the world, on the cusp of a war against fascism, may have felt a dangerous place into which children ought not to be brought. But their desire for children became so intense that on Francesca's return to England the conversations became serious. Michael, though rarely childish, was often childlike: physically boisterous, gleefully mischievous, facing life with a round-eyed joy that was half naive, half worldly-wise. He loved the company of children, and was adept at working with them, marshalling them, coaxing from them skilled performances of music that he refused to simplify, firmly insisting they step up to the mark. Neither he nor Francesca had had especially happy childhoods. Francesca's relationship with her father had been as difficult and damaging as Michael's with his mother. To create, as a parent, the domestic and loving security never known to them as children could have been one way of healing the wound.

A sexual relationship with Francesca was evidently still impossible, and they discussed having children through artificial insemination. Assisted conception was a relatively new procedure in the early

1930s. Such a course, undertaken soon after Francesca's goitre operation, may have required travel, would certainly have involved expense, and risked failure. In addition, hyperthyroidism can cause any number of complications to a pregnancy. They never went through with it. Their discussions appear only to have brought them closer together, but here is the first inkling not only of physical frailty in Francesca, but of the mental distress which would come to plague her over the following years, against which motherhood and a secure domestic life could have been a possible defence. To Bryan Fisher, Francesca already had "an air of fragility above a surface of robustness [. . .] longing for help and refuge in a turbulent world, both internal and external".[8] And in Michael too arose the first signs of the severe mental crisis that was shortly to hit him, as he realised the emotional costs of his sexual nature and his chosen profession, both lived out in a society that wouldn't countenance legalising homosexual adoption until seven years after his death. "I grew out of saying I wanted children," he later claimed, but in private it was a different story.[9] The "basic feminine reaction" that he had recognised in himself manifested itself in an impossible desire: namely to experience the physical sensation of childbirth. His publisher Sally Groves, asked whether she was aware that Michael wanted children, remembered:

Yes. Yes. Yes. We once got quite drunk together and he talked in tears about his longing to have a baby. Physically to have a baby. As I remember it to give birth to one, but also [to have a baby with a woman]. "I would so desperately like to have had a child." He was crying. He was lovely with children. He just treated them as they were, whatever age, and he didn't try and make things simple for them. They had to catch up, and children just adored him because he was this wonderful, charismatic, magical figure, full of laughter and joy.[10]

}

In 1933 Michael heard from W.H. Auden, who had written a play, *The Dance of Death*, in which music had an important role (there was to be an on-stage jazz band). Auden had yet to meet his soon-to-be collaborator Benjamin Britten, and was eager that Michael compose a score for the play. Michael later stated categorically that he had heard no suggestion of composing music for *The Dance of Death*, but his friend Douglas Newton later contradicted him with certainty: "[Apparently] Auden didn't offer Tippett *The Dance of Death* to set. Well, he did, because he sent Tippett a typescript of it which M later gave to me, and which I still have, with a note in it I made at the time about the circumstances. There."[11] The official reason given for Michael's lack of involvement was an unenthusiastic response from Rupert Doone, who with his partner Robert Medley was to direct *The Dance of Death* early the next year, for their recently formed Group Theatre company. As Medley remembered, "Rupert went off to listen to Michael Tippett's music, and said yes, it was very good, but the music is too important, it's too serious to stand, you know, and that he wanted something lighter. And so went to Herbert Murrill, and he wrote a very easy, very successful score."[12]

With Auden so keen, and with Michael in no position to turn down such a high-profile commission, it is strange that neither fought harder to secure this intended collaboration. Imagine for a moment that they had, and any number of alternative histories present themselves. An Auden–Tippett *Dance of Death* goes ahead in 1934 and is a success, followed by further collaborations in film and theatre . . . Michael adds his name to the Group Theatre's distinguished roster of collaborators, becomes close to its playwrights (Yeats and Eliot, Isherwood and Spender) and its set designers (Henry Moore, John Piper, Duncan Grant), settles comfortably into the left-wing milieu of the artistic scene in London . . . Auden meets Britten in 1935 but, distracted by any number of projects with Michael, the friendship doesn't develop . . . in 1939 Auden moves with Christopher Isherwood to America and invites Michael to join him for the war . . . Michael refuses . . . or Michael accepts. Or an Auden–Tippett *Dance of Death* goes ahead and doesn't quite come off, Michael producing a strange and not entirely convincing

series of jazz pastiches . . . Auden complicates the process with
dictatorial demands followed by an unsuccessful attempt to seduce
the handsome composer . . . the possibility of further collaboration
is made competitive and tricky by, three years later, the arrival in
Auden's life of Benjamin Britten . . . the whole situation ends in
reproachful difficulty . . .

Such things were not to be. Perhaps Michael foresaw them, and
already he may have begun to form the conviction that he was
not a composer to be hidebound by the demands of a headstrong
literary collaborator or of a play-script. He may have had doubts,
keen as he was on jazz, as to whether he were capable of the job.
Auden and his circle knew Rolf Gardiner, from whom Michael
wished to distance himself. And Michael's attention was already
taken up by a large-scale project. Orchestration lessons with Gordon
Jacob seem to have reached a natural stop halfway through 1933,
but having an orchestra of professional players at his disposal gave
Michael new impetus for his own composition. He returned to his
orchestrated string trio, to see what could be salvaged. He decided
that most of the central movement could be kept, and over the
year worked on new outer movements, to form his Symphony in B
flat (eventually withdrawn in favour of an official first symphony,
composed a decade later). He finished the score on 16 November,
and regarded it as his "Opus 1", an open rejection of some twenty
works that had gone before.

The Symphony in B flat was premiered, by his South London
Orchestra, on 4 March 1934. Evelyn Maude travelled to Morley for
the concert. "I like [the symphony] very much," she wrote to her
eldest daughter: "It's not terribly modern, not mad in any way and
really beautiful at times. [. . .] I do hope he will manage to get it
done again somewhere, if possible by a better orchestra. [. . .] At
the beginning of the symphony someone remarked 'oh, Michael
will get on all right if he doesn't get his legs tied into knots'. Which
was rather a just criticism of his conducting."[13]

The reviews were likewise happy with the half-hour piece: "a
remarkably capable piece of writing"; "a significant addition to
contemporary music". Scott Goddard of the *Sunday Times* afterwards

remembered the concert as "the first appearance of a big talent".[14] Michael had turned neither to a British inheritance (from Elgar or Vaughan Williams), nor to a European example (of Schoenberg or Stravinsky), settling instead for a well-upholstered neo-romantic idiom that he eventually considered too derivative of Sibelius. The Finnish composer had influenced every prominent British symphonist of the day, and Michael's effort followed hard on the heels of Arnold Bax's fifth, which was dedicated to Sibelius, while anticipating the first of William Walton, Edmund Rubbra, and Ernest Moeran. Of these Michael was eventually disparaging, and only Walton would stand the test of fashion.

Soon after the premiere of the Symphony in B flat, Michael professed its first movement "badly written", and the symphony's style "too new to me to be quite free of the scores I have looked at". But he was "prepared to stick by it", and sent it for various try-outs to the BBC who, true to form, thought a studio run-through (on 21 June) exposed it as imitative and feeble.[15] The symphony nevertheless received at least six further performances over the next two years, more in fact than the official Symphony No. 1 managed in the same period after its premiere a decade later. In 1940 Michael still considered the symphony one of the "early scores that matter" and had it locked in a vault lest it not survive the Blitz.[16] The war, forcing a hiatus in publication, would give him the peculiar privilege, unknown to most composers, of shaping his back catalogue in hindsight, and he withdrew the symphony, placing a legal restriction on its performance, as if refusing to show his working, to make public the stepping-stones on the journey to originality. His own reputation had by that time risen as firmly as Sibelius's had temporarily sunk, and finally to publish a neo-romantic symphony in the midst of the post-war avant-garde could have been greeted as a retrograde step. It was no mean feat to have written a well-received and full-length orchestral work before he was thirty, but he had plenty left to say that could not be said adequately within the limits of his talent, his musical articulacy not yet able to suit his intellectual needs.

Among the symphony's admirers was the composer Alan Bush,

with whom Michael spent much of his time in discussion.[17] Alumnus of conservatoires in London and Berlin, Bush was a committed Stalinist and conductor of the London Labour Choral Union, in which post he had met Francesca Allinson, who had made the introduction. Wilfred Franks turned out to have grown up as a near neighbour and good friend of Bush, in whom, underneath an often uncompromising and even forbiddingly stern exterior, there lurked kindness and warmth. Bush's communism was rigid and lifelong, and his political infamy often obscured his musical craftsmanship. He and Michael would soon diverge, with some violence, both politically and artistically, but Michael's imminent arrival at a new and inventive compositional voice was a clear offshoot of their friendship. As he acknowledged, since Bush "was five years my senior he was of necessity a much more mature composer. I learnt so much from him."[18]

It was to Alan Bush that Michael turned when life with Wilfred Franks became more difficult. By 1934 Wilfred had returned to London, and was in and out of Whitegates Cottage with a frequency that left Michael reeling. In June Michael admitted to Ruth Pennyman that Wilfred had "been much depressed and especially over a whole cart-load of unemployed play-acting rubbish which consisted in a group of Bloomsbury-ites and down-and-outs living emotionally on Wilf and financially through him and the rest of us". The details of the trouble are lost, but the fallout from "the 'gang' that were playing havoc with him" was intense, and Michael admitted that they had had "a bad row (trying my hardest not to let him see how much I thought his London lot were worthless!) and then a stay here [at Oxted] eating and sleeping more normally and living decently – but [it] does seem to me a hopeless way of going on".[19]

Michael had nearly bankrupted himself, not only by habitually paying for Wilfred when they were together, but by self-funding the performances of his symphony. He disliked the way Wilfred lived almost entirely on the charity of friends, and wanted to establish a fund in order to give him the dignity of, and the means to pursue, a career as an artist. David Ayerst agreed, and pledged

£10 a year. Michael hoped to get this up to an annual £50 (over £3,000 today), guaranteeing Wilfred a weekly pound. He assured Alan Bush:

> There is to be absolutely no moral obligation behind it. It is to be given out of straightforward love for him, for his own unwarranted self, and to work out his own destiny as best it seems to him. [. . .] I with a tiny amount of savings I no longer care to keep, will give him a lump sum down, up to £50 if I can, to set himself up with. Will you join us in this – £10 a year? You see, Alan, I can't take £10 p.a. as a more serious item than tobacco or any luxury, and goodness knows Wilf is a pardonable enough luxury to those of us who really care about him, and I think inside yourself you do, as I do. [. . .] Now, if you don't want to, curse me and say "no" bluntly – and anyhow it's all in confidence – but I'm too much in sympathy with you to be afraid of your wrath and so I've just written badly and boldly.[20]

To Ruth Pennyman, whom he also asked to fund the scheme, Michael admitted that he sounded "like a mama looking after her child's future – and it strikes myself as laughable – but really I have no hold on him beyond a fairly intimate friendship, which I am now determined if I can to use for stability and work of some sort – not philanthropic but because he's fundamentally unhappy".[21] Alan Bush, who had private means, agreed with the idea, and put forward a considerable lump sum of £30. Rolf Gardiner professed himself offended by Wilfred's departure from the Bauhaus and refused to participate. Ruth Pennyman also thought it best not to patronise Wilfred (in all senses). Michael replied to her:

> I appreciate what you say about the scheme, but I can't do anything else than we are doing, because it is not meant to be a moral scheme at all – quite the reverse. [. . .] I don't see any harm from people like Rolf and yourself telling Wilf how you think of him – I feel it does a bit to counteract my obvious inability to judge him. Wilf is quite unreservedly to me an equal

and so the whole question of tramp or child doesn't apply – I think fundamentally I'm prepared to give to any tramp. To one that I like I have no moral hesitation, because I am a very very bad moralist. The charge that I am furthering "tramp and child" behaviour by this I don't think holds. If he wants to waste his life let him do it as a man of leisure – a *rentier* – not as a beggar, who has to seek shelter over my doorstep. Quite immoral I'm sure – but then I am a product of the leisured class and live in the thick of it – (but alas my argument is quite inconsequent and unsound!)[22]

To be calmly certain of doing something "quite immoral", of having an argument "inconsequent and unsound" . . . Michael states the defects in his views as if he were helpless to prevent them, aware but unconcerned that love had sent his reasoning off course. His attempt to help Wilfred was born of so genuine an empathy that he avoided the charge of self-congratulation in this public display of generosity. Money would offer Wilfred independence, away from the shared life Michael partly desired, and in this lay the scheme's true selflessness.

He and Wilfred became further intertwined by Michael's embarking on another passion project for Boosbeck, which he appears not to have visited since *The Beggar's Opera* two years before.[23] He and David Ayerst were no longer involved in the work camps after the row with Rolf Gardiner, and decided to branch out on their own. Determined still to help the mining communities in any way they could and to replicate the success of *The Beggar's Opera*, they had begun to collaborate on a theatre piece that could be performed by the locals. Together they alighted on a story that would be well known by the villagers: Robin Hood, the legendary heroic outlaw who with his highwaymen robs from the rich to give to the poor. The "opera", Michael's first full-scale work for the stage, was really to be more of a play with music. Ayerst went away and by October had written a script that was to be punctuated with various arrangements of folk-songs. For these he and Michael asked Ruth Pennyman to write new lyrics, and the three spent almost a

year working with care and seriousness on numerous drafts and
rewrites. As if to make time for his new priorities, Michael formally
resigned from the Oxted ensembles he had conducted for almost a
decade, and reluctantly combined his orchestral rehearsals at Morley
College with teaching a clutch of harmony classes: "awful grind –
but I'm in debt".[24]

Oddly, given its aims and intentions, Robin Hood started out as a
tragedy: "you will see", Michael wrote to Ruth, "that the scenario
gets serious in the last act – and is quite tragic – so that the whole
thing will have to be kept as much as possible away from musical
comedy so that the transition to a serious setting of Robin's death
comes naturally".[25] But this plan was soon discarded in favour of
a comic and romantic piece, foregrounding the character of Alan
a'Dale, who finally becomes free to marry his sweetheart after Robin
and his outlaws rescue her from an unwanted marriage to an evil old
knight. Ruth Pennyman proved an adept and lyrical librettist, creating
a proper character out of Alan a'Dale's beloved (whom she named
Marret), and writing some Audenesque verses for their love duet:

When cockle shells turn silver bells,
And mussels grow on every tree,
When ice and snow turn fire to burn,
Then will my heart be turned from thee.

When sun and moon come tumbling down,
And waters flow into the sky,
When lilies grow within the sea,
Then will my love grow old and die.

Where'er I go, where'er I stay,
Over the land and the water wide,
Thy love shall hold me on my way,
Death then will lay me by thy side.[26]

Michael and David were determined to fold in a political bent.
Although neither was (yet) a card-carrying communist, their Labour

ideals were moving further to the left, spurred on by continued exposure to Boosbeck poverty. Joseph Stalin, General Secretary of the USSR, had just embarked on his second "Five-Year" economic plan for the Soviet Union, the first having been publicised as a rapidly successful period of industrial and agricultural growth. So, like hidden vegetables in a child's mashed potato, David tucked into Act One a rousing chorus:

> Oh God who made the cottager,
> He made him strong and free;
> But the devil made the landlord
> To steal from you and me.
>
> So God he made us outlaws
> To beat the devil's man:
> To rob the rich, to feed the poor
> By Robin's ten-year plan.

Michael scored the opera for a five-strong band, and almost every number is an arrangement of a traditional folk-song (the few tunes he spun from wholly new cloth sound convincingly authentic). Inspired by Francesca, who was researching the origins of such music, he had begun to think seriously about folk-song not as the foundations of a "national" identity or as a means to catch in music some rural idyll, but as melodies that could be used for their own beauty and proven to stem from any number of locations beyond England. He was now well versed in opera and its dramatic needs, and he arrived easily at the practicality of writing the scene-change music, the entrances and exits and sound effects. The scattering of the songs through the two acts was done with careful structure and variety, and with an eye towards theatrical effect: at the height of the opera, when Marret is led to her unwanted marriage, he placed the medieval carol "*Angelus ad virginem*", which processing local trebles were pressed into performing after being phonetically taught the words.

One of the few entirely original pieces of music in *Robin Hood* was the overture. Performed by the skilled professionals who made up the band, it was the one chunk of music on which Michael could unleash his fast-coagulating invention. The rhythmic freedom and suppleness he had discovered in his string trio and the symphony suddenly burst into life when harnessed to the dramatic necessity of indicating forthcoming excitement. Garlands of notes are draped over the bar lines like lengthy swatches of vivid material, resulting in a kind of merry war between the music and the staves on which it is written: a beating pulse is vividly discernible at the overture's heart, with which the accented notes joyously refuse to coincide. It is half folk dance, half jitterbug.

After a few false starts, two performances of *Robin Hood* were scheduled for 8 August 1934, the venue to be the small Miners' Hall on the edge of the village.[27] Wilfred went up to Boosbeck in late June in order to start designing the set and costumes, and to begin casting and rehearsals. He had a tricky time of it, going through three Robins before they had a competent performer. Marjorie Bradley (star of *The Beggar's Opera*) was persuaded to be one of Marret's bridesmaids, Michael brought up some musical friends, Wilfred opted to play Friar Tuck, and somehow the thing came together. Wilfred wrote to a friend of Michael's arrival (in his only surviving letter from the time): "Michael is not too well & has gone to bed thats why he hasnt writen this."[28] It was a bad bout of influenza and Michael was taken in by the director of the miners' male-voice choir, Tommy Taylor. Taylor's daughter, another Marjorie, retained vivid memories of that summer.

My mother used to mother him; I do remember him coming down with 'flu and packing him off to bed for about a week. He stayed with us for about a fortnight and offered to pay for me to have piano lessons. My mother's proudest boast was that. Tippett was always so nice with me, and he always spoke to me, always drew me into things. I do remember his manservant Wilfred – I can remember his hairy legs, real hairy legs! And they wore sandals and no men we knew wore sandals in those days. They held a musical evening in our Institute Hall in Charltons:

I remember his shock of wavy dark hair flying as he conducted [the Labour Party anthem] "The Red Flag". [For *Robin Hood*] he once stayed up all night to compose one song as a late addition. Tippett and Wilfred went to the local butcher and got a carcass and strung it on [the set], made it very realistic. He wasn't a chap who conformed a lot, that was the impression, but he was held in a lot of respect in the village, I'm sure he was. My father used to be very very proud to talk of him.[29]

The performances of *Robin Hood*, all agreed, were not quite the success that *The Beggar's Opera* had been. Michael had called in favours and exploited contacts to collate a remarkably distinguished band. At the piano was James Robertson, then a Cambridge undergraduate, later musical director of Sadler's Wells Opera. The oboist was the esteemed player Sylvia Spencer, and the cellist was Jasper Rootham, who went on to become Neville Chamberlain's private secretary. Frida Knight, eventually an eminent author and political activist, played the violin, and thought they had "put on a quite respectable performance of *Robin Hood*: if it was not up to Covent Garden standards we blamed the village upright, with its many missing notes, and the Boosbeck stage, which creaked and rocked beneath the weight of the chorus; the main thing was that everyone enjoyed themselves".[30] Wilfred blamed the eventual Robin Hood, an actor friend of Ruth's whom the villagers took against, "and this is one of the main reasons, I think, why it didn't go down well".[31] Michael, in his turn, quietly blamed Wilfred, who had got into a row with the Pennymans: "we ended up rather in the shadows because Ruth and Jim were so 'off' Wilf it became rather difficult – 'Everything good was Michael, everything bad was Wilf' – which got tiresome to me in particular – so we two got rather isolated, Wilf was of course quite difficult, and Ruth and Jim returned into conventionalism".[32] Wilfred and Michael escaped, going off hiking together across Yorkshire and through the Lake District, and although Michael wrote to the friends he had made there for some years, that was the last time he saw Boosbeck until a nostalgic visit four decades later.

He was disdainful of Robin Hood both at the time of its composition, when he thought it was "deplorable", an "unfortunately
romantic hotch potch operetta", and much later, when he described
it as a "tricksy piece of nonsense" with portions that were "quite
absurd".[33] There were four revivals in London, the last in 1940, and
one in Leeds. David and Ruth even published the libretto, under the
entwined pseudonym of "David Pennyless", and Michael wrote to
Ruth that "it'll be Boosbeck's own show and in their possession for
ever an age".[34] Soon after the Boosbeck performance he asked David
to overhaul the dialogue, remove what he considered the more
saccharine side of Ruth's additions, and then attempt to get the
opera published. But eventually he refused the score's publication or
performance, most likely feeling that the opera presaged a time of
intense political involvement from which, in his successful old age,
he wished to distance himself. Wilfred Franks believed that, if the
Boosbeck experience opened a door for Michael, it wasn't musical
but political: "he realised that the working class were contactable,
talk-to-able, work-with-able, that was the pivot".[35] And from this
pivot Michael soon bounced into several years of left-wing activism, which would certainly throw his music, and arguably his life,
off-course.

After the songs of Robin Hood had died away, Michael returned
to Oxted in late August 1934 to work on a string quartet he had
begun before his trip north, while Wilfred spent most of his time
in London looking for employment of one sort or another. Michael
best described how things stood between them in two letters to
David Ayerst, writing in stops and starts of a relationship that played
out in alternate stripes of argument and aggression, before settling
onto a calmer plain, physical infatuation lessening to a degree that
made Wilfred's paler sexual enthusiasm more manageable. Almost
in the same contradictory breath, Michael speaks of "heartbreak"
and of being "happier than I've ever been":

Wilf has become a pivot point for me and it's got its touch of
heartbreak – but I think probably invention on my part – I don't
like his being away, because I torture myself with difficulties

and moralities about him – and get long moments when I feel
I'm hemming him in, like I did Christopher [Fry] – and yet he
himself is so manifestly fond of me beyond the common lot – far
worse of course, he has a habit of sharing beds, though not
sexual commerce, with almost anyone who wants him to [. . .]
don't think this is tragic – not a bit – I'm really happier than I've
ever been – and the holiday was the happiest I've ever had – the
"Wilf" mood is only in spasms.[36]

And then:

Slowly but surely also we come to grips with the extent and
methods of our friendship. I've been facing up to the inevitable
heartbreak side of it and for the moment have relinquished things
for a sort of compromise. [. . .] I shall be glad as the fervour of
physical desire dies away to something more placid – which it
is doing slowly. Wilf is a hell of a mixture of love and altruistic
friendship. Sexual expression has to be wilted away to its least
sensual because that's the only bridge between our difference
in intensity and it also leaves least aftermath – and gradually
even my impulsive release of emotion will tend to grow rarer.
But I do not think we should have got to where we are without
travelling this path, either for Wilf or for me – we are both of
us less "repressed" if you like – remembering that Wilf broke
a four-year continence of mine – consequently [we are] more
open and frank to one another and with a great deal of give and
take and mutual forbearance at the back of things by now.[37]

And so they went on.

The Boosbeck performances with which Michael was involved were
still happily talked about by the locals half a century later, as they
read about Sir Michael Tippett in the newspapers and watched him
on the television. Ruth Pennyman had professional photographs

taken of the cast, in which German and Scandinavian students had mingled with the villagers. To look at the grainy young faces is to be haunted by their unknown fates, by those shortly to disappear into the uncertain future of their countries – to die on the battlefield or in the death camp; to face their former castmates in the skies and at the front line; to be etched into the memorial that lists the twenty-five Boosbeck dead; or to survive the war, widowed, orphaned, unscathed. Marjorie Bradley is kneeling at the bottom right. For years afterwards she kept the photographs. But during the Second World War her mother destroyed them. There had been Germans involved, and that was that.

Robin Hood, Boosbeck, August 1934

DIARY:

Glasgow – North Yorkshire

In Glasgow, on 1 February 2018, twenty years and a month after Michael Tippett died, I find myself at a Tippett premiere – or a premiere of sorts. The Tippett Foundation has decided to let the conductor Martyn Brabbins and the BBC Scottish Symphony Orchestra exhume Michael's all-but-forgotten Symphony in B flat, over eighty years after it was last performed. Snow threatens but never quite appears; suddenly even Radio 4's *Six O'Clock News* are interested in this symphony that has been recalled to life.

Sitting in the City Halls as the orchestra begins to rehearse a piece I have heard only in my head or bashed out at the piano, I feel as if I have tasted real Tippett coffee after months of instant, as if monochrome has bloomed into technicolour. Hard to know what to do: burst into tears, yell for joy, or sit quietly. I aim for the last, and settle for the first. There is a slow introduction, kicked off by a solo clarinet, seemingly a refugee from Sibelius's first symphony, alone and eerie and pregnant with mystery ... then the symphony oozes into D-flat major, golden with harp. It would be shameless, were it not beautiful. Martyn Brabbins takes the orchestra through the three movements without a break: the first craggy and shadowy, developing two contrasting subjects, one vigorous, one graceful. The central movement is woven from two melodies, reminiscent of folk-tunes, that Michael has let roam where they will, while despatching a chromatic clarinet to send the whole thing harmonically haywire – to what purpose, on this first hearing, I can't discern. The final movement tugs the symphony into a sunlit world, not without its oddities: at the climax, amid cymbal-clash and passionate strings, a trumpet seems to have wandered in from another piece entirely.

Much of the music has a strange inertia, and often seems all treatment and no material; but much of it is beautiful, and underneath its surface, like water lilies under a frozen lake, are hints at the invention that was to come.

It would be hard to call the symphony a lost masterpiece, but it is neither juvenilia nor agitprop, and is struck through with hopefulness, and a well-earned joy. And it occurs to me how often it is remarked that Michael's music, even his compositions from great old age, remained youthful – when, conversely, we had never heard the music he wrote in his youth. On the manuscript score, in Michael's own hand, is a quotation from Hölderlin's poem "Vulcan": "And there's always at least one friendly spirit who gladly blesses him, and even when the fierce, uneducated spirit-powers are angry, love still loves." It's a tribute to the symphony's dedicatee, Michael's beloved Evelyn Maude, but is also a reminder that he composed the piece in the first throes of his love for Wilfred Franks, and with the feeling that he and those with whom he was politically in sympathy were going to rebuild the world. If the piece shares anything with his later work, it is less in its technique than in its spirit, its capacity to respond to a darkling world by leading the listener through struggle and flight into the realm of exultation.

Whether *Robin Hood* is an opera worth reviving is a question that also raises its head, buoyed on by the success of the symphony. Two years earlier, I visit Boosbeck and the surrounding area; it is the winter of 2016, just a few months after the Brexit referendum. Middlesbrough has recently been found to have the worst unemployment rates in the country, and the newspapers already speak of Europe's political shift to the far right.

It's a short drive from Middlesbrough Station to Ormesby Hall, which is now put to sleep for the winter and free of visitors. A gardener nods knowingly at the mention of Tippett. It will have seemed the lap of luxury to Michael: inside is a riot of plush and plasterwork, jib-doors opening onto yet more rooms, each furnished by Ruth with a writing desk so that guests could attend to their correspondence in comfort. Some areas look as if the Pennymans have just popped out for groceries, others are strangely haunted and forlorn. In the hall stands a grand piano Michael will have known, and by it the visitors' book, where he marked his night here on 4 September 1932.

Michael went on to Boosbeck the next morning, and so, the next day, do I, travelling first to Margrove Park, where a caravan site has taken over what used to be one of the four patches of land leased for cultivation by the miners. A short drive along the road is what became known as Heartbreak Hill, the second site, now host to a small coop of chickens and strewn with sheep. Then comes Boosbeck itself, a high street with a few tributaries, the houses that spread beyond newly built since the 1930s. It is eerily quiet and deserted, its post office and two pubs shut for the day, the houses small and shabby, at their centre a large Methodist hall. The Miner pub, where Michael and Wilfred would gather with the villagers to sing songs in the evenings, is long gone. The English Defence League recently organised a protest in Boosbeck, and the place has an air of being worn down by years of continued unemployment. Standing on the cold high street gives me the clearest sense yet that Michael's trips were no picturesque holidays to the north, but periods lived for many weeks amid severe poverty in a remote community. I find what used to be the Miners' Hall, site of *Robin Hood*, right on the edge of the village, along the road that leads to Heartbreak Hill. Now converted into houses, it's strikingly small for such an ambitious production. And so I go on, to further work sites at Busky Fields, where in the distance the cliffs give way to a blue slice of the North Sea and a clump of tall smoking chimneys.

In 2009, seventy-five years after *Robin Hood* was first staged, a group of Cleveland residents came together in Boosbeck to sing some of its songs. BBC Radio made a documentary about the project – *Reviving Robin* – which I play on the car stereo. The weather puts on a spectacular display, and the sunset hems the clouds with pink during the drive through the North York Moors, quite the wintry wasteland, with great billowing waves of black where the heather has been scorched away to encourage new growth. When Michael was here, in the height of summer with the heather coming into bloom, the moors would have been turning into a spongy mass of sunny purple. The hillsides, now crowded with golden larch trees, were much less picturesque in his time, with the remnants of recently closed iron mines likely still smoking. Here and there I can still see more densely clumped trees that have grown over spoil heaps from the abandoned mines. As the evening is inked over, the songs of *Robin Hood* peal out from the car stereo just as I pass through these vistas, moving from bleak to uplifting with a shift of the cloud, that became familiar to Michael for a few years in the early 1930s. And it feels newly remarkable that a small opera staged just twice in a tiny hall in a remote mining town in the north-east of England should still be talked about, even eighty years later, should still seem so joyfully to sum up a spirit of resilience and community in the face of unimaginable change and hopelessness.

The music in *Robin Hood* was thrown like a handful of sparks into the darkest of times. It seems to have seared itself on the local consciousness. Stowed in the Teesside Archives is a taped interview, made in 1990, with Marjorie Taylor, whose piano-playing Michael had so much admired when staying with her family during rehearsals. Does she, the interviewer asks, remember any of the music from *Robin Hood*? In response, she goes to the piano and accompanies herself in the opening chorus, sung to the tune of the "Helston Furry Dance":

> Robin Hood and Little John, they both have gone to the fair, O,
> And we will to the merry greenwood to see what they do there, O.
> And for to live with them to chase the buck and doe;
> With hal-an-tow jolly rumble, O, to chase the buck and doe.
> And we were up at the break of day to fetch the summer home.

It was sixty years later. She was word-perfect.

PART THREE

SONGS OF LIBERTY
1934–1939

TEN

Machine Gun

Hitler had been anointed the supreme leader of the German people after the Night of the Long Knives. France shakily withstood an attempted coup by the far right. Spain wobbled on the brink of war and in England an increasingly anti-Semitic membership of the British Union of Fascists became ever more sympathetic to the Nazis. Michael and many of his friends would have been persecuted under fascist rule. Francesca Allinson was Jewish by descent; David Ayerst had published against the evils of Nazism; many of their circle were bisexual. How to fight authoritarianism was one of the major predicaments of the time.

In May 1934, while preparing *Robin Hood*, Michael had written to the composer Alan Bush, "I am growing more revolutionary now again − my revolutionary cousin [. . .] is living with me, because she is out of a job for the moment and is teaching me a great deal of 'technique' on the subject."[1] Michael's "again" is intriguing, for any revolutionary activity in his life prior to 1934 appears to have been of the mildest kind, his politics expressing themselves in a support of the Labour Party and in his work, political only to a degree, in Boosbeck. But these revolutionary sparks became a steady fire as he approached his thirtieth birthday. The fire was fanned by his cousin Phyllis Kemp and by Bush, both passionate Marxists. Through Bush, Michael served as the adjudicator of a London Labour Choral Union contest, and found himself disdaining as irreparably capitalist the Renaissance music he had previously venerated. Later in the year he chaired a "concert demonstration" of workers' songs, and when giving a plenary speech about the class struggle became so overwhelmed that he had to leave the platform.[2] On a less porous character the influence of Bush or of Phyllis may not have been so marked. But Michael was not an empty vessel waiting happily to be filled with the views of others. He was an independent spirit who would soon forge his own, diverging, political path. October 1934 was a decisive month in Michael's life, and can be seen as the high-water mark in the slow build of his revolutionary fervour. The last pieces were fitted into his political jigsaw.

All through that year Alan Bush had been working on the score for a musical drama called *The Pageant of Labour*, intended to celebrate the history of trades unions and the British Labour Movement, in music, short plays, and dance. Bush was to conduct the massed ranks of various Labour choirs and orchestras, and asked Michael to loan players from the South London Orchestra and to take over as conductor for two performances. Pageants had been all the rage since the beginning of the century, of a scale and community involvement paralleled today only by the opening ceremonies of Olympic Games. *The Pageant of Labour* was a colossal affair of six acts and nearly forty scenes, and the writer (Matthew Anderson) and director (Edward Genn) were well practised in using the form to focus on the plight of the working classes during a depression. Their scenario followed several generations of a working family, from eighteenth-century slavery to the First World War, via appearances from William Wilberforce, Adam Smith, the Tolpuddle Martyrs, and Mosley's blackshirts. There were ballets of deprived child workers, scenes of riot and violence, and a closing chorus of Bush's "Pageant Song". Bush thought it all "so wildly seditious that I doubt whether it will be allowed by the police", but it was, and a week's run was scheduled for 15–20 October 1934, each performance featuring nearly 2,000 actors, singers, and dancers.[3] The *Pageant* was to be mounted under a majestic ceiling of glass: five stages were erected in the central transept of the Crystal Palace at Sydenham, just two years before it was destroyed by fire.

So adept at conducting large ensembles had Michael become, especially those mounted for a greater political good, that it is hard to imagine him nervous. But when, on 16 and 18 October, he led the crowds of performers of all ages through Bush's music, his waving arms the focal point of a 9,000-seater auditorium, the sheer scale of the enterprise must have been daunting. For his efforts he was paid the princely sum of £2 18s. 6d. He will have seen mainly empty seats. The show was a critical hit, and spurred both Alan Bush and Michael on to further large-scale dramatic projects. But the expected crowds did not flock to Sydenham, and Oswald Mosley's rallies at Olympia earlier in the year had been far better attended. Financially the whole thing was a disaster, and years of legal wrangling followed as the accounts were sorted out. What Michael remembered afterwards were the chaotic rehearsals and the "ice-cold Crystal Palace", all the while praising this contribution to his "necessary education in the needs of a modern composer".[4]

On the very day that he took over Bush's baton for the *Pageant*, 16 October 1934, a newspaper article was published that would shape the course of Michael's life. A canon at St Paul's Cathedral named Hugh "Dick" Sheppard, who had spent the First World War sat beside dying soldiers in a French military hospital, wrote a letter to a number of publications. *The Times* rejected it, but many papers took it, and in one of them Michael read the following:

Sir. – The main reason for this letter, primarily addressed to men, is the fresh urgency of the present international situation and the almost universally acknowledged lunacy of the manner in which nations are pursuing peace. The situation is far graver than we allow ourselves to acknowledge [. . .]. Would those of my sex who so far have been silent, but are now of this mind, send a postcard to me within the next fortnight addressed to East Lodge, Ashley Park, Walton-on-Thames, to say if they are willing to be called together in the near future to vote in support of a resolution as uncompromising as the following: "We renounce war and never again directly or indirectly will we support or sanction another"?[5]

Tens of thousands of postcards arrived on Sheppard's doorstep within weeks, and the stream continued. Among them was one signed "Michael Tippett". Whether Michael attended the resulting demonstration at the Albert Hall the following year is unknown, but Sheppard's words cemented a philosophy Michael had held since childhood. Here was his public propagation that, aghast at the horrors of violence and conflict, he would renounce war.

A matter of days after *The Pageant of Labour* and the publication of Sheppard's letter, Michael attended a performance of his own work. This was not a piece of music but a play that he had written at some point that year called *War Ramp*, spurred on by his friend Jeffrey Mark, who had been a fellow student at the Royal College of Music and was now combining composition with the study of economics. The play propounded the idea of paying a National Dividend to all citizens, following the "social credit" theories of C.H. Douglas (which had led the Kindred of the Kibbo Kift, of which Wilfred Franks had been a member, to develop into the Green Shirt Movement for Social Credit). *War Ramp* was an angry protest against capitalist economic policy, and in its first act is the clearest statement of Michael's economic and political views in the mid-1930s: there was too much dominance by the banks amid an unsustainable cycle of generous credit, and unnecessary wars were funded by a "ramp" of bank loans that had to be repaid by a starving population. The play was influenced by scenes from *The Pageant of Labour* and by the techniques of Bertolt Brecht, with whom Alan Bush had been in close contact when training in Berlin. A Brechtian figure known as the "Announcer" arrives to introduce various masked personages ("Mr War Profiteer, Mr International Financier") and to announce the declaration of war. The government demands that all gold coinage be handed in to the banks, which are represented by a sinister unseen character called Pluto, heard counting his money beneath the stage floor. A band of war-wounded mud-stained soldiers then returns from the front to a future of unemployment and hyperinflation, only to find a collection of business and political profiteers negotiating and gloating over their spoils. The first soldier, who was played by Wilfred, proclaims:

this gun now that killed many a fine young German lad . . . what did we do that for when there was such damned devilry behind our backs . . . I can't see clear . . . Perhaps we haven't learnt our real enemy yet . . . what's that they did in Russia in 19-- (*begins to lift gun*).[6]

A policeman relieves the soldier of his weapon, allowing for the young soldier's final call to arms: "There's a job for me to do yet. I've got to get my gun back somehow." Michael often had to cadge two shillings from Alan Bush to cover the hire of a prop gun, and eventually Wilfred made one to save expense, as the play continued to be performed on and off all through 1935 and 1936, mainly in association with the Labour League of Youth.[7] Michael told Bush after the first performance that there were worries the play

might get us all into prohibition difficulties before we're properly under way [. . . in Oxted it] was extremely effective – that is it provoked real discussion on revolution and we were at it till eleven doing so – it actually woke Oxted up even if it shocked a good many pacifists. So don't despair – whatever the play does not do artistically it does get over ideologically and provokes the issue to a realistic discussion – I'm very delighted. [. . .] It's good revolutionary propaganda and I'm all for it anywhere.[8]

For this was where Michael's politics now explicitly stood, by October 1934. Rather than employing weapons to mow down innocent enemy soldiers, guns were better used to overthrow the capitalist system in a revolution. He had been casting around for a political allegiance that would fight not only the threat of fascist dictatorship but what he perceived as an out-of-control capitalism that had Britain in the grip of an exploitative social injustice. The Labour Party had won only a tiny number of seats in the National Government, and although its fortunes improved in the 1935 election, it had initially refused to forge an alliance with communist parties, and was suffering the aftershocks of a split (a breakaway group had formed the Independent Labour Party). An alternative was needed.

Phyllis Kemp had been an on-and-off lodger at Oxted, but, newly unemployed, she paid her rent in persuasive lectures on Marxism rather than hard cash. Both she and Alan Bush believed wholeheartedly in Stalin's interpretation of Marxism as exemplified in the Soviet Union. But once he was well versed in Marx, Michael's reading settled his fast-forming communism not on the side of Stalin but with the views of Leon Trotsky, who was then living in exile in France. For Michael, the news that slowly reached Britain of the true goings-on in the Soviet Union was incompatible with communism or workers' interests, and he recoiled in horror at Stalin's reign of terror and reversal of Lenin's reforms. (One potential attraction of Marxism was that the Soviet Communist Party had never criminalised homosexuality, which was outlawed by Stalin in 1933.) It was Trotsky's definition of Leninism that fired him, and for many Trotskyists of the time the Russian Revolution – the only communist revolution to date – was thought of as an unquestioned triumph, whose true direction had been shunted off-course by Stalin's tyranny. Michael and David Ayerst had hymned Stalin's agricultural policies in the libretto to *Robin Hood*, but the stark reality of such policies became evident in the Russian famine that killed millions. Soon Stalin's campaign of repression was to begin: the "Great Purge" of so-called "enemies of the working class", the gulags, the executions, the torture.

The clearest difference between a Stalinist and a Trotskyist ideology was in the efficacy of revolution. Stalinists such as Phyllis believed in a policy of "Socialism in One Country", whereby the Soviet Union would not incite revolution around the world, preferring to maintain its position of influence without rival socialist states in power, and to ensure good relations even with capitalist countries. Trotsky advocated perpetual revolution worldwide, and a refusal to co-operate with non-communist nations. In his Trotskyism, Michael was unusual. Trotsky was relatively unsupported, especially by the intellectuals of the British left wing, who were uneasy at criticism of the Soviet Union, with whom they believed the powers of the West could potentially join in order to fight Hitler. Antifascist alliances, even with right-wing democratic parties, were of paramount importance for Stalinists. For Trotskyists, fascism was a real danger, but one endemic in capitalism, and any and all mergers were dismissed as cowardly desertion. Michael's fast-forming view was that the overthrow of England's economic system should be prioritised above the overthrow of Hitler or Mussolini.

The natural path for Michael would have been to join not the Communist Party (which was Stalinist), but the Communist League, a group that had formed out of the original "Balham Group" of British Trotskyists. A member of the League named Albert Bilson spent much time at Morley College distributing propaganda, and sold Michael a copy of the League's paper, The Red Flag. One of the League's leaders, Reginald Groves, remembered that Michael then "came along to several of their meetings and took part in their discussions".[9] But by the time Michael was ready to become a member, the Communist League had dissolved, and instead of following one of the various branches into which it had splintered, he was persuaded by Phyllis that membership of the Communist Party was the best option. In November 1934 he and Phyllis travelled to London to be interviewed for membership of the Hampstead branch of the party. They were accompanied by two others, one of whom was Monica Felton, later an eminent town planner and activist. All were accepted, though Michael was the only one of the four to register in his own name (Phyllis gave the pseudonym "Mary Michaels").[10] He went to Camden to attend his first meeting, in early January 1935. Membership mainly consisted of a great number of missionary conversations with workers and, as he described, "doing the odd menial tasks of the party – canvassing house to house – I've lost all my shyness now – it's the harvest from the Wilf tuition".[11]

But, for Michael, joining the Communist Party was not an act of allegiance, either to the Soviets or to his cousin. Nor was it a method of making inroads into any left-wing literary set, and he wrote crossly of "the Bloomsbury arty lot who are unfortunately allowed membership".[12] (The poet Cecil Day-Lewis joined the party that year; Stephen Spender and Eric Hobsbawm the next, and almost all the poets in Auden's circle had left-wing political views of one persuasion or another.) A fair number of composers were card-carrying communists – Rutland Boughton, Bernard Stevens, and eventually Alan Bush chief among them – but Michael's Trotskyism set him apart. He was trying deliberately to infiltrate the party with his own more revolutionary brand of communism. He openly stated his conviction: "Russian foreign policy and native revolution are both necessary and possible in the present state of affairs."[13]

Suddenly to champion revolutionary violence was a strange move from someone who had so recently sent a postcard to Dick Sheppard renouncing war. But Michael's schoolboy pacifism was submerged entirely by his new-found allegiance. The postcards sent in response to Sheppard's article were used as the basis for "Sheppard's Peace Movement", which, in May 1936, would become the Peace Pledge Union. To this organisation and its beliefs Michael would eventually devote much of his life, but in the years of his Trotskyism, his own postcard to Sheppard notwithstanding, he remained dubious. He was fiercely opposed to any international capitalist-funded warfare, but was sure that absolute pacifism would obstruct the needful violence of revolution. "Can you not see, David," he wrote to Ayerst, "that pacifism alone is just a hypocrisy and as such can never have the moral force it thinks it has – it's simply false ethics."[14] On 4 March 1935 the government released a defence white paper that announced new expansions of Britain's Armed Forces. Many on the left opposed British rearmament, but Michael saw it as an opportunity to be welcomed, in that it could arm the working class for revolution: "I say and those like me, 'by all means prepare your white paper and when we get the guns so built, we will shoot you with them'."[15] Elsewhere he was even more explicit: "I am not a pacifist but a military enthusiast – for the war on capitalist ideology, frustrations, injustices, hypocrisies, etc etc – and war to the knife, to the death if need be – not by any means individual Terrorism, but conscious revolutionary action – one brings the house down in order to clear the ground for a 'better' one."[16]

In part this was just so much high talk (perhaps to rile his correspondents), and there is no evidence to link him even to the organisation of violent activity, let alone its carrying out. "The really skilful thing", he claimed, "will be to guide the revolution towards abolishment of an iniquitous system and to leave the people intact [. . .] a peaceful revolution? – yes – if we will sacrifice our class interests for it."[17] In calmer moments he admitted: "I am quite certain my views will never prevail in time." But he nevertheless swore that he was interested only in "warning the working-class, class-conscious element in time to organise themselves to use the beginning or end of the war to seize power". As he wrote to David:

> I don't care a damn almost what are the causes of this coming war – my energy is directed to "what can we get out of it" – the answer – the final collapse of a disgusting state of affairs, a fine civilisation grown overripe and decadent and crying out for the new syntheses – an appalling simplification – I know – it's dreadful – but then bombs and guns are simplifications of life! Grim ones – so are malnutrition deaths, and stagnation of all the lovely hopes and courage of the children [. . .] it doesn't follow that wars will cease after capitalism – but capitalist wars will and what is more, capitalism will have gone, with its gains and victories handed over to the economic-democratic community.[18]

To Alan Bush he offered the hand of friendship, sure that they should bury the political hatchet, so as to make "us all better revolutionaries, when we sink our differences behind the same machine-gun".[19]

ELEVEN

1935

JANUARY

On 2 January 1935 Michael Tippett turned thirty, a personality fixed and fluid. He had spent much of the winter conducting and introducing a series of children's concerts with the South London Orchestra. These were huge affairs held all over the capital, with nearly 1,000 schoolchildren at each one, whom Michael guided through a series of classics, always giving a tour of the orchestral instruments.[1] The easy, vivid way in which he communicated music to children was his best qualification for another job, one that would lead to a seminal meeting in his life, and it was all down to W.H. Auden.

The writer and mathematician Frank Morley, a director of the publishing house Faber and Faber, was on the lookout for a piano teacher for his second son, Hugh, known as Oliver. Oliver was profoundly and innately musical, with perfect pitch and a virtuosic skill at the piano. He was also severely autistic, and although he could be endearingly mischievous, had retreated into an almost silent social unease and inarticulacy. Frank Morley was casting around for a teacher who might bring Oliver out of his shell, and asked Auden, whom he published, for advice. Michael had yet to be superseded by Britten as Auden's go-to composer, and leaped at the chance to spend time with a musical child in a literary and well-connected household. Lessons began in early February at Pike's

Farm, the Morleys' large house in the little village of Crowhurst, a few miles inland from Hastings. Michael had on his hands a brilliantly talented six-year-old, as he told Alan Bush: "Oliver, my boy prodigy, is quite balmy – he spends all his time practising the Hammer-Klavier,* complaining that he can't stretch the ninths and tenths – but he reads the stuff much as you or I – having taught himself so to do [. . .]. As soon as he gets normal he ought to be taught properly."[2]

Michael was hugely affectionate towards Oliver, and Oliver towards him: "I had a lovely lesson with Michael Tipet last Friday," the boy wrote to his grandmother.[3] Michael coaxed both music and words out of him at the piano right up until 1939, when the Morleys emigrated to America. They did not return until after the war and contact wasn't renewed. So Michael may not have known that Oliver ended up first at the Juilliard School of Music in New York and then at the Royal College in London, eventually becoming a Fellow of the Royal College of Organists; nor that Oliver died suddenly in a residential home of the National Autistic Society, aged fifty-nine.

In order to vet the prospective teacher and to discuss terms, Frank Morley had paid a visit to Whitegates Cottage and brought with him his co-director at Faber, who waited outside. Michael could see "through the window, mooching about the minute grass frontage, the famous figure in the clerical hat".[4] And so T.S. Eliot mooched into Michael's life. This first exposure to Eliot was recalled by Michael at a time when his meetings with famous figures were two a penny, and his memories are somewhat matter of fact. But to have one of the literary world's great celebrities waiting outside the door of his cottage surely set Michael's pulse racing. His shelves contained well-thumbed copies of Eliot's verse and criticism. Now their author was standing just a few feet away. Eliot had returned from a lecturing spate in America and was fresh from the success of his dramatic work *The Rock*, a "pageant play" performed just a few

---

* Beethoven's impossibly virtuosic Piano Sonata No. 29 in B flat, op. 106.

months before Michael's own foray into pageantry at the Crystal Palace. When Eliot visited Oxted he was writing his verse-play on Thomas Becket's assassination, Murder in the Cathedral, and recovering from the breakdown of his first marriage. He had lodged in a house thirty steps away from Pike's Farm, and remained a frequent visitor, which was surely one of the reasons why Michael tried to spend as much time with the Morleys as he could. The artistic life in Oxted could be solitary, and Phyllis soon left Surrey for a job as a chemist's assistant in north London. Here was a family who welcomed Michael into the fold for a bit of ramshackle domesticity, and if this could be done in the company of a great poet, all to the good. Oliver was one of three (later four) Morley children, to whom Eliot was "Uncle Tom". It was a lighter, more domestic side of Eliot to which Michael was given privileged access. He remembered visits where Eliot

> divested himself of his poet's mantle and helped Morley's wife [Christina] in her domestic duties, both in the kitchen and in the garden (where once I found him studiously picking black currants). After supper in the evenings we all played monopoly. Eliot was, in fact, quite good at monopoly. The problem was always Oliver. If Oliver ever lost, it was simply calamitous. Eliot bore with it all, good-humouredly.[5]

Presumably Michael kept his political convictions quiet from Eliot as the poet trundled his boot or his thimble round the playing-board of the city in which much of The Waste Land takes place. Neither Michael's atheism nor his Trotskyism was an easy fit with Eliot's religion or politics. But Eliot, despite his previous career as a banker, was evidently too great a poet, too congenial a companion, too useful a contact wholly to be damned by Michael as machine-gunnably bourgeois. Michael was happy to run with the socialist hare while riding with conservative hounds. The two men saw each other intermittently at the Morleys' throughout the 1930s, but it would take some years for Michael to be in touch with Eliot on his own account.

MARCH

Michael may well have kept silent from the Morleys' conversation
the side of his musical life that saw him join with Alan Bush in
March 1935 to organise a demonstration of workers' music by the
Austrian composer Hanns Eisler. Eisler was a close collaborator of
Bertolt Brecht; their work had been banned by the Nazis and both
were living in exile. Eisler's political songs and ballads, written
for amateur groups and workers' choirs, had made him a role
model for Bush and other left-wing composers. The demonstration
was held at Morley College, and performed by various ensembles
from the London Labour Choral Union. In old age Michael pooh-
poohed Eisler, remembering that he "sang his songs and thumped
the piano, but left me unimpressed".[6] After the concert, however,
he wrote to Bush: "many congratulations about the Eisler – I did
not expect it to be so good or so worth it".[7] Later, when Eisler,
after a successful period in the United States, was blacklisted as a
communist and deported, Michael joined other British composers
in sending a protesting telegram to President Truman.[8]

Composition had begun to suffer badly in light of Michael's new
duties as a Communist Party member and the continued demands
of his conducting and teaching. But Hanns Eisler had posed one
answer to the thorny question as to how music might best respond
to the political views of its composer – or whether it should.
Eisler and Bush often followed the explicitly political path. "I think
music is there to serve the revolution," Bush would say to him,
and Michael would answer, "oh no, the revolution will serve the
music".[9] But he was in two minds, stuck between a rock and a hard
place, and he wrote to David Ayerst that he was "trying to wrestle
with 'bourgeois art' and the absurdities perpetrated as proletarian
music".[10] To align himself to almost any Western musical tradition
was to be bourgeois. To join Alan Bush in writing explicitly political music was to damage the art. The musical voice at which he
had begun to arrive in his Symphony in B flat was put on ice, as
his music began a wrestling match: artistic versus political merit,

attempting an uneasy truce. Of his compositions written during the mid-1930s, only a string quartet clung to its apolitical course.

MAY

In perfect illustration of how the worlds of political and Establishment music lay for him in uncomfortable combination, Michael would occasionally leave behind the stirring convictions of Eisler and Bush, and exist instead in a life of eccentric gentility. About half an hour's walk from his cottage lived the Harrison sisters: May (a violinist) and Beatrice (a cellist). Beatrice had gained notoriety for her live broadcasts on the BBC, sitting in her Oxted garden playing the cello in duet with the nightingales. She knew several distinguished musicians and Michael naturally became an occasional visitor, having tea not only with the sisters but with their menagerie: about fifteen dogs, any number of birds in cages, and two alligators (known as Jefferson and Virginia) in a tank on the dining-room table. The Harrisons had premiered works by Frederick Delius, whose music Michael had admired as a student, although it was hardly the sort of thing he went in for in these heady Marxist days. Delius had died the year before and, despite his wish to be buried in southern England, his widow's illness had necessitated a temporary burial near his home in northern France. The body was exhumed and brought, partly owing to the Harrison sisters, to the church at nearby Limpsfield, where it was controversially reburied under a necessary cover of darkness. The funeral was the next day, 26 May 1935, and there was Michael, sat in the parish church as Thomas Beecham conducted the London Philharmonic Orchestra in the work of the composer finally laid to rest, and walking among the congregation as they went to the graveside and heard Beecham's oration.

Nineteen thirty-four had brought the death not only of Delius but of Elgar and of Holst; the musical world found itself bereft of a senior triumvirate. Michael's presence at Delius's funeral is a remarkable moment in musical history, the younger composer seeing the baton of British music loosened from the newly interred hands of the older, but finding it yet out of reach. The ceremony is evidence too of how his life had divided into any number of contrasting worlds, the interlacing denoting both inconsistency and an all-embracing spirit. Much of his time was dedicated to canvassing and conducting, with chintzy interjections of tea in the Harrisons' fairy-tale world, or board games with T.S. Eliot. Folded into this rich mix was his relationship with Wilfred Franks, which stuttered unhealthily along, and then blew up.

Michael had become good friends with a man called Stanley Fisher, who had lived on David Ayerst's staircase when both were at Oxford. Stanley had started teaching at Little Missenden Abbey in Buckinghamshire, a small experimental school for mentally disturbed children; it was not uncommon for pupils to set fire to the buildings or to smash windows.[11] On his introduction Wilfred took a job as teacher at the school in late spring 1935. "The first six weeks of Wilf's job nearly brought me to ultimate despair," Michael wrote in anguish. "Ghoulish and very dreadful – Stanley is there mending the pieces."[12] What precisely was the trouble Michael's letters do not relate. Wilfred was suspended from teaching duties for a week, which he spent at Whitegates Cottage. At some point Michael then went to Missenden, which was disastrous for all concerned. A tumultuous friendship had quickly formed between Wilfred and the school's headmistress, Margaret Lister-Kaye, universally known as "Lissie", who had in some way poisoned Wilfred against homosexuality and made him determined to marry. Or so Michael thought: "if he could but make me and himself feel free of this 'must be married' dogma".[13] They had damaging rows all through the summer, and this was the start of Michael's internal crisis about his sexual nature, one he had previously greeted with concern but also with joy. Now the shadows of shame began to move inexorably in, seemingly cast by the school at Missenden and by Wilfred's time there. Michael wrote afterwards of the "endless Lissie complications", of the "Wilf–Lissie taboo", of his new but fast-developing worry at the "notion that arose from the Lissie business that the deepest and intensest love and fount of my life should be perversion". He had, he believed, been "put back a long way by the intensity and pain of that experience [at Missenden] and made less sure and happy about myself".[14] Wilfred would accuse him of being a "monster of double dealing", or speak in a combination of jealousy and anger of Michael's "clique of bum-boys".[15] At some point during one of the worst bouts of their rows, Wilfred returned one of Michael's letters with "To Mike, Bugger" written on the envelope – a public accusation of potentially catastrophic consequences. Michael's response was a startling lack of reproach. Towards the misdeeds of those he loved, forgiveness didn't apply. He had often regarded his own pain almost as a gift for Wilfred, a necessary, even needful product of the younger man's maturation. What did it matter "if my life does get buggered up a bit in consequence"?[16] Through all their turmoil, though he was doubtless more possessive than he realised, he tried to practise what he preached: "knowing as few the loveliness of a *grande passion*, I wish it [for Wilf] from my heart for whomever he may".[17]

Such a thing was not to occur for another few years. The Missenden school was soon closed down, and Wilfred had to cast about for another teaching job. He and Michael saw each other more frequently in consequence, and Wilfred would alternate bouts of their former intimacy with an insistence that permanent separation was the best way forward. The break, however, was never clean enough to result in anything other than Michael's emotional paralysis. He found refuge in frequent conversations with Evelyn Maude, who, he reported, "says that my 'shame' is much older than Missenden – it's simply the sensitiveness that I didn't have with Christopher [Fry], which has grown up with the awareness of the social life – that it springs really from the distress that the inside reality doesn't correspond to the outside social judgment".[18] In the 1920s, sexual experimentation had felt all part of the general mood; the 1930s attitude towards homosexuality was less tolerant. Michael wrote with deep concern at society's refusal to recognise his relationships: "a great deal of me emotionally is married to [Wilf] and has only an internal validity – as things are this internal grace can never be given outward form in present society – and

quite enough god-damn trouble that's caused us already [. . .]
the social bugger-lecher artificial partitioning of humanity."[19] He
had the outsider's acute combination of longing and contempt
for that indefinable and perhaps non-existent thing: the normal
life.

JUNE

Michael's autobiography is quite clear. The Spanish trip with David
and Wilfred in 1933 was "his last trip abroad until after the war".[20]
Whether evidence of the perils of ghost-writing, the hazy memory
of his old age, or a more purposeful decision to hide his political
activities, the statement is wrong. In the first week of June 1935
Michael accompanied Alan Bush to Strasbourg, where choirs from
the London Labour Choral Union and the Co-operative Society
were to participate in an International Workers' Music Olympiad,
of which Hanns Eisler was one of the judges. Here they competed
against choirs from all over Europe, although Russian competitors
were refused entry. Each entrant was required to state their opposition to fascism, to the exploitation of workers, and to war. The
English contingent, led by Michael and Alan Bush, achieved second
place. Over and above the competition, it was a chance for Michael
to see the workings of foreign Communist Parties and to visit a
region that, in the division of the spoils at Versailles, had been
returned to France. Two years before Michael's visit there had been
a strike in Strasbourg that had resulted in riots and a gun battle;
he was shown in triumph the evidence of the conflict. "To visit
Strasbourg", he wrote in a report of the competition,

> to stay with a working-class family, and talk to the men and
> women once German, now French, is to receive a lesson in
> international socialism which no books can teach. [. . .] I was
> taken round the town by two boys of eleven and sixteen. They
> were still at school: nevertheless, they gave me two or three
> hours of clear-cut teaching in international working-class history.

They showed me where the workers had torn up the cobbles to reply to the police rifle-shooting, a bridge where the workers had thrown cyclists into the river, bicycle and all, and a little narrow alley where the workers took their wounded comrades. They told me how the police tried to force an entrance to this alley, and how the workers, from first-floor windows, lifted up the police bodily and threw them out the other side.[21]

Such actions drew Michael's open support, and he found in the Olympiad an example in microcosm of a post-revolutionary society, free of class divisions, and dedicated to art. He returned with the sound of thousands of performers singing the "Internationale" ringing in his ears. "Alan", he remembered, "went off somewhere afterwards and I had to bring them all home, the whole choir, on trains – and of course being a rather maverick character I think we got a little bit excitable. It didn't quite turn into a football crowd going back, but it got near it!"[22]

JULY

On 12 July, he was back at the Royal College of Music. There was to be an open rehearsal with the London Symphony Orchestra under Malcolm Sargent's baton, and Michael called in a favour from his old conducting teacher. The rehearsal was organised as a showcase of rising talent, and to the list of works Sargent agreed to add the first movement of Michael's Symphony in B flat, though seemingly on the condition that Michael himself conduct. (Sargent was either generously allowing his former pupil a turn at conducting a leading orchestra, or grudgingly agreeing to include a work he wanted nothing to do with.) The movement from the symphony came off well in comparison to the other pieces and was reviewed as the star attraction, described by The Times as "the most significant" work in the programme. Although he found the climaxes unearned, and the themes a little undernourished, the reviewer thought the symphony showed "the crudeness of over-earnest youth, not of ineptitude".[23]

AUGUST

Michael let Whitegates Cottage for the first three weeks of August 1935, and spent much of the time working on his string quartet at Francesca Allinson's London flat. But he and David Ayerst, who had left journalism for teaching, spent the August bank holiday (then held on the first weekend of the month) in the village of High Hurstwood in Sussex, the home of Stanley Fisher's family. Here they met three more Fisher siblings. David was much struck by the youngest girl, Larema, and they were soon engaged to be married. A boy in his late teens called Bryan was openly entranced by Michael, and would soon follow him into various political movements and eventually into his bed, becoming an Oxted regular who adored spending weekends "with an extraordinary person, a genius where his music was concerned: [and] a wonderful man to know".[24] Finally there was Shelagh Fisher, the outgoing, heart-on-sleeve sister, not long returned from a job in Burma. And Michael liked her very much. He spent the rest of August travelling in the West Country with Stanley and, despite recent difficulties, with Wilfred. Then (the exact chronology is uncertain) Michael went to north-west Scotland with Bryan and Shelagh, driving from Fort William along to Arisaig for a camping holiday of lochs and mountains. His friendship with Shelagh strengthened quickly around the campfire as they batted at midges. They had much in common, and both were agonising over messy personal attachments, he with Wilfred, she with a lover in Burma whom she was to marry the following year.

Not long afterwards, ever itinerant, Michael followed David Ayerst to Devon. David was beginning his second year as history master at Blundell's School in Tiverton, where he had set up "The Friday Club", inviting distinguished friends to give lectures to the boys. Jim Pennyman and Rolf Gardiner came to speak on the miners' plight up in Teesside; Ayerst called in favours from his university poet-friends W.H. Auden and Cecil Day-Lewis, and now Michael was adding his own name to this distinguished roll-call, delivering a lecture on "The Artist and his Public".[25]

Ayerst introduced a delighted Michael to one of his sixth-form pupils, an eighteen-year-old called Nick Myant. After the lecture Michael wrote eagerly of what felt like a chance to break free from Wilfred. "Meeting new people and Nick especially made me see how much I wanted new life. [. . .] Blundell's is, as it were, a bit of the home that one is forced to find in bits when one is unmarried and temperamental. It's nice to know it's there."[26] Michael started an almost daily correspondence with Nick, admitting, "I have been strangely moved by him and frankly don't care to analyse it." He didn't take long to realise that the boy had fallen in love with him or was, at the least, in the throes of a devoted crush. The two of them shared much common ground: Nick was Francophone and well travelled (he had a Belgian father) and was loathing Blundell's as much as Michael had loathed Fettes.

Nick started to write more frequently, and then visited White-gates Cottage. To complicate matters, he was now competing for Michael's affections with a fellow pupil called Anthony Sedgwick, who was musically gifted and had composed a symphony for full orchestra. Michael enjoyed spending time with both boys, not entirely displeased by the way they fought between themselves for his attentions. But it was really Nick who most interested him, and Michael relished the opportunity to lend the boy a willing ear, and a bed for the night. Nick was, he thought, "laying bare his soul (and a very nice one)". He foresaw the potential dangers. "I don't really want to be his first emotional entanglement – I'm too old," he wrote, insisting he was staying "chaste and chastened" and would "consciously make no advances in behaviour and let him lead the dance entirely as it seems needful. [. . .] Evelyn has delivered me a short 'lecture' on not initiating adolescents into grown-up entanglements and subtleties of companionship before their time." But Evelyn Maude's warning didn't prevent Michael from falling in more deeply than he had planned, and he admitted his "direct, simple, love for Nick", a "nice, friendly warm love for him which he may accept or not as he will". The phrasing denotes affection more than passion, and Michael was keen that Nick wouldn't "take the 'wrong' place in my development, but the right-as-I-can place in his – i.e. he won't be a Wilf substitute, which he might have been".

The correspondence with Nick reached its soul-baring height; the relationship with Wilfred its soul-torturing peak. To David Ayerst, late in the year, Michael poured out his heart, recognising and trying to get to the bottom of the frequent shifts in his emotional and sexual needs, and reading with startling clarity the various unhappy stabs he had made at relationships. The abortive plans for married life with Francesca Allinson were still at the pained forefront of his mind:

> I have married crooks, cranks and strong men in an effort to establish the hero-worship, the child-parent relationship, the security and love – but it has always broken down fundamentally over that – not only is it unsatisfactory to the "parent", but being as I said extra abnormal I can't myself leave it at that – I must wean myself all the time – what I want underneath [. . .] is the full maturity of manhood and the marriage of equals [. . .] all the women relationships break down eventually while I cling to Evelyn who won't mother me more than I drive her to because she has the corresponding flash of the equality search – David, I don't see why one shouldn't marry one's mother and be happy – I can't be happy that way because the artist won't let me – it wouldn't even if I had done the Shelley trick and fucked women all along – there would always have been the same break downs. Now on the other side of things we buggers will persist in being ourselves the mothers, in some profound jealousy of child-bearing – it makes us good schoolmasters, but damned dangerous really – I know for myself that I am weaned to such a degree now that I really can be parent alone to the girls and boys of my junior class [with the Co-operative Choir] – they are nine to thirteen or so, mostly the sweetest wee girls – I can keep them to wean themselves and be secure and get independent and playing with one another – but as Evelyn says I am not out of the wood myself with the older boys (and girls?). I can so easily (you can't, mercifully) take a plunge and make the kiddy the old,

old hero. I have got to turn and turn about until it's really serene, without, I may say, running away. [. . .] See what idiotic distress of mind I have caused myself by trying to go a-whoring or marry against the inner light.[27]

NOVEMBER

On 14 November 1935, not long after Mussolini invaded Ethiopia, the reasons to fight harder for revolution increased. A general election in Britain resulted once again in a large majority for the Conservative Party in the National Government. The minority left-wing parties were splintering into groups mainly at war with each other. No general elections were held during the Second World War, and this 1935 house was to sit in Parliament for ten years. Two weeks after the election, Michael (fresh from a further performance of his Symphony in B flat, at London's North-Western Polytechnic) organised another concert demonstration, at Battersea Town Hall. One of the centrepieces was his play *War Ramp*. Wilfred Franks was once again lead actor, and responsible for sets and lighting. Bryan Fisher was in the audience:

The posters proclaimed "Workers Anti-War Concert Demonstration. Battersea Town Hall. Wednesday November 27th 1935. Novelties. Thrills. Plays. Ballets. Speech – Chorus. Choirs. Band. Over one hundred Performers. Come and learn the Battersea Anti-War Song. Propaganda – Entertainment. Comradeship. Admission Free. Collection for the South-West London Leagues of Youth. International Working-Class Solidarity means Peace. Concert Director Michael Tippett. Conductor Alan Bush." Over a hundred performers and all the stage hands; a disparate collection of individuals all united in a cause bigger than themselves, ardent, hopeful, talented artists moved by political fervour.

Fisher found himself hauled in to understudy one of the soldiers in *War Ramp*, and vividly remembered the end of the play: "Lights

out, actors line up behind the Concert Director, lights on. He makes
an appeal for the Leagues of Youth, ending with the point that
International Solidarity is the only defence against war, and then
calls upon everyone to sing the Internationale."[28]

Michael held two more similar demonstrations in venues
across London. That autumn, off the back of his success with his
Co-operative Junior Choir at New Malden, which invariably won
first prize in contests, he founded a "Federation Co-operative Operatic Society" that rehearsed in Abbey Wood. With its members he
conducted various light operas that drove him potty: *Iolanthe* by
Gilbert and Sullivan; *Dorothy* by Alfred Cellier. It may have been
through desperation that, the following year, he put on numerous
performances of his own *Robin Hood*. The venture angered Alan Bush,
in that many singers deserted the London Labour Choral Union,
preferring to have fun in Michael's operas. Michael felt wasted
in such jobs, but needed the money. After an abortive attempt
to form a communist cell in Oxted, his support for the Communist Party was waning. Wilfred Franks had been maddened by his
joining the party in the first place, thinking it a useless method
of furthering their mutual Trotskyism. Eventually, at some point
in 1935, Michael decided to leave, or may even have been kicked
out (his cousin Phyllis was temporarily expelled for her Trotskyist
connections).[29] He had made no headway in converting the branch
to Trotskyism, and had been sceptical from the start, never quite
giving off the courage of his convictions. Long and convoluted
arguments, remarkable in their fervour, are nevertheless undercut:
"treat this effusion as a 'flash in the pan'"; "the thing may wear
off". He described his membership as a method of channelling his
"bitterness about social injustice into even a ridiculous form".[30]
But it was precisely in leaving the party that he was soon able
to plough a more independent and dangerous political course. As
he wrote, leaving "does not mean we give up the revolutionary
idea".[31]

DECEMBER

At the end of September 1935 Michael had finished the string quartet on which he had been working for nearly eighteen months, heading the manuscript "Quartet no. 1 in A". Later, when the B-flat symphony was withdrawn, "Quartet no. 1" became the very first entry in Michael Tippett's official catalogue. The piece originally had four movements, running at roughly half an hour; but with the first two Michael was continually dissatisfied, and seven years later would replace them with a single allegro. So it is really with the opening notes of the two movements he left untouched that Michael's individual style begins. On a technical level, the recognisably Tippettian hallmarks are the sinuously lengthy melodic lines in the slow movement, and the quick-thinking rhythmical language of the finale, in which techniques visible under the surface of *Robin Hood* and the B-flat symphony suddenly break through. This rhythmic flair he described with the term "additive rhythm": out of the window goes a regular pulse, replaced by a flipbook of time signatures flashing by – two in a bar, five in a bar, three in a bar – while irregular groupings of notes ignore bar lines, are nudged out of kilter by rests, and are accented on the "wrong" beat. The musical achievement of such syncopation is that the apparent missteps make the music dance rather than limp. The music seems to move on springs, the rhythmical ground shifts beneath the listener's feet like quicksand, and the resulting energy is irresistible. The finale, a four-part fugue, gathers such momentum that when it stops suddenly it skids for a few bars, trying to slow itself down, before the musical brakes kick in.

Michael's new-found skill as a composer was assimilation, combining carefully selected musical ingredients not into a thick soup of leftovers but into an entirely original style. In his weaknesses lay his strength: he had not been able to study at Leipzig and had sniffed at hitching his wagon to the English tradition via lessons with Vaughan Williams; he had not gone to Vienna to study with Schoenberg, nor to Paris (as so many did) to learn from Nadia

Boulanger. Doggedly he ploughed his own musical furrow, creating, once again the autodidact, his own school, the Oxted school, weaned on Beethoven, and combining the techniques of Renaissance polyphony with those of contemporary jazz. His modernity lay in his dialogue with composers past: to revive and rework the structure and methods of Tudor madrigalists or Baroque oratorios was in its way as avant-garde for the time as a turn to atonalism.

Michael, analysing his path towards originality, was more interested in Wilfred's influence than in technical talk of rests and time signatures. He wrote to David Ayerst during composition that the quartet was "in some way the outcome of the Wilf affair"[32] and was later explicit that meeting Wilfred "was a major factor underlying the discovery of my own individual musical 'voice', something that couldn't be analysed purely in technical terms: all that love flowed out in the slow movement of my first string quartet, an unbroken span of lyrical music in which all four instruments sing ardently from start to finish".[33] To listen to the slow movement, to hear its heart throb so painfully on its sleeve, is to be almost embarrassed at its disinhibition. The melodies, long-breathed but never long-winded, rove up and down the stave as if in search of something (the first violin traverses two octaves in the opening bar), finally reaching a repose that, after such painfully scrunched harmonies, could suggest resignation rather than peace. The music is never self-pitying, but is woven both of love and of yearning for love. This, Michael soon decided, was his early music's weakness, and he wrote to his fellow composer William Busch that he believed the slow movement had "really gone too far", that he "thought it to be dead", that it "represented to me the *nec plus ultra* of my own romantic 'sensible' development – the attention to rhythm and clarity came next, afterwards".[34]

When the quartet reached its premiere the originality of its language went under the critical radar, which at the time was more attuned to harmonic innovation than rhythmic novelty. One of Michael's contemporaries at the Royal College, the conductor Iris Lemare, had fond memories of him from their student days. With the violinist Anne Macnaghten she had started a concert series designed to premiere new works, and programmed Michael's quartet for 9 December 1935, to be performed by the Brosa Quartet at the small Mercury Theatre in Notting Hill; capacity 150. Michael spent much of the run-up to the performance worrying that Nick Myant would travel up from Blundell's, which he thought unwise (he had nevertheless sent Nick a ticket). In the event Nick stayed away, but in the audience, alongside Phyllis and Francesca and Evelyn, David and Alan, sat Wilfred Franks, the quartet's dedicatee. He was accompanied by friends from the Missenden school, Stanley Fisher and Margaret Lister-Kaye. "What fun," Michael wrote in dripping irony. "You can all have a look at her."[35]

The Brosa Quartet was distinguished, with premieres of Prokofiev and others under its collective belt, but it is a mark of just how unusual Michael's writing was for the time that during the performance – as the composer later recalled with good humour – the players could be heard "madly counting quavers".[36] Also on the programme was Alan Bush's quartet *Dialectic* (1929), to the counterpoint of which Michael's piece certainly owed something. *Dialectic* was better received. About Michael's contribution the reviews were tepid: "Michael Tippett's quartet in A gave an impression of much less assurance, and suggested, generally, inspiration rather than the intellect as the source of its being" thought *The Times*. It was the finale that got up the reviewer's nose, and he bemoaned its "irritably smart, modern-at-all-costs nature, without any particular individuality".[37]

Reviews are not always indicative of a general reaction, but the premiere did nothing whatsoever to put Michael on the musical map, and the day jobs of teaching and conducting beckoned once more. The perceived difficulty of his writing was initially used, by performers and reviewers, as a stick to beat him with, and he was castigated for amateurish notation and eccentric technique – evidence of how he started with a musical idea heard in his head, before trying to find the means to take dictation from his imagination. He worked first in sounds, and then in notes, and it was only with the help of the Brosas that he found a more practical way of writing down the effects he was looking to achieve. The quartet is tricky and tricksy, the notes aligned like crazy paving: players and listeners snag themselves on quavers in unexpected places, before tumbling into oddly placed rests. After its wartime revision and re-premiere, it became prized for the passion and originality that its first performance had seemingly kept so hidden.

What might the sympathetic listener to the quartet, sitting at the back of the small London theatre, have predicted for Michael's compositional career? The twists and turns that were to come could scarcely have been prophesied, but evident in this first official work is a dense and bristling life force from which he was scarcely able to turn away. Rarely if ever would he write a "thin" work that didn't teem with ideas. In the quartet his brain can be heard, grinding its mental gears, and although his technique became less evident, the sense of effort in Michael's music is one of its defining characteristics. Just as seeing the brushstrokes in paint thickly and vigorously applied can remind the viewer of the hand behind the brush, so the personality in Michael's music, suffering, exulting, thinking, is always evident, in the brain behind the notes, in the muscles taut on the violinist's arm.

At the close of 1935 he went off to his parents' house for Christmas, joined by Alan Bush and David Ayerst. It was over twelve years since he had set his heart on being a composer. Thirty years into his life his official catalogue begins. Now he had done it; now he was there.

TWELVE

The Grim Nut of Fire

Early in 1936 Nick Myant and Anthony Sedgwick left Blundell's
School to join Michael on a hiking holiday in Yorkshire, accompanied by a younger school friend called David Temple-Roberts.
All three, and especially David, returned with a perceptible belief
in communism, and soon the boys' parents alerted the school
to the situation. Suddenly things turned nasty, not least because,
having become aware of Nick's intense liking for Michael, David
Temple-Roberts threatened to release details of the relationship in a
letter that didn't run far short of blackmail. Michael was outraged,
thinking the boy a "silly little devil" and "such a bloody liar".[1]
He fiercely denied having converted the boys politically: "I have
absolutely nothing to do with that side of David and don't let
anyone accuse me of it."

Michael quickly attempted to make his friendship with the boys
mature and above board, suggesting that he visit their parents to
assure them of his good intentions, and trying to persuade Nick
not to come to Oxted during term-time. He managed to patch
things up, but decided "the whole incident confirms my opinion
1) of my own immaturity, 2) of the bloodiness of public-schools
– or rather of Blundell's, 3) of the real division between class
divisions and culture". He blamed himself badly – "how deep this
bloody business goes" – and felt that he should have disillusioned
Nick "about the commonness and inevitability of reciprocal love".
Then his characteristic optimism kicked in: "All will be well." And

gradually Nick Myant's passion did fade, gradually he dropped from Michael's world, leaving Blundell's first for Oxford, and then to balance married life and fatherhood with a distinguished career as a scientist. (He died in 2015, aged ninety-seven, a committed socialist to the last.)

The mess was made worse by the fact that Wilfred Franks, for all his protestations that he wanted to leave Michael and get married, became madly jealous of the younger boys. In spring 1936 Michael admitted he was "absolutely lost. Suffice it to say that physically I'm very turned in on myself at home, very lecherous in the street after handsome young men, apparently longing to be married and with a home."[2] It was in this mood of self-recrimination and disorientation that his political life started up again after his abandonment of the Communist Party.

By 1936 there were various groups vying for the affiliations of a committed Trotskyist such as Michael. But, says Ian Kemp's authorised account of Michael's life in the 1930s, "he never joined a Trotskyist party and never got involved with sticky political in-fighting".[3] Neither statement is true. Either it was jointly decided that the reputation of a by-then-knighted composer would be damaged by a detailed exposé of his political past, or (more likely) Michael deliberately misremembered his own history. In truth, Michael Tippett spent the majority of the second half of the 1930s working at the heart of one of the major Trotskyist parties in the country. "Underneath my pleasant exterior and charm" he wrote knowingly to David, "is a grim nut of fire somewhere which burns all the time."[4]

During Michael's short-lived membership of the Communist Party, British Trotskyism had reorganised itself. The Communist League (in which he had originally expressed interest) had split, after lengthy wrangling, into various smaller cells. In February 1936 six Trotskyists entered the Labour Party, forming the Youth Militant Group, which grew its membership from six to sixty over the rest of the year.[5] And one of the fifty-four new recruits was Michael Tippett.

The group was initially much committed to harnessing the Trotskyist potential of the Labour League of Youth, with which Michael was already involved. He may have believed entry into the Labour Party the best way of furthering Trotskyism, and been swayed by the persuasion of the group's core members and its leader, Denzil Dean Harber. In October 1936 Michael wrote to Alan Bush about his "organizer Comrade Harber [. . .] a pure intellectual whom I react strongly against, though I have to admit his lucidity and clarity and coldness of judgement – Trotskyist though he is – he and I make rather a good pair – he controls my impulsive feelings".[6] Michael was one of the earlier recruits to the Youth Militant Group, for he published an article in its newspaper in June, fewer than four months after its foundation. *The Youth Militant* started life as a hand-stapled amateurish affair, produced on a typewriter with a hand-drawn front page, on sale for sixpence. Michael told Ruth Pennyman about "the little rag here for which I help to do news work", which was printed "by hand on a roneo".[7] Soon he was making regular contributions to the paper. What were known as "Notes of the Month" by "M.T.", usually focused on the Trotskyist situation in Paris, and Michael's language skills made him the ideal reporter of untranslated Marxist literature. He picked up the revolutionary tone in no time: "Lead the workers to take the offensive against Fascism with a workers' militia!" "The further the strikes spread the better."[8] From early 1937, the paper was revamped and began a series of articles by a news correspondent going by the name of "Mick", perhaps Michael, perhaps not. "To Action!" runs a typical sentence, "in this New Year of proletarian Revolution across the channel. To all comrades, we wish you Revolutionary Greetings."[9] Membership of the Youth Militant Group, which cost three shillings a week, otherwise entailed arduous meetings for which Michael travelled to Paddington: "we have ten compulsory books. In our aggregate meetings everyone is obliged to turn up or be expelled! And these meetings are five-hour, six-hour discussions on policy, tactics etc, training ourselves all the time – building up independence of character, to become responsible and make decisions."[10] But he revelled in it all: "I prefer the severe training of my present group to the Communist Party, that is what it comes to."[11]

The Youth Militant Group aimed to convert Stalinist communists and the Labour Party, and described itself as a "socialist organisation [which] has as its object the revolutionary overthrow of the capitalist system, and the establishment of the dictatorship of the new proletariat as the necessary first step towards the classless, communist society".[12] It was open in its belief that eggs must be broken to cook a utopian omelette, and called for "an armed insurrection to overthrow capitalism".[13] Denzil Harber would distribute rousing circulars to members, warning them that capitalism was not the "lesser evil" against fascism, and that it was "necessary at all times to combine illegal with legal work". Michael had been avowedly anti-war, but the convictions of the Militant Group were perilously close to welcoming international conflict as a chance to arm the workers. He received pamphlets in which it was argued that

> the working-class should regard defeat [in an encroaching war] as a lesser evil and not shirk action which will deliberately lead even to the victory of the enemy; for a military defeat resulting from the growth of the revolutionary movement is infinitely more beneficial to the working class than military victory [. . .]. A critical period, which of necessity arises, will then have to be used by the workers for turning the arms against their own ruling class and thus transform the imperialist war into civil war.[14]

Breathing the heady air of such rhetoric, Michael wrote to Alan Bush of his conviction that it was better to overturn the British Empire than the German dictatorship:

> my one hope is that the British Empire will go under and Hitler win, rather than the reverse and the whole business begin over again. I hate the Empire as I hate nothing else. It is the key pin of world capitalism and it's our job to bring it to the ground. [. . . Trotskyist] minds are on the concrete problem now. How to survive in the opening phases of the coming war and how to

organise illegal literature etc for the eventual turn against them, while shoot [those] who led them into it.[15]

So all-encompassing had Michael's political involvement become that his letters sent during his membership are bleached of his usual humour and lightness of touch, barely mentioning concerts or theatre or literature, the lodestars of his student life. His reading, bar a new-found interest in William Blake and Benjamin Disraeli, had been submerged with works by and commentaries upon Lenin, Marx, and Trotsky. He appears to have spent less time with David Ayerst and Francesca Allinson, closest of friends but calmer in their politics, and instead socialised with politically sympathetic Oxted locals, and with the comrades in party meetings. For his London musical work he sat on the executive committee of Alan Bush's newly formed Workers' Music Association. Bush and Phyllis Kemp were now his frequent sparring partners, on paper and in person.

In the fight against fascism there were glimmers of hope. In May 1936 the Front Populaire (an alliance of left-wing parties) had won the legislative elections in France, leading to the formation of a short-lived government headed by Léon Blum. But in this Michael refused to rejoice. So ardent had his Trotskyism become that Blum's government, and the formation in Britain of a similar Popular Front later in the year, were to him a "real danger", a "zig-zag to the Right", and he was convinced that there would be a civil war in France and that "only new parties and a new revolutionary International can effectively deal with the new revolutionary upsurge".[16]

Michael was referring to the "Fourth International", a worldwide union of Trotskyist parties that aimed to bring about global communism, in competition with the Stalinist "Third International". No such organisation would be formed until 1938, but Trotsky had long called for its existence, and from 29 to 31 July 1936 a conference was held to discuss its foundation. Known as the "Geneva conference" for security reasons, it actually took place in Paris. It was a small and badly organised affair for which the minutes have been lost, but it is known that Denzil Harber represented the British delegation. Once again contradicting the claim that he never went abroad between 1933 and the end of the war, Michael can be firmly placed in Paris, close to the time of the conference, in 1936. In mid-August he sent Ruth Pennyman a letter from Cassis-sur-mer in southern France, to which he had evidently travelled from the capital: "I enjoyed Paris".[17] Whether he accompanied Harber to the conference is uncertain, but he did once admit to having "visited the Trotskyist headquarters in Paris to offer help of some kind".[18] One clear motivation of the trip was to get a sense of the Trotskyist Movement in France, the machinations of which he reported to British groups. His letter to Ruth also makes clear that he had been despatched, either as an official Militant Group emissary or off his own bat, to deliver aid to fighters in the Spanish Civil War that had broken out just weeks earlier.

Like so many European countries, Spain was fiercely divided between right wing and left wing and struggling to recover from the depression. By 1936 the Republican Party, mainly formed of workers, trade unions, socialists, and peasants, held shaky power, but on 17 July a group of army officers launched an abortive coup against the government, triggering civil war between the Republicans and the Nationalists. Somehow Michael had raised or got hold of £5 (roughly £300 today), which he delivered to one of the Republican aid organisations that had sprung up in Paris and which he found was

passing men across the frontier into the militias in Barcelona. I can't get a very good view of things from here [Cassis-sur-mer] after all, because I can't find my way about the French papers as with the English. [. . .] The [Spanish] Trotsky-party, the POUM* is growing pretty significant and is putting out something like the real Bolshevik line. [. . . It] has grown to fifteen thousand members and thus a daily paper − it is also spreading to other

* Partido Obrero de Unificación Marxista (Workers' Party of Marxist Unification), a Communist Party formed, in 1935 and against Trotsky's wishes, by uniting a Spanish Trotskyist Party with the Workers and Peasants' Bloc.

parts and looks as if it might go a long way – if the Trotskyists
after all show themselves to be the real revolutionaries in this
case the Stalin-bureaucracy will receive a major blow.[19]

The POUM was the anti-Stalinist branch of the Spanish left wing, on
whose militia George Orwell served, as documented in his *Homage
to Catalonia*; he was one of many British volunteers who travelled
to Spain in the fight against fascism. The French Trotskyists, on
meeting Michael in Paris, mistook his support for the POUM as
an indication that he wanted, like Orwell, to join their forces.
But he admitted to Ruth Pennyman, who had taken child refugees
from Spain into Ormesby Hall, that he "could not agree to think
of going to Spain to fight because I am not a political professional
but one of the common lot that will fight it out when it comes to
all of us and ours".[20] To Alan Bush he wrote: "Funnily enough I
had been making a study of Spain for some time beforehand, and a
party sailor sent me every conceivable paper from the country just
before it broke out, so I have been able to find my way about in
the numerous parties, etc. [. . .] I can give you a very clear account
of Spain I think. It's tremendously thrilling. I can't do any music
at all."[21]

His music was indeed suffering. Shocked by Stalin's denunciation
of Dmitri Shostakovich's music in *Pravda* earlier that year, Michael
remained firm that the artist should be permitted freedom: "It is
quite certain", he avowed, "that the communist art dictatorship
is as radical as the Nazi."[22] But, certain as he was that art should
be beyond the strictures of politics, he now began to turn his
composition almost exclusively over to political statement. The
achievement of his string quartet went partly by the wayside, and
his music began to sound more and more like the agitprop of
Hanns Eisler that he had heard at Morley College the previous year.
He joined with David Ayerst to write an anti-war protest song (now
lost, assuming it was ever finished), and then turned his attention
to a large piece for the choreographer Margaret Barr.[23] Barr, whom
he likely met through work at Morley, had established a highly
successful school of dance and mime at Dartington Hall in Devon,

and was now staging polemical dance-dramas (she wouldn't use the word "ballet") in London. Michael had sat almost in tears through Barr's *Mothers*; the "lovely young ardent girls", he admitted, "went straight to my heart".[24] Barr wanted to rework a piece from Dartington called *Colliery*, and Michael agreed to write the music. The work was retitled *The Miners* and depicted the fallout from a mine explosion through song and dance, speech and mime. It was staged in London in the second half of 1936, and all that survives of Michael's contribution is a substantial choral ballad, for which he used a text by Judy Wogan.[25]

Wogan was a friend of Wilfred Franks (who had joined Barr's troupe and may have performed in *The Miners*). She was a tiny blonde Irishwoman whose husband had been killed in the First World War. An actress and a writer, she owned a small theatre on Tottenham Court Road and around this time met and began an affair with Francesca Allinson.[26] She wrote for *The Miners* a coal-blackened text of revolution, which Michael set to relatively simple music, accompanied by a complex piano part of shadowy chromatic hammering and numerous solo passages. A male chorus of miners starts things off: "Be this blasted world sunk, and all the coal, and all the blasted bosses." Then comes a rather stodgy anthem along the lines of the "Internationale": "Unite, fight, unite, fight, we haul in the new world which dawns on our black hands." The following year Michael worked again with Barr, on her *Dance of Two with Chorus*, which dramatised a conflict between differing attitudes to love. For this, wrote an audience member, "Michael Tippett contributed an interesting experimental score: his music for *Dance of Two with Chorus* was arranged for a very odd collection of wood blocks, tin cans, etc."[27] Not a note survives.

His ability to map out and stick to a compositional schedule many years in advance was already in place, and for two years he had been planning a setting of his favourite poet, William Blake. With Wilfred's help, he had selected Blake's "A Song of Liberty" from *The Marriage of Heaven and Hell*, almost certainly proof that his politics had got the better of his musical instincts, for the twenty long lines of free verse (which he set uncut) are unwieldy mouthfuls to recite, let alone to set to music. In choosing an eighteenth-century text, Michael was linking together two periods of revolution. His setting of Blake's poem, which calls upon France and Spain to break free from the shackles of Monarchy and Church, and for London's citizens to harness the revolutionary energy of Europe and America, was a call to arms. When asking Bush to take the piece for the London Labour Choral Union, Michael was sure that no "other group would do such violent words (or music)".[28] He predicted he would finish *A Song of Liberty* in the summer of 1936, and it is a mark of his life's other distractions that, usually so accurate at gauging his compositional speed, he took a year longer than he had expected.

There was one memorable disruption to the Oxted life. David Ayerst's soon-to-be sister-in-law Shelagh Fisher, to whom Michael had become close during their holiday in Scotland the previous year, married Ray Hobbins in August 1936. Ray went off to Burma, where he worked for the Forestry Commission, and Shelagh was to join him a few months later. She remembered what happened next in her private memoirs: "One day Michael Tippett asked me to meet him in the newly laid out Embankment Gardens. He was an unusual man. I remember him all these years later as tall, slim with tousled good looks. A fascinating character, very determined [. . .]. When we met in those gardens he asked me if I was happily married to my forest empire builder because . . . what he said was amazing but too late for me to consider."[29] Shelagh's brother Bryan was their shared sounding board, and he perceived a situation that went beyond the blurting of whims:

Michael asked Shelagh to give up her man in Burma and come and live with him but she said no – though his suggestion set the doves fluttering in the dovecot. [. . . He] gave the possibility of a lasting relationship with her a lot of cogitation. [. . .] In her state of anxiety I think she only flirted with the proposition of a relationship with Michael: she always knew that between the mercurial relationship Michael offered and the steadfast and pre-dictable husband that Ray turned out to be, it was her destiny to choose the latter. Marriage always lingered on in Michael's mind as an ideal, against the odds. There was enough attraction on both sides to wonder sometimes at what might have transpired if Shelagh had never met Ray in Burma and . . .[30]

It was a familiar dual-headed problem in which Michael was once again caught. He wrote to Bryan with a wistful, jumbled honesty:

Shelagh is a very great dear and the Ray marriage does not seem very sensible – but after talking to Larema I realised how much all the same many aspects of the outside world meant so much more to Shelagh than ever to me – that is – somewhere, at any rate, I need companionship on the mystical inside or else the intellectual-musical life and that trying to fit in with such an extravert person as Shelagh is – that is, one so dependent on the other person, his constant awareness of herself or her doings – if not of actual affectionate embraces and so forth, at all times – would mean a fair strain on both sides and one which could not be borne satisfactorily without the passionate physical attraction, which I never felt – that is I felt homely and happy with her, and sexually curious perhaps, but in no way at any time, in love.[31]

Soon afterwards Shelagh left England permanently for Burma. On her journey to the ferry she went to Michael to say goodbye. "I stopped the car," she remembered, "walked up the garden path, knocked on the door. Michael said 'come in'. He was in the bath in the kitchen. He climbed out, folded me in his arms. Back I walked down the path, climbed into the car with my 'beige two-piece going-away' all splodged with water. Mother who sat beside me never said a word. I haven't seen Michael since that day."[32] For his turn Michael remained thereafter silent on the matter, and never mentioned Shelagh in reports of his life; nor yet the Blundell's pupils – Nick Myant, Anthony Sedgwick – who had caused him such joy and trouble. The openness for which in old age he was famous masked some calculated self-editing. His heterosexual affairs, such as they were, were not politically useful in the later and more open decades of the century, and his political involvement would likely have been used against him in the eras first of nuclear threat and then of *glasnost*. The ill-fated proposal to Shelagh, tentatively intended to break another relationship without apparent scruple, was stowed away, shelved next to the closed mental boxes marked "Fettes College", "Blundell's", and "Youth Militant Group", and he moved on without looking back.

THIRTEEN

They Shall Not Pass

On the side of a building in Dock Street, east London, is a red plaque that reads:

THE BATTLE OF CABLE STREET
The people of East London rallied to Cable Street
on the 4th October 1936 and forced back the march
of the fascist Oswald Mosley and his Blackshirts
through the streets of the East End.
"THEY SHALL NOT PASS"

And they didn't. Oswald Mosley had sent his black-clad marchers through an area of the East End that had a large Jewish population, and although violence was foreseen, a police barrier was deemed preferable to proscription. Anti-fascist protestors, around 20,000 of them, organised roadblocks to hold back the fascists (whom they outnumbered ten to one). The police tried to clear the roads, charging on horseback into the fray. The demonstrators began to riot, throwing stones and broken furniture, until the march was called off. But many of the protestors were arrested, and among them was Wilfred Franks.

Three days later Michael wrote to Alan Bush: "Yes – Sunday was historic! Wilf is on remand for criminal assault – police perjury – and the family fortune has fallen heavily over a counsel for him. Thames Police Court Friday morning! So it goes."[1] At the trial, on 9 October,

Wilfred was "charged with insulting behaviour and assaulting P.C. Medley by kicking him on the shin and stomach". He was sentenced to "twenty-eight days' hard labour and bound over on the insulting behaviour charge".[2] Wilfred was adamant that he had been framed, and appealed. Michael bore the brunt of the financial and emotional fallout, calling on his old friend Aubrey Russ for legal expertise and trying to gather funds: "I have compromised myself so to speak for the whole amount and shall pay the remainder, whatever it turns out to be."[3] He could ill afford the financial strain, and that year totted up his earnings from teaching and conducting as £97 6s., an income of just under £6,000 in today's money, plumped out by parental contributions and generous friends but rendered down again by supporting Wilf. The worry took its toll. He is marked as being "indisposed" for all his Co-op choirs' rehearsals in October and November, and spent at least two days "in bed cracked up with it".[4] At the retrial, on 12 November, the original sentence was upheld, but no mention of Wilfred's carrying out his punishment survives. Michael wrote to Alan Bush that the costs had been "absolutely crippling", and that "though I live apart from [Wilf], I am still somewhat helplessly tied to him in some unexplained psychological-emotional way. His first trial made me ill for a night – this one has made me very depressed and lonely. [. . .] I am loyal to my support of Wilf, because that is my character."[5]

At Christmas, not long after the country had buckled in shock at Edward VIII's abdication, David Ayerst married Larema Fisher (sister to Bryan and to Shelagh). And it was not without a slight though affectionate contempt that Michael reported to a mutual friend that David was "out to get married as a goal".[6] In marrying a Fisher girl, David had succeeded where Michael had failed. On the day of the Ayersts' wedding, Michael stubbornly refused to leave the couple alone in the bedroom while Larema changed out of her wedding dress.[7] His behaviour was typically eccentric and rebellious, but indicates not only his desire to be close in some way to such a union but his fear of losing a dear friend. Such a fear proved needless, but bespeaks a man aware that his social circle and emotional life were under strain. Francesca and Wilfred he saw only intermittently. Alan and Phyllis were increasingly lost to Stalinism. Composition and teaching, politics and personal life, were intermingling and boiling over under the pressure. What he ever afterwards depicted as a clean break with Wilfred in 1938 that led to a mental crisis and a period of therapy, was in truth a breakdown ragged and prolonged, during which even the Trotskyist politics to which he had clung could seem in their violence nothing but a projection of inner turmoil.

Evelyn Maude had introduced Michael to Carl Jung's *The Psychology of the Unconscious*, one of the Swiss psychoanalyst's earliest works. Intrigued, Michael – never one to explore a subject only at a surface level – had read deeper and deeper in Jung's writings, finding much that chimed with his own situation. He soon became enough of a "Jungian" that he could lecture extempore on Jung's categorisation of people into psychological "types".[8] Many of Jung's beliefs and ideas had a decisive and fundamental influence on his creative and psychological life. Underpinning a great deal of Jung's thought was the belief that mental illness is characterised by disunity of the personality. "Personality", for Jung, was neither organic nor inherent, but to be achieved by those individuals who were happy to undergo an inward-looking journey, termed the "individuation" process. This process of psychological integration required accessing and acknowledging the "personal unconscious": a store of memories forgotten or suppressed, and festering in consequence. Deeper still lay the "collective unconscious", shared alike by every member of the human race, a level of mind common to all, consisting of mythological motifs and images that he named "archetypes". Dreams were communications from the unconscious and, coded in symbolic language as they may be, could be carefully analysed and understood, leading to a full integration of the self.

Michael began very tentatively. David Ayerst knew a famous Jungian analyst named John Layard, to whom he had introduced Michael a few years before: "hawk-eyed and hawk-beaked", as David vividly described him, "with a hawk's swift swoop on his prey".[9] Layard, who was bisexual, had turned to Jung's writings in order to solve personal crises of his own in the wake of the First World War. He had twice attempted suicide, and received treatment from Jung himself. He would eventually author a renowned work of anthropology, *Stone Men of Malekula*, to which T.S. Eliot acknowledged a debt. When living in Berlin in the late 1920s, he became the model for a character in Christopher Isherwood's novel *The Memorial*, and an inspiring mentor to W.H. Auden, who turned down Layard's sexual advances but acknowledged his deep influence on early works such as *The Orators*.

Michael, although too impoverished to pay for any formal therapy sessions, would spend many years recounting his dreams to John Layard, in long and involved letters, each of which Layard carefully annotated in red pencil. As early as October 1936 Michael had sent him a dream to consider, and around the same time persuaded Wilfred to meet with Layard and his wife.[10] Then in January 1937 Michael wrote to Alan Bush:

> Am going through a very exciting sort of re-birth – a sorting out of things inside. [. . .] I have been playing a false role and have got to learn to behave myself. [. . .] What I have been trying to express is that I <u>know</u> now that arguing with you is really inside myself all the time. [. . .] the phase is only now beginning, and will mean some certain withdrawal into myself to attain a necessary balance – so that it seems rather as if the political quarrels no longer were of such consequence. [. . .] I realise what a ghastly projection the whole theory [of Trotskyism] has been (and still can be) for me, of things inside myself which are at war.[11]

Six months later Michael finished *A Song of Liberty*, surely noticing or even planning the synchronicity with which he wrote the last notes on International Workers' Day (1 May), an important Marxist holiday. Almost immediately he began to sketch out another choral work, and in May or June wrote to Frank Morley (whose son, Oliver, he was still teaching piano) to see if T.S. Eliot could suggest a likely poet to provide a text. "The theme I have in mind", he explained to Morley, "is the descent into the unconscious [. . .], the idea of acceptance personally and collectively of the chaos from which a new courage can be born – the idea of the Shadow, as I call it. A man can have no depth, nor stand in the sunlight, without a shadow – until the shadow is accepted there is no spiritual substance that is not as hollow as the nineteenth-century romanticism." The work was to conclude with a "sort of memorial to the [First World] War – as it appears to my generation, to whom the War specifically is the start of things – we were <u>born</u> into a mass struggle as into our fated element".[12]

On the top of Michael's letter, Frank Morley wrote: "TSE says George Barker". Eliot admired George Barker's poetry enormously, had published him at Faber and even organised a fund so that he could write full-time. Much of Barker's poetry was written in response to the Spanish Civil War, but eventually he became associated with the New Apocalyptics Movement, whose work reacted against gritty 1930s realism by moving into the worlds of myth and surreality. Morley wrote off to Barker suggesting the collaboration. Meantime Michael, waiting for a reply, was not "able to prevent my fertile mind pursuing things further".[13] His planned work grew, and acquired a title, Nekyia, referring to an Ancient Greek rite in which ghosts of the past were questioned about the future. (In autumn 1935 Jung had lectured in London on the concept of the Nekyia allowing the conscious mind to rove into the unconscious.)[14] Michael's Nekyia was to be a tripartite choral work on Jungian themes, explicating the necessity of acknowledging the darkest reaches of the human psyche. Here, in the spring of 1937, is the first inkling of his oratorio A Child of Our Time.

The first part was to use lines from Blake's The Book of Thel; the second to be a scene from T.S. Eliot's Sweeney Agonistes.* The third

---

* Tippett planned to use Eliot's "Fragment of an Agon", and wanted to set it "word for word – (provided this is not sacrilege) – using a sort of song-speech which I have been at work on in my own art". The "Fragment" is the second scene of Eliot's Sweeney Agonistes, an incomplete verse-drama written in the late 1920s and first performed in 1933. The prose combines the rhythms of jazz and music hall with those of common speech, and Eliot had considered having the lines punctuated with drum beats. (Tippett to Frank Morley, June 1937, Morris Library, Southern Illinois University; see Eliot, Poems, 1, pp. 121–7.)

and final part was to incorporate Wilfred Owen's "Strange Meeting" and Walt Whitman's "Ode to Death", before concluding with the Jungian message as fashioned by George Barker, who Michael hoped would be able to provide words that would transmute the following passage of Jung into singable words for a "chorus of mankind":

> I always thought, when we accept things, they overpower us in one way or another. Now this is not true at all, and it is only by accepting them that one can define an attitude toward them. So now I intend playing the game of life, being receptive to whatever comes to me, good and bad, sun and shadow that are for ever shifting, and, in this way, also accepting my own nature with its positive and negative sides. Thus everything becomes more alive to me. What a fool I was! How I tried to force everything to go according to my idea![15]

The quotation is from a letter sent to Jung by one of his patients, and included in his commentary (1929) on the seventeenth-century Taoist text *The Secret of the Golden Flower*. In alighting upon it Michael was fully aware of its relevance to his own situation. George Barker wrote offering a poem for the third part of *Nekyia*. Michael arranged to meet him either in London or in Oxted, and they became reasonably good friends.[16]

But *Nekyia*, and Michael's mastery of Jung's individuation process, soon stalled amid a resurgence of political pressure. Despite acknowledging his Trotskyism as a "projection", he couldn't give it up, and his involvement with the Youth Militant Group instead grew more intense. Just weeks before he wrote so openly and excitedly to Alan Bush of his rebirth, a statement released by the Youth Militant Group (on 29 December 1936) had listed Michael as a member senior enough to take part in discussions of policy at the very highest level, his name bracketed with the leader, Denzil Dean Harber, and with C.L.R James,* who was influential in another

---

* C.L.R. James (1901–89), Afro-Trinidadian historian, author of a seminal history of the Haitian Revolution, *The Black Jacobins* (London: Secker and Warburg, 1938).

Trotskyist group.[17] Such activity quickly led to violent fracture in his friendships with both Phyllis and Bush, who were maddened by the mismatch between Michael's actions and words. Michael was the most diplomatic of the trio in his attempt to save the friendships, but all three had missionary zeal and none would capitulate. It was, Michael later thought, "the Trotsky purge trials which split us all apart".[18] Between 1936 and 1938 Stalin instigated a series of show trials that charged secret-police officials and Bolshevik leaders from the 1917 revolutions with conspiring to assassinate him. Most were executed, as part of Stalin's violent attempt to rid the party of any opposition. Trotskyists suffered badly. Many were accused of being in contact with Trotsky and shot. Michael found it hard to forgive any such as Bush or Phyllis who refused to denounce Stalin once and for all in the face of the trials. His "re-birth" fell by the wayside and he was once again aflame, writing of a necessary "revolutionary terror of the elimination of the bourgeoisie", after which

> greater and greater democracy and liberty of opinion, parties and all, are to be allowed and encouraged. The shooting of leaders of the Revolution: men who have spent their lives for the revolution, who have ruled Russia, the exile and imprisonment of thousands upon thousands of workers is an indication to many of us that it is a travesty of the dictatorship of the proletariat [. . .]. For ages I hoped that we could get away without dealing with the truth about the Soviet Union [. . . but] – the longer we delay facing the truth, the worse will be the disillusion.[19]

Neither Bush nor Phyllis would listen. Michael took to giving speeches at Bush's Choral Union concerts that Bush angrily believed were intended to convert the singers to Trotskyism. Michael hastily denied this, claiming few members of his own choirs knew his political affiliations, but the rift grew more intense. "Have you seen Michael lately?" Bush had written to Phyllis in December 1936. "He misbehaved himself badly the last time I saw him. I am going to make one last effort to rescue him from his present parlous state, and if unsuccessful I shall have regretfully to avoid allowing him to take any part in what we are doing because on this last occasion he undoubtedly did a great deal of harm."[20] Phyllis, in one of her few surviving letters, replied with aggrieved affection: "Micky seems to be going from bad to worse. [. . .] With him it is more and more obviously a subjective attitude of his own, the result of his isolation."[21] Phyllis had moved to a flat in St George's Square in London, and was trying to hold down her job as a chemist's assistant in combination with her political activity. But she was beset by a chronic illness that infected her eyes and made professional life difficult (eventually it gave her a pronounced squint). Bush snapped dismissively back: "it is rather difficult to make out what he does think. Anyway he is impossible for our purposes at present."[22]

Michael and Phyllis tried to patch it up, and he was temporarily apologetic. But their differences were too ingrained, and Phyllis was, or so Michael thought, held under the thumb of her boyfriend, David Petruska, an exiled White Russian who had converted to communism, and who treated Michael with undisguised and reciprocated dislike. From 1 January 1937, the British security service had opened an extensive file on Phyllis, and her political activism would be closely monitored by the government for some decades.[23] The cousins had seen nothing of each other for the first half of that year, until, in July, Phyllis turned up at Whitegates Cottage with an official from the Communist Party. "There is blood between us," he remembered her saying. "We shall never see each other again."[24] It was a bad blow, and one of the continuities of his episodic life had been suddenly removed in a storm-cloud of bad feeling. "Even myself," he wrote sadly to Ruth Pennyman, "absurdly inadequate as I am as a comrade, find that my cousin of longstanding, an intimate friendship since childhood, comes here after six months' more or less silence, to declare our friendship closed and outside the pale, because I cannot give up my [Trotskyist] class-internationalism."[25] Relations with Alan Bush were also shaky, and although the friendship survived their differences with the passage of time, tempers flared on paper and in person. Wilfred continued to threaten permanent separation. The moorings of life were loosening dangerously. Rather than going back to Jung or to John Layard, Michael clung steadily to politics. On 29 October 1937 he gave a talk at the Oxted Congregational Hall, in which he said that he "wanted the world to know that the Labour Party in the final issue was prepared to back its ideals with armed force".[26]

In Spain, General Franco had active support from Italy and Germany, and the effect on leftist parties in Europe was cataclysmic. Temporary unity against the Nationalists dissolved in a welter of in-fighting as feelings pro- and anti-Republican took wing. Communists in Spain were taking the opportunity to annihilate Trotskyists, and Michael, through the Youth Militant Group, became involved in British aid not for the Republican cause, but for Trotskyist factions in Spain, who were being hunted down by Russian secret police. Soon after the break with Phyllis, he called once again on Ruth Pennyman:

> I've had an urgent appeal about Spain [. . .] for funds to <u>feed</u> these people in hiding – a very grim affair. What do you feel about it? I want to pass some money collected from England through channels of our own, to these comrades in distress. [. . .] Every penny that helps them weather this preliminary hunt is to my mind the one chance to keep internationalism afloat concretely in coming submersion. [. . .] I am so clear myself, but it is not easy all the same to stand one's ground in the general drift towards war and the fratricidal mania against those revolutionaries that will not give in. In Spain it's already like the early days of the war. Only the best will stand fast (the masses are not yet disarmed). Meanwhile the hunted and proscribed ones are close on starvation. Let me know if you feel you can help. Ever yours fraternally, Michael.[27]

On 7 November 1937 came the premiere of *A Song of Liberty*. Michael had produced a large choral piece, stretching to sixty-three pages of, mainly, recitative for a four-part choir. The score retains William Blake's capital letters in the line "FOR EMPIRE IS NO MORE"

(introduced with a *fortissimo* D-major chord and cymbal clash). Only at the poem's final line, "For everything that lives is Holy!", does the music incorporate the rhythmic technique Michael had developed in his string quartet, audible for the first time in a vocal line and thus shunting madrigalian influences to the fore. The line is endlessly repeated so as to be spun into a fugue, the word "holy" stretched into bouncing affirmation, all finally uniting in a blaze of E major. The demands of the piece were such that it had taken half a year for a specially formed choir to learn, and three years all told in thought and execution.[28]

Shortly after the performance, and with the Moscow show trials at their height, the Militant Group began to implode. (It had dropped the "Youth" from its title in order to move its focus towards an older demographic.) The group had been much bolstered by the arrival of a band of Trotskyists from South Africa, among whom was a man called Ralph Lee. In October rumours began to circulate that Lee had stolen strike funds from a band of workers. At a group meeting in November the allegations were made formally. Lee demanded an inquiry and there was a row. Several members left the meeting in support of Lee and in their absence were instantly expelled by the leader, Denzil Harber. The group was riven down the middle by what became known as the "Lee affair". The charges were eventually proved false. Michael was one of those who walked out in support of Lee, and he soon wrote a long statement that was read out to the group's executive committee on 26 November. He damned the leaders for their "petty-bourgeois habit of gossiping", believing the group to have suffered from "continued, personal, intimate associations becoming reflected in opinions", which placed "a severe limitation on our obtaining a leadership we can trust, not only now, but in the future illegal work of the rapidly approaching war".[29] On 8 January 1938 he delivered another long statement, damning the general behaviour at the meeting ("not being able to contain my disgust, I left"), and openly stating that "I, personally, must plead guilty to a continued distrust of the leadership". His speech was nearly 1,500 words long, and must have taken nearly a quarter of an hour to deliver, evidence of his senior position in the group, which now numbered several hundred members nationally. His conclusion was that the "behaviour of the Militant Group through its Executive Committee is inimical to the British [Trotskyist] movement, and is perpetuating feud and temperamental jealousies. I am not prepared to be a party to it, and intend to look around, therefore, for means to assist, in what small way I can, the production of general Fourth International propaganda, especially with regard to the 'International Offensive Against Stalinism'."[30]

Arguments over the Lee affair reached Leon Trotsky himself. Denzil Harber responded angrily to Michael with a five-page refutation, in which he made a telling comment: "I know that, in private, comrade Tippett will readily admit that he himself is not a revolutionary and is not fit to be a member of a revolutionary party."[31] This throws up the possibility of Michael's revolutionary politics waning perceptibly by early 1938, although Harber may only have meant it as a jibe. In March the inevitable happened, and the Militant Group split. Nineteen of Ralph Lee's supporters departed, and Michael was among them, signing his name to a statement that claimed the group had been "equivocally destroyed", and condemned "the present leadership and the majority membership". Their intention was "to make a new beginning in the fulfilling of the duty placed before us of striving towards the building of a nucleus for the revolutionary workers' party in Britain".[32] David Ayerst's brother-in-law, Bryan Fisher, also signed the document, an indication not only of his membership, but of Michael's persuasive influence.

Rather than join any pre-existing Trotskyist groups, the nineteen names, alongside supportive members from regional branches of the Militant Group, formed yet another revolutionary party: the Workers' International League. This group remained in the Labour Party, refusing any merger with other parties, and staggered on until late into the war. One of the founder members, Ted Grant, remembered Michael as being a supporter of the League for a short time, and becoming close to a French Trotskyist within it named Betty Hamilton. Certainly, Michael remained in touch with Grant and Hamilton for at least another five years.[33] Wilfred Franks, who despite never joining the Militant Group appears to have had connections to the Workers' International League, remembered Michael's maintaining a friendship of reasonably long standing with a member named Gerry Healy:* "Tippett [met] with Gerry Healy. Tippett used to come to London from our cottage in Oxted in Surrey to discuss with Healy, whom Tippett had the greatest respect for."[34]

Although Whitegates had never quite been "our cottage", as Wilfred would later claim, it had frequently been a domestic base for any number of Michael's friends in need of a roof over their heads. Even when sharing it with nothing but a piano and a tin bath, Michael was cramped. One reason for a retraction in his political activities after the split may simply have been that he took on a massive project of domestic upheaval that restricted his time. At some point in 1938 he persuaded his father to help him purchase the entire building of which his cottage had been half, and a chunk of the surrounding land. He then decided to rent out both cottages, and erect alongside them a new home for himself. Family support ran out, and it was via Evelyn Maude's husband, who was president of a philanthropic housing society providing low-interest loans, that Michael set about designing and having built a new red-brick bungalow on the site. It was a light-filled but ugly building, squat and square, with a pyramid of a roof that, with a single chimney right at the centre, looked like the lid of a tagine. The broadcaster John Amis became a frequent visitor during the war:

It was an ordinary and not particularly comfortable little bungalow: kitchen-dining area, two bedrooms and a living room containing armchairs, an animal rug, an early wireless with record player, a black grand piano with just a few remaining ivories

---

* In the 1980s Gerry Healy became the leader of the Workers' Revolutionary Party, which imploded amid accusations of Healy's sexual abuse and links to extremist governments. It was in this political environment that the first detailed biographical portraits of Tippett were published, creating yet further reason to play down his early political activities.

[. . .] and a work table strewn, like the top of the piano, with correspondence, pamphlets, concert notices, manuscript paper, books and scores, all in great disarray and with a considerable overflow on the floor.[35]

The bungalow also became known as Whitegates Cottage, and it satisfied Michael's need for a fortress of solitude in order to compose away from the world's encroaching madness, while remaining a continual reminder of the life unshared. He was now able to draw a small income by renting out the two original cottages, the first to a Trotskyist ex-coal-miner and his wife, Ben and Miriam Lewis, and the second to their daughter Bronwen and her husband Jack, who were hoping to start a family. The arrangement was one way to fend off loneliness, as suddenly he had near neighbours and good friends a few steps away. Years before, Michael's opera *Robin Hood* had included the pointed line: "But the devil made the landlord to steal from you and me." Somehow, he accepted the fact that family money had made him a landlord in his turn.

Through the letterbox of both his old and his new house had arrived official documents to do with the Ralph Lee affair on which Michael's name had appeared undisguised. Copies of these had been sent on to the Secretariat of the Fourth International. At one point a bundle of letters from Trotsky himself, written to his prominent French supporter Gérard Rosenthal, turned up by accident at Whitegates Cottage. Michael sent them on to comrades at the Trotsky Defence Committee with a covering note that makes plain he was already in correspondence with Rosenthal.[36] That the mistake was able to be made is some indication of an involvement, albeit peripheral, at the highest levels of the revolutionary left, and in the same month as the split in the Militant Group, March 1938, Michael's political involvement hit what could have been a frightening crisis. The noises he had made in Trotskyist parties both in England and in France threatened real danger. Bryan Fisher remembered receiving a worrying letter

from the British Trotskyists Secretariat saying that Michael's address was known to the G.P.U. (Russian Secret Police) and apparently under their surveillance. The letter asked me to convey this information to MT and tell him to observe the utmost caution, especially in correspondence with abroad and in keeping any important internal material there. It asked me to do this personally and not communicate it to anyone else as the Secretariat was investigating the sources and did not wish any English agents to be forewarned. We did not take this matter light-heartedly but we did have some fun imagining Russian agents quaffing vodka behind a hedge in a deserted field in Surrey. But the matter had serious undertones of the states to which politics can descend.[37]

It was in Michael's nature to scoff at such a threat; it was perhaps in the Secretariat's nature to be paranoid. The Trotskyist Movement and the Soviet secret police had their headquarters in Paris, and Michael's interest in French journalism, on top of his visit to Paris in 1936 and his various articles on political machinations across the Channel, had likely not gone unnoticed. Bryan Fisher had followed Michael to the Militant Group's meetings in London, and had received from him "long letters as to the stratagems and tactics to be advocated". But his own political involvement, which was a product of Michael's influence as much as of idealism, was on the wane: "I came to realise I was not a party political animal, that I had no heart or natural inclination or talent for party politics."[38] Michael had had all three, but he was slowly coming round to the same view in those last eighteen months of peace. But Fisher was right to recognise the "serious undertones" that played out like a ground bass beneath the political activism that Michael was so keen to forget as he grew older.

Somehow or other Michael was back in touch with Christopher Fry, his fellow teacher from Hazelwood, a man whom he had loved. Already Fry was having success as a man of the theatre, had directed and acted in a British premiere by George Bernard Shaw, and written the first of the many verse-dramas for which he became famous. Michael's professional reputation by contrast had progressed little, and his musical life was now crammed into the time he could spare from talks and meetings and writing. One of the mainstays of the last decade had been his conducting of choirs for the Royal Arsenal Co-operative Society. He had suggested to the RACS committee that he might compose an opera to be performed by all the Co-operative junior choirs. Christopher Fry agreed to write the libretto, basing it on a story from Longfellow in which foolish King Robert of Sicily, swapping places with an angel, goes on his travels disguised as a jester; arriving in Rome, he refuses to kneel for the Easter service, before the chanting voice of the angel makes him see the light. Given that the choirs were dotted all over London and the expense of endless journeying could not be met, the idea was that the children could be divided into groups with separate parts to rehearse: the Emperor's train, the Sicilians, the Romans, and so on. Michael scattered arrangements of well-known songs between the scenes of Fry's script, with the odd bit of original scene-change music, and he finished the score on 1 March 1938. There were opportunities for canons by William Byrd, for a rousing chorus of "Jerusalem", for vibrant tunes by Purcell that Francesca Allinson had sought out especially, and for three numbers – songs from Scotland and Ireland, and a French lullaby – that would return in his later compositions.[39] Michael and Christopher Fry called upon techniques they had seen used in theatre productions by the Austrian impresario Max Reinhardt, sending the choirs marching in procession down the aisles. Fry even found an opportunity to add an ape to the cast list.

In that decade of rallies and pageants, the Co-operative Movement was well used to the organisation of vast events, with choirs and audiences of thousands. At least 200 children were involved in Robert of Sicily, which was performed sometime in May 1938, first at the Co-operative Hall in Peckham, then again at Woolwich Polytechnic. The show was a great success, and a few months later a third performance was mounted at Shornells, a country house in Abbey Wood that boasted a large open-air theatre in its grounds. It was nice to be back with Christopher Fry and surrounded with children once again, and they began to make plans to repeat the process on a larger scale. Michael wrote to Ruth Pennyman, who had introduced him to such ventures, that he was "getting quite used to these sorts of productions" and could make "a moving show of them".[40] The Arsenal Co-operative naturally agreed, calling the opera "an event of signal significance", and thinking that "the choirs gave two magnificent performances. We wish to take this opportunity of offering our thanks to Michael Tippett, the composer and conductor of this work, and to Wilfred Franks, who acted as stage manager."[41]

Michael had used a tune from *Robert of Sicily* ("Ca' the yowes", a Scottish song with words by Robert Burns) in a four-movement piano sonata, on which he had been working intermittently for nearly two years, and which he finished on 1 July 1938. The sonata proves that the temptation to read Michael's music as explicit autobiography should often be resisted; composed throughout the breakdown of a relationship and finished at the height of his revolutionary fervour, it is memorable mainly for its technical dazzle and its bursts of joy. Michael's piano skills, at their peak when he was a student, had lapsed into an eccentric technique exploited just enough to serve his compositional needs. But his lack of proficiency widened the parameters of his imagination when composing for the instrument. And while his piano compositions are often said not to fall easily under the fingers, this is less true of this first official sonata than of its successors, its difficulties lying in the rhythmic independence required of each hand, and the sheer speeds necessary for the music to glitter as it should. The first movement is formed of variations on an original theme that is worryingly bland, but the worries prove needless as the variations become ever more inventive, never more so than when the two hands begin a dance of syncopated octaves, tumbling around one another in joyous independence, meeting occasionally before bounding off again on their own separate course, and finally ending in a series of cock-a-hoop chords. Alan Bush was privately rather peeved that the mournful, Wilf-ful slow movement was partly based on a phrase from one of his own piano pieces, for Michael had neither concealed the burglary, nor highlighted it to the point where it could be passed off as humble tribute.[42] In the same allusive vein, the sonata marks one of the earliest attempts by a British composer to incorporate the sound of gongs from an Indonesian gamelan orchestra, of which Michael had heard recordings. The piece is spun through with folk-songs, delicate wisps breaking free from a whirlwind of unrelenting quavers in the third movement, before the finale arrives, a cheeky jumble of hoe-down and ragtime.

The composition of the sonata overlapped with Michael's embarking on a Concerto for Double String Orchestra, which he began early in 1938 and on which he was still working when, one summer's evening in the first weeks of August, he met Wilfred Franks in a café in London. His autobiography reads: "I reached the café ahead of him and sat with my head in my hands, brooding on the section I had reached in the slow movement of my Double Concerto. When Wilf arrived he said, 'I have decided to marry this girl.' I went completely cold. At the very moment he said that, I cut off relations absolutely. Wilf was deeply hurt."[43] Wilfred had been exploiting his uncanny ability to master any art form he put his hand to, and following another teaching job had made an abortive attempt to work, on Michael's introduction, at the General Post Office Film Unit (where Auden and Benjamin Britten were collaborating on documentary films). More successful was his work with Margaret Barr's dance troupe. Barr's theatre pieces were garnering considerable acclaim and were used for some of the BBC's first television programmes, broadcast live from Alexandra Palace, and often featuring Wilfred.[44] Among the dancers was the woman he decided to marry, Margarita "Meg" Masters. In the event he never married Meg, though they did have a daughter together. They spent the last years of the 1930s living in Highgate, and working for whichever Trotskyist faction Wilfred had joined in London. He was taciturn in remembering his side of the break: "I got fed up with Mike because we were not the same kind of person."[45] The split was not so decisive as Michael remembered, for he and Wilfred worked together on further projects in 1939 and in 1940, meeting occasionally and exchanging letters and Christmas cards long into the war.[46] But the intense relationship that had caused such joy and pain for the best part of a decade was at an end.

Michael's Trotskyism had not entirely rested on the three-headed catalyst of Alan Bush, Phyllis Kemp, and Wilfred Franks. Within the space of a year his close friendships with all three had faded almost to nothing, but he lost neither his revolutionary zeal nor his love for Wilfred overnight. The sharp break of Wilfred's departure nevertheless caught Michael's passion before it could be subjected to the quotidian weathering of age, of domesticity, of fame. Wilfred was for ever preserved for him in a delicate amber of youth, barely aged from when he had first clapped eyes on what he described as Wilfred's "coal-black hair". The similes of his memory were woven from that revolutionary time in the mining villages of the north. Half a century later Michael began his final opera, *New Year*, in which a young "coal-haired stranger", from another world and of impossible beauty, visits the heroine, and they fall in love.

Across the Channel, Hitler was pushing to invade the Sudetenland region of Czechoslovakia, and Britain threatened to join France against such aggression. Armed conflict felt inevitable, and the country watched anxiously to see how Neville Chamberlain, who had become Prime Minister the year before, would deal with the situation. Michael was no longer an active force in any group that saw the conflict as an opportunity to arm the workers and bring about capitalism's downfall, and his emotional and political distress, long simmering, long contradictory, boiled over completely. "A breakdown of a relationship", he recounted, "happens to me with great violence, [producing] a break in your interior world, when what has been put upon someone else comes back like *that*, and it came back on me."[47]

His earlier attempts at dream analysis and a Jungian rebirth had been short-lived, and only the odd dream had found its way by letter to John Layard since 1936. When Wilfred's bombshell was finally dropped, Michael went straight back to Layard, who took notes of two formal analysis sessions, on 16 and 17 August 1938; there were then a further two in November.[48] Michael's dreams had begun to dig right down into his sexual past, and one figure about whom he dreamed vividly was Herbert Sumsion, his first love, from Royal College days. But the dreams had also turned disturbing, recounted for Layard in a bleary, agitated handwriting with startling violence. One of his first after losing Wilfred to Meg Masters was of watching from a high window, but as if in close-up, two foxes mating. "Vixen covers him," he wrote, "draws him over, bit by bit, till vixen is on her back below window, so that I can see the udders – as yet, I notice, no entry of penis into cunt. Fox comes to the final charge – notice his snarling jaw and teeth."[49] Often he wrote to Layard of his distress, whether in dream worlds, or the real world, or both: "feeling of being useless", "no job to do", "everyone else seems positive, myself alone negative, inferior".[50] Even before Wilfred's engagement, Michael's dreams had become feverish and frightened, not only in response to his personal life but in fear at the world's situation. On the night of 24 January 1938 he had dreamed of chopping wood with an axe. "Suddenly a voice speaks from the roof: 'Hitler is Lord and Master of us all, now.'"[51]

In many ways Michael was a prime candidate for Jungian analysis. His class; his complex sexuality; the violence of his schooldays; the intermittent breakdown of relations with his mother – all lay to differing extents unacknowledged. Jung believed that the "individuation" process could be achieved only by those willing to remove themselves from the safe architecture of convention prescribed by family or Church (or political party), and instead undergo a process in which elements of the personality are integrated into a healthily functioning whole. The process was lonely, and required parting from the crowd, a good fit for Michael, who had always felt in himself an acute sense of unbelonging, and who was on the verge of moving away from the Trotskyist shoals with which he had temporarily swum in political togetherness.

But journeys to self-knowledge and self-acceptance, via whatever road, can be tortuous and slow, and the last four months of 1938 were ones of loneliness and of mental crisis. Once again Michael considered a shared life with Francesca Allinson in the hopes of domesticity and children, and they trialled cohabitation. As he remembered, "when we ever tried to live together the problem was [. . .] that I had no money, I couldn't support her; she wanted a social life, and I was locked in this everlasting obsessive bloody music – so she'd be there for a fortnight and then go away".[52] The impression is of a man groping for solutions to psychological quandaries, none of which was entirely successful in satisfying his three-pronged desire for emotional, sexual, and domestic content-ment. Around this time came an affair with Bryan Fisher, who admitted that, though on the verge of meeting and marrying his wife, he "went to bed with Michael for a short time because he wanted me to and I was more than grateful to him for the loving and fresh air he had brought into my life. But I soon found it was not a satisfactory means of expressing my feelings for him, so I returned to my single bed."[53] Eleven years younger than Michael, ostensibly heterosexual, alight with revolutionary fire, Bryan may have seemed a potential Wilfred substitute. But when, all too simi-lar to Wilfred in other ways, he visited Whitegates Cottage with his fiancée in tow, the situation became tense and awkward, and was never again repeated.

It was not that Michael took refuge in promiscuity, and he openly admitted that he "saw little value in sex as sex".[54] Nor did he thrill to the ostensible unavailability of the heterosexual, for any lack of reciprocity or longevity in an affair was a constant pain. Sex was for him a way of demonstrating friendship, as well as love; or rather it was the fact that almost all of his friendships were conducted with such loving intensity that sex seemed their natural expression. When his offering of it proved irresistible to some of the young men he took under his wing, it was less a question of their sexual orientation than of grateful affection or tentative experimentation. For the sake of self-preservation Michael soon lessened his hopes that these brief dalliances might result in anything other than the usual pattern of departure to married life. His relationship with Nick Myant had led him to describe his "love with young people as a sort of warming the heart for the bride or bridegroom" that would inevitably follow.[55] Love made him generous even as loss, which is stitched into the fibre of such relationships, threatened. From the sidelines his friends watched in concern, foreseeing the inevitable abandonments. Michael once wrote sadly to David Ayerst: "I've had to renounce everything I most long for – a shared home etc."[56]

By late September 1938 the war appeared to be upon Britain. Reneging on previous agreements, Hitler had demanded the Sudetenland entire, and Chamberlain had refused. Children were sent out of London. Pits for air-raid shelters began to be dug, and at zoos across the country preparations were made to shoot the most dangerous animals lest a bomb facilitate their escape. At his piano in Whitegates Cottage, Michael's response was to jot down a shuffling, unnerving little motif that lay dormant until it became the theme for a string quartet begun some years later. On 29 September Chamberlain went to Munich. By the small hours of the next day it had been agreed that Britain and France would permit Hitler's annexation of the Sudetenland, and the Munich agreement was signed by Chamberlain, Hitler, Mussolini, and the French Prime Minister, Édouard Daladier. Hitler then signed a peace treaty between Britain and Germany, which Chamberlain brought back to rejoicing crowds. It would be "peace for our time". On 4 October Michael wrote to Ruth Pennyman that it had been a "nightmare week" that had "laid all my plans in ruins".[57] The family of an unemployed comrade, presumably evacuated from London, had descended upon his bungalow. Michael's hospitality indicates a not entirely unfaded Trotskyite tendency, which could have had a new surge of energy in light of the formal declaration of the Fourth International the previous month. Michael had written of military conflict with anticipation verging on excitement, a sense that the war was inevitable and should be used as a means of arming the proletariat. Nevertheless, he had been anti-war at all costs, and most Trotskyists differed from Stalinists by believing that capitulating to Hitler was a necessary spoke in the more important wheel of internal revolution. Later he described, with no concession as to the suffering of the Czechs or the weaknesses of appeasement, "the extraordinary moment of September 1938 when the four men sat round a table, representing the Ideal, the Dream, the way that might have been".[58]

Michael held fast to work and continued his Concerto for Double String Orchestra, but, at the grand old age of thirty-three, felt he wanted to write a "major artistic statement of all that I felt about the state of the world".[59] Ambitions for his Jungian choral work, Nekyia, began to fade, not least because his intended collaborator, the poet George Barker, was soon to depart to a professorship in Japan, and thence to America.* Laying this choral work aside, Michael turned instead to a piece for the stage. He began to plan very roughly an opera that would combine his complex political views with his new phase of psychological rebirth. It was a figure from his childhood who surfaced to inspire him: Charlotte Despard, whom his mother had followed into prison all those years ago. Despard was living in London, and had stayed politically active long into her nineties. She mooted the idea of an opera based around the events of the Easter Rising in Ireland, the armed rebellion of 1916 in which Irish Republicans attempted to emancipate themselves from British rule. The uprising had been the inspiration not only for Yeats's poem "Easter, 1916", but also for a 1935 play of the same name by the writer Montagu Slater (with incidental music by Benjamin Britten, who would soon invite Slater to write the libretto for Peter Grimes). Slater was a Communist Party member who had written the scenario for an enormous Co-operative Society pageant in which Michael had conducted his New Malden choir; it was held in Wembley Stadium that summer, with music composed by Alan Bush.[60] It was either in direct emulation of Slater, or just as a consequence of inhaling the same political air, that Michael thought Despard's suggestion a good one. The Easter setting could be a symbol of rebirth and a new world order, committee meetings paralleled with the Last Supper. The lead character would be Roger Casement, who had played a major role in ensuring German support for Irish

---

* Where his affair with the writer Elizabeth Smart became the subject of her 1945 novel, By Grand Central Station I Sat Down and Wept.

independence and was executed for treason. The opera was to be largely set in the submarine in which he travelled to Ireland hoping to postpone the uprising until greater aid could be provided.[61] Homosexual, anti-colonialist, and revolutionary, Casement would doubtless have been the wronged hero of the piece. And that was the opera Michael wanted to write, as the country breathed slowly out, granted its year's reprieve, the war clouds held temporarily at bay, that autumn, in 1938.

FOURTEEN

The World Turns on its Dark Side

On the morning of 7 November 1938, 300 miles from Oxted, a seventeen-year-old boy crossed the Boulevard Saint-Germain in Paris and walked towards the Seine. He passed the Gare d'Orsay, and turned left onto the Rue de Lille, heading for the German Embassy. On his arrival the boy claimed to have important information he wished to impart to the ambassador. He was shown to the office of a junior official named Ernst vom Rath, whom he shot, five times, wounding him in the spleen, pancreas, and stomach. When the police arrived the boy made no attempt to run, confessed openly to the crime, claimed his motive was to avenge the persecution of Jews, and gave his name as Herschel Grynszpan.

Born in Germany to Polish Jews, Grynszpan had moved to Paris to live with his uncle and aunt. Denied Polish citizenship and official residence, he drifted, stateless and illegal, around the coffee shops and cinemas of Paris. In October 1938 his parents, still living in Hanover, were arrested and deported to Poland, becoming stranded on the border in barely human conditions. Herschel's sister sent him a postcard pleading for help. In response, he asked his uncle to send money, and on his uncle's refusal there was a row that led to Herschel's walking out of the house to spend the night in an hotel. The next morning he wrote a card to his parents and went to buy a revolver, before taking the métro to the embassy.

It took Ernst vom Rath, who was twenty-nine, two days to die, in which time he was treated by Hitler's personal doctors. He died on

9 November, at half past five in the afternoon. Later that evening the Propaganda Minister, Joseph Goebbels, made a speech in Munich in which he said that any acts of revenge taken against Jews would not be opposed or prevented. It took just hours for the Nazis to unleash vengeance (thought to have been long-planned, vom Rath's assassination a handy pretext), in which Jewish communities throughout Germany were attacked. Tens of thousands were arrested and sent to concentration camps. Shops, homes, offices, synagogues were burned or attacked in their thousands, and, later, insurance claims for the damage were ignored. Germany's cities blazed and glittered in the violence, and the streets of shivered panes gave the riots their collective name: Kristallnacht. The Night of Broken Glass.

Back in England, Michael followed the case in the newspapers, and read about the country he loved being set alight. In Munich, the location of his first trip to Germany, over 1,000 Jewish men were arrested during the riots and taken ten miles north, to the concentration camp at Dachau. Frankfurt an der Oder, where he and Francesca Allinson had visited Georg Götsch's music school, now lay on the railway route of locked train carriages crammed with Jews en route to Poland. The violence of Kristallnacht ended in the early morning of 10 November. The very next day Michael travelled to Bloomsbury to hear Phyllis Sellick give the premiere of his piano sonata, providing him with immediate access to a wider range of reports and conversation than was available in the solitude of Whitegates.[1] British papers were mainly outraged at the attack, the national mood becoming gradually more critical of Chamberlain's appeasement policy. Michael faced with increasing disgust the reality that even left-wing political parties in Britain, let alone the government, were going to do little in the way of helping Jewish refugees. The country's immigration policy was liberalised as a result of Kristallnacht, and Jewish children began to arrive on the Kindertransport, some of them billeted with Michael's parents in Somerset. But for every arriving child there were parents left behind in Europe. By the outbreak of war nearly 70,000 Jews had been admitted to Britain, but nearly half a million were turned away.[2]

Michael had started to lose faith in the idea of a dramatic work on the Easter Rising and may already have been casting about for a subject that could be treated in a more contemplative form, or hoping somehow to return to his earlier plan for a tripartite choral work on Jungian themes. In his mind began to form a secular oratorio, taking as its models Handel's *Messiah* and Bach's Passions, with Grynszpan cast as "the protagonist of a modern passion story".[3] A few weeks later, Michael's attention was drawn to a review in the *Times Literary Supplement* of two novellas by the Austro-Hungarian writer Ödön von Horváth. The first was *Ein Kind unserer Zeit*: "A Child of Our Time". Its protagonist was a young German soldier, brought up in unemployment and degradation, who becomes easy meat for the Fatherland's ideals and, brainwashed, turns to murder. At the end of the book the soldier staggers to a park bench, frozen half to death. A child approaches, thinking him a snowman. "Your children will tell you that this soldier was a common murderer – but don't revile him. Just think, how could he help himself? He was a child of his time."[4]

Reading von Horváth's novella eventually gave Michael the title for the work he came to write on the Grynszpan story. The book provided not only a prophecy of Herschel Grynszpan's actions, but a way of viewing them – with pity, even sympathy. Michael had a pronounced capacity to side with the underdog, and saw in Grynszpan a man driven to desperate action by the times in which he lived. Years before, he had admitted to finding "the archetype of the prisoner, scapegoat, crucified, and so on" to be "the totally powerful one".[5] Baldly, even beautifully, he had conceded his capacity for empathy above all else: "Here is the real revolutionary kernel in me – sown by Blake and more disastrous than Marx-Lenin because it thrusts the luring branches up through the most sacred institutions of the whole kingdom – church, state, law, morality, crumble before the child's tear."[6] Later he would admit that he had "taken Grynszpan as hero", and it is possible that he thought he had witnessed – with something approaching approval – the trigger for international revolution.[7] After all, Grynszpan's actions had been propagated by Michael as the ideal: the youth who turns a gun on authority. In February 1939, Leon Trotsky circulated an essay in which he stated his "open moral solidarity" with Grynszpan. Despite thinking the boy's act unwise, in that mass revolutionary forces were far preferable to lone acts of violence, Trotsky wrote that "all our emotions, all our sympathies are with self-sacrificing avengers, even though they have been unable to discover the correct road", believing that Grynszpan should be "torn out of the hands of capitalist justice". And he concluded that Grynszpan's attack "may serve as an example for every young revolutionist".[8]

A month before this essay was published, Michael heard a broadcast of some African-American spirituals on the crystal wireless set he had purchased. It is a mark of spirituals' popularity at the time that the exact performance he heard can only be guessed at out of a great number, but it was likely by the Northern Ireland Singers conducted by James Denny, put out on the BBC National Programme at 12.45 p.m. on 10 January 1939.[9] Michael had known spirituals since his schooldays, and a concert devoted to them had been given at the Royal College when he was a student (on 5 March 1925). James Weldon Johnson's two volumes of spirituals, for which Michael sent away in high excitement, were often to be seen on the pianos of amateur musicians such as he had known and worked with in Oxted. He thought he had found a contemporary musical parallel to the Lutheran chorales with which Bach had punctuated his Passions. Spirituals expressed a collective suffering that could speak not just for the African slaves who had created them, but on a more universal level. In Nazi Germany, they fell under the title of *Negermusik* and were banned in an attempt to censor foreign infiltration of Aryan culture; to place them within a British oratorio was not only a musical innovation but a political statement. They had been used in political pageants over the last decade: Edward Genn and Matthew Anderson, with whom Michael had worked on *The Pageant of Labour*, included them in their *Lancashire Cotton Pageant*, performed in Manchester in 1932.

It is a possibility that at the turn of the year Michael was contemplating a revolutionary oratorio, a series of short scenes in which choruses could take on many parts, with Grynszpan proffered as the revolutionary turning his gun on the fascist Establishment, and the spirituals included almost as political anthems, universalised versions of the "Internationale" such as could be sung by massed forces of Co-operative Choirs at some stadium or other. Alan Bush had devoted much time and energy to enormous stagings of Handel's oratorios reconfigured as political pageants, most notably *Belshazzar* at the Scala Theatre in Camden, in May 1938. Michael's planned scheme for *A Child of Our Time* has to be understood as emerging from five years of intense political engagement, and from his involvement with large-scale political-musical projects. He referred to the character of Grynszpan's uncle as a "comrade", and wondered about the effect a performance would have on "party members".[10] But as the work progressed, and as he cast around for a writer who might provide a text on the story, his emotional realignment continued.

He had been teaching Oliver Morley piano in Sussex for nearly five years, at the house in which T.S. Eliot was a frequent visitor, but it wasn't until early in 1939 that Michael plucked up courage to be directly in touch with Eliot, asking him to write a libretto for this modern oratorio. It was an ambitious and self-confident request, given that his own reputation – as compared to Eliot's – was scant. On one level it was shrewd, as Eliot's name on a work would all but guarantee interest and performances. Eliot had never written for a composer and Michael confidently thought the oratorio's novel combination of contemporaneity and tradition might appeal to him. On 8 February, Eliot replied. "Thank you for your very interesting letter. I should be delighted to see you and talk about the possibilities."[11] They arranged to meet in March, at Faber and Faber's offices in Russell Square. At one stage Eliot, who had quoted from a spiritual in *Murder in the Cathedral* and was said to sing them aloud in unguarded moments, appears nevertheless to have had the wrong end of the stick about their inclusion in the oratorio, apparently enquiring, "Are the chorus going to black their faces?"[12] Michael left the meeting "tempted to whoop like a schoolboy", for Eliot had tentatively agreed to write a text, and asked for an outline of the overall scheme.[13] Yet to decide on using von Horváth's title,

Michael began to write draft notes for Eliot that he called *Sketch for
a Modern Oratorio*.[14]

In the sketch, as Eliot would perceive, much of the work that
became *A Child of Our Time*'s libretto is there in embryo. Michael
got carried away with himself and attempted to jot down the odd
line or two, either in the hope that Eliot would polish them up, or
with the hunch that Eliot's involvement, should it transpire, would
be of the most cursory kind. He gave his modern oratorio a three-
part structure based on Handel's *Messiah*: the first part preparatory
prophecy and scene-setting; the second "telling the story"; the third
moving towards redemption. The work was to begin up above the
clouds. Three years before, Michael had seen *The Green Pastures*, a film
depicting Bible stories as visualised by African-American characters.
Angels run to the gates of heaven to look over into space, and the
earth spins into view. It gave Michael his first image, crystallising
the accruing horrors of the decade: "The world turns on its dark
side." Many ideas and quotations from the oratorio's progenitor,
Nekyia, survived intact. He depicted a godless world in which men
proclaimed themselves deities; he wrote of morals turned topsy-
turvy; he wrote words for a chorus "led to a great slaughter", "cast
out by authority and tormented", suffering from "purges in the
east, lynching in the west". There was to be a young woman trying
desperately to comfort her children in the face of low wages and
encroaching violence; and a young worker, an echo of the unemployed Boosbeck miner, stunted and made bereft by his misfortune.

As Michael moved on to Part Two he began to tell the story
of Herschel Grynszpan, proceeding with a potent combination of
timeliness and timelessness that would translate the work from journalism to parable. No name, no country, no period is mentioned.
Grynszpan was to be a "young lad", Paris merely "a great city"
from which choruses of oppressed peoples clamour for "sanctuary", and choruses of oppressors proclaim: "We cannot have them
here in our just Empires. They shall not work, nor draw a dole."
The moment of the assassination is outlined with biblical simplicity. Studded through it all would come the spirituals Michael had
selected: "Steal away to Jesus" to end Part One, and "Deep River"

to end the whole thing. "Nobody knows de trouble I see, Lord" for the boy's anguish. "Go down, Moses", to be sung in response to the violence of *Kristallnacht*. And, to finish Part Two, a flicker of hope: "O, by an' by – I'm gwinter lay down my heavy load."

Michael was wringing the story dry of its politics, and to Eliot he wrote that any polemic in the work would be a "danger zone".[15] Even as he wrote his outline he was maintaining links with the Workers' International League (the party that had sprung up after the split in the Militant Group). As late as November 1939 he admitted that he was "in touch vaguely with the group" and "an unrepentant admirer" of its leaders.[16] But Michael's embryonic oratorio was taking on a life of its own, one that stretched wider than his personal situation. The work was getting carried away with itself, becoming more mature than its composer. He was not a man of regrets, and rarely one of retractions or apologies. He moved on; he looked forward. He was self-professedly "unrepentant". But although *A Child of Our Time*, even in this earliest form, cannot be read as an explicit withdrawal of his revolutionary views, it comes from a political mind on the cusp, daringly sympathetic towards a murderous figure, portraying an act that, just months before, its composer would have believed justifiably violent, but inviting the conclusion that no good political effect has been achieved bar further suffering.

The *Sketch for a Modern Oratorio* was being written for Eliot alongside Michael's Jungian analysis. On 4 January 1939 Michael took a dream to Layard in which his fears of war interrupted an embrace with Wilfred Franks:

I dreamt I was crouched under Wilf's legs, with my head just touching his balls. Looking out across fields towards my old home (childhood). I liked being there. I wanted to draw his legs in together closer to me. When I did this, the magic broke. Then the attack began. Huge aeroplanes like great white kites flying down from the right. Then we were in a sort of hut, shed. A girl is brought in slightly wounded by the splinter of a bomb.[17]

Layard, solemnly linking the spherical bombs to Wilf's testicles
when annotating the report, took this (and other dreams in which
young women were injured or killed) as a sign that Michael should
give up same-sex affairs. He proclaimed the women to be manifestations of Michael's soul, soon to be irreparably damaged by sexual
relations with men. Michael reached his own conclusion, taking the
girl to be his soul falling dead in consequence of his hesitations,
and feeling her appearance was a sign that his sexuality should be
embraced. He gave up on the sessions with Layard, and thereafter
became his own psychotherapist, recording and analysing his own
dreams.

Michael's dream diaries are formed of 364 pages, written almost
every morning between 30 January and 31 August 1939.[18] They
ring with startling vividness, so remarkable was his ability to
remember and recount in great detail his night thoughts, although
it is impossible to know, in the recollection of a dream, what is
the construction of the waker. The clearest conclusion to draw is
that Michael's sleep was fitful and feverish, or as he put it "not
always either fast asleep or slap awake – often inhabit the halfway
land and don't much worry".[19] Reading the diaries we must tread
softly, for we tread on his dreams. They are intensely private documents, although he would occasionally show excerpts to Evelyn
Maude, and sanctioned their partial inclusion in his autobiography.
But they are more disturbing than their selected publication would
have readers believe. There are very few of the expected "classic"
dreams: acting a part without knowing the lines, appearing naked
in public, losing all one's teeth. In his dreams Michael retreated
into childhood, finding himself back at Rosemary Cottage, or at his
prep school, or in the frozen Fettes dormitory awaiting the clang
of a morning bell. As he dreamed of childhood, so he physically
re-entered adolescence, and he would meticulously record waking
to find he had ejaculated in the night, experiencing once again
the "wet dreams" of puberty. He dreamed in vivid colour and in
detailed sound, able on waking to recollect the precise intonation of
a trumpet, the first phrase of a Vaughan Williams symphony, tunes
from *Robin Hood*, hymns on a church organ. Many of the dreams

were mundane, but occasionally he would suffer almost Dalí-esque visions of half-sexual nightmare, in which he would see, to quote a single example, "a woman's lower body from the waist face down on the ground, the legs slightly apart, a man's form in between the woman's legs trying to get back from two red tongues coming from the woman's behind".[20]

The presence of children (and especially of Oliver Morley) in the diaries week after week is no surprise, and Michael dreamed frequently about babies, delighting in the rituals of fatherhood: garden games, nappy-changing. Equally unsurprising is the frequency with which the dreams become sexual, often recounted with careful, physiological explicitness. In some, his relations with children move from the paternal to the sexual. A few years before, Michael had read an article by the artist Eric Kennington that had led him to think Kennington could offer useful thoughts on sexual crises. Michael requested and won a meeting that was awkward and unhelpful, but he took a shine to Kennington's "gentle son", Christopher, who turned fourteen in 1939.[21] Michael barely knew Christopher, but the boy sometimes became the object of his dream-desires.* Dreams may offer an environment in which we can test that which we would never experience or attempt in life, and many a night thought has contained the unsettling and the dangerous, depicting fears as well as cravings. The sleeping world is one beyond blame or judgement. There is no evidence to suggest Michael slept or wished to sleep with anyone under sixteen, and the accounts of such dreams, which focus on burgeoning adolescence rather than any childish physique or innocence, are less startling and illuminating than the fact of their frank recounting and careful

---

* "In or on a bed with Kennington's young son, Christopher (aged thirteen) [actually fourteen]. Perhaps we are both clothed. [. . .] his sexual parts [. . . seem] bigger, more adolescent than I expect. [. . .] I am a bit surprised at myself. [. . .] a sexual dream with a boy – fifteen or so. [. . .] it was not sexually aggressive – on the contrary, gentle, but very passionate and mutually desirous." Dream diaries, pp. 118–19, 229–30 (Wright collection). Christopher Kennington was born in March 1925 and died in October 2015.

1. Michael's father,
Henry William (Tippett) Kemp.

2. Michael's mother, Isabel Clementina
Binny Kemp. The family took Isabel's
maiden name in the 1920s.

3. Michael Tippett (right) with his brother, Peter, c.1910.

4. Artist Wilfred Franks, in costume for amateur theatricals. "Meeting with Wilf", Tippett wrote, "was the deepest, most shattering experience of falling in love."

5. Wilfred Franks as Autolycus in a production of *The Winter's Tale*, staged in the grounds of Ormesby Hall, Middlesbrough, summer 1933.

6. Tippett conducting the South London Orchestra at Morley College, 1930s. Second-from-the-left is leader Fred May, who accounted Tippett a "genuinely fine conductor"; in the background are murals by Charles Mahoney that were lost in the Blitz.

7. The cast of *Robin Hood*, a folk-song opera written by Tippett in collaboration with David Ayerst and Ruth Pennyman.

8. The cast were photographed, at Ruth's expense, outside the Miners' Hall in Boosbeck, Middlesbrough, in August 1934.

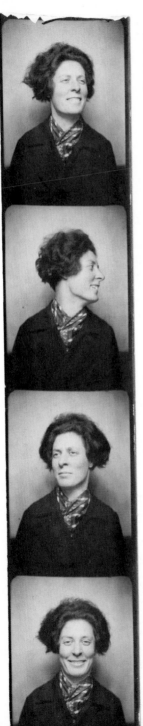

9. Writer and music-editor Enid "Francesca" Allinson, whom Tippett "was closer to than almost anybody". He recalled: "It was a strange, tender, extremely tender, gentle relationship."

10. Evelyn Maude, Tippett's "guardian angel".

11. Priaulx Rainier, composer. "It's always a great love I have of you," Tippett told her, "however ill expressed."

12. Michael Tippett, photographed in 1929, all but unknown as a composer. The following year the *Telegraph* would praise a concert showcasing his early pieces: "Not all young musicians have the remarkable gift of Michael Tippett."

13. Poet and curator Douglas Newton. "I love you in my own funny way," Tippett told him during the Second World War, hopeful that they might collaborate on the opera that became *The Midsummer Marriage*.

14. Artist Karl Hawker, with whom, in 1958, Tippett began a "relationship as near to marriage as these relationships can be".

15. At a rehearsal of Symphony No. 2 at the BBC Studios in Maida Vale, 4 February 1958. From left: conductor Adrian Boult, who led a premiere that broke down after a few bars; Tippett; composer Ralph Vaughan Williams with his wife, Ursula; and John Minchinton, whose affair with Tippett drew to a fiery close just six months later.

16. Tippett with his "step-daughters", Sarah (left) and Susan Hawker.

17. With Benjamin Britten, celebrating Tippett's sixtieth birthday at Morley College, on 2 January 1965. At the party Tippett was presented with a book in which Britten had written "I am proud to call you my friend".

FRIENDS AND FAMILY

18. George Tippett

19. David Ayerst

20. Christopher Fry

21. Ruth Pennyman

22. Alan Bush

23. Phyllis Kemp

24. Oliver Morley

25. Bryan Fisher

26. Shelagh Fisher

27. John Layard

28. Edric Maynard

29. Anna Kallin

preservation. They are forged of the quality remarkable in Michael's correspondence: the fierce and unafraid attempt to acknowledge everything; to leave out nothing; and to see and know himself in every detail.

The year and its dreams continued, but his mind had turned inwards from events on the world stage. His diaries do not mention Madrid's surrender in March 1939, which ended the Spanish Civil War; nor Hitler's renunciation of Germany's non-aggression pact with Poland, which led to conscription in Britain for men aged twenty to twenty-one. Michael was working to complete the *Sketch for a Modern Oratorio*, and in early summer sent the typescript off to Eliot, who held on to it, ruminating, almost until the end of the year before giving any definitive answer.[22]

Michael then turned to another children's opera, once again written with Christopher Fry for the Co-operative Society choirs, and intended to repeat the success he had scored with *Robert of Sicily* the year before. This second venture, called *Seven at One Stroke*, had better funding, and Michael risked a mass performance rather than dividing up the choirs into separate groups. He and Christopher turned to a Grimm fairy tale about a tailor who killed seven flies "at one stroke", before going out into the world and winning the inevitable princess and half the kingdom. Christopher had great fun with the text: "I'm tired of eating frugal fare | And sitting on my derriere"; "And my ambitions churn up | While I complete the turn up."[23] For the music Michael arranged a handful of nursery rhymes, and, neatly coinciding with his work on *A Child of Our Time*, incorporated a spiritual that is now far beyond the bounds of political correctness: "Go to sleep my little piccaninny [. . .] Mammy's little Alabama coon." The opera was performed in Peckham on 15 April 1939, and then again at Woolwich on 10 June. Michael himself joined in. As he wrote in an advertisement, "there is a novelty this time in that the choirmasters appear on the stage as the giants. They have some remarkable and ingenious masks to wear, made by Wilfred Franks, who makes masks for television."[24]

Separated as they were, Wilfred and Michael were still frequent collaborators, and after *Seven at One Stroke* they moved swiftly on to a project designed to raise funds for a children's hospital: the Symphony of Youth, a "musical spectacle in two acts expounding the progress of youth and dedicated to its spirit".[25] The score was made up of arrangements by the organist Frederick Holloway and the critic Edward Lockspeiser, but the scenario, following children through infancy to adolescence with scenes of playground games and physical exercises, owes much to Michael, who had devised and produced the whole affair in collaboration with the producer Carrington Wood and the novelist Louis Golding. The evening concluded with a torchlit procession to "symbolise youth's spiritual awakening", the children "on the verge of dreams". The Symphony of Youth ran from 21 June to 15 July 1939, in the since-demolished open-air theatre in Brockwell Park, south London, specially extended for the occasion to accommodate a 5,000-strong audience; the park even installed an organ. Michael conducted the orchestra and the cast of 1,000 locals, aged between five and twenty-one. Wilfred rehearsed the children and provided masks and puppets, some based on Mickey Mouse. In the end it was British weather, rather than the spirit of youth, that triumphed: on most evenings the heavens opened, and the venture lost a huge amount of money.

In between Seven at One Stroke and the Symphony of Youth, and at the height of his dreams, Michael finished his Concerto for Double String Orchestra, on 6 June 1939. He had expected his self-analysis to lead him towards a more socially permissible sexual and domestic life. But as the diaries went on he was led to accept the facets of himself he was discovering anew, and it was in this mood that he finished the piece, spurred on by faint glimmers of success in his compositional life. Earlier in the year an article had been published in Monthly Musical Record praising Michael's small but striking output; and in February Phyllis Sellick had broadcast his piano sonata on the BBC Regional Programme.[26] At a concert a year or two before, Michael had met Wilhelm Strecker, the head of German publisher Schott Music, who offered to look at a portfolio of scores. Thrilled to be considered by a European publisher, Michael waited until he had finished the concerto before sending Strecker the five pieces that he regarded as his "official" catalogue: the concerto, the symphony, the string quartet, the piano sonata, and *A Song of Liberty*. These had been rejected by various British publishers, but at a meeting in Schott's London offices just weeks before the outbreak of war, Wilhelm Strecker's son Hugo agreed definitely to publish the concerto, and (provisionally) the piano sonata. Meanwhile Wilhelm sent a message from Germany expressing his agreement, "if we are all alive when the fighting is over". This card was one of the very last letters to reach London from Germany before the war began.[27] Conflict between the countries had become inevitable, and it made the Streckers' offer unfeasible. Paper-rationing threatened, and any printing of contemporary music by Schott would have had to be done in Germany. The agreement was put on hold, and the manuscripts went into store. Back to square one – although Schott did offer an annual retainer of £100 per year, a vital addition to Michael's depleted resources.

It is no surprise that Schott had firmly singled out the double concerto for publication. Not a concerto in the sense of a soloist pitched against larger forces, the piece is a Baroque-inspired "concerto grosso" of two string orchestras, placed in complementary partnership rather than argument, kicking the music back and forth, each winding in and out of the spotlight, first one in clearer focus, then the other, occasionally uniting. The score places its individual talent in the tradition of English composers that had gone before: Elgar and Vaughan Williams are vivid influences. But Michael had incorporated the techniques of jazz and blues, adding to his seductive rhythmic gallop a new spikiness redolent of Stravinsky and Bartók, and bearing aloft his long, long phrases with no visible means of support, like birds floating on some invisible current.

Michael had written to Alan Bush: "my job now is really to get myself straight – to disentangle my Logos self from the mastery by Eros".[28] (Jung had suggested that a masculine "Logos" – rationality – was a counterpart to the feminine "Eros" – love – and that the two needed to be accepted and balanced.) One reading of the concerto's three movements is as a commentary on this very disentangling. The thorny energy of the first movement, modelled on the layout of a Beethoven string quartet, epitomises the struggle in the head; the yearning bluesy lines of the central movement form a great cry of the heart; and, in the third and final movement, head and heart unite. Michael's college friend Jeffrey Mark was convinced that the concerto should incorporate melodies and rhythms of English folk-songs and dances. So, for the climax of his ebullient finale, Michael introduced snatches of a Northumbrian bagpipe tune, which, as each orchestra spurs the other on to greater heights, leads the concerto to bursting point. The strings tighten and tauten, as if winding up an internal spring that, when released, propels the movement to a free-wheeling burst of melody that ends the piece in burnished joy, after a final whoop from the cellos.

The concerto is steeped in Michael's political thought, wiped clean of the politics. He was able to take the revolutionary theories in which he had saturated himself, blow off the political dust, and use what was left behind for composition. Alan Bush had titled his early quartet *Dialectic*, as an explicit reference to Dialectical Materialism: the Marxist theory that political and historical events result from a constant conflict between opposites. Michael's music takes the theory, wringing it dry of overtones from Marx and Engels, and tussling instead with the Jungian dialectics between Logos and Eros, masculine and feminine, conscious and unconscious, light and shadow. In dramatising such tussles in music, his love of counterpoint, a technique defined by setting one line against another, found its natural expression.

The concerto marked Michael's decisive move from political specificity to human universality (or universal humanity) and, later, became the first piece he permitted to appear unrevised in his published catalogue. The two children's operas for the Co-operative Society, his music for Boosbeck, works such as *The Miners* or *A Song of Liberty* – performances of these he expressly forbade. He resisted too all efforts in his lifetime to publish his correspondence with Alan Bush and David Ayerst, and never spoke of his collaborations with Margaret Barr. This was more than a simple refusal to show his progression to maturity; it was a calculated wiping-clean of his life in the 1930s, a period of global and personal crisis, of fire and revolution, of love and distress. In 1937 W.H. Auden had written

in his long poem *Spain* of the "conscious acceptance of guilt in the
necessary murder", altered the line to "the fact of murder", and
then withdrew the whole work. Benjamin Britten likewise retracted
his *Pacifist March*, a strangely militant song composed for the Peace
Pledge Union. A generation of artists had been caught between a
past of unknowable violence and deprivation, and a future that
threatened similar horrors on an even wider scale.

Among the final entries in Michael's dream diaries are those
headed "Special Dreams during Holiday, 22 July–8 August".[29] The
holiday was with Bryan Fisher, and they went off together to stay
with Francesca Allinson, who was living with her lover Judy Wogan
in the village of St Osyth, close to the Essex coast. The four of them
spent a happy week on Judy's yacht, which was moored nearby.
For the second week, Michael and Bryan went to the Lake District,
joined by Anthony Sedgwick (one of the Blundell's pupils to whom
Michael had been close). The train on which they returned from
Penrith to London was crowded with soldiers, and they emerged
into a city that, Bryan remembered, was "turbid with tensions,
evacuations, ugly and cumbersome barrage balloons floating on
their cables, black-out, fears and bonhomie".[30]

The Emergency Powers (Defence) Act 1939 was passed on 23
August, giving the government unprecedented powers of defence
and attack. When Michael made one final visit to London in the
last week of August, "in full preparation for war nightmare", there
were fleets of buses conveying children out of the city.[31] The underground was at a standstill; hospitals were cleared and windows
fortified against attack. Coffins began to be stockpiled.

On 31 August 1939 Michael dreamed that four men were going
to strangle him to death. During the dream he heard himself say:
"Let what must be happen."[32] He interpreted the men as benign
spirits, throttling the final vestiges of shame and fear within him.
He took his sanguine reaction to possible death as a sign of the
calmness with which he could now accept himself and his place in
the world. "I knew that the outcome was that I was not going to
come out married and with children, which some part of me would
have loved, but that I was a better artist."[33] Finally the passage from

Jung that had struck him two years before could truly apply to his own situation: "being receptive to whatever comes to me, good and bad, sun and shadow that are there for the shifting, and, in this way, also accepting my own nature with its positive and negative sides". Two years earlier he had asked the poet George Barker to transmute the sense of this passage into a singable libretto. Now, for *A Child of Our Time*, he dipped Herschel Grynszpan in the Jungian philosophy he believed to have been his own salvation. Grynszpan, in shooting vom Rath, had projected an inner psychological turmoil onto an external figure, rather than acknowledging and unifying it within the psyche. The oratorio concludes with what Michael believed to be an important truth: "I would know my dark side and my light, so shall I at last be whole." Eventually he altered it: "I would know my shadow and my light, so shall I at last be whole", cross-stitching two vowel sounds, i and o, all through the line, like conflicting entities trying to unite in one self.

The oratorio, even in its earliest sketches, is too outward-looking to be reduced to self-portrait. But in its portrayal of Grynszpan – rumoured homosexual, and certainly society's outcast – there is something of Michael, as he came to believe that his own political violence had been a release of repressed turmoil. The dream world had not been a repository from which he drew musical inspiration. But he had delved into and acknowledged memories he didn't know he harboured. He made peace with what he discovered, but in this psychological peace-making there arose what was nearly a second crisis, for the entirely equable mind gave off, or so he thought, little creative energy. Self-acceptance had to stop short of sinking into a mundane serenity. Acceptance came in embracing life's troubles as necessary for creative work. Although he continued for years to send intermittent reports of his more confusing dreams to John Layard, he gave up the diary and analysis. At thirty-four, he had made life's transition from becoming to being, from preparing to living, and had the rare privilege of knowing the exact moment of juncture.

Michael's long and hard-won journey to musical and psychological maturity had coincided with the dark and now certain prospect of a second world war. He made his final entry in the dream diaries on 31 August, just days after the Molotov–Ribbentrop Pact, in which his fears of the Soviet Union proved founded, as it agreed to non-aggression with the Nazis. The next day, 1 September, Hitler invaded Poland. Far across the ocean Wystan Auden, who had moved to New York earlier that year, sat in one of the dives on 52nd Street in Manhattan, "uncertain and afraid, as the clever hopes expire, of a low dishonest decade". On that same day Michael wrote to David Ayerst in despair: "It seems to be going over the edge. I lose all my jobs in London. Composition isn't a social possibility in war."[34] The Morley family planned to emigrate and Oliver no longer needed a piano teacher. A concert in which Michael's Concerto for Double String Orchestra was to have been premiered was cancelled. Blackout curtains were being sewn, gas masks of pungent black rubber distributed as a possible defence against a war that would be fought for an unknowable time, and waged with who knew what lethal weaponry. Mustard gas, perhaps, that would float on the streets in yellow clouds from high-explosive shells. *Hitler will send no warning*, the posters read. *So always carry your gas mask.*

Britain had agreed a pact of mutual assistance with Poland, and on the morning of 3 September gave Germany an ultimatum to cease military operations. At quarter past eleven Neville Chamberlain broadcast to the nation. When Michael heard that Britain was at war for the second time in his life, he was presumably glued, like most of the country, to his wireless. He remembered "being alone in my cottage and saying 'it'll be like this for a long time. Looking out and hoping to survive.'"[35] He may have heard a distant wailing in Oxted just before half past eleven, as the country's air-raid sirens began to go off in warning, and in rural areas wardens bravely ran to wind the alarms by hand, or to drive past secluded houses making sure that residents were indoors and under cover.

What use is music if the world is on fire? Michael found some manuscript paper and wrote down the first notes of *A Child of Our Time*.

DIARY:

Manchester – London

I had given up hope of ever seeing filmed footage of Michael as a young man. Then, suddenly, two discoveries. The first is a brief piece of colour footage taken of a performance of *Robert of Sicily* at Abbey Wood in 1938: a forest of a thousand hats watches choir after choir of children processing down the aisles in medieval dress, carrying banners onto the simple white stage, with its backdrop of crudely drawn pillars, followed by small scenes of duel and drama. A tall, dark-haired man stands in the corner in front of a small band, waving his arms maniacally.[36] Later, in a small office at the National Co-operative Archives in Manchester, I find him again, filmed, also in 1938, for *People with a Purpose*, a documentary to advertise the Royal Arsenal Co-operative Society. About halfway through, Michael, thirty-three years old, rehearses actors and singers in a performance of *Robin Hood*. He is far more natural and at ease than everyone else, and he conducts up on stage as he rehearses, moving amid the singers. His posture is ramrod-straight and as his dark-haired head floats, weirdly disembodied, high above the performers, I see clearly just how tall he was. He looks informal but less eccentric than I had expected, in trousers and a tank top, with his sleeves rolled up. It is Michael that starts things off, shouting: "Where is Alan a'Dale? Is he delivering milk again at this hour?" Enter Alan a'Dale, in contemporary dress as a Co-op milkman, while everyone else is in medieval mummery. The orchestra and singers sound professional as they embark on the overture at impressive speed. Michael's conducting technique is precise, until there is some kind of game or riot on stage and he doodles the air with twice as many movements as are necessary or clear to follow

– but it doesn't matter, because nobody is watching him anyway.

It is under a neon glare in London's British Library that Michael Tippett clicks yet further into focus, in thousands of silent-speaking words. His childhood nickname had been "non-stop" and he proved unstoppable as a letter writer: "Don't be worried by these rows of letters. I get into the habit of writing a whole batch to someone and then stop for a bit."[37] A steady flow of letters projects his voice across the decades, the loose knitting of his speedy italics frequently dropping stitches or unravelling across the page, six words to a line, in order to catch up with his thoughts. I find myself sneaking up on words unawares in the hopes that the jumble of marks might arrange themselves into recognisable English. Mostly they do, and I get faster as, not entirely immune to a kind of voyeuristic pleasure, I rummage about amid the flimsy sheets in which Michael Tippett's private life lies preserved. Sentences twist and turn and tangle, divided more by dashes than by commas, no more than epistolary gulps for air. The letters verge on self-obsession, their recipient almost incidental to their content: "I am writing this really to clear up my own mind as I so often have to – I only think with difficulty!"[38] He used his correspondence as a means of filing his thoughts and relating his life, as if a diary, adding courtesies just at the last minute. "Remember to me your wife" is often scrawled in another pen just before the paper reached the envelope. "As usual," he admitted, "one writes letters to oneself!"[39] Eventually he purchased a typewriter, but the tiny number of typed documents are almost harder to navigate than the handwritten ones, the words disappearing beneath layers of misprints and his haphazard attempts to correct them. The declaration of war instantly makes itself felt, as watermarked notepaper gives way to a pile of lemon-yellow sheets, tissue-thin, and his handwriting shrivels further into illegibility in an effort to save space.

The writer that emerges is winningly informal, never frightened of asking favours, adept at requesting money, and secure to the point of manipulation in the efficacy of his charm. He is also indiscreet: "this you must keep to yourself – in fact you oughtn't to know, so forget it at once".[40] He offers frequent verbose apologies for his verbosity, and is startlingly blunt on matters financial, emotional, and all else that he might have been expected to starch into discretion under the stiffest of upper lips. Mentioning masturbation as a cure for insomnia, he drops the remedy into the written conversation as if recommending the counting of sheep. He wrote letters on Christmas or

New Year's Day with no mention of festivity; he wrote letters to the newest of friends addressed lavishly to "dearest", "mine", "angel". Documents from the 1930s are dense with political acronyms and Marxist theory, contain many arguments but no quarrels, point out failings but never bear grudges, and happily sweep aside lengthy and tangled disagreements with a cheerful "anyhow, much love". Amid the fuzzy mass of sentences and names, of dates and political parties, is a sharp clear-sightedness.

Slowly I begin to realise that Michael wrote as he spoke, and spoke as he thought. His speech was fast and emphatic, dashing across his already wide range of knowledge and reference, with thoughts trailing off as new ones rushed in to take their place, his brain always slightly ahead of his mouth. He gave an interview later in life in which the journalist described him "saying the punctuation of a sentence, quite unaware that he was doing so, as if he were writing the words down".[41] His written English is a strange combination of unconscious idiosyncratic elegance and sheer verbal gawkiness, as if translated from another of the many languages he spoke: "I use much a thesaurus indeed!" And there is a strange sprung rhythm in the letters, a verbal syncopation. The composer Alexander Goehr says to me: "He had a mode of speech very much his own. It was high-pitched and it sang, it sang exactly like his music sings. Tippett had this idea, which I'm afraid I've inherited, of putting the [accented notes] on the wrong beat. And that's Tippett's voice again, you can hear Tippett talking, that's how he talked, he put things on the wrong beat." And indeed, Michael's pronunciation was always etymologically convincing but strangely off kilter: "ambi-*vay*lent"; "perseverence"; "*con*-dolence" . . .

Frequent in his correspondence are little rug-pulls and undercuts, turned on himself as well as on others in jibes of self-mockery, a caustic snap against any potential self-importance. A long artistic credo is appended with the sceptical giggle, a written raised eyebrow: "Well, well!" Haranguing John Layard, he finished with "Well, well – that's quite enough!", and in another letter "but enough of that".[42] Such phrases are scattered through his correspondence like stubborn knots tied at the end of topics over which he'd brook no further discussion, a shrug at his own troubles, at once laying them out as an impermeable barrier, and swerving them in side-stepping avoidance. "So it goes." "So that is over." And, many times: "So that's that."[43] Partly this was a determination to ensure that, just as his work warned against self-appointed prophets, he himself did not become sanctimonious. Often his music seems to destabilise itself with a chuckle, a musical wink, passages so vividly out of place that they seem purposeful self-sabotage, interruptions as surprising as Beethoven's use of a Turkish march must have seemed to the first audiences of the Ninth Symphony. Michael's Triple Concerto, finished in 1979, contains a dawn-chorus interlude, barely a minute long, which makes a sharp rip in the concerto's soundworld, led by a jaunty rhythm from the hi-hat, as if a mischievous poltergeist has descended to wreak havoc before as quickly departing. A tinkling or even bawdy passage from his Fourth Symphony seems suddenly to introduce a fairground band, like a cartoon musical pratfall. Or he could make the point with reticence, half resigned, half despairing, as in the final lines of a choral work he would write in the 1960s, *The Vision of Saint Augustine*: "I count not myself to have apprehended." As he once explained: "I have to put a pin in my own balloon so I'm down on the ground."[44]

It is as if the letters and the music convey a tone of voice: Michael Tippett, speaking.

PART FOUR

WAR
1939–1945

FIFTEEN

Pacifist

On 4 September 1939 Evelyn Maude wrote to her daughter: "I have just been with Michael and as always returned cheered up about this war which is no war – he believes that <u>nothing</u> is going on at the 'front' at all, nor will now that each side is within its own frontiers [. . .] he holds that any bigscale attack on either side is an impossibility and bombing alone no earthly use. It sounds more cheering than one might imagine and he has been usually a wise prophet."[1]

Over the next weeks the bureaucracy of the war came into force, the filling-out of registration forms so as to obtain buff-coloured identity cards or booklets of ration coupons (not needed, in the event, until early the following year). On 29 September came National Registration Day. In the census Michael gave his profession as "Instructor, Technical Institute, Private Tutor and Child Psychologist". Registered as living with him was his sometime lover and friend Bryan Fisher. Meantime the Western Allies did nothing to prevent Poland's being quickly overrun by the Nazis and the Soviets, and only minor skirmishes broke out in Europe. What became known as the Phoney War lasted for over eight months, until the German invasion of France in May 1940. When it became clear that bombs were not raining from the skies – at least not yet – many evacuees returned to their families in London. "We are having children on us," Michael wrote, presumably meaning evacuees were expected at Whitegates Cottages, but no mention of their arrival survives.[2]

Michael had not lost all of his conducting jobs at war's outbreak, and although his Co-operative Choir at Abbey Wood had disbanded, he still went to New Malden every Sunday to rehearse his choral society in Charles Stanford's opera *The Travelling Companion*, and in his own *Robin Hood*, which was to be revived the following spring. His priority was to compose, and to ensure performances of his music as best he could while London's cultural life adjusted to the war. Phoney as the conflict seemed, and optimistic as Michael usually was, the prospect of escalation was real. Wanting to write a piece for piano and orchestra, he had begun a quasi-concerto, based on a theme of his beloved Handel. But, fearing that he might not survive the war, he put the piano work aside and instead ploughed on with *A Child of Our Time*, which he considered more personal and more pressing. He had started the music of the opening chorus, but hadn't yet heard whether T.S. Eliot was willing to write the libretto. Late in September Eliot sent him a presentation copy of *Old Possum's Book of Practical Cats* inscribed "to Michael Tippett with the compliments of O. Possum" – use of the nickname was an intimacy Eliot did not mete out with abandon.[3] On 6 October Michael wrote to Alan Bush: "I am contemplating an oratorio on the Grynszpan story and it seems probable that T.S. Eliot will write the words for me."[4] Despite the contrivedly blasé name-drop, Michael still thought the possibility of collaboration was real enough. Then, a month or so later, he paid a visit to Eliot. "I realised he had played a trick on me," he told Ruth Pennyman on 16 November. "He had got me really to do the whole thing myself, and now I am wrestling with the polishing of words and a definitive version, it's no use sending you the old version, which though very nearly right has many ineptitudes, because I was not considering it as anything but a sketch for a poet to embody. However it's very exciting now, putting it out myself."[5]

That Eliot had kept the sketch for the best part of a year could indicate that he was giving it careful consideration; or maybe it had been forgotten in a pile of paperwork. A busy and acclaimed poet, he may have been groping for an excuse not to get involved. But asking Michael to outline a structure could well have been a conscious trick, for he believed that "the words of an oratorio should be either very familiar to an audience [or] very simple. It seemed to me that there was no point in getting me or any other poet to provide words for that purpose."[6] Michael remembered that Eliot "made the lovely remark: 'Anything I add to it will stand out a mile as so much better poetry.' But his whole advice was, 'don't let the poets loose on your librettos, on anything, because they are going to do with the words what your music should do'."[7] It was advice to which Michael would mainly stick throughout his career, rare among his contemporaries in setting only a small number of poems, believing that the sonic effects of great poetry should not be put into competition with music. The relationship between words and music became a chief topic of conversation between Michael and Eliot. Eliot guided Michael's newly apolitical reading list, suggesting the poetry of W.B. Yeats, and sending him volumes from the Faber catalogue. Michael, for his part, thought that Eliot "(above all others) helped me clarify my notions of the aesthetics of theatre and opera. Unwittingly he became my spiritual father."[8]

Michael spent the rest of 1939 top-and-tailing *A Child of Our Time*'s libretto. Seemingly he never considered going against Eliot's advice, neither sounding out Christopher Fry nor asking any literary-minded friend to take on the job. But he welcomed detailed advice from all who would give it, chiefly Francesca Allinson. "Will you ponder over it?", he wrote to her about a troubling line, and often implemented her suggestions: "I will put back the order you suggest is the better (and I agree now) and leave them be." Even Eliot himself offered occasional help. "I don't like 'slaughter'," Michael avowed, although the word eventually made the cut. "Nor did Eliot."[9] The libretto was finished by the end of the year, and the pared-down result shows that Michael had taken Eliot's advice to heart, the style partly arrived at by accident, in that he had initially sketched the libretto in note form and then found that little more was needed.

One of the friends to whom Michael turned most for guidance when finishing the text was someone he had met earlier in 1939.

Brean Leslie Douglas Newton – who went by the name of Douglas or "Den" – was tall and thin, with a sharp nose and large forehead underneath an eruption of black hair, and he turned nineteen just weeks into the Second World War.[10] Born in Malaysia (then the Malay States), he came to England aged six, left school at fifteen, and promptly immersed himself in the worlds of music, literature, and art. The outbreak of war and subsequent closure of a number of museums curtailed his ambitions to work as a curator, and he turned instead to writing; he was a fine though unprolific poet. To make ends meet he joined an accountancy firm, where he found Bryan Fisher among his colleagues; the two eventually shared a flat in Muswell Hill. Inevitably Douglas was introduced to Michael, and he remembered one conversation, in August 1939, that ended with Michael's saying "That's settled, then, there won't be a war. Let's have tea."[11]

Douglas, blessed with a photographic memory and measuring six foot five, was a match for Michael both intellectually and vertically, and they were soon planning a collaboration. By November Michael was asking Douglas for help with *A Child of Our Time*'s text, and beginning to ponder an opera, to be called *The Man with the Seven Daughters*, for which he considered Douglas a potential librettist. The work's unlikely scenario – seemingly an original one, its plot summed up by its title – hovered about at the back of Michael's brain for a year or more before the tempting prospect of a sevenfold female ensemble bit the dust.[12] By 1940 Michael and Douglas had become fast friends and frequent correspondents, fiercely united by their opposition to the war, and most of all by their mutual determination to refuse military service.

Pacifism was a conviction that Michael had held since his schooldays, aghast at the carnage of the First World War. His immersion in Trotskyist Marxism had diverted his world view to the extent that he had maintained a political objection to a war with the Nazis, while advocating the use of violence in other, more vital, conflicts. "I am not a pacifist but a military enthusiast," he had written, damning anybody who would obstruct a British revolution. The

Jungian dream therapy eased his heart, and the looming spectre of war's destruction concentrated his mind. Having spent extended periods of time with German children in orphanages and schools throughout the 1920s, he faced the reality of being called up to an army that would be required to fight, metaphorically speaking, those very children. His anti-Nazism precluded neither an intense sympathy for German civilians nor criticism of the British government, which he blamed fiercely for past colonial misdeeds and for its treatment of Jewish refugees. It seemed to him hypocrisy that Britain should now denounce in the Nazis actions of which it itself had been time and again guilty. On the outbreak of war he repudiated violence in all its forms – whether Trotskyist, Hitlerian, or, eventually, Churchillian – and turned once more to the loose threads of his teenage pacifism, gathering them together into a tight knot of formal absolutism. His was no longer a political objection to a specific war against fascism, but a conviction that war was wrong, under any circumstances.

His rejection of violent revolution was made with no great fanfare or apology, although the ardour of his pacifism, to which he had reverted with speed, may have shone the brighter in compensation. By 23 October 1939 he was chairing a series of discussions arranged by the Oxted and Limpsfield branch of the Peace Pledge Union. A fellow member thought he was a "good pacifist speaker", sure that "we knew him more as a pacifist than a musician".[13] On 4 December Michael gave a lecture on "Pacifism and Humanism" and the local paper wrote it up: "What was wanted, said Mr Tippett, after dealing with the totalitarian forms of government, was a form of society in which no one was either excluded or exclusive."[14]

As news emerged from Germany of continued Jewish oppression and Nazi atrocity, the number of pacifists had dwindled. In the 1930s most anti-fascists believed pacifism was the natural course against the Nazis, until the Spanish Civil War led to some searching questions about whether and what force was justified in the face of dictatorship. The novelist Storm Jameson was one of many who, avowed pacifist in the First World War, renounced their views in the Second, believing that, this time around, the fighting was warranted. The Peace Pledge Union nevertheless maintained a small but vocal membership, among them Vera Brittain, Aldous Huxley, and Bertrand Russell. Some members were part of the British Union of Fascists, while others had devoted much of their lives to the opposition of Mosley and his followers. The Union had been determinedly pro-appeasement and encouraged the sponsorship of Jewish refugees fleeing Europe, arguing that the war facilitated their persecution. Its official stance was that Hitler's claim to the Sudetenland was entirely justified, and its paper, Peace News, had (like Michael himself) often placed the evils of the British Empire above the evils of Nazism. The pacifists of Michael's generation had encountered at first hand, though only as children, the carnage of the First World War, and were determined that it shouldn't be repeated. Their protest against the second war was arguably a vicarious protest against the first.

Michael himself was certain that compromise was necessary to broker peace. The relations between means and ends tumbled about in his brain. Having once openly believed that violent revolution was a necessary means to a utopian end, he now turned such a view on its head, stating himself to be one of a group "forced by the necessities of their make-up to feel that good ends" – a world without Nazism – "could never make up for bad means" – a violent war.[15] Once, but only once, he admitted that he had to "accept the guilt and shame hidden in the outer clothing of pacifism".[16] But his absolutism on the question of a just war was soon like a lump of granite: solid, impermeable, there. Often he had spoken of his own actions or views as ones against which he had no defence, however convincing the opposition. "Quite immoral I'm sure," he had once written without qualm of his scheme to fund Wilfred Franks. Comparably, in a wartime letter to his one-time analyst John Layard, he laid out his views as something almost separate from himself:

Comes the war! For me it is a civil war between brothers, and in it I feel neutral. Further, I am a pacifist in the roots of my being somewhere. This may be scandalous, adolescent, immoral, but I have no will to tamper with it. In fact I know it can't be tampered with. [. . .] I have no doubts on this matter, except artificial doubts produced by arguments. I can be argued into doubt, but I can't be argued out of the experience, it always returns, and with a feeling of great peace, and strength and guidance [. . .]. This war that no-one wants can only be conducted at all by a complete abnegation of individual responsibility and will, under total conscription powers [. . .]. Against this mass bestialisation, as on the Eastern Front in *excelsis*, as you say: the still voice of conscience. Among thousands of others I will take my place there. My technique of witness may be faulty, I can well believe. But you are wrong if you think I blame society – or myself. I simply know that "society" is doing the will of the devil, not of God, and that is the reason for the self-destructive nature of this war. Civilisation and society is attempting to destroy itself, and has, on the continent, succeeded to a very large extent.[17]

The final links to his Trotskyist politics were speedily severed. He had been a founder member of the Workers' International League in 1938, but at some point in 1940 he was kicked out. Fellow member Ted Grant recalled that Michael had "developed pacifist leanings, for which he was expelled in 1940. I know we were still in touch with him [for a few years afterwards]. Looking back on it, we may have been a bit hard on him."[18] It was unusual for someone as avowedly anti-war as Michael to be expelled from the League, whose members were against capitalist warfare and had opposed Britain's joining the conflict from the start. But as Ted Grant explains it, "we also wanted to defeat Hitler, but with our own means and programme. This could only be achieved by the carrying through of a revolutionary war against fascism, which meant the working class taking power."[19] Leon Trotsky meanwhile disapproved of any among his followers who wouldn't join military forces in order to prepare for revolutionary conflict.

Trotsky's murder, in August 1940, barely appears to have registered for Michael, who was distracted by the plight of a group of
young men that had sprung up in the face of the war. The National
Service (Armed Forces) Act had enforced conscription of men
from the age of eighteen to forty-one, an age range wide enough
to encompass not only Michael himself but most of his younger
friends, including Bryan Fisher and Douglas Newton. The Act gave
men the right to apply on grounds of conscience for exemption
from conscription, and Michael, Bryan, Douglas, and many in their
circle were to become conscientious objectors.

In the First World War conscientious objectors had been exposed
to ridicule and public accusations of cowardice. They were reliant
on unofficial help from small organisations such as the Women's
Freedom League, of which Michael's mother had been a member,
to combat unsympathetic official judgement. Such judgement often
resulted in a harsh prison sentence, or even, as for the group of
absolutist objectors known as the Richmond Sixteen, penal servitude. But for conscientious objectors to the Second World War,
the government actively made efforts to provide a more humane
system. Objectors had no legal status in France, and in Germany
were often executed. But in Britain those who wished to apply
for exemption could visit their local employment exchange and
were entered on a special register. They then had to await a
tribunal, at which a decision would be made as to the sincerity
of their objection. Non-combatant duties, if any, would then be
assigned.

In the last months of 1939 men aged twenty to twenty-three were
called up. Of those in Michael's immediate circle determined to
register as objectors, only Bryan Fisher qualified (Douglas Newton
was a year too young). Michael himself was granted a respite until
late in 1940, allowing him a period of more or less uninterrupted
composition. But he threw himself quickly and wholeheartedly into
supporting a number of objectors in their early twenties. More than
8 million men registered under the Military Training Act during the
Second World War, and of these just under 60,000 were conscientious objectors.[20] It was a tiny percentage that, despite the newly

humane governmental provision, was in opposition to the prevailing public mood and, often, to the views of friends and family. The likelihood of social ostracism was pronounced, and over and above the necessary courage needed to follow such a course, the system required a coherent written statement, the gathering of testimonials and supporters, and the ability to stand up calmly and lucidly to cross-examination at a tribunal. Michael cast himself as an unofficial one-man advisory bureau, actively searching out communities of objectors in need of moral and practical support. He would help to write statements, and often appeared at the tribunals to deliver testimonials. In December 1939 he told Douglas Newton that he had had "tea with two young conscientious objectors – this week we are discussing the final shape of one application".[21] And the previous month he had written to his old friend from Yorkshire, Ruth Pennyman, about the lay of his new psychological and political land:

I have ceased to be a rigorous political (if I ever was) since eighteen months or more. I have been drawn much more since the war myself towards the more intimate and personal stand made by the young COs of twenty [years old] and the dim sense that the best of them have of being pioneers in a new outlook, as yet only in its babyhood. The right, as one put [it] in a Tribunal Court when I was there "to live a human life as meant to by God" – or some such expression. He was a young journalist on a local paper, of twenty [years old], and refused any alternative service – he used the word "pioneer" of himself, and expressed the conviction that the answer to totalitarian war and usury, was totalitarian refusal, and to take the individual consequences. This outlook (which is my own) has led me towards the Gandhi method [of *satyagraha*, or civil disobedience], and to the Peace Pledge Union, and the odd effort to try the experiment of working through inclusiveness, not exclusiveness, as in a revolutionary organisation. [. . .] I have come to feel the fight as back against a wall – the rock-bottom wall of personal liberty anywhere and everywhere before the advance of totalitarian nonsense. [. . . I have only] slight Marxist

tendencies – the spiritual-aesthetic problem lands one where I am
now – fighting for music, liberty, conscience, simplicity.[22]

Other areas of life continued almost as normal. Michael still commuted weekly to London to rehearse his Co-operative Operatic
Society and to conduct the South London Orchestra, although both
were stuttering to a halt. His domestic set-up, while not exactly
primitive, had always been sparsely furnished and reasonably basic,
and wartime austerity may not have changed his routine overmuch.
Nevertheless he had to navigate the practicalities of ration books, or
of wandering in the blacked-out darkness of London streets in the
winter twilight, amid the dead bulbs of switched-off street lamps.
At home there was the gloomy exasperation of sealing oneself in
with the light each evening, laboriously covering the windows
with heavy blackout curtains, and taking them all down again next
morning to reveal windowpanes patched with tape against a possible blast. The cold quotidian grubbiness of wartime existence
kicked in, as soap and coal were rationed, and a thin reproving
line drawn five inches from the bottom of the bath offered a bald
reminder of the week's hot-water allowance.

Michael sat in his freezing and isolated bungalow and composed
Part One of *A Child of Our Time*. He fashioned the opening chorus,
where the line "the world turns on its dark side" corkscrews down
through the four-part choir in aghast *pianissimo*. He created ugly
fugues of disunity: "we are gathered to a great slaughter". And he
came to the arias for tenor and for soprano, the first ("I have no
money for my bread") accompanied by a seedy Weimar tango,
the second an impassioned cry from the soul: "How shall I feed
my children on so small a wage? How can I comfort them when I
am dead?" The soprano's lines give way to a wordless cry of pain
as, gently stealing in beneath her, the chorus washes and stills the
oratorio with the first of the spirituals, as if to comfort her, not
with the religiosity of the text, but with the cool balm of its hopefulness for a better world. "Steal away, steal away, steal away to
Jesus. I han't got long to stay here." The lines of this spiritual take
on a darker resonance when read from within the unpredictable

world of wartime Britain, in which so few people felt certain of an abiding stay. But Michael determinedly banished fear. On 7 January 1940 he wrote to his oldest friend David Ayerst, who was now the headmaster of a grammar school in Lancashire, "I have for the time being begun to live for periods in a considerable degree of serenity – whether specious or not, I don't know. It is a necessity, of course, for the production of the oratorio, and may be no more than that – however something has healed inside and I feel less wounded than since adolescent days."[23]

On 27 January 1937 Virginia Woolf had written in a letter to the composer Ethel Smyth: "A perfect stranger is coming at 4.30 [tomorrow] for a long business talk about her book."[24] The stranger was Francesca Allinson, Michael's closest of friends for some fifteen years, whose first and only novel, A Childhood, had been accepted by Leonard and Virginia Woolf for publication by their Hogarth Press.

A Childhood, which was published in October 1938, is a strange, sickly book in which it is impossible to discern the extent to which autobiography poses as fiction, and fiction as autobiography. It owes less to Virginia Woolf (for whom Francesca and Michael had a mutual passion) than to Proust, in its evocation of a childhood spent half in wonderment, half in a sick-bed. The novel shares with A Child of Our Time a structure based on the year's seasonal cycle, although by the end of the story's single year the child, called Charlotte, has mysteriously aged. So had Francesca, who, despite being only in her late thirties, had white hair and was perceptibly frail. While delighting friends with her outward gaiety, she was badly depressed by the war, and at some point underwent psychoanalysis with Woolf's brother, Adrian Stephen. Francesca considered herself heterosexual and was troubled by her affair with the actress Judy Wogan, which was alternately placid and tormenting. She loved Judy passionately, and blamed herself for the relationship's failure, becoming sharply self-recriminatory.[25] Often-severe stomach pain and continued thyroid trouble (her operation had removed only part of the gland) led to frequent hospitalisation. With so many German friends and relatives, she felt torn to shreds as to where her wartime sympathies should lie.

Francesca and Michael were frequent correspondents, but her letters to him are lost. Those he wrote to her are devoid of passion but glowing with warmth. They chart Francesca's continual ill health, and Michael's desperate longing to see her: "It's when you are away like this that I miss you most. I suppose by now we belong to each other in some particular way."[26] They were vicariously living out the nags and needs of the shared domestic life they had once wished for, not within the walls of the bungalow, but within the freedoms and restrictions of ink and paper. "The Dufy looks very gay on top of the bookshelves," he would write to her of a framed print. Or "shall we have the triangular corner-cupboard painted?"[27] In some ways she was his wife in all but name, however frequently they were separated by life's disruptions, and he would write to her, with husbandly pride: "I think that dress is OK. I like you to be *auffallend* [striking], especially [for a] first public appearance after a long illness."[28]

Michael's need for Francesca's financial support became acute. He escapes by a whisker the charge that he was taking advantage, by dint of the generosity with which he'd share his own resources when flush. Already he had fewer conducting jobs to help pay his way, and in February 1940 admitted he was living "very close to the bone now as my father has stopped his assistance to me, to the lattermost farthing".[29] He barraged Francesca with requests for tea and oatmeal, eggs and jam; his dependence on coffee was unthreatened, as the beans were never rationed. Privately wealthy from the fortunes of the family mill, she became nothing less than his benefactress, and as Michael grew ever more friendly with Douglas Newton, who had left the accountancy firm and was unemployed, he would grandly offer to "spare you I expect the necessary pocket money – I have a bit now from Fresca to help in this sort of matter".[30]

Francesca had often loaned Michael and his friends the use of her

London flat just off Baker Street; by the time war was declared she had moved to a nearby house, at 23 Mornington Terrace. But she spent most of her time with Judy Wogan in Essex, where she had purchased a small wood called Martin's Grove (she was a brilliant arboriculturalist). The couple took in evacuees: "We have three lovely boys," she wrote in her journal. "I feel a mixture of despair, apathy, and a desire to be swallowed up in activity [. . .]. Jude's artistic projects and mine are both knocked on the head."[31] The two women had recently travelled to Ireland together to research a monograph that Francesca and Michael were planning to co-write, focusing on the Irish influence on British folk-song and hoping to rebut the views of Vaughan Williams. The reality was that Francesca did much of the donkey-work and Michael then commented on drafts and wrote out music examples.

As 1940 dawned Francesca began to throw herself into the conscientious objectors' cause, of which – although she herself escaped the maximum age of thirty for female conscription, which came the following year – she was entirely and ardently supportive. Her London house became a base for unemployed objectors, many of whom needed an address to register for the dole. She bought shares in two Quaker-run land schemes in East Sussex, founded to allow objectors, many of whom were ordered to do agricultural duties, to carry out their work in safety and sympathetic company. Taking a flat on East Grinstead high street, she became involved with the day-to-day running of the two sites. Michael suggested that Douglas Newton, although not yet registered as a conscientious objector, might work on one of the schemes and live among the community there. The objectors had to pay their own way and Michael promised to foot all Douglas's bills. "East Grinstead is a crack concern", Michael wrote to him persuasively, "and is the high light of the country. [. . .] You will enjoy it very much I think, though it's a hard-working life at the moment."[32]

Michael, at thirty-five, had slipped comfortably into the role of senior supporter, to which the groups of young people determined to refuse military service looked up. He combined composition on *A Child of Our Time* with visits to the sites in Sussex, and he and

Francesca formed an unofficial first couple to the two communities, offering what help they could. In a way it was an indirect experience of the parenthood of which they had dreamed. But Michael, attracted as always to the ardency of youth, hovered between father figure and lover to the young men. As ever he was casting about for a partner, and, by spring 1940, was trying once again to rekindle his affair with Wilfred Franks, writing him forthcoming letters which Douglas Newton, who for a time became a kind of go-between, was asked to deliver. Michael may have been consciously trying not to fall too deeply in love with Douglas, wary that overbearing affection might frighten him away, or fearing a hurtful repeat of being abandoned by a younger man intent on marriage. It was in the spirit of reassurance that he told Douglas he had written "a very gentle [letter to Wilfred], telling him I'm always here and can wait without forgetting – it will help him. You see, I am still nearer in 'language' to him than anyone when I need be – have no fear."[33] But this letter is signed, with love, "Mike", a nickname hitherto reserved for Wilfred. And in pushing for Douglas to join the objectors' community, Michael was ensuring their proximity. Whitegates Cottage was only an hour's cycle north of East Grinstead, and soon he was suggesting that he and Douglas might set up house together: "As long as you were away playing the husband and I am at home as the wife, I don't see why it shouldn't work at least for a bit." He made sure to add "and if you have the spare room you can be in there to your heart's content".[34] But such open-armed gestures failed to produce the desired effect. Wilfred slipped yet further out of Michael's life, and Douglas, who did decide to join one of the Sussex schemes, ended up working on the land and living happily at Francesca Allinson's flat for the rest of that year and into the next.

While waiting for his summons to military service, Michael's musical work continued. In April a production of *Robin Hood* had been mounted in London without a hitch, but played to tiny audiences; this was seemingly Michael's last venture with the Co-operative Society after nearly a decade's involvement. He had made little headway in getting a leading ensemble to premiere his Concerto for

Double String Orchestra, and wasn't able to resist trying it out with his own South London Orchestra at Morley College, on 21 April 1940. The few reviewers who attended the concert were impressed ("a serious, passionate work, full of contrapuntal resource"), but the BBC reading panel greeted the score with open dislike.[35]

Three weeks later, after an ill-fated Allied campaign in Norway that led to the resignation of Neville Chamberlain, Winston Churchill became Prime Minister of a coalition government. That same day, 10 May, Germany began its invasion of France and the Low Countries, and the war was phoney no longer. Allied soldiers were evacuated from Dunkirk, over 300,000 of them. In less than two months Paris was occupied by the Nazis, and an armistice declared that was effectively a French surrender. The Germans pushed for a peace deal that the British refused to negotiate. In response, Hitler began to plan an invasion of Britain, but first needed to gain control of the skies over southern England. By July the Battle of Britain had begun. After bomb raids on several towns throughout August, the German planes moved towards London, and the air offensive known as the Blitz began. On 7 September, at about five o'clock, the night was clouded over with planes, nearly 1,000 German and Italian aircraft, as London suffered the first of fifty-seven near-continuous nights of bombing.

In Surrey several factories and dockyards were targeted. Oxted lay further south, but Michael's bungalow and cottages were just six miles from Biggin Hill aerodrome, then an RAF base. Residents of Oxted and Hurst Green would count the planes out and in again, and some fights in the Battle of Britain took place above their heads. Over in Limpsfield Michael's cellist friend Beatrice Harrison began what had become her traditional BBC broadcast, duetting with the nightingales in her back garden, only for it to be terminated mid-transmission: the live recording had picked up RAF planes in the Surrey skies, en route for Germany, and would have alerted German spies to the impending attack. Further south, in East Grinstead, Francesca Allinson "would drown the noise by playing and singing the most bawdy drinking songs on the piano".[36] During the Blitz she wrote in her diary: "I hear the German planes

overhead now, passing on their way to London, and in the afternoon saw ghostly streaks in the sky [. . .]. There are several girls
in the town, their faces torn and rendered hideous for life. I feel
excessively for them. And there is no prospect of a peace for years
and years."[37]

September 1940 was unusually hot. That month Michael wrote
to Francesca of a raid he had witnessed with his tenant Ben Lewis
and Ben's twenty-four-year-old daughter, Bronwen. He was sketching out the fugue in *A Child of Our Time* that depicts *Kristallnacht*, when
he "heard the sound of German planes and firing – I had the oddest
of feelings as I deliberately completed the twenty-four bars and
then the restlessness was too much and I went to chat to Ben – the
warning then went and Bron next suddenly cried 'look at those
things dropping from a plane over there' and to the sound of gun-
firing a fight began over Oxted and over our heads, as it seemed".[38]
Likely they had witnessed the evening of 17 September, when a
German bomber was intercepted right above Oxted and chased by
a Hurricane. The bomber caught fire over Esher but flew on until
Leatherhead, at which point the crew baled out, three to become
prisoners of war; the fourth fell out of his parachute harness and
was killed.

Aside from rogue skirmishes, Surrey found itself on the receiving
end of accidental attacks. London was often missed and Surrey close
enough to take the hit. German planes frequently offloaded any
undropped bombs in order to lighten their aircraft for the return
journey, and Surrey came soon on the home straight eastward.
Michael cleared a space under his grand piano so as to hide beneath
it for the worst of the raids. "There were two big bonks here last
night", he told Francesca, "which turn out to be bombs beside the
Hurst Green factory – unloading, I fancy. Sooner or later I feel we
shall [at the] least be shot out of our beds! [. . .] Not that these bonks
affect me very much, having got very fatalistic and re-believing in
my star and that of my nearest and dearest."[39] The danger was
nevertheless such that finishing *A Child of Our Time* became urgent,
as did preserving the parts of it already completed, and Michael
decided to store various copies away from the bungalow for safe

keeping. He was profoundly conscious that composition of the oratorio's central section – depicting Herschel Grynszpan's attack and its aftermath – was bound up with the bombing, afterwards remembering "some very evil moments, when the day and night raiding exactly corresponded to the work on the pogrom and the boy's shooting".[40] He finished Part Two amid the opening weeks of the Blitz, as the country fought hard against the very real threat of enemy occupation. Each day was passed expecting the invasion, and newspapers carried instructions on what to do if, or when, it arrived. Around 18 September, just after the plane fight above Oxted and the bombs on the Hurst Green factory, Michael began to arrange the "Spiritual of Anger", "Go Down Moses".[41] The singers are confined to the seething tread of the vocal line, while the strings and brass, permitted freedom, surge in desperation on the voices' behalf, above a death-knock of timpani:

When Israel was in Egypt land
Let my people go
Oppressed so hard they could not stand
Let my people go

The night of 15 October 1940 saw an especially heavy raid on London. A bomb fell on a shelter in Kennington Park, killing over fifty. Then, at quarter to eight, a 1,000-kilogram high-explosive demolition bomb, painted blue with a yellow strip at one end, hit the Prince of Wales Hall at Morley College, the room that had hosted so many of Michael's concerts. The explosion destroyed the entire college building, three-quarters of its whole site. Its force was such that bricks and concrete were thrown so high in the air they demolished houses in the nearby streets. Every piece of paper inside was lost, as were the college's murals by Eric Ravilious, and one of the manuscript scores of Michael's Concerto for Double String Orchestra. The large proscenium arch of the concert hall was left standing, undamaged and frighteningly devoid of context, and through it could be seen, like a stage-set, a black tangle of blasted trees. The college was hosting a small school for non-evacuated

Morley College, late 1940

children, and the gym and refectory had been turned into a dormitory for bombed-out Lambeth residents. And so there were nearly
200 people sheltering from the Blitz at Morley College the night the
bomb struck. Many had fled to the basement, and as the wreckage
of rubble and glass was slowly cleared away in the following days,
the injured and the dying and the dead were found crushed. It took
three weeks to recover the fifty-seven corpses, many of which had
to be cut out with saws.[42]

Michael had been using Morley College as a professional base for
nearly a decade, and earlier that year had served with the artist John
Piper on the board of its new Theatre School. In the fallout from
the blast, his South London Orchestra disbanded (its loyal leader,
Fred May, ended up in Wormwood Scrubs as a conscientious objector in 1942). At the outbreak of war the college's courses for adult
education were flourishing under the visionary leadership of its
principal, Eva Hubback, who, suffragette, feminist, and economist,
had been a brilliant and sympathetic friend to Michael. After the
bomb and the resulting damage, Hubback worked hard to ensure

the college's teaching programme was up and running again as quickly and as normally as possible. Almost straight after the explosion the college's director of music, Arnold Foster, was evacuated with Westminster School, where he also taught. Hubback didn't have to cast her net wide to find a suitable replacement.

Michael took over the music directorship at Morley College just days after the bomb blast, taking his first class on 1 December, and his first orchestral rehearsal the week after. He was given the use of the college's modern extension, which had survived, though it had to be vacated for temporary use as a mortuary when, in January 1941, a hostel nearby collapsed and the seventy-one dead were laid out in the Gustav Holst Music Room. In March the college formally reopened and the Holst Room was designated as a possible concert venue for the tiny orchestra (nine students) and choir (eight students).

This new job paid £125 a year, which, combined with his Schott retainer and with Francesca Allinson's stalwart support, kept Michael afloat for the duration of the war. In addition, for the autumn term of 1940, he found himself once again on the staff of Hazelwood School in Oxted, in order to bolster a common room vastly depleted by army calls-up.[43] The weeks were full, and his new responsibilities at Morley involved taking music classes every Sunday, and rehearsing the orchestra and choir every Friday. Soon he would plough ahead with an ambitious concert series, meaning further trips to Lambeth. So it was at the height of the Blitz that Michael commuted to London twice or thrice weekly, travelling from Hurst Green to Victoria on a train with blacked-out windows, before going on another two miles, perhaps by tram but more likely on foot, to Morley College.

As Elizabeth Bowen described it, to walk through London the day after a raid, in streets full of sandbags and tired faces, past windows covered in mesh and public squares spiked with wire to disrupt enemy landings, was to traverse "the moon's capital – shallow, cratered, extinct".[44] Skeletons of buildings made dark lattices against the sky, and the bombs had skinned houses of their brickwork. Single walls stood perilous and strange, and the fronts of houses were blown away as if on hinges, like the front of a doll's house, leaving wallpapered interiors indecently exposed. Fires were still being put out, and hard-hatted workmen dousing buildings, or the remnants of buildings. In the city you could smell the war: the throat-catching reek of fire and smoke; the odour of the acrid glue that stuck a temporary patchwork of sheeting over bomb damage; and the scent of the London parks, pungent with sap, after the bombs had stripped bark from the trees. Pedestrians got used to the icy crunch of glass underfoot, always in quantities too vast to be wholly cleared away, and witnessed the barrage balloons hovering above the city in the hope of obstructing enemy aircraft, like silver whales swimming in the vapour-trail scribble, absurd and frightening. Michael became familiar with a world whose seasons were knocked out of kilter, its trees wintry and bare of leaves, its lawns scorched as if by the summer sun, and everything about frosted with the surreal pink powder of exploded plaster.

In the first week of November 1940 Bryan Fisher came to meet Michael in London. His tribunal as a conscientious objector had been in May, and despite Michael's appearing on his behalf, he had not been granted exemption from military duties. Now he was due in London to appeal the ruling, with Michael's help. The pair met at Victoria Station amid the chilling wail of an air-raid warning, and visited the ruins of Morley College, from which bodies were still being dug out and carried off. "As I sadly looked at it", Bryan remembered, "I saw in retrospect all the concerts and occasions I had enjoyed there, a whole phase of my life intimately connected with the place."[45] Bryan's appellate tribunal that afternoon, at which Michael spoke, led to the offer of agricultural work in place of military service, which was accepted gladly. They went back to Michael's bungalow, where Bryan noticed that the fields between the station and Whitegates Cottage had been churned into muddy bogs by tanks, driven by the hundreds of Canadian servicemen billeted at Leatherhead that year. The two spent the evening listening to "the anti-aircraft guns firing consistently, shaking all the fittings in the room".[46] The next morning they went to Oxted Station to meet Francesca and Douglas Newton, who had travelled over

together from East Grinstead, and the four of them went to London.
Michael rushed off somewhere, but Bryan and Douglas went with
Francesca up to Camden Town. A bomb had recently fallen near
to Francesca's house in Mornington Terrace, and the windows had
been blown to shards. Together, as so many were doing all over the
country, they started to clear up the damage.

On 16 November 1940 all British men born between 1 January
and 30 June 1905 were required by the National Service Act to
register for military service. Michael qualified. The time had come,
after a year helping others to register as conscientious objectors,
to do so himself. That very day he went to a local register office.
Objectors were directed to a separate table, given a case number
(his was L15870), and handed a two-page form in order to apply
for a tribunal. This had to be filled out with a personal statement, and sent within two weeks to the Ministry of Labour and
National Service at 59–62 Queen's Gardens, W2. Nine days later
Michael threaded the form into his typewriter and wrote out his
statement:

> People of my age entered adolescence as the Great War ended.
> We grew up into a war torn and war weary world. My first
> political act was to attend an International Congress of Youth at
> Brussels in 1922 called by the Jeunesse Suisse Romande to discuss
> methods of raising money to send child victims of the Great War
> to sanatoria in the Swiss mountains. I was seventeen years old.
> It is not now possible for me to be at war with what amounts
> to those same children or to take part in a state of war which
> will result in the same victimisation. When I was eighteen I saw
> the war film *The Four Horsemen of the Apocalypse* which ended with
> photographs of the vast Flanders grave yards. I and the student
> friends with me, made a sort of vow, or promise afterwards to
> see that such a thing could never happen again, that promise was
> quite real to me then and still is so now, though I do not now

see the matter so optimistically. At no time has my opposition
to war been a merely personal matter. There is some sense of
a dedication to the memory of those who did horrible things
last time in the belief that they fought a war to end war. Not to
stand against a repetition is to make a mockery of their sacrifice.
Our present day pacifism holds that the present horrors and evil
results of modern total war are far greater than the evils which
the wars hope to eradicate. The Great war was a War to End war
and it left the world afterwards one vast mad arsenal. The present
war threatens to engulf the whole world in what Dean Inge* calls
co-operative suicide about a European dispute. War has its own
logic of madness but the pacifist is in some degree dispassionate.
I think we feel the virtue of peace as an enduring state which
must be struggled for even in war itself. Values, especially the
good ones, cannot be scrapped one day and replaced the next.
Some people feel they have a necessity, a duty to serve those
values in times when they are in general danger. There is no
confusion between my professional life as a musician and my
political life as a pacifist. There is certainly confusion between
the world of imagining music and the world of co-operative
suicide. In the Napoleonic wars there were many great artists
alive in Europe, Beethoven, Schubert, Schiller, Goethe, Shelley,
Keats, Wordsworth, Byron, Blake. None of them except Goethe
was conscripted into that madness. Total war, in wishing to conscript every man and woman alive, forces the struggle for liberty
back on to the individual, whether it is Ossietzky in Germany,
or Nehru in India.† I imagine that only by the endurance of

---

* William Inge (1860–1954), Dean of St Paul's Cathedral, who opposed Britain's
entry into the war in a number of essay collections, on the grounds that she
had no quarrel with Germany.

† Carl von Ossietzky (1889–1938), a German pacifist and winner of the Nobel
Peace Prize, detained in concentration camps for his opposition to the Nazi
regime. Jawaharlal Nehru (1889–1964), eventually first Prime Minister of India, whose calls for Indian independence were often carried out in the spirit of
Mahatma Gandhi's satyagraha.

individuals who refuse (non-co-operation) can the madness of
the war be in any degree shortened.[47]

The form asked the applicant to strike out any of the statements, *a*,
b, or *c*, which did *not* apply to him. Michael objected to all three,
but, seemingly misunderstanding the instructions, struck through
each one.

> I conscientiously object
> (a) to being registered in the Military Service Register
> (b) to performing military service
> (c) to performing combatant duties

He then signed the form. "Michael Tippett, 25th November 1940."
Now he had to wait for his tribunal, which would decide his
fate. Such was the bureaucracy of the system that it was to take
fifteen months for such a call to arrive. He went with Bryan Fisher
to Francesca's flat at East Grinstead, where Douglas Newton was
still living, and they all spent Christmas together, celebrating as
best they could. Across the country church bells were silenced.
Christmas Eve had brought an unofficial truce, but by 29 December
the bombs were falling once more, producing one of the heaviest
raids of the Blitz, and London burned.

SIXTEEN

Conchie

Success against the odds was Michael's speciality, via a combination of talent and confidence, graft and patience. In the grinding war years he fashioned from Morley College's Music Department one of London's most distinguished concert series. The city's cultural life had clung on during the Blitz. The Proms season, still held at the Queen's Hall, had been cancelled when war was declared, but soon resumed under private sponsorship. Eventually the hall was destroyed by a bomb, and the Albert Hall was suggested as a substitute. Meanwhile the BBC Symphony Orchestra continued to perform despite constant evacuation, from London to Bristol, from Bristol to Bedford. Most orchestras suffered from a loss of manpower. But defiant wartime seasons were launched, most famously by the pianist Myra Hess, who played in or organised hundreds of lunchtime concerts at the National Gallery. Michael quickly set about expanding the Morley choir, and how he did so during the Blitz, which continued for the first seven months of his directorship, is anyone's guess. Sleepless nights led to days in which energy and free time were at a premium; the streets and buses and tea-shops were full of people snatching dozes. But membership of the choir more than trebled within a year. By the end of the war there were around seventy singers.

He was helped immensely by some distinguished European musicians who in ordinary circumstances would have been pursuing prominent careers, but who had escaped the Nazis and took what jobs they could. About this foreign influx Ralph Vaughan Williams, who was intermittently involved with the college, had strong reservations, but Michael stood firm, inviting the Hungarian composer Mátyás Seiber, who had immigrated to England in 1935, to teach composition. Walter Bergmann, a musician trained at Leipzig, had been working as a lawyer in Germany, but his defence of Jewish clients led to his arrest, and he escaped to Britain. On his release from the Isle of Man, where he had been held as an enemy alien, he got an editing job at the British branch of the Schott publishing house, and Michael soon had him teaching several courses at Morley, in recorder and early music. "Tippett had two principles," Bergmann remembered, "never to miss a choir rehearsal (unless one were dead or in prison), and to foster a loyalty among the choir members to the choir but not to the conductor. [. . .] in spite of great linguistic difficulties on my side, [he] offered me friendship; nor do I forget the help he gave me and many others."[1] Most important would be the German composer and conductor Walter Goehr, who had studied with Arnold Schoenberg, and who had been fired from his job at Berlin Radio owing to his Jewish ancestry. By happy chance he had already been invited to London to work for the record company that became EMI, and was soon appearing frequently on the BBC. Goehr understood the European and early-music influence on Michael's composition, and became one of its first and most consistent defenders, at a time when others found its techniques hard to accept. Michael soon persuaded him to take over the Morley College Orchestra, meaning that the tiny amateur ensemble was now run by a fine conductor who would later give the British premiere of, among others, Messiaen's *Turangalîla-Symphonie*. It was a cosmopolitan and prestigious team and, with Michael retaining responsibility for the choir and teaching a few classes, they began to put together concert seasons that lasted through the war and beyond.

After a year to settle in and to get new recruits, Michael scheduled the first concert for 22 November 1941, and the choir marked the day, St Cecilia's, with a performance of Purcell's *Hail! Bright Cecilia*, substituting recorders for trumpets. There were then three or four concerts each term, held in the small and often stuffy Holst Room, where planets were muralled on the ceiling and seats laid out for

150. Many of the performances left a lot to be desired technically, and had to fight against the clatter and clank of trams wobbling along Westminster Bridge Road. But the spirit of the music-making, caught from Michael's infectious passion, began to attract considerable attention, and the hall was often packed, especially when raids on London became less frequent. Loyal audiences picked their way to evening concerts through the dark streets of rubble and glass, following the dim light of small torches and directed by policemen with uniforms daubed in luminous paint.

Michael and his team programmed an exciting repertoire that far outstripped the narrow range of professional music on offer elsewhere. The season's backbone was the early music about which Michael and Walter Bergmann were knowledgeable and passionate: madrigals and anthems by Tudor composers (Gibbons and Wilbye, Tallis and Dowland), moving on to key figures of the Renaissance and Baroque such as Bach and Handel, Monteverdi and Purcell. (Michael had fished miraculously intact volumes of the Purcell Society's complete edition of its namesake from the wreckage of the Morley library.) The college was one of the few places in England where such a repertoire was being performed, and although there was little emphasis on historically informed presentation, Michael's Music Department, in combination with the recently founded and similarly focused Schola Cantorum Basiliensis in Switzerland, should be considered a key part of the century's Early music revival, paving the way for future generations. Michael was careful not to produce endless showcases of his own work, and Vaughan Williams was only a token presence. Other British composers were all but ignored. Instead the programmes were punctuated with pieces by pre-eminent figures at work on the continent, such as Bartók, Stravinsky (whose "Dumbarton Oaks" chamber concerto was given its British premiere at Morley), and the German composer Paul Hindemith. Hindemith's star has faded since, but his neoclassical combination of muscular counterpoint with folk-song was one of the greatest influences on Michael's early pieces. Morley's focus on such figures, many of whom were living in exile and had had their music denounced by the Nazis, sent a clear political message.

The repertoire and enterprise brought newspaper critics to the concerts, which only helped spread the word. As an audience member recalled, Michael took to giving pre-performance talks, "with sentences often left unfinished, with one finger poking at eye, ear or nose", but somehow putting everyone "in the right frame of mind to grasp what was going to be played".[2] The *New Statesman* eventually eulogised Michael for having transformed Morley's "little choir into one of the best ensembles in the country".[3] Soon there were performances not only at Morley but at the National Gallery, and eventually at the Wigmore Hall. How had he done it? Not through conducting technique, all agreed, and with considerable help from Walter Goehr and others on the staff. It was Michael's eclectic taste and adventurous programming that, combined with charm and diplomacy, made him an adept and inspirational leader. The ladies of his choir, who far outnumbered the men, adored him to the point of infatuation. As Walter Goehr's son Alexander, often roped in to sing, remembers: "Tippett was fascinated by women and women loved Tippett. Tippett was very very attractive to women in the Morley choir – all the girls and the ladies were completely flattened by him."[4]

Through Morley Michael made two close friends, who became part of the bevy of young men – conchies, composers, and choristers alike intermingled – in whose company Michael throve: "they have minds like sinks", he told Francesca, "and are enchanting and fresh and young".[5] The first was John Amis, a round-faced boy in spectacles, who was eighteen when Michael joined the college's staff. He was exempt from national service owing to his partial deafness, and although neither a composer nor a performer, was hoping to put his love for music to good use. One of those people who seems to know everyone, a master of the art of networking and persuasion, Amis would forge a career that seemed to encompass music critic, writer, arts administrator, and broadcaster (most famously on the BBC radio quiz *My Music*). It wasn't long before he was working more or less as Michael's unpaid secretary, and spending a great deal of time at Whitegates Cottage. He had an insider's view of Michael's compositional process: "After breakfast Michael would shut himself up in the living room to compose and then a noise would ensue of singing, groaning, shrieking, laughing, a curious declaimed humming and much crashing on the piano." Michael had, Amis thought,

> a wonderful way of being at ease with his fellow men and women, friendly with anybody and everybody, never patronizing the humble, never sucking up to important people. [. . .] he knew his worth, knew that his music would eventually win through. That showed incredible confidence. So did his habit of writing on to the full score and publishing his works before the premieres. Like all great artists, he had his ruthless side, and that sometimes meant sacrifices for some of us that knew him well, but, since we loved him and his music, we were happy to serve him. After all, *he* has sacrificed everything to his muse. And he is a genius.[6]

The second close friend met at Morley College was Antony Hopkins. No relation to the actor who shares his name, Hopkins was a twenty-year-old student at the Royal College of Music, hoping to compose and perform (eventually he became famous for his long-running series of radio lectures for the BBC, *Talking About Music*). He too was declared unfit for military service, after a botched cartilage operation. With his girlfriend, Alison Purves, Hopkins joined the Morley choir in 1941, and soon found in Michael an informal composition teacher and musical mentor. "If I were asked who taught me the most about music," he later said,

> I would answer without hesitation, Michael Tippett. [. . .] His method of teaching was quite unusual but most illuminating. Instead of saying this harmony or that sequence was *wrong* [. . .] he would simply say, "I think you could improve that; let's see how someone else coped with a similar problem". He would go over to the bookcase and pull out a score – it could be Beethoven or Bach, Stravinsky or Hindemith. "Ah, here it is . . ." With that peculiarly intense gaze he would peer at the page, making little humming noises to himself, as though to check that he had indeed found the passage he wanted. "Look – do you see how

he avoided a cliché there? The obvious thing would have been to have gone da-bada-dah but he went da-bada-da bada – *deepa-bada-dah*. Makes all the difference doesn't it?" The blue eyes would twinkle and he would burst into his infectious giggle.[7]

Michael had to be cautious, lest he be over-eager to harness the near-erotic charge that can exist at the heart of intense teacher–pupil relationships. John Amis often found himself having to protest that he was neither homosexual nor Michael's lover, and it is true that the relationship was friendly but no more. But Michael found Antony Hopkins sweet and attractive, and while he was careful not to disrupt Antony's relationship with Alison Purves, meticulously taking care to include her in his arrangements and affections, he admitted that he entertained fantasies and had to restrain himself from acting on them.[8] Occasionally he wrote to the couple to check he hadn't overstepped the mark and that all was well, which it usually was, and they took his confessions in good humour. In the end, Michael admitted that his feelings for Douglas Newton kept him "from hankering after Tony, who knows, I fear, that he can nearly twiddle me round his finger".[9]

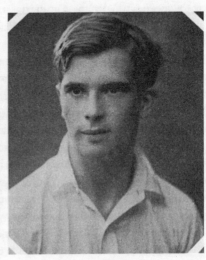

John Amis   Antony Hopkins

By 1941 Douglas had been living with Francesca Allinson in East
Grinstead for over a year. An unhappy love affair with one of the
older men in the objectors' communities had left her distressed
and wanting to move away, and the situation was complicated
by the fact that Douglas, as he admitted, now "loved her a great
deal".[10] His love, perhaps perceived by Francesca as an overwhelming dependency, caused some unknown problem. "I expect you
enjoyed your visit away to Fresca", Michael wrote to Douglas
later in the year, "and became thereby a trifle solaced for all the
goings-on before. To be in love is certainly to make a fool, if not
an abjection, of oneself – but it's part of man's horrible heritage
to disappear down the slippery slope, even if slimy."[11] Whatever
the "goings-on", it prompted Douglas to leave Sussex, a move so
abrupt that the workers left behind cursed him for what they saw
as a thoughtlessly sudden departure.

Every county in England had a War Agricultural Executive
Committee, an organisation backed by the government to foster
agricultural self-sufficiency. Numerous conscientious objectors
were set to work by such committees, and early in 1941 Bryan
Fisher became the warden of a hostel at Lilley Farm in the hamlet
of Caldecote, run by the Cambridgeshire committee for objectors
working on a nearby land scheme. Douglas Newton, on leaving East
Grinstead in February, went to live at the hostel and work on the
land. It was a punishing schedule, and each day lorryloads of objectors were bussed in so as to clear the fields of deep-rooted trees
and scrub. Solace came in a long correspondence with Francesca.
Her letters to Douglas are wrapped in a film of stylish bantering
eloquence, through which can be caught glimpses of her deep
unhappiness: "what with the spring rattling one up, drawing attention to the great open spaces in one's bed and so on, or what with
one's longing for a nice tidy cheerful world – well, one's a little out
of shape. I also feel as thirsty as a sponge for affection and human
contact. I also want someone to play with. Oh lovey."[12]

Her gloom was to intensify. Just as Michael was nearing the end of
A Child of Our Time, around the Easter weekend of 1941, which came
in mid-April, the communities at East Grinstead were threatening

to break apart. One of the workers was a friend of Bryan Fisher's named Edric Maynard. He was twenty-four, born into rural poverty in Yorkshire (today he lies in the shadow of his sister Joan, who became a renowned and infamously left-wing Labour politician). He fell in love with Bryan and his feelings became damagingly intense. Soon he was diagnosed with schizophrenia. His condition led to frequent episodes of mania, of which Michael somehow ended up bearing the brunt. Edric would cycle to the bungalow, and Michael would do what he could. Helplessly he acquiesced to Edric's physical desires and went unwillingly to bed with him: "I let him do whatever he wanted, but afterwards made him sleep in the spare bedroom. Lying awake, I could hear him singing to the full moon shining outside and became desperately worried."[13] With Francesca's help Michael funded psychiatric treatment for Edric. The situation dragged on into the summer and became increasingly difficult. On one occasion, in search of Bryan, Edric went to Francesca's flat and threatened violence. Michael wrote to John Layard for advice: "I had to hold [Edric] in my arms against very deep-seated physical antipathy, in order to keep him human. He went into a Mental Home for a time, is now out again, and leads me a devil of a dance. I am not a little frightened at times." Edric was, he thought, "an extraordinary Hitler type".[14] It was a nasty and prolonged situation, but after the war Edric recovered enough to start studying for university entrance, for which Michael wrote him a reference. In 1947, a few weeks after his thirtieth birthday, he died suddenly of a ruptured appendix.

The weeks after Easter 1941 brought some of the last raids of the Blitz. Francesca Allinson's house in Mornington Terrace had had its windows blasted out four times. In the raid of 10 and 11 May, which gutted the House of Commons and flattened the Queen's Hall, the house was blown to pieces. By some miracle nobody had been inside. "I'm really frightfully cheery," Francesca promised Douglas as she rushed from Sussex to London, arriving to find Regent's Canal full of rubbish, and the city with "no buses, no water, no telephones, and you walk a mile so as to reach the next street". Little could be salvaged.

Tell Bryan that in my room the fireplace is still in the wall and
his dress suit hangs upon a nail – about fifty feet in the air. [. . .]
The piano appears to have tobogganed down subsiding floors
on its backside and was proud in the garden being played by
the demolition squad. [. . .] Just as I was leaving, having put
a fine toothcomb through everything, I caught sight of a rag
mashed into the ground. Behold my favourite pyjamas. The squad
had decided they were too small to be mine and consequently
tramped them in. I made no comment as to the size of my
person, as I didn't fancy half-a-dozen chaps getting fresh on its
account.[15]

There was little the owner of a bombed house could do other than
submit a claim for compensation to the War Damage Commission,
hope friends or relatives would open their doors, and wait. The
tobogganing piano soon joined Michael's inferior instrument in
Oxted, and he used it to compose for a number of years. Francesca
meanwhile kept shares in the Sussex land schemes, which continued successful, and divided her time between a life in Essex with
Judy Wogan and long periods spent with her brother Cyril in his
large house outside Cambridge.

The *carpe-diem* spirit of the war, seizing the day at a time when
days seemed numbered, led to entanglements that might have been
rejected in peacetime. Suppressed longings were recklessly indulged
behind the smokescreen of the blackout curtains; a desperate excitement could kick in during the fire-drenched nights. By June 1941
there was a feeling of relief in the air: the Blitz was over and
the Germans were distracted from their plans to invade Britain,
having launched an attack on the Soviets. It was in this fraught and
heady atmosphere, and off the back of Francesca's departure, that a
number of objectors from East Grinstead moved to Cambridgeshire
to join Douglas Newton at the hostel of which Bryan Fisher was
warden, and to work on the land. They formed a new community,
staying together until the closure of the Agricultural Committee
early the following year. Soon it was in a complex tangle, and
Michael was at its centre.

An objector friend of Michael's named Karl Hawker (twenty years old, handsome, reckless, charming) arrived at the hostel. Bryan, who was deeply unhappy in his marriage, fell in love with him. As Michael reported, "Bryan suddenly had an overwhelming homosexual affair, during which he feels that sex and love met."[16] During and after this relationship with Bryan, Karl spent more and more time at Oxted in Michael's bungalow. His similarities to Michael's first love Wilfred Franks were striking: he came from an impoverished background in Wales, and was an immensely talented draughtsman and painter with ambitions for an artistic career. He and Michael had shared the odd night together when introduced before the war by Michael's friend Aubrey Russ, but by the spring of 1941 they too had begun an affair, meeting when they could at weekends. Michael had once offered to play wife if Douglas Newton took the role of husband, and again he reached longingly towards vocabulary that was then a heterosexual privilege:

> I've grown very fond of Karl, but I can't bear the thought of the intensities of cross love affairs and jealousies. I find that after Karl was here over Whitsun I had re-reached a sort of gay and sensual notion of sexual life and the darknesses of Wilf have receded into the past. I don't know if it has any sense but I'm inclined to dream of a more prolonged liaison of this sort if Karl were to be in such circumstances as made it convenient to make here his chief home for a bit. In fact I've more or less proposed to him! – all providing he has some outside job and isn't emotionally dependent entirely on my attending to him in the daytime.[17]

But Karl was footloose and could settle neither at the hostel nor at Michael's bungalow. He worked on the land only in fits and starts, and frequently received fines for dereliction of duty that were usually paid on his behalf. By July Michael wrote with apparent resignation: "The little Karl seems intending to go to London on the run for a bit [. . .]. As far as I am concerned, in Papageno's words:

'*Ich bleibe ledig!*'* A gentle and occasional liaison shall we say."[18] And that was all it stayed, until, when the Agricultural Committee closed down, Karl moved to central Cambridge, met and then married a young actress called Anne, and the two set off to make a life in London.

That a relationship with Karl never quite reached fruition was perhaps due to the fact that Michael's feelings for Douglas Newton were fast intensifying. They saw each other infrequently, but when they did the friendship began to find expression in physical affection, initiated by Michael, but evidently accepted without rebuttal by Douglas. Where Karl had been unhappy and sexually conflicted, Douglas went to bed with Michael – sometimes no more than that – in the spirit of affection and experiment. Michael himself recognised that he was back in the familiar pattern of "warming the heart for the bride" whom he thought it inevitable Douglas would eventually find. With Douglas it was not a full-blown physical affair, a fact about which Michael was quite open, admitting that he had now accepted the "once shameful buggery", but making sure to qualify the statement: "I hope I haven't raised misunderstandings when I said buggery. I didn't mean the thing itself (no one has taken Wilf's place)."[19]

Douglas Newton's one surviving recollection of the relationship was wry, acidically unregretful, and slightly dismissive, as if looking back on youthful folly. There appears to have been a genuine friendship among the young men in Michael's orbit, and Douglas remembered Wilfred as "a sort of intuitive genius", and Karl as "that teddy-dear – I mean it nicely". He continued: "Was not getting into even an innocent bed with our old friend Michael Tippett not a sign of a certain juvenile-delinquent-ism? Surely so. Even though I can assure you it wasn't an erotic riot at any time. Respectful yes, and if he likes to munch away, why not?"[20]

Michael meanwhile was happy to compartmentalise his emotional life, which for a time had stood divided between Douglas and Karl.

---

* "I stay single!" (from Mozart's *The Magic Flute*).

He wrote to the former – nicknamed "Den" – to say so: "As you say, Den is Den and Karl is Karl and that's very satisfactory. I am not one of the people much gone on the usual Freudian theories of repression and see little value in sex as sex. [. . .] So there's not much to worry about, and for more people than appears at first sight, sex is only a deluding cover for deeper and more spiritual things."[21] Michael put out of his mind the inevitable day when Douglas would meet someone else, likely a woman, and instead, invoking in his letters on some six or seven separate occasions a phrase from William Blake, determined to seize with him the "joy as it flies".*

Completing *A Child of Our Time* had taken roughly the first four to five months of 1941. The third panel in the oratorio's triptych was written during the height of the Blitz, the destruction of Francesca's house, and the trouble with Edric Maynard. Part Three dramatises the Jungian journey into what the libretto calls the "icy waters" of the unconscious, at which point the strings surge upward, as if indicating the positive outcome of the necessary but difficult self-analysis. The bass becomes a prophet, to whom a lost chorus poses desperate questions. His answers, set to music as Britain faced a serious threat of invasion, are ones of comfort: "The man of destiny" – a title to which Hitler laid claim – "is cut off from fellowship. Healing springs from the womb of time." After an orchestral prelude, in which two flutes dance around each other like shadow and light trying to combine in one self, the tenor is permitted to soar: "I would know my shadow and my light, so shall I at last be whole." The four soloists are tightly laced into a quartet of reconciliation, wordless and rapturous, before the final

---

* From "Eternity" by William Blake: "He who binds to himself a joy | Does the winged life destroy; | But he who kisses the joy as it flies | Lives in eternity's sun rise."

spiritual, "Deep River", offers a glimpse – but only that – of a "land where all is peace". While the oratorio can inspire scepticism in all but the most Jung-steeped, the closing numbers sweep away doubt, shining hopeful beams into the dark. But the final moments are tinged with desperation. While the lyrics of the spirituals should not be taken too specifically, those of "Deep River" – "I want to cross over into camp ground" – bespeak a longing for death sung by an enslaved race. "I want to, I want to", never "I will", is yearningly and endlessly repeated by the chorus, forming a reminder of the precariousness of peace and renewal, and the price at which either is achieved. The singers end *A Child of Our Time* on an unaccompanied minor third. Michael had written a pacifist oratorio with the shadow of war and violence vivid on its lungs.

A Child of Our Time had been two and a half years in the conception and eighteen months in composition, but there was little prospect of performance or publication. Phyllis Sellick made a recording of Michael's piano sonata, which was issued, in August 1941, by the record company Rimington Van Wyck, who had to spread the twenty-minute piece over no fewer than five twelve-inch records. The release made a splash, and off the back of it Michael acquired two important supporters, eventually friends, in the form of critics William Glock and Edward Sackville-West, who put him pride of place in the pantheon of promising contemporary composers they admired. (Sackville-West urged him to cut the spirituals from *A Child of Our Time*.) In response to such attentions, Schott rushed through a printed edition of the sonata the following year, and then agreed, for a fee of £10 10s., to publish the string quartet and Concerto for Double String Orchestra as soon as possible.

With air raids much less frequent, the crushing tiredness of the previous year had mainly abated. In September Michael could finally turn his attention back to his work for piano and orchestra, the *Fantasia on a Theme of Handel*, which had lain abandoned since his cursory work on it in 1939; he finished on 11 November. The piece is formed of variations on a strangely stolid and unyielding phrase of Handel's, chosen for its appearance in a novel by Samuel Butler. Each variation depicts, in the tradition of Elgar's "Enigma"

Variations, one of Michael's friends.[22] The first is Francesca, painted in a wash of bright watercolour, a soaring, sunny theme on the violins bearing aloft a fizzing soloist. The second variation is a portrait of his friend from student days Jeffrey Mark, sprigged with snatches of the dance and folk-song rhythms in which Mark was a specialist. After this the portraits are unidentified, but matching them up is a fun game to play: a slow passage aglimmer with trills could be a love song for Douglas Newton; a boisterous and almost raunchy variation perhaps the youthful ardour of Antony Hopkins. Cadenzas for the soloist bring each variation to a frustrating halt, as if revealing the personalities' darker sides: for Francesca some funereal chords in the shadows of C-sharp minor; for war-traumatised Jeffrey Mark a jangling explosion of octaves.

Underneath the fantasia's surface gaiety lurks a reminder that composition was overshadowed by the constant threat of Michael's objector tribunal. And in September 1941 he had heard news of an old friend, Anthony Sedgwick, one of the pupils from Blundell's school to whom he had remained close. Sedgwick had been study-ing at Oxford when he was called up, and sent Michael desolate letters from his training courses in Lancashire and Plymouth. But then the letters stopped. On completion of his training he was sent abroad as a private in the Royal Army Ordnance Corps. Crossing the Mediterranean, his convoy was torpedoed. Michael lived in hope that Sedgwick had been picked up by the Italians and taken prisoner, but knew this would be an unlikely outcome. So it proved. Anthony was not killed instantly in the attack, and drowned as the ship sank. He was twenty-two. Bryan Fisher, a mutual friend, was distraught. "I grieved over his death and wondered how many more humane, endearing and worthwhile young men were going to be damaged and killed as the price to be paid for an ungodly war."[23]

The news can only have made Michael yet more resolved to oppose the fighting. But his registration could cause friction with friends. The composer Alan Bush, anti-war as he had been, was called into the army and assigned to the Medical Corps. David Ayerst had left teaching, been commissioned into the Royal Artillery and then sidetracked at the last minute into the War Office in London.

David, who was respectfully troubled by absolutism against the war, was living in Kensington with a number of soldiers (his wife and children had gone to Canada). He frequently hosted Michael, who did not miss the irony of being the only conscientious objector amid a group of uniformed men.

On 24 November 1941 the rise in Michael's musical reputation was proved when, much to his surprise, he received a letter from ENSA, an acronym lovingly said to stand for Every Night Something Awful, but actually referring to the Entertainments National Service Association, which provided entertainment for the Armed Forces. The letter offered him the job of musical organiser of the Northern Irish command. This meant not only potential security against imprisonment or land work, but a generous salary: £500 per year, of which he'd never seen the like. It would also entail giving up London musical life and moving to Londonderry. Michael instantly refused. "It meant retrograde music to what I am doing, and no composition at all – and merely for money. It wasn't me at all. But it's nice to know one's 'market' worth."[24] Turning down the money meant relying as ever on Francesca's financial help. "Is it very wrong", he asked her, "to refuse ENSA and depend on good friends?"[25] In a letter to John Layard, sent late in November, he best described his standpoint:

> It's not only that I can't morally or physically do what they want – but I only understand the way of love as a method of dealing with the renegade personality, even that of a whole nation. I don't presume to think this attitude objectively right for us all – it's just my fate in some absolutely clear way and so far I have never had a shadow of hostility – on the contrary – soldiers and civilians often force me unwillingly to say what I feel because it seems to give them some comfort to hear a point of view and feeling that is outside the emotional melee. [. . .] I am not in the least afraid of the consequences of my view.[26]

Just over a week later, on 7 December, the Empire of Japan attacked the American naval and army base on Pearl Harbor in Hawaii, and

Hitler promptly declared war on the United States. The Allies now had American support, there was a distinct lull in aerial attacks (fewer than thirty raids on London over the following two years), and it was hoped that the war would soon be at an end. GIs began to appear in London, bringing with them Coca-Cola, nylon stockings, and chewing-gum. Two of them even found their way to a Morley concert, and Michael overheard with glee their appreciation of the programme: "Monteverdi! Attaboy, Attaboy!"[27] He spent the first months of 1942 scrambling to gather testimonials for his tribunal, which, over a year after he had registered as a conscientious objector, had been set for early in February. Ralph Vaughan Williams duly sent a supportive statement, but made no bones about his disapproval:

> I will not argue with you about your pacifist scruples which I respect though I think they are all wrong. [. . .] you are not the only composer in this predicament. What about Rubbra and Finzi and Bush who have all temporarily given up their creative work and gone on to various kinds of "war-work". If you are to be exempted so as to carry on your composition, why not they? However wrong and dreadful we think war (and we all do) − here it is and we can't shirk it − and surely we can all do a little bit to try and bring it to an end.[28]

On 3 February 1942 Michael came up before the South Eastern Counties tribunal at Lambeth. He gave his profession as "Institute Instructor (Music Teacher)", and the statement that he had submitted on his registration form was read out. He was then questioned by the chairman, and by a board made up of three men: a lawyer, someone from the army, and a representative from a trade union. The following notes were made of the evidence he gave when cross-examined:

> Object to non-combatant duties. Witness. Not on religious grounds in general sense though close to Quaker point of view and my experience is a spiritual one. Refused to join Officer

Training Corps but parents and teachers over-ruled me.* [. . .]
It's not wrong to do the non-combatant duties but it's wrong
to conscript me to do it. I would object to doing it voluntarily
because I have a definite job to do. If I were a doctor I would
probably not be a doctor in R.A.M.C. You are asking me to give
up my job just because of a war. I am called to witness to the
wrongness of conscripting people for military service. War is
illimited evil. [. . .] I must do my best to secure that there shall
be more Pacifists next time. [. . .] No previous war has been of
use; total war infinitely more grievous. Refused job in E.N.S.A.
primarily because of loyalty to Morley College. Object to Air Raid
Precautions because it is expressly arising out of war. Could not
do combatant duties. Obviously because it's wrong.[29]

Six letters of support were then read out, from David Ayerst, Aubrey
Russ, Eva Hubback, Ralph Vaughan Williams, a Mr A.W. Bing-
ham (unidentifiable), and J.F.R. Buttle (senior in the Co-operative
Society).

There were four possible outcomes. The most desirable but
least likely was that Michael would be registered unconditionally
as a conscientious objector, and exempted from military or any
other service. Another option was to be conditionally registered,
providing he undertake war work of a civilian character, such as
work on the land, in the Fire Service, in hospitals, or with the Air
Raid Precautions organisation. Otherwise he could be registered for
military service but only employed in non-combatant duties. Or he
could be struck off from the Register of Conscientious Objectors
completely.

The chairman of Michael's tribunal, a Mr D. Davies, delivered the
board's unanimous decision: "The applicant was clearly sincere but
the Tribunal felt considerable doubt whether his objection was based

---

* A manipulation of the truth, perhaps; elsewhere he remembered that he had
flatly refused, with his parents' support, to join Stamford School's Officer
Training Corps, and was allowed to parade instead with the juniors.

upon a sense of moral objection to abstain from military service, or upon an objection to conscription or a desire to demonstrate his detestation of war and to continue his work as a musician. On the whole they came to the conclusion that he had a conscientious objection to combatant duties." The ruling was that "the applicant shall be registered as a person liable under the [National Service] Act to be called up for service but to be employed only in non-combatant duties".[30]

Bar being struck off the register altogether, it was the worst possible outcome, and gave him just two options. He could join the Non-Combatant Corps, which comprised not only objectors but those who hadn't passed their medical exams, and which had relatively little stigma attached to it. Most members worked in bomb disposal, others in transport, agriculture, or forestry. (Christopher Fry, also an objector, was ordered into the Corps and found himself cleaning out sewers underneath bombed London docks, which gave him first double pneumonia and then a nervous breakdown.) Otherwise it would have to be the Royal Army Medical Corps, where a period of training would usually result in a nursing and military qualification, and then a posting abroad. Few conscientious objectors made it into the RAMC, as doctors had a right to handle weapons so as to defend themselves and their patients. But any non-combatant military duty still entailed being called up into the army, being given a rank, and wearing a uniform. The tribunal's decision sent Michael reeling, and back in his bungalow he sobbed. "When I got home", he told Francesca, "and began to realise in my body that the music must go, whichever way I travel, I cried like a child. Now I feel better, but lost. David and [almost everyone] else, is trying to get me to compromise – but I am realising that mere social work won't replace the music – only pacifist witness against the whole madness can do so. I am going through a considerable moral crisis."[31]

Michael was determined to appeal, and the matter was made more urgent when, just weeks after his tribunal, the Empire of Japan captured Singapore, resulting in what Churchill deemed the "worst disaster" in British military history. The prospect of peace

seemed far off. Michael thought it doubtful that another tribunal
would change his ruling to unconditional exemption, but hoped
that his duties would be downgraded to civilian work. "I dare say
it all seems crackers to you," he wrote to John Layard, "but my
serenity and gaiety have always been at a price – the price of sitting
also with the scapegoats and the outcasts – I am learning to do it
willingly and joyously, and because, with a world going awry and
gearing itself up for even greater destruction, I must take my stand
where I truly belong."[32] It was a view that, then as now, many
struggled to understand. David Ayerst was chief among his friends
in trying desperately to persuade Michael to take whatever terms
were offered him. Michael stood firm.

> I don't pretend to see things in their only true light [. . . and]
> have submitted to everyone else's argumentation from the other
> side [. . .]. David wants me to go into the National Fire Service
> with Stephen Spender to carry on adult education there – but
> exactly what is the point of giving up adult education in the
> Co-Ops and Morley College to do it in Fire depots, I fail to see,
> except to evade the real show-down between my feelings and
> principles and those of the authorities. In any case I can't really
> desert my own, however peculiar and cissy and shadow-like they
> are – because it is now for the first time given me the power to
> do so without shame or distress.[33]

While waiting for his appellate tribunal, Michael juddered between
a kind of exultation and a deep depression and isolation, starved
of affection and sex. It had been a bitterly cold winter and spring,
and the bungalow, heated only by a coal fire, was often icy. Karl
Hawker had disappeared into London; Douglas Newton was living
in central Cambridge and Michael was only an occasional visitor;
Francesca was recuperating in Cambridgeshire. Michael wrote to
her: "I was thinking last night before I went to sleep and with a
pang how much I have missed you all these long months."[34]

John Layard, now living in Cornwall, had become by letter an
almost weekly confessor, one of many older men whom Michael

was actively hunting out for support. The artist Eric Kennington had now met Michael on a number of occasions; he approved neither of homosexuality nor of conscientious objectors, and they had parted on bad terms. A war artist in the First World War, Kennington had spent the 1930s reasonably committed to pacifism, before a visceral response to the bravery of individual soldiers had led him to return to war art. "If Kennington could but once paint the young conscientious objector [. . .] among his blue boys", Michael wrote, "I should feel England were safer."[35] On 4 February, the day after the tribunal, he and Kennington, whose shifting viewpoints had got under Michael's skin, arranged to have a peace-making tea. "EK was not upsetting," Michael reported to Douglas. "I tried to make him my father-confessor but it was no go. However some irrelevant thing he said did help. He is preoccupied with his own problem: he feels it his duty to prepare himself inside to shoot his fellow men for England's sake, and the authorities will only let him paint! [. . .] Anyhow, we're all as mad as each other."[36]

Last in the trio of "father-confessors" was T.S. Eliot. Michael visited the Faber offices in the week following the tribunal, "to announce the decision [to appeal] and [Eliot] seemed both to expect it and to agree".[37] The poet was training to be an air-raid warden and, although tempted by pacifism in the First World War, feared the triumph of the Axis Powers. In 1939 he had written: "I cannot but believe that the man who maintains that war is in all circumstances wrong, is in some way repudiating an obligation towards society."[38] But Eliot's willingly lent ear to Michael's troubles proves him, if not a supporter, then distantly sympathetic to such a position. He sent Michael a warm and understanding letter, with an offer of help on which, surprisingly, Michael never took him up:

I hope you will let me know when any more of your compositions are available in recorded form. I very much like the one I have. I have often wondered since I saw you how your affairs are going. Of course, I am sorry that you hold the views you do but I respect them and if you hold them at all I respect them the more for being thoroughgoing. Of course, if I can help at a

later stage I shall be very glad to do so, but I do not believe my
name carries very much weight with military authorities. [. . .]
If you have a chance before the worst happens, do look in one
day and see me.[39]

Composition continued, the music untouched by Michael's slow
and upsetting progress through the bureaucracy of conscientious
objection. Just two days before the tribunal he had finished work
on a madrigal (setting Edward Thomas) for his Morley choir; in
the weeks afterwards, he completed another (setting Gerard Manley
Hopkins). On 7 March came the first performance, at the Wigmore
Hall, of his Handel fantasia.[40] The concert was the biggest premiere
he'd yet experienced, but the work didn't quite come off, as not
only reviewers but even his friends admitted. His close circle gathered at a party afterwards; even Wilfred Franks and Meg Masters
attended. But just a few months later Wilfred was, Michael thought,
"going dead on me" and he had to rely on hearing second-hand
news of his former love. Wilfred had registered as an objector, and
was ordered to teach at the Tavistock Clinic (an institute of medical
psychology). Eventually he spent a month in prison for refusing,
as many objectors did, to submit to a medical exam.[41] But Michael
did no more than look on from a distance. Late in the war Wilfred
and Meg had a child together, but the intended marriage that had
caused Michael such pain never took place, and Wilfred soon separated from Meg and their daughter. It would be forty years until
he met Michael Tippett again.

In April 1942 Michael conducted his Morley choir in a production
of Purcell's Dido and Aeneas, staged at the Arts Theatre in Westminster and accompanied by a single piano, with costumes made of
dusters and towels to save on clothing coupons. Soon afterwards,
he holidayed in Cornwall. As he reported to Francesca, who was
suffering a bad relapse, "there is no one about, and no soldiers
and such heavenly colouring and things just as they ever were".[42]

Then, in early May, he was summoned to his appellate tribunal at a building on the King's Road in Chelsea. He called Aubrey Russ as a witness, and produced a statement from Evelyn Maude. "The Appellate Tribunal was yesterday," he told John Layard (to whom he was now reporting events almost daily), "but the decision is to be by letter, which has not yet been delivered [. . .] the good-versus-evil nature of the experience yesterday [. . .] was so extreme and unequivocal at a certain moment that I lost all sense of my self and the consequences and knew that I had absolutely no option but to go forward."[43]

Finally the letter came, and on 24 May he could update Layard that the ruling had been softened to civilian work. "Full time Air Raid Precaution, Fire Service, or Land. The first two are impossible, the last a discreet 'way out'. But I am inclined to offer school-teaching and to stand pat. If they refuse to accept, it will take six months or so to reach quod." (Quod he frequently used as a nickname for prison, which beckoned for any who refused to comply with a tribunal's ruling.) "Meanwhile the music is so active publicly and creatively that I think on the whole this is the way through. I shall treat the probable four months shut away as a meditation exercise!"[44] Then there was further news, reported to Francesca: "Have had an order to become a labourer in Buckinghamshire and refused. I suppose this is the usual procedure. It all feels so much like an enclosing prison, and I think I hope very much for a sentence or a finality if only that is possible."[45]

Over 6,000 objectors refused to comply with the terms of their exemption. Many thought even civilian tasks were too closely linked to militarism; others argued that by taking such jobs they were freeing up another worker for conscription. Some reasoned on grounds of conscience that they would undertake civilian duties voluntarily but not compulsorily. Michael's argument was common: civilian work would not be as useful as the job he was already doing. He believed passionately that his maintenance of Morley College's Music Department would be of more value than working as an agricultural labourer, but most of all was determined to make a stand at what was, he felt, a damaging and potentially lengthy interruption to his own music-making. His foremost task was to compose, and abdication was unthinkable. In descriptions of his composition his metaphors frequently turn to the obstetric, and his greatest fear was a forced prevention of musical birth, although he conceded that this experience was "no different from the experience of artists who fight in wars".[46] In one letter he placed the stultifying of the creative impulse as a worse result of the war than killing: "I could get out of this private impasse if I would agree to turn my gifts exclusively to entertainment and the making of morale and propaganda (T.S. Eliot does it) – in the BBC feature programmes. But that is for me the real 'sin [against] the Holy Ghost' – I could more easily go into the army and kill. Unfortunately I can't do that either. So it has to be lumped."[47]

He had spent three years helping younger objectors through their own tribunals, had watched many of them go to prison through his example, and was determined not to let them down. "If I do a voluntary political act for pacifism, it is for the sake of the six hundred and fifty lads in quod."[48] Though he attempted to be disciplined with himself in refusing any sense of martyrdom, trying to avoid any "spiritual pride at being 'taken'", he may have been guilty of cultivating a "celebrity conchie" status: "I'm sort of a general favourite".[49] Either way, he had made up his mind. "The way I intend to go is both proper to my character and certainly more sensible than to enter the network of conscription laws. So that is over."[50] Thirty years later he insisted in interview: "I would have been shot rather than be compelled to fight. But I didn't really believe in a damn thing. My only job is to write music and that is that."[51] A call to trial could come at any time. But determination to go to prison in political protest did not prevent his making what efforts he could to fight the authorities. The case would drag on for over a year: thirteen months during which the threat of incarceration hung over his head like a dark cloud, and in which almost no arrangement could be made without the qualifier "unless I'm in prison".[52]

Composition became pressing in consequence and he was determined to work as much as he could. He had begun his String

Quartet No. 2 in around April, hoping in emulation of Eliot eventually to create a series of four, and worked on it all through the year (he would finish on 5 December). Proving Michael's striking ability and determination often to separate his life and his music, three of the quartet's four movements are joyous, even graceful: a lyrical opening, a jaunty quicksilver scherzo, and a dramatic finale that eventually finds peace. But most memorable in the quartet is the shambling fugue of its slow movement, based on the five-bar shard of a theme he had jotted down in 1938 during the war's false start. The hopeless trudge is exacerbated by a carefully marked awkwardness in the bowing, and the voices shackled into the fugal lattice are soon scrunched with pain, before giving up the fight and resignedly abandoning themselves to the cold comfort of a minor chord. During composition Michael updated Francesca: "Work has gone very well and the quartet moves. But the prison walls worry me and sometimes dry everything up. I am frightened in my body, though unafraid in my mind."[53] Come 2 September, soon after a snatched holiday with David Ayerst to the Black Mountains, he could report that the Ministry of Labour were "making a final investigation before either leaving me alone or sending me to prison for a term. It's an awful matter of luck."[54] Still he was writing to John Layard almost every day, as on 25 September: "Of course I am afraid of prison – it's always been for me the symbol of all that is most horrible and inhuman. As a young man I used to get into an anarchistic passion over prison walls and tales of sufferings from that quarter."[55] Michael's correspondence of the second half of 1942 glitters with an honestly admitted dread: "The trouble with the authorities is advancing with seven-league boots, and what is more it looks as if there is a real danger of cat-and-mouse imprisonment, *ad eternitam* so to speak. All very frightening. [. . .] For the moment I write all I can, awaiting the evil day of prosecution."[56]

One bright spot on the horizon was the friendship of Benjamin Britten and his partner, the singer Peter Pears. Michael had long been aware of Britten, who had already produced over forty film and theatre scores, and nearly thirty official works, with some of his most lasting pieces – the Simple Symphony, *Variations on a Theme of Frank Bridge*, *Les Illuminations*, and concertos for violin and piano – already premiered. Britten was far better known and more frequently performed than Michael, but had had similar battles to fight, against carping critics and imperfect performances. Britten (born in November 1913) was nearly nine years' Tippett's junior: the difference between remembering the First World War and reading about it, being an Edwardian or a war baby, and coming of age in a London booming or busting. Two years after graduation Britten had been invited to write music for documentary films at the General Post Office Film Unit, where he had befriended W.H. Auden. In 1937 Britten had met Pears, and the distinctive metallic gleam of Pears's tenor voice was an instantaneous inspiration. Their relationship turned into a lifelong love when, five months before the outbreak of war, the two men travelled first to Canada and eventually to join Auden in New York. The British Embassy in America encouraged their presence as artistic ambassadors, but eventually some MPs and the right-wing press began to unleash their fury at the group of young artistic Englishmen who had "fled" to America. Feeling deracinated and longing for his beloved Suffolk coast, Britten returned to England, with Pears, in April 1942.

Michael was due to conduct the Morley choir in a concert, on 7 November, that lacked a soloist for some anthems by Orlando Gibbons. Walter Bergmann suggested Pears, who gamely bolstered the tenor line of the choir as well as singing solo. Pears and Britten became reasonably frequent performers at Morley, and gave in quickly to Michael's gift for friendships speedily made and intensely lived out. Michael was keen to tell all to Douglas Newton: "PP and BB are become two very good friends – BB was apparently jealous of me at first! Saw my name only on the Handel-Fantasia in America."[57] Soon Britten presented Michael with a copy of *The Sonnets of Michael Angelo Buonarroti*, portions of which he had recently set to music, inscribed "To Michael, with love from Ben." The explicitly homoerotic poetry made for a pointedly intimate gift.[58]

Like Michael, Britten had struggled with what role music might play in expressing his political convictions. He and Pears were pacifists and pro-appeasement. Both had managed (Britten at a second attempt) to become one of the 4.7 per cent of conscientious objectors who were registered unconditionally, and thus given complete exemption from war service. Before Michael had met either man, he allowed himself a little moan: "Benjamin Britten, the young composer of the Wystan [Auden] click, back from America and a C.O., gets the head of the pacifist Union to represent him, William Walton the composer to speak for him, and gets unconditional exemption! Poor little me can't manage to have such publicity or throw his weight about. But I don't mind, all the same."[59] Elsewhere he admitted, not without slight disapproval: "I was not able to 'flee' to America with the others and I know then the consequences."[60]

But on meeting Britten, what few doubts and jealousies Michael was harbouring quickly fled. Their similarities were as uniting as their differences were complementary. Both were influenced by Purcell and his contemporaries; both had fought against a perceived anti-intellectual folksiness in British music; and both were alive to musical development in Europe. Britten found in Michael a fierce and all-encompassing intellect, and the true warmth of creative passion. And Michael instantly recognised a musical facility and technique that seemed to pour from Britten's very soul. Where Britten could write a three-act opera in seven months (as in 1960 with *A Midsummer Night's Dream*), a work of comparable length would take Michael many years. Britten had a fine-tuned ear and could compose more or less in his head, whereas Michael was reliant on manuscript paper and the piano. Neither Britten's creative toil nor Michael's fluency (especially with counterpoint and fugue) can be ignored: the effect of struggle can be effortlessly achieved, just as apparent effortlessness is often the result of laborious work. But it was not out of false flattery that Michael wrote time and again of Britten's facility: "I sigh all the time for your wonderful ease of composition, and what I can steal, I do."[61] His admiration was reciprocated. "Glad you like Michael Tippett," Auden wrote to

Britten, "and to hear that he has talent."[62] And Britten had reported to Elizabeth Mayer, at whose house in America he and Pears had lived: "One great new friend Peter and I have made, an <u>excellent</u> composer, and most delightful and intelligent young man, Michael Tippett is having a bad time and may have to go to prison (you can guess what for) – but he is brave and says he won't mind, but nevertheless we're all fighting to keep him out."[63] Pears was no less enthusiastic, writing independently to Mayer that Michael was someone "we can both wholly admire and love".[64] By May 1943 Britten was banding Michael with Pears as the duo of "rigorous critics" whose opinions most mattered to him.[65] The two composers believed themselves to be at the forefront of their musical generation in England, and took the responsibility seriously. Many critics would link them together as the white-hot hope, a pair who could drag British music out of what was often appraised as a century's stodge.

Britten became notorious for dropping his friends after quarrels, leaving a trail of so-called "corpses" in his wake. Some testified to his lack of humour, but Michael's often knockabout lack of seriousness evidently brought out the best in him. That their friendship was to endure a number of creative and personal differences is testament to its closeness. Their correspondence reveals a sentiment unchanged through the decades, and rare in the intensity of its expression, though in some ways they made an unlikely pair. Pears was the natural friend for Michael: the more sophisticated letter writer, the more convivial and witty, and the more comfortable with his homosexuality. But although Michael's true feelings need to be picked out of his natural gregariousness, it is no exaggeration to say (and eventually he would say it himself) that he loved Benjamin Britten, drawn irresistibly to his evident musical talent. Britten, Pears, and Michael lived out the war a close trio, frequent visitors to each other's houses. Odd to imagine them all in Michael's cold and sparsely furnished bungalow. There was a strange contradiction in the friendship, in that while Britten's career and composition had forged ahead, Michael could look upon Britten's arrested and arresting boyishness with almost avuncular affection, nowhere better illustrated than in his observation of Britten, one cold spring morning in Oxted. "So like Ben – waiting for breakfast and seeing the streaming window frames of the door, I saw he had written in each with his finger, P.P., M.T., B.B. It just expresses his small boy side."[66]

On 15 November 1942 the church bells rang all over Britain for the first time in eighteen months, in celebration of victory at the Second Battle of El Alamein. In the weeks afterwards, small victories were all the time being achieved in Michael's career. "I'm still unaccountably at liberty," he wrote to John Layard on Christmas Day, omitting any festive greeting, "it only adds to the general feeling within of living at the periphery or near-centre of an outer whirlpool, where all the usual values are confused together and the gods are turned arse-upwards."[67] After the final Morley concert that year and the completion of his String Quartet No. 2, he was invited by the BBC to give a radio talk on Stravinsky. *Portrait of Stravinsky*, the first of his many broadcast lectures, went out on the BBC Home Service on 31 January 1943, and Michael was grateful for the pay cheque, being overdrawn that month by nearly five pounds (hundreds today).[68] He insisted on rehearsing with Douglas Newton, whose opinion he trusted, and who was one of the main reasons for the parlous state of his finances.

It was to Douglas Newton that Michael wanted to dedicate a cantata, intended for Pears and Britten to perform, on which he began composition early in 1943. He had earmarked a long prose passage from the memoirs of the naturalist William Henry Hudson, *Far Away and Long Ago*, depicting Hudson's childhood in Argentina, perhaps feeling that there were parallels with Douglas's upbringing in Malaysia. Douglas rejected the idea of dedication, either in worry that it would be too binding a love token, or owing to his sense that the prose did not lend itself easily to musical setting. The 500-word chunk of the memoirs does indeed turn away from T.S. Eliot's advice that composers should use simple or serviceable words, and Michael would have to do battle with the verbiage and foliage of the text: "to let my sight dwell and feast on the camalote flower amid its floating masses of moist vivid green leaves, the large almanda-like flower of a purest divine yellow," and so on. But the passage was a vivid gift to its intended performers in the way it teeters on the fulcrum between childhood innocence and the sadnesses of adult experience. Such were topics close to Britten's heart, and Michael – using the title of the relevant chapter in Hudson's memoir – called the cantata *Boyhood's End*.

"I'm afraid somehow that I won't come up to expectations," he wrote at the outset of composition, "life is too restless. I've been depressed at the exceeding slowness of getting one's music out and about – so that Britten's apparently genuine consideration has been a blessing and encouragement. I'm still rather down in the dumps and wonder what I'm up to."[69] Work on the piece was slow, interrupted by continued visits to conscientious objectors in prison, planning a joint radio talk with Pears on Beethoven's *Fidelio*, and handfuls of Morley concerts. Francesca Allinson stayed with him for an extended period, but Michael admitted that he "may have half resented her being here [. . .]. I'm a horrid person inside, like most artists."[70] And the horrors of the war were sometimes very close.

In 1939 or 1940 Michael's parents, Henry and Isabel Kemp, had downsized from their large manor in Somerset and moved to a house on the seafront in Exmouth, east Devon. In later life Michael was quick to characterise his wartime relationship with both (but especially his mother) as almost beyond repair. Difficulties had not vanished, but his letters depict softer and more forgiving feelings. Exmouth was a convenient pit stop on the way to Cornish holidays, and although he was only an intermittent visitor, he made sure to check in when he could, and was growing rather fond of them: "They're a remarkable old couple."[71] Henry Kemp, the man who had once gone adventuring in South America, had by 1943 reached the age of eighty-five. Isabel, in her early sixties, was still vigorous and spent most of her time seeing to his care. Meanwhile Michael's brother, Peter, long since invalided out of active service after losing his leg at naval college, had been working as a sports journalist for

The Times; on receiving his call-up he had joined the Naval Intelligence Division of the Admiralty, where he ran the Radio Direction Finding section, developing an invaluable tool for locating the position of ships and submarines. His work made him privy to the best-kept secrets of the naval war, and he was "one of the few who knew of the remarkable work of the Bletchley team and their Enigma decoding machines".[72] The brothers met at their parents' house on high and holy days but were not close, and Peter's distinguished war service was in sharp relief to Michael's pacifism. Peter seemed to Michael something of a model son, not least because, although Isabel, ever the political protestor, was proud of Michael's objections, Henry supported the war. Peter had also provided three grandchildren, to whom Isabel was devoted.

On 26 February 1943, at around noon, eight enemy planes flew above Exmouth, and each dropped a bomb above the town while firing with machine guns. In the Exmouth Strand one of the bombs demolished an entire row of shops. Twenty-five people were killed and forty were seriously injured, among them Henry Kemp, who got caught in a blast while working in the garden.[73] He sustained what appeared to be surface injuries, but was suffering from internal bleeding, and would never truly recover.

Michael stayed in London, in low spirits, struggling on with *Boyhood's End*. "Life is fearful," he told Francesca on 9 March, "composition hopeless."[74] He took solace from Douglas, who was still working on a farm in Cambridge, and now lodging nearby in the house of the philosopher G.E. Moore. Douglas had finally been called up and had registered as a conscientious objector; his commitments on the land, and the pressure of his upcoming tribunal, made him an intermittent correspondent and a flighty keeper of arrangements. "Had set my heart somewhat on your coming," Michael wrote to him on the last day of February, "so had a momentary pang when there was no Den. Vision of a long-wanted day off, and spring-like weather, and a person I'm very fond of. Still there we are – you'll appear sometime. [. . .] Miss you."[75] In early March Douglas did in fact turn up, much to Michael's relief. "Did so enjoy your being here. I don't know what I should do if I didn't feel you'd be there from time to time. It's when we haven't seen each other for some time that when it happens I feel as if someone very near and dear had arrived – and nothing else matters and life becomes refreshment."[76]

On 27 March came the premiere of Michael's String Quartet No. 2, given by the all-female Zorian Quartet, at the Wigmore Hall. It was this piece, scheduled for a large number of performances over the following months, that really turned the tide in his reputation. William Glock wrote in the *Observer* that "a new composer has emerged in English music", and the composer Lennox Berkeley produced a glowing report recommending it for broadcast by the BBC.[77] But there was little time to enjoy the success. On 2 April Michael made a final push against a criminal trial, and went nervously to the Westerham Employment Office for an interview with Cyril Phillips, an official from the Ministry of Labour whom he found "kindness itself".[78] Michael made a single, important, concession, by offering to take part in civil defence work: "my pigheadedness seems to have fastened on fire-watching now".[79] But such an offer did not, it seems, cancel out the fact that he was due to be prosecuted for refusing to work for the Buckinghamshire Agricultural Committee.

His case was now reaching the very highest levels of government and he found a valuable supporter in Sir Stafford Cripps, the Minister of Aircraft Production, who was often mentioned as a rival to Churchill for the top job. Cripps wrote a letter supporting Michael to Ernest Bevin, the Minister of Labour. For a while there was hope. Michael wrote to William Busch (a fellow pacifist composer on the Schott list) that "correspondence with the Ministry of Labour is long-drawn out and the sentence might not come for six months or more. I am not worried. Too busy."[80] But by May he had to tell Busch the bad news. Ernest Bevin, who was known for his antipathy to pacifists, had "refused all the letters in *toto*".[81]

There was no more to be done. To David Ayerst, who was increasingly upset at Michael's stance, he stood firm in his belief that the Allied actions seemed as ruthless as Hitler's:

There is nothing to do but await prosecution. Personally I am glad. We had begun to lose sight of the actuality, responsibility indeed, of conscientious objection. Turn about how I may, total war and such particular attributes of it as the British (or Axis) night-bombing, and the square miles of terror involved, is as far removed from the life of the gospel as anything I can imagine. Archbishop Spellman blessing the American bombers which carried out the Antwerp daylight raid and its attendant horrors is a mockery which organised Christianity must atone for if it can.* [. . .] At present the issue is a coarse and brutal one. For or against the 1000-bomber raid – and the answer is: against. Where this central refusal lands you depends on temperament and other considerations. However I feel very much at peace and ready to go.[82]

In the second week of May he was called to trial, and the date was set for 7 June 1943.[83] *Boyhood's End* was due to be premiered by Britten and Pears at Morley College just two days earlier, and Michael had to scramble all through May to finish it in time, all the while making preparations for the trial and a possible spell in prison, obtaining and poring over a copy of Bach's *The Art of Fugue* so as to continue studying it from memory in a cell. He sent a letter trying to make peace with his cousin Phyllis Kemp, to whom he hadn't spoken since their political rows in the 1930s, but it went unanswered. John Amis agreed to keep Morley up and running, and Imogen Holst (Gustav's daughter) was booked to rehearse the choir. Meanwhile Britten tried to obtain letters of support for Michael's trial: the composer Arnold Bax wrote encouragingly, and so did the conductor Adrian Boult.[84] But Michael was advised

---

* Francis Spellman was Archbishop of New York and Apostolic Vicar for the US Armed Forces. In the Vietnam War, as in the Second World War, he would sprinkle guns and bombers with holy water. On 5 April 1943 the US Air Force had attacked Mortsel, a city not far from Antwerp, without warning and in daylight. In the space of eight minutes nearly 1,000 people were killed, and twice as many again were injured.

that Ralph Vaughan Williams would be thought a bigger name
when it came to an actual appearance in court. Vaughan Williams
grudgingly agreed to appear, "on the understanding", Michael told
Britten, "that he can say how much he disapproves of my being a
conchie!"[85] At the end of May news came that the trial would be
delayed by two weeks, and it was rescheduled for 21 June.

Boyhood's End was finished just in time for its premiere. Michael
had fixed with glee on certain words of Hudson's text and stretched
them over Monteverdi-inspired cascades that dramatise the action
they describe: the single word "dance" is an extended frolic of
sixty-three notes. In the finale the voice describes the "ecstasy" of
being at one with nature in an ululation full of tension and release
that John Amis described as "like a much-to-be-enjoyed orgasm"
and Evelyn Maude found "too physical".[86] Michael dashed off a
card to Britten and Pears, both of whom admired the piece a great
deal: "Have only just recovered from your dual performance. It
was a knock-out for many besides myself – ever so many heartfelt
thanks. As I told Peter before, it is indeed a love song – or the
exuberance of love turned into sound. [. . .] I long to hear it again
soon. Goehr thinks it the best thing I've done. And done it was for
you both."[87] On 6 June Michael rushed to London to give a radio
talk. Twelve days later he went to Bedford to discuss a broadcast
of his music by the BBC Symphony Orchestra. On the same trip
he visited Bedford Prison – known to have a harsh regime – to see
a conscientious objector serving time. The young man, on seeing
Michael, burst into tears.[88]

"If I'm shut away on Monday don't take it to heart," Michael
told John Layard the next day. "To be forced to leave go may be
a salvation and a great peace. [. . .] It is not at all an act of insub-
ordination to me now, but an act nearer to dedication."[89] It was
two and a half years since Michael had provisionally registered as
a conscientious objector, in which time his musical reputation had
changed utterly. At the outbreak of war he had been little known,
but three reasonably high-profile premieres in London, and the
successful series of Morley concerts, had changed all that. Newspapers were beginning to talk of him as a leading British composer.

Hyperbolic advertisement this could have been, but he had become famous enough that his trial was reported in some detail up and down the country. He was a national news story.[90]

At half past ten on the morning of 21 June 1943 he arrived at Oxted Police Court, which was two miles away from his cottage, and housed alongside the police station in a large red-brick building that, with its mock-Tudor gables and chimneys and tiny cupola, looked like nothing so much as a large country house. Inside was the small, oak-panelled courtroom. Gathered in the room to testify on his behalf were David Ayerst, going strictly by the title of colonel and in full military costume; Eva Hubback, Morley's principal; Ralph Vaughan Williams; and Peter Pears (who, having had an easier time than Britten in gaining unconditional exemption, was thought a more useful presence than his partner).[91] Evelyn Maude watched from the gallery. First a manslaughter case was heard, trying a young soldier who had run somebody over with an army vehicle. Guilty. Then it was Michael's turn.

The case was outlined. Michael pleaded not guilty.[92] The prosecuting lawyer appearing for the Ministry of Labour, Captain W.R. Howe Pringle (decorated for his war service), called as witness Cyril Phillips, the official from the Ministry of Labour who had interviewed Michael in April. Phillips confirmed that at the meeting Michael had frankly stated his views and claimed to have "been commissioned for additional work by the BBC, radio talks and incidental music for news reels". (Spurious perhaps: there is no evidence of Michael's having composed for the latter.) An army officer called John Falmingham then gave corroborative evidence.

Michael, on the advice of his lawyer, Robert Pollard, had engaged the services of a barrister and Peace Pledge Union member named Gerald Gardiner. Gardiner was a humane and distinguished man, who eventually defended Penguin Books when they were prosecuted for obscenity after publishing *Lady Chatterley's Lover*, and who became Lord Chancellor in Harold Wilson's 1964 Labour government. He argued that refusing to comply with conditions of exemption was not an offence should the defendant have a reasonable excuse. In Michael's case, this was the public recognition he had only recently won for his composition. Even Ernest Bevin, the Minister of Labour, had – so Gardiner argued – recognised that the performance of serious music was grounds enough not to prosecute those who refused to comply with registration conditions. (Peter Pears was the unnamed example.) "The only difference here was that while other people performed serious music, Tippett composed the music they performed."

Michael was then cross-examined, and listed his recent professional engagements. Eva Hubback was called, and said that Michael had convinced her absolutely of his pacifism and deep sincerity. Ralph Vaughan Williams then took the stand: "I think Tippett's pacifist views entirely wrong, but I respect him very much for holding them so firmly. I think his compositions are very remarkable and form a distinct national asset, and will increase the prestige of this country in the world. As regards his teachings at Morley College, it is distinctly work of national importance to create a musical atmosphere at the college and elsewhere."[93] David Ayerst spoke of Michael's long-held pacifism, saying "there was no question of his complete straightforwardness". Peter Pears said that "Tippett was one of a very small number whose work would have great influence on the future of English music."

The chairman of magistrates was a Mr F.H. Elliot and it was he who delivered the verdict. "The magistrates are not satisfied you have a reasonable excuse for failing to comply with the condition on which you were registered, and they sentence you to three months' imprisonment."

Michael was taken to a room to wait and then, when the day's trials were over, was handcuffed to the young soldier whose case had been heard before his. Whenever Michael recounted this fact in later life, a friend remembered, "each time it brought tears to his eyes".[94] Nor did the irony – of the objector coupled to the soldier – escape him as, along with a young man sentenced for stealing rabbits, they got into the back of a police van, known as a Black

Maria, and were driven through the evening sunshine of the year's longest day. They went thirty miles north, a journey of some two hours, to Shepherd's Bush in west London. "During those months of calm", Stella Gibbons wrote of the pendulous mid-war hush when the bombing raids on the capital were temporarily stilled, "London in ruin was beautiful as a city in a dream."[95]

His Majesty's Prison Wormwood Scrubs, brown and austere, was formed of four wings laid out side by side, with a large white chapel at the centre, and, at the front, an incongruously ornate red-brick gatehouse patterned with white stone. In the open meadows beyond, four anti-aircraft guns had been erected. The easternmost wing of the prison had been damaged by a high-explosive bomb, forcing out the government's War Department, which had requisitioned some of the building for office space. Around the whole site stretched a high and impenetrable wall. The soldier was led away. Michael was given a medical examination, interviewed by the prison governor, and then taken to a cell.

SEVENTEEN

Prisoner

It was a strange submarine world, populated by ghosts. The corridors of cells had great skylights in their roofs, in need of blacking out. Some humane psychologist had warned of the damaging effect on inmates of large black windows looming above them, and the skylights had instead been painted over in blue. In those summer months of 1943, as the sun beat down on the roof, the whole prison was cast in an eerie blue glow. Walking in the blue light were the prisoners, bleached into dusty monochrome by their ill-fitting uniform: jacket, trousers, shirt, tie, poorly sewn canvas shoes, all made from the same grey material.

Wormwood Scrubs was used mainly for first offenders, and had roughly 800 prisoners. It often served as a halfway house for men sentenced to penal servitude and awaiting transfer. "Among these PS-men", Michael wrote, "I got to know some very nice soldier fellows back from the Middle East, some with sentences up to fourteen years (!), one of whom described to me the physical and moral sensations of seeing the man you have shot 'crumple and fall like a flower', and begged me to stick it out."[1] Sticking it out with him were about 150 conscientious objectors, who formed a strong bond. Among them was the artist Arnold Machin, who spent much of the war in and out of prison, and had been transferred to the Scrubs from the harsher regime at Bedford. He became a distinguished sculptor and eventually designed effigies of Queen Elizabeth that were used on British coins and continue to be printed on all British stamps. Michael's arrival made an impression on Machin: "He was on top of the world when he came in, and had an irrepressible personality, as we were soon to discover."[2]

Of his entry into prison Michael often said: "I thought I had come home."[3] And while he revelled in the unexpectedness of such a remark, he truly felt, alongside the fear and boredom, an exhilaration at this apotheosis of three years' protest. To be finally on the other side of the visiting box's glass window felt like a natural progression. T.S. Eliot wrote that "pacifism can only continue to flourish so long as the majority of persons forming a society are not pacifists", and Michael felt he belonged to any group (regardless, almost, of its convictions) that society, rightly or wrongly, had ostracised.[4] Since early childhood he had naturally fallen, again and again, in politics as in sex, into a world of outcasts, swimming against the tide. Here, in prison, was a large community swimming with him.

Michael was moved to his permanent cell on the first morning of his incarceration, 22 June. Some prisoners had to share, but Michael appears to have had a cell to himself, with his own sliver of sky. The cells were accessed by balconied walkways that were painfully narrow, to avert riots, and strung with nets, to prevent suicides. Each cell had a small window, too high to be looked through easily, which let little light into the room even with the blackout curtains undrawn. The sun would shine an oblong patch of light into the cell, chequered by the window bars. There was a chair, there was a table. There was a wooden pallet with a straw mattress on top. The cell walls had never been plastered, and their open brickwork, in a strange token effort at decoration, was painted green to waist height. Each cell had a bucket-cum-chamber pot, which had to be emptied each morning. Doors had spy-holes to observe prisoners, and were occasionally left unlocked by the gaolers as a reward for good behaviour. Although it was forbidden to walk out, the psychological benefit of sleeping behind an unlocked door could be considerable.

It may be that the discomfort of prison meant little to the alumnus of a British public school, although the clang and echo of the corridors was surely an assault on the sensitive ear. A strict routine was adhered to, enforced by the warders, who answered to the taciturn prison governor. The cells were unlocked early in the morning, and each prisoner given a bucket of water to pour over the hard cell floor, wiping down the walls and furniture as best he could. The plumbing was old and insufficiently maintained, pipes would block, and the floors were most mornings awash with sewage and waste that didn't drain properly until lunchtime. Baths were only weekly occurrences; uniforms rarely washed. In those hot summer months, as the prisoners queued to slop out their makeshift chamber pots while meals were prepared, the smells of prison life throbbed and drifted on the air of the unventilated corridors.

For breakfast the men stood in their cell doorway, holding their bowls out for porridge. They were then let out for exercise, either in pairs or trios: objectors and rapists could be grouped with black marketeers and murderers. They marched round the barren yard, which the twice-daily tramping of 800 prisoners had, especially after rain, churned into deep mud. During the summer, irises grew in the cinders on the path, and the branches of a single talismanic tree poked over the prison wall. A meagre lunch was eaten around large refectory tables, a single bulb hanging dimly over each. "Sea pie" was usually followed by a kind of suet pudding known as "floating duff". All food had to be eaten with shaped pieces of tin, cutlery being forbidden. There followed another bout of exercise, and then the afternoon's work. Conscientious objectors were permitted to refuse tasks that contributed to the war effort, and instead were set to sewing large canvas bags for use by the General Post Office. For this they were paid a weekly allowance of three shillings. Thimbles were not provided for the two hours' sewing in the dim light of the workroom known as "Mail Bags Two", in which the rule of silence was never upheld. On one memorable day the work was changed to packing up swatches of vivid-red flannel. So blanched of colour and light was prison existence that Arnold Machin, with his artist's eyes, found this crimson interruption "unbelievably startling".[5] A small cob loaf and a cup of oily cocoa were doled out at half past four, and the prisoners were locked back in their cells at half past five, to read, to brood, and eventually to sleep as best they could amid the noises of prison life.

Each evening came an eerie twilight chorus, a dreadful nocturne. First there was the rattle of the Central Line trains as they emerged from underground at nearby White City Station. And there soon followed, as remembered by the actor Edward Petherbridge, who served time in the Scrubs as an objector the following decade, "shouts and screams such as you could imagine coming from a human zoo. No one was being tortured except by silence and solitude."[6] During wartime the noise was doubled, in that soldiers imprisoned for desertion preferred to stay in the Scrubs rather than face a court martial on their release. Fearing the shorter sentences that resulted from good behaviour, they created a rumpus in their cells, hammering on the doors and shouting. Each cell had an electric bell that could be rung in an emergency, or to inform the warder of a need to use a proper toilet. Soldiers intent on misbehaviour rang the bells as a prank, and the result was that any prisoner genuinely trying to call attention to emergency or illness was ignored. Warders gave up responding to requests for lavatory trips, and the bucket, which stayed in the tiny airless room overnight, had to be used for any and all toiletry needs.

The routine was interrupted by treats that took on vast importance: the weekly bath, the screening on Sunday evenings of biblical films provided by a missionary prison visitor. Quakers from the Society of Friends were frequent callers, and one of them, seeing that Michael was less traumatised than some by incarceration, enlisted his help in offering support to younger inmates. Each Sunday every prisoner was allowed to attend a morning service in the chapel, one of the largest prison chapels in England, of which the wide central transept and vaulted ceiling, the sun pouring through the rose window behind the congregation and illuminating the rows of white pillars to either side, became a light-filled sanctuary punctuating the week's grey corridors and shadowy brickwork. The prisoners would stand in serried rows and sing the hymns lustily: a highlight of Michael's sentence.

He soon became au fait with prison existence, in all its quirks and hierarchies. He learned not to leave food in his unlocked cell during work hours, as it would instantly disappear; he learned to keep valuables under his shirt, safe from prying hands; he learned to respect the more senior prisoners in exchange for his share of goods stolen from the kitchens. His was an observant and non-judgemental eye, taking in his neighbouring prisoner sentenced for the rape of a daughter; the double standards of some of the warders; and the wealthy black marketeer at the end of the corridor who paid others to do his sewing. Objectors had to stick together against the ill will of the warders, many of whom thought their "crime" was unforgivable and treated them accordingly. But the ratio of warders to prisoners was small, and objectors, for whom good behaviour was of paramount importance, caused little trouble and more often than not were left in relative freedom, moving unsupervised from cell to workroom. Michael even found himself being asked for advice on the music lessons of a warder's daughter. Books were passed secretly around, and an underground magazine was formed, titled *The Flowery* ("flowery dells" was Cockney rhyming slang for "prison cells"). Articles were scribbled on the crackly brown toilet paper, ranging from parodies of Shakespeare speeches relocated to the Scrubs – "Oh that this too, too sullied fish would melt, thaw, and resolve itself into a stew" – to thoughtful pieces on their collective stance, or wryly witty news bulletins: "The rectory cat's five kittens have now been reduced to three. No news has been received of the missing. We know, however, that the meat on a recent Sunday was highly seasoned."[7] The loosely stitched pamphlet was surreptitiously handed around each month, risking the penalty of solitary confinement should its existence be discovered. When a smuggled-out copy of the magazine was formally published after the war, Michael was persuaded to review it (favourably) for *Peace News*.[8]

Prisoners were permitted just one correspondent when in Wormwood Scrubs, to whom they could write every Monday fortnight. Michael took the choice with immense seriousness. Francesca Allinson was in poor health, and would have been thought unsuitable by the authorities, given her record of supporting objectors. Douglas Newton, facing his own court case, was hardly in a position to be burdened with keeping Michael's professional and personal life afloat. Isabel was far off in Devon, looking after her ailing husband. So it was to Evelyn Maude that Michael wrote his four long letters from inside prison. Little did the authorities know that Evelyn considered herself a conscientious objector, was a regular reader of *Peace News*, and had to be prevented by her husband from selling copies of it at Oxted Station.[9] Michael's letters to her get straight down to business without formality or, often, gratitude, flinging out a jumble of instructions, as he tried vicariously to organise the Morley concert series, to keep abreast of the young objectors whose cases and appeals he was continuing to support, to make plans for the weeks after his release, and to send good wishes to all he knew. Evelyn followed his directions assiduously, finding him the right kind of razor blades and searching for books he wanted to read (specific titles could be sent to the prison library via the Society of Friends and then be nonchalantly borrowed as if picked at random). She passed on messages, fielded mail, arranged concerts in his absence. Only when inventoried for another does the full scope and busyness of a life become evident.

His first letter to Evelyn was sent on the very evening he arrived in prison, and written on a desk in his temporary cell. The paper is marked with his prisoner number, 5832, and headed with the list of official regulations. Letters were to be sent only to "respectable friends", all communication would be read by prison authorities, anything "of an objectionable tendency" would be suppressed. Money, stamps, food, tobacco, clothes – sending such items was forbidden. "Evelyn dear," Michael wrote, cramming tiny handwriting into the official prison form,

It's rather like the first days of term before the days begin to move. In the good mood it's rejoicing, it is – as you can tell everyone – comradeship, peace and a full heart. On the recoil it's somewhat of a waste, negative and like being unwell in a foreign hotel. [. . .] It is only gradually that one takes on the new life.

Write straight away if you can, I'll get it quickly then. Tomorrow is Quaker meeting which I look forward to. There's also a baby orchestra I hope to be allowed some time to help on its way.[10]

In an attempt to provide some sort of education in the Scrubs, the authorities had suggested that instrumentalists among the prisoners should form a small orchestra, which rehearsed on and off. It soon got round that a good musician was in their midst and could become the orchestra's conductor. John Amis's memory that Michael was "tickled pink to take over the prison orchestra from Ivor Novello, who was in for petrol-coupon diddling" has become legend, but the chronology doesn't add up: Novello wasn't imprisoned in the Scrubs until the following year.[11] Naturally persuasive, Michael somehow got the deputy governor to bring in more instruments, and began rehearsals. Arnold Machin, not a player himself, was permitted with others to sit in, and he remembered that Michael

> did a remarkable job and displayed great skill with [the orchestra]. If their playing didn't come up to his expectations he would say, "If you can't do better than that I shall go home!", which of course caused great hilarity. He also persuaded the Governor to allow Cyril Smith, and his wife Phyllis Sellick, to come in and give us a piano recital. He was full of life and vitality with an absorbing love of music and through him our exceedingly drab lives were enriched.[12]

On 5 July, a fortnight into his sentence, Michael wrote again to Evelyn Maude: "It hasn't worked out quite as I expected. One gets not only fallow but sluggish. We're all the same. You can't manufacture the proper conditions and there's a lot of internal strain – a great deal of dreaming and inner adjustment – and the weeks inside seem monstrously lengthy and disproportionate, so that you fail to realise how easily they pass to those outside or how little one might oneself get done outside."

When alone in his cell Michael spent much of his time pondering composition, but he admitted to Evelyn (by now indicating his paragraph breaks with vertical lines to save space):

> I don't think it's any good trying to make things move when the circumstances forbid any real output or creation. Prison is not a creative experience at any point – except perhaps in human contacts. I dare say it will seem less wasteful when one looks back – perhaps it may be a real holiday mentally. It's difficult inside not to give exaggerated importance to its actual length of days – and to brood on them so that they go slower. In fact I am pretty active and the time passes somehow. | [. . .] One has moments of nostalgia, but not too many. I shall come through. It's boring of course. It is good to know things happen outside. Much love to all friends – and specially to you. Michael. I dreamed of a green flowering olive tree in spring last night. Good.[13]

Benjamin Britten and Peter Pears had for a year or so been giving joint recitals for the Council of Encouragement of Music and the Arts (a precursor of the Arts Council). As part of this series, they had been booked to give a recital in Wormwood Scrubs chapel, and they made sure to coincide with Michael's prison term.[14] The date was set for 11 July. Michael looked forward to the pair's arrival with excitement and nervousness, fearing their reaction to the prison orchestra, due in the same concert to perform a Bach chorale and Handel's "Largo" (from *Xerxes*). The piano was moved out of the recreation room into the chapel, and when he was caught playing it by the prison governor, Michael had to think on his feet when asked what he thought he was doing: "Tuning the piano, sir."[15]

Pears and Britten arrived. Afterwards, Britten remembered how disturbing he had found the smell of the prison. John Amis came with them, ostensibly as a page turner. What followed became such a good anecdote that, typically, everyone had a slightly different version. As Michael told it, he had made his own arrangements to turn the pages. "And what the prison service teaches you is to lie! So I said that nobody could turn the pages for Ben except me.

Well, they believed it, for some extraordinary reason. What I didn't foresee, of course, was that Amis was going to be there! He went out, naturally, and there I was, sitting beside Ben."[16] John Amis, meanwhile, recast the story giving himself a more prominent role: "I asked if we could borrow prisoner No. 5832, Tippett, M., who was known to us and could read music. The chaplain said it was against all the rules but he would see what he could do. So Michael came on to the platform with us and we turned alternate pages. It was a very moving occasion."[17] Amis or no Amis, Michael was permitted to perch, still in his prison uniform, on one side of Benjamin Britten at the clangy upright, which had yet to be replaced by the grand piano that Ivor Novello would donate the following year. "The concert here", Michael reported to Evelyn Maude in his next letter, "was a terrific success, and to be next [to Britten] at the piano was absurdly deep-going. The orchestra did not function."

He was coming up to the halfway point of his sentence, and release was on the horizon, a month early for good behaviour. His mind whirred away at music, and he had started to plan out a symphony in his head. His letter to Evelyn continues: "What you wrote about 'endless patches of time' was extraordinarily helpful. I do believe in it, and it gives strength to endure the apparent wastage. (Incidentally the symphony is gestating alright, almost consciously. I shall have the whole form mapped out in my mind by the time I come out. It's going to be a big thing.) I am only really close to you, Benjamin Britten and John Amis – no one else." Here he tells Evelyn, despite their intense bond, a strange white lie, for it was surely Francesca Allinson and Douglas Newton who were engraved deepest on his heart. He had a skill at making the person he was writing or talking to feel most important in his affections – witness his writing to David Ayerst in 1936: "I have you so much nearer and dearer than anyone else."[18] That said, letters from prison were written with a mind to the censor who would read them, and mention of any love for Douglas, an objector known to the authorities, was unthinkable.

Ben is very near, just because he is himself, I sense, so moved by my imprisonment. You of course are something almost eternal ! ! and the closeness is more to be expected. [. . .] | Later this week I go on "association" as it is called, and have meals at tables in community, and move to another cell – the Upper School! and that marks my exact half-way, which will seem better afterwards I think. | Could you get me a fresh tin of Calverts tooth-powder, and send in for me. | I have my specs in fact – but the truth is that the strain of the eyes is very great, and I shall have to do exercises in all seriousness this autumn to try and undo the damage. | [. . .] I'm very thin and bony – if not haggard! | [. . .] It's all very dreamlike – as indeed freedom often is to me. But here it's stronger. I, actually in prison; seems something so natural and yet so like a dream existence. That's enhanced, you see, by not feeling or being a criminal. [. . .] Wonderful moments like the hundreds of men's voices singing the Old Hundredth* – and that brings tears. One is rather emotional, naturally: and fearfully self-conscious. We all are. That takes a bit of time to go afterwards I believe. Quaker meeting means a lot. One is also closer to the spirit in here, by the act of cutting off. I've never felt it more strongly, though I can't as yet go the violent ascetic way – but I have a sense of cleansing the grossness, by means of which the spirit shines clearer through one – it may affect the music, I think; gradually. [. . .] Give my love to all and at this moment I am at peace – god bless you.[19]

With a move of cell came permission for visitors, and on 12 August John Amis came once again, bringing Walter Bergmann from Morley, and Felix Aprahamian (the director of the London Philharmonic). The days passed. Mailbags and meals, orchestra and

---

* A sixteenth-century hymn tune, usually sung to the words of Psalm 100 in the translation "All people that on earth do dwell . . .". In Benjamin Britten's cantata *Saint Nicolas* (1948) the music comes to a rousing climax with this very hymn, inserted just before Nicolas is imprisoned. The congregation is directed to join the singing.

exercise. Michael read what and when he could, and lived in the music of his mind. Once or twice he climbed up onto some kind of prison landing for a glimpse of the continuing world: "there I could see the crudely built yards of the Great Western Railway near Paddington. My sense of being in a community disrelated from the rest of society was acute."[20] He had become in prison something of a ringleader, offering special support to Arnold Machin, who was wobbling badly under the strain. He remembered joining in wholeheartedly "to help the illegal feeding of the comrade on bread-and-water and in solitary confinement (as punishment for refusal to work), which was going on while I was inside".[21] John Amis had twice witnessed Michael's effect on his fellow prisoners: "I know for a fact how much his presence and counsel meant to some of the bewildered and distressed young people in the Scrubs at that time."[22]

In the middle of August Evelyn Maude caught pneumonia. She told Michael not to worry, but during his final week in gaol the illness developed into a severe case of pleurisy, for which she was hospitalised. On 16 August Michael wrote her his final letter from prison, unaware of her situation and hoping that she would be among his welcome party in five days' time. His handwriting is slack with fatigue.

As this letter tells you, I'm already living outside the prison – I try not to get in a fever – but occasionally I do; though not for long or seriously. By the time this gets you, if it does in time, the thing will be virtually over – and I have little wish to repeat it – but of course will do so if driven.

Have made some very good friends and seen a great slice of life so to speak. Extraordinarily childlike, if not frankly childish. But all of a piece with the army, factory life and all other mass phenomena. We are indeed "such stuff as dreams are made of" – I become more drawn to Shakespeare and his viewpoint – only in another age's setting.[23]

Evelyn remained in hospital and was unable to get to the Scrubs, but at Michael's request she had placed an advert in *Peace News*: "Michael Tippett's release from Wormwood Scrubs Prison will take place on August 21st, coinciding with a performance. He hopes to make this concert the occasion for reunion with many of his friends."[24] He had been in prison for sixty days and sixty-one nights: some 1,500 hours. He was released at half past seven in the morning, let out through the small door in the enormous prison gates, and there were Benjamin Britten and Peter Pears at the front of a crowd of supporters waiting to meet him.

Months later, Michael wrote to thank Ralph Vaughan Williams for appearing at the trial, and attempted a summation of his imprisonment:

A great sense of comradeship and a sweet tolerance overriding the general social tragedies. [. . .] the experience is a deep-going one. I grieve for that strange community – and I grieve for all the coming nations of outcasts. It will need, in those of us who are sensitive, a tolerance, an understanding springing from depths "too deep for taint" as Wilfred Owen put it during the last war* – and which did not obtain then. I know of no duty more binding on myself than this increase of understanding – I can well believe that voluntary prison is a way through for people like myself, meaning much more than the negative withdrawal from general acts which one cannot take part in, but a positive searching for that deep level from which even criminals are our brothers. I might remark that with some of the older ones, long-term married men and some of the soldiers who had destroyed human life and wondered at it, there were occasional moments of spiritual apprehension we shall never forget.[25]

---

* "Then, when much blood had clogged their chariot-wheels, | I would go up and wash them from sweet wells, | Even with truths that lie too deep for taint." (From Wilfred Owen's "Strange Meeting".)

EIGHTEEN

Survivor

Evelyn Maude had sent news through the prison gates, while the outside world had carried on through the summer. At a performance of Michael's Concerto for Double String Orchestra at the Wigmore Hall on 17 July, it had been announced that "circumstances beyond his control prevented the composer attending". Walter Goehr had then made a recording of the piece at Levy's Sound Studio, supervised in Michael's absence by Benjamin Britten, who could hear without looking that a single viola player had his bowing direction out of sync with the rest.[1] Meanwhile, arguments over Michael's case had raged in the correspondence pages of the national newspapers. "I do not know Mr Tippett," a man named Roger Marvell had written to the New Statesman, "nor do I understand the workings of a conscience that allows a man to consume food but not to produce it. But is it not reasonable to ask what useful purpose can be served by sending him to prison?"[2] Another reader responded: "There is no conscientious objection to growing food; there is a conscientious objection to accepting a condition of exemption. If a tribunal accepts that a man is a genuine and sincere C.O., can they not accept the fact that he will be likely to undertake freely the work in which he can best serve his fellows?"[3]

Michael may never have known the exact goings-on in the corridors of the BBC. The composer Arthur Bliss, director of music at the Corporation, had sent out a statement: "MICHAEL TIPPETT. The governing body wish that the works of the above composer should be kept out of broadcast programmes until his release."[4] Bliss, who was following standard practice in not broadcasting the work of prisoners, made sure to keep a close eye on the case, and reinstated Michael's music in the schedules as soon as possible. But Michael's stance had made enemies of certain BBC employees, not least the conductor Clarence Raybould, once a tentative supporter, who now could not "help expressing my disgust that the gang [. . .] of Conscientious (!) Objectors and general slackers should have such prominence", thinking "the unbalanced adulation of one or two of these people is enough to make a normal person rather sick".[5] Then came the expense of Michael's legal fees, his lawyer Robert Pollard having charged eighteen guineas (equivalent to some £750). Michael's annual income was around £15,000 in today's money; large bills were difficult to pay, especially given the high taxation of wartime, and friends had to rally round.[6]

But for now, everything could wait. Britten and Pears, on the morning of Michael's release, went with him and a group of supporters to a nearby café, where Michael regaled them with prison stories. Among the avid listeners was the prominent suffragist and peace activist Sybil Morrison.[7] He then went with Britten and Pears for a proper breakfast, and that very afternoon the three of them attended a performance of Michael's String Quartet No. 2 at the Wigmore Hall. Straight after the concert, and with nothing but the single backpack of belongings that had been handed back to him at the prison gates, Michael departed by overnight train for his long-planned Cornish holiday, accompanied by John Amis, and by Antony Hopkins and Alison Purves. It was only en route, drowsing in the dim light of the overcrowded carriage, that someone bothered to open the telegram informing them their lodgings had been taken over by the RAF and were no longer available. Eventually they arrived at St Austell, a town on the south coast of Cornwall, and went by bus a few miles south to the village of Mevagissey. Here they lunched with the local poet and historian Leslie (A.L.) Rowse, with whom Michael had recently begun a correspondence. The two men had homosexuality, support for the Labour Party, and a love of Cornish history in common. Rowse sorted them all various

lodgings in the village, and they were soon joined by Francesca
Allinson's oldest brother, Adrian, a successful artist now in his
fifties, who, a conscientious objector in the First World War, had
become a war artist in the Second.* The eclectic collation of people
made for a happy holiday. They missed only Douglas Newton, held
up with his agricultural work at Cambridge. "It is pissing with
rain," John Amis wrote to him. "We miss you brother, and are sad
at your absence."[8] The weather improved, but sea-swimming and
beach-lounging were made all but impossible by the barbed wire
that was coiled along the Cornish sands to prevent enemy landings.
Eventually they found an inlet, and at Michael's instigation threw
off their clothes and jumped into the water. Afterwards they shivered on the rocks, persuading themselves they were sunbathing,
and watched with consternation as a policeman rowed laboriously
towards them. Studiously ignoring their nudity, he asked to see
their identity cards, and revealed that a coastguard had thought
them a landing party from a German submarine. Michael had not
had his ration book or identity card returned, and may rather have
enjoyed explaining that his "previous residence" was Wormwood
Scrubs.[9]

Clashes with the authorities aside, it was a time for Michael to
breathe clean air and to recuperate. He was sombre, ravenous, and
his eyesight was suffering badly. But the holiday was restful and he
defrosted slowly. He also took the opportunity to visit John Layard,
who was on the verge of finishing his famous book of dream
analysis, *The Lady of the Hare*, and who had settled in Mevagissey.

---

* Tall and willowy, with a face that could have been painted by Modigliani,
Adrian trained at the Slade (where he grew close to the poet and painter Isaac
Rosenberg), before becoming a founder member first of the Camden Town
Group (alongside Walter Sickert, Wyndham Lewis, and Augustus John), and
then of the London Group. A fine artist, of classic posters for the London
Undergound, stage-sets for Thomas Beecham, and evocative depictions of his
travels, he is perhaps destined to be always a footnote in other people's biogra-
phies; also among his friends were Dora Carrington, Stanley Spencer, and Jean
Rhys, with whom he had an affair.

Michael had had a bad row with Layard in the weeks leading up to
the imprisonment. Speaking at a conference at Oxford, Layard had
apparently used Michael as a case study without altering names or
swerving the issue of homosexuality. "I was somewhat shocked,"
Michael had written to him. "It is a criminal matter. I may already
be an outlaw as a conchie, but I can't see what point you can
have in risking my reputation further."[10] Layard denied the charges,
demanding to know Michael's source, and annotating the margins
of the lengthy who-did-what-to-whom correspondence in jabs of
angry red pencil: "conceit", "patronising". Michael's confusion
went hand in hand with his almost pathological avoidance of quarrel: "I am not really complaining, John, and in any case it's over
and done with, and please don't worry"; "you must believe me (or
not if you can't) when I say that I do not change in my feelings
towards you, nor my gratefulness, nor my belief in the truth as
you see it"; "it'll all come right in the end – don't worry". Visiting
Layard on his home turf was a successful attempt to make peace,
and Michael updated Francesca Allinson in relief: "made it all up
with John Layard and parted on the warmest terms".[11]

On the way back to Surrey he went via Exmouth to see his
parents, his mother declaring his prison sentence to have been "her
proudest moment".[12] Nothing survives of his father's reaction to yet
another family member having been sent to prison. From Exmouth
Michael went to Taunton, where David Ayerst, who with his family
had house-sat for Michael in Oxted, was now living. And finally, on
or just before 3 September, Michael arrived at Whitegates Cottage
for the first time since the morning of his trial. "It's wonderful to
be back," he wrote to Douglas Newton. "I've thawed out now after
the complete askesis of all bodily affections in prison."[13]

It was some months since he had seen Douglas, who had been
ordered by his own tribunal to do civil defence training, which he
refused, seemingly escaping a prison sentence, although he spent
much of the year fearing a summons.[14] The enforced hiatus in their
friendship seems only to have increased the intensity of Michael's
feelings, and there is no doubt that by late 1943 he was very much
in love with Douglas. The strange comradeship of prison made the

bungalow seem solitary. "Frankly I'm longing to be beside you and no one else seems to be able to make up [. . .] I wish you were here now."[15] They met on 6 September, and Michael wrote to Douglas in joy at their "double union – of the day and the night. And just as I fear less in my own pleasures, I joy in yours in the measure as you want. I can't see much point in stinting ourselves of anything we have for one another, whether spiritual or sensual. Nor I hope do you. Either one lives or one doesn't."[16] While proclaiming that Douglas shouldn't worry "about queerness or not", he told him that "for some reason of circumstance relations with you are more satisfying in fact than ever before with anyone. I seem to know more or less what I want and you seem to know how to give it me."[17] By October the two had had some sort of mild row, owing to the fact that Douglas, predictably, had fallen for a woman. Michael wrote to him about "the very little storm in the tea cup":

> I feel extremely little possessiveness, I dare say none at all – nor any jealousy or any loss – [. . .] There ain't going to be no sticky end in Lust and Rage.* Can you really imagine it? Are you leaping to the awful conclusion that because I'm a "sexy piece" with you, I lie with everyone? or even that I want to? Life of this frankness is something that for a while is possible with you – and it's not because either of us is wicked or debauched or sunk in buggery or what not and which not. Let us not worry.[18]

His responses lost, Douglas is silent. Sometimes Michael would write to him twice a day in those last lonely months of 1943. It was a barrage of affection, as on 17 October: "I love you for yourself very much, and with the better part of me. It's a pity perhaps that being what I am, all the traditional expressions of union come to be desirable – mercifully though the more violent ones aren't the essential ones, nor do the desires ride me – for the moment it's

---

* "You think it horrible that lust and rage | Should dance attention upon my old age" (from "The Spur" by W.B. Yeats).

very serene." And then later that day: "It's a portentous sign that I write a second letter in one day – the odd thing is that for the first time for a long while – years indeed – I've felt lonely – and that always means for me, lonely for one particular person. [. . .] The only good sign from it is to show that the dopey organ of the heart be still green."[19]

Might Michael have agreed with Auden's couplet: "If equal affection cannot be, | Let the more loving one be me"? It was a state to which he was becoming used, although the tables were turned and complicated by his having to deal with the affection of a local young woman, Rose Turnbull (daughter of the Oxted signalman), who had made her feelings for him known. He wrote of her plight with sympathy, for it was one with which he was familiar, and in relating the situation to Douglas he appears to be laying out his own position: "I'm a bit jangled again by trouble with Rose – and having had to withdraw and cut off – and so give her the hurt which I have sustained so often myself. [. . .] every time the imagined response from the other doesn't come, then it stabs through the stomach like a knife."[20]

With the authorities held at bay for the moment, Michael could return to music with full focus. His work was more scatter-gun over the six months following his sentence than it ever would be again. Following the acclaim of his second quartet had come a small number of commissions. Michael was used to writing at his own pace, and although commission fees were welcome, the deadlines weren't. One piece had been shunted his way by Benjamin Britten, who had been contracted to write a cantata for the fiftieth anniversary of the consecration of St Matthew's church in Northampton. Sharing his fee, he arranged for Michael to write a fanfare. Michael was hard pushed to finish in time, despite the work's brevity. He went to Northampton for the performance, on 21 September, and sang tenor in the premiere of Britten's festival cantata *Rejoice in the Lamb*. But, grateful as he was, he couldn't help admitting some disquiet: "I was B.B.'s 'younger brother', asked to show 'his' talent and promise – all out of B.B.'s unconscious and sincere desire to help me win recognition. [. . .] I come up with a shock against the refusal of my creative activity to function except for its own values, and they are just hopelessly at variance with the complete industrial, mass-entertainment set-up."[21] He was annoyed not to be able to go to Wormwood Scrubs to meet Arnold Machin, due for release that day after nine months' imprisonment. Machin arrived at Whitegates Cottage two days later with a fellow prisoner in tow, to be looked after and to recuperate.

The solitude of Michael's cell had given him ample time to plot and to plan, and he had mapped out in detail the structure of a symphony, and formulated a major revision to his first string quartet, which was now nearly ten years old. He had begun to think the first two of its four movements unsatisfactory, and wanted to replace them with a single movement, which he began in earnest at the end of September 1943 and finished in November; the quartet was re-premiered in January the following year. He then planned a number of pieces that were never started (a setting of T.S. Eliot's "Coriolan" poems; a chaconne for string quartet; a piano sonatina for Antony Hopkins) and began pieces that were never finished, including a setting of Wilfred Owen for Peter Pears.[22]

The final and largest musical plate of the many Michael had spinning was an opera. *A Child of Our Time* had temporarily shunted aside his ambitions to write a work for the stage, but now he was longing to begin an opera in earnest, and in Douglas Newton he believed he had the ideal librettist and collaborator. His plans had drifted vaguely during the years of the war. Chief among his passions at the time was the ancient Chinese text the *I Ching*, and he had sketched out a music-theatre piece, tentatively titled *Octett*, that would use the eight basic "trigram" figures of the *I Ching* to link seasons and instruments.[23] The structure of this quickly abandoned work lay behind what he was calling, by late 1940, "the slowly maturing conception of the 'masque'".[24] This was to be, in the tradition of Mozart's *The Magic Flute*, a *Singspiel*, with arias and ensembles interspersed with spoken dialogue, all existing within a magical world of symbolism and ritual. Its form came not only from Mozart but from any number of possible sources, not least the festive court entertainments of music and dance popular in the

sixteenth and seventeenth centuries. Once again he was reworking
a traditional form in a contemporary way, and, in shaping out the
Masque (soon a working title) from the depths of wartime, was
turning away from a realistic or autobiographical narrative that
would convey the horrors of conflict and the necessities of pacifism.
Nor yet was he choosing to tell, even metaphorically, the story of
the conscientious objector. Instead, as he told David Ayerst, "the
Masque will be an attempt to deal with this matter of the healing
symbol, or symbol of healing".[25] Little has survived of the *Masque*
in its earliest incarnations, though by September 1943 Michael was
confident enough about it to meet the soprano Joan Cross, director
of Sadler's Wells Opera, to see about a possible performance. He
was also constantly trying to set up meetings with Douglas in order
to hammer out a scenario, so that Douglas could make a start at
turning it into speakable and singable words.[26]

The *Masque* was intended to dramatise Jung's individuation process, the assimilation of facets in the personality that Michael had
felt so vital to his own psychological development. In his own
recollection: "I *saw* a stage picture (as opposed to hearing a musical
sound) of a wooded hilltop with a temple, where a warm and soft
young man was being rebuffed by a cold and hard young woman."[27]
The interruption of a marriage is a trope of any number of comedies, not least his opera *Robin Hood*, and Michael was searching for
a way to display theatrically the couple's psychological journey, as
if following the trials undergone by the hero and heroine of *The
Magic Flute*. From the numerous letters concerning the *Masque* that he
sent Douglas in the last years of the war, and using the notebooks
containing the plot's earliest outlines, the scenario as it then stood
can be tentatively reconstructed. It was to be a masque-within-a-
masque, in which two mysterious "Ancients" – inspired by similar
figures in a play by George Bernard Shaw – act as masters of
ceremony, and put on a show for a young chorus. This show was
to be an I Ching-inspired octet of four couples: the main couple
who were to undergo the Jungian trials; a mysterious couple in
the magic wood; a prophetess out of T.S. Eliot (Madame Sosostris)
paired with her polar opposite, a vulgar business tycoon; and finally

the counterbalancing "lower" couple (descendants of Papageno and Papagena in *The Magic Flute*, or Audrey and Touchstone in *As You Like It*). The cast list was set for a dreamscape of revelry and mischief, trial and confusion, in which the worlds of realism and fantasy would collide in truly masque-like theatrical spectacle, enjoyed either for itself or for its Jungian symbolism.[28]

There is no indication of what Michael's musical plans for the *Masque* yet were, although opportunities were rife – in a work about marriages psychological and romantic – to make a union of musical styles old and new. But the midsummer setting that would provide the final title (*The Midsummer Marriage*) had yet to be decided upon, and Michael and Douglas's plans would undergo numerous changes before they could begin to be realised. By February 1944 they had a detailed scenario of the first act and much of the second down on paper, and farmed everything out to close friends, who were divided in their reaction and often chipped in with suggestions. Benjamin Britten, or so Michael believed, was jealous of their plans when comparing the *Masque* to *Peter Grimes*; but such assurance seems misguided with the hindsight of the phenomenal success Britten was to achieve with his opera about a Suffolk fisherman the following year, as opposed to the decade's delay and eventual, troubled, performance that awaited Michael.

By spring 1944 Michael and Douglas had come up with a title that stuck for some years: *Aurora Consurgens, or The Laughing Children*.* The work was taking a distinct shape, and Michael was keen to press Douglas into making a start on the libretto and dialogue. Knowing that Britten was working away at *Peter Grimes*, he felt the pressure was on, not necessarily to beat Britten at his own game, but to be a part of a new generation of opera composers. The difference between *Aurora Consurgens* and *Peter Grimes* was at one stage

---

* The Latin phrase ("Rising Dawn") is from a treatise sometimes ascribed to Thomas Aquinas, and mirrored the Latin titles of Renaissance court masques. The subtitle, suggested by the troubled conscientious objector Edric Maynard, is a reference to T.S. Eliot's *Four Quartets*.

going to be made humorously explicit, and Michael and Douglas planned for the two Ancients to announce that "they have no truck with 'that ... Suffolk Grimes | or those sickly children of our times'" – this to be accompanied by musical quotations from *Peter Grimes* and from *A Child of Our Time*.[29] Soon Michael sketched out the title page for a printed libretto that makes explicit how seriously he took the fact of the work's being a collaboration:[30]

Douglas Newton

An Opera

in 2 Acts

AURORA CONSURGENS

or

The Laughing Children

MICHAEL TIPPETT

But with no prospect of Douglas's being ready to begin the text straight away, Michael turned to the symphony he had planned in prison, which he began in March. But he worked slowly, distracted by a more exciting project.

There was still the possibility that Michael might face further prosecution. The government threatened cat-and-mouse tactics, which would have seen him in and out of prison for the duration of the war. On 31 December 1943, four months after his release, he had been called to interview at Westerham. Writing that day and the next to update his friends, he did not pause to wish them a happy new year. "I had an interview at Westerham today – with Ministry of Labour official – nature of work? Would I persist in refusal? I'm very frightened, to the extent that I've been crying – the usual bout of self-pity. It appears a lot worse the second time."[31] He refused once again to work on the land, but made one major concession, agreeing to do any musical work required of him for the war effort. The file was sent off to the Ministry of Labour, and Michael was soon afterwards informed that he was free for the rest of the war's duration to work as he wished.

First up was a motet that had been commissioned in the autumn of the previous year by Canterbury Cathedral, which by some miracle had mainly escaped the damage Hitler had inflicted during the "Baedeker" raids on cathedral cities in 1942. Michael finished the piece, *Plebs Angelica*, in January 1944, choosing to set his liturgical text in its original Latin, despite the Anglican choir that would perform it in September. The real pleasure of his visits to Canterbury was in meeting one of the lay clerks and hearing his high, haunting, singing voice, androgynous and bell-like, that didn't appear to be falsetto.[32] Canterbury's lay clerk, Alfred Deller, had described himself as an "alto", but Michael instantly recommended Purcell's term, "counter-tenor". The voice had barely been heard in England since Purcell had written for it in the late seventeenth century. Michael, who had returned to his job at Morley, soon had Deller singing Purcell with the college choir, and at the original pitch.

On finishing *Plebs Angelica* he could turn to a more important matter. Not long after he had left Wormwood Scrubs he had decided "to float the oratorio willy-nilly".[33] It was now over four years since Michael had begun *A Child of Our Time*, and although the libretto had been published back in 1940, the score had lain, almost forgotten, in a drawer. Walter Goehr had suggested Michael wait until peacetime to organise its premiere, but on 28 November 1942 Michael had played the oratorio to Benjamin Britten, who, after suggesting a tiny and soon-implemented emendation in one of the spirituals, thought a performance should and could be arranged, with Pears a natural choice for the tenor soloist. Michael reported happily that Britten was "mentioning the oratorio" to all and sundry.[34] It was no easy task to put on such a large-scale work, which required a choir and orchestra able to navigate its complexities. There were a few false starts, and finally it was John Amis who persuaded the London Philharmonic Orchestra to programme *A Child of Our Time* in one of their Sunday afternoon concerts at the Adelphi Theatre (with so many concert halls destroyed, orchestras often took up residence in theatres during the afternoon). It took months of preparation to

ensure not only audiences but performers and scores. Walter Goehr
was to conduct, and he convinced Michael that it was vital to aug-
ment the Morley choir with professionals; the London Region Civil
Defence Choir was hired. Benjamin Britten persuaded the soprano
Joan Cross to sing (she would premiere the role of Ellen Orford in
Peter Grimes the following year), and the concert was scheduled for
19 March 1944. The total cost of mounting the premiere was £83
9s., nearly £3,500 today. Much of this came from Michael himself,
draining his savings. Britten and Pears footed a third of the bill.
With all hands to the pump, some publicity was drummed up,
and Michael was photographed by Cecil Beaton, who, running late
for the session, found the composer fast asleep and, on waking,
"sensitive, highly-strung, and somewhat inclined to giggle", with
"dark pansy-like eyes" – presumably a nod to their shared sexuality
rather than a floral simile.[35]

Michael Tippett by Cecil Beaton, 1944

It was an exciting and busy time. A few days before the concert
Michael wrote to Pears: "Peter my dear – shall be thankful to have

you down here standing by my side and giving some much needed support. I <u>do</u> look forward to your being there. I am at times a little tiny boy wanting a big brother."[36]

The premiere of *A Child of Our Time* fell in the middle of Hitler's Operation Steinbock, known as the "Baby Blitz", which lasted from January to May 1944. The Allies had been bombing German industrial cities day and night and were gaining ground. Hitler retaliated by targeting southern England. It was not an entirely successful operation but caused extensive damage, a horrific shock after a lull of nearly three years since the Blitz. On the night of 14 March 162 tons of bombs were dropped on London by the Luftwaffe. On 21 March Paddington Station sustained a direct hit. But on 19 March, the date of the concert and the day on which the Nazis occupied Hungary, the planes left London alone in favour of the north of England. At half past two that afternoon Michael and many of his friends made their way to the Adelphi Theatre on the Strand, which was strewn with the detritus of war: sandbags, rubble. The Blitz had left a vast crater just a little further up from the theatre; across the way the basement shelter of the Savoy Hotel hosted society grandees in style. At one end of the Strand was the wreckage of St Clement Danes church, flattened in 1941; at the other was Trafalgar Square, where a large air-raid shelter had been erected, and the plinth of Nelson's column, up which Michael's mother had climbed all those years ago, was now emblazoned with propaganda. Isabel was stuck in Exmouth, caring for her husband, who was too ill to attend the concert or to be left alone. "My mother," Michael wrote, not without tenderness, "to try and clear her disappointment about not being able to leave my father and get to the show, has sent me their best set of dessert knives and forks. Very touching of them."[37]

Theatres in the war were shabby and under-staffed. Programme books were printed with instructions on procedure during an attack, and as the noise of the performance usually drowned out the warning sirens, most auditoria were hung with signs that would light up during a raid. *A Child of Our Time* went ahead without a hitch, although it had been a fearfully cold March, its average temperature five degrees, and the building was likely underlit and barely heated.[38] The Adelphi could seat 1,500 in the sleek wooden tiers of its Art Deco auditorium, and was hosting a wildly popular revival of Ivor Novello's 1939 musical The Dancing Years. It was not incongruous to host The Dancing Years and A Child of Our Time in the same week, for apart from the composers' mutual experiences in Wormwood Scrubs, in many ways they shared a theme: Novello's musical follows a Jewish composer through the years of Nazi persecution. There was a shortage of black cloth in theatres during the war, owing to the blackout, and the set for The Dancing Years could not be covered up for Michael's premiere. And so it was that the performers of A Child of Our Time "took their places in front of a colourful though antiquated backdrop representing a Victorian conservatory".[39]

The first half was Mozart; A Child of Our Time came after the interval. There was a rousing reception (not surprising, given the audience was full of friends and supporters). "I've had such moving letters from varying people generally pouring out a sort of diffident gratitude," Michael happily told the critic William Glock afterwards. "For myself, it's the fairly objective wonder at the stimmung [mood] created at the concert, and the response to the things which are publicly repressed in this holocaust – so that I had a sense of immense life underneath the destruction – and for a moment, a unity between composer, performer and the 'folk'. I think it was helped by the large number of young people in the theatre, and quite ordinary people too."[40] He was also struck by the number of audience members in army uniform. The success of the concert was such that printed copies of the libretto soon sold out, and the takings (£130) made a tidy profit that could be divided between the investors, not least Britten and Pears.[41] Three days later Michael turned pages for Britten during a piano recital, and the two went back to Whitegates Cottage – without Pears.

While Pears is thought occasionally to have pursued sex elsewhere, Britten was, his biographers agree, faithful and eventually celibate during their partnership.[42] But that spring evening, as Michael remembered it, Britten "thought it would be nice if we slept together, which we did, though I drew back from sexual relations; Peter was nevertheless quite disturbed at our intimacy on that occasion".[43] This memory is taken from Michael's autobiography, which, never above gossip, was published long after Britten or Pears was alive to read it or contradict. An account of the evening Michael wrote a fortnight afterwards may be more reliable: "I went to bed first and B.B. hovered about in loaned pyjamas, till I said: 'if you want to be matey you'd better sleep in the big bed mit mir' [with me]. So he did. Whereupon I got a fit of distaste, withdrawal, virginity, coldness or whatever, and tried not to make it obvious, except that there it was."[44] He awoke the next morning feeling troubled and sick. That night Britten stayed in the bungalow's spare bedroom, and "matey"-ness never again occurred. The letter is not an admission of an affair, but does seem to imply that the night could have taken a different turn, had Michael been more willing. A few years later he admitted he had detected in Britten's sexuality a "curious sterility", finding him "woefully un-grown-up in these ways".[45]

The awkward bed-sharing was perhaps part of the heady excitement of A Child of Our Time's premiere. Reviews, as they came through, were divided but mainly positive, and The Times thought the oratorio "strikingly original alike in conception and execution". The Daily Star acclaimed the libretto as a greater achievement than the music; others found the idiom of Michael's text hard to take, and the spirituals poorly incorporated. But most agreed: "The words are of effective simplicity, and the music has a highly individual quality that reveals great skill." "The choral work for which we have been waiting since the outbreak of this war."[46] Eyebrows were raised at this success among Michael's fellow composers, and the seeds of the intense dislike in which his music was to be held were already being sown. The composer John Ireland wrote to Alan Bush (with whom Michael was now only intermittently in touch) that A Child of Our Time was "childish stuff", that it "astounded me by its utter ineptitude, and musical and psychological banality – not to mention the incompetence so freely displayed".[47] Bush had pronounced himself impressed when he heard the oratorio played through at the piano, but was not altogether loyal in his reply: "I must say that the rage for Tippett is rather astonishing [. . .] I was very disappointed. There seemed no force. It was emotional but very formless."[48] John Ireland was twenty-six years Michael's senior; it was always, Michael believed, a generation younger than himself to whom his music spoke most clearly and movingly.

Various offers arrived in the wake of *A Child of Our Time*'s success. In April Michael was commissioned to write incidental music for a production of Marlowe's *Dr Faustus* at the Liverpool Old Vic. He enlisted Antony Hopkins to "do the dirty work" when it came to instrumentation and copying, and then, just as rehearsals were due to start, handed a marked-up copy of the play to Antony, saying: "Oh, I can't be bothered; you do it instead!"[49] More of a priority was a request to write a pamphlet on pacifism for *Peace News*, and after much proof-reading by Francesca and Douglas, *Abundance of Creation* was published in July, arguing that to contract-out of a war-torn society was to contract-in "to something more generous", a world of gaiety and peace and "an abundance of creation, whether of values or works, in a world of destruction".[50] Only in revising the pamphlet fifty years later did Michael allow himself unequivocally to state that pacifism was "the only stand compatible with a belief in creativity".[51]

There was quickly talk of further performances of *A Child of Our Time*, and the piece was broadcast by the BBC Home Service on 17 January 1945. There were some dissenting voices at the Corporation who disliked the music, thought the performance abominable, and were highly critical of a well-known conscientious objector being supported in this way.[52] But this was a minority view, and the work was soon chosen to be the centrepiece for a concert at the Royal Albert Hall, on 28 February, to raise money for the Polish Children Rescue Fund. Michael jumped at the invitation, though conducting the work himself for the first time was nerve-wracking: "I care tremendously for this gesture to that 'scapegoat' of a country."[53] Although there was still much debate about whether Michael had entirely succeeded, in some quarters the oratorio was already acclaimed as a masterpiece and spoken of as a major contemporary work. The influential magazine *Picture Post* devoted pages to the Albert Hall performance, speaking of Michael as a well-established though controversial figure, and arguing against any notion of his musical ear being unsatisfactory or sloppy:

> The younger critics had no doubts of the distinction which lay in *A Child of Our Time*. As a technician, Tippett's skill in the use of polyrhythm, the assurance of his counterpoint, and above all, the aptness of his orchestration, indicated his usual merits. [. . .] To see Tippett at a rehearsal, is to repeat with him some of the birth-pangs of his oratorios. He twists in his chair, clutches his head with his hands, then walks around the empty hall with his eyes shut. His whole body becomes tense, as the voices of the choir swell out. In the middle of a passage for muted violins, Tippett hears a wrong note. He jumps like a man who has been insulted, and hurries to the conductor's dais. [. . .] What is there in *A Child of Our Time* which received such an instant and vibrating answer in the feelings of the ordinary man and woman? Perhaps it is that Tippett's oratorio, with its pain, its ecstasy and its theme – "The simple-hearted shall exult in the end" – speaks the inexpressible thoughts of us all, children of our time, brothers and sisters in the modern agony.[54]

The spring and summer of 1944 were some of the hardest months of Michael's life. His eyesight was deteriorating badly after months of ill-lit sewing work in Wormwood Scrubs, and he was working frantically to preserve it. Francesca Allinson had another serious bout of illness in April. The relationship with Douglas Newton rocked complicatedly about, and Michael wrote him endless assurances that he was free to meet and marry, while at the same time hemming him in: "I get scared that you won't get away: scared because I need a holiday so much and there seems no one anywhere to take your place." He was explicit: "I love you in my own funny way, and what's the good of denying it while it be there." [55]

Michael was more upset by the progress of the war than he had been since its outbreak. Kneeling at the hearth as he screwed up newspaper to make firelighters, he found that even a glimpse of headlines or casualty lists produced in him instant nausea. On 6 June came the Allied invasion of Normandy, when British and American troops landed in France, the first step in liberating the countries of northern Europe. The end of the war seemed to be in sight. But just a week later, on 13 June, the Nazis fired their secret weapon: small pilotless planes that flew across the sky like malevolent comets, engines buzzing. The sound was terrifying, and gave the planes, called V-1s, their blackly ironic nicknames: buzz-bombs, doodlebugs. More chilling still was the silence when the engine cut out, and the hushed uncertainty as to where the plane would fall. Then the explosion. The renewed attacks were especially crushing in that the Normandy landings and the prospect of Allied victory had changed the strangely exhilarating fatalism of the Blitz into a desperate wish to live and witness peace. Once again people began to leave London. The familiar crocodiles of children with brown labels around their necks were again formed at train sta-tions. Michael briefly hosted a thirteen-year-old, and he tuned the wireless to *Monday Night at Eight* while learning to cook for two. But the arrangement became awkward and was short-lived: "An intel-lectual bachelor alone in a cottage is hopeless host to a small boy."[56] The bombs were so frequent – more than 100 dropped daily over southern England at the height of the attacks – that shelters became almost useless. The corrugated-iron cabins of Anderson shelters often flooded, and had been surpassed in popularity by the smaller steel cages of the Morrison shelters, which, kept indoors, could be used as a table during the day and a shelter during the night. There was a new mood of serious fear, and it hit Michael badly.

On 21 June he wrote to Douglas Newton: "The combination of recording, concerts etc in London and these uncanny machines of destruction has made me feel worse than I did a year ago today when I went to the Scrubs. I'm quite suddenly badly *énervé* [on edge]. Tonight I have to sleep in town and am feeling like death about it."[57] For the first week of the V-1 attacks there were few over

Surrey, but soon the bombing reached Oxted. Huge anti-aircraft guns were sent down from London to shoot the V-1s out of the air, and a barrage balloon was erected on Limpsfield Common, just two miles from Michael's bungalow: "very uncanny and no one has liked it".[58] News began to reach him of the homes of friends and neighbours being blown up, and Evelyn Maude's house had its windows blasted out. He tried to focus on composing his symphony, and thought it best to stay put. But, as he wrote to Francesca: "When they let off what seems to be a fortnight's savings of bombs, as they appeared to do last night, it makes one doubt the wisdom of staying. I can't make out whether the fall of one of those abortive glass shades of this room is a good or a bad omen! The blast from quite distant bombs draws the windows outwards – we leave them on the latch, so they fly open at a touch. [. . .] Want to see you frightfully badly."[59]

After getting through the last two concerts of the season at Morley, Michael appears to have suffered the strange freeze born of panic. In the face of serious danger he was pinioned to the bungalow, and turned down the offer of a month's job in Canterbury, covering for a lay clerk. He still had five tenants lodging in his properties, whom he felt uneasy abandoning. Ben and Miriam Lewis continued to share the double cottage with their daughter Bronwen and her husband Jack; now there was a three-year-old grandson, Ian. During the V-1 raids Miriam suffered a stroke. Bronwen was heavily pregnant with her second child. Feeling responsible for the family amid the continual bombing made Michael ill, and John Amis had to take him to Cambridge for a few days' recuperation with Douglas Newton, on whom his reliance was becoming severe. He returned to Oxted for more sleepless nights of heavy bombardment.

Then a letter arrived from his mother. His father, whom he knew to have faded badly over the last couple of weeks, was unlikely to live much longer. Michael went to Exmouth in the last week of June, and found Henry, now eighty-six years old, trying to hasten his death with sleeping tablets. Michael sat by the bed and held his father's hand. Neither he nor his mother was willing to procure further tablets, or help Henry take them. Henry faded over the following week, and it was only now, lying on what he knew to be his deathbed, that he told his family the truth about his own father's imprisonment and the court case both of them had faced. He died on 6 July, "as peacefully", Michael thought, "as can be imagined".[60] In the days that followed, Isabel and her younger son argued as never before, each airing grievances long pent up. Peter arrived and, to Michael's admiration, could let their mother's difficulties wash over him and attend to everything needful despite the discomfort of his wooden leg. Henry's financial savviness had left his widow in comfort, and carefully tied-up investments promised greater riches after the war (his estate was valued at £14,592, over half a million in today's money).[61] Isabel promised to divide up income she no longer needed between her sons, and Michael could accept the generosity only grudgingly. Peter was called away, Isabel professed herself uninterested in organising a funeral, and on 10 July it was left to Michael to take his father's body in its coffin on a train to the Plymouth crematorium. Alone, he scattered his father's ashes on the border between Devon and Cornwall.

He returned to London on 12 July, arriving at Waterloo in the middle of an air raid, and made a sticky journey on the train down to Oxted while the guard announced over the tannoy: "Your attention please! Your attention please! Hostile aircraft approaching . . .".[62] He made it home to find that the impact of a V-1 rocket brought down nearby by an anti-aircraft gun had damaged the cottage. Bronwen was lying "upstairs in much mental distress clutching the new babe, born on Sunday – a girl". The rockets continued to fall. "I just sat staring out of the window when one stopped," he told Francesca, "until brought to earth by the bang." His correspondence took on a chill immediacy: "There's one just gone over now."[63]

A day or so later he was able to depart for a holiday. Travel had been made tricky by the air raids, and nobody could journey into or out of Devon or Cornwall without a valid reason. A dying father would get you through the check at the station, but a holiday would not. The ban was suddenly lifted and Michael – who had planned to go to Wales with John Amis and Douglas Newton – delightedly decided to throw all their carefully laid plans up in the air, and instead go to Mevagissey for ten days. They got back on 24 July and he sank yet further over the next two weeks and their rocket-filled nights. "I can't see what to do except to stick it out like everyone else and try to write in the intervals. But it means work on the Big Symphony is desperately slow."[64]

Early in the morning of 8 August, at five minutes to six, he was woken by the familiar ghastly noise of a buzz-bomb, and heard the silence. Then he dived for cover as best he could as the windows shattered, the doors were blown from their hinges, and bits of his bedroom ceiling fell on top of him.[65] He waited until he was sure that another hit wasn't imminent, then extricated himself from the bed and managed to get a dressing gown from a wardrobe that had stayed standing. When he got outside he found the cottages more or less in ruins, crushed by a felled tree. The bomb had fallen in the field opposite. Today the land is still mounded in one corner, the grass allowed to grow over the pile of thrown-up soil. Miriam Lewis, who had managed to scramble out, was standing in front of the ruins. She and her husband Ben were uninjured, protected by the Morrison shelter.

Bronwen and her family had also rushed for the shelter in their cottage, but it was a tight and stifling fit. Thinking the danger had passed, she and her husband Jack had left their two children inside the shelter, while they slept on top of it. When the bomb hit, the ceiling of the room fell down upon them. Almost immediately members of the RAF Balloon Command, controlling the nearby barrage, were on the scene. Families often chalked their identity numbers on the front door or gatepost to let such helpers know how many survivors, or bodies, to dig for. It took one hour to dig out Jack, alive but badly wounded, and he spent a long time recovering in hospital. The little boy, Ian, also managed to escape the wreckage, and his month-old sister, Sheila, was carried out safe and well. But Bronwen had been killed instantly. She was twenty-eight, and had lodged with Michael for six years. "We are all pretty tearful," he told Francesca. "A real tragedy. I felt it like my own."[66] David Ayerst remembered, forty years later, that for Michael the whole Lewis family "were far more than good neighbours, [but] real friends. I can never forget the break in his voice on the telephone as he told me that Bronwen was dead."[67]

Among the preparatory interviews made for Michael's autobiography are some telling comments that did not make the final cut: "I would agree that I get all the credit [for making a political stand against the war] and those who grovelled in the bombed-out ruins to save children were unsung." Here, and here alone, he admitted the blast of shame that hit him as he watched men from the Auxiliary Fire Service, into which some conscientious objectors had been drafted to carry out their non-combatant duties, begin to dig about in the rubble of his home. "I must admit that when the bomb fell in the garden and killed the little girl next door, I came out from under my bed and went indoors again. I realised that the men who were doing things [to help] were good enough. I felt ashamed that I wasn't contributing; that was at the heart of it all."[68]

A week after the blast Michael wrote to Douglas Newton, trying to organise a visit to Douglas's Cambridge digs, where the beady eye of a landlady precluded their sharing a room:

I feel I must see you. It will seem odd not sharing a bed with you and shall hate it, as things are. But it can't be helped and must be lumped, like everything else. [. . .] I suppose it's a weakness and imposition to want to be sometimes in your arms and you're wonderfully gentle and good about it. I wish it didn't mean so much, but it's one of the few unadulterated things I ever experience. Because it's you, the pleasure is pure and unmixed and I lie on happy as a child. [. . .] So you shall yet be gentle with me for a while – much-loved Den. [. . .]

I spent the first two days practically fed by the Balloon Site chaps. Got to know them well and regaled them with the prison stories! They hope to be there till end of war and to come to a concert of the Child or some other. Grand folk. And carrying baby Sheila down the road in the morning sun: fantastic symbol of vitality ever-renewed. She's a beautiful babe. It all adds up to what Yeats called an "experience" and will surfeit the biographers. But it was gruesome and frightening.[69]

A Child of Our Time's premiere had evidently cemented Michael's certainty that he would in due course be the subject of fame and interest; he evinces the artist's strange detachment, the ability to live life from within and to observe it from without, to focus on the day lived, while considering its place in history remembered. Practically speaking, he was homeless. The cottages had been completely destroyed. Baby Sheila was fostered with relations. Ben and Miriam Lewis found a home with family in Wales. Michael's bungalow was stuffed with salvaged furniture from the cottages, but it could not be lived in. Most of the windows were empty sockets and the building itself was thought liable to collapse. Precious food rations were speckled with glass, and there was a yawning hole in the ceiling. The bomb had lifted the ivory from the keys of Francesca's piano, which was full of debris that rattled and thrummed against the strings. Rebuilding took time, windowpanes were hard to come by, and there was little point mending anything with the V-1s continuing to buzz themselves across the sea. So the bungalow was patched up as much as possible, and left empty, standing forlorn opposite the ruins of the cottages.

Friends rallied around. In the fortnight after the bomb Michael lived at a farm in Sussex owned by some old Oxted friends, Dorothy and Eric Shaxson, who had a grand piano at which he could continue composing the symphony. Benjamin Britten and Peter Pears instantly offered him use of their flat on St John's Wood high street for the rest of the year; William Glock and his wife did likewise with their Hampstead apartment. Somehow Michael managed, and with remarkably little self-pity, although he was desperately looking around for a place of his own, never quite daring to tell Douglas Newton except in subtle hints that what he really wanted was to move in somewhere with him. He spent much of the time staying with Francesca Allinson in her brother's house outside Cambridge, but she only added to his worries, having suffered such a bad attack of illness that she had fainted and nearly died (a result of a flare-up of her overactive thyroid, known as a "thyroid storm"). She weighed around six stone and was desperately frail.[70]

Michael spent much of the autumn dealing with glaziers and builders and insurers, and although he began camping out in the bungalow about six weeks after the bomb had hit, there was still much work to be done to get him properly up and running before the much-dreaded winter. "Victory!" he wrote on 5 October; "I've just got permission to have ceiling-board and to use my neighbour carpenter. Money repaid by the government – hip hip."[71] The Morley concerts had started up again that month, by which time an even more advanced weapon was being dropped by the Nazis: the V-2, a long-range ballistic missile that travelled faster than sound. The explosion was often heard before the noise of the engine that brought it, a single hit destroying dozens of buildings. The attacks lasted almost seven months, killing or injuring thousands.

Amid all the turmoil, Michael managed to finish the first movement of the symphony, with which he'd been struggling since March (in hindsight he thought it the weakest of the eventual four). The music contains nothing of its unhappy birth: its beginning is almost chirpy. Two sumptuous chords unleash a flock of string-birds that soar briefly aloft; but the severer side of Paul Hindemith's counterpoint was never more of an influence on Michael than here, as if Michael had purposefully set himself a technical exercise, lest a too-willing reflection of wartime troubles led him to self-pity.

Finishing the movement meant that, by November, he hadn't even begun work on a major commission, his first from the BBC, organised by Edward Sackville-West for a Christmas broadcast. Five composers had been paired with five poets, and Michael had been asked to set a new work by Edith Sitwell, "The Weeping Babe". He put his head down and finished just in time for the broadcast, *Poet's Christmas*, which went out on the Home Service that Christmas Eve. He was in good musical company, joining Britten and Lennox Berkeley, while among the writers were Laurie Lee, Vita Sackville-West, Louis MacNeice, and Cecil Day-Lewis. That very day thirty V-1s hit the north of England, and it was one of the most joyless Christmases of the war – although for the first time in four years churches were permitted to illumine their stained-glass windows. Sitwell's poem is a lullaby, a wartime nativity, sung by the Virgin Mary to the baby Jesus as the flowers of spring start to poke through the winter snow. "Why dost thou weep, my little child? For the winter heart of the world." Michael wove from the poem some aching harmonies, a soprano solo emerging tenderly from the choir – "lullay, lullay" – and he headed the score "In memory of Bronwen Wilson".

Just over a week later, on 2 January 1945, he wrote to Francesca Allinson as if in surprise: "Am forty today!"[72] In the absence of the Lewises, he had employed a charlady, Mrs Brown, to help him with the endless work the bungalow still required. He hoped she would move her large family into the cottages once they were rebuilt. "Then I shall be in the centre of a baby farm. Isn't that grand?"[73] But there was no prospect of the rebuilding at present, and he devoted himself to the second movement of his symphony during the seemingly endless winter. He had begun to correspond and meet more frequently with the composer William Busch, now a good friend, to discuss music and their mutual pacifism. Busch's music was just on the cusp of recognition, and his cello concerto was performed at the Proms during the war. On 26 January 1945, Busch visited his wife and newborn daughter in a nursing home in Devon amid heavy snowfall. All transport was cancelled and he elected to walk the six-mile cliff path to their home, only to find the way impassable. Hypothermia led to a major internal haem-orrhage, and no doctor could reach him. He died on 30 January. Michael sent his widow a letter of condolence "out of my love for William", in which he wrote: "I for one can't yet adjust to his not being there."[74] It was a bad shock; another figure on his landscape had dropped away.

Over the next months, as the Allies advanced, pictures of devastated German cities began to appear in the newspapers. In mid-February came the Allied bombing of Dresden, in which tens of thousands were killed. Many thought that such large-scale attacks would do nothing to forward the Allied victory, which was already more or less assured. Michael had visited Dresden with Francesca, who was still living with her brother and sister-in-law, Cyril and Veronica, at The Mill House at Streetly End, a few miles southeast of Cambridge. Her bouts of illness were now frequent and severe, and she was often bedbound. Still her self-recrimination over the messy affair with Judy Wogan raged round her, as her one surviving letter to Michael proves: "I was lying in bed thinking what scum I was and wondering if I couldn't even begin to be good."[75] The pages of her brief wartime journal are bruised with unhappiness: "My only method of living is through loving and I do not yet know how to love. Loving as a state of being, as an activity which is a final end in itself. My attempts to find good men, saints shall we say, are abortive. The two that I cast for that role have proved equally inappropriate. They both turn out to be professional good men."[76] Nevertheless, she and Michael (presumably one of the men to whom Francesca refers) were still pondering the life that might have been. Late into the war he wrote to her: "The vision of joining my music and your children by the acts of marriage is not a neutral vision, nor simple, nor easy – though it has its pros as well as its cons." And, at around the same time: "It's downright stupid to rationalise the fact that we feel close to each other."[77]

The last weeks of March brought the Allied invasion of Germany, and the final bomb attack on British soil. The newspapers were already talking of victory celebrations. On Saturday, 7 April 1945 Francesca was left alone in The Mill House. She wrote letters to her closest friends and made up parcels for them, which she left in her room with a request that they be posted. She wrote to her brother Cyril that she had gone to die at Martin's Grove, the little wood she had purchased not far from the Essex village where she had lived with Judy. Then she left the house, wearing a small china crucifix around her neck, a gift from Michael.[78]

She travelled five miles, presumably by cab, from The Mill House to the nearest station, at Haverhill, where she boarded one of the infrequent steam trains on the Stour Valley Railway. Suffolk was studded with small stations, most of them now closed. She was heading east, likely towards Marks Tey at the end of the line, whence she could have got herself to the grove. The train stopped at small villages every two to three miles.

Haverhill. Sturmer. Stoke. Clare.

At Clare, overcome by panic, or pain, she disembarked. Many in Britain with Jewish ancestry had obtained suicide pills, fearing a Nazi invasion. Francesca appears to have ingested cyanide as she made the short walk from Clare Station to the banks of the River Stour. Here she walked onto a bridge, and from the bridge she jumped into the river.

Cyril and Veronica Allinson, on returning to The Mill House to find Francesca's letter, drove straight to Martin's Grove, but did not find her.[79] Her body was soon discovered and taken to Addenbrooke's Hospital in Cambridge. The cause of death was pronounced as "cardiac failure due to shock from complete immersion in cold water", and as "suicide whilst the balance of her mind was disturbed". A post-mortem found she had suffered not only from hyperthyroidism, but from prolapse of her abdominal organs. It noted a distinct smell of almond, indicating cyanide, on her heart and spleen.[80]

Late on the evening Francesca had killed herself, Cyril telephoned Michael with the news. When the phone rang, Michael was writing the final pages of his symphony's slow movement. On replacing the receiver in its cradle, he went back to its composition. Its music emerges out of the deep, with a sonorous introduction that becomes a *passacaglia*, literally a "walk in the street", describing the endlessly repeated tread of a ground bass. Michael's innovation was to have the repeated bass line not supporting but disrupting the music above. Resisting as best they can, voices drift out of the mist like birds singing on a bombsite: a mournful clarinet solo; a falsely soothing flute trio. The intensity that builds is plunged into disunity. The final bars, written late on the evening of 7 April, contain a last call from the clarinet, echoed by the horn, before the very lowest strings – viola, cello, bass – fade away to nothing.[81]

The next day Michael, alone and in a coil of grief, had to inform friends of the news. "Don't grieve, Den dear," he told Douglas Newton, who had loved Francesca so much. David Ayerst thought she was "as much a war casualty as if she had been killed in an air-raid".[82] Judy Wogan rang a number of times in severe distress. From Adrian Allinson, Francesca's artist brother, Michael received a letter of condolence addressed "as to a brother-in-law – really kind and good. Surprising."[83] He himself, as he admitted to David, was

> too out of mind to be very coherent just yet. [. . .] I can't adjust
> to it easily. Her gaiety and gentleness and even her waywardness
> and her love of pretty things all seem irreplaceable values. I
> loved her more deeply than I knew when she was there. The
> memory is extremely sweet and fragrant. [. . .] We were both
> marked as so many of our generation have been – but perhaps
> my career especially got in the way and she is part of the price.
> We never learn about real loss till it is there in our persons.
> Her going is less perhaps than the maiming and death of so
> many young folk, children, mothers, in this lunatic power-driven
> world. But I know it sharper. She was a lovely lovely creature
> as I feel, and lived her birthright out with courage – poor
> lamb.[84]

On either Monday, 9 or Tuesday, 10 April, he received the package Francesca had put together for him. She had left him a copy of Shakespeare's sonnets, marked at number fifty-seven: "Being your slave, what should I do but tend | Upon the hours and times of your desire?" It was a painfully charged token, as if admitting herself weary of a slavish and unreciprocated devotion to one whose attentions were elsewhere; but it may also have been beseeching Michael not to "think the bitterness of absence sour | When you have bid your servant once adieu". There was also a tiny photograph, taken on their holiday to Germany and Czechoslovakia thirteen years before. In it Michael sits on the floor, all ankles, his long legs awkwardly folded. Close to him is a small, fair-haired

child, perceptibly smiling. A tangle of limbs is all that can be seen of another child sitting close by. And there was a letter:

Darling – It's no good – I can't hold on any longer. One has to be a better and a stronger character than me to be able to face a life of invalidism – the monograph has kept me going these years – and now I am too exhausted to give it the finishing touches and see it into print. Will you and Den do so for me. You don't know how long and ardently I have longed to die. I should love to have talked it over with you – but that would have involved you in responsibility for my suicide and so it could not be. I have thought endlessly about whether it is wrong – and perhaps it is. But one would have to feel very sure of its wrongness to go on existing as a helpless unhelping unit in the terrible post war years that are to come. I am glad to be going during Germany's agony and don't want to survive it. If we have to live many lives, may I live near those I now love again and make a better job of living. And may I love a bit better. I can't live without the warm enfolding love of another person – and in this life I have smashed up my chance of that. Give my love to Judy. Darling, forgive me. I am so tired and have been for so many years.

    All my love

      Fresc

On the other side of the paper she had added a note:

> If I had the courage to hold on for another few years, I might emerge into health and strength but I doubt it. I've never been strong and the amount of trouble it has been to keep my machinery working is idiotic. If I had been poor I should have died ages ago. And anyhow I am such a rotten person, it's not worth wasting all that trouble on me. But oh I have tasted the good things of being alive and am glad I was born. I would love to give you a great good-bye hug. Keep a little place warm for me in your heart.[85]

Had Francesca failed in her attempt to kill herself, she could have been prosecuted and imprisoned. Had there been any evidence that friends or family were aware of her intentions, they too would have been liable for prosecution (the maximum prison term for aiding or abetting suicide was fourteen years). Such would be the law in this country until 1961. That Francesca had died alone caused Michael lasting distress: "Poor sweet sweetheart. [. . .] But if she were cold and level then I would have held her hand at least."[86]

Francesca had wanted her body donated to science or buried where she believed she would be found, in Martin's Grove: "I don't want any kind of funeral. If the hospital won't take what's left of me, have a hole dug near where they find me and put some lime in. I'll help something to grow."[87] In the event she was taken back to The Mill House and buried privately under an elder tree in the garden, on 13 April. Her grave is unmarked, but Cyril and Veronica covered the patch of earth with flowers.

In her will, Francesca gave "all the residue of my real and personal estate and effects [. . .] to Michael Tippett absolutely".[88] He also received her Parker pen, her *Times* subscription, a caravan, and the china crucifix she had worn to die. As he told Cyril, "I hadn't known the contents of the will, which is a bit of a surprise, in a way."[89] Martin's Grove and the rubble of her London house were both left elsewhere, but after various bequests had been paid, Michael received the best part of £9,000 (some £350,000 today).[90]

Post-war interest rates were low, but it was a life-changing sum, and one never mentioned by Michael in his autobiography. In many ways he buried the memory of Francesca. The caravan arrived in due course – "it's rather a pet" – and was made good use of.[91] He went to pick up her papers, but never managed to publish their folk-song monograph as she had requested; after a refusal from Oxford University Press he deposited it in an archive, where it lies still, its arguments mainly disproven. He found she had kept the letters he had sent her, and was shocked: "they are wildly unfeeling – there is nothing whatever in them, except occasional gentleness to her, but everlasting accounts of the music: reads like a mono-mania".[92] No photographs of her survived among his papers or were included in his books. "Were you ever close to a woman?" he was asked, for a ninetieth-birthday interview. "Oh yes. Indeed. All through my life. Francesca Allinson, who I was closer to than almost anybody. It was a strange, tender, extremely tender, gentle relation-ship. And of course she took her life eventually. [. . .] Anyhow that's rather a closed book, love. I can't go very far down that road."[93]

In the shadow of Francesca's death, the concentration camps began to be liberated. With friends and family in Germany, and rumours of the camps dripping into Britain all through the war, neither she nor Michael can have been entirely ignorant of their existence. But she did not live to read reports of the piles of skeletal bodies, or to see the newsreels filmed at Bergen-Belsen, where British soldiers, just days after her funeral, discovered thousands of unburied corpses. She did not live to read of Hitler's suicide on 30 April, or of the ruins of Berlin as it was overrun by the Soviets, or of the final document of unconditional German surrender, which was signed on 7 May.

The war, in which Michael had been arrested and imprisoned, in which Francesca Allinson had committed suicide, in which Bronw-en Wilson had been killed, in which his house had been bombed, in which his parents' house had been bombed, in which Morley College had been bombed, in which his father had died, in which he had composed and conducted so much music, in which he had moved from obscurity to fame, in which he had loved and parted from so many, in which so much had been killed and destroyed and created, was finally at an end.

DIARY:

Suffolk

It is over seventy years since Francesca Allinson walked out of The Mill House in Streetly End for the last time, but the house has since changed hands only once, and is lived in by a couple to whom Cyril bequeathed it after many years of friendship.

The air is dense, and luminous bruised clouds promise a storm, much needed by the extraordinary garden, where there are trees planted or suggested by Francesca, gingko and hazelnut and a weeping lime. The house from the outside is picture-book perfect, as a child might draw a house: door, four windows around it, roof and chimney, and a rose climbing all over the Suffolk-pink walls. The grounds are scattered with outbuildings, one of which was a small consecrated chapel that the Allinsons used for storage. At the bottom of the garden is the large mill from which the house took its name, long bereft of its sails; now a store-room and studio, it contains the Allinsons' telephone, and the couch on which Francesca's father, Thomas, would treat his patients.

Inside is a treasure trove. Much remains unchanged since the 1940s. There are piles of papers and photographs; chunks of the folk-song book that Michael and Francesca wanted to write together; and, excitingly, the manuscript score of Michael's first piano sonata, lost for half a century. Most moving is a picture of Francesca at sixteen, her gaze disconcertingly appraising and intense under an astonishing helmet of hair.

There is a letter sent from Michael after the suicide, his pencil scrawl already fading on the yellow paper. There is Francesca's will. Oil paintings by her mother hang on the walls. The whole place feels as if it would have been

Francesca Allinson, aged sixteen

an enchanted refuge for Francesca from wartime London, but in truth there was an aerodrome nearby, and she would sit and watch the planes overhead, driven to distraction by the noise. Growing more and more unwell, she became nervous and neurotic, and after a day left alone in the house would sit by the gate waiting frantically for Cyril and Veronica to return home from London. After her death the villagers claimed they could hear her whistling. There is nothing but birdsong on the air when I walk to a patch of lawn under which Francesca is buried, the grass allowed to grow long, and dotted with cow parsley. She is near to, or perhaps underneath, the weeping lime, cascades of heart-shaped leaves reaching gently down towards the ground.

The village of Clare is twelve miles east from the little hamlet of Streetly End. The train station is long since closed, but its buildings are preserved: a stationmaster's house with ticket office and waiting room; a goods shed a little further off. A shard of train track has been laid in the grass. The air now crackles with storm as I walk where Francesca walked, overlooked by the ruins of Clare Castle, high on its motte, with the station built within its bailey. No more than twenty steps away from the station, towards the village, on a dirt track canopied with ash and elder and birch, through fizzing clouds of midges, is the river, smelling of sulphur and mud, and popping with insects. There has been no rain here for days, but it threatens now. The water is brown and shiny, about eight metres wide, and although it doesn't rush it is not sluggish. I can barely see the bottom and poke a stick in. A person could wade through it with ease, but it would submerge a horizontal body. The track through the woods forces the walker first onto an iron bridge; there is then another a little further in. The first is higher and sturdier, shrouded in branches, and has a step that could help a person up and onto its ledge. Both are overlooked by a row of red-brick Victorian houses on the banks of the river. It is when I am standing on the bridge that it begins to pour, although the trees on either side make their sycamore handshake, green upon green, to mask me from the rain, and the sun still shines through the leaves. I wonder if Michael ever came here.

PART FIVE

———

PEACE
1945–1962

NINETEEN

The Wonderful Truth of Overness

In Muriel Spark's novel *The Girls of Slender Means* there is a vivid description of war-torn peacetime London, its rows of houses "like giant teeth in which decay had been drilled out, leaving only the cavity", the "surviving staircases leading up and up to an unspecified destination that made unusual demands on the mind's eye".[1] It comes as no surprise, reading this passage, that Michael Tippett was beginning work on an opera that, while ostensibly leaving realism aside for a world of symbolism and magic, was dreamed up in a time when surreality was commonplace. The opera's stage directions would eventually describe "an ascending spiral stone staircase", standing alone and unexplained in a forest clearing, and seeming "to break abruptly in mid-air".[2]

It is hard to imagine Michael joining the victory celebrations on VE day, 8 May 1945, as the country erupted in a welter of bunting and euphoria, rejoicing in what the writer and editor Diana Athill remembers as "the wonderful truth of Overness".[3] The dead were somehow more irrevocably absent in peacetime than in war, and Francesca Allinson's fear of "Germany's agony" was doubtless at the forefront of Michael's mind. With the night raids gone for good the country could be illuminated without anxiety, and the moon became once again a thing of beauty rather than dread. Rationing persisted, and in some cases became stricter. But brightness mingled with the drear, and when the first general election for a decade was held in July, the Labour Party won a landslide victory.

The new Prime Minister, Clement Attlee, was not unsympathetic to pacifists, having had a brother imprisoned as an absolute pacifist during the First World War. In just over a year the National Health Service Act would provide free universal healthcare, one example of the government's expansion of the welfare state. Most of Britain's major colonies began their slow journey to independence, and the coal industry was nationalised. Michael's social ideals were more aligned with government policy than ever before. But the glimmer of progress, as the country put itself back together piece by piece, continued alongside the last cataclysms: the dropping on 6 August of an atomic bomb on Hiroshima, and, three days later, an even more powerful explosion in Nagasaki, which led to Japan's surrender. "I couldn't believe it," Michael remembered. "I read the *News Chronicle* headline. I just did not take it in. I thought, it's impossible."[4] On 2 September a surrender document was signed that marked the end of hostilities.

All of these events Michael's music would address explicitly, but not for some decades. It would be years, too, before Francesca's death found its place in his composition. Trauma needed to bury deep into his mind before he trusted himself to respond. The final devastations of the war had, he thought, changed his creative life for ever. *A Child of Our Time* had tentatively tendered hope from horror. Later he admitted that this optimism had been tarnished:

> What I'm sure about is that Hiroshima, and the worldwide concentration camps, made it impossible for me to be as naïve as I had been perhaps, about the possibility that paradise was just round the corner, and that by this-or-that we might find it. And yet, the dream [of peace] is real – we dream it, even if we are in concentration camps. And so, what was I doing? I had to sing always ever anew. I have to sing as Blake put it: no longer the songs of innocence but the songs of experience.[5]

But Michael emerged from six years' arduous slog of survival a man frequently capable of great joy, the needle on his emotional scales flicking always back to merriment, as if he were wired for happiness.[6] Friends delighted in his company and found him unwounded, high-spirited almost to a fault, even-tempered and hard to offend. The dazzle of his charm could lead to suspicion, and he was shocking to those easily shocked. He proceeded with a calmly cheerful effrontery, mischievous rather than malicious. His attitude delighted some as it horrified others. "I mean if he came and kissed you on the lips," remembers the singer Raimund Herincx, "that was just Tippett saying hello, you know; every time I got a smacker I didn't find that was offensive in any way." Alexander Goehr admits: "I objected to being kissed by Tippett on the lips – he didn't know when to stop."[7] In what may be a glimpse of masochistic sexual tastes, or merely proof of his delightedly brazen irreverence, Michael reported with undisguised glee meeting the chief executive of the Royal Opera House, David Webster, and refusing to attend a party at the Savoy Hotel "because the only sort of party I wanted was where I should be undressed, thrown on a bed, and raped".[8]

Optimism; joy; a teasingly merry equanimity: these facets of his character are not the less genuine for being in some ways a coping strategy. Pessimism may be the privilege of the content. He had written of Francesca's suicide: "Our own gaieties [and] light-heartedness cover the inner sensitiveness to her memory."[9] The bitterness of absence could have sounded in his life like a ground bass, but aware of his ability to survive trauma seemingly unscarred, he admitted: "I have the rather unpleasant capability of forgetting a past experience on the instant, and fully entering on a new, with no regrets."[10] He rushed into all his projects with the dedication of one hoping to form professional scabs over emotional wounds, and underneath the not inconsiderable hopefulness and gaiety of his nature there lurked deep guilt about the dangerous implications of his artistic obsession, his sense that to pursue a much-desired domestic relationship was in some way to be adulterous to his music. All was crystallised in Francesca's death, to which one of his immediate reactions was to write: "men with careers are often just monsters it seems to me".[11] Even before her death, he had told John Amis that "an artist is hopelessly dubious as a social being. Creative activity will knock every social and erotic demand sky high and leave the other person or persons in the lurch – and then when that ceases, the poor artist finds himself only too anxious to play – but the companion is not there – and this is [the] general problem whether one is 'normal' or not. Well, well, one is what one is."[12]

"One is what one is." "I accepted it. It was myself." In these and other phrases Michael shows the clear-sighted acceptance of who he was, or believed himself to be, and his self-professed inability or refusal to change the facets of his character he disliked. It was an attitude that stemmed from his devotion to Jung, an attempt to know his shadow and his light. On such terms, hard-won self-acceptance would seem to cancel out efforts at self-improvement; the shadow is to be acknowledged, not removed.

In his surviving correspondence sent during the spring and summer of 1945 Michael is completely silent on global developments, never mentioning the bombs on Japan, and touching on the victory in Europe only to say that "everyone is a trifle emotionally deflated by the peace".[13] The silence seems to indicate not apathy but numbed retreat into music. More than anything else the war had been for Michael an interruption to a soul-deep creative impulse. He might reasonably expect to be coming up to a halfway point in his life, but his catalogue ran to a grand total of just eleven pieces, and to create the body of work of which he thought himself capable was now his most driving force. His job at Morley College continued, and financially he was more secure than he had ever been. All this was a springboard from which he could leap into composition, which would now stretch, uninterrupted by even a single year's pause, across the rest of his life. The peace declared, his first priority was to finish his symphony, so as to move on to a third string quartet, and then, at long last, to *Aurora Consurgens*, the opera on which he had been working with Douglas Newton.

The symphony's first two movements had taken over a year; the third and fourth were composed in five months or so, and the piece was finished in September 1945.[14] The third movement is a Beethovenian scherzo and trio, a one-in-a-bar eruption with a rhythm (placing a strong accent on the first note of each bar) that

Michael took from mediaeval polyphony. The final movement is a double fugue that shoots the orchestra through, between, above, and below the bar lines with unbridled momentum, before spinning out and away, the strings dancing off into the distance in a quiver of trills far above the stave. But the prevailing mood is one of abandonment and invasion. Far from being a depiction of victory, the movement is kicked to death by the intermittent slam of a bass drum and timpani. Michael had not set out to emulate Shostakovich in using music practically as a dispatch from the front, nor to unite with Vaughan Williams in providing balm during war or rage at its fallout. But Michael's symphony had been mapped out in prison, and composed on a piano twice bombed, its ivory blown off and its strings rattling with broken glass. It was an instrument inherited from one he had loved, who was now dead. He came to think the music "sprang more than I knew from the experiences of general catastrophe".[15]

The premiere was given by the Liverpool Philharmonic Orchestra, on 10 November 1945.* The London concert scene was suffering from bomb damage and conservative programming, and provincial orchestras and concert halls began to steal a march on the capital when it came to contemporary premieres. Malcolm Sargent was engaged to conduct, though Michael thought his old mentor had not bothered to study the score in advance and was confused by some of the techniques drawn from then-obscure composers such as Monteverdi. John Amis was at the concert, and, believing it to have been conducted "extremely badly", watched with amusement as Sargent, pen at the ready, instructed autograph hunters to be let into the dressing room, only for them all to troop across to Michael, all but ignoring Sargent, who flew into a fury.[16]

---

* The work was begun under the title "Symphony No. 2", following the Symphony in B flat, from 1933; come the premiere Tippett was apparently yet to decide how the two works related to each other. Schott suggested the premiere be given the title of "Symphony 1945", as if making explicit the year of war and peace from which it had sprung. In 1948 it was published as "Symphony No. 1", the Symphony in B flat having finally been dismissed as juvenilia.

The reviews started to come through. "I gather amongst other things the [Times critic] thinks the work 'drab!'", Michael wrote. "I shan't change a note of the symphony because I can't."[17] But the concert had been anything but a critical failure. The Times had in fact praised the "composer's sincerity" and found the symphony a greater achievement than the Rachmaninov piano concerto that followed it. "Tippett is truly a modern among the present-day British composers," remarked the Birmingham Daily Post, hearing in the piece "a new kind of beauty to be rising like a sap in a young tree".[18] The orchestra repeated the symphony the following week, to a full house, and the work then received the odd performance or broadcast over the next few years, under the more sympathetic baton of Walter Goehr.

The sense of Michael's music having been almost universally derided in the first decades of his career has been tacked on in hindsight. William Walton had produced no major work since 1939, and in the decade following the first performance of A Child of Our Time Michael's reputation was outclassed in his generation of British composers only by Benjamin Britten, who had soared to fame with the premiere, in June 1945, of Peter Grimes. There were naysayers, but real mistrust and dislike were yet to come. For now, a popular survey of British music published in 1946 proclaimed A Child of Our Time to be of "outstanding importance", and concluded that "the unique art of Michael Tippett springs from phenomenal gifts which in their highest application are expressive of sheer genius".[19] The New Statesman declared his best work to be "as good as anything being written today", and soon, following in the footsteps of Elgar and Vaughan Williams, Michael would be awarded the prestigious Cobbett Medal for chamber music.[20]

With the symphony out of the way by late 1945, Michael was longing to turn his attention towards his long-gestating masque-opera Aurora Consurgens, and – already having noted down a possible musical scheme – began to push Douglas Newton to make a start on the libretto (which was still to contain spoken dialogue).[21] Their relationship was beginning to fade, and Michael had written to him in June: "you may at times feel worried that I shall grieve when the time comes for you to go off with your proper partner. There's no need to worry over much, even if I do let on occasionally how much I care for you [. . .] after all it's bound to happen – it's only a fact finally, like Fresca's death, and one just lumps it without ill feeling or self-pity. I've had the experience before."[22] By February 1946 Newton had come up with various drafts and a rough version of the first act.[23] Michael thought the drafts had "tremendous possibilities" and confirmed "my confidence in your ability to do the needful, if you could but do it before the few months left run out". Pressing Douglas forward was his constant theme: "Gather yourself together and begin Act 2 and all power to your elbow!"[24] Silence from Douglas. Michael began to badger him.

> For heaven's sake don't give up now. Can you do Act 2 this spring? I think it will have to be. I must begin laying out the musical pattern at once, more or less. [. . .] I'm still continually frightened that circumstances will trip us up, either by delaying you (who are slow enough as it is!) or by hurrying me – both of which are fairly likely. So I think about three more months at the most is a sort of date-line. After that I'd have to look around I suppose for a script in a hurry.[25]

By March it had become clear that Douglas was never going to have the time or inclination to get going. "I do like what you have done," Michael told him,

> but it's no use disguising the circumstantial difficulties – and temperamental ones also! I have got a great deal myself out of your co-operation so far – in ideas and discussion. I must acknowledge that in any case: and handsomely as appropriate. But I often get the feeling that it were almost better for both of us to leave straining and worrying and let me see what I can do either alone or with help between now and the summer. This indeed would be easier for me, if perhaps not a gain for the work itself.[26]

By late April Douglas had dropped out.[27] He had agreed with
Michael's view that good poetry didn't make for good librettos;
hoping to make his way in the literary world as a poet, he may
have started to believe himself disqualified for the collaboration.
But there was also the fact that, late into the war, he had met
a strikingly bright young woman from America called Mary Lee
Settle.

Settle eventually became a well-known novelist; her ambitions to
be an actress had led her to be tested for the part of Scarlett O'Hara
in *Gone with the Wind*. At the beginning of the war, having divorced
her husband, she moved to London to serve in the Women's Auxiliary Air Force and then the Office of War Information.[28] When
the fighting was over, she returned to America to collect her baby
son; soon back in England, she met Douglas, and they fell in love.
Michael had long been preparing himself for such an event, and
made purposeful efforts to welcome Mary into the fold. "Best of
love, poppet," he told Douglas, "and I'm terribly pleased for you
that you are having the experience you are."[29] Mary for her part
remembered with affection the three of them hearing a concert at
the Wigmore Hall and then going on to an Indian restaurant, walking along the freezing street, Michael "wearing my white gloves
over his ears".[30] The couple had moved to a flat in Camden Town
and Michael was initially a frequent visitor. But hopes for a happy
post-war community began to sour, during months as hard as any
winter since before the war, cold for lack of fuel, malnourished for
lack of food. On top of such hardships, the happy trio soon became
a fractious quartet, with the arrival in Michael's life of a young man
called John Minchinton.

Minchinton is the most inscrutable of Michael's close friends.
Little information, and no correspondence, survives to reveal him.
He was born in 1928 and appears in Michael's letters as a new
face late in 1945: "I have a notion that I may get a silent SOS for
temporary house room for that T.B. [top brass?] youngster, John
Minchinton, coming up to term at the Guildhall soon." Michael
thought him "so young he's rather lost" and "far too serious –
but with guts".[31] Minchinton was studying music and wanted to

conduct; he had worked as page-turner for Benjamin Britten and got hold of Michael's address. Evidently impulsive, the seventeen-year-old simply took leave from his school, hitch-hiked from Bristol to London, and turned up without warning at the bungalow, finding it unlocked (as it almost always was, Michael priding himself on not having a key, so that friends could come and go). "To be picked out as a mentor by one so determined and so young was a bit worrying," Michael admitted. "But somehow I couldn't just refuse to help."[32] Michael may have thought the young man could fill the void in his life that Douglas Newton's absence was soon to leave. Irresistible and persuasive but seemingly unpredatory, Michael began, despite the twenty-three-year age gap, a half-hearted affair with John, who thenceforth lived on and off at Whitegates and quickly received the customary baptism of being taken to Cornwall for a walking holiday. In private interviews Michael remembered: "When I walked into the cottage and this figure came out of the bedroom – a school kid – I accepted it. We went to bed together. At once his problems began. I didn't want to live a celibate life. I wanted sex."[33]

With his dark curly hair, John was not physically dissimilar to Douglas, although his chiselled face was more conventionally handsome. Douglas, an equable middle-class intellectual, had been an anomaly in Michael's love life. John Minchinton, evidently escaping a difficult home, was working-class, and had a temper as well as talent. Michael was fond of John, and, while more willing than others to tolerate his difficulties, he was not blind to them. The affair was an expression of friendly affection and practical support rather than of love or passion. Sex likely took second place to the furthering of John's career and Michael's offering of musical assistance. Instantly clear is that few of Michael's friends found John likeable, or especially gifted. Alexander Goehr thought him "clearly a crook", "a great poseur" with "fairly primitive" musical abilities, and "surely not a homosexual – he was of proletarian origin and this was a step up in the world – that was the price to pay".[34] Evelyn Maude's daughter Alison still remembers her mother muttering darkly about "nasty little Johnnie".[35]

John's arrival on the scene surely contributed to the collaboration over *Aurora Consurgens* falling through. Douglas dealt with difficulties by going silent, and it was Mary who wrote to Michael to air their grievances, troubled not only by John's behaviour, but by the homosexual group with which Douglas had been involved during the war. Much later, Douglas admitted that Mary "believed me to have been ruined by quote Michael Tippett, bugger, end quote". He added: "I didn't think so at all."[36]

Michael was willing to concede that John Minchinton was causing all sorts of difficulty, and told Mary that the temper tantrums were a result of John's finding that

> his hero, artist, conscientious objector going to prison, and all that, is at the same time what is called "queer". None of these shocks is simple – because all the present social problems get quickly involved. Minch is no exception [. . . and] he is not pleasant company while it lasts. No one is. Here it really is easier for me to tolerate this because I am factually older by so much, even if it may not appear in behaviour. [. . .] I won't nursemaid him. He must fall on his head or his arse as it may happen.[37]

But Michael did little to prevent relations between the four of them going from bad to worse. He admitted to Douglas that "the best thing to do would be to tell Minch to move", but professed to having "no control over him". The difficulty was, he thought, John's "imaginative quality, which enters into his relation of facts and events. I'm seldom sure what he has done or not, because he has confused by then his dreams, aspirations and actualities."[38] Mary and Douglas were losing patience, and Michael missed hearing from them. He told Mary: "You are in no way the reason I haven't seen Den – far from it – or why should it? I am extremely fond of you. But, you see, if Den and you both keep the silence of the grave (nothing has passed between us three but my last visit to you in early August) and you have no telephone, what is to happen?"[39]

Tellingly, it was a letter from Mary, rather than Douglas, that arrived in autumn 1946, bearing news of their marriage. "Dearest Mary," Michael replied, with an offhand briskness that he may not have felt. "I suppose the great occasion was on last Saturday – I was a bit puzzled by the letter, but that's how I read it. I couldn't get [away] anyhow – I was tied up in rehearsal for choir broadcast. [. . .] I'm terribly glad about the settlement of you two. That's excellent as well as being proper. Love to you both."[40] And that, as Michael might have put it, was that, and just had to be lumped.

It may be that Douglas simply didn't keep any of Michael's letters sent after 1946, but it may be that there were no letters to keep. Michael's episodic love life had moved on without obvious regret, as if an affair at its peak during the war could no longer be sustained in peacetime, or as if his love were an outward and visible expression of their collaboration, physical and artistic unions somehow fused. There is little evidence of a major bust-up. Douglas and Mary were on the ascendant in their respective careers: travelling to Paris, where they met the composers John Cage and Pierre Boulez; mingling with sculptors such as Eduardo Paolozzi; working in the reopened British Museum, which encouraged Douglas finally to pursue his long-held ambition of being a curator. In 1948 he published a short article for children on Michael's music, in which he seemed still to have a working knowledge of the composer's life and ambitions, and argued that Michael had "already earned his place among the English composers who show most clearly the marks of genius".[41] Whether he followed the developments of *Aurora Consurgens* as it morphed into *The Midsummer Marriage* and received, in 1955, its premiere at Covent Garden, is unknown. In 1956 he and Mary Lee relocated to America, where their marriage quickly broke down. Douglas had already embarked on a career that saw him become one of the most respected curators in New York. There is nothing to suggest that he ever saw Michael Tippett again.

In Ian Kemp's major study of Michael's music, the name Douglas Newton is tucked into a lone footnote. And Michael's autobiography runs: "I tried to collaborate on the text [of *The Midsummer Marriage*] with Douglas Newton, but we were soon at cross purposes."[42] This single sentence does scant justice to a project that was discussed between them for at least six years, and worked on in some detail for over two. Michael had at one point gone so far as to ask Schott about Douglas's copyright in the work, and the scenario of the finished opera owes a great deal to the younger man's poetic instincts and literary knowledge. Perhaps it was curatorial compulsion that led Douglas to haul nearly 200 of Michael's letters over the ocean and keep them for some decades, but when he asked his old friend John Amis to ensure their safekeeping in London's British Library, he may have been quietly making sure that his contribution was preserved for posterity. Whether Michael's silence on the matter was maintained to protect or to ignore Douglas, we cannot know.

Back in the spring of 1946 Michael found himself without a librettist for a work he desperately wanted to write, its scenario ready and raring to go. It is far from the case that he was instantly happy to write the words himself, and despite his view that librettos should have little to no literary quality, he contacted a number of authors with the suggestion of immediate collaboration. He had had enough recent success that even well-known writers might not have dismissed out of hand such a suggestion. But they may have baulked at being asked to fill out a detailed pre-existing scenario, rather than start from scratch. Likely in 1946 Michael arranged to meet the poet and playwright Ronald Duncan, who seemed an ideal candidate: a pacifist and conscientious objector, he had recently authored a "Masque and Anti-Masque" called *This Way to the Tomb*, for which Benjamin Britten had provided incidental music. Duncan met Michael in a London tea-shop and soon realised he had a back-seat librettist on his hands, as Michael excitedly discussed endless possibilities over the tea and buttered toast. Duncan was at work on the libretto for Britten's opera *The Rape of Lucretia*, and Michael liked the topic. "Would you mind if I set it too?", he suddenly asked. "In the eighteenth century composers often set the same libretto." Duncan said he would have to let Britten know, and Michael agreed. "Of course he'll finish his score a couple of years before me," he said. "It's all so easy for him." Britten's reaction was to be crestfallen, and rather jealous. "I suppose you think Michael could make a better job of it than I can," Duncan remembered him saying. "Well, you may be right."[43] This spur-of-the-moment idea soon died a death, as did a Tippett–Duncan masque; they went their separate ways.

Christopher Fry, Michael's beloved friend from Hazelwood School, would have been an obvious candidate and was back in contact after a difficult war; but he was distracted by the premiere of his breakout play *A Phoenix Too Frequent*, and self-professedly a slow and dogged worker. George Barker, with whom Michael had wanted to collaborate some years earlier, was back in London and hoping to move in his writing from poetry to drama, but he had to go abroad in the summer of 1946.[44] Finally there was A.L. Rowse, the historian with whom Michael had holidayed when released from Wormwood Scrubs. Rowse could be difficult and bitter, and Michael privately thought him "a queer cuss", but the two had got on well enough, and Rowse was an evocative poet with a professional interest in Cornish mythology.[45] Michael sent him a letter: "I have a scheme for words and music you might like to think about."[46] Maybe Rowse did think about it, but, living 300 miles away and churning out a book a year, he was far from an ideal collaborator.

While Douglas Newton was casting off both *Aurora Consurgens* and his relationship with its composer, Michael had written a third string quartet, commissioned (back in 1944, for £50) by the American arts patron Mary Behrend, a friend and sponsor of Britten, who had likely made the introduction: "That you also believe in Michael, helps too," he told her, "because I know him to be so frightfully good."[47] Michael had planned to leave work on the quartet until after the opera, but with the libretto still unwritten, he had started his String Quartet No. 3 sometime in the autumn of 1945 and finished in early September of the following year.[48] The work moves away from the four-movement classical model of his previous quartets and, inspired by the quartets of Bartók, into a five-movement club sandwich of fugue. Interspersed between the three fugal layers are the two slow movements, pools of respite, of which the second nudges into an aural vision of some other world. The two violins and viola slowly enter, one by one, until a chord has been floated unsteadily on the air; the cello, through a gradually ascending and accelerating bass line, leads this first verse of the movement to breaking point, and the three other players abandon ship, leaving the cellist sawing away, like some odd parody of a child practising scales. The pattern is repeated three times, ending in kaleidoscopic rotations, seemingly eternal. The last movement caused Michael endless problems as the quartet returned to earth. The Zorian Quartet gave its premiere at the Wigmore Hall on 19 October 1946 (the first violinist, Olive Zorian, soon became Mrs John Amis).

Three weeks later came another premiere, of Michael's speedily despatched *Little Music for String Orchestra*, commissioned by the conductor Reginald Jacques, who had been a support in the lead-up to Michael's trial. As ever with money-earning commissions, Michael was contemptuous: "This damned piece for Jacques! Prelude, Fugue and Air are not so bad – Finale is poor stuff. Lack of time and energy."[49] Performed with sufficient vigour, the romping finale can be the *Little Music*'s most winning movement, in that the piece ends three times, the culminating phrase returning like a cheeky child who refuses to be sent to bed. The quartet and the *Little Music*, Michael's first two works of peacetime, form a final burst of indefatigable counterpoint, flinging out fugues by the fistful, and tie a knot around Michael's first musical "voice". The opera would require something different, and his pressing need to compose it had him in an iron grip. Librettists, he had found, did not grow on trees and could not be conjured out of thin air. As so often throughout his life, he decided to do the needful himself. Later, firm in the belief that his theatrical works required composer and librettist to be one and the same, he made a proud virtue of what had originally been mere necessity. "I can't now wait on librettists," he wrote in December 1946.[50] It would take him six years. He began.

TWENTY

Off the Hook, on the Air, in the Air

As the years went by, normal pre-war life was parcelled up and returned, slowly and incrementally, in small portions: the forgotten glow of street lamps, the reductions in rationing, the first drive in a car newly full of petrol. Life was becoming warmer, better fed, better slept. Michael's attentions in the late 1940s were turned mainly towards the opera, its composition necessitating periods of deep isolation at Whitegates Cottage: "I'm horribly single-minded, mono-maniac, and have next to no energy for the outside public life which I'm reducing to a minimum!"[1] Such was his hope. But professional demands continued to require his time and attention. His social and public life were split between worlds old and new, and his political involvement and responsibilities at Morley College continued alongside the blossoming of his career in broadcasting, and a rediscovery of the European travels that the war had denied him for so long.

Early in 1946 Mary Lee Settle, living with Douglas "Den" Newton in a small flat in Camden Town, was weeping over the ironing board. "Our apartment", she remembered,

> was also the "address" of fourteen or fifteen conscientious-objector friends of Den, who were spread all over the south

of England, on the run. The government had been too slow in releasing them from their assigned farm work when the war was over. When Den decided to report, expecting to go to jail, I remember ironing his one shirt, and crying. He came back an hour later and said he was off the hook. They weren't interested.[2]

Many objectors who had served a prison term for non-compliance made the transition from war to peace with no change in their legal status. Douglas had escaped prison, but his work on objectors' land schemes had been in an unofficial capacity, and having refused the Civil Defence training assigned him he was still liable for prosecution. One reason why Michael had been keen to push him into writing a libretto, and fast, was that an enforced absence from a lengthy prison sentence seemed more than likely. The release of objectors from the terms of their tribunals was done in batches, dependent on age and on length of service or imprisonment. Many faced difficulties in returning to their pre-war jobs or in finding replacement employment, and ex-servicemen were usually prioritised. Others found themselves rejected by their families. The last of the Second World War's conscientious objectors was released from his terms of registration in 1947, but Michael didn't have to wait so long, and in June 1946 received a letter: "National Service (Release of Conscientious Objectors) Act, 1946 [. . .] Michael Kemp Tippett, of Whitegates Cottages, Oxted, Surrey, a conditionally registered conscientious objector [. . .] shall as from the date hereof be released from the obligation to undertake work subject to which he was so registered."[3]

It was soon announced that conscription would last a further fourteen years. There was much opposition to this extension, especially when, on 18 November, the Chancellor of the Exchequer declared that no objector would be excused from some form of alternative service. On 12 December the Central Board of Conscientious Objectors sent a deputation, of which Michael was part, to Downing Street for a meeting with George Isaacs, the Minister of Labour.[4] Three months later it was announced that unconditional registration would in fact be retained as a potential outcome from a tribunal. A further 9,000 men registered as conscientious objectors until, in 1960, conscription was abolished.

Michael had been one of the more high-profile of the country's objectors. Peter Pears and Benjamin Britten believed they had suffered some mild animosity for their stance and for their support of Michael, but the success of Peter Grimes mainly gave them general acceptance and celebrity. Michael, despite mingling in his professional life with numerous distinguished veterans, likewise faced very little hostility. The trio's public reputation remained surprisingly secure, amid a traceable shift away from jingoistic nationalism. Fighting in Europe was stilled, and integration of the Continent's countries was seen as an antidote to conflict. From the rubble of the League of Nations was built, in October 1945, the United Nations; NATO followed in 1949 and, the next decade, came the beginnings of what was eventually the European Union. In laying out his case to David Ayerst during the war, Michael had held few illusions about pacifism: "I am pretty sure it will be politically a failure [. . .] but despite the weakness of us pacifists, we have managed to keep a challenge alive. The harvest will come later."[5] One of the major legacies of the Second World War's conscientious objectors was to pave the way not only for the next generation of consciences, but for the political protests against the wars the century would continue to witness: in Korea, Vietnam, Yugoslavia, and the Middle East. In 1944 Michael had issued a statement: "Much more has been accomplished by our witness this time than we know, or perhaps than we deserve."[6]

His own political activities lessened after the war. In 1944 he had written to Alan Bush, who would remain a lifelong communist, that he had "lost all interest in 'opposition' politics or their writing". But the following year he admitted: "One doesn't cease to be in some senses always a political animal. [. . .] For me the language and ideas of Marxism are only one, and not the only, apprehension of present social life. The centre of gravity, so to speak, has for me shifted. [. . .] Very crudely I might put it that the moral ends of Marxism are good, but the methods are by now so uncivilised that the ends envisaged cannot any longer be encompassed."[7] Trotskyist violence was a thing of the past. True, an early draft of his libretto to *Aurora Consurgens* contains the line: "Take care! In an age of revolution, the past has a way of coming back in a most violent form." But to this the hero replies: "What nonsense."[8]

Michael's new-found reputation led to any number of job offers, almost all of which, including the invitation to become chorus master of the Philharmonia, he turned down. He even refused the lucrative offer of a weekly column at the *Observer*, despite being wined and dined at the Waldorf by its editor. He did, however, sit on the musical advisory committee of the British Council, and on the board of the Freedom Defence Committee, set up in 1945 to protest the raiding by Special Branch of the anarchist newspaper *War Commentary*, and committed to upholding freedom of speech and civil liberties. The vice-chairman was George Orwell, and alongside Michael on the board were Britten, E.M. Forster, Henry Moore, and George Bernard Shaw. On 1 May 1946 the board sent an open letter to President Truman (which T.S. Eliot also signed) calling upon America to release some 2,000 of its conscientious objectors still serving heavy prison sentences.[9]

But it was only to the Peace Pledge Union, in the years after the war, that Michael entirely committed himself, and with a resolution that lasted for the rest of his life. In 1945 he had become, alongside Britten and others, a "sponsor" of the Union (essentially an honorary vice-president), and two years later joined its council, annually addressing the general meeting. In November 1947 he conducted a choir at the memorial concert to its founder, Dick Sheppard, and throughout the 1940s attended peace demonstrations and addressed the quite sizeable crowds, calling, as at Bristol in February 1947, for a speedy withdrawal of British Armed Forces from Europe, the Middle East, India, and the Far East.[10] He protested fiercely against the use of napalm in the Korean War, joined the editorial board of *Peace News*, and found himself, on 21 January 1949, at yet another rally, where he and Vera Brittain spoke alongside the actress Dame Sybil Thorndike, whose performances had so entranced him during his student theatre-going.[11]

This surge in activism may have been spiked by the fact that, in

1948, his cousin Phyllis Kemp telephoned him after a wounded and wounding eleven-year silence, fiercely maintained since political disagreements had destroyed their friendship. Phyllis had spent the war working in a car factory, becoming more and more embroiled in the highest levels of left-wing politics. After the war she lived for a short while in Yugoslavia, befriending the revolutionary leader Tito and translating his speeches. On her return to England she sank into penury and was under more or less constant surveillance. It may only be thanks to a fuzzy phone line that Michael himself escaped investigation. Secret agents at MI5 transcribed a bugged conversation in which Phyllis explained to fellow party members that she had "joined the [Communist] Party in 1934 with MICHAEL TIBBETT (phonetic), who is her cousin [. . .] he was a musician and used to 'organise the music at MALVERN ?? College'. He was very well known in the early days of the war, but has been very quiet ever since."[12]

In 1948 Phyllis married a Marxist historian, Kunwar Muhammad Ashraf, who had been a secretary to Jawaharlal Nehru and became a leading member of the then-illegal Communist Party of India; he had been held for two years in a Delhi internment camp, and on his release lived in exile in London. Eventually he and Phyllis applied unsuccessfully for repatriation in the Soviet Union, before moving first to India and then to East Berlin. Both continued to publish major works of left-wing scholarship, and Phyllis's politics were now so at odds with Michael's that their rejuvenated friendship could be maintained only with unease. She was, he thought, still bitter that her hope of starting a family with him had gone unfulfilled, and he believed her true reason for making contact was to forge links between the Peace Pledge Union and the Communist Party of Great Britain. The party was at the height of its influence, and had yet to see the mass walkouts that would greet the Hungarian Revolution in 1956. But Michael was now openly and publicly opposed to its policies. What influence he had he used to argue fiercely against the Union's joining with the communists in any unified peace movement. Prospective pacifists, he maintained, would reason that "joining the peace movement means appearing on platforms with people who uphold the political tyrannies of Eastern Europe".[13]

Sure enough, not long after Phyllis was back in touch, his suspicions proved founded. His Trotskyism seemingly water under the bridge, he duly received invitations from the Russian Embassy. The first was to a World Congress of Intellectuals for Peace, held in Poland, in August 1948; the second to a Cultural and Scientific Conference for World Peace, held at the Waldorf Astoria in New York, in March 1949. The former was attended, among others, by Picasso, Brecht, and Aldous and Julian Huxley; the latter by Leonard Bernstein and Arthur Miller. But Michael refused to go to either, perceiving that beneath the conferences' surface commitments to world government and pacifism lay a darker purpose, namely the intention of proving that intellectuals could thrive not under Western imperialism but under the Soviet system. In so doing he turned down the invitation to meet and to question Dmitri Shostakovich, correctly predicting that during the New York conference the beleaguered Russian composer would be compelled to condemn self-exiled figures such as Hindemith and Stravinsky, to much applause. The conferences were early stirrings of the World Peace Council, which Michael thought was blind to Soviet horrors. As he wrote in the PPU [*Peace Pledge Union*] *Journal*, to which he was now a frequent contributor:

> I prefer to bargain with the CP thus: "I will come on to your platform if you will state your case frankly as I state mine. You cannot have my public co-operation in less terms. That is to say you cannot use my good name to cover your bad name, and make your true policy of Russia-sponsored police-state appear as 'renunciation of war'. For me to allow you to do that would show me to be more politically naïve than I am. My message is 'Truth and non-violence'. We will begin with Truth. Good day."[14]

The work at Morley College produced under Michael's musical directorship was continuing to cause a stir. On 19 March 1946 the singers took part in a performance of *A Child of Our Time* at Central Hall, Westminster. It was this performance that T.S. Eliot attended, but his opinion of the oratorio has not survived.[15] John Amis, still working as Michael's secretary, appears to have got badly overwhelmed by the organisation required for the Westminster concert, or was just fed up with working for nothing. He had left bills unpaid, gone on to another job, and abandoned Michael to the pile of lawyers' threats that ensued. Michael's letters of recrimination are among the crossest and most wounded he ever sent: "To be candid John I have been badly shaken and badly hurt. Beginning with great affection and confidence in you, [this has] ended in something very different." It was a letter of dismissal. Michael was not a man of quarrels; his friendships could fade, but they rarely exploded. And while John Amis never worked for him again, Michael had made sure to end his letter: "I remain both as affectionate as before and as interested in your career; though I can't recommend you in the same way, I do wish you success."[16]

Soon afterwards came an important and ambitious performance of Monteverdi's *Vespers* of 1610, which had only been available complete since the early 1930s and had never been performed in Britain. The concert, which owed much to the knowledge and contacts of its conductor, Walter Goehr, took place on 14 May 1946, was repeated and then broadcast. Vaughan Williams thought that Michael was "wasting his efforts over the dreary Monteverdi stuff"; the concert was acclaimed as "the outstanding musical event of the year".[17] The following year, on 21 November 1947, Michael conducted the choir in Thomas Tallis's forty-part motet *Spem in alium*. The singers had taken years to learn its complex interweaving of eight five-part choirs, and rehearsals had gestated alongside Michael's plans for an opera that would be structured, with help from the I Ching, in an octet. The Tallis performance was broadcast and a recording, the piece's first, released to the public. In 1948 Michael directed a production of Monteverdi's *The Coronation of Poppea* that pushed the opera back into musical consciousness after centuries of neglect. Eventually a Morley College Concerts Society was formed, boosted by funding from the newly founded Arts Council.

Purcell and his contemporaries remained a staple in the repertoire, and Michael and Benjamin Britten were tireless in their efforts to secure Purcell a lasting place in the British musical canon. "Have they won their case?" pondered the *Observer*. "I do not on the whole think that the verdict of the last quarter millennium on Purcell will be reversed."[18]

Morley obligations, much as Michael tried to lessen their number, necessitated frequent trips to London. He had moved into a different social circle in the city, his name suddenly a password into new dining rooms. As well as the company of musicians there was the friendship of poets. He had set to music Edith Sitwell's "The Weeping Babe" back in 1944, but had still not met its author. After a second performance the following year, Sitwell wrote to him of her pleasure at the piece. "I'm glad you liked it. Not everyone did!" he replied. "Will you come and have lunch with me somewhere? I have lots and lots to say. [. . .] Your poetry and Eliot's are my two loves."[19] Sitwell's fluctuating reputation had been restored by her war poetry; she could be haughty but was loyal to her inner circle, and on Michael's request had read some of Douglas Newton's verse, pronouncing him to have "a real gift".[20] Of Michael's forays into literary commentary, not least a pre-concert talk for *The Weeping Babe*, she had been dismissive, but her pacifist inclinations and taste for eccentricity meant that the composer, something of a hot new thing in the musical world, had piqued her interest. He flicked in and out of favour, as many did: "As far as I can make out I am also discarded by Edith," he wrote in autumn 1946, soon after meeting her. "I don't really mind much – perhaps she suddenly feels she has picked up too many new admirers and that they need sloughing off. However, sloughed off we are."[21] But soon Michael was again taken up, and paraded at some of Sitwell's literary soireés at the Sesame Imperial and Pioneer Club, the women's club in Mayfair that she used as a London base.

Anyone interested in the colliding worlds of post-war literature and music might have paid a great deal to be a fly on the patterned wallpaper of the Sesame dining room, watching the party assemble around Edith Sitwell, who was approaching sixty, all nose and pencilled eyebrows. Adaptable as ever, Michael enjoyed breaking into the hushed atmosphere of the club with tales of prison life or diatribes on left-wing politics, all of which were received in good humour. He may have been there more as curio than companion, exhibited in the same spirit as the fireman that Edith had once brought subversively into the dining room. The gatherings stopped when she embarked in 1948 on a two-year tour of America, but started up again on her return. Frequent among the guests was the poet Stephen Spender, not long married to the pianist Natasha Litvin. T.S. Eliot came, and Michael remembered the poet entertaining the group with self-deflating tales of his by now considerable fame: "Eliot had just returned from collecting the Nobel Prize in Sweden. Drily he told of his discomfiture when, just before dinner with the King, he had received back his only spare woollen underwear from the laundry, in an impossibly shrunken state."[22]

Nineteen forty-six was a golden year for British culture. The government had speedily recognised that funding for the arts was vital in those broken times. August brought the royal charter for the Arts Council of Great Britain, and then, on 29 September, came the launch of the Third Programme (eventually BBC Radio 3, though with a higher proportion of spoken word than today). The station was on air for six hours each evening, and three days into its existence broadcast Michael's cantata *Boyhood's End*. Two weeks later he gave a talk for the Programme on the contemporary music scene. It was the start of a reasonably regular series of radio talks, which allowed him to continue, in his clipped energetic tenor, his rejuvenation of Purcell, while at the same time focusing on contemporary repertoire. Fees for talks, usually twenty guineas, were far higher than for conducting or composing. He turned down an approach to write a piece for the Third Programme's first anniversary, but when, in July 1951, Arnold Schoenberg died, agreed to deliver three radio talks pondering the Austrian composer's career. His salary, set at £210, was vast: over £5,000 today. The musicologist Hans Keller raged in print that a Schoenberg expert had not been chosen: "Tippett tries his pathetic best [. . . but] more than half of his facts are wrong, and less than half of his thoughts are baked. He dabbles here, he dabbles there, he leaves a muddle everywhere. [. . .] I have the greatest respect for Tippett the composer and Tippett the thinker, but none for his accepting this job."[23] The row, which reached the correspondence pages of the *Radio Times*, stemmed from Michael's having mentioned a letter that, so the superstition ran, contributed to Schoenberg's death. Keller wrote to Michael directly, complaining the letter was apocryphal and mention of it offensive. Michael responded calmly, unbothered: "don't let us get it out of proportion".[24]

Less divisive were the extra-musical panels on which Michael appeared, speaking alongside Graham Greene and Elizabeth Bowen about a book that had triggered a crisis in his life (his choice sadly lost); reading favourite poetry and prose aloud; and moving from the Third Programme onto the BBC Home Service to appear on *Women's Hour*, where he discussed moving house, the Seven Deadly Sins, and "the imaginative life and its relation to everyday things". In a debate about corporal punishment, so angrily did recollections of his schooldays lead him to refute the efficacy of the cane that he knocked the microphone off the table.[25] Absent from this diverse list of topics is pacifism.

For television he would have to wait, but Michael took to radio broadcasting with immense seriousness and industry, and was rewarded by his music's becoming something of a fixture on the Third Programme. *A Child of Our Time* was featured on the station almost every year after the war. Michael wrote of the power of radio to his producer George Barnes, in unashamed support of the new channel's perceived "elitist" content:

"Nation shall speak peace unto nation"!* At least we might be able to begin with "person shall speak truth unto person" – and I

---

* The motto of the BBC's coat of arms.

mean by truth, for the moment, honesty, dignity, goodwill, and a few other imponderables. [. . .] When person speaks distinctly and singly to person, from studio to fireside, there seems to be extension of our humanity – in contrast perhaps with the fictitious means by which the BBC brings us into contact with the Grand National. [. . .] To draw men of goodwill and integrity into any fruitful relation to itself is a tremendous step that luckily can't be assessed by listening figures or otherwise.[26]

Michael made close friends of his radio producers, not least the Russian-born Anna Kallin, who had recently moved to England after decades in Germany. Kallin had been the lover of the Austrian painter Oskar Kokoschka, who agreed to provide the poster for the Polish-aid performance of *A Child of Our Time*, and eventually to paint Michael's portrait, becoming a vocal supporter: "I should dearly love to see Austria acquire [Tippett] for good [. . .] as a kind of national musical adviser."[27]

Anna Kallin was now living with a famously beautiful Russian socialite, Princess Salomea Andronikova, in a Chelsea flat gifted them by the philosopher Isaiah Berlin. Before the Russian Revolution the princess had been friends with poets such as Anna Akhmatova and Osip Mandelstam, and the influence of such writers on Michael's later music likely began with conversations in Broadcasting House that were continued in Chelsea, over the chocolate truffles that Kallin would offer her distinguished guests.

One pleasure returned to Michael was travel, after a decade spent landlocked. In 1947 or 1948 he had rekindled his friendship with Bryan Fisher, David Ayerst's brother-in-law, whom he had barely seen since the early years of the war. Bryan had since married his second wife, Irene, and they were living with their children in Corsham. He and Michael went on holiday to Ireland together; it was the first time that Michael, in his early forties and a seasoned traveller, had ever set foot in an aeroplane. As Bryan remembered,

Michael was "erratically nervous" but "after one duty free single
gin and tonic (all we could afford), as long as those engines went
droning on it all seemed tranquil".[28] Droning is an understatement
for the engine noise of 1940s planes, and cabin crew were forced
to yell at passengers through small megaphones. Bowls were placed
under every seat in readiness for the motion sickness that ensued
when aircraft dropped hundreds of feet at random, and the small
cabin was likely full of cigarette smoke. It was by the tried-and-
tested method, longer but cheaper, of ferry and train that Michael
then began to reacquaint himself with the countries of Europe. He
had the privilege, when recreational travel remained impossible for
most, of going abroad by official invitation. It was an expensive
business, exchange rates were all over the place, and only restric-
tively tiny amounts of money could be taken out of the country. But
he could now run to, or be reimbursed for, the luxury of a bunk,
even a sleeper, as he ticked off frontiers. In 1948 he went twice to
Budapest, first in June to conduct the Hungarian premiere (given in
Hungarian) of *A Child of Our Time*, and then again in October, with
the music writer Edward Dent, to sit on the international jury of
the Bartók competition and judge string quartets.[29] On the first visit
he changed trains at Prague, and while waiting for his connection
met a musician he had known previously in London, who was
desperately trying to escape Czechoslovakia, which lay behind the
Iron Curtain, for a life in America. He implored Michael to smuggle
a letter out of the country and Michael agreed, albeit nervously,
being an official visitor. On finally reaching Budapest, Michael was
invited by a singer's husband on a reckless drive along the Danube,
and the car quickly ended up, its passengers unhurt, in a ditch.
The performance of the oratorio nearly had no conductor. "Thank
God you're alive!", the British consul exclaimed. "There could have
been a serious diplomatic incident!"[30] Given the Soviet military
occupation of Hungary and the first stirrings of the Cold War, this
was very likely true. Michael was later told by a Hungarian refugee
that she had been cross-examined by secret police in a room that
lay below one of his frequent walking routes through the city.
Budapest was visibly devastated by both Allied and Axis Powers: the

bridges that spanned the river to connect Buda and Pest had been exploded by the Nazis as the city had buckled to Soviet attack, and were only partially rebuilt.

Europe's ruin, and a guilt-ridden dismay at the Holocaust that had taken place in its midst, may explain the Continental popularity of *A Child of Our Time*, which in 1946 had been twice broadcast on European radio: from Belgium in January, and from Hamburg in September. For the Hamburg performance Michael was not granted a permit to travel. Not that he minded, and he would anyway have refused to wear the army uniform required of visitors to occupied Germany. "Hamburg is not very pleasant," he wrote, "either for the conquerors or the conquered."[31] On 12 September 1947 he went to Arnhem, Holland, to hear the oratorio in a concert commemorating the battle fought in the town. He returned via Belgium for a wildly popular performance in Brussels, and two years later went to Lausanne to hear the piece on Christmas Day. *A Child of Our Time* was beginning to cement Michael's reputation abroad, and he was happy to be thought of as a European, rather than a British, composer. The oratorio had come to be considered not as music that had unforgivably advocated inaction during a necessary war, but as a work that, as once it had captured hope and desperation from within the heat of battle, could now call for a preservation of peace, and serve as a reminder of a horror to which the world should never return.

TWENTY-ONE

A Continuous High Pressure of Creation

On 13 May 1948, excerpts from Michael's new opera were performed on the Third Programme. The listing of the broadcast is the first appearance of its final title: *The Midsummer Marriage*.[1] Its composition was now the substance of his life: "Oh my! What a curious affair! Heaven knows what anyone will make of it. But it has to come."[2] Back in the early summer of 1946 he had begun to write the libretto for the first act, jotting it down in a series of thin blue exercise books. At first he planned to interleave music with spoken dialogue, but by September had changed his mind; the work was shifting towards a conventionally through-composed opera. By the end of the year the text for Act One was complete, and he began the music in the very last weeks of 1946, during a freezing winter that brought much of the country to a standstill. "The music has begun," he told William Glock at Christmas. "Season's greetings. Am rapturously happy."[3]

Unusually for Michael, who for most of his career would have the text entire more or less set in stone before starting the music, he proceeded act by act. It would take him six years to finish, composing directly into the hundreds of pages of full score, its leaves scattered with thousands of notes and furry with rubbings-out and corrections, words scrawled messily beneath the staves. He had no commission, no payment, no firm prospect of staging. This was a situation to which he was entirely used, although the promise of an opera from Michael Tippett was now all but guaranteed to arouse interest. The Royal Opera House and some European companies were asking to be sent updates on its slow progress. Act One was completed on 3 June 1949, after two and a half years' work; there followed a three-month break to finish the next chunk of the libretto, and the music was taken up again in November. Schott had by then committed to publishing the score, which soon grew to encompass three acts, of which the second was finished on 12 October 1950. Michael moved straight on to Act Three, this time working scene by scene: libretto, music, libretto, music.[4] Peter Brook, newly appointed director of productions at the Opera House, had begun to talk seriously of a staging for 1952, hoping that Benjamin Britten's successes had triggered further interest in a British opera revival. But the third act would be slow, delayed by domestic and personal upheavals.

Michael was producing a work similar and different to the one he and Douglas Newton had dreamed up together. As sole librettist he removed their play-within-a-play framework (in which two "Ancient" characters were to have presented a masque to a young chorus) and binned the partner of the mysterious forest dweller Strephon, thus losing sight of the planned octet structure. But his finished version of the first act, on which Douglas had worked the most, preserves much intact from their joint efforts, and in other places does nothing but reduce Douglas's dialogue to shorter, singable lines.[5] The original intention remained, as he wove his strange concoction of myth and reality, dream and fairy tale: to dramatise on stage a Jungian journey, in which a young couple (Mark and Jenifer), unhappily in love, cannot be married until each acknowledges the shadow and light of their own psyches.[6] Michael maintained that refusing to acknowledge the shadow, and instead projecting it on others, had been one of the causes of the recent war: "total war on its present scale is only possible because everyone is able in entire unconsciousness to project his inferior side on to the enemy."[7]

Michael was reaching for concrete images with which to reify such abstract psychological ideals. He sent Mark and Jenifer each

individually up a staircase to the light-filled sky, and through deathly
gates into the shadowy earth. Whether the metaphor be King Lear
roaming across the heath through the storm, a quest for the holy
grail or the golden fleece, or the lovers' travels through Michael's
magical forest, the journey expressed is the same: the journey to
self-knowledge, grasping at a moral or psychological framework in
a violent world. In this the opera shares the theme of much great
art: how to live, and how to be. But, like all symbolic works, it
exists on the plane of metaphor and literalness, and in this is its
magic. The symbolism stands for something, but has ultimately to
be accepted for itself.

It was soon into the writing of the first act that Michael chose to
unfold the action across the longest day and shortest night of the
year, and in alighting on 21 June he was, wittingly or unwittingly,
recalling not only the setting of his children's opera Robert of Sicily,
but also the very date on which he had been sentenced and driven
to Wormwood Scrubs. Later he said that a line from T.S. Eliot's play
The Family Reunion – "I remember a summer day of unusual heat for
this cold country" – had been "the beginning of the long adventure".[8] The setting nodded not only to A Midsummer Night's Dream but
to Wagner's Die Meistersinger; as in Shakespeare's play, the magical
and the real are intertwined. Surviving from the original scenario
were Jenifer's violent and plutocratic father, and his secretary Bella,
in love with a mechanic named Jack.* Of the magical forest dwell-
ers, there were to be the silent figure of Strephon, represented by
a dancer, and the clairvoyante out of T.S. Eliot, Madame Sosostris,
transformed into a powerful sorceress whose grand third-act aria
would bring the opera to its spectacular climax around the midsummer bonfire. After the short night's journey into day, Mark and
Jenifer realise that everything and nothing has changed all at once,

---

* Alexander Goehr comments: "Bella was modelled on my father's secretary, Pam
Hunnecks. Pam was beautiful, and at that time during the war they didn't have
any stockings, so she painted her legs with the seam. She is Bella – I know that
from Tippett himself." (Author's interview.)

that they have been given a second chance, and it is midsummer morning once more.

The central act is almost entirely taken up with a series of "Ritual Dances", featuring Strephon, transformed into hare, fish, and bird, ritually re-enacting with a female dancer a sequence of pursuit and near-capture, with the female pursuing in each case. (The sequence is an unlikely precursor of Philip Pullman's "daemons", external manifestations of the self in animal form.) The dances are strikingly reminiscent of Michael's vividly recorded dream, over a decade before, of a male fox dominated by a vixen, so clearly Wilfred Franks being "stolen" by a fiancée. And maybe the wounding departure of beloved young men to their respective wives hovers behind the dances, just as the possibility of autobiography raises its head elsewhere. Michael had split himself into four when creating his two couples, granting each, via different routes, the rapturous union and domestic harmony that he himself craved: Jack and Bella weave dreamy coils of lullaby to the children they will soon parent. It was not that his opera mirrored his life; rather he was hoping that life might conform to the opera. But just as the Ritual Dances stand for more than Michael's personal situation (they depict nature's mating game, red in tooth and claw), *The Midsummer Marriage* employs what personal resonances it contains to speak more widely. In a sense the whole opera was to be a renewing ritual: of the ancient ceding to the young, of earthly love ceding to the divine, of knowing oneself, and knowing another.

Michael called on any number of literary traditions to serve his vision of renewal and psychological healing, producing a rich melting pot of allusion to dozens of books and mythologies, some only half remembered. As a younger man he had laid down a cellar of intellectual memories from which he drank deep in later life, while frequently failing to check the labels. He toiled with some care over the libretto, now sure that he was right to undertake the text himself: "I'm learning the technique of juggling with words and music at once, but naturally words don't leap so immediately to my mind. I use much a thesaurus indeed! – but the peculiar world I am creating seems to preclude, *ab initio*, any collaboration with another. A nuisance – but one which being there, must be made a virtue of, as far as one may."⁹ As he concluded: "everything depends on getting the script right".¹⁰ Happy to profess himself an amateur when it came to libretto-writing, he welcomed the views of friends, many of whom read and commented upon drafts with such frequency and helpfulness that their advice bordered on collaboration. They were offered businesslike thanks, rather than gushing gratitude or formal acknowledgement. The arts administrator Eric Walter White, whom Michael had met via the various incarnations of the Arts Council, was the most frequent sounding board by letter, and suggested major structural alterations that Michael soon incorporated, making a close and lifelong friend in the process. Michael wrote to him: "This process of getting things right by common consent was widely followed, and successfully, in Child of Our Time. I value it very much."¹¹

But he knew that he was taking a huge risk in relying on the music to put flesh on the bones of his symbolic text, and in leaving characterisation to notes as well as to words. Not for the last time, a stage work was dictating a change in his style: the music of the opera has a new climate. Michael moved into fresh zones of musical colour to depict the magic wood of his setting, orchestrated with thick impasto, yet somehow translucent, with bubbling undercurrents of woodwind and brass audible beneath the surface layer of melody. Clearly discernible is the influence of the early ballets of Stravinsky, the woodwind fizz of Petrushka adding brightness to Michael's palette. And where once the music of Paul Hindemith could inspire in him a slightly greyscale focus on counterpoint, now it was the embellished chorales of the German composer's Mathis der Maler symphony that sang in his work. But the opera's style was Michael's own, lushly melodic and freshly luminous, seizing hold of certain words, "love", "dance", and lavishly dilating them into rapturous outpourings. New in his orchestration was an attention not only to notes but to their resonance and afterglow: sunspots from the celesta or glockenspiel, flutes and oboes ruffling the lakes, the sun and moon emerging from the clouds in great rays of brass. After a dawn chorus from the strings, delicate and dewy, the chorus dances off singing the opera's final words, taken from Yeats's "Lapis Lazuli": "All things fall and are built again | And those that build them again are gay." As the words fade into the distance, a chorale is steadily unspooled beneath whizzing strings, before a culminating burst of A major for full orchestra. It was the key signature that, in his *Fantasia on a Theme of Handel* ten years before, Michael had chosen for the variation depicting Francesca Allinson. The opera's music is so redolent of sheerest joy that it could only have been written by one who had experienced the deepest grief.

The score has the spontaneous quality that denotes years of revision and hard work. What gives the impression of having poured from Michael in a dazzling stream, described by the critic David Cairns as a "flood of lyrical invention rarely equalled in twentieth-century art", was an intense agony of creation.[12] *The Midsummer Marriage*'s 150 minutes of music were composed (roughly speaking, and allowing for holidays and distractions) across 2,000 morning sessions of work, meaning that Michael wrote about five seconds of music, a matter of a few bars, each day. Proceeding in such tiny stitches, he had to hold the larger musical canvas in his head for many years, composing on a scale at once epic and miniature. Where lack of facility might have deterred another with similar skills and weaknesses, once again subservience to inspiration won through, by sheer grit, and his characteristic mixture of self-confidence and uncertainty. One year rolled into the next and the slow pace at which he worked necessitated major revisions to earlier scenes, as his thoughts and style developed over time. He composed with the body as well as the mind, and his deep-seated sense of purpose lay beneath a surface of nerves and frustration that frequently made him ill, more so for *The Midsummer Marriage* than for any other work he had yet written. Prolonged sitting damaged, or so he thought, his digestion, but he was willing to admit the psychosomatic nature of his illnesses, brought on by overwork and a fear that he could not do justice to the opera that had lain excitedly dormant for so long. As if searching for a friend who would understand the labours of composition, he wrote most openly of the toil to Benjamin Britten:

I find I suffer now from a deep-seated fatigue that's always round
the corner, waiting to pounce. I have never kept so long at one
huge continuous invention. It isn't complicated. I don't seem to
use anything but common chords. And there's no counterpoint!!
[. . .] I've never (since the Child) been so cursed by a work,
which seems to live [inside] me, with all its stage trappings into
the bargain. [. . .] I'm very happy and cheerful, though I get
depressive moments due to this so unexpectedly long wait – I
imagined it would have been quicker. But there's been no stop-
page, only a continuous high pressure of creation.[13]

Michael was as ready and willing a collaborator as he had ever
been. John Minchinton was his lover in private and assistant in
public; in this latter role he was immensely helpful, and did a great
deal of copying from Michael's pencil score into ink. There was
also Michael Tillett, a student at the Royal College of Music who
had been roped in to play viola in the Morley College Orchestra,
before being persuaded to join the choir and – as he remembered
it – "sing under the baton of its persuasive conductor, hitherto
unknown to me, whose name my own so ridiculously resembled".
Eventually he left the choir to take up a teaching job in Highgate,
and Michael soon asked him whether he might "have a crack" at
a piano reduction of The Midsummer Marriage. Tillett examined the
orchestral score with excited alarm, but agreed:

It amazes me to remember what casual treatment the various
sections of this precious manuscript received, going to and fro in
the same large battered envelope, the address continually being
changed, but only the l's and p's of the surname being altered
and the original "Mr Michael . . ." remaining constant! [. . .] A
great shriek of laughter is my earliest recollection of working for
Tippett, a shriek provoked by the composer hearing the great A
major choral outburst greeting the sun in the first scene of The
Midsummer Marriage being played mistakenly.[14]

Tillett ended up an assistant to the composer for life, a musical mid-wife, quietly indispensable during the difficult birth of numerous pieces, proof-reading, editing. He was a constant sounding board, and "the only other person in the world", Michael admitted, "who knows the music as I do – or even better".[15] Michael was willing to concede mistakes and agreed readily to the corrections and suggestions of Tillett and others, almost as if he were the ringleader of a group effort to realise the opera he had imagined. The notes were barely the point, merely a written means to an audible end. "I shan't mind what you say," he told Tillett, "so long as you speak your truth."[16] He proceeded with a kind of slapdash punctiliousness, splashing about with any number of suggestions or ideas, no detail too small, until he had reached the effect he wanted.

Also of importance in the opera's long creation was Walter Goehr, Michael's loyal colleague and supporter from Morley College, now living with his family in Buckinghamshire, whither Michael often made the train ride north-west to visit him, attempting frequently to dodge the fare, with mixed success. Goehr's son, Alexander, turned eighteen in 1950, and had compositional ambitions that his father largely scorned. It was Michael whom he found the more supportive and persuasive presence:

> I became a composer – or largely – because of Tippett. [When called up in 1950] I went and became a conscientious objector, rather under his influence, and he sent me to the Peace Pledge Union. Tippett was incredibly contagious from when I was a schoolboy – he had an irresistible personality. My father – and this I know both from having watched it, and also I can *hear* it – was instrumental in the orchestration of The Midsummer Marriage. Tippett came every three weeks with the latest bit of score, and my father – who was a better composer than Tippett, but with no talent and no originality – reharmonised, redid the voice parts, and above all he reorchestrated.[17]

Alexander Goehr, now an eminent composer, admits his "family prejudice" (the score of The Midsummer Marriage is in no hand other than Michael's own). But it is highly likely that Michael willingly took advice or imbibed techniques from Walter. Their relationship, however, was not to last. It had been Walter's suggestion to extract the four Ritual Dances into a separate concert work, of which he became the dedicatee. "I am shocked by the cavalier treatment of my father," says Alexander. "The fallout was very simple. At that time Tippett was flirting with Paul Sacher and gave Sacher the first performance of the Dances, which he did the day before my father had arranged to give the first performance [at the BBC]. And my father found that unforgiveable. And that was that."[18] Paul Sacher, a rich and influential Swiss conductor, premiered the *Ritual Dances* on 13 February 1953, in Basel. Privately Michael began to profess himself unsure of Walter Goehr's abilities, and although he proclaimed in 1950 that "from Goehr alone in this country have I received, without asking for it, just this unfailing effort and pains", by 1956 he was describing Goehr as a "very odd conductor", and finding his performances "rather horrid".[19] Walter Goehr died, suddenly, just four years later, and Michael travelled to York to attend his memorial concert, at which *A Child of Our Time* was performed.

Michael allowed just two pieces to interrupt composition of *The Midsummer Marriage*, and both were in some way owing to Benjamin Britten. Mainly he had turned down all commissions, refusing to write a piece for the Third Programme's first anniversary, and rejecting an approach "from York Minster (for 1951) and the horribly tempting fee!"[20] In 1948 Pears and Britten, who still performed intermittently at Morley College, had joined with the librettist and producer Eric Crozier to found the first Aldeburgh Festival of Music and the Arts. Michael's dedication to the opera led to his rejecting their offer to write a piece for the opening season and his String Quartet No. 2 was programmed instead. He had become newly wary of Britten after the success of *Peter Grimes*, thinking the resulting fame had made its composer rather precious. Aware that their compositional lives were diverging, he was also suspicious of Britten's ever-growing circle of admirers, finding them a rather dubious clique liable to poison the mind of their god against his perceived competition. He disagreed with the critics' view that Britten had returned opera to England, and admitted experiencing "momentary returnings and twinges of adolescent envy" at *Peter Grimes*'s success, but "being me, it's all pretty mild!"[21] He had reservations about the opera – "*Grimes* libretto is bad I think" – and was prophetically concerned about a possible backlash over the title character's complex relationship with juvenile apprentices and by implication Britten's own tangled affections for pre-pubescent boys.[22] His objection to Britten's operas, as they appeared over the next thirty years, was less to the music than to their topics. For him, childhood had been something to escape rather than preserve, and Britten's veneration of innocence could be the polar opposite of Michael's journeys towards knowledge. Principally, they disagreed on the very nature of opera libretto. Michael wrote to the radio producer George Barnes:

> What I want for Ben is that he should come to grips a bit more with the technique of "libretto", because I suspect that lies behind the technique of opera itself: for the composer as well as the librettist. For heaven's sake don't turn his attention back to good poetry and high thinking! [. . .] *Herring** is in trouble largely from the flatness – so that the music seems always to be "setting a play to music", not to be the principal vehicle of the comic imagination.[23]

After the premiere of Britten's *The Rape of Lucretia* in 1946, Michael had cheerily savaged Ronald Duncan's libretto both in person and by letter. Specifically, he suggested a "discussion of one scene: the arrival of Junius and Collatinus", which he thought could be further

---

* Britten's opera *Albert Herring* (1946–7), with a libretto by Eric Crozier after de Maupassant; the work depicts a grocer being elected May King by a band of eccentric locals, after no young woman is found worthy to be May Queen.

exploited: "I have told you a lot of good things [. . . and] don't suppose they'll get all over to you, because our mental processes are so different. But I should feel lacking in friendship if I didn't hand you over all I have, as far as I can."[24] Britten was wounded by the response to *Lucretia* in general, but, far from bridling at Michael's somewhat lordly tone, was soon writing to a friend of the changes he wanted to make in "the scene between Junius and Collatinus, Act I".[25] Three months later, on 27 January 1947, Michael conducted Britten's *Rejoice in the Lamb* for a radio broadcast. The friendship seems to have been in nothing but good repair, and Britten continued to pass commissions Michael's way. When in the autumn of 1948 he was unable to accept an invitation from the BBC to write a work celebrating the birth of Princess Elizabeth's first child, he suggested Michael might welcome the opportunity (and, by implication, the fee). Come October, Michael, the one-time Trotskyist, had agreed to write the piece, and with the royal arrival due in a matter of weeks, time was tight. The five movements of his *Suite for the Birthday of Prince Charles* were mainly produced by plundering his back catalogue, and he interwove material from *Robin Hood* and *Robert of Sicily* with arrangements of lullabies, fertility songs, and the hymn tunes and trumpet fanfares heard at Elizabeth's wedding. Suspicions that rehashing material from his intermittently communist early opera was intended to undercut the royal birth are stilled by a few moments in the suite's company: it contains nothing but delight. If its origins were a private joke, they were no more than that, and in fact the material from *Robin Hood* that Michael used for the finale eventually dissatisfied him so much that he composed an alternative using Welsh folk-songs, before returning to the original and revising it into submission.

The commission was surely accepted in the spirit of furthering his reputation rather than of dedicated royalism. His revolutionary past was well behind him, and he was evidently thought by the BBC a suitable composer, even though a second choice, to mark such an important occasion. The sleeping dog of his conscientious objection was allowed to lie, and he had made the leap from left-wing rebel to uneasy Establishment figure. The suite was finished in time for Adrian Boult to pre-record it with the BBC Symphony Orchestra, and was broadcast on 15 November 1948, the day after Charles's birth. It featured in a concert early the following year and the *Times* reviewer, who Michael was coming to think bore a distinct grudge against his music, found it the least successful piece in the programme. But the audience response was ecstatic, and there were calls for an encore. Michael was delighted, feeling it a good omen for the shift in his music that *The Midsummer Marriage* had engendered.[26]

Nineteen forty-nine he dedicated as much as possible to the opera, while lessening as best he could his commitments to Morley College. Then, in March 1950, he began to plan a series of songs for Peter Pears to perform with Britten. Michael was at last turning to a memorial composition for Francesca Allinson, as the fifth anniversary of her death loomed ahead. He obtained a volume of Second World War poetry published that year called *For Your Tomorrow*, and picked out two poems by Sidney Keyes, who, sent to fight in the Tunisian Campaign, had been killed in 1943, aged twenty. Poets were eligible for inclusion in the anthology only if they had been to public school and, suspicious of such exclusivity, Michael looked elsewhere and chose two further poems, by the Welsh poet Alun Lewis. A grammar-school boy, Lewis had originally been a pacifist, willing only to join the army's Royal Engineers, but a change of mind saw him commissioned to a battalion and sent to Burma, where in March 1944 he was shot in the head, sustaining a wound from which it took him six hours to die, four months before his thirtieth birthday.

So much post-war music, including Michael's own, had been dedicated to renewal, that there was little composed following the Second World War to match the slew of commemorative pieces that emerged from the First. Michael now had words for a quartet of songs that would go some way towards restoring the balance, and he intercut Alun Lewis's poems of hopeful compassion with the dread resignation of Sidney Keyes. The fates of the two poets hover behind the music as much as the fate of Francesca, the three united as war casualties. The songs were to be a requiem both public and personal, gathered under the working title of *For Your Tomorrow*. There survives in Michael's sketches for them a musical refrain using the epitaph on the Kohima War Cemetery: "When you go home, tell them of us and say, For your tomorrow, we gave our today."[27] The refrain was soon discarded, and the cycle renamed after one of the poems: *The Heart's Assurance*. The first two songs were completed by April 1950. "Though death taps down every street", as the opening song runs, we are to remember that "life has trembled in a kiss | from genesis to genesis, | and what's transfigured will live on | long after death has come and gone." Michael strung these lines along the delicate branch of a resolute and unchanging high E natural, supposedly Pears's best note. Soon a Keyes poem states with certainty: "O never trust the heart's assurance | Trust only the heart's fear." (Here a jagged dance of a vocal line.) Michael worked dispiritedly, and was dismissive of what he had achieved so far: "it's no major work". Maintaining a consistent voice throughout *The Midsummer Marriage*'s lengthy composition was, he thought, constraining his development. The cycle "doesn't reach an inch forward, and that's that. All that can be said is that the years at the opera have produced an easiness, of which I suppose the songs may be a hangover."[28]

In May, seemingly overwrought by work, he was hospitalised with hepatitis and took most of the summer to recover, nursed back to health by John Minchinton's mother.[29] He returned to work slowly, prioritising the opera's central act, the music of which bears no trace of the forced interregnum. He spent much of his recuperation with Britten and Pears, going with John Minchinton in early July to Crag House, the couple's home on the pebbled Suffolk seafront of their beloved Aldeburgh. Britten was deep in the first act of his seafaring opera *Billy Budd*, and its co-librettist, E.M. Forster, was also staying. A conscientious objector in the First World War, Forster had much in common with Michael, and sexually they were more united than they might have admitted to each other. "I want to love a strong young man of the lower classes," Forster had confided in his journal, "and be loved by him and even hurt by him."[30] The admission encapsulated Michael's own situation to some degree, and afterwards the two retained an affectionate acquaintance. "I haven't grown to your kind of sensibility yet," Michael later told him, "but guess a bit what may be the 'extended universe' into which you push your mind."[31]

Forster was in considerable pain from a recent prostate operation and his collaboration with Britten was not plain sailing. It is hard to imagine the atmosphere in Crag House was made any easier by Michael's pointing out, amid gales of laughter, the double entendre in an early draft of Billy Budd's libretto: "Clear the decks of seamen!"[32] But the visit, which coincided with that year's Aldeburgh Festival, was evidently an enjoyable one, Britten composing in his studio, the North Sea rolling beyond, Michael and Morgan (as Forster was known) deep in discussion the while. Michael paid another visit to Crag House in the autumn, arriving on 16 October. He was between the second and third acts of The Midsummer Marriage, and after so long spent in the isolation of Oxted was pondering a house move. On 22 October he and Britten went house-hunting in Sudbury, a Suffolk town just close and distant enough to suit their deep but now slightly careful friendship. "A nice thought", Britten told a friend, "that [Michael will] be near, and a nice acquisition for Suffolk music!"[33]

On returning home, Michael finally went back to work on The Heart's Assurance, and finished the third song early in 1951. Setting Lewis's "Compassion", it depicts the nursing of a wounded soldier by a brave woman, with "lucid simple hands". The song, which manages to be both tender and monolithic, suddenly made the cycle so heavy as to be imbalanced, and Michael quickly decided to insert a fleet-footed scherzo using Alun Lewis's "The Dancer", before embarking on what was now the fifth and final song: "Remember Your Lovers", written by the eighteen-year-old Sidney Keyes in an exam hall after he had finished a paper early. Michael completed The Heart's Assurance not early but just about on time, in the first days of April. The premiere was at the Wigmore Hall on 7 May. The Times considered some of the vocal writing overdone, but believed the music "developed after its own fashion the incandescence which is one test of a song's quality".[34] Peter Pears found the songs overwrought, with a fuzzy piano part, and Imogen Holst recorded in her diary that Britten also had doubts about the piece, that the songs "didn't always make sense" and that the ending "was impossible vocally [. . .] the <u>notes</u> were wrong – it was a weak cadence".[35]

In 1952 Elisabeth Schwarzkopf agreed to record *The Heart's Assurance* after Michael suggested a woman's voice might better suit the text. But when timetables clashed Peter Pears stepped into the breach.[36] Britten, however, relinquished accompanying duties to the Australi-an virtuoso Noel Mewton-Wood, who had played for demonstrative run-throughs of *The Midsummer Marriage*, and would have become an ideal pianist for Michael's music. In 1953, distraught by the death from appendicitis of his lover Bill Fedricks, Mewton-Wood killed himself, and *The Heart's Assurance* became inexorably linked to another suicide. In a painful echo of Francesca Allinson's death, Mewton-Wood had drunk cyanide. It was "difficult not to be despairing about Noel", Michael thought, "what a waste! Those records become precious."[37] He was asked by his old friend John Amis to write a piece for Mewton-Wood's memorial concert, but replied: "All that I could say of Noel and his tragic death is already in *The Heart's Assurance* – especially song five, that's the last. I cannot recreate the emotion in a lesser, or more personal, form now. So I must leave it."[38]

Each verse of the fifth song opens with an address to the fallen "young men", which the tenor sings in a phrase that quotes the opening notes of the "Last Post". The poem concludes:

> We led you out of terror tenderly
> And fooled you into peace with our soft words
> And gave you all we had and let you die.
> Young men drunk with death's unquenchable wisdom,
> Remember your lovers who gave you more than love.

The music mirrors the falsely soothing tenderness with which this verse opens, before blazing: fearsome in its anger, overwhelming in its grief. The refrain ("young men . . .") appears three times unaccompanied, the voice widowed from its partner, but on the final call of the tenor the piano explodes beneath, before the song retreats into the hollow-eyed resignation of bereavement. In stark contrast to The Midsummer Marriage the conclusion of The Heart's Assurance is achingly bleak. The tenderness and optimism of what has gone before must remain in the memory if we are to believe that the cycle's theme may not only be, as Michael described it, "love under the shadow of death", but also death under the light of love.[39] The music must bravely contradict the verses and remind us that the heart's assurance might be trustworthy after all, even in the face of deep grief. The songs were a cry from the heart for what had been lost, and for what Michael believed. He told Britten:

> In this last song, "Remember Your Lovers", I seem so clearly to hear Peter calling to the young men in the fields of death, even though formally it may be supposed to be a woman. I can't quite tell why, but the man's voice seems right-er — and Peter's voice particularly. There are one or two happy "quotations" from you — turns of phrase which strike my ear as having been learnt from the master! Anyhow Francesca would bless you for it. In the letter she left behind for me she wrote: keep a place warm for me in your heart. That's just what happened and what the songs express — but for all of us lovers, so to speak. I think it could only be possible now that the wound is healing and I can think of her death without resentment.[40]

Forty-four years later, a concert was held at the Wigmore Hall in celebration of Michael Tippett's ninetieth birthday. One critic praised The Heart's Assurance, which concluded the evening, as "a great work: one of the finest song cycles in the English language".[41] White-haired, frail, and with, by then, a number of departed lovers to remember, Michael was helped from his seat and onto the platform, where he stood amid the applause, and wept.

TWENTY-TWO

Nel Mezzo del Cammin
di Nostra Vita

Not for the first or last time in his life, Michael was seriously in debt. Over the course of five years he had eaten through his inheritance from Francesca Allinson, having provided financial support not only to friends but to the Morley College concerts. His ruthless and unpaid dedication to the opera had led him to neglect money-earning work, and he paid for the assistance of John Minchinton and Michael Tillett out of his own pocket. He wrote to his loyal friend David Ayerst with a brisk and unwheedling request outlining the seriousness of the situation: "what really, without sentimentality, can you manage about my debt settlement? I shall be short of a clear £500." Today the sum would nudge £16,000. Michael told David that he had had to give notice to the bank of his

intention to clear the guarantee (which costs £1 a week) and settle – pending bankruptcy petition. If you can lend me something at a fixed rate, that would be more than nice. I would, I admit, much prefer, if that's not too selfish, to carry the debt for a while, and try to pay it off when (*hoffentlich*) [hopefully] lump sums come in from the first broadcasts of the opera. I don't know whether I'm very extravagant, but I realise that I'm living a very regular regimen, which is more continuously applied to composition than ever before.[1]

It is hard to imagine David Ayerst's teacher's wage and growing family allowing him to help all that much, though nor will he have begrudged Michael the assistance.

The pressure to move had become acute, in that if Michael bought a house with his mother, running costs could be shared. He had lived in Oxted for over twenty years, and had outgrown his bungalow. In November 1950, while in the middle of *The Heart's Assurance*, he had put Whitegates Cottages on the market, offering the now-renovated buildings at £2,500 for a private sale. It was perhaps through an unconscious sense of self-preservation that he abandoned the idea of moving to Suffolk (although Britten had sent him details of a house even closer to Aldeburgh, in East Bergholt). Eventually Michael settled for a large manor near the town of Wadhurst in East Sussex, a few miles south of Tunbridge Wells, whence a train, steam at first, but soon a diesel locomotive, could speed him to London.

All that can be seen of Tidebrook Manor from the surrounding valleys of the High Weald is the large cream box of its north-west wing, the Victorian frontage hiding its original fifteenth-century timber-framed building. It was surrounded by a wealth of grounds, outbuildings, even oast houses, much of which could be let to raise income. The manor had cost £5,350, of which £3,300 was provided by Isabel, and Michael paid the balance with the capital raised from the Oxted sale, leaving him barely enough for the expenditure of the move and the endless renovation and repair that such a large property required. (It had been bought from the Canadian army, and was badly dilapidated.) He and Isabel had moved in mid-December 1950, and despite the lack of heat or furniture Michael was deliriously happy with the new domestic set-up, and with his large composition studio, in which he soon finished the last three songs of *The Heart's Assurance*, while through the window were what estate agents call "far-reaching views" over the South Downs and Ashdown Forest.[2]

One of his first visitors was Evelyn Maude, beloved friend and supporter for some three decades. Pushing sixty and with children flying the nest, she and her husband had downsized from their large family house but remained in Oxted, and were enjoying grandparenthood. She wrote to her daughter:

> The house is <u>huge</u> [. . .], with plaster falling off in all directions, a wilderness of a garden, about eight or ten acres of "grounds" or "park", rather like Sleeping Beauty's must have been, quarter of a mile of drive, two enormous rooms (one each) on the ground floor [. . .] and the first floor of the main house completely uninhabitable with water coming through the roof! [. . .] At present [Michael] is thrilled with it all and doing a lot of writing and not going to London more than once in ten days or so. For heating they have endless quantities of dead trees which go on to the fire in pieces weighing about half a hundredweight at a time, and coke and Calor gas for cooking. Lamps at present, but electricity on the way from the next door farm.[3]

John Minchinton and his mother, never permanent residents, paid frequent visits. The house had a healing effect on Michael, whose affection for his nearest and dearest redoubled: "I love [John] very dearly and am endlessly loyal." And although later he complained about Isabel's eccentricity, insisting that she had mixed laxatives into visitors' food and generally behaved badly, for a while at least, bathed in the newness of Tidebrook, his feelings softened: "I find that I've become unexpectedly close to my mother [. . .] I do believe the new move to be a symbol of new life. Very exciting."[4]

Michael's vision for the manor was clear enough, and emerges from his attraction to the counter-communities of conscientious objectors that had sprung up during the war and which, in other guises, were remaining popular throughout the 1950s: a large house with many rooms, a music studio, and an unlocked door, full to the brim with like-minded thinkers, and Michael as the benign patriarch, earning enough, or so he hoped, to make sure everyone was comfortable. James Hutt was thirty years old, and had been a conscientious objector during the war, helping with the rebuilding of Michael's bungalow after the bomb. He moved into the farmhouse at the back of the manor, with his wife Thelma and their three children. In exchange for low rents and a small wage the couple acted as workmen, housekeepers, and cooks. Michael adored watching the junior Hutts queueing to catch the bus to school: "I was enchanted to see them all line up to be embraced by their parents – something I hadn't experienced in my childhood."[5] The first months in the new house were characterised by the hard work of unpacking and household maintenance, and by composition and illness. Not long after an early summer holiday with John Minchinton to Portofino, a glandular swelling in Michael's groin led to an incapacitated foot and the usual stomach trouble, confining him to bed. So low did he sink that he appears to have embarked upon another period of dream analysis. "I'm having to get internal things free again," he wrote that summer, "which I try to do just by observation and cogitation of dream material."[6] He considered his mental state a result of stresses domestic and professional, and was "getting very nearly bored" with The Midsummer Marriage – "must finish it now or never" – professing he wouldn't be "surprised if in the end the opera is a white elephant! But one never knows. And it might come to mean something to a public not yet born."[7]

That was in early July 1951. The century was at a midpoint. Michael, forty-six and a half years old, was also at the exact midpoint, could he have known it, of his ninety-three years. Slowly he was making the inexorable shift that comes to all successful artists: having spent time earning money in order to be able to work, he could now work to earn money. His fame was increasing. On 24 August his music was played at the Proms for the first time. That summer the Festival of Britain was held, its epicentre a national exhibition on the South Bank of London attended by millions. It was a last gasp of the stuttering Labour government, organised to prove the country's recovery from the war, and to promote advances in arts and science. An aluminium obelisk, like a huge metal blade of grass, nearly ninety metres high and known as the Skylon, was erected by the Thames, looking as if it would spring into the air. As part of the festival, in the concrete cube of the newly opened Festival Hall, Michael led his Morley choir in A Child of Our Time and the British premiere of Stravinsky's Babel. But his loyalty to Morley was wavering. Eva Hubback, the supportive principal to whom he had owed a great deal, had died in 1949, and the commitment had become an expense and a distraction. The college was still using much temporary accommodation after the bomb, and the Ministry of Education rejected its repeated requests to rebuild. After twenty years' involvement with Morley College, Michael resigned as director of music in the autumn of 1951, handing over the post to the composer Peter Racine Fricker.

Back at Tidebrook there was the addition of an eighth permanent resident in the form of Paul Dienes, a Hungarian mathematician and poet whom Michael had known since the 1930s. During Hungary's unstable years between the wars Dienes had been charged with restructuring university education in the short-lived communist government of the Hungarian Soviet Republic; on the Republic's collapse he fled to western Europe. His influence on Michael's work had been important, from his contagious enthusiasm for Bartók, whom he had known personally, to his recommendation of the von Horváth novella that gave *A Child of Our Time* its title. He had written entire lines of the oratorio's libretto, and in suggesting Valéry's poem "La Pythie" had crystallised the scene of *The Midsummer Marriage* featuring Madame Sosostris.[8] Now nearing seventy, Dienes had separated from his wife (the influential artist Sari Dienes), and was recovering from a series of heart attacks. Michael had extended the invitation in the hopes of lessening Paul's loneliness, but Paul threw himself into housework and gardening with such energy that Michael thought he was trying to provoke a fatal attack and end it all. Soon the inevitable happened. Paul died on 26 March 1952, after only six months at Tidebrook, just as Michael was composing the third act of *The Midsummer Marriage*, in which King Fisher falls dead: "For which of you", says the She-Ancient, as if addressing her creator, "do minister with love to the dying under the broken house?"[9]

The practical realities of lived-out fantasies began to afflict the broken house of Tidebrook. The Hutts found themselves continually unable to pay their rent, the bills went unattended, and the house crumbled and froze. Nor could James Hutt – known as Jim – take in his stride the increasingly irascible behaviour of John

Minchinton, and the eccentricities of Isabel. "I had to take the Hutts mildly to task, or to enquiry at least, as to the mounting unpaid bills," Michael admitted to David Ayerst. "The upshot is that they want to go. The reason being that they can't make an economic go of it at the present rate of living and out of what they get. That John has emotionally poisoned the atmosphere for them, and Jim believes 'gets all the money'. Jim doesn't wish to go on 'under the same roof as John'. In this respect he feels he has been 'let down', etc, etc. That's that."[10] The resulting financial strain did little to assuage Michael's desire, bordering on need, for frequent holidays. Travel was, he believed, almost the only cure for the composition-induced illnesses that had followed him from Surrey to Sussex, and hang the cost: "It'll mean a major financial crisis, [but] I feel I shall never get to the South and the remains of Greece unless I just go."[11] Eventually he realised he would have to "sell up securities to keep myself at least in the next five years or so; to use my energies for composition while I am in my prime – and risk being penniless afterwards. It's a somewhat frightening decision – but I can't see how else to go forward."[12]

After the Hutts, who left in September 1952, came the Berberichs, a German family who had escaped occupied East Germany, and who brought with them their young son, Horst. "How equable and satisfactory life has been, and seems in prospect of being," Michael thought, hopeful once again. "The Berberichs are really turning out trumps – the garden is stocked – cockerels fattening – pullets' eggs to come – and with a very gracious atmosphere that is a great comfort and pleasure."[13] There were arguments and battles, as in any large household, and Isabel, arthritic and querulous, limped around the house complaining that the dogs were underfed and the housekeeping shoddy, all the while sniping at Mrs Minchinton, whose eccentricity she seemed to take as a challenge to outdo. Matters became bleakly farcical. "My mama", Michael moaned to his radio producer Anna Kallin, "blew up with the Berberichs and they wanted to go. I made a fearful scene, and felt quite stuck, and everyone recovered themselves, and my mama fell in the drive and may have fractured her shoulders and is slightly incapacitated,

while John's mama, whom he has been treating – I consider mis-
guidedly – with molasses, has just gone to bed at 9.30 in the
morning."[14] But even in hot-headed rows there was a reminder of
companionship, and Michael suddenly found himself experiencing
the domestic contentment he had always craved. For the very first
time in his letters there is evidence of his marking festivities, as on
Christmas Eve, when he anticipated in quasi-paternal pleasure the
celebration with the Tidebrook family, delighting in the newness
of decorations and gifts and ritual, all in the company of an excited
child: "Today I have stopped all thought of music – though John
doesn't come till the evening. Then we have a German Christmas
eve – with a tree and holly and a crib and presents – Horst counts
the hours, and will soon count the minutes. His bicycle stands in
John's room."[15]

"Finishing *The Midsummer Marriage*", Michael wrote, "is like coming
out of a long dream into a grey reality."[16] The last nineteen months
of composition had been at Tidebrook, where he had made a final
push in a plague of dizziness, stiffness, and a stomach pain so bad
that he had consented, feeling sure he had cancer, to have an X-ray
– which showed nothing wrong. "I wrote to my German publisher
and said 'I can't go on'."[17] He couldn't go on, but he went on, and
at half past seven on the evening of 11 October 1952 completed the
six years of work and thirteen years of thought that had produced
his first major opera. The following day he found a large postcard
of a rather garish toucan and sent it to Anna Kallin with just three
words written on the back: "It is finished."[18] The paper-and-ink
scores ran to a total of 1,140 handwritten pages.[19] There was soon
to come the long, steady slog of putting it on stage, but first
there was an endless round of musical bureaucracy, of orchestral
parts and piano reductions, of proof-reading and publishing, and
all amid the strange anticlimax of completion. Returning to a score
after it was finished was, Michael thought, "rather like the return
of a dog to vomit".[20]

The tension in *The Midsummer Marriage* between the theatrical magic of its setting and its atheistic humanist psychology had resolved itself into a commitment to and reminder of the healing power of art, at a time when the idea of a national culture, and the role of art in society, was in flux. Dreamed up on the cusp of war, prepared throughout the conflict, and composed for all but a year during the post-war Labour government, the opera had ended as an expression of psychological renewal, indelibly of the post-war period, and an anomaly amid much post-war art, still dark with the horror of war. Its embrace was wide, covering its present, past, and future: it expressed the rebirth of the 1950s, while being struck through with the horrors of the 1940s, and predictive of the freedoms of the 1960s. A tonic for the age of austerity, it also caught the ebullient mood of renewal and is bathed, like the years in which it was composed, in the glow of peace, the shadow of war, the prospect of renewal, and the memory of loss.

There were dents in the social altruism of the post-war years. A colder wind began to blow, and health charges were imposed to meet increased defence spending. In October 1951 Winston Churchill had led the Conservative Party back into power. The Skylon, considered a symbol of the short-lived Labour government, was dismantled and sold for scrap. While enough steam had been generated by Labour's social innovations to carry things forward, social services were deprived of resources. In October 1952, just eight days before Michael finished the opera, the first British atomic device was successfully detonated off Western Australia. At none of this could Michael rejoice, and he worried about the "deep, deep malaise in society that's throwing everything, even art, into question".[21] But this was a minority view. The year had brought a new queen. It was a new Elizabethan age. To many the young monarch seemed the perfect emblem of the country's growing prosperity. Michael's music, so well suited to celebration, so expressive of new dawns, became bound up in the country's rejoicing. In December 1952, as a Great Smog descended on London killing thousands, he and Christopher Fry suggested to the BBC that they might collaborate on a cantata to celebrate the coronation, with an idea it could

be sung by Kathleen Ferrier. Fry penned some suitable verses about
past queens of Britain, and the BBC accepted at once. Ferrier said
she was "very much intrigued" and "ready to learn it and sing it"
for a concert just after the coronation.[22] But Michael's most pressing
concern was a piece he had already begun for the Edinburgh Festival to celebrate the tercentenary of the Italian Baroque composer
Arcangelo Corelli. He decided to abandon the cantata, despite its
being the more high-profile commission, and by the time of the
coronation Ferrier was dying of cancer in a London hospital.

At the end of April 1953, Michael's *Suite for the Birthday of Prince
Charles* was used for a new ballet in honour of Queen Elizabeth's
birthday, conducted by Norman Del Mar, one of a younger generation soon to discover Michael's music anew.[23] And Michael did
manage to collaborate with Christopher Fry in celebration of the
coronation: they were one of nine composer–poet pairings asked
for a contribution to a series entitled *A Garland for the Queen*. Fry wrote
a verse called "Dance Clarion Air", from which Michael fashioned a
jubilant madrigal, full of echoes and peals. *A Garland for the Queen* was
performed at the Festival Hall on the eve of Coronation Day, which
dawned on 2 June 1953. It seems unlikely that Michael rushed
to purchase a television set in order to watch the service, which
was viewed by an estimated 20 million. In the days following the
coronation, he went straight to St Ives in Cornwall, and it was all
because of the composer Priaulx Rainier.

Priaulx was a vital figure in Michael's life, and another who has
been given short shrift in accounts of it. Born on 3 February 1903,
she was six months Francesca Allinson's junior, and although she
was nothing so crude as a replacement, she filled the Francesca-
shaped void in Michael's life; nevertheless he was quick to point
out that "Francesca, by the way, was all almost that Priaulx is not:
fastidious, elegant and feminine."[24] He had met Priaulx on the
musical scene in the last years of the war, and although she had
flicked in and out of his social circle, it was not until 1947, when
Michael commissioned her *Sinfonia da Camera* for Morley College, that
they became close.[25]

She was born in a village in Natal, a British colony in south-eastern

South Africa, and a childhood spent among sunlight and rainstorms, listening to the clicks and cries of calling insects and spoken Zulu, had a great influence on her compositions. Despite spending most of her life in Britain, she retained a foreign unease, a sense of being at right angles to British music and society, which surely struck a chord with Michael. At seventeen she had won a scholarship to study violin at the Royal Academy of Music. Soon she settled permanently in England to teach violin, until a bad car smash left her temporarily unable to play, and she turned, now in her late thirties, to composition. After a bout of intensive study with Nadia Boulanger, Priaulx wrote a string quartet; its eventual premiere, at the Wigmore Hall in 1944, was immediately well received. "Had Miss Rainier written nothing but the first movement," wrote William Glock, "she would still be one of our best composers."[26] At Michael's recommendation Priaulx was signed by Schott; its eventual director, Sally Groves, remembers her as "very beautiful, quite masculine, and openly lesbian, in a very quiet, dignified way. I think of a very poised, calm, beautiful woman. Quite quizzical. She had quite a high voice, from another age, quite clipped and precise."[27] Others remember her sense of fun, and vivid, snorting laugh. In 1949 she was introduced to the sculptor Barbara Hepworth, and soon became an integral member of the artists' community that Hepworth, with her husband Ben Nicholson, had formed in St Ives.

Like Michael, Priaulx was a slow worker, and, as for him, the process of notating sounds she heard in her head was an arduous one. He wrote to her conspiratorially of "our general inadequacies compared with the great", and while the phrase may contain a knowing swipe at composers whose facility covered a perceived thinness of vision (Britten the obvious candidate, though they were mutual in their admiration of him), it nudged at a truism.[28] Michael would later remember Priaulx as her own worst enemy, setting herself impossible goals to which she could not live up, leaving her depressed and the music unfinished. She lacked, he thought, "the necessary obsessive single-mindedness" that composition required, and her scores were often chaotic.[29] Today a diagnosis of dyslexia might explain the slips and stumbles in Priaulx's manuscripts. The

organisation of day-to-day life could likewise defeat her, and her
vagueness and eccentricity could madden as it could enchant. Her
catalogue is not long, and the scale of her pieces usually small.
The sharp granite edges of her music, beautifully as they can catch
the light, were dismissed with the casual sexism of the time: "I
really think Miss Rainier must have barbed-wire underwear!" was
William Walton's appraisal.[30] Critics often reached for words along
the lines of "tough" and "uncompromising" to describe her work –
apt terms for soundworlds carbonated with percussion and sparely
orchestrated, aerated with silences but blaring with visceral attack.
Jacqueline du Pré, faced with the task of performing Priaulx's gong-
tormented Cello Concerto, found rehearsing the piece heavy going.
Yehudi Menuhin, for whom Priaulx would write two violin concertos, pronounced her to have "a musical imagination of a colour and
variety scarcely to be believed".[31] Priaulx's correspondence with
Michael – disorganised as she could be, she lovingly preserved
hundreds of his letters, each carefully paperclipped to its envelope
– makes clear that his career-defining shifts in musical voice were
often following her lead.

Their closeness became such that they appear very seriously to
have considered marriage, or at least a *mariage blanc*: a union that
would allow domestic companionship, the freedom to pursue
independent affairs, and public respectability when needed. Evelyn
Maude's daughter recalls that Michael "almost got married to Priaulx Rainier, but then she was very nearly a man anyway, really. I
even wondered if they *had* got married very briefly. Certainly, the
question arose."[32] The question never quite became a reality. But
although the relationship could not be sexually fulfilling, in its first
flush it was one of, as Michael would sign letters to her, "heaps and
heaps and heaps of love".[33] When he first made a will, she was to
receive half of his estate. He became her sponsor, and (symbolical-
ly) suggested that he make her a gift of Francesca Allinson's piano.
But such generosity, and the friendship in general, was complicated
by John Minchinton, who visited Tidebrook most weekends, doing
a great deal of work on the score of *The Midsummer Marriage*. Michael
wrote to Priaulx, who was in financial distress:

He is amusingly jealous of you (!), which I encourage rather selfishly because it gives me an easier emotional way out, for the break, which must come. Actually the emotional or other pull with him is very small, and I am much relieved when he keeps to himself, but I'm not hard-enough made to "blacken" him sufficiently to myself to throw him off at this stage. I mean throw off my financial and moral responsibility. [. . .] if you can help me to see my way through to setting a time limit for the boy that is reasonable and doesn't cripple him, then we can add up the capital expenditure needed to find you what you need during that time. And I don't mean by increasing your overdraft, but by direct gift from me – after a joint discussion. [. . .] unless we appeared to the outside world married, there is no automatic protection.[34]

Michael's love for John Minchinton was colder-blooded than for Wilfred Franks, and less affectionate than for Douglas Newton. But once again he was in thrall to a younger man whose demonstrably difficult behaviour he professed himself powerless to call out. He appears to have had a very genuine wish to help John, who was the first of his lovers to have serious musical ability, forge a career. But it was almost with relief that he reported to Priaulx, in March 1950, the inevitable complications:

I think it's possible, if not probable, that John is moving over on to the other ground and, as I always imagined and really hoped, will fall for someone of his own age – and a girl. This idea oddly enough seems to delight me, deep down, though I dare say in another mood it may not. I don't think he can stand on his own quite yet – so that I am still very necessary to him – perhaps entirely so, even now. But I doubt if he is really "necessary" to me, though I don't know if I am ready to make any move to be colder to him – unless it comes mutually. Because I fancy it will happen very easily, at the right time.[35]

Michael's secret hope that John might jump ship, although he made
no move to push him, was in part a desire to be closer to and
spend more time with Priaulx; they even considered purchasing
a home together. Her Cornish life, and their mutual devotion to
composition, led to long periods apart. "You know my darling,"
he told her,

> what I miss is not our musical doings, but just our companionship
> – you yourself. I grudge music – St Ives too if you like – taking
> this away and wasting its precious time. There's so much I'd love
> to talk over with you – probably in my usual everlasting selfish
> way. But also, when I'm with you in a personal way, rubbishy
> sides of my nature fall away – perhaps not absolutely – I suppose
> they never will – but in a measure. It's that I miss so much. It
> doesn't happen with others, so I just miss it. [. . .] It's always a
> great love I have of you, however ill expressed.[36]

The light-saturated town of St Ives juts out into the Atlantic in
a jumble of lichened roofs and golden sand. Virginia Woolf had
spent much of her childhood there, and the wink of the white
lighthouse perched on an island at the entry to St Ives Bay inspired
one of her most famous novels. The town had long been a draw
for artists and by 1953 Barbara Hepworth, recently divorced from
Ben Nicholson and grieving the death of one of her sons in a plane
crash, had been settled there for over a decade, sculpting in her
studio while Priaulx composed in a hut in the garden, which was
studded with Hepworth's large-scale bronzes. So close had the two
become that their work almost intermingled, and Priaulx's notes
seemed to catch the knock of chisel on metal or wood, while the
smooth and almost melodic lines of Hepworth's sculptures were
often strung like instruments.

The St Ives Festival of Music and the Arts, which opened on 6
June 1953, was co-founded by Hepworth, Priaulx, and Michael,
and somehow permission was received to perform "under the
patronage of H.M. The Queen", a photograph of whom adorned
the programme book, which stated that the festival had been

formed "to commemorate the two Elizabethan ages, to enjoy the achievements of each epoch in music, drama, and the visual arts". Raising funds had been an arduous task, the list of donors was long, and Michael and Priaulx had been scrappy with one another in the stress of organisation. "I know my letter was troubling and uncalled for," he apologised, referring to a lost quarrel. "I write these stupid and even distressing and hurtful letters to people, only when I get at cross-purposes somewhere with myself." The festival was, he reassured her, "an excuse to be ten days together!"[37]

Programming the contemporary with the Tudor was second nature to Michael, and he and Priaulx, jointly in charge of the music, persuaded numerous friends and colleagues to travel to St Ives for a packed week of performances. There were stagings of Shakespeare's history plays; artists such as Terry Frost opened their studios to the public; Michael gave a number of lectures and persuaded A.L. Rowse to come across from Mevagissey and do the same. Peter Pears gave a recital, including *The Heart's Assurance*, on 14 June. On paper it was an exciting programme, but there was little hope of the founders having created a viable tradition to match the Aldeburgh blueprint, and not just because of the town's distance from London. The whole thing was slightly cursed, partly by Priaulx's tremendous scattiness, and Michael was not much better organised. Peter Pears, driving back to London after the performance, had a bad car crash from which he emerged unwounded but shaken. Michael composed a fanfare to open proceedings, written to be performed from the four corners of the church tower, but had to write a replacement at top speed as players and instruments came and went. He was one of the driving forces behind the festival, but in his autobiography is quietly edited out of proceedings: "When [Priaulx] and Barbara tried to organise a festival at St Ives, in 1953, the administration was hilarious." He recalled that "madrigals were to be sung from a boat in the harbour" – more likely one of the harbour-front concerts given by the St Ives Town Band – "but Priaulx and Barbara forgot to check the tides: in the event, the tide went out, taking with it the boatful of inaudible singers!"[38] But he had spent the festival in high spirits. Eric Walter White was there:

"At the end of an evening concert of part songs and choruses held on the terrace of the Tregenna Castle Hotel with its fabulous view of the north coast of Cornwall, [Michael] suddenly seized me by the arm and with a whoop of abandon rushed me off headlong down the precipitous slope that leads towards the harbour."[39]

Back at home, Michael had to complete his *Fantasia Concertante on a Theme of Corelli*, which he had begun late the previous year; he finished in a scramble around July 1953, with Schott and the Edinburgh Festival breathing down his neck.[40] The fantasia is written for a solo group of two violins and cello, accompanied by string orchestra, and begins by laying out the original Corelli theme (an adagio in F minor from a concerto grosso), before frothing it into rapture over a series of variations, culminating in a fugue (based on Bach's *Fugue on a Theme of Corelli*). Michael's counterpoint is newly imbued with the teeming ecstasy of *The Midsummer Marriage*: it became typical for him to set satellite pieces into orbit around the bright sun of a stage work. Over its spinning and ornate terrain, the fantasia ushers listeners into the realms of the sublime, the tender melodies of the two violins coiled together in a gently rotating double helix. Of all Michael's works, the fantasia is the one most often and most easily identified as "English", although the word is too frequently equated merely with the pastoral, a nostalgic depiction of rolling hills and sceptred isles. The joy and the melancholy of the piece amount to more than a landscape painting, its Englishness deriving from composers past (Vaughan Williams, Elgar) and combined with flourishes entirely Mediterranean. The director Peter Hall, eventually to become a friend and colleague, chose it to score his film *Akenfield*, a depiction of an English village made in 1974 that brought Michael's music to an audience of 20 million. When, in 2017, Hall lay dying in his hospital bed after a long illness, it was, as per his instructions, the fantasia that played on a loop beside him.[41]

Michael only just finished the piece in time for the premiere, on 29 August, which he conducted himself. The concert had been offered to Malcolm Sargent, who, no champion of contemporary music, complained about the score to the publishers and at a public press conference: "I intend to get the intellectuals out of music."[42] The reviews were equally dismissive, hearing little but mess, and although the *Manchester Guardian* avowed that "one could call it intellectual if that did not generally imply that it was not beautiful", *The Times* deemed the fantasia a "grand confusion". When a few weeks later it was heard at the Proms, it was described as an "involved sonorous mesh, which all but succeeds in hiding the essentially fine and moving quality of its thought".[43] The piece requires a performance more lucid and cohesive than Michael and the first performers were evidently able to give, partly as a result of its densely layered and intricate lacework: so much is going on, and so close together, that players, acoustic, and conductor must all be perfectly judged so that the music can swell as it should, rather than bloat.

The press reaction quickly undid the success of a London concert by the conductor Hans Schmidt-Isserstedt who, a vital supporter of Michael's music in Germany, led a performance of the Concerto for Double String Orchestra with such sympathy and rhythmic understanding that the work was newly revealed and acclaimed.[44] But the Corelli fantasia and the pieces that followed began to be treated with, at best, suspicion, and at worst, contempt. Such an attitude was to endure throughout the 1950s. At the *Ritual Dances'* premiere, the players of the Swiss orchestra had complained bitterly about the orchestral parts. Even *A Child of Our Time* had begun to suffer, for although it was now performed by some of the stars of the day, they failed to recognise the references and allusions that stood behind its structure. Michael tended to think that European conductors understood better what he was getting at, sure that Sargent made an utter hash of *A Child of Our Time* whenever he got near it. But when in 1952 Herbert von Karajan had led a radio performance of the oratorio with Elisabeth Schwarzkopf and Nicolai Gedda among the soloists, the renowned Austrian conductor explained to a flabbergasted composer that the work would be divided into four parts, rather than the *Messiah*-inspired three. Karajan nevertheless liked Michael's music enough that he agreed to record the *Ritual Dances*, and although finance for this project fell through, he took on John Minchinton as a conducting pupil.[45]

When the ideas flew in Michael's head it seems they had to be quickly caught and pinned before they flew away. Barely weeks after finishing the fantasia he began a piano concerto. His commitment to established forms of music – concertos, symphonies, quartets – was strong, and the piece had likely long been an ambition. Towards the end of the war he had planned a work for two pianos and orchestra, but now he embarked with a single soloist, inspired by hearing a performance of Beethoven's Piano Concerto No. 4. It was an undertaking that he wouldn't finish for some years, partly because he was composing it concurrently with a five-movement divertimento on an Elizabethan dance tune, and all the while seeing *The Midsummer Marriage* into print and onto the stage. As he told Anna Kallin in November 1953, "I'm writing so many pieces I'm apt to add bars to the wrong score."[46]

The divertimento was finished in July 1954, and had begun with Benjamin Britten. Michael had been one of six composers invited by Britten to provide a variation on an anonymous Elizabethan dance tune ("Sellinger's Round"), while weaving in another quotation of their choice. Michael went to town for his contribution, using the ground bass from an aria in Purcell's *Dido and Aeneas*, a solo violin weeping above. At the premiere the Aldeburgh audience was asked to guess which variation was whose, but nobody identified each composer correctly. Michael had enjoyed the speed and ease with which he had composed his variation, was pleased with the result – "Mine was the best!" – and decided to extend it into a five-movement divertimento so as to satisfy a commission from Paul Sacher, who gave the premiere, in Zurich, on 5 November 1954.[47] A fragment of the original dance tune appears in each of the five movements, which skim through periods and pieces, quoting composers from Orlando Gibbons to Arthur Sullivan. Michael sent Britten a copy of the piece as a gift with a cheery covering note, and thought no more about it.

As far as Michael was concerned the drawbridge was fast being pulled up around Aldeburgh, although in October 1954 he had turned down a commission from Peter Pears for a vocal work. "I just can't see how I can <u>truly</u> serve you at this time," he wrote

apologetically. "I see a lovely Yeats (unpublished) poem for you
– but it must wait. [. . .] Don't be too disappointed." He signed
the letter: "Love, dear love."[48] The regret and the affection were
genuine, but this was the scratchiest period in Michael's relationship with Britten and Pears, no doubt exacerbated by the fact
that, in the time it had taken to compose *The Midsummer Marriage*,
"the curly cherub", as he had nicknamed Britten with astringent
affection, had written two major and successful operas: *Albert Herring* and *Billy Budd*. Then, in the time it took *The Midsummer Marriage*
to be staged, Britten premiered two more: the huge success of
The Turn of the Screw followed *Gloriana*. "Another thin opera" was
Michael's appraisal of the latter, a view with which many of
the critics had agreed.[49] But he was in an increasing panic as he
witnessed the success of Britten's dark psychological studies, and
realised how his own topic and its treatment would go against the
critical grain.

On 15 December 1954 Britten wrote to Michael of his displeasure
at the *Divertimento on "Sellinger's Round"*, in a letter (omitted from his
published correspondence) formally typed on headed notepaper:
"I must say that the thing came as a complete bombshell to us at
Aldeburgh. [. . .] I really think either you or Schott's might have
warned us about this. Is it not possible at least to make some
mention of Aldeburgh in the score? It might even have been more
considerate, if not to have asked our permission, at least to have
consulted us."[50] Twelve days beforehand the two men had met
at the Royal Opera House for the premiere of Walton's *Troilus and
Cressida*, but, as Michael told Anna Kallin, Britten "cut me twice
dead. So I've had it. Er ist äusserst empfindlich!"[51] His German translated into an appraisal of Britten with which few disagreed: "he's
extremely touchy". The description of being ignored aims at non-
chalant apathy, its German something of a mask. For a short while
it seemed as if Michael would join W.H. Auden, Montagu Slater,
and others in the line of friends who had fallen permanently foul
of Britten's capacity for offence. But after sleeping a few nights on
his response, he wrote lengthily to Britten, by hand. The fulsome
tenderness and apology of his *mea culpa* letter are uncharacteristic,

born from a worry that so close and important a friendship might come to an end:

> Seen from your letter my conduct seems quite different and quite wrong. That it didn't seem so before is one of those mysteries that I can only <u>now</u> wonder how they were. I thought something would be to you a pleasurable surprise and it is a "bombshell". [. . .] I wouldn't let Schott's tell you, because I had determined to do it in my way – make you a present, personally to you, of what I was so excited had come to me through doing a variation for you. [. . .] All this is quite secondary to my real present distress that I have by deliberate misconceived action appeared to do something harmful to Aldeburgh or yourself, through whom something good came to me. I merely wish, rather like a child, that I had not done it. That I am sorry is just an understatement. I have been looking forward to Jan 2nd and to seeing you. As I always do. I was excited by Turn of the Screw – I marvelled anew at Peter's tour-de-force in Troilus* – but even these things aren't the only source of some absolutely enduring affection. And to be with you both under [the] same roof is something I go on looking forward to; as I do now.[52]

A week or so later, on 2 January 1955, Michael turned fifty. At the celebratory concert that evening, held at Morley College, Britten and Pears loyally appeared, despite Britten's being in poor health, to perform Boyhood's End. "You should not have been out and about for my sake and so ill," Michael wrote the next day. "I was deeply touched, but also deeply worried. Of course yours and Peter's contribution stood so out, that that was all there is to it. [. . .] Boyhood's End stood up so well, I thought, from the far away and long ago days when I wrote it for you both; and Fresca was still alive. Bless you both."[53] Britten replied curtly that the concert "was not exactly the moment to raise the matter of your previous letter which, of

---

* Singing Pandarus in William Walton's opera.

course, was received with affection and sympathy; but you did not in replying make any comment on our idea of putting a note in the score [. . .] to clarify the confusing situation".[54] A credit was duly added, the piece was programmed at the Aldeburgh Festival the following year, and no more was said. The letter-writing tone of the two composers is so different that it is partly fruitless to compare correspondence as evidence of true feeling, and the stiffness of Britten's letters apparently masked continuing genuine affection. That the argument was forgiven and forgotten is evidence enough, when compared to his behaviour with others, that he felt Michael too good a friend to lose. A wedge of unease may have been driven between the two men, but Britten made sure to attend the premiere of *The Midsummer Marriage* when it came round, on 27 January 1955. "It meant a lot to have you there," Michael told him, "however the music takes you or not. Most deeply it meant an outward sign of affection. And then it is that for better or worse, we two are the most interesting English music has at the moment."[55]

TWENTY-THREE

Equal to All Reasonable Demands

On 27 January 1955 London was shivering in the first weeks of that winter's "big freeze". Just ten days before, the wind and pollution reached such a pitch that the city, its Clean Air Act not yet in force, had been swathed in darkness at one o'clock in the afternoon, triggering a slew of calls to the emergency services and a general panic. In the light and warmth of the Royal Opera House a respectable audience had gathered, full of the great and the good. *Tatler* wrote up the list with glee: Cecil Beaton, Ninette de Valois, a smattering of MPs, and a viscount or two.[1] The programme book solemnly informed the audience that the auditorium had been sterilised with Jeyes fluid, and asked ladies to remove their hats. Finally the violins scurried and the curtain rose to reveal a towering henge of wooden blocks, painted in green and blue, while men and women in contemporary dress flooded the stage: "This way, this way . . ."

That *The Midsummer Marriage* had finally reached performance, fifteen years after its conception, was something of a miracle. It had been an arduous process. Michael's growing success in Germany led to the Bavarian State Opera making a concrete offer of a first production, and the Hamburg State Opera sent over to London its celebrated chief director, Günther Rennert, to discuss a possible staging. But Michael was sure that his opera, "like *Grimes*, [had] to make its first bow in native dress".[2] A number of premieres by leading British composers were already scheduled for the 1954–5 season. Sadler's Wells had committed to Lennox Berkeley's *Nelson* and were to give the British premiere of Britten's *The Turn of the Screw*; meanwhile the Royal Opera House had agreed to stage William Walton's *Troilus and Cressida*. It was doubtless in such company that Michael thought his own work should belong, but Sadler's Wells soon refused *The Midsummer Marriage*. Michael held out for the Opera House, but trod carefully, sure that Walton's *Troilus* was being put on "to annoy Britten – by staging a kind of rival show. Which is exactly what MM is <u>not</u> about. So I want my decision to be made for sensible reasons and not in a hurry."[3] By late 1952 the Opera House's chief executive, David Webster, had all but agreed to a 1954 production of *The Midsummer Marriage*, which was eventually shunted by Walton's opera into the following January.

Although Michael would later decide to take a back seat when his operas were staged, a lot rode on this premiere, and he got heavily involved in finalising almost every aspect of the production. The first issue was casting. Elisabeth Schwarzkopf was approached to sing the role of the secretary, Bella, but the dates were impossible. Birgit Nilsson, the famous Wagnerian soprano, was Michael's first choice for the lead, Jenifer, and he was tremendously excited when Kirsten Flagstad (another great Wagnerian) was raised as a possibility for Madame Sosostris. But the Opera House soon made it clear that, for a risky new work, they were unwilling to pay the fees demanded by such performers. All this was complicated by the fact that, for Walton's *Troilus*, an international star (Magda László) had been flown in at great expense to sing Cressida, and Walton, being on the board of the Royal Opera, had some say in the casting of *The Midsummer Marriage*. Eventually Michael had to settle for a cheaper though not undistinguished cast. It took an age to find a singer for Madame Sosostris, and at a panic-inducing last minute a Mexican mezzo who spoke barely a word of English, Oralia Dominguez, agreed to perform, learning the words phonetically. And Michael was mightily unhappy with the soprano eventually chosen for Jenifer: "silly stupid girl, and ugly – but a wonderful voice".[4] Hard now to believe that Joan Sutherland, later a legend known to adoring audiences worldwide as "La Stupenda", was only reluctantly cast in *The Midsummer Marriage*. She had performed in major roles for a few seasons at the Opera House, but in 1955 her name did not guarantee sales, and Michael was privately disappointed.

Nor did he get his first choices where the production team was concerned. For director he pushed hard for either Peter Brook or Günther Rennert; for conductor he wanted Paul Sacher; and to choreograph the Ritual Dances he was sure that Frederick Ashton, soon to be principal choreographer of the Royal Ballet, would be best. He had eventually to settle for the conductor John Pritchard, and, to choreograph, John Cranko, with whom he never really got on. When it came to the sets, almost every major British artist of the period was briefly linked to The Midsummer Marriage: Duncan Grant, Henry Moore, Graham Sutherland, Ben Nicholson.[5] (Sutherland jumped ship on receiving an official request to paint the Prime Minister, producing a portrait so honest and penetrating that Clementine Churchill had it destroyed, after much controversy.) With less than four months to go before the first night, Michael asked his friend, and Nicholson's ex-wife, Barbara Hepworth, to design all the costumes and sets, even offering personally to top up Covent Garden's fee, and she agreed.[6]

But still they had no director. Everyone seemed perfectly happy to carry on without one. Almost as a last resort, the house director Christopher West agreed to take it on. He and Michael, who was still gunning for Günther Rennert, made their peace, and at the end of September 1954 went together to meet Hepworth in St Ives. Michael was thrilled with what he found: "Dearest darling Barbara – I came back on air – because I think the costumes absolutely right, and very lovely. It seems to me we're set now for something really remarkable – and I'm too grateful to be articulate."[7] He then proceeded to bombard Hepworth all through October with some of the longest letters he ever wrote, outlining his vision for the production. Timber from the Tidebrook grounds soon found its way to Cornwall for her sculpture.

The fact that The Midsummer Marriage was following hard on the heels of Walton's Troilus and Cressida led to competition at the Opera House, and there was a general sense that sides had to be taken. For every problem that beset Michael's opera, the unspoken inference was that Walton was always receiving preferential treatment. Mainly this was nonsense, as *Troilus* was having more than its fair share of hold-ups and disasters. "It's only a momentary mood on my part," Michael wrote to his assistant Michael Tillett, "that Tippett is being hard-done by against Walton. I hope you haven't come across a sense of rivalry outside? I haven't yet myself. The proper view, which needs to be put over where possible, is that with Berkeley, Britten, Walton at the least, all in the field together, it's a great season of hope for English opera."[8] But as Michael dutifully sat in the audience for the British premieres that came before his, he found little of value. Berkeley's *Nelson* he left at the interval in favour of supper, thinking the music imitative, the libretto dreadful, and the production "awful, dowdy to the nth degree". By December *Troilus and Cressida* had opened with a lacklustre production only politely reviewed, and Michael found the music "horribly poor".[9]

Rehearsals for *The Midsummer Marriage* were done at speed and in a scramble. The chorus had had their parts long in advance and knew them well, but Michael thought little of John Cranko's choreography, and said so. It was only by threats from the management that John Pritchard was persuaded to learn the score properly, rather than conduct it from sight. "There's no doubt Covent Garden wishes I'd never been born," Michael told Peter Pears during rehearsals. "Sometimes I think that myself too!"[10] Complaints about the music came thick and fast, the vocal writing for Jenifer being described as "beyond any known voice".[11] Everything had to be worked through, and cuts (mainly to the Ritual Dances) implemented. Michael, no Tippett purist, came to think them improvements. Joan Sutherland was deeply unhappy in the role of Jenifer, and found Michael's cheery dismissal of her queries no help at all. "The plot was unfathomable," she insisted later, "nothing seemed to come together and one went through the motions and sang the music hoping the audience might comprehend what was going on."[12] The unhappiness behind the scenes was ripe for press intrusion, and the day before the first night the *News Chronicle* published an article under the headline: "This opera baffles us too, say singers – bewilderment at Covent Garden." There were interviews with disgruntled cast members. "I don't know who I am and that's the truth," said Edith Coates, playing the She-Ancient. Michael gave an interview but did little to elucidate: "The opera means what it says – nothing more."[13] He insisted afterwards that many in the cast had tearfully denied saying what was attributed to them.

The article seemed to set the stage for a disaster of epic proportions. But it was an exception in a torrent of optimistic publicity. The score was favourably reviewed in the Listener, and papers looked forward to "one of the most exciting and incalculable first-nights in the whole history of British opera".[14] Michael was interviewed on Panorama, a current affairs programme then just fourteen months old, seemingly his first television appearance. But he began to have little hope of success. "I'm a bit down at the thought of all the snooty comments we shall get for the whole opera . . . however it was to be expected, and it has to be sustained when it comes."[15] The production had run out of time, the third act was barely rehearsed, and the choreography for the fourth Ritual Dance proved problematic. Michael was jangled with nerves, despair, excitement, delight, relief. He liked the stage team, had fallen completely for the young soprano, Adele Leigh, who was singing Bella – "just ravishing" – and adored watching Hepworth at work.[16] She had made of the stage a kind of magical timber-yard of glowing and intersecting blocks, looking more like a Ben Nicholson abstract in three dimensions than a Hepworth sculpture garden, and gave the dancers cane structures swathed in vividly coloured gauzes that were then lit from within. Much of this proved impractical, but Michael was thrilled, and left the dress rehearsal "saying to myself, take it or leave it, if you can't be moved by things like Jenifer's aria, then you are a moron!"[17]

The morning after the first night brought the reviews, and two days later came the Sundays. A lack of surtitles meant that critics had read advance copies of the text, unharnessed to the music and unprotected by translation (the usual armour of librettos). Worst was the write-up by the influential critic Ernest Newman, the sting all the sharper because Michael had enjoyed a cordial correspondence with him while writing the opera. "Let me say here", Newman began, "that I am writing the first part of the present article before the performance: for the moment I am concentrating solely on the text of the work." It was precisely what Michael had not wanted to happen. Newman expended one single sentence on the music. He was not cruel: "I have the greatest respect for Mr. Tippett, whose mind is of an exceptional range and acuity in other spheres beside the musical." But the review professed itself "unable to make head or tail" of it all. Others followed suit. The *Daily Telegraph* thought that the music could not "wholly redeem this hotchpotch", and the American musicologist Cecil Smith was apoplectic. "I consider this libretto", he wrote in the *Daily Express*, "one of the worst in the 350-years history of opera. And what a pity: for Tippett's music is often astoundingly beautiful, and the stage production is worthy of a dramatic masterpiece."[18] Many reviewers had decided that because they did not understand the opera, it was unintelligible. The product of six and a half years' work had been subjected to three hours' scrutiny and found wanting. Evidently the production, while often beautiful, had not put across satisfactorily Michael's scenario, and many complained at the singers' poor diction or thick foreign accents, which obscured things yet further; nor had Hepworth's abstract set clearly demarcated the forest, the staircase, and the temple that had been specified.

There was also the fact that Michael had dropped somewhat off the critical radar. "The last decade has been marked by silence", wrote the *Observer* of his career.[19] His re-entry was suddenly suspicious. This fifty-year-old, while not exactly coming from nowhere, was offering up a first opera at an unusually advanced age, seemingly a lone late starter in a generation of prodigies. Almost nothing was publicly known about the details of his long and sincere record of music-making or his extensive back catalogue of withdrawn pieces, and there was little biographical information available to explain his dilatoriness.

The opera had been conceived, in its earliest incarnation as the *Masque*, just four years after the Surrealist Movement in Britain had reached its height, with the London International Surrealism Exhibition of 1936; artists such as Paul Nash had painted mystical landscapes, dotted with everyday objects and rich in the symbolism of death and rebirth, that could almost be stage designs for *The Midsummer Marriage*. But the surrealist work of Michael's friends such as the poet George Barker or the painter Cecil Collins (with whom he had corresponded) was fast going out of fashion.[20] Michael had also been determined for his opera to spring from the world of theatre, and believed the prevalent theatrical movement of his time to be "as I saw it, verse drama: the theatre of Auden, Eliot, and Fry".[21] Verse-dramas of the 1930s, which thanks to Auden and Isherwood largely expounded a Marxist analysis of society, had been superseded by Christopher Fry's poetic affirmations of life and love: between the first year of *The Midsummer Marriage*'s composition and the year of its premiere, Fry wrote three translations and seven major plays, most staged to critical acclaim with starry productions in the West End or on Broadway. His verse, rich with seasonal symbolism, could transcend the drabness of post-war Britain, when theatregoers had little stomach for realism.

But *The Midsummer Marriage* took so long to reach the stage that tastes began to change, and abruptly, *during* composition. Theatrical revolution was in the air. The Angry Young Men were arriving, disillusioned, often working-class, committed to harnessing the gritty poetry inherent in everyday prose. A year after *The Midsummer Marriage* was first performed, the Royal Court Theatre's curtain rose on a cramped attic flat, a woman ironing, men reading the papers: John Osborne's *Look Back in Anger*. Poor as the reviews were, theatrical taste was transformed by the play. The dramas of Christopher Fry and T.S. Eliot were quickly consigned to a cold storage from which they have yet to return.

In opera the turn to realism had arguably arrived even earlier. Arthur Bliss's *The Olympians* (1949), with a libretto by J.B. Priestley, had combined the worlds of opera and symbolic drama, depicting a group of strolling players who briefly become gods – it is even set on midsummer's day. But it had not been a success. Benjamin Britten had moved the country's opera into a world of verismo. His librettist for *Peter Grimes*, Montagu Slater, had emerged from the age of verse-drama, but the opera is anchored in Suffolk realism. Even in Britten's supernatural operas, ghosts haunt an ostensibly realist and temporally grounded world. Walton had turned to Chaucer; Berkeley to historical drama. *The Midsummer Marriage* fell between two stools, coming too late to join surrealist operas of the 1930s such as Martinů's *Julietta*, but too early to hold hands with the mythic rituals of Harrison Birtwistle, which, at least theatrically, it anticipates. Its symbolism was completely out of place amid the operatic or theatrical worlds of the mid-1950s.

But there were among the reviewers more than a few praiseful voices. The *Observer* complained of the libretto, but was sure that "its bare bones are as old as the hills", its very complexity "the best proof that the subject [Tippett] has chosen is well fitted for opera". The score was of "intoxicating beauty", had "miraculous power", and "a richness of invention that has few equals in modern opera". Scott Goddard of the *News Chronicle*, long an admirer, wrote: "The plot was said to be complicated. Really it is clear, though very unusual. But what else should one have expected of one of the most individual composers among us today? There is more originality in this work than in any new opera I have heard in the last twelve months." The *New Statesman*, voicing thoughtful criticisms of the text, wrote that "the level of inspiration in this long score is astonishingly high", and the *Spectator*'s reviewer, Colin Mason, devoted pages to an out-and-out rave of the opera's words, music, and staging. This "astonishing new work", Mason argued, was a "perfect integration of libretto and music", "an overwhelming experience that, it is to be hoped, there will be many opportunities to repeat".[22] A recording of the first night has captured not only the orchestra's mastery of the score and Joan Sutherland's jaw-dropping coloratura, but the warm applause at the curtain call, in which a group of booers does battle with rousing cheers.

That the premiere of *The Midsummer Marriage* was a major disaster for its composer is little more than legend. For a new opera it had, from the outset, a respectable innings. For a new opera that was predominantly tonal in an age of the avant-garde, predominantly symbolic in an age of realism, and written without commission or fee in a six-year, white-hot surge of creative endeavour that surmounted any number of practical and physical hardships, it had quite remarkable success. While some found it hard to get to grips with, others were held in its grip. Word of mouth spread, the whole run was well attended, and the final two performances were all but sold out. *Troilus and Cressida*, by contrast, had played to ever-dwindling ticket sales. Michael avowed the critical hoo-hah would dissipate:

> It'll all die down. Covent Garden do <u>not</u> regard it as a flop at all – but a great success. And the man most outspoken publicly and privately in favour is Walton! He simply proclaims to us all, and to BBC, and Opera House, and what have you, that this is the best music of any English opera to date, including his own. So what! Most moving of all has been very young people, in their twenties, who have come unsolicited and tried to pour out their sense of excitement. Obviously it's quite carried them away into some incalculable magic world.[23]

The production was revived for two performances in February 1957, which were cast with a higher proportion of English speakers, and had a restaged third act containing new machinery of some kind for Madame Sosostris. Michael resisted fierce calls from the Opera House to cut the final ten minutes of music, but agreed to small and effective tightenings.[24] There was then a gap of only three years before excerpts were given at the Proms, with Janet Baker as Sosostris; Baker sang the role again in a wildly popular broadcast on the Third Programme in 1963, which led to a second production at Covent Garden five years later. Compared to most of the decade's opera premieres, these are respectable figures.[25] Further revivals throughout the 1970s elucidated the opera yet further. Even the libretto gained its critical studies and admirers, among them the conductor Andrew Davis, who can quote from memory long chunks of the text for Sosostris's aria: "If that isn't great poetry I don't know what is."[26]

But the criticism clung to Michael like bindweed, and the view that the opera was nothing but the ramblings of a confused old hippie was hard to dispel. A history of the Royal Opera House written half a century later can be found claiming, quite falsely, that during rehearsals for *The Midsummer Marriage* Michael "slept in a hovel and was likely to turn up in open-toed sandals".[27] The description of the production in a biography of Joan Sutherland is more or less fiction, reporting singers disdainfully chewing gum throughout the performances, and the audience roaring with laughter following the phrase "What's he saying now?" The line is not present in Michael's libretto.[28] Worse difficulties were to beset Michael's music and reputation in the years that followed. Typically, he was calm, excited by the opera's having finally come alive, and sure, whatever the criticism, that it had had to be as it had had to be. Certain that the libretto contained some "shuddering doggerel", he was equally certain that it didn't matter, and that the music could not have existed without the words.[29] It was a necessary learning curve, and perhaps his next opera would be better. The breezy tone of his reaction may have been partly in the spirit of self-preservation, but he was not unhappy, and was looking forward to a rest, a time to contemplate, the quietness of Tidebrook. He wrote to David Webster with certainty that the opera would "grow in esteem gradually all the same".[30]

In the summer of 1955, with the reviews of *The Midsummer Marriage* behind him, Michael was still embroiled in his piano concerto, which he had been composing on and off for eighteen months. At Easter a young Swiss couple had moved into Tidebrook Manor to keep house, replacing the Berberichs. Michael had spent the summer "fattening cockerels for the market and growing a gigantic garden of vegetables – in consequence I am badly in debt".[31] He took a loan so as to be able to take John Minchinton abroad to Italy, and on his return rushed to complete the concerto so as to cash the commission money and pay off his creditors. He finished, finally, on 20 August 1955. The concerto was scheduled for a premiere at Birmingham the following year, although the choice of pianist

proved a tricky one. The piece had been vaguely intended as a
vehicle for Noel Mewton-Wood, who had committed suicide in
the early stages of composition. Michael thought the concerto was
"made for Noel to grow up into. How sad!"[32]

He moved immediately on to a Sonata for Four Horns, due for a
concert at the Wigmore Hall in December. His heart wasn't really in
it, and he admitted to being "disturbed by the horn piece", wanting
"to throw it overboard".[33] His dissatisfaction was exacerbated by
the players of the Dennis Brain Wind Ensemble, who received the
score just days before the premiere. They quickly insisted that the
work was unplayable as written, and he had to transpose the parts
down a tone for the concert. (Subsequent performances restored
the original pitch.) Then, just days later, the pianist who was to
give the premiere of Michael's concerto, Julius Katchen, pulled
out, declaring the score impossible. Michael, who had in any case
suggested that Paul Baumgartner should play it, wrote on 2 January
1956 in uncharacteristic anguish and from the depths of a winter
cold: "all is in turmoil!"[34] He was badly affected by what appeared
to be yet another crisis, and was generally a bit all over the place,
turning up for a lunch at the French Institute "one week too late!"[35]
It became clear that Julius Katchen had only allotted three weeks
in his schedule to learn the concerto, and likely realised he would
not be ready in time for the concert, which was postponed. By
February the pianist Louis Kentner, who had two Bartók concertos
under his fingers, had been booked, and at the eventual premiere,
on 30 October, played Michael's piece from memory.

But the shadows of these difficult births were hard to banish. A
generally accepted sense of Michael's amateurishness was bedding
in. The reviews of the piano concerto spoke of its striking colours
and sonorities, but also of its incoherence, though many noted
that Birmingham Town Hall's acoustics did it no favours.[36] Michael
himself found it "a strange piece", as ever managing to hear his
music with startling objectivity. "Too much Beethoven in it!"[37]
Subsequent performers, including Kentner's wife, Ilona Kabos,
quickly convinced him (and others) of its worth, and the composer
David Matthews has described it as "the outstanding piano concerto

since Bartók's Third".[38] The three movements are awash with the instruments of The Midsummer Marriage, glimmering with celesta and harp, and the piano, as if in direct renunciation of its often percussive employment in the works of Bartók and Stravinsky, soars and sings and sparkles amid an orchestral heat haze. Paul Crossley, the pianist who became most associated with Michael's music, remains convinced that the concerto is one of Michael's few failures, and never recorded it: "I like bits. I like the opening, I like the cadenza of the first movement, I like the end of the slow movement (though it takes a long time to get there). And I hate the last movement with a passion, except for the duet between celesta and piano. And I do know the last movement was a rush job."[39]

On 29 October, the day before the piano concerto was premiered, Israel invaded the Egyptian Sinai. On 30 October, the day of the performance, Britain and France issued an ultimatum to both sides to stop the fighting. The Israelis continued their advance, and by 5 November an Anglo-French assault on the Egyptian city of Suez was launched. It emerged that the Israeli invasion, and the attack by Britain and France, had been co-ordinated in an effort to regain Western control of the Suez Canal, recently nationalised by President Nasser of Egypt. The invasion was halted after nine days but British credibility was damaged and in January 1957 the disgraced Prime Minister, Anthony Eden, was replaced by Harold Macmillan. The British Empire, and deference towards its Establishment, were fast disappearing. But the fairer and more peaceful world for which Michael had fervently hoped had not materialised. The new opposing ideologies were capitalism and communism. The Communist Party of Great Britain, which had survived the death of Stalin, now suffered major losses, its members largely aghast at the Soviet invasion of Hungary in November. Michael's composer friend Alan Bush did not renounce his communism. Neither did Michael's cousin Phyllis Kemp, who was now living, appropriately enough, on the Karl-Marx-Allee in East Berlin.

In Britain, Harold Macmillan strengthened the economy, and told the British people that they had "never had it so good". He strongly supported the country's nuclear weapons programme.

Michael's response was to become a sponsor of the Campaign for Nuclear Disarmament, and to join Forster and Britten in backing the National Committee for the Abolition of Nuclear Weapons Tests. His name can also be found on the list of sponsors of the Direct Action Committee Against Nuclear War, a small pacifist group that organised, in Easter 1958, a march from London to the Atomic Weapons Research Establishment at Aldermaston. CND then took over the organisation of annual marches from Aldermaston to London, culminating in mass protests, and hundreds of arrests, in Trafalgar Square. "CND marchers?" Michael said. "Thank God for them."[40] In 1958 he became the president of the Peace Pledge Union, an honorary role, held until he died, that consisted of writing a few articles and cheques and giving an annual address.

As the Suez Crisis was playing out, and the old world order seemingly disintegrating in front of his eyes, Michael was writing his Symphony No. 2. Composition was now for him a means of keeping "the whirling world at bay", and the late 1950s' concatenation of rebellion and suppression, of atomic threat and never-had-it-so-good prosperity, speaks very little in the symphony, which seems to be a direct riposte of jubilation to a world that was, by some estimates, turning once more on its dark side.[41] For the moment Michael's continual preoccupation was rapture, and each of the symphony's four movements he linked to a specific state: joy, tenderness, gaiety, and fantasy.

The symphony had begun in Switzerland. He had travelled to Lugano back in December 1951 in order to conduct the first Italian performance of *A Child of Our Time* with a choir linked to Radio Monteceneri, a station for Italian-speaking Swiss. He had then returned every spring to conduct an annual concert for the station, and it was in May 1953, sitting in a studio overlooking the lake on the border between Switzerland and Italy, with mountains to either side, that he heard a tape of Vivaldi, with pounding Cs in the bass. As so often, a specific sound burrowed into his mind and hibernated for some years before it emerged in his music. Not until December 1955 did he begin Symphony No. 2, hoping to have another shot at the challenges of the form.[42] The piece had been commissioned by the BBC to celebrate the Third Programme's tenth anniversary, in September 1956, and as was becoming an uncomfortable custom, Michael did not finish in time, completing the symphony, a year later than planned, on 13 November 1957.

The first movement bursts into life with a thump of quavers on a low C. Gyrating strings romp in above, before a second subject is introduced in the woodwind: graceful, elegiac, polished to a sugar-plum-fairy sparkle by the celesta. The two subjects are spliced and intercut within an overall sonata-form framework, building the dialogue of contrasts inherent to Michael's music, the friction between them providing inexorable momentum, cast each as you will: man and woman, earth and heaven, body and soul, shadow and light.

Or so it was meant to be. The premiere of the symphony was entrusted to Michael's great mentor from student days: Adrian Boult. The concert, given at the Royal Festival Hall on 5 February 1958, was broadcast on the Third Programme, and the recording survives. After a few coughs from the audience the BBC Symphony Orchestra begins, and at a greater lick than any subsequent recording. All is excitement and promise, the strings rushing just slightly ahead of the brass. Trumpets and strings fall headlong into the softer second subject, all a bit of a scramble. Then suddenly everything grinds to a halt – and this just sixteen pages into the score, about two and a half minutes into the performance. There is barely a second's pause, then Boult's voice, sanguine, unruffled, is heard: "Entirely my mistake, ladies and gentlemen."[43] There is a rustling of pages, a murmur from the audience, and within seven seconds the piece has begun again.

What had happened? Michael was sure. The leader of the BBC Symphony Orchestra, Paul Beard, had made his distaste for Michael's music known during rehearsals for the Corelli fantasia, when he had refused to be one of the soloists. Then, at a run-through of the symphony at the BBC's Maida Vale studios, Beard had argued that the violin parts caused the players needless difficulty, Michael having banded the notes together across the bar lines, rather than grouping them more conventionally within the bars. Michael Tillett was present and remembered "Sir Adrian soothing [Beard] down by saying properly written parts would be made before the next rehearsal." The message got back to Michael, who was reasonably contrite. "Can we let the ligatures remain as I originally had them? Or do you think the vexed passage after [figure] 8 needs any kind of re-grouping?" The parts were regrouped. This seemed to be *carte blanche* for players to take matters into their own hands. Tillett remembered a percussionist "showing me the 'new' timpani part he had made for himself".[44] Ever afterwards, Michael blamed Paul Beard for the breakdown of the performance, believing the strings had not been able clearly to follow the hastily emended parts. Alexander Goehr, employed by Schott as a copyist at the time, wonders whether it was *his* fault: "I was actually the one to blame, because I wrote the parts out, and I don't know that I was a terribly accurate copyist."[45] But, as meticulous study of the first performance by the editor and musicologist Jonathan Del Mar has shown, "the note-groupings in the violins were a colossal red herring".[46]

The recording of the broadcast leaves no room for doubt. The woodwind, in the bubbling second subject, came unstuck from one another, a flute entering too early and leading a chain reaction of false cues. By the time the low strings and the horns return with the first subject, they should be a bar apart, but are actually playing together. When Beard leads the higher strings back into the fray they are where they should be, playing what they should be, and with total accuracy – but no longer fit into where the rest of the orchestra has got to in the meantime. The published score of the symphony stuck to Michael's original notation, but some orchestras have since deemed Beard's alterations easier to follow.

At the premiere, Boult began the symphony again, and this time it went without a hitch. The slow movement laid out its sensuous lapping sea of strings beneath a sky spangled with oboe and clarinet, its pulsing wash reminiscent of the "Moonlight" interlude from Britten's *Peter Grimes*, or of Elgar's *Sea Pictures*. Michael later claimed that "Beard slowed down his violin solo in the scherzo", but the recording proves that the leader played hell-for-leather, spinning like a whirling dervish out of a rhythmic maelstrom.[47] The finale is a fantasia, composed of four unrelated sections. Here, in embryo, is the start of the mosaic technique that Michael would come to use in works that lay just around the corner, but he thought the lack of transition between the sections had yet to move from weakness to strategy: "It doesn't entirely succeed. The four bits aren't properly welded or whatever."[48] The symphony ends with a single passage, a brass build-up that sends the strings flying, which is five times repeated to form – in the composer's words – five "gestures of farewell".

The applause was polite. The damage had been done. No shouts of acclaim greeted the composer's presence on the platform. The cut-glass tones of the Third Programme announcer rounded the broadcast off inscrutably. Ralph Vaughan Williams wrote to Adrian Boult in calming support: "It was a fine performance of a fine work, played by a fine orchestra under a fine conductor."[49] The next morning The Times gallantly omitted the false start, but branded the symphony "abstruse", claiming that "Tippett's mind is always bursting with ideas, which he is not always successful in controlling."[50] The Daily Mail had a field day – "Sir Adrian Misses the Beat" – while the Spectator blamed the orchestra for the problems, and argued that the impracticalities in the writing were all part of the point: "There is no voice in English music today more worth listening to."[51] When the piece was performed again, on 8 February, there were further mistakes, with an audibly false string entry on the very first page. Michael tried hard not to get into a rage: "The critics are fools – one, I should guess, perhaps schizophrenic!"[52] Soon Richard Howgill, the BBC's controller of music, felt the need to write to The Times: "The music critics of at least three journals have implied that [the orchestra] was unequal to the correct performance of certain passages in Mr. Michael Tippett's new symphony. [. . .] The comprehensive technique of the BBC Symphony Orchestra is equal to all reasonable demands."[53] Howgill's inference was clear: Michael's symphony did not make reasonable demands. The musical world began to take sides. Michael received letters backing up the orchestra, though Benjamin Britten wrote to say just how much he had liked the work, especially the first two movements. Michael was able to escape to Germany to conduct, and remained characteristically sanguine, writing cordially to Howgill and apologetically to Boult.

But matters got worse before they got better. The Hallé Orchestra cancelled a scheduled performance of the symphony, its conductor John Barbirolli having (as Michael Tillett remembered) "dumped it mid-rehearsal saying 'not worth the bother getting it right'".[54] Michael was due to conduct a performance at the Proms on 15 August. In light of the general furore he offered to stand down, and Boult was once again engaged. The rehearsals threatened to descend into recrimination, and Michael was asked to attend, but only on the condition, so cross were the players, that he would not come within forty feet of the platform. He agreed, trying to keep things civil, but instructed the conductor to walk to the back of the auditorium should discussion be needed, and was not invited to take a call after the performance.[55] Conversely, after all this farce, Boult and the orchestra were now, thought a reviewer, "without any fear of the technical hitches that robbed the initial performance of confidence". Suddenly the symphony was ranked "as the out-standing English symphonic achievement of the year to date".[56] It was becoming a tiresome pattern for Michael that success in subsequent performances failed to eclipse the initial difficulties of his premieres.

For many, however, it was nothing but proof that Michael Tippett was a cack-handed amateur. The esteem in which he was held a decade before, so long awaited, was threatening to melt. And true dislike came not from the concert-going public and reviewers, but from fellow composers. Most who had spent time with Michael were soon charmed into something like submission, but those who knew him more distantly professed sharp antipathy. As Alexander Goehr remembers: "People really had it in for him – Elisabeth Lutyens and people – they loathed Tippett."[57] Most vicious was Constant Lambert, who had nothing for Michael but coldly fierce contempt. Lambert had been star composition pupil in Michael's year at the Royal College, but his career had never lived up to its early successes, and he was eaten up with a sense of failure and with the alcoholism that killed him. Not long before his death he had met John Amis, and happened to pick up a book Amis had borrowed from Michael, whose name was scrawled on the fly-leaf. On seeing this, Amis remembered, Lambert "rapped the book shut, finished his drink in one gulp and bustled out of the pub without ever uttering another word to me". Another composer of the same generation was Lambert's friend Alan Rawsthorne, who after a number of notable successes in the 1930s and 1940s had turned to writing for films. "One of the very few times that I have found Tippett being nasty to a colleague", John Amis remembered, "was when he and Rawsthorne were together."[58]

In the gossipy crucible of post-war British music, it is almost impossible to work out what each composer truly thought of the other. "I think X or Y overrated" usually meant "I think my own music is underrated." In William Walton Michael supposedly had a supporter, but Walton, although his love of puns may mask his true feelings, was more than capable of damning behind a fellow composer's back what he had praised to his face. He had spoken at Benjamin Britten's conscientious-objector tribunal, and raved to the younger composer about *Peter Grimes*, but in private could speak bitterly of "Grimy Peter". Michael he evidently liked as a person – "I'm very fond of him" – but he professed himself "more often than not completely baffled by his music". Vociferously praising *The Midsummer Marriage* at the time of its premiere, in private he called it "Midsummer Madness", and when the opera was revived to a chorus of praise, wrote to a friend that its success "is one of the mysteries of life".[59] Partly this was in annoyance that *Troilus and Cressida* had been forgotten, and that, despite their closeness in age, Michael was appearing to cast Walton into the ranks of the old guard.

Rawsthorne and Lutyens, Walton and Lambert had all enjoyed considerable acclaim in the 1930s. Here was a giggling man in ill-fitting clothes, who had spent his youth on the peripheries of the musical scene conducting amateur choirs, suddenly getting a great deal of attention. Constant Lambert had been profoundly interested in African-American music, and had pushed unsuccessfully for his work *The Rio Grande* to feature a black choir, yet it was Michael receiving praise for the inclusion of spirituals in *A Child of Our Time*. Unavoidably, there was an intense dislike of both Tippett and Britten, now frequently banded together as the country's leading musical figures, for their sexuality. Neither Lambert nor Walton was sure which of them had invented their nickname for Michael, "Arse-over-Tippett".[60] This was either jesting word play or homophobic swipe, but, although we only have Michael's memories for evidence, Walton was apparently more and more convinced that there was homosexual conspiracy in British music, and he attempted to block Britten being appointed music director at the Royal Opera House: "there are enough buggers in the place already, it's time it is stopped". In Michael's presence he apparently shouted: "Everyone is queer and I'm just normal, so my music will never succeed."[61] Michael had little time for any of this, told Walton he was being ridiculous, and the two maintained, somewhat against the odds, a cordial friendship. Walton and his wife had eventually moved to the volcanic island of Ischia, off the coast of Naples, and Michael was to spend some happy holidays there.

Walton's attitude, shared by others, was indicative of a wider movement in the classical-music world. The Royal Opera House had long been an accepting refuge for homosexuals. Of the production team behind *The Midsummer Marriage* the director, Christopher West, and the conductor, John Pritchard, were openly gay (the latter had been a conscientious objector), and the choreographer, John Cranko, was soon to be prosecuted for homosexual activity. Michael's friend and supporter Edward Sackville-West, who sat on the Opera House's board, was gay; and the chief executive, David Webster, had long been in a loving relationship with another man. Some saw this as a cabal, with Webster prioritising jobs for attractive young males. The singer Steuart Wilson had been music director of the Arts Council prior to becoming the BBC's director of music, in which role he had supported the broadcast of *A Child of Our Time* in the face of concerns regarding Michael's prison sentence. He moved to become David Webster's deputy at the Opera House and had interviewed Michael on the radio.

But Wilson, resenting his subordinate role, soon resigned under a cloud of ill feeling and quickly announced his Campaign against Homosexuality in British Music. "The influence of perverts in the world of music has grown beyond all measure," he was quoted as saying in the tabloid newspaper *The People*. "If it is not curbed soon, Covent Garden and other precious musical heritages could suffer irreparable harm. Many people in the profession are worried. There is a kind of agreement among the homosexuals which results in their keeping jobs for the boys." A further interview in *The People*, with the film composer Walford Hyden, whose sole claim to fame was a cameo role in David Lean's *Great Expectations*, continued the diatribe: "Homosexuals are damaging music and all the other arts. I am sorry for those born that way, but many acquire it – and for them I have nothing but contempt. Singers who are perverted often get work simply because of this. And new works by composers are given preference by some people if the writer is perverted."[62] David Webster, about whom rumours of indecent activity began to circulate, acted fast to tamp down Wilson's campaign, and no other newspaper picked up the story.

But the situation was all too typical of the national picture. Wartime attitudes towards sexuality had given way to fearsome intolerance, and the illegality of any form of same-sex activity, whether in public or private, could be upheld with all the panicked persecution of a witch-hunt. It was a time of suicides among the young, of unpredictable attacks by the police, and in the artistic communities of theatre and opera it spawned considerable fear.[63] In 1953 John Gielgud had been arrested for cottaging in a public lavatory amid swirls of rumour and publicity, setting off what is often argued to have been a concerted effort to ensnare famous or aristocratic homosexuals. There were raids on public toilets and underground clubs, with the handsomest policemen pushed forward as bait, and by the end of 1954 over 1,000 men were incarcerated for homosexual acts. A conviction of sodomy led to a life sentence, and "gross indecency" two years. There were calls for Britain to follow the lead of the many European countries that had legalised sexual acts between consenting men in private, and on 4

September 1957 a committee led by Lord Wolfenden had published a report on homosexual offences recommending just such a legalisation. It took a decade for the recommendations to become law. The manuscript of E.M. Forster's love story between men, *Maurice*, lay in a drawer, unpublished, unpublishable.

Michael cannot have been unaware of the plight suffered by so many who shared his sexual nature. Benjamin Britten was interviewed by Scotland Yard (no charges were brought). That Michael had had homosexual affairs was an open secret. Those who knew, knew; others didn't think to ponder. In concert halls and opera houses a don't-ask-don't-tell attitude prevailed. But whereas Britten and Pears were evidently partners, who visitors could see clearly shared a bed in their Aldeburgh house, Michael's situation was more complicated, and he could easily be appraised as a bachelor, married to music. John Minchinton could be passed off in public as an eager conductor, helping to prepare scores and rehearse orchestras. He was only an intermittent visitor to Tidebrook, with his own bedroom and his own flat in London. The relationship was faltering badly, and for years Michael had been "getting myself ready for the bump, if I do have to be alone". John had begun a relationship with not one but two women, and Michael's response was calmly to take them all on holiday, and to revel in their youthful company. He was sure that he and John "would need a further *éclaircissement d'amitié*" – a clarification of friendship – "because I want to leave him all of himself, that he needs for his real life".[64]

All this helped Michael escape the more rabid homophobia that afflicted so many throughout the 1950s, and apart from the jibes and dislike of his contemporaries he suffered relatively little. The closest he had got to any public "outing" was in a satirical broadcast on the Third Programme by the dramatist Henry Reed, who created a series of radio plays featuring the outlandish figure of "twelve-tone composeress" Hilda Tablet, an amalgam of Ethel Smyth and Elisabeth Lutyens. One features a dramatised reading from a novel called *The Arse and the Elbow* (parodying Graham Greene), in which a rather gnomic elderly priest named "Father Tippett" scratches at his groin and mourns a handsome young airman.[65] It was a thinly veiled appearance, but one of Michael's most marked characteristics was an ability to take a joke. Another was his resolution against self-pity. His music continued its apolitical course, and there is nothing in his piano concerto or second symphony that rages against a homophobic Establishment, although the music may be said to extend a comforting hand to those suffering. His optimistic and patient nature stood him in good stead as he weathered the critical attacks. Nevertheless, it was in the prevailing wind of suspicion against his music, and amid the persecution of homosexuals, that he would actively transform both his compositional and his personal life.

TWENTY-FOUR

Unexpected Flowering

Michael was now unarguably middle-aged, though few who met him believed he could be so old. His hair kept its colour, his posture was unstooped, his energy undimmed. Long countryside walks were still vital to his disciplined Tidebrook routine. "He is fifty, but looks thirty," thought one interviewer. A profile in the *Observer* was more insightful: "In spite of an almost boyish physique and a rich head of jet black hair that belie his years, the face itself is ravaged beyond its age by the agonies and discipline of creation." He was a strange mixture now of levity and seriousness, of self-assured authority and self-sabotaging breeziness, though underneath both was a likeable warmth and complex mind. "It is indeed", continued the *Observer*, "from this almost disturbing originality of mind, and not from mere eccentricity, that there stems an impression of individuality so intense as to amount to oddness."[1] He had an otherworldly haphazardness, his mind seemingly holding so much music that it excluded the practicalities of daily life. He got into the habit of posting cards to himself; on one, addressed to "Michael Tippett", is written "a) Mama's birthday, b) Menuhin". It is signed "M".[2]

Major figures from his youth were dropping away. On 26 April 1957 his old, troubled friend Aubrey Russ, who had guided his student days in London, had died aged sixty-six in a hospital in Redhill, after a long decline into early-onset dementia. The following year, Michael's first partner, Roy Langford, also died, of unknown causes, only as old as the century. Michael had broken with Roy twenty-five years before, but never again had he lived permanently with any of the men or women he had loved. A taste of family life he gleaned from old friends and their children, who were invited to Tidebrook Manor with a frequency bordering on pressure, though most readily took up the offers of hospitality. Michael's nieces would visit with their parents, though the family was grieving for the death of Michael's nephew, John, aged just twenty-three. (Born intersex, he had suffered a number of operations and was eventually diagnosed with cancer.) There were camping holidays to Cornwall with the Ayersts, and with the family of Bryan Fisher, who became proficient in rescuing dripping tea-towels from Michael's gesticulating hands, the washing-up forgotten in the face of philosophical or political discussions.[3]

Michael was on the cusp of tremendous change. His mind was full of a new opera, which eventually became *King Priam*, although its gestation was long and convoluted. In an early draft of *The Midsummer Marriage* is the scenario of a ballet for the character of Strephon entitled *The Windrose*, referring to an eight-pointed tool used by meteorologists to measure the direction of the winds.[4] This ballet was eventually replaced by the Ritual Dances, but Michael did not want to abandon the idea completely, and in 1950 had mentioned that he was soon to embark upon "a new choral and orchestral creation with a probable title of 'The Windrose'".[5] Plans to extend this discarded scene of *The Midsummer Marriage* were soon abandoned, as was a long-discussed collaboration with David Ayerst that in April 1950 was to have been a cantata on the poet Caedmon, which then morphed into a piece using biblical quotations, written for male solo and chorus, and designed to express "the idea that the rebuilding is finer than the building".[6] In May 1953 another piece had flickered in Michael's mind: an oratorio on the Italian author Cesare Pavese who, arrested as an anti-fascist during the war, had committed suicide. The story was, Michael thought, "the way forward to my second *Child* [of Our Time . . .] all very exciting".[7] But soon he had discarded Pavese's story in favour of an opera documenting the life of Edith Cavell, the British nurse executed by a German firing squad for helping Allied soldiers escape from occupied Belgium during the First World War. By January 1954, though: "Nurse Cavell has gone down the drain in the sense of an operatic possibility."[8]

That same month Michael had begun "sketching out the shape of a strange choral work, that has the eight fundamental hexagrams of the I Ching at its base".[9] Two years later he was still deep in this planned work, and on 3 January 1956 told Priaulx Rainier that "the next choral work I am already meditating is all embedded in the archetypal images – if I can successfully awaken them". As if stung by the reaction to The Midsummer Marriage, he had wanted to try collaboration with a librettist. "I am imagining that I am going this time to try to work with a poet – and I have spoken of it already to [Christopher] Fry. [. . .] I'm afraid of the more obvious poet – like Kathleen Raine* – because I must have great clarity of image – a deceptive simplicity à la Chinese. For at the back of my idea is a Chinese book."[10] Fifteen months later, in March 1957, a vocal piece based on the I Ching was still Michael's priority. "I'm full of a new work for the theatre," he had told Anna Kallin. "The Flowering of the I Ching (that's not the title) – in the end, as some kind of choral ballet or mime. [. . .] I don't suppose anyone will know how much, if at all, that book has given me stimulus to write." His plans had almost interrupted work on his second symphony, which was then nearing completion. "It's all slowly taking shape and taking fire," he wrote of what he had now tentatively titled Festival in the Humane City. "It's apt to overwhelm the symphony every so often."[11]

Festival in the Humane City was to have been a huge creation, seemingly for dancers, choir, and orchestra, more pageant than opera. The twelve-page sketch is of the most cryptic kind, with the earlier scenes the most detailed. Laid out in eight sections and with

---

* The visionary poetry of Kathleen Raine (1908–2003), who was an expert on any number of Tippett's literary gods, including Yeats and Blake, was imbued with a love of nature, an interest in Jung, and an intense mysticism. The titles of her poems read like a potted synopsis of The Midsummer Marriage: "The Locked Gates", "The Hollow Hill", "The Pythoness".

frequent reference to the I Ching, the piece forms a life cycle, from childhood through education and maturity, eventually reaching a harmonious old age. Opening "in the mountains [as] spring melts the snow", a number of vignettes flashes past: a little boy works with his father to take the cows from their winter byres, while a little girl "is going to school with her brother", and "sits in the light wind hugging her adolescence". Startlingly autobiographical, the sketch moves through an unhappy experience of schooldays, with "submission to priest"; the "humiliation of repeated penetration (too forced, not gentle)"; the boy witnessing "some (horrible) image of 'propaganda'". Eventually childhood is subsumed by scenes of war and destruction, with a central section designed to depict "science – techniques – precision – war". Michael even went so far as to sketch one scene featuring "a jet plane with A-bomb".[12] The piece was to be "on an apocalyptic theme".[13] A finished work can scarcely be imagined from such intriguing and daring jottings, but the Festival in the Humane City indicates a firm step away from the buoyant renewal of The Midsummer Marriage into a consideration of what Michael perceived to be the dangerous precipice on which the ostensibly optimistic world of the late 1950s was actually poised. The Festival had been a serious intention for at least three years, and the Edinburgh Festival had expressed interest in its premiere. Its ideas haunt Michael's later works: the life-cycle structure of his fourth symphony, and, most of all, his enormous piece for choir and orchestra, The Mask of Time, begun in 1980, which mentions atomic bombs and the I Ching.

Plans for the Festival had been full-steam-ahead in March 1957. But in a matter of months a blazing new inspiration for an opera had knocked them aside. The future of opera had seemed uncertain in the late 1950s. Many avant-garde composers in Europe – Hans Werner Henze being a notable exception – remained suspicious of the form, feeling it had had its day. Lennox Berkeley never produced another, and Walton only a one-act chamber piece. Benjamin Britten composed nothing for the operatic stage between 1954 and 1960, and the country's younger generation of opera composers had yet to begin. Michael meanwhile, caring little for fashion, kept

faith in traditional forms. David Webster, director of the Royal
Opera House, thought the *Festival*'s scenario had potential for a more
conventional operatic work, perhaps hoping to net a successful, not
to say lucid, premiere. In August 1956 Bertolt Brecht had brought
his Berliner Ensemble to London with productions of his *Mother
Courage* and Farquhar's *The Recruiting Officer* (updated to the American
War of Independence). The epic stagings were typically "Brechtian"
and made Michael aware of the operatic potential in Brecht's self-
conscious theatricality. A few months later he was likewise struck
by a revival of Paul Claudel's play *Le Livre de Christophe Colomb*, and by
its technically complex production, with mime, processions, and
projection.[14] Most important was the advice of Peter Brook, now
working in theatre and film. In the spring of 1957 Michael, bold
as ever in seeking advice, had taken his ideas to Brook, and they
had a stimulating and vigorous discussion. "Brook was forthright
and theatrically concrete", Michael thought: "The real thing that
seems to emerge is that whatever mistakes were made with the
choice of *handlung* for *The Midsummer Marriage*, they sprang from a very
early 'mistake' – when I got a fixed idea of something, and got
too far involved too soon. So then I dug my heels in and built the
tremendous façade of the music to carry the strange (*Willkuerliche*)
Handlung." Michael's German translates as a remarkable casting-off
of *The Midsummer Marriage*'s scenario: *arbitrary action*. He thought the
discussions with Brook "may be going to do some of the functions
of a collaboration", and that "the core of the thing, according
to Brook, is that, with a mind like mine that is almost over-rich
[. . .] it's essential to reduce to an action that is, in the face of it,
simple".[15]

Certainly it would have taken an audience with more than a
working knowledge of the *I Ching* fully to grasp the *Festival*. Michael
was persuaded. As he reached the final movement of the second
symphony, things had begun to rush. By May 1957 he had alighted
on the "simple" scenario that would form the basis of an opera:
the Trojan war, as depicted in Homer's *Iliad* and a handful of other
sources. Ancient Greek literature had been an infectious love of his
father's, read since his childhood, but the idea could have been

prompted by any number of circumstances: a chance meeting with the eminent mythologist Gertrude Levy; a noted production of Berlioz's *The Trojans* at Covent Garden in 1957; and most of all the work of Christopher Fry, whose play *Venus Observed* (1950) had retold the Judgement of Paris. In 1955 Fry had written a celebrated adaptation of Jean Giraudoux's *The Trojan War Will Not Take Place*, and invited Michael to provide the production's incidental music. Michael eventually declined, but the suggestion had planted a seed.[16]

Impetus to continue with a Homeric opera was furthered, in July 1957, by the prestigious offer of a commission from the Koussevitzky Music Foundation: $1,500 for a choral-orchestral piece lasting no more than half an hour, with no deadline. The Foundation was persuaded to accept an opera in lieu of a choral piece, and as Michael came to the end of the second symphony he decided, undaunted by criticism and itching to begin, to write the libretto himself. After completing the symphony on 13 November, Michael had moved straight on to a two-movement violin sonata. But the tug to the opera was now irresistible, and by 22 November he had given in, and given up. "Alas, the new opera has swept the violin sonata aside – I'd begun it, but couldn't sustain it against the pull of the other. Perhaps just as well, as it had got promised to Edinburgh for [Wolfgang] Schneiderhan. But Ben and Yehudi" – Britten and Menuhin – "would have been much nearer to me."[17] Nothing of the violin sonata survives.

Four days later, on 26 November, he was sitting in T.S. Eliot's office in Bloomsbury, eager to discuss the new opera's libretto. Eliot had recently remarried and was writing a final play, *The Elder Statesman*. Michael had seen little of him since their meetings around Edith Sitwell's dinner table a decade before, although he had continued to invite the poet to various concerts. "It is always a pleasure", Eliot told him, "to admire your back in a tail coat."[18] He and Michael had rejuvenated their acquaintance at the Sound Broadcasting Society, which both had joined to protest the BBC's cutting of the Third Programme's output in favour of the newly launched and more populist Network Three. They met at least three times in the space of a few months that autumn.[19] Michael always claimed that it was Eliot who had persuaded him that a composer should write his own texts, but in private Eliot clarified the situation, and wrote to Eric Walter White:

> My advice was specifically directed toward oratorio [. . .] opera is a different matter, and while I don't think that a really poetic gift is necessary, I do feel that the author of an operatic libretto should have some theatrical gift. I have not seen *The Midsummer Marriage*. I have only listened to some of it on the wireless, and while I enjoy Michael Tippett's music, I suspect from the reviews of the opera that I have read, that he might have been well advised to secure a good librettist.[20]

Nevertheless, Eliot made no attempt to dissuade Michael from writing another libretto – or if he did, he was ignored. Eliot had less than a decade to live and was soon plagued by health problems caused by heavy smoking. He and Michael were to meet for the last time in August the following year, at the premiere, in Edinburgh, of *The Elder Statesman*. Dining at the hotel where Eliot and his wife were staying, Michael watched them walk in, "hand in hand, as was their custom, and go to their table". By happy coincidence, at the play's performance he was "sitting right next to Eliot, who was also on his own". Eliot had not published a major poem in many years. "Would he move back once more towards poetry?" Michael asked him. "He said it was possible. If that was truly in his mind, it was not in his fate."[21]

The first half of 1958 was taken up with the premiere of the second symphony and the fallout from the performance's breakdown. There was no chance of beginning serious work on an opera. Michael had also accepted a commission from a girls' school in Bristol, a setting, with instrumental interludes, of Christopher Fry's poem "Crown of the Year".[22] This was finished in late spring and Michael then turned his attention to seeing a collection of his radio talks into print (for the essay volume *Moving into Aquarius*), and worked on the opera's synopsis and libretto, dithering for many months over its title. Eventually he decided: *King Priam*.[23]

It was to take place in the margins of the *Iliad*, of which much was pared away. His libretto would be by no means a simple translation or adaptation of Homer, and makes no mention of the Trojan Horse. He turned also to the plays of Euripides, and Hyginus's *Fabulae*, weaving from his source materials a deeply personal gloss on the Trojan War. His visceral recoil from violence and conflict rings in every scene, both on the plains of battle and on the home front, as women wait at home, keeping baths hot for husbands who might never return. Descriptions of war are combined with precise domestic details, and patriotic duty is put into conflict with personal loves. For his cast list Michael maintained the octet of four couples that had stood behind many of his earlier ideas for stage works: Paris and Helen; Priam and his wife Hecuba; their son Hector and his wife, Andromache; and, of the Greeks, Achilles and Patroclus. Encircling this eight-pointed compass is the messenger-god Hermes, and a choric trio: a guard, an old man, and a nurse. (Originally these were cast explicitly as a composer, a poet, and a theatre director, but Peter Brook persuaded him against this idea.)[24] Michael humanised the drama by doubling the three women in Paris's life – Hecuba, Andromache, Helen – with the goddesses Athene, Hera, and Aphrodite.

The scenario was a means by which to ask from the midst of battle how humanity had descended to such a state, charting a series of pivotal moments that are the result either of fate or of choice. Michael, in his love affairs as in his politics, had often felt himself unable to resist urges that he believed almost foretold for him. "I have another fate to live out," he had written of his pacifism, or, on the same topic: "I can go forwards according to my fate." The word piles up in his self-analyses. "It happens to be my fate to incarnate [pacifism] to a certain degree [. . .]. I cannot evade the fate for fear of the consequence." "It's my fate, in some absolutely clear way."[25] He placed his tug of war between human agency and human destiny at the heart of his opera. Priam, warned that his newborn son Paris will cause his death, chooses to have the baby killed. A young guard chooses to save Paris, entrusting him to the care of a local shepherd. Priam chooses, on discovering

Paris still alive, to return him to Troy. Paris, now a man, is asked to choose between three goddesses. And so the dominoes topple, and the long, stagnant war begins.

"All hands on page eleven!" is a typical example of Michael's attitude towards the text.[26] Conversations with Peter Brook continued on and off throughout the year, and Günther Rennert, whom Michael had wanted to direct *The Midsummer Marriage*, also offered advice. It is true to say that great swathes of *King Priam*'s libretto — especially in the third act — were taken in by Michael verbatim from others' suggestions. The opera's three-act structure, consigning the war scenes and their spare instrumentation to an act of their own, was a proposal of Eric Walter White's, and it was Christopher Fry who persuaded Michael to leave the slaughter of Achilles's lover Patroclus in the wings, so that the explicit depiction of Priam's murder in the final moments of the opera might rip through the Greek convention of off-stage death all the more effectively.[27]

King Priam was becoming an explicit rejection of Utopianism, be it political, religious, or the drug-fuelled peace-and-love culture of hippiedom that lay just around the corner. Before beginning the libretto Michael had been sure that the opera would have "no chiliastic* philosophy, whether of a classless society or a heavenly reward".[28] He had once devoted many years of his life to Marxist parties that sought to rebuild society into an idyll of equality. In the closing scenes of *King Priam* can be found his retraction of these views, the calcifying of his hopefulness, as the Greeks finally lay waste to Troy, and Priam's family is murdered or sold into slavery one by one, and Andromache sees Achilles's son "raging through the town swinging my own dead child as club". An early draft of the libretto had Priam as a blazing King Lear figure, quoting Shakespeare explicitly: "Howl, howl, howl, howl! O you are men of stones".[29] But soon Michael made of Priam, hiding somewhere in Troy, growing frailer and frailer, a figure imbued with the

---

* "Chiliastic" refers to a religious belief in a 1,000-year period of peace and prosperity.

chilling calm of hopelessness. Dismissing his family, he will agree to see only the curiously blank figure of Helen, onto whom men have projected any number of fantasies. She is made peculiarly transcendent by dint of being the opera's only character who has had to make no choice.

It was sometime in 1957 that Michael, walking in Bloomsbury and pondering *King Priam*, had bumped into a figure from his past. It was Karl Hawker, with whom he had had a brief affair during the last months of the Blitz, when Karl was working on a land scheme in Cambridge for conscientious objectors. They had not met for over fifteen years. Michael was running for a bus and Karl joined him. In September 1945, after leaving the objectors' land scheme, Karl had married. He and his actress wife, Anne, had had their first child, Susan, in 1947; two years later their daughter Sarah was born. The marriage had ended in 1953 and Karl, who had trained at Hornsey College of Art, was attempting to make a living as an artist and teacher. He was now thirty-six, and had grown into his looks. He visited Michael in Sussex, and the attraction between the two men was revived. In June 1958, as work on *King Priam*'s libretto began, Michael wrote to Karl to declare his love, found it requited, and a few months later Karl came to live at Tidebrook Manor.[30]

It was a brave decision to begin a relationship with another man that would be more evident to others, given the new domestic set-up, than any Michael had yet experienced. For a while Karl lived in one of the outhouses, but soon moved, not into Michael's bed, but to a room of his own in the main house. Secrecy had to be maintained given the predatory atmosphere in the country towards such relationships, and only carefully chosen friends were informed of the change. It had happened with great speed, and necessitated what Michael had long predicted: a separation from John Minchinton, after a thirteen-year affair. John's emotional life was now focused mainly on his girlfriend, Jessica Jenkins, and Michael had hoped for and expected a smooth transition. But John's rage in the face of the new arrival was very terrible. His life had crumbled. In July he had conducted the premiere of Michael's folk-song arrangements, *Four Songs from the British Isles*, but soon afterwards the Third Programme, citing lack of technique, had suspended him from conducting duties for a year.[31] He likely realised that without Michael's support his career would suffer further.

August 1958 was an impossibly difficult month. Michael narrated the difficulties in a series of letters to Priaulx Rainier, still one of his most intimate friends:

3 August 1958

I can't help him over the matter except by speaking the truth if demanded, and being patient to listen when he needs to talk. I don't think I see the outcome yet. As to myself, I am sore inside because of John's violences, and happy in a new warmth in Tide-brook and with someone who, for example, is looking forward to your coming, because you are close to me, and not unsure of your coming because close to me! I really can't go much back into the thrashing, jealous world. In fact I can't go back at all. But poor John is in the very heart of it. [. . .] I get moments of guilt about John turned out of his supposed home, but they only are moments which don't hold against (though they hurt me) the sense of having to go forward in myself, even if down the wrong path – whatever "wrong" means in such a context.

11 August

Life here varies between happy times when things seem peaceful, and dreadful, and times when John (on the phone) goes nearly mad. Or so it seems. It is just the way the world is, that new life has to fight its way out of the old. But we (particularly Karl of course) get to being resentful of John that his unbalance is so extreme he will not let me be [. . .]. When [I refuse] to let John go on shouting, he slowly calms himself and is forced into a new life rhythm. And even for myself – the new came so unex-pectedly it has to slough off the past – and there are pangs, as when a child misbehaves and won't go out into the world on its own and won't let one be. Don't worry too much – I shall come through. This morning has been, in myself, a bad morning. Sense of all the worst in John; and of deep disillusion.

24 August
Poor John is still in grave difficulties. When we meet in person we can get through to some sense, control and contact – but the phone is a devil. He becomes vituperative and bitter and rude. He made a visit down last weekend over a night, with Jessica. I think it helped, in that he had to see and find out for himself how it is here under the new dispensation. But it ended not so well, after a good beginning. There is so much *amour propre* tied up in it, as well as the sense of betrayal and loss. As he went away in a huff, Jessica looked back at me and smiled and almost winked. So I took heart. She knows it is her chance, and her responsibility to try and get him onto a new life. This period is practically difficult in any case, because his professional life is in abeyance. He has too little to do, I guess.

4 September
I had a terrible last scene with John. [. . .] He was so violent I had to leave, to a slammed door. And I just won't go to see him if that is all he can manage. I neither wrote nor rang afterwards; till today, when a reasonable letter came. [. . .] My new life is very happy and peaceful; though it is a new adjustment, long hoped for I think, but unexpected. A throw towards the male in myself; with thereby a tremendous enrichment of my *sensibilité* – and direct perception of relationships and character. Interesting in that way. The sensual [in Karl] very developed compared with me.

Eventually John calmed, and his relationship with Michael became one of distant civility. He continued to work intermittently as a conductor, but his career never took off. Jessica Jenkins did not become Mrs Minchinton until 1974. The couple had sixteen years of married life together before John died, in 1990, after a long illness, at the age of seventy-two.[32]

For a while Michael found himself deliriously happy at life with
Karl. At fifty-three he was finally sharing his life, permanently, with
someone he loved, and who loved him. Karl introduced Michael
to his daughters, Susan and Sarah, then aged eleven and ten, and
Michael fell for them instantly. Relations were cordial with Karl's
ex-wife, and Michael enjoyed sorting out the girls' drop-offs, paying
his share of uniforms and school fees. The girls spent their holidays
at Tidebrook Manor, and the Hawkers, father and daughters, got
to know Michael's friends, who accepted them gladly, privately
relieved that John Minchinton was no longer around. "Some of my
friends", Michael admitted, "find new life here, without John. He
didn't please all of them."[33] The house could be full to the brim
with children, junior Ayersts, junior Hawkers, junior Fishers. As
David's daughter Caroline says, "we were always hordes. Karl was
the one who would engineer the games and do things like that.
He was a good raconteur and Michael would have a sort of stooge
relationship to him, so he would sort of feed Karl a line, and Karl
would run with it." Alexander Goehr agrees: "Karl was marvellous,
I liked him best of all the Tippett men that I knew."[34] Most of the
children were rather terrified of Isabel, elderly and arthritic in her
private rooms. She had taken up painting, producing not charming
watercolours but bewitched oils of shrieking heads that haunted
the dreams of visitors. Michael wrote of the new life to Benjamin
Britten: "The moment of change isn't a pretty story, I suspect – but
the outcome is that someone lives here with me, in a relationship
as near to marriage as these relationships can be. [. . .] The pull is
quite mutual. Something I've never known before in this continuous way – and have consequently often envied you and Peter. So
it's a totally unexpected flowering into a union I'd quite decided
was not due to me. We are very happy."[35]

Time and again the twists and turns of Michael's musical style
had been bound up in his personal life. Time and again he had
reinvented himself musically just as he could calmly reinvent himself personally, seemingly turning his back on past lives, past loves.
The synchronicity is striking. In 1932, on meeting Wilfred Franks,
he had rejected a number of compositions and begun his grand

Symphony in B flat. Wilfred's departure had led to the Concerto for Double String Orchestra, the first unrevised piece in Michael's official catalogue. The affair with Douglas Newton coincided with work on *A Child of Our Time*; the move into the glowing world of *The Midsummer Marriage* and its successors followed hard on the heels of John Minchinton's arrival. And now, Karl was the catalyst for Michael's embarking upon a new opera that would be tougher, darker, more violent in topic and treatment than anything he had yet written. This new relationship had, Michael thought, brought about an emotional and sexual recalibration, and he believed himself "to have flung round on to a more masculine road". If, with lovers past, his emotional and maybe his sexual role had been subservient, now things were different: "suddenly [I] won't be pushed around, whereas before I have wanted to be. [. . .] It has all happened with astonishing speed. And coincides with a growing obsession with the new opera. Mixed up I dare [say], somewhere, somehow."[36]

Although it was *King Priam* that truly fired the starting pistol, a change had been coming for some while. It was a time of musical experiment, most evidently in Europe, where a new generation of composers – among them Pierre Boulez and Karlheinz Stockhausen – were coming to the fore, many experimenting in individual ways with the serialism of the Viennese School, or with music for electronically created or modified sounds. Michael had been dogged by a growing dissatisfaction, a nagging sense that *The Midsummer Marriage* had taken him so long to complete that it was threatening to ossify his style into one that would be left behind by the decade's musical developments. "I think the present trend in my music is leaning too much over towards the expected and too little adventurous," he had written during composition of the piano concerto. "Maybe it'll swing back again soon. A bath of Stravinsky – even a dose of Hindemith, perhaps."[37] As happens so often with composers who are known especially for one early work, he was beginning to resent the popularity of *A Child of Our Time*, and wrote of its "shocking technical conservatism", eventually deeming it "the silly old Child".[38] He was experiencing an acute sense of unbelonging. His style could be dismissed by musicians reactionary and experimental, falling neither into the British pastoral school, nor the worlds of atonalism or serialism.

Michael spoke praisingly of Vaughan Williams, who died on 26 August 1958: "I loved him for his generosity as a human being, and within that love I realised that all the so-to-say rejections which had come from the arrogance of my youth no longer had any interest or consequence whatsoever. [. . .] I think now that through him, as well as through others, but through him especially, we were made free."[39] But Michael had not forgotten how dismissive he had initially been of his musical ancestor, and even in middle age could be heard referring to Vaughan Williams's orchestral suite *Flos Campi* as "camp flossy".[40] He was likely aware that, were he not careful, he too could be confined by a new generation to the world of the fuddy-duddy. Nevertheless, he was adept at positioning himself as a bridge between warring factions. He listened with open ears to the second Viennese school, and helped to bridge the divisions in British music. Leading British composers, including Vaughan Williams, had publicly declared their continued antipathy to serialism; William Glock was fired from the *Observer* for focusing too heavily on the Continental avant-garde.[41] Figures such as Elisabeth Lutyens and Humphrey Searle were meanwhile becoming leading pioneers of British serial music. Michael had chaired a composers' conference on Schoenberg and, "with Tippett presiding", wrote the *Observer*, "the two armies drew themselves up to give battle. Had it not been for the unquestioned authority of the chairman, who sharply told musical eminences when to speak up and when to sit down, an irate lady composer" – Lutyens – "would certainly have smashed an eminent critic's skull with an umbrella."[42]

Michael had told Benjamin Britten: "you are the only English composer of nowadays I care at all about".[43] The statement was more flattering than true. He could be sharply dismissive of his contemporaries, as when, towards the end of the war, he had lunched with Gerald Finzi, who believed Michael a superior talent to Britten, and had campaigned on his behalf prior to his trial. But Michael found Finzi "a hopelessly old-fashioned, folksy composer, and talkative".[44] He had continued to keep an admiring ear on the output of Alan Bush and his Royal College contemporary Elizabeth Maconchy, and above all there was Priaulx Rainier, who during the 1950s was producing some of her most original work, mainly for Peter Pears, who had to navigate a wild unaccompanied recitative that intermittently settles into icy lakes of melody, floating between pebbled shores. Priaulx was moving further away from tonality, and discarding conventional ensembles. Michael professed himself "moved" by her music "in a way I seldom am nowadays", and was sure that she had solved "a technical problem of unaccompanied song that I hadn't seen how to. I shall have to imitate you!" Flattery again perhaps, but he was more honest with Priaulx than with others, and his praise was consistent. "Compared with you," Michael told her, the songs of The Heart's Assurance seemed "too civilised"; he was sure that "one's best work lies elsewhere – more in the region that you usually inhabit". He read Theodor Adorno's polemical Philosophy of New Music, which focused on the work of Schoenberg and Stravinsky, and it put the wind up him. Soon he was worrying, only half in jest, that there would eventually be "nothing of our day left but the major works of Schoenberg, and a few bars of Rainier!"[45]

The figure Michael and Priaulx had most in common was Igor Stravinsky, whom Priaulx openly professed her musical god. Michael agreed: "Stravinsky is a giant and the rest of us more or less pygmies."[46] He and the Russian composer met just once, on 11 December 1956. He was with Priaulx, at a dinner in London to celebrate the London premiere of Stravinsky's Canticum Sacrum. At the table Priaulx demonstrated to Stravinsky the clicks of the Zulu she had picked up as a child, and he delightedly tried to imitate them. Michael wrote to her afterwards: "Yes – meeting Stravinsky was memorable. I'm glad it happened."[47] His music had been audibly shot through with the neoclassical vigour of Stravinsky's orchestral symphonies. But the 1950s had seen Stravinsky beginning to employ techniques first devised by Schoenberg. The British premiere of his ballet Agon was given by John Minchinton at the Festival Hall in May 1958 and had a remarkable effect on Michael, who was struck especially by Stravinsky's renovation of the orchestra (which never

once plays all together) into smaller ensembles of vividly imaginative instrumental combinations. Flicking through the influences
on his own music, Michael admitted that Britten had a lucidity he
aimed always "to go towards", that Shostakovich had "never drawn
him", and that Stravinsky, above all others, "was the master who
mattered".[48]

Agon had slotted into the jigsaw of influences that was moving
Michael's music into new worlds. The change is evident from the
first bars of *King Priam*. Michael began the music early in October
1958, with a fanfare for trumpets punctuated by sharp blasts of
gunfire from the timpani, and a wordless off-stage chorus.[49] The
cries seem to denote celebration at the birth of Paris, but when they
return at the end of the opera, we know them for what they are:
the screams of the dying, as the Greeks lay waste to Troy. Michael's
music has darkened in colour, gone matte, its edges sharpened. Soft
curves have hardened into angularity and the leaves fallen from his
hitherto lush musical branches. It is as if the orchestra has been
combed through. In contrast to the thickly scored verdure of *The
Midsummer Marriage*, the blasted soundscape of *King Priam* has been
laid to waste. In the central, war-torn act the strings abandon the
pit altogether, as the women have abandoned the stage, leaving
only a scorched accompaniment of brass, mottled with percussion.
Michael's orchestra is no longer a sea on which the voices might
sail, but a Greek chorus in its own right, commenting, goading,
lamenting. Key signatures wobble and disintegrate, hide behind
rogue accidentals, are overlaid one with another or simply absent.

Most obvious is a new structural technique. Development and
exuberance have given way to a score that splinters into a tough
mosaic of motifs, juxtaposed or intertwined, each linked to a specific character: mournful cellos for Andromache; a blizzard of violins
in panicked judder for Hecuba. Paris's instrument is mainly the
oboe, while the Old Man is accompanied by a foreboding trio of
low woodwind. But the "mosaic" metaphor (Michael's own) is
only half apt. There is no grouting in the score, no bridge passages
to ease the transition from one motif to another, and instead the
musical tiles scrape up against one another.

30. The premiere of Tippett's first major opera, *The Midsummer Marriage*, at the Royal Opera House, Covent Garden, in January 1955. Lead singers Richard Lewis (left) and Joan Sutherland (right) stand in front of the central arch. "Barbara Hepworth's scenery will divide opinion," wrote *The Times* (it did). The set was painted in an array of greens and blues, with a bright blue cyclorama at the back.

31. Sam Wanamaker directed the premiere of *King Priam* in 1962; the production is shown here in its 1985 revival, with Alexander Malta as Priam and Kim Begley as Achilles. The *Spectator* thought that Sean Kenny's sets heralded "the coming-of-age of operatic design in this country".

32. *The Knot Garden* was premiered to rapturous acclaim at the Opera House in 1970. Peter Hall's production featured sets by Timothy O'Brien, with photographs of sunlight and leaves projected onto hanging nylon ropes.

33. *The Ice Break* had a more difficult premiere (Tippett's last at the Opera House, in July 1977). Sam Wanamaker, a last-minute replacement for Peter Hall, was unable to depict the other-worldly visitor, Astron, with holograms, and had to settle for laser beams.

34. The first revival of *The Ice Break* in nearly half a century, Graham Vick's promenade production with the Birmingham Opera Company, in April 2015, was staged in a disused Birmingham warehouse.

35. Tippett's final opera, *New Year*, was directed by Peter Hall with sets by Alison Chitty (the British premiere was at Glyndebourne Festival Opera, shown here in its touring revival in 1990, with Marie Angel as the heroine, JoAnn). Tippett told Hall that the production was "the most magical presentation at premiere of any theatre piece".

36. Michael Tippett, photographed in 1955. "He is fifty, but looks thirty" thought one interviewer, but the *Observer* found that "in spite of an almost boyish physique and a rich head of jet black hair that belie his years, the face itself is ravaged beyond its age by the agonies and discipline of creation".

37. Meirion "Bill" Bowen, who became, after a long and initially illicit affair, Tippett's partner and assistant.

38. On holiday with Bill (right), who found Tippett "as confident directing a group of friends around the Arizona desert as he is navigating an orchestra through his Fourth Symphony".

39. In Turkey, photographed by architect Graham Modlen, who thought Tippett "wanted to see the world and see everyone".

40. Sir Michael With-it? Modelling trousers designed by Philip Griffin for the British premiere of *Byzantium*. "Our distinguished octogenarian composer looked like a bird of paradise that had accidentally navigated a few thousand miles off course," wrote the *Telegraph*.

41. Sir Michael Tippett, OM.

42. "Tippett's age-spotted hands were slim and delicate", one interviewer described, "and at other times wove expressive movements to complement his words."

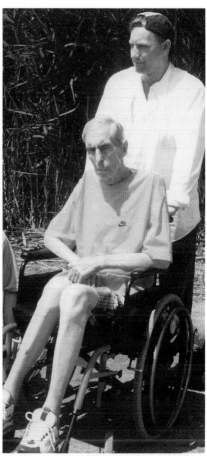

43. At Isleworth, c.1997. "The old Michael has gone," John Amis found, "leaving a wraith with sunken face and fairly useless limbs."

44. With friend and carer Andrew Coster: "Straight away we had this rapport. I learned so much from him."

45. Lake Retba, Senegal, photographed by Graham Modlen during his visit with Tippett in 1990.

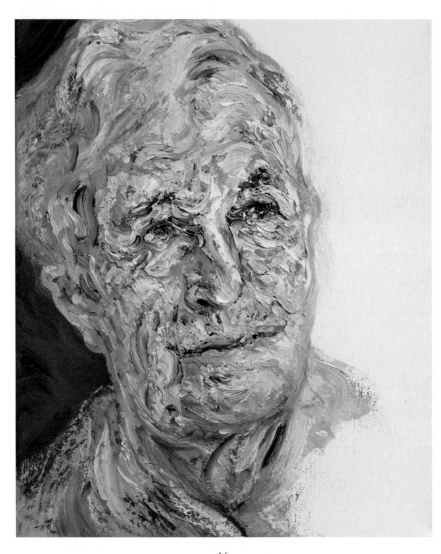

46.
Michael Tippett
Maggi Hambling
oil on canvas, 2017
12 x 10 inches

The change is not a hinge at the centre of Michael's catalogue, dividing his music into before-*Priam* and post-*Priam*. His had been a voice of frequent changes, and the shift in his career from the romanticism of the Symphony in B flat to the tough counterpoint of his first mature works was in its way as pronounced. Still to come was a yet more seismic change, when he would introduce the world of jazz and pop to his operas. And just as *The Midsummer Marriage* has its moments of startling violence, *King Priam* has moments of startling lyricism, glinting from within the angular lattice: from the dark plush of the string motif that cushions Priam's internal monologues, to the tightly plaited ribbons of the third-act trio for the women left behind in Troy. The Greek hero Achilles ends the first act with the chilling ululations of his war-cry, electronically amplified, as brass pounds into the earth beneath, but soon, accompanied by a lone guitar, sings a sinuously lyrical song, yearning for his homeland.

In May 1959 Michael wrote to Priaulx Rainier: "Just so that you can know, but no-one else (I haven't told mother yet even) – I've decided to accept a C.B.E. in the Birthday Honours." Michael may have been expected to turn down any suggestion of adding the initials of the British Empire to his name. "I hate the Empire as I hate nothing else" had been his constant theme as a younger man. But his reluctance to accept the award was not for anti-colonialist reasons, nor yet in dislike of the Tory government that had offered it. "At first I wanted to hang out for something better – a Companion of Honour like Benjamin Britten's, and then I felt that was unworthy and petty." He was sure that "there are many counts on which I could be faulted (going to prison, general outspokenness, etc) and this shows some kind of recognition, even if it has little to do with final artistic values".[50] Accepting the award was a means of joining the Establishment, but also a way to probe it from within, and most of all to further performances and funding. "I'm not an establishment composer," he later said, "but I belong to an

establishment." Composer Alan Bush had clung to the Marxist doctrines Michael had long since rejected, and was, Michael thought,
"nearer [to being] within an establishment than I could ever be".[51]
Back in 1955, during a raid on the flat of a Communist Party
member known as Operation Party Piece, MI5 had got hold of a
document written by Bush in which it was clearly stated: "I had also
got to know the composer Michael TIPPETT [. . .] it is not widely
known that Michael TIPPETT was for some time a Party member
about 1934–35."[52] But Michael appears to have escaped any kind of
investigation and it is a mark of his reputation's growing security
that a government honour had followed only a few years later.

Karl Hawker accompanied Michael to his investiture, and they
evidently felt happy enough appearing in public. King Priam was
flowing more easily than had The Midsummer Marriage, for the simple
reason that Michael was happier during the writing of it. He was
much more certain of the opera's quality, sure that he was achieving
what he had set out to achieve. By the end of 1959 the Royal Opera
House had agreed to a performance. There was an unforgettable
holiday with Karl in Venice, lovely weeks with Susan and Sarah,
and the purchase of a car brought a new freedom. A housekeeper
arrived, whom they thought a wonderful cook. "It's too good to
be true," was Michael's contented sigh. "An enrichment I'd never
imagined as coming my way. It's certainly no virtue in me that
has brought it, but the run of the luck. The 'troubles' are so minor
compared with the joys. And so, of course, the music prospers."[53]

The novelty of the relationship had seemingly kept at bay Karl's
intermittent bouts of depression. But as the months went past he
sank into crippling mental illness. By 1960 he was in the grip of
a bad depressive episode, was severely nauseous, and the doctors
could prescribe nothing to alter his mood. The affair had started
when King Priam was only words on paper, words on which Karl's
advice was often sought. But now a year had gone by with Michael
deep in the grip of composition (he began the second act on 29
February 1960), and the realities of sharing life not only with a
composer but with his opera and its demands, the music acting like
a lover living openly in the house and needing constant attention,

exerted fierce strain.[54] An affair with a man was not a novelty for
Karl, but a domestic life with a man, married in all but name, was.
The age would not allow him to move into such a set-up without
anxiety. Denied the dignity of being recognised as Michael's partner,
he found himself often described as an "assistant" or "secretary".
Michael had barely driven since his holiday to Spain in 1933, and
had never got a driver's licence, which was now required by law.
Karl became more or less his chauffeur. He was a talented and
ambitious artist, and found it hard to be content with a life spent
facilitating someone else's creative urge. Michael, who was privately sure that Karl lacked the real drive and application that led to
success, did not take Karl's career entirely seriously. "K has gone off
by train today to near Leeds to a small 'job'," he wrote – his use of
quotation marks is telling.[55] An inspiring and devoted teacher, Karl
remained unprolific as a painter, although he produced a number
of intense, melancholy portraits, clearly influenced by Cézanne. His
style was hard to place, and may have seemed conservative amid
the prevalent artistic fashions of the 1950s and 1960s.

A black cloud descended on Tidebrook Manor. Isabel, who never
made her peace with Michael's sexuality, caused further difficulty. "Quite grotesque rumpus with my mama," Michael wrote to
Priaulx, who was recovering from a fractured skull after being
knocked down by a lorry in Cornwall. "I've not seen such an
extraordinary melodramatic affair with her for years. Like a difficult
and spoilt child." Over Karl he professed himself "very patient,
but I don't know always how to disguise my own drive (to work)
and so not to let my real care and affection and love seem just
a demand".[56] Karl retreated into silence. "I don't really know",
Michael told David Ayerst, "whether I can stand this complete
refusal to communicate. [. . .] It's so wildly unnatural – to live
together in one household and to behave as if the other person
didn't exist or made a bad smell. And it's got so illusory for the
children now – 'our home' is at Tidebrook – 'Daddy's car'; all on
the basis of a union which no longer exists."[57]

In May 1960 Karl had a breakdown. He would spend days in
bed, was vomiting daily, and threatened suicide. "K has had a

terrible time," Michael wrote. "We all feared he might end his life even. But he has promised me he won't do anything suddenly."[58] Karl was convinced he was having a heart attack, "thinks indeed he's slowly dying!" He had a scan, which "showed nothing", and "brought everything to a break. Indeed apparently to a breakup. From this agreed end we found, at K's suggestion, a kind of compromise, that he would have a place in London as his, and from that try, slowly, to refind some shared life. But he is very down. Everything seeming to fail at once."[59]

A tiny flat was found in west London that Michael could use for any necessary overnights, but which would be Karl's own space and refuge, where he hoped to paint. Renting the flat was really an unaffordable expense, and would mean, sooner or later, the sale of Tidebrook, which continued to eat money. But Michael pinned his hopes on this new set-up. "If all comes out gradually and well it will be wonderful. Both K and I are fiercely tenacious and loyal people – so I guess it will." And he hoped "the new pattern of life, or of place, will set some kind of seal on the growing and deepening relationship. It will be what we have designed and discussed together, for our life together."[60]

Karl's departure from Tidebrook was messy and prolonged. After spending a period in London he would return helplessly to Michael. They could not be together, and they could not be apart. "He 'hates' and 'resents' me and Tidebrook," Michael reported, "yet it's a grievously difficult business to get away. I am gently 'freeing' him, of course, because it's essential." He admitted: "I can't bear to see him thus because of my presence."[61] In the autumn, and at Michael's suggestion and expense, Karl left more permanently to spend a period of time being treated in a London clinic. And Michael found himself again alone.

It isn't at all certain the outcome of this climacteric will be (for him) a final turning to life with me, with tensions more or less resolved. It may well be a fresh attempt at marriage. It's fairly certain that both of us need feminine company very much – i.e. real women, not the feminine in men. If we did come to live together again this problem would need to be solved as well. But it's equally probable that Karl's need is a more radical one – finally more physiological, leading to marriage or a mistress (in the best sense of the word). I am not imagining any certain future for myself with him any more – and have told him so.[62]

It was in this mood of hopelessness that Michael finished the second act of King Priam early in September 1960, while Karl was in the clinic. The Riley was replaced with a Morris Minor, and Michael learned to drive it, badly. Unexpectedly, he bumped into Karl in London, and Karl admitted that the analysis had persuaded him to return to his ex-wife. "Wonderful for them all," Michael reported to Benjamin Britten.

I have been overwhelmed by it, as you more than another will know. We had three months when we chose each other and loved each other and by some transformation all seemed possible. Then the old life pulled poor Karl and the long descent into resentment and introversion began. Now, he at least feels new life again. I wanted a home so much (I've never found anyone before, I loved, who wanted to make a home together) that I've done a lot of crying – but that's passing. Everyone showers love on me, even Karl himself! – and I am only alone in the loneliness of an unfulfilled want. And there it is.[63]

His usual stoic crust began to form: "I'm a tough bird inside! I know quite well that what we call suffering is mostly self-pity, and seldom indulge in it for more than a very little while." And then his habitual phlegmatic phrase: "So that's that."[64] Karl meanwhile, who in the event did not return to live with Anne, was more hopeful, and wrote to Michael: "Have patience. If I can come back to you again, it will be worth it, and of course if I cannot come back in the previous way, I'll be there for you in another, all my life."[65]

A period living apart, as they had hoped, did allow the relationship slowly to heal and to find a new footing. Karl responded well to his treatment, returning from time to time to Tidebrook.

By 1961 he and Michael were determined to move, thinking they might risk a joint domestic life once again if they could find a more suitable house and start afresh, but with the proviso that Karl might always be able to spend time in London should he need to escape. It was Isabel who forced them into action by deciding that she could no longer be forever caught in the middle of the rows, and she left Tidebrook at Easter for a village in Norfolk.

The manor had been on the market for months when suddenly, late in April, the actor Rex Harrison, flush with the success of playing Henry Higgins in My Fair Lady on stage, turned up for a viewing.* He had his fiancée, the actress Rachel Roberts, in tow, disguised as a sister-in-law replete with false name. "I must say," Michael told the Daily Mirror indiscreetly, "I thought it amusing to have the actress introduced as a Mrs. Evans because Rachel Roberts is so well known." Harrison made an offer for the manor on the spot, and gave the Mirror their headline: "Now Squire Harrison has a £14,000 retreat."⁶⁶ It was a considerable sum, nearly seven times the average house price of the time. Michael owed his mother over a quarter of the money, and had a heavy debt to pay off, but there was enough left over that a monthly income could be drawn to rent a new house. Michael finally had a steady cash flow, no obligations, and was nearing the end of a new opera. He was, he told Priaulx Rainier, "immensely looking forward to a new adventure in living".⁶⁷

The house they had chosen they already knew well. The town of Corsham lies north-east of Bath, and at the end of its high street is the building known as Parkside, an architectural wonder, its main body Tudor, its third floor Queen Anne, all wrapped in a Regency frontage of honey-coloured stone. For years Parkside had been rented by Bryan Fisher, whom both Michael and Karl had known since their days as conscientious objectors during the war. They had been frequent visitors to the house, at which Bryan had started a small school. When Bryan left to found a larger school nearby,

---

* On Broadway Harrison handed over the role of Higgins to his understudy, Michael Allinson, Francesca's nephew.

Michael and Karl determined to move in, and to leave Tidebrook Manor behind them, with all its seclusion, responsibilities, and trouble. They were able to arrange a good rent from Parkside's owner, Lord Methuen of Corsham Court, and he made extensive renovations and generously arranged for the installation of a large composition studio.

Michael and Karl left Tidebrook for Corsham on 22 June 1961, but had to oversee a great deal of the building work before the house was habitable.[68] Michael spent the nights staying with one of David Ayerst's daughters, and the days in Parkside's exquisite walled garden, composing on a hired upright piano he had had installed in the ornate stone gazebo with its ogee roof. Suddenly creature comforts could be afforded, white carpets laid, walls painted and furniture chosen. The low beams of the upper rooms, which Michael surely spent much of the next decade ducking beneath, were painted black; the bathrooms became a 1960s symphony of orange and brown tiles; and storage heaters were installed that reliably ran out of heat come the cold winter afternoons. Eventually everything was finished, and Corsham life proper began. The window by Michael's piano looked out on, and a door in the garden wall opened directly onto, the grounds of Corsham Court, laid out by Capability Brown and host to Michael's daily walks, past the lake, past the peacocks roaming and calling. With the Fisher family living nearby there was a ready-made social life on the doorstep, all a far cry from the rural isolation Michael had hitherto known.

King Priam, an opera begun in new-found happiness, and continued through stress and upset, was finished at Parkside amid investment in a new life. The final note was written on 14 October 1961, and the score dedicated to Karl Hawker. The century's sixties had started, and Michael's were not far off, as was revealed only by the crow's feet at the corners of his eyes. Behind him lay some not inconsiderable achievements that, had he somehow died or retired in late middle age, would have guaranteed him a respectable place in the annals of British music. But in the thirty years of composition that still lay ahead he was to journey into other worlds. Really, he was just beginning.

DIARY:

London

I had given up hope of ever finding Susan and Sarah Hawker, to whom Michael Tippett referred as stepdaughters. Descriptions of his love for the girls pile up: "They are really lovely children," he writes, "very grown up, self-possessed and some of the nicest-behaved ever."[69] But maiden names have ceded to married names, and the Internet cannot help. Someone remembers that one of the girls had moved to Brazil.

It all started with marmalade. There is a correspondence in the *Telegraph* about the best recipe, and someone writes in to say how much Tippett had adored marmalade, and did anybody have his recipe? It so happens that Michael had reviewed C. Anne Wilson's *The Book of Marmalade* for the *Guardian* in 1985, and let slip that his preferred recipe came from his copy of *Minnie, Lady Hindlip's Cook Book*, which he'd bought in 1925: "just bitter (Seville) oranges, sugar and water". He opened with the memorable line, "If there's no marmalade in heaven, I shan't want to go."[70] I send all this off to the *Telegraph* and think little more about it.

Two days later there is an email from Susan Barlow, née Hawker, nonchalantly saying she had seen my name in the paper, that her father was Karl Hawker and did I want to talk to her about Tippett? "Some of the memories are painful," she writes, "but there is much that is not. Sarah and I were dearly fond of him. He was a large part of our formative lives. I loved Michael, and I loved my father." Sarah has indeed lived in Brazil but is now in New York, and is coming to visit in a month's time. And soon I am sitting with both of them around Susan's kitchen table in London, with the sun coming through a skylight, grandchildren pottering in the background, and an ancient cat miaowing for food. In the hall is the original sketch, long thought lost, that Karl made of Michael for one of their Christmas cards, which catches some essence of the man he loved, some melancholy behind the bright eyes, their vividness apparent even in dusty grey charcoal.

Michael Tippett by Karl Hawker, 1964

Together we work through their father's life. As Susan says: "His dad was killed down the mine when he was six, he was one of seven children and there was no welfare in those days. Then he had TB of the neck. For two years he was in bed – no doctors, nothing, he just lay in bed for two years. I think at eleven he did get a scholarship to the local grammar school. Then he had an older brother who was killed in a motorbike accident. The next brother down got one cap for rugby, for Wales presumably, but he was off playing – this is a horrible story – his wife had an affair with the local butcher; he came back at one point, found out, chopped the wife and butcher up, and stuffed himself in the car and gassed himself. This is why I think my father was such a damaged person. I used to think he was a manic depressive, but then realised he never had the manic episodes." It is possible to see why Michael fell for this troubled and talented artist, who had so much in common with Wilfred Franks.

Occasionally memories clash good-naturedly, over dates and details; the slight age difference between Karl's daughters, and the fact that Sarah worked abroad, has given them varying slants on things. But they both have vivid memories of Tidebrook Manor: "They couldn't kill the chickens – they'd try and strangle them and neither of them could do it." "They had a cockerel that was blind. What was he called?" Both burst out laughing. Nobody remembers the name of the cockerel, though they do remember (from much later on) the name of the dishwasher, purchased at great expense with the proceeds of a television interview and referred to ever afterwards as Bernard Levin. The car that Michael and Karl bought usually failed to make it up the hill to Tidebrook, so the girls would have to get out and walk; when Michael learned to drive it he would forget to put the brakes on, and on one occasion the vehicle rolled down into the fields behind the house. Otherwise it is Michael's recipe for Welsh rarebit that has stuck in their memory, and (more gales of laughter) his appalling table manners while eating it. "The best thing was his mother!" Sarah says. "Oh my god, she was incredible! She would, in the middle of winter, sleep with the French doors open, and she'd be in bed piled up high with quilts. She was an amazing woman." "She was scary," murmurs Susan. "Was she?" Sarah says. Susan thinks she's prejudiced: "I had to take my cat to Tidebrook and she made me lock him in the garden shed. But Michael used to get the cat out for me. I don't think [Karl and Isabel] got on well at all. My father hated her, basically."

Both talk openly about Karl's sexuality. "His identity was complicated," Sarah says. "He would never actually speak about it. My mother knew. But he desperately wanted a family and a normal sort of life – he tried very hard." Both confirm that the two slept in different bedrooms. "My father" – this is Susan now – "was very muddled about who he was and what he was. In those days it was difficult to talk about what your home life was." And she remembers that both her parents became worried when, as a child, she spent a great deal of time with another girl – a friend, only, but Karl panicked. "My father took me to a restaurant" (a rare occurrence) "and said 'I don't want you to have a life like mine.'"

The word nobody ever used was "homosexual". Sarah is sure, though

Susan knows little of this, that "Dad got arrested once or twice. He was accused in Wales of soliciting and it wasn't, it was in some public toilet. They were fearful when it wasn't in that big music world" – where homosexuality was more openly tolerated – "and I can remember picking up on that very early. I think they were both, if you could label them, probably bisexual in some way."

Wasn't it hard, in the late 1950s, one's father leaving one's mother for another man? Did they know what was going on? They both agree: "I think we just sort of knew." What they remember is that, of all the trio responsible for their upbringing – Anne, Michael, Karl – it was Michael who bothered to make sure they were informed and all right.

Susan: "We came home from school and Mum said, 'Michael's in the sitting room, he wants to talk to you.' And he then explained to us the relationship between him and Dad. Neither of us were interested, we were both hungry, just come home from school. 'Oh, we know all that Michael.' Michael was fantastic – neither my mother nor my father had been bothered to tell us. They were scared, presumably. He was the one. Everyone was kind of worried that maybe we hadn't twigged, or that nobody had talked to us about anything. It never occurred to me that it was illegal."

Was Michael a father figure, I ask them? Susan isn't sure. But Sarah says she was "closer to Michael in many ways" than to her father. "I mean Michael would talk for hours, he was more open. Dad was never really open about what was going on, he tried to hide it. Michael was very authentic, a very authentic person." Susan agrees that he was "very gentle. He never forced his thoughts onto anyone. But if the conversation started going the way he didn't want, he would shut you down. Very gently." Their mother and Michael got on well. Anne was a "very complicated person, a very fearful, anxious person, and that coloured her entire life". But "she was accepting of all of this because she loved the people involved. It's as simple as that."

What they both remember was the dedication to composition. "There was a side of Michael's personality," Sarah says, "that my father used to talk about. He could be as ... it's not cold-as-a-fish, but he would cut himself off from emotions, you know? Things that really upset him – either he just couldn't cope with it, or he couldn't express it. Somehow you couldn't reach him, as a person." During big pieces, "he could drive people a bit nuts. Some people say he was self-centred or whatever, but his work was so all-absorbing and all-involving. You just couldn't get through to him at times. So if you were living with him, you just felt that you weren't yourself, you didn't have a life, you didn't have anything of your own. I remember Dad saying that, always." Both remember Michael's nervous attacks when pieces were due for completion: "very trembly". He would go to bed and stay there.

Both are open about how difficult their father could be when in the blackness of depression. As premiere followed premiere, and Michael's success grew, Karl found it harder to cope. He was musical, taught himself to play the flute, and "was incredibly proud of Michael", Sarah thinks. But there is no doubt that some jealousy set in, and it was hard to maintain the relationship as Michael's fame soared upward, and Karl's mood plummeted downward, with little hope of the artistic career at which he had aimed. Susan is sure, however: "The problems that Dad had were very separate from Michael. I don't think Michael was the cause. He [Karl] always was a difficult man. Difficult in the sense that he could be fine, some of the time, he was a very kind, very warm, very generous person – but then he could just go, like that. He had a bad temper, though was never violent. Soon he wasn't eating meals, and he'd given up travelling with Michael a long time before."

This meant that the girls and Michael would go off without Karl, and when Susan puts a slideshow of photographs on her laptop, I see various shots of the three of them, looking for all the world like two daughters curled around a proud father, with the sea or the mountains behind, buckled shoes and cardigans giving way to short-skirted dresses, their dark hair differentiated as now, Susan's in a bob and Sarah's much longer. Once, they all went to a freezing-cold hotel in Aldeburgh and spent each day with Britten and Pears. As boyfriends arrived, they came too. On one occasion, when they were all on holiday in the South of France and en route for a rental property, Michael calmly let them all into the wrong house and began to unpack. More memories. Mahjong, Racing Demon. Getting stuck with Michael in a boat (this is Susan's husband John, now, joining us) and the by-now-knighted composer calmly peeing over the side, uncaring.

We watch a clip of Karl Hawker on YouTube, the only footage I have ever seen of him. It is a piece of silent film taken in the beautiful walled garden at Parkside, with Michael and Karl greeting various suited dignitaries and playing croquet on the lawn, a game at which, many tell me, Michael cheated with aplomb. Karl is in a red V-neck jumper over a white polo-neck, and he is smiling, undoubtedly handsome, laughter lines around kind eyes, prominent ears. "Our dad was an incredibly good-looking man." Susan adds that she didn't realise that for a long time. "I was so pleased to see a clip of him on YouTube, because he looks happy in it. You could see that he and Michael were happy at one point."

And Sarah adds: "They were happy, for a long time."

PART SIX

———

THE CURTAIN RISES
1962–1977

TWENTY-FIVE

A Timeless Music Played in Time

On 2 May 1962 an audience of 3,000 people gathered in Tel Aviv. The Kol Yisrael Symphony Orchestra and the Tel Aviv Chamber Choir were giving the Israeli premiere of *A Child of Our Time*, a piece inspired, all those years ago, by Herschel Grynszpan's assassination of a Nazi official. Press reaction was mixed, but one newspaper, *HaBoker*, found that "the composition had moved everyone to the depths of his soul", concluding: "no Jewish composer had ever written anything so sublime on the theme of the holocaust".[1] Sitting in the audience was a seventy-six-year-old man, with a long white beard, little spectacles, a kippah on his head, apparently deeply moved. His son Herschel had been declared legally dead two years before, but Sendel Grynszpan had lived to hear *A Child of Our Time*.

Michael was unable to travel to Israel for the performance, presumably because he was deep in preparations for the premiere of *King Priam*, due at a theatre in Coventry just a few weeks later. During the Second World War, Coventry Cathedral had been destroyed by a bombing raid so severe that over 4,000 homes were flattened in the course of its single night. The ruins of the cathedral stand in the city still, with the words "Father Forgive" inscribed on the wall behind the altar. Not until March 1956 was the foundation stone for a new cathedral laid, and over the next six years Basil Spence's modernist sandstone building was erected, soon becoming a symbol of the country's renewal. The cathedral was consecrated on 25 May 1962, and a festival held in the city to celebrate. On 29 May, at the Belgrade Theatre Coventry, came the first performance of *King Priam*, heralded by a strangely out-of-place overture in the form of the national anthem. It had been suggested that the opera could have a preview run of performances in Coventry, before coming to the Royal Opera House on 5 June, and Michael was all in favour, having worked briefly on a documentary about the cathedral's reconstruction, arranging passages of his music for its score. As he had once written, he tried to express in his composition "the idea that the rebuilding is finer than the building".[2]

Getting Michael's second opera onto the stage was a much less arduous process than for his first, partly because the composer himself decided to take a back seat. None of his first choices for director – Günther Rennert, Tyrone Guthrie, and above all Peter Brook – was available, and he instructed Covent Garden that he wanted someone with a background in theatre or film. The job fell to Sam Wanamaker, most famous today for pioneering the reconstruction of Shakespeare's Globe in London. Wanamaker's left-leaning politics had led him to leave his native America during the McCarthyite witch-hunts, and he was dividing his time between acting and directing. *King Priam* was his first opera, and he relied not on the score, but on records of a piano reduction and on Michael's resolute faith in the piece. They went off together to see Lionel Bart's musical *Oliver!*, which featured spectacular sets of rotating scaffolding by the designer Sean Kenny, who was promptly hired for *King Priam*.

Kenny abandoned the idea of any specific sets or scene changes, in favour of a makeshift revolve of two spinning discs, on which the cast – which featured leading singers of the day such as Forbes Robinson (Priam), Marie Collier (Hecuba), and Josephine Veasey (Andromache) – could appear, encumbered by very few props or furniture, and moving between towering columns or forests of wooden planks that descended silently from the flies to indicate the walls of Troy, the tents of the Trojan camp, or some war-blasted terrain onto which a cannon-like gun trained on the Greek lines was wheeled in the central act. Stylised make-up and costumes gave the singers the appearance of having stepped from a Greek vase.

The lighting designer, William Bundy, created elaborate effects that were a first for the Opera House. A cluster of silver masts from the Greek ships was projected onto a night sky, sailing from the distant horizon until they dominated the entire stage. Late in the opera a serving-maid billowed a scarlet sheet like a splash of blood against a muddy backdrop of browns and ochres, and a burning ball of fire hovered and blazed above the city as it gave in to its ruin.[3] It was precisely the sort of production that Michael had hoped for: epic yet simple, and a new terrain for design in British opera.

The production team had offered Michael absolute commitment to the work from the outset (the night before the opening in Coventry, Sam Wanamaker was to be found up a ladder painting the proscenium arch). Only on the musical side did the performance suffer, and Michael had not yet managed to throw off the view that he produced scores of fumbling and unnecessary difficulty. The new idiom of King Priam, which gave almost every player a virtuosic moment in the spotlight, produced challenge after challenge. As for The Midsummer Marriage, the conductor was John Pritchard, who in 1958 had led the first commercial recording of A Child of Our Time. But Pritchard made a large number of amendments to the score of King Priam, which Michael was evidently powerless to prevent. The frenzied motif for the character of Hecuba, intended for all violins to play together, was heavily cut and given to the orchestra's pianist, John Constable, who was startled to receive so much additional music to learn on top of his part: "Pritchard never asked Tippett, not at all. When Tippett came to the general [rehearsal], suddenly it was all on the piano. I would say eighty per cent of the violin parts, which were for Hecuba. Nowadays probably people could do it. I think times have changed. It did sound a terrible mess in rehearsals, so out of tune – but very few people have written an opera in which one instrument is paired with one particular character."[4]

There were more last-minute changes to come; a list of Pritchard's numerous alterations spreads across many pages.[5] Members of the orchestra refused Michael's request for prominent solo instruments to appear on the stage, and Pritchard tried to orchestrate the guitar solos, fearing they would be drowned by the voice. Michael stood firm, even suggesting an electric guitar be used. In the event John Williams performed the part without difficulty on an acoustic instrument, but was available only on the first night, after which his part was transferred to harpsichord. And a broadcast of the Coventry premiere reveals a change that casts a light on the times in which the opera was first performed. Richard Lewis, playing Achilles, sings to his fellow warrior Patroclus of their beloved homeland, and those left behind: "Shall we kiss, after the war, my tall son again?" The syntactical oddity is deliberate: after the words, "Shall we kiss" the guitar makes an extended interjection, and for a long and charged moment the line seems to be an invitation to Patroclus, undeniably homoerotic. But in 1962 the Lord Chamberlain's Office had powers over opera and theatre productions, and homosexuality was to remain illegal for another six years; the words "Shall we kiss, my tall son" were crammed in *before* the guitar entry.[6]

Changes aside, the first production of *King Priam* was a happy one, with Michael an admired but reticent presence. As John Constable remembers:

> How could you take against him? He hardly ever criticised people – some composers can be very very picky and pull you to pieces the whole time, but he hardly ever made suggestions. The thing which I must get through, which is important: it was so different from anything that had been done before. Sam Wanamaker was a wonderful producer, and we all got on so well. However difficult people found the music or whatever, it's a very dramatic piece – a wonderful production, everything about it, everybody enjoyed being on it, oh yes.[7]

Two decades later Michael can be found, on *Desert Island Discs*, reminiscing about the reviews. "The bad patch really ended with your next opera, *King Priam*?" asks Roy Plomley. "Well yes and no, love," is the reply, as Plomley, not routinely addressed as "love" on Radio 4, chuckles good-naturedly. "On the contrary, another bad patch began like crazy. By this time they thought: oh *The Midsummer Marriage*, nice lyrical work, that's the work he should be doing. When I didn't, and went the other way – a forceful dramatic work where I changed my style and a real heroic world was put before you – they said Christ, let's have none of that."[8]

True, the opera raised some sharp disapproval, not least from Priaulx Rainier, who told a friend that the opera "interests me, but doesn't move me", sure that "all who appreciate [Michael's] greatest qualities hope that this is an intrusion period".[9] But most critics instantly acclaimed King Priam as a great work. Michael had, thought the Standard, "struck a reverberating blow for the glory and genius of English opera". The differences to The Midsummer Marriage were noted, but more than one critic remarked on how Tippettian were the utterances, sure that the style "need not really surprise. It is a new style because it is a new subject."[10] The Financial Times and New Statesman voiced more doubts than some, while the Telegraph hailed a "master of opera". All were certain that the production was "the coming of age of operatic design in this country".[11] In the Spectator David Cairns praised the "superb libretto" as "amazingly sure in dramatic instinct, unerring in detail, economical, exact, cunningly proportioned from first to last". He concluded: "The notion of Tippett the inspired amateur, the eccentric stumbling on moments of perfection, was always three-quarters due to shortcomings of performance. If there is sense and sanity in our musical life, King Priam will come to be generally recognised, as it must surely now be recognised by all who have believed in the unlimited potentialities of his genius, as a great opera – great in idea, great in working out, great in fulfilment."[12]

Now, at last, Michael's reputation was bedding in. More than one newspaper documented the roaring ovation the composer received when taking a call on the first night. Some critics began to talk of a figure such as Igor Stravinsky composing at his most "Tippett-like", rather than the other way around.[13] That year Michael was the subject of a documentary for ITV and an episode of the BBC arts programme Monitor. The Third Programme's broadcast of The Midsummer Marriage in 1963 grabbed listeners, not least Michael, by the scruff of the neck, and reviewers ate humble pie: "The charge of obscurity is not so much a condemnation as a confession of one's own inadequacy," read the *Times* review of the broadcast. "It is not really so obscure after all [. . . and] demands to be experienced in the theatre once again before an audience which may now be ready to receive it more humbly and gratefully."[14] *King Priam* was revived twice more that decade and twice more the next, and commissions were offered thick and fast. The scene was set for Michael's sixtieth birthday to usher in a period of celebration and reappraisal. Michael himself was thrilled with his second opera, and ready to admit it. "I think *King Priam* is tops," he told his publisher, and to the composer Alan Bush, with whom he was rejuvenating a cautious friendship after the political rows of their youth, he wrote: "I was bucked by its manifest success. Over-sold-out on the last performance! I think it may go to West Germany in the spring."[15]

Trips to Germany, either on musical business or to visit his cousin Phyllis Kemp in East Berlin, meant that Michael frequently saw the country's division at first hand, as he went through the concrete barrier of the Berlin Wall at one of its several border crossings, passing the guard towers, the trenches on either side, the armed soldiers, the beds of nails on which those attempting to climb over would land. "I intend to cross through the wall to see someone beloved on the other side," he wrote in May 1963. "My going through the wall with permits will help no one who feels they must risk their lives to cross."[16] *König Priamus* reached West Germany as early as January that year, in a new production at Karlsruhe that projected photographs of a "bomb-shattered twentieth-century city" above the stage.[17]

On the surface, it was as if the liberation and security of the 1960s had allowed Michael to turn away from the optimistic glow of his earlier music. But *King Priam* was composed and performed against a backdrop of dangerous instability, in his personal life and in the world at large. "He might", wrote Andrew Porter of the opera, "have written about a para in Algeria having to choose between obedience and humanity when ordered to torture a prisoner; or about a King forced to choose between his throne and exile with the woman he loved; or about a president deciding whether any circumstances could justify the dropping of an atomic bomb."[18] All such choices were implied by King Priam's scenario, which was sharply prescient of the global crises that followed just a few months after the opera opened in London. In October 1962 a thirteen-day stand-off between the United States and the Soviet Union over the deployment of ballistic missiles saw the Cold War threaten to escalate into full-scale nuclear conflict. The threat was real; the terror and subsequent relief were palpable. In an interview the following April, Michael looked back on the Cuban Missile Crisis with a calmly stoical scrutiny that few had shared: "I remember I walked over to the bank, and the bank manager said something like, 'I suppose we'll still be here at 3.10', or whatever time it was the Russian ships were going to meet the Americans. [. . .] The Campaign for Nuclear Disarmament is struggling against a deep-seated sense of false security. [. . .] If you think as the Americans do that Communism is the devil, then you're prepared to do anything, however horrible, to remove it."[19]

In January 1963 he appeared with Alan Bush at a conference organised by Marxism Today, though spoke as a non-Marxist devil's advocate. And to a request from Bush to appear at an event for the Workers' Music Association he replied: "I haven't had 'owt to do with the WMA for thirty-five years at least. What might you not have all gotten up to! I don't like even letting my name be used for outside-of-music bodies as e.g. Peace Pledge Union and Amnesty International. Though that's being pedantic. Or else simply a 'cover-up' for self-protective laziness as I grow older!"[20] He continued to work for and finance the Union intermittently, giving an address each year, in which he remained outspoken against Soviet actions but was likewise determined that nuclear weapons could not be the answer: "Modern methods of war – the use of the atomic bomb and bacterial warfare" were, he argued, "so debasing and so horrible that their use could be justified only if those things we were fighting against were even more debasing and more horrible. Unless the things we hope to remove are worse than the things we do, then we should reject even a moral fight by these methods; and that means we should reject war itself."[21]

There is a moment towards the end of King Priam when time

stops. The king is in hiding as the Greeks rampage through Troy, slaughtering men, women, children. Hermes, the messenger god, sings an ode to music. His melody unspools itself over high, icy strings. Eventually a piano enters, as if accompanying a song rather than joining in with the opera. A flute and harp begin a *pas de deux*.

I come as messenger of death.
For the story will soon end.
A timeless music played in time.   [. . .]
O divine music,
O stream of sound,
In which the states of soul
Flow, surfacing and drowning   [. . .]
Melt our hearts,
Renew our love.

"A timeless music played in time." The delicate symmetrical phrase, a strange concoction of Proust and Eliot, encompasses a great deal. The creation of music "for all time" that will still resonate within the time in which it is performed. The music that attempts to evoke the timeless while still being "in time": three in a bar, four in a bar. The sense that Priam could be saved by music played, as it were, just in time. But at the moment of Priam's murder there is nothing but a few bars of casual ugliness. The music is recycled from earlier in the opera: almost dull in its workaday desolation. Violence is unoriginal, however novel its methods. Only the memory of Hermes's words can be any comfort. Priam dead, Troy fallen, the opera offers just five bars of painfully abbreviated compassion at the waste and violence wreaked by calamitous human decision. A few instruments emerge from the wreckage, and what Michael described as teardrops splash metallically onto the stage from a xylophone. The opera ends with the speedy, banal savagery of war's necessary violence: not a transcendent tragedy or religious martyrdom, not a glorious demise for the greater good, but merely the squalor and waste of conflict. The ability of music to "melt our hearts, renew our love" seems, at this midpoint in Michael's career, with the world perched precariously on an abyss of nuclear warfare, very dicey indeed.

A remarkable convergence of people had descended on Coventry at the end of May 1962. In the audience for *King Priam* were E.M. Forster (who liked it), and Stephen Spender (who had mixed feelings).²² The town was host to the birth not only of Michael's opera but the next evening, 30 May, of Benjamin Britten's *War Requiem*. Michael had seen very little of Britten in the years since *The Midsummer Marriage*. In 1960 Britten had premiered his opera *A Midsummer Night's Dream*, but Michael, who went to stay with Britten and Pears at Aldeburgh for the first performance, felt the piece had crystallised their differences as composers. "We got less than hoped for from *The Dream*," he admitted. "It didn't <u>seem</u> to extend Ben's range at all, though much of it lovely. The magic wood music is the best, I think. (I didn't really like the yokels at all.) But it's <u>possible</u>, when we're all dead and buried, that the magic wood of *The Midsummer Marriage* will prove more enriching and lasting."²³ Britten's ever-increasing reputation was, as Michael admitted to Priaulx Rainier, beginning to grate. "I think B.B. is temporarily overvalued and hence, maybe, overplayed. I imagine it will last a time yet. To put it rather personally: I think a work of mine like the first symphony, which hasn't been played in England for twelve years at least, contains better music than, say, the B.B. *Sinfonia da Requiem*, and should therefore be given a rehearsing."²⁴ In March 1961 he had confided once again in Priaulx: "B.B. really is overrated at the present time, I've come to the conclusion. It's not any grudge against it all, so much, as a feeling it's got out of hand, and will need some time to readjust itself. This may be long delayed all the same."²⁵ Having Peter Pears as constant and exclusive muse had hemmed in Britten's imagination, Michael thought, and it was Britten's orchestral music that he admired most, especially the 1957 gamelan-infused ballet *The Prince of the Pagodas*: "a marvellous score! Wish I knew <u>how</u> many of the sounds were made."²⁶

His relationship with Britten and Pears evidently remained secure, however, and their correspondence (at least on Michael's side, the only to survive) was warm and intimate. In January 1961 Michael had asked Pears to sing the role of Hermes in *King Priam*: "Do please consider it. No one else could do it so well."[27] The *War Requiem* made Pears's involvement impossible, but in spring 1961 Michael had paused his opera's composition in order to extend Achilles's dramatic life: he took the guitar-accompanied song from its central act, and added two more dramatic monologues for the character, also with guitar, also to his own words. "I fancy I may have gone a bit wild for the guitar this time!" he told Pears, who premiered the *Songs for Achilles* at the 1961 Aldeburgh Festival, with Julian Bream the guitarist.[28]

Britten, rehearsing the *War Requiem* at Coventry, was unable to attend the premiere of *King Priam* and Michael was privately upset that he made no efforts to see it in London: "those two have never attended my operas except very occasionally, *Priam* not at all I think".[29] But in an interview the following year Britten loyally named Michael as one of the four living composers he most admired. Michael, his own first night out of the way, did hear the *Requiem* and found its combination of the Mass for the dead with Wilfred Owen's poetry deeply moving: "we were already overwrought and tired," he told Britten, "exhausted from responding – so we got deeply moved still further, but could hardly fake it!"[30] This wasn't mere politeness, nor even gratitude that the crowd flocking to Britten's premiere had bolstered his own ticket sales. He told Priaulx: "I was very impressed and moved when I heard it on the radio. One of his best things I think."[31]

Nineteen sixty-three brought Britten's fiftieth birthday, and 1965 Michael's sixtieth. Each made the necessary tributes to the other, perhaps showing only a public face, but honest as to their differences, and generous. "We have known each other now for more than twenty years," Britten wrote in an open letter to Michael:

we have been very close often, at other times we have seemed to be moving in different directions. But whenever I see our names bracketed together (and they often are, I am glad to say) I am reminded of the spirit of courage and integrity, sympathy, gaiety and profound musical independence which is yours, and I am proud to call you my friend.

Your devoted

Ben.

P.S. I wish your piano parts weren't so difficult.[32]

Songs for Achilles was not the only work to emerge in the wake of King Priam's new style. During the opera's composition Michael had despatched a flurry of occasional pieces in which he could flex his new musical muscles. The poetry of W.B. Yeats was an abiding passion, and in 1959, for Alfred Deller and his ensemble, Michael had produced a setting of Yeats's "Lullaby", in which the counter-tenor soloist intones the words amid a swirling choral mist of echoes and repetitions. But, despite then writing a Purcell-like setting of Shelley's "Music" for choirs in Sussex and Kent, Michael remained uncomfortable as ever with setting great poetry. He attempted a compromise when, in 1960, he was asked by the Third Programme to provide bursts of instrumental music, to be interleaved with spoken recitations of Yeats. The result, Words for Music Perhaps, eventually led to an invitation from the BBC to repeat the experiment, with Eliot's Four Quartets. Eliot's widow, Valerie, notoriously protective of her husband's legacy, was said to be "enthusiastically in favour". But Michael rejected the offer, along with a number of other invitations from the Third Programme and a proposed ten-minute piece for the Philadelphia Orchestra for which a $1,000 fee was suggested.[33] Still he yearned for the freedom to write what and when he wished, and at any cost to avoid deadlines.

On completing King Priam (in October 1961) he had not paused for breath. The routine of composition continued, six mornings a week, four hours a morning.[34] First there was a setting of the Magnificat and Nunc dimittis, to show off the trumpet organ stop in the chapel of St John's College, Cambridge. Then came a second piano sonata, completed two months before the opera's premiere, and first performed, by Margaret Kitchin, in September 1962. The sonata had been composed on a hired upright in the gazebo at the bottom of Parkside's garden, while workmen completed improvements in the house, and something of their hammering may have found its way into the piece: in an early draft the player is instructed to thump the wood of the instrument with a fist, an idea that Michael soon rejected. The mosaic arrangement of King Priam is still to the fore; the one-movement sonata quotes the opera directly, and breaks down into a heap of musical tiles that demonstrate almost every sound and technique – percussive, lyrical, clear, murky – of which the piano is capable. Michael was unsure. "I don't think the piano piece a very good one," he admitted. "More experimental (to me) than compelling."[35] But the sonata has a great deal to say in its twelve-minute span.

Then there was a rush job for the theatre. Just two weeks before the premiere of King Priam Michael was to be found straining to finish incidental music for a production of The Tempest at the Old Vic in London, setting Ariel's three songs and scoring Prospero's fourth-act Masque. His love for the play had led him to accept, for the only time in his career, the invitation to write for the spoken theatre. It had left him stressed and unhappy: "I got the last of the Tempest music into the post," he told Priaulx on 16 May. "Ouff! Ouff! And that's that. Never again!!"[36] The play, directed by Oliver Neville, opened just days later; it starred Alastair Sim as Prospero and, as Miranda, a young Eileen Atkins, who remembers the production as indescribably dreadful, a view with which the critics did not disagree.[37] Of the settings of Ariel's songs Michael made a separate work, which soon became a staple of Peter Pears's and many others' repertoires. By August 1962 he had completed a five-minute Praeludium for brass, bells, and percussion, commissioned for the BBC's fortieth anniversary and performed by the BBC Symphony Orchestra later that year. "Nothing tremendous" was the appraisal of its composer and of most critics, but the piece wasn't helped by the conductor, Antal Doráti, deciding to alter the composer's dynamics from forte to piano.[38]

The following month Michael could finally begin in earnest on a work he had had in mind for some twelve years: a Concerto for

Orchestra, which had been commissioned for the 1963 Edinburgh Festival.[39] Of this he was confident, and he would be better served by its conductor. Still extending and experimenting with the mosaic-like soundworld of *King Priam*, he split the orchestra yet further into its constituent parts, laying out the separate self-contained blocks side by side, overlapping, or on top of one another. So multi-dimensional is the structure of the concerto that a Rubik's cube may be a better metaphor than mosaic to describe its layered and variously coloured blocks, endlessly twisting. The piece is in, as it were, three acts, the first for brass, woodwind, and percussion; the second for strings only; and the third for full orchestra. The drama lasts some thirty minutes, each movement beginning and ending in *medias res*, mid-breath, almost arbitrarily, as if the music were continuing eternally in some other world. In the first movement Michael divided the players into nine highly contrasting separate ensembles, which might be imagined, in some ideal performance, spread out in a circle around the audience, the music ricocheting between them like the ball in a pinball machine. In the slow movement the strings take to the stage, an endless coil of melody passed from instrument to instrument, striving resolutely upward towards the light, and disproving the notion that Michael's music had entirely sacrificed the lyricism and rapture of his earlier pieces. The first months of 1963, as the country emerged from the coldest winter on record, were taken up with the German premiere of *King Priam* and a conducting trip to Belgium, and Michael fell badly behind schedule when completing the concerto, working late into the night, 'flu-ridden and being treated for a frozen shoulder. He finished, in June, just about on time, only by cutting small portions from the score of *King Priam* and arranging them into the propulsive finale. This gave more prominence to the one freshly composed motif: a pulsing canon, graceful and courtly, that seems to still the brass-led militarism and which, begun by a high flute, nods to the first Sea Interlude from *Peter Grimes*: a hidden gift for Benjamin Britten, from whom Michael asked (and received) permission to dedicate the score "with affection and admiration".[40]

The London Symphony Orchestra premiered the Concerto for

Orchestra in the Usher Hall in Edinburgh, conducted by a thirty-five-year-old called Colin Davis, who after a period of freelance struggle was gaining huge acclaim as the director of Sadler's Wells Opera. It was the start of one of the most important professional relationships in Michael's career. Davis had heard *A Child of Our Time* in Westminster as a student, and "knew that here was a fateful turning point". He was, he told Michael, "mad about your music".[41] Davis would become one of Michael's most enthusiastic advocates, bringing seven new Tippett pieces into the world, and returning to works such as *A Child of Our Time* and the earlier symphonies to offer them, new-minted, to a fresh audience in the concert hall and on record. Stunned by the 1963 broadcast of *The Midsummer Marriage*, he was soon active in efforts to revive the opera and, a voracious reader, he could follow Michael's wide range of reference with ease. With careful rehearsal and preparation Davis was able, as few others were, to navigate Michael's music with clarity and energy, to whip his players into the necessary vigour without sacrificing lyricism. When Davis first got to know Michael he had, by his own admission, a very short fuse, but made a conscious and successful effort to mellow into patience, and was soon a rock of support. He was not without humour, but had little of Michael's frivolity, and it was a chalk-and-cheese friendship, eventually deeply felt but not without its awkwardnesses. When Davis came to make a studio recording of *The Midsummer Marriage*, a behind-the-scenes documentary was filmed that catches Michael leaning over and tweaking him on the nose, in mock punishment at some tease or other. A look of sheer anger flashes on Davis's face, before he takes a breath and smiles away his irritation. Initially Michael trod very carefully. "I don't really know Colin in that intimate way," he told William Glock: "He said one half-bitter thing [. . .] in answer to a half-bitter thing I had said! Such things (even half-bitter!) being out of my line we both withdrew hastily. And that has been all – one <u>minute</u> minute. [. . .] Colin is angelic with me – but I'm careful never to see or talk with him beyond the absolute minimum. I <u>very</u> rarely go to any rehearsals. It's a sort of instinct. But then I am <u>very</u> well served."[42] Critics agreed that Michael's concerto could not have been served better by Colin Davis and the orchestra. And while Peter Heyworth in the *Observer* professed grave doubts about Michael's new direction, most deemed the piece important: in the *Sunday Times* Desmond Shawe-Taylor wrote that it had "extended the frontiers of orchestral colour".[43]

Travelling up to Scotland for the concerto's premiere was Evelyn Maude, Michael's beloved guardian angel of three decades. They went off to tea together. A slight unease had arisen in that Evelyn, her daughter thinks, was "unconsciously jealous about all of Michael's friends" and "'Karl' eventually became a dirty word in our house". But she paid Michael an annual three-day visit for the last eight years of her life, and died in a nursing home in January 1971, aged seventy-eight.[44]

Nineteen sixty-three was the year sex began, Philip Larkin said, "between the end of the 'Chatterley' ban, and the Beatles' first LP". Michael's Concerto for Orchestra was played again, at the Royal Festival Hall, on 21 November that year. The following day the Hall hosted a concert performance of Britten's *Gloriana*, and whispers began to shoot round the auditorium saying that President Kennedy had been assassinated as he travelled in his motorcade along a boulevard in Texas.

TWENTY-SIX

O My America!

It is difficult to push open the door of Parkside and peer in. Michael clicks just a little out of focus, no longer laying out his detailed feelings or itemising his movements in correspondence. His life from the 1960s onward necessitates a gear change in its telling. His days, more than ever, were lived on a piano stool. A constant stream of friends visited the house, children in tow, and it was made clear that the top floor, on which he and Karl had separate bedrooms but evidently a shared life, was out of bounds, even to the housekeeper, Lily Speirs. Closest to Michael at this time, both geographically and emotionally, was Bryan Fisher, but between Bryan and Karl relations were becoming more than awkward. Lovers during the war, and with too much history, they were wary of one another, and Bryan's is one of the voices of disapproval amid the many memories testifying to Karl's attraction, finding him "inconceivably jealous of us and nearly all of Michael's friends". Bryan had been dismayed by Karl's rearrival in Michael's life, and thought Michael in dangerous thrall to his new love: "the relationship did not show up as happiness but as an alarming compulsion".[1]

Karl was on a steadier mental footing as a result of psychiatric treatment, but the relationship with Michael had not regained its initial fervour, and it remained a possibility that he might return to his ex-wife. Both men, Michael thought, needed feminine company, and Michael became close to Bryan Fisher's second wife, Irene. They took to sharing long walks around Corsham together.

As Bryan remembered:

> Perhaps it was [Michael's] last attempt to come to terms with
> the possibility of a relationship with a woman, to move towards
> a solution to the servitude in which his homosexual alliances
> tended to engulf him, to strengthen the assertion in his life which
> would influence the music he wrote, when, on one of his walks
> with Irene, he asked her if she would take him to bed with her;
> not for an emotional relationship with him but, as a sympathetic
> person, to help him break down the barrier he had against having
> a physical union with a woman and because he did not know
> what went on, or how he had to behave physically, or how he
> could respond in the circumstances. Irene was the only female
> he knew whom he could trust to ask this favour and to whom
> he felt sufficiently attracted to do so. [. . .] She told him that she
> would not be happy endangering her relationship of trust with
> me by going to bed with my best friend and felt, anyway, that he
> would solve his problem only by first forming a relationship with
> a woman with whom he could, even if he subsequently found he
> could not, anticipate a lasting partnership.[2]

But Bryan and Karl never made their peace, and the Fishers were
hurt not only by Karl's perceived rudeness, but by Michael's lack
of effort to improve the situation. Eventually matters became irreparable, and the Fishers permanently broke off the friendship with
both men.

Another friend to whom Michael had become close was the poet
Ursula Wood, Ralph Vaughan Williams's widow. She adored Karl,
with whom she maintained a quite separate friendship. Michael
had, since 1956, been a committee member of the Vaughan Williams Trust, and after Ralph's death intensified his relationship with
Ursula, sending her drafts of *King Priam*'s libretto for comment. And,
likely in the early 1960s and at around the same time as his suggestion that he might experiment sexually with Irene Fisher, Michael
proposed marriage to Ursula. Her close friend, the musicologist
Oliver Neighbour, wrote up his memories:

The proposal had come in a letter "not long" after Vaughan Williams's death. It was unquestionably intended seriously, but had absolutely no basis in the nature of their friendship. [. . .] She took Tippett's proposal as a sudden rush of blood to the head and made no mention of it in replying to his letter, which contained other things to which she could respond. She destroyed the letter. [. . .] Ursula was undoubtedly attracted to Tippett [. . . but] his affection for Ursula, though no doubt genuine enough as far as it went, can have had very little to do with it.[3]

Given the destruction of Michael's letter, the truth is hard to discern amid these gossamer memories, murky and recycled. Oliver Neighbour thought the proposal was a means of showing publicly that Michael had inherited Vaughan Williams's mantle. But, given that Vaughan Williams had fallen quickly though temporarily out of fashion, and that the name of Tippett was steadily in the ascendant, it seems unlikely that Michael, who was assured of his own abilities, would need to take so drastic a step merely to cement his own reputation. Homosexuality remained illegal, and he could have planned the marriage for public display. A "sudden rush of blood to the head" the letter may have been, but, considered in the light of Michael's love for Francesca Allinson and for Priaulx Rainier, his request to Irene Fisher, or his long-ago proposal to her sister-in-law Shelagh as they sat together on the Victoria Embankment, it is more clearly the step of a man emotionally adrift, a last-ditch attempt to secure, amid his faltering and mercurial relationship with Karl, an abiding union of companionship and affection.

Amid these personal crises Michael had reignited his friendship with the analyst John Layard, whose psychiatric guidance he had sought during the late 1930s. Layard was still wrestling with his own demons, but quickly fell back into the role of Michael's confessor. "I permitted myself some exasperation this morning," Michael wrote to him around 1964,

in that [Karl] expects his breakfast every morning from me on a tray with no return courtesy of any kind whatsoever. [. . .]

For though we don't eat together or sleep together (and there's a total taboo on his side of all tenderness and cherishing; he's not smiled or been easily friendly to me once in years) we do sometimes talk together when he's so disposed. [. . .] I keep the problematic in my relationship to him suppressed and at bay, and live, so far as I can, as it were on my own. [. . .] It seems to me now very possible that he can't ever be himself when near me — absolutely. The identification and all the resentment that that fosters is just too bloody powerful. So that I have "given him up" inside myself some long time ago. The heart break, such as it was, came at the first time he went, four years ago or so. It's in the past.[4]

He and Karl were locked in an unbreakable cycle. In August 1964 they separated once again: "we parted as easily as possible," Michael told Layard, "on my side very little pang, indeed almost relief".[5] But soon Karl was again living at Corsham much of the time, and friends knew them as a couple once more.

The rush of compositions in the early 1960s, combined with domestic volatility and the necessary press junket, had left Michael mired in "abysmal tiredness".[6] He was desperate to begin work on a third opera and, an even greater priority, a choral work based on the Confessions of Saint Augustine, which he had planned since late 1962. There was a slight delay, in that he began a small choral piece for Amnesty International, using a Spanish religious text, "but had to throw it in — text wouldn't work and it altogether got me into a mess, really because I was all set inside for Augustine".[7] Work on what became The Vision of Saint Augustine had begun on 30 September 1963, and continued uninterrupted until its completion, on 10 April 1965.

Augustine's Confessions had been an enthusiasm of Michael's since boyhood, and he knew chunks of the original Latin by heart. His own copy of the text, from which he selected portions to set to music, is barely annotated. The piece, for baritone, orchestra, and choir, uses the techniques of King Priam in order to achieve the ecstasy of The Midsummer Marriage, and seeks to convey in music

Augustine's description of two visions: the first in a Milanese garden with his closest friend, and the second with his mother en route to Africa. The first vision was of a child singing, and the second a glimpse of eternity. Once again Michael was attempting to create what he had described in *King Priam* as a "timeless music played in time". Returning to the piece some decades later, he was rather shocked. "What crazy worlds of music I got into then," he wrote in hindsight. "The sheer exultation of the sound seemed ready to put me under the seat! Whatever does a stranger to the work make of it?"[8] *The Vision* almost requires the audience to exist among the players, to swim inside rather than sit in front of it. Long conversations with Priaulx Rainier were also at the back of his mind, and he paid careful attention to her sculpted and non-developing blocks of sound. "All you say", he had told her in 1962, "about [. . .] your spatial preoccupations is more than interesting"; "your own singular ways of approaching ensembles of instruments are always fascinating and very stimulating".[9] Michael seems to create a universe in a single score, in which a choral hymn, a densely layered orchestral outburst, and the wild ululations of the baritone part, as it leaps in ecstasy or drills repeatedly into a single note, are all simultaneous happenings. Two of the three movements climax with an epilogue for instruments alone that (to quote Wallace Stevens) "whip from themselves a jovial hullabaloo among the spheres". Michael had written an impossible piece, of which a performance seems simultaneously necessary and destructive.

At the premiere, on 19 January 1966, many critics heard cacophony. The soloist Dietrich Fischer-Dieskau combined unearthly beauty of tone with some scrambled passages, and afterwards deemed the work "problematical", but "to be taken seriously".[10] Michael himself was forced to conduct, taking over from an indisposed Hans Schmidt-Isserstedt, and lacked the baton technique to keep the vast scale of the work in check. Reacting to a sniffy review in *The Times*, Eric Walter White wrote, with a fervour that seems to supersede mere loyalty, that the work was a masterpiece, unique in its "ability also to stand back and contemplate the vision as well as to be involved in it".[11] An attempt to express the inexpressible, *The Vision* concedes both its own failure and the hubris of embarking upon the endeavour. It ends with a repeated passage of "glossolalia", a musical rendition of ecstasy via torrents of vowel sounds, before the choir seems to discard the piece altogether, conceding that even music, in the end, gives concrete voice to the unvoiceable. Quietly and in rhythm the performers whisper: "I count not myself to have apprehended."

The *Confessions* had been a surprisingly religious topic for an avowed humanist, but are really a metaphor for Michael's primary concerns. The fact that he kept the words in Latin and Greek shows him more concerned with the sonic attempt at revelation than the semantic meaning of the text. Once again the poetry of T.S. Eliot seems to have been at the front of his mind: *The Vision of Saint Augustine* may be thought of as a musical gloss on the *Four Quartets*, and on Eliot's contrasting of unredeemable time with the beauty of eternity. Michael prefaced the score with a quotation from "Burnt Norton": "And all is always now." Eliot died, wracked with emphysema, on 4 January 1965, just three months before Michael completed *The Vision of Saint Augustine*, which is dedicated "to my mother, and in memory of my father". It is not impossible that Michael meant the dedication to encompass the poet he frequently called his "spiritual father".

Isabel meanwhile was now eighty-four, living in retirement flats in Essex. She had become a follower of the philosopher Rudolf Steiner, and converted to a mystical brand of Christianity with a passionate fervour of which her younger son surely disapproved; she published a religious tract called *God Within*, its royalties going to Amnesty International. (The copy that survives in Michael's library is in suspiciously pristine condition.) On 20 February 1964 Michael was awarded an honorary doctorate from Cambridge University, the citation reading that he was a "producer of delectable sounds". Isabel attended the ceremony; asked whether she was proud of her younger son, she was heard to say that she was prouder of his prison sentence. E.M. Forster was also there, now eighty-five and living in King's College, his novelist days long behind him. "Was a joy to see you at Cambridge for my degree," Michael wrote to him. "Just a line to underline my affection."[12]

On 2 January 1965, four months before completing *The Vision of Saint Augustine*, Michael had turned sixty, in a whirl of tribute and celebration.[13] The conductor Norman Del Mar wrote in the *Radio Times*: "I know of no one who seems so to bear the imprint of perpetual youth, not only in his physical appearance and manner, but in the fantastic liveliness and originality of his mind."[14] Michael was in danger of becoming a venerable institution. A new generation of British composers had emerged, many trying to reconcile their national inheritance with European modernism. Harrison Birtwistle, Peter Maxwell Davies, and Alexander Goehr were leading figures of the so-called Manchester School, a group of composers and performers who had studied at Manchester University in the 1950s. Maxwell Davies remembered: "For composers like me, Birtwistle and Sandy Goehr, Tippett was a wonderful example of somebody who was totally himself, which took a great deal of musical courage." Goehr, close to Michael since childhood, is happy to concede he was "influenced by Tippett in almost every respect – in the case of literature, politics, music. I wouldn't deny it for a minute."[15]

In many ways there was a sharp divide between the generations of British composers, and Michael had become an important bridge between older and younger. Maxwell Davies had found Benjamin Britten an appreciative support, but they met only twice; Britten would be seen walking out of Birtwistle's first opera, *Punch and Judy*, and Goehr believes himself to have been sharply dropped from the Aldeburgh circle. Unlike Britten, Michael would live to witness the leading composers of the younger generation blossom and bloom, seemingly without any excessive concern that he was being superseded, a (qualified) admirer of their music.[16] His own success had come late and showed no signs of fading: security made him generous. In April 1963 Boosey and Hawkes had tried to poach Maxwell Davies from Schott. To match Boosey's large financial offer, Schott suggested reducing its list of contemporary composers to just two, Maxwell Davies and Tippett, so as to pay them both highly and in kind. This would have vastly increased Michael's income, but meant Schott's dropping figures such as Priaulx Rainier, Alexander Goehr, and many others. Michael refused. Maxwell Davies went to Boosey and Hawkes.

Supporting the younger generation remained a primary concern. In 1965 Michael agreed to become a patron and director of the Leicestershire Schools Symphony Orchestra, approving wholeheartedly of the bountiful arts patronage that had sprung from Harold Wilson's Labour government: there was money enough to bus in the young players, all in their mid- to late teens, for tailor-made summer schools close to Michael's house in Corsham. He had not taken on the commitment lightly. The LSSO had already been an impressive force, and under his now splashy but communicative baton it flourished further. Twice Michael led the orchestra on European tours, taking along the composer Richard Rodney Bennett as pianist. What he most enjoyed was programming a typically adventurous and stretching repertoire, and the company of the children in the orchestra; footage from a television documentary shows him leading them as he would any professional ensemble. For their part, the players sheepishly admit to the camera how dissimilar Michael was to most of the adults in authority they knew, and how much they liked him.[17] For a concert in the LSSO's first season he wrote a Prologue and Epilogue for the programme, the first a strident version of "Soomer is icoomen in"; the last an arrangement of a "*Non nobis, domine*" then attributed to William Byrd. To these he planned to add further movements, but nothing emerged for a number of years. His compositional priorities lay with a third opera. Another seismic change in his personal life was on its way that would threaten to destabilise his already rocky emotional state. Meanwhile, amid the rows, he and Karl pinned their hopes on America.

America hadn't exactly been a closed book for Michael. Schott had made intermittent attempts to publicise his music there, and some recordings were already available. In April 1952 *A Child of Our Time*

had been given its American premiere, at Columbia University, New York. Michael had steeped himself in American literature, and the country's music had permeated even the earliest of his compositions. In May 1949 he had met the eminent American composer Aaron Copland, who recorded in his diary just how "un-English" he had found Michael; on hearing a broadcast of the Concerto for Double String Orchestra, which he eventually conducted, he assumed it American, and drafted a sixtieth-birthday tribute to its composer under the title "Cousin Michael".[18]

Through Copland, whose music was programmed in concerts with the Leicestershire Schools Symphony Orchestra, Michael began to feel an irresistible tug to the country that had hosted and assimilated figures such as Stravinsky, Schoenberg, and Hindemith. In downtown New York the Minimalist Movement was burgeoning, led by figures such as Terry Riley, Steve Reich, and Philip Glass. But Michael (who may confidently be called a maximalist composer) was more interested in exploring the work of Gershwin and Bernstein, or discovering the experimental music of Elliott Carter and, especially, Charles Ives, who had died in 1954 and whose pieces were becoming celebrated, after much neglect. It was the counter-tenor Alfred Deller who arranged for Michael's first trip to America, recommending *A Child of Our Time* be performed at one of the country's leading music festivals, in Aspen, Colorado. Michael duly booked a flight for the summer of 1965, planning an ambitious tour of the States on which Karl was eventually to join him.

America was a country half hope, half despair; half joy, half rage. That year President Lyndon B. Johnson, who had recently led a Democratic landslide, had proclaimed his "Great Society", aiming to eliminate poverty and racism. But in March the first American combat troops had been sent into Vietnam, just a day after violent riots had broken out between civil rights demonstrators and state troopers in Selma, Alabama, whence Martin Luther King Jr was leading protest marches to Montgomery. While Michael was travelling through the States for the first time, legislation was passed prohibiting racial discrimination in voting.

It was Michael's first long-haul flight, his first experience of jet lag. Leaving London in early July, he flew first to New York, then had to take a long connecting flight west, to Denver, Colorado. His final destination of Aspen was still 200 miles away, and the next day he set off on the long train journey south-west, and was carried up into the Rocky Mountains. "The setting inside huge snow mountains is better than the little town, which is colonial-type wood and brick and 'Swiss' chalets," he wrote in a postcard sent from Aspen. "Am still very confused by gaining seven hours' daylight (five thousand miles west), and also the altitude (eight thousand feet). But everyone is mighty nice and music should be good."[19]

He spent ten days in Aspen, much to the initial displeasure of the festival's composer in residence, Darius Milhaud, who smelled rivalry. Matters were made more complex by Karl's eventual arrival, for unlike Michael he could not talk to the Milhauds in French, and was often bored during rehearsals or study sessions. But the festival was a success, the performance of *A Child of Our Time* went well, and the Amadeus Quartet (old friends from Morley College days) were also in residence. That season Duke Ellington performed a benefit concert with his orchestra.

Michael and Karl now had a proper holiday to look forward to, and on 19 July they left Colorado, driving south to Mesa Verde National Park, where they saw some of the best-preserved cliff dwellings from communities of early Native Americans; across into Utah and Monument Valley, a desert of red sand on the border of Arizona, with huge sandstone buttes glowing in the incredible summer heat; and from motel to motel, canyon to canyon, new vista to new vista, Bryce Canyon, Grand Canyon, and the Canyon de Chelly National Monument. On the advice of a local couple, Michael and Karl drove a little way west and reached First Mesa, an area on the Native American Hope Reservation in Arizona, spread across three villages perched high on flat-topped cliffs. There they watched the dancing of the Native American communities, but found the heat and the litter unbearable.

There followed, as July turned into August, a huge drive, some 600 miles, across the deserts of Arizona, its rock striped with red and gold, its uninhabited stretches of land punctuated with cactus, the temperature staying resolutely at forty degrees Celsius. Michael and Karl arrived in Los Angeles just a week before the Watts riots, where racial tensions in predominantly black neighbourhoods reached such a pitch that six days of violent protest erupted over the south of the city, with buildings looted and aflame and guns firing, leaving thirty-four dead. After Los Angeles came, from 4 August, two days in a mist-shrouded San Francisco, and then four days in New York. The experience of these two vibrant American cities, polyglot, multicultural, at the height of the 1960s' radicalism, hit Michael with full force. It was a time of fierce protest, against the Vietnam War, against discrimination racial or sexual. Hippies gathered in Golden Gate Park in San Francisco, where just a few months earlier the Grateful Dead rock band had been formed. The city had recently been dubbed the "gay capital of America" and the Summer of Love, which saw the gathering of 100,000 people in one of its neighbourhoods, was just around the corner. In New York Michael ticked off the tourist attractions, climbed skyscrapers, walked through the streets, soaked up the pulsating energy, the soundscape of horns and engines, the pop music that people were beginning to listen to on new, compact, cassette tapes. He and Karl flew home on 10 August 1965, high on travel. "America was terrific," Michael concluded. "A holiday in a million."[20]

It was the beginning of a love affair with a country he had taken to his heart in all its infinite variety. America had acted on him almost like a drug, and, craving its Technicolor energy, he longed to return. He had considered himself, as a composer, European. But the sounds he had heard in America were burrowing indelibly into his music, as he began to turn his attention to a third opera. He had been attracted not only to the landscape of America, but to its youth culture, its internationalism and multiculturalism, the babel of languages he heard on its streets, a kind of indefinable urban energy that, conversely, he would begin to recreate in music composed in rural solitude. London had offered him all of this to a certain degree, but not on America's scale. He had not fallen head over heels for the American dream, and his work would eventually be sharply critical of the country's subculture and political divisions, as the supposed freedoms of the 1960s tipped over into a sharper reality, and the Vietnam War dragged on. But the trip rapidly consolidated his ideas about the necessary internationalism of culture, and bolstered his rejection of any especially "British" idiom in his own work: "my concerns as a composer bear no relation at all to my passport nationality".[21] In an interview that decade he said: "I can never get away from the conviction that the most immediately momentous thing that is happening, is not the exploration of space, but the making of one world on this planet, through the interaction of cultures."[22]

Even in England the younger generation of the "swinging sixties" delighted him. He who had been born into a world of bustles and petticoats was now enthralled by his concert audiences: "jeans, mini-skirts, long hair, the lot!"[23] And at the back of his mind, all through the American trips, was someone who was not Karl. He was in the middle of a double existence. Back in September 1962 he had received a letter from Meirion Bowen, whom, like everyone else, he soon came to call "Bill". It was an innocuous letter, pointing out a mistake in the score of the second piano sonata, and professing much admiration of Michael's music. Michael responded gratefully, and, as was his usual answer to such communications, offered to meet.

Bill Bowen was born in Wales in 1940, and studied music first at Birmingham University and then at Cambridge. The thirty-five-year age gap between him and Michael was soon to mean very little. They had first met at the studio recording for the Third Programme's broadcast of The Midsummer Marriage in January 1963, but barely talked. Continuing to correspond, they met occasionally, listening to records and watching That Was the Week That Was on the boxy television at Parkside. Bill was lonely, shy, idealistic, left-wing, a CND member. A strong friendship was developing. Michael wrote to him in December 1963: "I wanted to draw you out to become and to experience all you have to."[24]

For a while Michael told Bill that Karl Hawker was merely a "friend of mine".[25] It cannot have taken long for the true situation to emerge. Bill was an outlet for Michael from an increasingly troubled personal life. At first Michael trod carefully, flirtatiously: "I wish you every luck in your loves and hope you succeed – for to excite someone and be excited by them is a naturally given joy. And I'm sorry not to be in the running as I like you very much!"[26] But soon he *was* in the running, soon they were spending the nights together as well as the days, and by the time Michael had returned from America, they were, as Bill remembers now, "head over heels in love with each other".[27] Michael wrote to him: "I think, incidentally, for a while I may sleep the first sleeping bit of our nights together, in the next room, partly I'm sure so as to be fresher when I come to you in the morning! I find our times together – warm, loving, sensual – as you might say, gorgeous. And I soon miss you again when you're gone." They were, he thought, "involved in some voyage of discovery together", a "gradual and extraordinary concentration of all the body into one channel. It immensely extends us and as immensely releases us – into the 'home' of someone's arms."[28]

By this time Bill was lecturing at Croydon Art College, his ears open to the pop music of the 1960s as well as to the classical. He was musically gifted and practically helpful. Michael, porous as ever to the views of those he loved, took his suggestions seriously. As early as 1963 Michael's musical sketches had begun to contain the initials "MB" in the margin, as if acknowledging the provenance of a particular suggestion.[29] Uniquely among Michael's lovers over the previous forty years, Bill was openly homosexual, and was not tugged back and forth between Michael and a woman. By the time he was twenty-seven the country would legalise homosexuality, and the generational gap had given him a different attitude to sexual politics. With Bill, Michael enjoyed a reciprocal and joyous sexual life that he had not experienced for many years, if ever. "I'm still bemused, in the nice sense, by sharing a bed with you all night," runs one letter. "Warm and comforting and intimate – with time to make love and time to sleep as it comes to us. It seems like the natural fulfilment of intimacy – to both of us I guess."[30] Or another: "Perhaps [. . . my happiness] is just the consequence naturally of joyful giving and being given sexual pleasure. And thinking of ourselves incidentally it's clear now I generally need a swift premature ejaculation, which often happens of itself, before I can enter with you on the proper, prolonged rhythms of sex, where all is possible. Love and desire are tremendous things – to be taken, even though gently, 'with both hands'."[31]

Karl was in and out of Parkside, as were his daughters, Susan and Sarah. Gran Hawker and Gran Tippett, as they were known, paid long visits, and nights with Bill had to be kept secret even from the housekeeper and cook. "A couple of times", Bill says now, "when Karl was there, and I was there . . ." He sighs. "It was very difficult."[32] If Michael divulged the affair to his closest friends it can only have been in conversation, as Karl was dealing with all correspondence. Given that most of their friends liked Karl enormously, it is more likely that Michael held this secret relationship close to his chest. He was no stranger to overlapping affairs, but they had taken place in the strange and open atmosphere of the war. Never before had he had an affair with one person that he needed to keep secret from another, and he was not impervious to its excitements. There survive in Bill Bowen's papers a myriad restaurant receipts, hotel bills using false names ("Mr Michaels"), hundreds of cards and notes, all documenting a period of snatched nights and illicit embraces, of secret calls made from high-street phone boxes, life playing out in a double secrecy, from Karl, and from the world at large.

The stage was set for an opera more personal than any Michael had yet written.

TWENTY-SEVEN

Seven Characters in Search
of an Opera

In a large and labyrinthine walled garden, with urban towers in the distance beyond, a woman named Thea, green-fingered, unhappy in her marriage to a civil engineer called Faber, tends to the roses. Evidently unable to have children, they have adopted a troubled girl named Flora. Life is tense and unhappy. Thea and Faber have grown apart, and Flora flees from Faber's touch, finding him lecherous.

Four guests arrive in the course of the day. Dov, a musician, is there with his male partner, Mel, a black writer – their own relationship is shaky. A strange psychoanalyst called Mangus hovers in corners, watching. And as the day continues Thea's sister, Denise, arrives after a long absence: she is a devoted activist, and during a long period of arrest in some foreign prison was severely tortured. Twisted with anger and maltreatment, she is unforgiving, afraid of love.

That night the garden becomes a strange dreamscape, a maze of unhappiness. Some unnamed terror lurks beneath the surface of life. The two sisters are at odds. Faber, bruised and alone, speaks with Dov, to whom he has always been attracted, and eventually makes a pass at him. Dov and Mel, still deeply in love, argue bitterly as they realise their relationship may be breaking down. Everyone is in flight: from each other, from themselves, from fear itself.

Soon the psychoanalyst, Mangus, has them all re-enacting Shakespeare, specifically *The Tempest*, casting himself as Prospero, and

Flora as Miranda. Dov and Mel are Ariel and Caliban. Dov watches helplessly as his lover turns to Denise for tenderness.

Suddenly Mangus halts proceedings, disillusioned. Mel and Denise go off together. Flora goes off alone, newly radiant. Dov, his relationship with Mel seemingly at an end, trails after them. Thea and Faber stay behind in the garden, in the darkness. Overcome with a reignited desire, they move towards each other.

Such is the plot of the opera that became *The Knot Garden*, not premiered until December 1970, but the main focus of Michael's composition for the second half of the 1960s. He had begun cursory work on it as early as August 1962, soon after the premiere of *King Priam*.[1] That month he told Priaulx Rainier he was going to throw everything else aside "and begin the opera. That is, the text proper; while hammering out musical conceptions in my mind. It's all very exciting – a strange, weird world again!!"[2] These plans had to be put on hold while various commissions were attended to, not least the Concerto for Orchestra and *The Vision of Saint Augustine*, but throughout 1963 and 1964 he had worked intermittently on the scenario and libretto, once again asking all and sundry for advice, relying on Ursula Vaughan Williams and most of all on his friend Eric Walter White. He did not finish the libretto until he had returned from America, and what had begun as a country-house drama out of George Bernard Shaw or Noël Coward was speedily shaken up with a quotation from almost every American idiom of the last half-century.

The scenario went through various changes and alterations as he went on, most notably, and at White's urging, the cutting of an eighth character (Michael had once again started an opera with an octet). The figure of Claire, a hospital doctor and potential love match for Mangus, was removed, as was an idea of ending the opera with a mime, while the closing paragraph from a Virginia Woolf novel was read into a microphone: "Left alone together the first time that day, they were silent. Alone, enmity was bared; also love. Before they slept, they must fight; after they had fought, they would embrace. From that embrace another life might be born. [. . .] Then the curtain rose. They spoke."[3] This portion of *Between the Acts* may hold the key to unlocking *The Knot Garden*. Woolf's novel depicts a gathering in a country house on a day when a pageant is to be performed. The house's owners are a couple living unhappy separate lives, and flirting with visitors, one of whom is homosexual. When the pageant is over, the characters hover between fragmentation and togetherness. Music from a gramophone plays: "Dispersed are we who have come together. But let us retain whatever made that harmony."

The Knot Garden ponders how people might know themselves, and know each other, in a deadened world. Michael was returning to the theme of *The Midsummer Marriage*, but with a less optimistic temper, bringing together seven unhappy and lost people through the power of art. It was a reaction to the divided world, to the supposed freedom and optimism of the 1960s. *The Knot Garden* is a warning, and sets its unhappy characters adrift in a maze around which some nameless terror lurks, bursting into moments of violence. The opera exposes the isolation of the human condition, and tentatively offers a proposed remedy, though its conclusions are far from blanketly hopeful. The moments of love obtained are radiant, brief, transitory. The characters come together in a union they know to be temporary, and no less genuine or valuable for it, singing a final ensemble of reconciliation, a hint of a new togetherness in society, a possibility of mutual forgiveness and love, or a positing of the *need* for such a thing. Michael had written a comedy of forgiveness, as if in dialogue with Shakespeare's late plays, or with Mozart's *Così fan tutte*. As in both Shakespeare and Mozart, a shadow is cast over the ostensibly happy ending and the neatly knotted couples. Michael wrote to Priaulx Rainier during composition: "You know, I don't know at all <u>why</u> I seem to remain positive or affirmatory, in so far as I do. I regard the whole temper of the present time as especially difficult and 'insecure' – and it affects us <u>all</u>, whether we <u>appear</u> to be 'successful' or whatever. And the wrestling with this 'blackness' is almost the only activity for creative artists and others at all."[4]

The Knot Garden was an odd fit in the British operatic world of the 1960s, which had turned dark and ferocious. Britten was at work on Owen Wingrave, an adaptation for television of a Henry James story depicting the disintegration of an ex-soldier who rejects the military life. Younger composers, in their different ways, were exploring an often playfully macabre realm of murder and madness. Michael's opera fitted more snugly into the worlds of theatre and literature. John Fowles's novel The Magus (a smash hit in 1965) features a mysterious psychoanalyst living on a remote island, who attempts to bring a young and lost man to self-knowledge via the reconstruction of theatrical masques, including The Tempest. Michael was fashioning a markedly similar tale, making a psychological cyclone out of the literal storm of Shakespeare's play. Once again the work of Christopher Fry and of T.S. Eliot was a bedrock of his thought, from the wartime dreamworld of Fry's A Sleep of Prisoners to Eliot's The Cocktail Party, which depicts a couple on the verge of separation hosting a party in London, attended by a mysterious but healing psychologist.[5] Also in his mind were the philosophical farces of Iris Murdoch such as A Severed Head (her 1963 novel-turned-play in which the cast tumbles through almost as many love pairings as can be made from the seven characters, one of them a dubious psychoanalyst). And equally influential was Edward Albee: the unhappy central couple of Who's Afraid of Virginia Woolf, torturing guests with play-acting games so as to torture each other, was a clear inspiration for The Knot Garden.[6]

But the opera had arisen from within, as well as without. That Michael thought of it as emanating from the last novel of Virginia Woolf, published after her death by drowning, may have increased its haunting by the ghost of Francesca Allinson. There could be something of his fiery cousin Phyllis Kemp in the figure of freedom-fighter Denise, or of John Layard in Mangus. But each of the characters seems to reflect a facet of Michael's own personality, as if he had split himself into seven: the directorial figure modelling himself on Prospero; the troubled adolescent; the couple locked in a dysfunctional and unfaithful marriage who are unable to have children. Dov, a troubled musician, perpetually on the outside looking on, would seem to be an almost explicit self-portrait: he ends the opera rejected by a male partner in favour of a female lover, and left solitary. The libretto was a means of putting together the fragments of a broken life so swathed in secrecy that neither at the time, nor for many years afterwards, were people aware of the extent to which *The Knot Garden* was a *roman à clef*.

Back in 1944, an early draft of *The Midsummer Marriage* had contained a kiss between two men, eventually, perhaps necessarily, discarded.[7] Nearly twenty years later, planning *The Knot Garden*, Michael could try again. The open depiction of homosexuality and bisexuality, of a mixed-race relationship, of an implied sexual assault between father and daughter, are all present in the very earliest drafts of Michael's scenario, sketched out sometime in 1962: five years before the legalisation of homosexuality, six years before the abolition of censorship from the London stage, and seven years before the Stonewall riots in New York. As Michael began to circulate early copies of the libretto, he was not only writing something unprecedented in the history of opera, but was defying both convention and criminal law.

By 1965 he had a more or less finished text: "The libretto is so mad I'm getting a touch of cold feet!"[8] Once again a new operatic topic would need a new kind of music, and he was anxious to get going. In mid-1965 he began work on a piano trio, a fascinating might-have-been of a piece that Yehudi Menuhin and his pianist sister Hephzibah had agreed to premiere at the Bath Festival, joined by the cellist Maurice Gendron.[9] The piece was interrupted by the trip to America. Back in England, Michael caught bronchitis and then, in September 1965, had a bad car crash. "He escaped unhurt," Karl reported to John Layard, "but two men in the other car were badly hurt. Michael drove around a lorry at night, without being able to see the road ahead. I've always thought Michael's driving appalling."[10] All this put paid to the trio once and for all. The performance was cancelled, the score seemingly destroyed. But the piece can be reconstructed in some detail from plans sent to Michael Tillett, who was still as vital an assistant as ever. It was to have been in one movement, with four blocks of material: an energetic fugue; a sequence of piano chords; a melodic section "stimulated maybe by some Messiaen"; and, to finish, "my first blues (a try-out for the big blues ensemble of the new opera, which I begin immediately after the trio)."[11] Michael asked Bill Bowen to provide him with music "which would be unmistakably pop – in the very widest sense", wanting a "recognisable 'quote'" to be incorporated "either straight or changed, into one of the 'movements' of the new trio".[12]

Michael's standing in the British musical world was now such that he might have been expected to consolidate his achievement. Instead he was systematically picking it apart, taking, as his fame grew, one new risk after another. The Knot Garden brought about the sharpest reinvention in his career, as if unleashed by the affair with Bill. The presence of jazz and blues in his music was not new, but the extent to which they dominated The Knot Garden was unprecedented. His musical preoccupation was now a kind of urban pastoral, an attempt to see what lyricism might bloom amid the soundscape of the city. And stitched into the very fabric of his score came the blues, which he called "something that belonged to our century", with the ability both to portray and to heal suffering. The term was most likely derived from the dye "blue indigo", used by many West African cultures in death and mourning ceremonies. Michael began to dye his music blue to indicate the suffering of the century, and his tentative hope that, through singing the blues, such suffering could be alleviated: "one sings the blues", he wrote, "when one's mood is 'blue'".[13]

Into the orchestra pit he despatched a jazz kit and an electric guitar. Such instruments were commonly used in post-war compositions on the Continent but initially caused British orchestras numerous problems. Michael had to choose between rock musicians unaccustomed to playing in an orchestra and classical guitarists who couldn't navigate the electric instruments. As characters in the opera come together and are wrenched apart, musical numbers appear, fragment, and reassemble. The score cuts frenetically from jagged particles to heart-easing melodies. The orchestra becomes a maze in which the seven characters are caught. As, in The Waste Land,

T.S. Eliot quotes both from Wagner and from popular song, into *The Knot Garden* are woven quotations from Delta blues and 1960s civil-rights anthems, alongside shards of Schubert and fragments of Beethoven. A scene between Mel and Denise above a thick swirl of strings melts into a line from "We shall overcome", bound so firmly into the duet as to be barely recognisable. By the end of the first act Flora has performed a complete verse of a Schubert song ("Die liebe Farbe", from *Die Schöne Müllerin*), followed by a decon- struction of the original, in which Dov sings an English translation while icicles melt high in the piano. He then responds with a blues song of his own: "Play it cool, play it cool". It was an almost brutal cohabitation of the classical and the vernacular. From now on in Michael's music, Beethoven and the blues would stand cheek by jowl, and his constant preoccupation was how the two might coexist in a new synthesis.

This patchwork of different cloths, as vivid and varied as the cultural make-up of the decade, was shaped into an overall frame- work in which scene moved into scene with nothing but a brief blare of music. The opera was presented with a new tightness of structure, on which the world of film and television had been a strong influence. Michael had been dipping his toe into television more and more through the 1960s, and began to appear on arts programmes with some regularity. In 1964 a second, artistically more highbrow, channel had arrived in the shape of BBC2, and the television became a fixture first of Michael's evening entertainment, and then of his music. On no other composer of his generation did televisual techniques work so strongly.[14] The score of *The Knot Garden* seems not so much composed as, in the filmic sense, edited. Even a new shortness of scene seems to reflect the short, sharp packaging of television, and scene changes are marked with the vocabulary of the movie camera: "dissolve". At times the music seems to be channel-hopping. Conversely, Michael would never compose an opera specifically for television. The theatrical power of *The Knot Garden* would come in the peculiar magic trick of filmic techniques translated, live, onto the stage. There was no question of the work not being staged by the Royal Opera House, and he now had a close bond with the chief executive, David Webster, who became *The Knot Garden*'s dedicatee. On 30 November 1965 Michael told Priaulx Rainier: "The <u>music</u> has begun now for the opera, and it's always hard work hammering out the beginnings."[15]

The three years and three months which *The Knot Garden* would take to compose were a time of professional busyness and success, leading to exhaustion and crisis. There was a Labour government, after thirteen years of Tory rule. It was a period of change and liberty and protest, in which homosexuality would be decriminalised, censorship on the British stage abolished, and man would walk on the moon.

Foreign travel continued to influence the opera's progress. Exhausted from the premiere of *The Vision of Saint Augustine* and a conducting tour in Belgium early in 1966, Michael was nevertheless eager to get back to *The Knot Garden*. But an invitation to return to America had come quickly, and that year, in early spring, he went to Goucher College for Girls in Baltimore to make his American conducting debut with a performance of *A Child of Our Time*, and was delighted to find the choir a mixture of black and white singers. The oratorio would become more and more popular in America. And although some Americans felt that spirituals were not an English composer's for the taking, many performances were highly charged. "Tippett told me", remembers the singer Raimund Herincx, "how when he'd heard [*A Child of Our Time*] in America, of course all the audience started to sing the spirituals, and it made him weep apparently. Almost makes me weep to see him telling me."[16]

On this second American trip Michael witnessed segregation and the attempts to overturn it. London was no stranger to racism, and Karl Hawker kept a flat in Notting Hill Gate, the scene of race riots and racketeering landlords, where it was still common to see boarding houses reacting to the West Indian communities with signs in the window stating "No blacks". But the southern states of America had enforced the Jim Crow laws until 1965, and the Ku Klux Klan continued to oppose the Civil Rights Movement with violence and murder. Before the concert in Baltimore, Michael took Karl and his daughters on a driving holiday. They went first to New Orleans, melting pot of different cultures, city of jazz, and then travelled up north-east to Baltimore, through Alabama, Tennessee, and Virginia. Michael never kept a travel diary, but in April, soon after his return to England, he gave his annual speech to the Peace Pledge Union and recounted his experience:

> As we remembered when we got to Montgomery, Alabama, this is indeed where something extraordinary took place. We very rarely ever saw anything offensive: nothing, in fact. But we were driving eventually along a country road quite empty, and we overtook a man who obviously was trying to get somewhere, and I offered him a lift. He was a negro and when he understood what we wanted he did not very much want to get into the car. He said he was trying to find a garage in order to buy a spanner of some kind. However, we persuaded him to take a lift, and he turned out to be an elderly man, I would say an ardent Christian: or ardent is probably the wrong term: a convinced Christian. And as he began to talk he said "You are strangers. You could only be strangers because no white person from this locality could have offered me a lift." He then said, "but it is changing and in the last five or ten years it has changed so much I cannot tell you, and there is hope".[17]

On 11 June 1966 Michael was knighted in the Queen's Birthday Honours, an accolade he perhaps found easier to accept from a Labour government. His strange journey from traitor to national treasure seemed complete. "I tease myself about you-know-what," he admitted to Bill Bowen, "because it sits very oddly on my shoulders! On the other hand to get used to it is to accept the public persona honestly I dare say. Anyhow, 'tis done now."[18] There was little time to bask. By 28 June he was in hospital for an operation on his prostate from which he took some weeks to recover. He was nursed devotedly by Karl, who was now living at Parkside more or less full-time. The affair with Bill had to remain as secret as ever. By the summer Michael had recovered and was back at work, making his by now annual trip to the Edinburgh Festival, going in October to Berlin, back to Scotland in November, and finishing the year with one of his rare periods of composer's block, exhausted, and finding London "nightmarish".[19] He did manage to complete a five-minute contribution to the joint effort of the *Severn Bridge Variations*, for which six composers, three Welsh, three English, offered a variation on a rather awkward and asymmetrical Welsh hymn tune, to celebrate the opening of the Severn Bridge connecting England with Wales. Michael's variation juxtaposes strident fanfares and galloping strings with a haze of tuned percussion redolent of a much later period in his music. Adrian Boult, risking a brief Tippett premiere nearly a decade after his first had proved so disastrous, led the performance, on 11 January 1967, with the short-lived BBC Training Orchestra, whose first birthday Michael was happy to celebrate. Secretly, he may also have rejoiced at a bridge that would ease journeys between England and Wales, where Bill Bowen spent time with his family.

By spring 1967, Michael was coming towards the end of *The Knot Garden*'s first act, distracted only by having to nurse both his mother and Karl's, who were lying ill in two of Parkside's many bedrooms. But suddenly life began to reflect the opera, when Karl found out about Bill. He had been unhappily aware of the relationship, but not its full extent, and Michael had seemingly assured him that it was all over. Michael wrote to Bill:

Our garage gave Karl the monthly bill to give to me, and the taxi for you was itemised with your name. So we fell into a nightmare world from which we've only just gotten ourselves out again. K's nightmare (no quarrelling) is a terrifying fear that you are waiting so to speak to step into his shoes. He knows rationally this isn't true – but irrationally it's true enough for him and seems to echo what did in fact happen to his marriage. My nightmare was different, but terrifyingly real also. I have never had a secret relationship before, and on the face of it it's right out of character. So its positive side has a negative obverse: of a deep-seated guilt. Least I suppose that's what it is. And to practise deliberate deception in K's own home seems to give this irrational guilt its sharpest symbol. Maybe too there's an element of guilt towards you too. That I have somehow led you down the garden path. But I don't think either of us, you or me, regrets this.[20]

He wrote to Bill again, not long afterwards:

Part of Karl's extreme shock was that I had promised a year ago or so when it happened before that it would be the end. The broken promises and the lies were hard to take. Also, of course hard to give. It's something relatively unknown to me as an experience – and quite frankly I'm not at all sure about it. I know I never wanted you to have to lie too [. . .]. Karl now sees that it is partly his overwhelming "suspicion and possessiveness" as he calls it, that prevents him moving on to a more tolerant ground. But it's one thing to recognise something in oneself and another to grow out of it. And even then, what is the nature or extent of tolerance between partners so close and fundamentally united as we are? I am myself an almost ridiculously unjealous person – possibly just complacent – though not quite, for I've had *crises de jalousie* in the past of Proustian violence. [. . .] It's pretty unclear yet how much deception I am able and willing to practise in the future – so one needs time to let things settle a bit before testing what one feels. This playing it cool is part of the quality and success of what you and I have known and enjoyed together. The price (for me) in deception has been high but worth it. But it's not to turn round now into tragedy.[21]

The row settled; the affair continued. If Karl knew, he somehow found a way of blocking it out from his life with Michael at Corsham. If Bill resented having always to be, as it were, "the other man", it didn't damage the relationship. Now working as a radio producer at the BBC, he established an experimental music group called The Electric Candle, whose repertoire found its way into Michael's new musical world. Bill was able to help write out blues lines and boogie-woogie, and advise on the use of instruments novel to Michael, such as the drum machine or electric guitar. On 27 July 1967 the Sexual Offences Act was passed, after intense debate and much opposition, decriminalising homosexual acts, in private, between two men over the age of twenty-one. Michael and Bill had to be doubly careful, in that courts took the wording of the act to exclude sexual activity between men in hotel rooms, in which, by necessity, they often met. It was far from a new dawn of tolerance, and when on 28 July The Times reported Royal Assent to the Bill, Lord Arran asked homosexuals to "show their thanks by comporting themselves quietly and with dignity".[22] Bill Bowen remembers that "when the news came out, Michael left me an answerphone message which said 'now we can tell the world!'"[23] One day short of an exact year after the Sexual Offences Act, on 26 July 1968, the Theatres Act was passed, abolishing stage censorship. The Knot Garden would become one of the first new operas in Britain to be untroubled by the prurient pencil of the Lord Chamberlain's team, its depiction of sexuality mirroring, with a kind of self-conscious casualness, a new world.

By the spring of 1968 Michael was deep into the opera's central act. On 10 April a new production of The Midsummer Marriage appeared at Covent Garden, and, with Colin Davis devotedly at the helm of the orchestra, audiences and critics alike rejoiced at the music. The production, by a resident producer, Ande Anderson, had been hurriedly redesigned at the last minute – his widow Josephine Barstow describes it as a "great big compost heap" – and it was not thought a success in all circles. "I liked the idea of the prehistoric mound," Alan Bush told Michael, "even if I could not quite stomach the prehistoric mini-skirts."[24] But the cast, led by Joan Carlyle and Alberto Remedios, was thought impeccable, and the choreography of the Ritual Dances (by Gillian Lynne, later famous for Lloyd Webber's Cats) a huge success. Copies of the libretto sold out and had to be reprinted at a mad dash, and within two years there was a revival.

Michael rushed from first-night party to aeroplane. An indisposed

Igor Stravinsky had left a concert by the St Louis Symphony Orchestra without a conductor, and Michael was flown in at short notice, rather thrilled to find in the orchestra a Native American trumpeter. This performance led, after an introduction from Aaron Copland, to his signing with an American agent, Herbert Barrett, and offers of work in the States soon came thick and fast. He returned to England on 23 April, before going, in May, to Israel. He and Karl went from head to toe of the country, from Galilee down to Masada, an ancient fortress to which the Six-Day War of the previous year had finally granted public access, and then to Eilat, a port city near the Jordan border, which prior to the war had been blockaded by the Egyptians. But Michael was on holiday: "I swim in the wine-dark sea under a hot-blue sky."[25] His reputation as a conscientious objector had preceded him, and many, still numbed by the Holocaust, found his stance hard to take. "How is it that you could not fight?" an Israeli woman asked him in distress. "I could have said," he remembered, "'well, I don't see how burning people in Dresden makes up for burning people in the concentration camps', but that wasn't the issue. I tried to comfort her. I didn't do it very well."[26] He and Karl returned via Norway, where they sat through no fewer than four banquets with the King, salmon at each. Back at Corsham, Michael was at last able to begin the final act of The Knot Garden. Karl remained anxious and manic, driving off in his car not to return until morning, but Susan and Sarah (whom, that September, Michael took to visit William Walton on the island of Ischia) were frequent visitors, and they all spent Christmas together.

Nineteen sixty-eight was the year of rejected invitations. The first was from W.H. Auden, of whom Michael had seen little since their brief acquaintance in the 1930s. Auden, who was living in New York, had enjoyed a broadcast of The Midsummer Marriage and suggested to Michael that they might work together on an opera. This was partly a project to occupy his friend and sometime lover Chester Kallman, with whom he had collaborated on a number of librettos; both had strong feelings as to the structure and mood of the music to which their words would be set. Michael was now used to acting as his own librettist, had already outlined the scenario for a fourth opera, and was immediately sure that Auden would be too domineering a collaborator. The poet moved on to Harrison Birtwistle, who rejected the proposal on similar grounds.[27]

The second invitation came in the autumn. The Soviet Embassy in London asked Michael to be guest of honour at a congress, to be held in Moscow in December, of the Union of Soviet Composers. Michael refused, partly because he had no time, partly from political principle. In August the five nations of the Warsaw Pact, led by the USSR, had invaded Czechoslovakia. The official stance of the Union, founded in 1960, was to approve of the invasion of Czechoslovakia; speakers at the congress would attack not only Western art for its individualism, but even Soviet music for its importation of jazz. Dmitri Shostakovich had been unanimously elected as the Union's secretary, necessitating his joining the Communist Party. Michael was conflicted about Shostakovich's later music, perhaps thinking it indissolubly bound to the world of Russian politics from which he had so categorically turned away, and hoping to avoid the did-he didn't-he arguments over Shostakovich's complicity. He may have wished simply to keep away from a composer who had become close to Benjamin Britten, and part of the Aldeburgh world. He would now never meet Shostakovich, who was profoundly depressed, under intense political blackmail, and beset by the ill health that would kill him seven years later. "I am glad I did not go to Moscow", Michael wrote afterwards. "I would not have wanted to see him like that."[28] So resolutely against the Soviet bloc had Michael become that he initiated almost no friendships or collaborations with its musicians, even those who had fought fiercely against the regime. His name is a notable absence from the list of over 100 composers who wrote works for cellist Mstislav Rostropovich.

A rare exception came via the Bath International Music Festival, of which, in 1968, Michael took over from Yehudi Menuhin as an artistic director. He already had strong links with the festival, having conducted concerts there, and Menuhin's Bath Festival Chamber Orchestra had combined with the Moscow Chamber Orchestra in a vibrant recording of Michael's Concerto for Double String Orchestra, led by the Soviet conductor Rudolf Barshai. Bath's proximity to Corsham made directing the festival a viable proposition, though Michael soon found the burden immense, despite splitting directorial duties three ways with Colin Davis and the arts administrator Jack Phipps. Menuhin had left a mountain of debt, which they worked hard to pay off, Michael occasionally using his own funds. He was facing the challenge, common to every artistic director, of having to attract a new audience without losing the old, and was already well versed in the art of combining early with modern, and of sandwiching "challenging" premieres between some guaranteed crowd-pleasers. Placing a strong emphasis on young composers and performers, he made the Georgian city a place of pilgrimage for music-lovers half his age. He invited Elliott Carter over from America, and was generous to composer friends, programming premieres by Elizabeth Maconchy (which he privately deemed "flimsy"), by Priaulx Rainier ("by far the best"), and by Alan Bush ("dire").[29] A number of social fixtures were organised – tours of local churches, art exhibitions, film showings, wine tastings – and Morris dancers and brass bands played in the shadow of Bath Abbey. There were weekends devoted to rock and blues, one headlined by Led Zeppelin, and Michael insisted that the audience should wear jeans if they wished. All this was brilliantly received by the press, but sold badly. In 1969 Davis and Phipps resigned from the festival, seemingly without rancour; both had found their obligations too difficult to combine with their London commitments. It was not long before Michael, going it alone, began to find the bureaucracy and financial constraints a drag. He would stick it out, not without success, for six years, but kept vowing to abandon the commitment. Only one of his own works received its premiere at Bath during his tenure.

Come 1969 he was on the finale of *The Knot Garden*, and in breaks from its composition was already sketching out the scenario of another opera, and planning a third symphony. On 20 February *The Knot Garden* was finished. Its reconciled couple, Thea and Faber, move off to make love, singing together, in the hope of a new life and a new age: "The curtain rises." The orchestra bubbles upward into the flies. Michael may have been hoping for such a reconciliation with Karl, but his thoughts were elsewhere. "I thought of you", he told Bill as he shared news of the opera's completion, and of Thea's and Faber's love-making, "and felt (in a dream way) we'd have done the same had the opportunity served – and all night if we felt like it! Though we're a stranger couple than is often found."[30]

There followed the usual depressive anticlimax, and within three days he began sketching out another work. The new musical style of an opera, as with his first two, continued to have a kind of after-birth, and he needed somewhere to put it. Following the pattern of Songs for Achilles, but using a full orchestra, he wrote (again to his own words) Songs for Dov, extending the life of the character in The Knot Garden who had been in so many ways a self-portrait. Startling in an early draft of the opera's libretto is a moment, soon discarded, in which Dov rolls on the floor shouting, "I want to be raped!"[31] The line may be indicative of Michael's sexual tastes, recalling his proclamation to David Webster, if it can be taken at face value, that he wanted to be "thrown on a bed, and raped". Sexual submission had been a means of going to bed with heterosexual men; meeting Karl Hawker, he had once admitted, moved him away from want-ing to be "pushed around". Rape fantasies, if such they are, might indicate lingering guilt and shame at his sexuality, as if his sexual distress could be reduced by abnegating responsibility. Two of the Songs for Dov open with a cacophony of percussion and electric guitar while Dov howls like a dog in a painful portrayal of unhappiness and submission. Accompanying the tenor is a strange honeycomb of quotation, from Beethoven, from Dixieland, from Wagner, from Tippett. Recalling his urban upbringing and his world travels, Dov becomes the archetypal wandering Jew, a strange cousin to Her-schel Grynszpan: the scapegoat who reinvents himself in exile. But he is also the solitary artist seeking to arrive at maturity through journeying and experience, and endlessly trying and then discarding the illusions and temptations of fashion, portrayed with a daring and deliberate tackiness.

The songs were a self-corrective to the energetic delights of the sprawling urban jungles that had so entranced Michael on his travels.

How, amid the new speeds and ever-growing industrial cities of the century, with their endless and ephemeral fashions and tribes, could the permanent landscape that shone through his Wiltshire windows each day find its way into art without cliché? How could the century allow Michael to return to the lush and innocent worlds of his earliest pieces? Dov quotes from Boris Pasternak: "Surely it is my calling to see that the distances should not lose heart, and that beyond the limits of the town, the earth should not feel lonely?" The songs are none too sure that such a thing is possible, ending in bitter irony. Dov reverts to the fashion-led temptation of sultry, slangy disillusion: "Sure, baby." The percussion chuckles sardonically.

But the triumph was in the attempt. Of all Michael's "Desert Island Discs", *Songs for Dov* was the only piece of his own that he chose to hear, as a reminder, amidst the solitude of the island, that he had composed music at all.

Over the summer of 1969, after a trip to Philadelphia, Michael's heavy schedule caught up with him, and he began to experience what would today be called panic attacks: he found himself shaking uncontrollably, his heart banging, and was plagued with diarrhoea. All the symptoms are medically explained by a surge of adrenaline and other stress hormones in the bloodstream, putting the body into emergency mode. The emotional explanation was the completion of a major and deeply personal opera amid his by now international conducting schedule, and his double life with Bill and with Karl. The nervous attacks continued for the rest of the year, much of which Michael spent in bed, composing on calmer days when his medication kicked in (atrial fibrillation was diagnosed). On top of everything else, his mother was suffering a series of strokes, one of which left her totally debilitated. Isabel died at midnight on 29 November 1969, eighty-nine years old, a suffragist who had lived to see the women's liberation movements of the 1960s. Michael's relationship with her had been loving, thorny, tangled by turns. She had never truly accepted his partners, which meant, in a way, that she had never truly accepted him. One reading of his productivity would be as a means of gaining maternal approval, just as the messes of his personal life could be seen as an attempt to recreate the love he had felt absent from his childhood. All too crude perhaps: Isabel's death seemed neither agony nor release for Michael, and did not interrupt or alter his compositional dedication. Her estate was valued at £3,772, of which a half-share would be worth about £26,000 today. Driving away from Chelmsford Crematorium with his brother Peter, Michael had little time for pleasantries: "How do I get my hands on the money?"[32] Only in a tiny phrase in a card written years later did he concede: "loss of a parent is always sharp".[33]

If his body was in fight-or-flight mode, then so was he. Once again he pinned his hopes on a change of scene. He laid plans to reduce commitments to the Leicestershire Schools Symphony Orchestra and to the Bath Festival as soon as possible, and he and Karl began to house-hunt. The festival had made Michael too much of a local celebrity, and living at the end of a high street had led to frequent unannounced visits from admirers and administrators. The rent on Parkside had risen considerably, and a multi-storey car park (never built, in the event) was being planned by a local supermarket. The inheritance from his mother was a help, and he needed it. He was earning well, but spending more, helping Bill, helping Karl, and laying out thousands a year on holidays, on which he often took friends at his own expense. His manuscript scores could now sell to American collectors for five-figure sums, and he raised enough funds to a purchase, for £26,000, a four-year-old timbered box of a house, ten miles east of Corsham, close to the village of Calne. Nocketts, as the house was called, was an exciting prospect for Michael, offering a cleansing world of seclusion, and in a solarium close to the house there was a heated pool where he could swim away the tension in his muscles. "A feeling of a fresh period (the last obviously!)," he told Priaulx on 20 December, "in which to do some few good things if I can – but without pressure or haste." After a Christmas with all the Hawkers, Michael managed to finish *Songs for Dov* on 9 February 1970, still ridden with anxiety and nerves.[34] He and Karl moved into Nocketts on 24 March, and sent joint change-of-address cards. Bill or no Bill, Michael was evidently thinking of the move as a joint one with Karl.

No fence or wall divided the house's twenty acres of land from the endless stretch of countryside that lay beyond. Visitors to Nocketts marvelled at the outlook from the music room that was added to the back of the building, with its large glass doors and patio beyond. The house is perched, secluded, at the end of a long road and on one of the few hills in the area, and the view from it is seemingly endless, encompassing counties, with little clusters of villages and towns floating amid green fields underneath the great vault of sky. It was the first house Michael had ever lived in that was well insulated and easily heated, and he kept it boiling-hot in winter. But Nocketts could not offer all the answers. The affair with Bill was continuing in secret. In May, both of Michael's eyes were suddenly clouded with small cataracts that eventually had to be removed, and it was the beginning of his vision's slow degeneration.

There was good news on the professional front. In 1969 and in 1970 Michael had finally got round to extending his piece for the Leicestershire Schools Symphony Orchestra and he conducted the premiere of what he titled *The Shires Suite* on 8 July 1970. It had become a five-movement riot of rounds and canons, evidently the work of a composer enjoying himself, and determined that his young players should enjoy themselves too: in the cacophony of the central cantata, woven from hunting and drinking songs, the singers must make cork-popping noises through loudspeakers and throw trays of cutlery to the floor, an electric guitar playing furiously amid wild percussion.[35] The orchestral writing, often quoting from *The Knot Garden*, made few concessions, but the players had developed into a crack team under his leadership and rose to the challenge. That summer, Colin Davis's full-throttle recording of *The Midsummer Marriage* was released and became a bestseller, the LPs being handed round in university towns. It was at a university, Cardiff, that *Songs for Dov* was premiered on 12 October (whetting critics' appetites for the new opera), and Michael was already making arrangements, half canny, half generous, to ensure that the American premiere of The Knot Garden was given to university students.

As the first summer in the new house faded into autumn and the view from Nocketts changed colour, the premiere of The Knot Garden was finally on the horizon. There was a long advance puff in The Times and Michael was excited. It was "back to composition, and the laborious but <u>only</u> life, to sitting on my arse before the piano".[36] In May 1970 he had admitted: "My nervous bouts still come every week at least and are a bit depressive."[37] Colin Davis wrote to him: "I'm sorry you've been depressed: so have I been. When the fires run low it is hard to sustain one's vision of anything except minus 273 degrees centigrade. The pendulum swings again as it must and we must be patient as we 'turn on our dark sides'. [. . .] If my faith is of help it is there, although in the freezing dark one is beyond help."[38]

TWENTY-EIGHT

Freeze and Thaw

December 1970. Edward Heath had led the Conservatives to a shock victory at the June elections. Hippie culture seemed to be waning, the optimism of free love having curdled into dangerous drug use and violence. Jimi Hendrix was dead and the Beatles had disbanded. Frequent industrial strikes and lengthy blackouts from power cuts were already a way of life.

The audience gathering at the Royal Opera House for the premiere of *The Knot Garden* knew only to expect nothing. There was a new regime. Colin Davis was about to take over as principal conductor, the plan being that he would work in equal partnership with Peter Hall, late of the Royal Shakespeare Company. Davis had been thrilled with the score. "I can't wait to turn that place upside down!" he wrote to Michael acknowledging its receipt, sending "all my prayers for your health, your spirit, and your new works. Love, in fact."[1] And in Peter Hall, who as a child had been "excited beyond belief" by a recording of *A Child of Our Time*, Michael had made a lifelong friend, who would speak of working with Tippett in the same breath as his collaborations with Beckett and Pinter, and who, much later, told Michael that directing *The Knot Garden* was "one of the best experiences of my theatrical life".[2] In the event it was a short-lived dream team. Davis's career soon settled after a few poorly reviewed and loudly booed productions, but Hall was to depart within three years, lured to the National Theatre to take over its directorship from Laurence Olivier. *The Knot Garden*, the pair's first collaboration, was intended as a manifesto (received as a gimmick in some quarters): "opera is being dragged into the 1970s".[3]

Michael had composed, as ever, with no specific singers in mind, but as casting was under way he asked Peter Pears to sing the role of the Prospero-like psychoanalyst, Mangus.[4] Pears replied that the role lay outside the tenor range (eventually the baritone Thomas Hemsley was cast). This may have been a convenient excuse, and the clash with Britten's Owen Wingrave, recorded for television during rehearsals for The Knot Garden, was anyway unavoidable. Pears was more concerned by an early draft of the libretto that dithered between naming the homosexual musician either "Dov" or "Piers". Michael's claim that he had not noticed the homonym seems genuine enough (although Dov's nickname for Mel, "honey", was often Britten's and Pears's term of endearment for one another):

> My dear, dear Peter, I also prefer Dov to Piers! To be accurate, I only realised how the latter would appear slowly, after Karl or my mother and others explained . . . I had started off with Piers Plowman, the visionary poet. Dov I saw later by accident, as the son-in-law of General Dayan.* But in fact, in Hebrew, it means a bear. Now I've got so used to it I've forgotten there was ever a Piers years ago. I think I like now too the small implication that he is, maybe, a Jew. [. . .] It's a splendidly mad opera.[5]

Peter Hall had in any case been determined to work with young actor-singers, and rehearsed the drama as he would have done a play. As the maimed activist Denise he cast Josephine Barstow, who had a fiendish time learning her huge first-act aria, which does not require singing so much as vomiting forth from the soul. But she made a vast success of the role, and enjoyed the rehearsals immensely:

---

* Dov Sion, the husband of Israeli Defence Minister Moshe Dayan's daughter, Yael.

I loved doing it. We were all very serious about it. The thing about Michael was, when I think about him in rehearsals, everybody loved him. He was loveable. Don't forget that I was a baby, and I was completely wide-eyed about the whole thing. But to be treated as an equal by somebody like Michael Tippett . . . You could go and ask him about something in the score, and he gave me an answer, and then he said: "You see that? That's *brilliant*." About his own work. And it wasn't remotely arrogant. Once he'd given birth to it, there it was on the page, it had nothing to do with him. And he could look, with this intellectual height, and think "how fantastic". When you spoke to him, it was like speaking to a library. He would be able to call on Chinese literature, German literature, anything. He would fetch these examples from the world's knowledge. He was the most intelligent man I ever met, the person that you felt had really tried to think about what being a person, and what life, was about.[6]

The role of Dov was given to the British tenor Robert Tear; and Faber, the engineer who clumsily tries to seduce him, to Raimund Herincx. The abortive seduction is only innocuously indicated in the libretto, but the production allowed matters to progress further, and the two men kissed. The depiction of a gay couple on a stage was nothing new to audiences who had seen the plays of Christopher Hampton, Simon Gray, Joe Orton and others in the late 1960s. But portrayals often stayed within safe or even cruel stereotypes, and moments of physical intimacy were rare (Tear played Dov with a campery not present in the libretto, wearing pink socks and a feather boa). The kiss between two men in *The Knot Garden* was a first for opera, and would have been unusual even in the theatre of the day. No gay kiss would be seen on British television until 1987. Raimund Herincx:

They said, "Would you do this?", and I said, "If I can experiment, and we're not going to be made fools of, then *yes*." Of course, it could come to any person – we don't know, do we, how we're going to feel about another person, any of us? (That

I think is what Tippett believed, I don't think he was gender-conscious particularly. I think he made relationships with *people*.) We got over it in rehearsal with a digestive biscuit. We knew that everyone was going to groan in rehearsal. So I said to [Tear], "I'm going to make out I've got a digestive biscuit in there." So I passed him the biscuit, he said "Urgh, a biscuit", and everybody laughed, and we heard no more about it.[7]

In 1967 the French composer-conductor Pierre Boulez had famously said that the most expensive but also the most elegant solution to the mismatch between eighteenth-century theatrical architecture and the twentieth-century operatic imagination would be to blow up the opera houses. *The Knot Garden* seemed to do just that. Its production fought against the very fabric of the building, doing battle with its proscenium arch. England had seen many provocative opera productions over the previous thirty years, from Peter Brook's blood-drenched *Salome* to Peter Hall's orgiastic British premiere of Schoenberg's *Moses und Aron*. Audiences in London and Edinburgh had recently been stimulated and challenged by the plays of Beckett and Albee, and the music of Boulez and Stockhausen featured with some regularity at the Proms. But this was something different again: the uniting of radical theatre with radical music. That something new was going on was evident as soon as the audience entered the auditorium. Many of the seats in the stalls were missing, allowing for cheap promenade tickets to lure in younger audiences. The stage had been built out across the orchestra pit, and the prompt box banished. Most crucial was the role of the designer, Timothy O'Brien. The challenge was, in O'Brien's words, "to fill the stage with nature", to create the fluid garden that would allow scene to dissolve into scene without break, with the characters caught up in its labyrinth. The swirling maze of stage machinery was the easy part: four coils of aluminium rods criss-crossed under a bright light, the singers having to time precisely the minute at which they would throw themselves into its revolutions. Then O'Brien fashioned a backcloth and wings from eleven miles of hanging nylon cords, onto which were projected photographs of the sun shining through a high canopy of beech leaves. When air was blown through the cords, the garden was brought to life in unreal shimmer. It was an enormous technical challenge: twenty-four seats were removed from the grand tier to make way for a temporary soundproof projection room, containing no fewer than six tailor-made projectors. The set and lighting required weeks of preliminary tests on a quarter-full-sized model in a warehouse. Hall claimed he had "seen projections used in theatres all over the world but I have never known it possible before *The Knot Garden* to give performers strong lighting without making the projection disappear".[8]

The soprano Jill Gomez was brought in at a frighteningly late minute to sing Faber's troubled ward, Flora (she had replaced Elizabeth Harwood, who was pregnant), and remembers the difficulties and excitements of the whirling set, into which a misjudged leap once knocked her out cold. "It was such an era-breaking thing. There was an excitement in the air. You couldn't buy a ticket for love nor money." With the re-enactment of *The Tempest* in the third act, Gomez, playing Flora, had to be assaulted by Thomas Carey's Mel, and suggested, half in jest, that Carey might rip off her bikini top. Nudity in opera was more or less unheard of, as Gomez remembers:

> Of course the other singers creased themselves laughing. And Peter said: "Brilliant. That's perfect." I thought, what have I done? Tom was very embarrassed by this – "Oh I can't do that Peter, I can't pull her top off, I can't do that." I used to giggle because he'd start creeping along towards me, and as he got nearer to me he'd say, "Don't worry, Jill, I'm not going to be able to pull it off, I'll miss, I'll protect you Jill." He muffed it every time, he never got that thing off.

Unbeknownst to Gomez, surreptitious alterations were made to her bikini behind the scenes:

> Come the first night, Tom comes towards me – "Don't worry Jill, it's OK" – he pulls, and there's a loud screech of velcro and the

damn thing came off. I got such a shock. And then lo and behold came the tinkling of the coins into the opera glass dispensers, suddenly, all around the opera house, and then a grabbing of glasses, but it was much too late, they'd missed it. Of course once it was known, the press had a ball with it. So every night, before this happened, the audience lunged – you'd suddenly hear in the middle of a scene – ding-ding-ding-ding – everybody getting their glasses ready, before The Happening. And of course the boys were very ribald about it. Peter came up to me and said, "Jill, I've got a big favour to ask from you. When he pulls it off you, with that delicious tearing sound of velcro, will you count at least to five before you scream and run away?" It was hysterically funny. They were just so silly.[9]

Thomas Carey had a hard time in rehearsals, aware of the sensitivities in playing a black homosexual character (he was born in South Carolina in the 1930s). "The charge was felt more by him than by us," remembers Gomez. "He suddenly realised that he was playing the part of the monster, Caliban. And this upset him terribly. I remember a whole morning of rehearsals was lost because he was so upset, he was practically in tears." For a revival in 2005, a reviewer suggested that equating "the 'moronic' (according to the libretto) Caliban with a black, bisexual man is highly questionable".[10] Alternatively, the opera may be said to presage productions of The Tempest that, in casting black actors as Caliban, used the play as a metaphor for colonialism and oppression.

The opera ended with Mangus revealing the charades for what they were. The projections were suddenly switched off. The quintet of reconciliation was sung by the cast advancing on the audience, with the house lights up. Hall scattered a chanting chorus of spirits and sprites around the auditorium. As the act closed and the cast abandoned the stage, Faber and Thea were left alone on the stage singing "The curtain rises", just as the red-and-gold swathes of the opera house curtain fell in front of them. The next day the reviewers, more than one referring to "the gay boys", praised the design and production, and most hailed a masterpiece. "Oh we knew it was a success," says Josephine Barstow. "It was hugely exciting. It felt wonderful – I was terrified, but also in heaven."[11] *The Times* thought the blues ensemble that closed Act One so powerful as "to drain the blood from your cheeks".[12] The *Observer* proclaimed the work "unlike any opera ever written", and mainly meant it as a compliment: "the most marvellous achievement of this score", wrote the reviewer, was that it "breathed life into seven living people", with a depth "unequalled in my experience by any composer since Alban Berg".[13] Views on the libretto ranged from "a fearsome brew of dated slang, unabashed cliché, sub-Eliotese and flashes of real poetry" to "one of the best librettos I know".[14] Even naysayers gave the opera the benefit of the doubt. *The Knot Garden* had been, concluded the *Telegraph*, a "triumphant example of musical theatre concerning itself with genuinely human values".[15]

Word of mouth quickly spread around a younger group of operagoers, who were thrilled to encounter scenes more suited to television serials and current affairs documentaries, and to register the delicious shock of seeing the inner lives of contemporary society reflected in the music of a composer some twice or even three times their age. The production had been determined to look contemporary experience in the face, and the costume department had gone off to Miss Selfridge and Laura Ashley to buy clothes. For audiences to see themselves reflected on the Royal Opera House stage so vividly was unprecedented, at a time when Britten was basing his last two operas on novellas set in the preceding century. Someone wrote in to the *Sunday Times* to say that his paper had been "delivered by a lad who entertained the whole street with the first act of Tippett's *Knot Garden*".[16] Older members of the audience could be much less sure, as could Michael's contemporaries. Lennox Berkeley wrote in his diary of his intense dislike of an opera that was "the opposite of what I believe in both musically and philosophically".[17]

At the centre of the labyrinth was Michael, enjoying one of the biggest successes of his career. He pronounced himself "more excited inside than I can ever remember. I <u>think</u> it's the immense disrelation between success and one's puny realities."[18] His appearance on the stage for the first and last nights was greeted by roars and stamps of approval. He wrote to Eric Walter White, just before Christmas: "*The Knot Garden* does seem very much like a double six. I'm glad, too, for everyone's sake that it packed them in. I went to the final performance, and then began at last to feel the relief of knowing it was safely and successfully launched. My mind goes over to the next one!"[19]

The "next one" was an opera with its scenario already finalised, but composition would not begin for three years. Off the back of *The Knot Garden*'s success Michael, aged sixty-five, could happily have retired, and was eligible for a state pension. But the music couldn't help but come, and he composed at a faster pace in the new and secluded world of Nocketts. There were still frequent visitors, who would find him curled up on the enormous sofa in his living room, one arm hooked over his head as if for safe-keeping, talking at a pace and breadth matched only by the landscape behind him, shifting and vast. As his fourth opera gestated, he fitted in two "thirds": a symphony and then a piano sonata, both finished within just over two years, during which Karl Hawker had another major breakdown, what Michael called a "bad go – looking over the self-destruction edge – which is never anything but agonising".[20] To Bill Bowen he wrote that "there have been moments, during this 'bad' time, when I have wished K totally not there. Not as surprising, I dare say, as my seemingly unshakeable loyalty. But what is to be done after fifteen years of being together? Or even not together? For I keep hearing the inarticulate cry for help. [. . .] Being with you on the other hand . . . That needs no expression beyond itself."[21]

The third symphony had all begun with Pierre Boulez, for whom Michael felt only tentative admiration, disagreeing not with Boulez's views so much as the exclusivity with which they were upheld.[22] Michael professed himself to be losing patience with what he was now calling "the 'artificial' modern systems, such as serialism" and branded "the breakdown of the tonal system" a "fallacy and a red herring". *The Knot Garden* had opened with a series of all twelve notes in the chromatic scale, as if promising to be a tone row, the basis for the twelve-tone technique, devised by Schoenberg. But the technique is never applied, and the twelve different notes prove to be no more than that, as if the opera had entered in a soon-abandoned disguise. "I've seen composers judged", he railed in the *Observer*, "because they haven't become fragmented or haven't gone electronic; and in every case judgement on these terms is pretence."[23] Boulez, who became chief conductor of the BBC Symphony Orchestra, never once programmed or conducted a work by Britten or by Tippett. In the 1965 Edinburgh Festival he and Michael had been scheduled to debate the state of classical music on television. "He'll eat you alive!" was the gist of Michael's friends' ironic good wishes, mindful that Boulez took few prisoners, but the two men got on well: "Fun in Edinburgh meeting Boulez," Michael told Priaulx Rainier. "We 'confronted' on TV – but this was nicely mild, as I knew it would be."[24] On 29 August 1965 Boulez had conducted his setting of Mallarmé, *Pli selon pli*, at the Usher Hall, with Michael in the audience. "I found myself saying", Michael remembered, "that if ever I wanted to use that kind of music, I would have to match it with something extremely sharp, violent, and certainly speedy." (This assessment of Boulez could be easily argued with.) He turned to Karl, who was sitting next to him, and said: "the Third Symphony has begun".[25]

Composition proper started in the autumn of 1970, and was finished on 30 March 1972. Michael was simultaneously attempting to keep the symphony alive as a form, and asking whether it could live at all. The piece explodes into being, with music of stuttering compressed energy pitched against surging semiquavers, both continuing to do battle before moving, without break, into the slow movement: a wasteland, where fragments of music drift in the ether. A small ditty for solo viola. The calls of a distant oboe duet, over harp and percussion. Eventually the strings grow to a pitch of almost unbearable density before going out with the tide. The third movement is a frantic collage of sheer anarchy, redolent of

Charles Ives, as if five pieces are playing at once, and culminating in a quotation from Beethoven's Symphony No. 9 that unleashes the finale.

In *Songs for Dov* Michael had examined how artists might fight against the urban explosion of the century. The third symphony goes further, dramatising an agonising struggle between a composer and his times. During composition Michael worked on the voiceover for a television documentary, eventually broadcast on 19 February 1972, in which he would pose the question: "What does this music – or any music – do within our present society and what do I think I am doing by composing it?"[26] He had been inspired by discussions with Colin Davis after a performance of Beethoven's Ninth, in which Davis had questioned what resonance Beethoven's affirmations could have amid the traumas of the twentieth century. Michael put his symphony directly into dialogue with Beethoven's setting of Schiller's "Ode to Joy". After two world wars, Auschwitz, Hiroshima, the use of napalm on children in Vietnam, how could the "Ode to Joy" continue to have value, in its claim that all men are brothers, and that voices should be raised only in joyful sounds? Michael wrote a text of his own that fiercely condemns Schiller's compassionate God, and questions any possibility of universal brotherhood:

> They sang that when she waved her wings,
> The Goddess Joy would make us one.
> And did my brother die of frostbite in the camp?
> And was my sister charred to cinders in the oven?
> We know not so much joy
> For so much sorrow

He quickly sent the words to Colin Davis. "Your songs of Innocence and Experience", Davis replied, "caught me in a mood that made me want to weep: I suppose because I do not know how to sustain that vision. [. . .] It is extraordinary how you draw all the threads of my own reading together: there is a community of spirit that is our only hope."[27]

The verses became the symphony's final movement in the shape of four blues songs for soprano, modelled on Bessie Smith's *St Louis Blues*. Michael added a virtuosic flugelhorn in parallel to Louis Armstrong's cornet. In the last song, the so-called "terror fanfare" from Beethoven's Ninth is three times quoted. Michael put a match underneath the third quotation, as if to crack the dream. The soprano must pick her way through broken bits of Beethoven. But the symphony does not end in despair. "Must I stop singing", Michael asked, "because of the fragility of all aspiration?"[28] The blues are to stop us feeling blue. The soprano explicitly quotes Martin Luther King in her final lines:

> I have a dream
> That my strong hand shall grip the cruel
> That my strong mouth shall kiss the fearful
> That my strong arms shall lift the lame   [. . .]
> What though the dream crack!
> We shall remake it.   [. . .]
> We sense a huge compassionate power
> To heal
> To love

The voice peals out above whirling strings. The flugelhorn returns, as do memories of the slow movement. The orchestra spins itself into a final antithesis, pitching brash *forte* brass chords against answering *pianissimo* strings. The argument could go on for ever, but it's the gentler voice of healing and love with which the symphony ends.

Michael's music showed no signs of taxing players any the less. "I've been getting alarmed," Davis wrote to him in panic, on receipt of the score. He showed the parts to the leader of the Boston Symphony Orchestra: "he, who can play anything, was stopped dead in his tracks! It took him five minutes to work it out! Just think of the moderate players in the London Symphony Orchestra." But instead of dismissing the writing as wilfully impossible, Davis had a different attitude to Michael's music: "I hope this is not a worry or distraction," he wrote. "It just means that I'm getting excited about 'how'. [. . .] You know what I wish, which is to please you and do for your music all I can."[29] He arranged extra rehearsal time, worked through the piece with a toothcomb, and at the premiere, on 17 June 1972, wrought from Heather Harper and the London Symphony Orchestra an apparently incandescent performance. "Oh God," says publisher Sally Groves at the memory, "I was just . . ." Words fail. Asked what he makes of the third symphony in hindsight, Alexander Goehr pulls no punches: "loathsome".[30]

Michael spent the summer of 1972 on tour in Canada, returning on 7 August, and then launched himself into the three sections of his third piano sonata, in which toccatas of impossible virtuosity whip the pianist's hands into independent tarantellas across the keys, in Beethovenian frenzies of counterpoint organised in fearful symmetry. The almost arbitrary turmoil of the finale threatens to blot out the rhapsody at the sonata's centre, which draws out a theme of spread chords into smoky variations. In the sonata's first performer, Paul Crossley, who gave its premiere on 26 May 1973 at the Bath Festival, Michael had a new muse. For his turn Crossley was thrilled to have got to know a figure he had long admired, and noticed how spontaneously and happily Michael, for whom composition was often a fraught and carefully planned process, wrote for the piano. Crossley and his partner, Michael Vyner, had met the composer a few years earlier, prior to the legalisation of homosexuality: "I didn't know Tippett was gay, I had no idea. This extraordinary man whom I hero-worshipped was gay. Extraordinary meeting one of the heroes of your life and realising: it's not just me. The complete and utter normality of it. I think it was the same for him. I don't think he'd met a young couple like Michael [Vyner] and me. We were very young, part of a new generation for whom this was going to be perfectly straightforward."[31]

Michael's fourth opera, he told journalists, would be his last. Instantly the Royal Opera House tried to persuade him to collaborate with a writer. "In a way those of us who pressed him to change

were probably being a bit wrong," remembers John Tooley, who
had taken over as director in 1970. "But nonetheless we wanted
intelligibility! But he said, 'Absolutely no, I couldn't start if I wasn't
writing the words for an opera.'"[32] As early as March 1970 Michael
had written the scenario, and could tell a journalist the whole story
by December: "It concerns a father who has spent all his son's
lifetime in a prison camp, and comes to find his son in another
land."[33] His musical starting point was the booming crack of frozen
rivers in northern Russia, as the ice began to melt in springtime.
Stravinsky too had been stirred by the sound, and Michael sent off
to the BBC for audio recordings. He had found not only a musical motif but the opera's primary metaphor: of the ice breaking
between human relationships, of the cyclical nature of the world,
the shift from winter to spring. He seemed to be translating into
opera lines from Christopher Fry's play *A Sleep of Prisoners*:

> Dark and cold we may be, but this
> Is no winter now. The frozen misery
> Of centuries breaks, cracks, begins to move;
> The thunder is the thunder of the floes,
> The thaw, the flood, the upstart Spring.

Soon Michael had his title: *The Ice Break*.*

He began the libretto late in 1972, thrilled that, in September,
the opera had started "to engulf all again, praise be!"[34] The libretto's first draft is dated 6 March 1973, and thirteen days later he
began the music, with a low blare of ice-cracking brass, hardened
by the piano. It was his old friend Priaulx Rainier to whom he
wrote announcing that composition had begun. On the envelope of
the letter is a stamp featuring the UK as a piece of a jigsaw puzzle
fitting into a map of Europe, to celebrate the country's having

---

* In 1940 Alan Bush composed a song called "The Ice Breaks". The words are by
  the communist playwright Randall Swingler: "The ice breaks and the fields are
  flooding, on the unbound lakes [. . .] The sign of Spring."

acceded to the European Economic Community on 1 January 1973. During composition a referendum would be held to gauge support of Britain's continued membership. The Ice Break is a work of unification and split, of freeze and thaw, and would turn out to be one of the most violent and upsetting operas of the 1970s. Michael predicted, with some accuracy, that it would take him three years. By the time the opera was finished his life had undergone another sea-change.

In the spring of 1974 he was back in America, for a tour in which his music was performed by three major American orchestras and The Knot Garden was given its American premiere at Northwestern University, Illinois. At performances of the third symphony, in Boston and Chicago, the critics were ecstatic: "no more important work has been written during my lifetime". Michael was, thought the New York Times, "England's greatest living composer".[35] He had gone alone to America, and was sharing very little time with Karl Hawker, who in the summer went to Cyprus, getting caught up in the violent Turkish invasion of the island on 20 July.[36] Karl got back to Nocketts badly shaken, and it became finally clear that a shared existence was no longer possible. Michael had decided, after many years of secrecy, that living a dual life was dishonest and harmful. It was a talk with Karl's daughter Susan and her husband that decided him, as Susan recalls: "He was worried about Dad and he was worried what would happen to him. So we just said to him, look, you have to do what you have to do, and if that's the result, that's the result, we're not going to tell you not to." For a while, she and her sister were "quite in touch" with Michael, "but we didn't really go and stay there".[37]

The permanent break came in late summer. "This is to say," Michael informed Anna Kallin in September, "shortly, and <u>confidentially</u>, that K and I are separating out. I've come to my end."[38] The fallout was bloody, for a time. "The wrenching has been rather horrible – predictably – but it's kind of over. Now there's an interim to get it actually to happen."[39] Michael was determined to set Karl up with an income for life, to pay what was, to all intents and purposes, alimony. Karl wrote to him on 7 September 1974, in some anguish. It is the first of just two surviving letters written to Michael in which Karl and his viewpoint tumble into the light:

> I still cannot decide yet if I can accept money from you. It's true that step by step I gave up my earning power as your life engulfed me, without receiving a real wage for what I was doing. But I did it without thought of self protection, I decided your life and work was of great importance and gave what I could. Anything else in me demanding attention I fought down, it had to be utterly worthwhile to exist for you, but it backlashed, and this grew in violence in me as I got older, and I made an historical judgment on my life. I found I'd left talents behind, certainly left property behind, and could be turned out legally by you on a months "wages". I got the skids, despair set in, and my only hope was that somehow I could get through, but you moved further away and again the old process in you arose, it was Karl being neurotic! You never seemed to be able to conceive that I too could be at the mercy of a "drive" – an obsession such as you claim for yourself. The vast difference between us was that I couldn't afford it, that had to be resisted in order for me to be here at all. Previous attempts to remake life for myself (and I did those with little or no support from you) failed abysmally – I was hooked. It was never in your books that I could follow my own star. [. . .]
>
> But back to now – as I say I find it very difficult to accept your own power over me, to be able as you are to dispose of me, along with Francesca Allinson, Wilf and [John] Minchinton. To me it is the utmost humiliation to be so in your hands, to have lost control of my life. I have to a great extent brought it upon myself but I did it with near worship of your work, not in any self-seeking way. Had I any real self-seeking qualities I would not now be in this position.[40]

Michael's replies were loving, brief, distant, although he made sure to keep in touch with Karl, scrawling him letters on headed notepaper from the bland luxury of the foreign hotels in which so much of his professional life was now spent. "You've got it a bit wrong, you know, love," was the extent of his written recrimination, though there were spurts of argument by phone: "Sorry about the phone call," he apologised. "I was growing ever more tensed and hostile. Going back into the 'bad old'. Quite a shock. A kind of emotional STOP sign. I daresay my easiness of manner is deceptive – and the real has to be spelled out again."[41] Eventually Karl agreed to a financial arrangement. "It's all OK and allowed for," Michael told him. "Monthly sums (plus 5 per cent annual increment) till you die." Later he wrote: "I don't think of it as _my_ money but as _your_ money. Agreed, meant, personal." A will Michael made at this time names Susan and Sarah Hawker as the main beneficiaries. But the payments to Karl began to set Michael on the inexorable spiral of debt from which he would never really extricate himself, as he bedded into the pattern of living extravagantly on forthcoming earnings and on credit. His fees from American concert tours and manuscript sales were now large, as were his royalties from international performances. But his holidays were lavish, his wine cellar first-rate, his generosity deep. He was well into the top bracket of income tax, which in 1974, with an added surcharge on investment income, could reach 98 per cent. Soon he had to admit he was "£23,000 in the red! Already!!" Today this sum would nudge six figures. To Karl's repeated requests for more money his responses were initially sharp: "I don't intend now to increase my present over-large debt for anyone except myself!! To secure good conditions for my last decade of composition. But you will get your money to the end, even when I'm dead . . ." Soon, though, he agreed to increase the sums as much as he could.

Finances aside, they worked out a new way of communicating. "Thanks for letting go so gently," was the gist of Michael's attitude:

The good memories will stay, the bad will fade – give them time. I think what _is_ good is that the old lovable Karl has returned (or the new has been born) and so relationships flower independently – for their own sake, so to speak. Something of the sort is happening to me – facets of myself are flowering which have

been severely inhibited – and independently. I need time for
this independence to feel secure – I can't yet put it into hazard.
I guess you understand.

He was aware, however, that he had emerged from the "divorce"
more easily than Karl, and had a lover, a home, a career, ready and
waiting. "It is more difficult for you," he admitted, conceding that
he was "driven as ever into composition (a burden and a joy, I
suppose)". He had, he wrote, "an imperious drive for a new life-
phase, which, once it declares itself, I guess will be seen to have
been forced by the music. As ever, everyone goes to the wall." He
had used exactly the same phrase when writing about his guilt over
Francesca Allinson's suicide thirty years before: "Men with careers
are often just monsters it seems to me. Everyone can go to the
wall." Karl replied to Michael in seeming content:

I am "through" to love for you and joy that I did help in some
way, and that all was utterly of value, even though I felt I would
not survive. Indeed I would not have, but could not reconcile
the hovering death with not hurting you. All now past, I'm on
my way again in painting, but short time for the great work it
is. I'm steady and gay (in your Midsummer Marriage sense – in fact
that is my guiding belief) and full of vitality and as I used to
be. I'm remaking health – extraordinary – glowing and alive. All
stimulants have gone and my old "the world is my oyster" is
back – I dance along as before. So my love be happy take care
of yourself.[42]

Michael forwarded the letter to David Ayerst (hence its survival),
writing on the envelope: "For your curiosity. Am not replying of
course."

Bill Bowen was now in his mid-thirties, and working as a music
journalist for the Guardian. He had no wish to leave London to live
in the country with a lover forty years his senior, and Michael did
not ask him to. Their affair moved slowly and naturally into a deep-
going friendship, and Bill became a frequent visitor to Nocketts.

"My professional life", Michael told him sadly, as if in warning, "just 'eats up' the other person – be it man or woman. The 'eater up' can't prevent it, but can be gentle." It was a soft insistence that Bill was free to pursue relationships elsewhere. "Your own drive and youth and promise are the true vital safeguards however – and that's what I know I prize for you. Within, that is, the possibly selfish sides of my affection."[43] He was uncertain of his own future. "I don't think I know yet who my 'family' is," he wrote to Karl. "With tension lifted from the house, people of all sorts come and go, free and easy. That seems enough for the time being. That, and to complete another work!" The shift in his personal life did not escape gossip in the musical world. "Back to square one, retrograde perversion like M.T.", William Walton wrote to a friend. "At his age getting himself a new boy-friend – he ought to be ashamed of himself!"[44]

As Michael progressed through *The Ice Break* (he finished Act Two on 17 February 1975, and began Act Three the following day) life was moving into a new phase, old friends departing, new ones from Bill Bowen's younger social circle taking their place. On 26 November 1974 his mentor and psychoanalyst John Layard had died. Michael had gone with David Ayerst to say goodbye. "John was in hospital terminally ill," Ayerst remembered: "When Michael gave him a gentle farewell kiss, it was not what John wanted. 'Give me a real kiss', he demanded. His was a sad, broken life, a man of unfulfilled gifts. Yet he helped many, not least Michael and myself."[45] Then, in May 1975, Barbara Hepworth died, killed by an accidental fire in the St Ives studio that Michael had often visited. "The shock of Barbara's death has been too sharp for writing about," he told Priaulx Rainier, who was similarly bereft.[46]

In January Michael had turned seventy, and a piece of his was performed somewhere in the country almost every day of that month, a pitch of celebratory coverage that didn't let up for much of the year. Robert Ponsonby, a loyal friend and supporter, had taken over directorship of the Proms two years before and would programme Michael's music annually until his departure. Michael meanwhile resigned the directorship of the Bath Festival, its deficit paid off, and was succeeded by William Glock, who led the festival into its golden age. In the spring Michael went to Zambia, to attend, on 18 April, a multiracial performance of *A Child of Our Time* in Lusaka Cathedral in the presence of the country's President. He returned for a final push to finish *The Ice Break*. The effort led him to a nervous collapse in October, and he cancelled his conducting commitments. Finally the opera was finished, on 27 January 1976, and a performance scheduled for the following year, to reunite the director–conductor pairing of Peter Hall and Colin Davis, to the latter of whom Michael dedicated the score. But before the opera reached the stage another major player in Michael's life made his final exit.

One result of the success of *The Knot Garden*, and the promise that surrounded *The Ice Break*, was that the name of Tippett had risen above that of Benjamin Britten. While Michael was still basking in his reviews, Britten's penultimate opera, *Owen Wingrave*, was generally thought to have been a damp squib when broadcast on BBC2 in May 1971, as recalled by Josephine Barstow: "In those days all we musicians used to say, 'Well, of course, Tippett is so superior to Britten.' There was a huge amount of snobbery: Tippett is the real McCoy, and Britten was just commercial. I went along with the general feeling, but that was the attitude: that Britten wrote commercial pieces, and these operas [by Tippett] were going to live on into the future. It's exactly the opposite of what's happened."[47] A younger generation of listeners, passing around recordings of Michael's music on university campuses or studying his pieces at A level, professed to preferring Tippett to Britten, who had begun to be dismissed as old-fashioned. The music of seventy-year-old Tippett had somehow clinched the zeitgeist for a younger generation. There arose talk of a rivalry between the two leading British composers that has still not been dispelled. The name of a road-haulage company in business at the time, Tibbett and Britten, did not escape people's notice. The two men were destined to be forever compared to one another, and listeners felt, perhaps still feel, compelled to take sides. The comparison between the two is in a way useless, so different, by now, were their compositional styles. Michael's music of the 1960s and 1970s may more fruitfully be banded with and compared to the jazz-inflected collages of the German composer Bernd Alois Zimmermann, to the visionary glow of Olivier Messiaen or the orchestral invention of Witold Lutosławski. But, just as the similarities were over-egged, so too were the differences, made all too neatly: between Michael's warmth and Britten's coolness, between Britten's facility and Michael's amateurism, between Michael's sprawl and Britten's economy.

Gatekeepers and cliques on both sides did much to foster supposed divisions. Michael's fans would be photographed with Britten LPs while holding their noses. In New York Michael had once found himself hoisted by two friends over the balcony of a skyscraper: "We've been asked to do this by Benjamin Britten!"[48] The jokes were in good part, but Michael's recounting of them could be rather too gleeful. One of Britten's executors, Donald Mitchell, would abruptly cut off comparisons between the two composers – "not to be mentioned in the same breath" – and was apparently seen walking out of Aldeburgh concerts before a work of Michael's was performed.[49]

Clearing away the undergrowth of gossip to get to the roots of the two composers' thoughts and feelings is a difficult task. Michael had made clear, to Britten and to others, his doubts about some of Britten's music; these he raised above a ground level of unwavering admiration. That Britten was critical of Michael and perturbed by his success is widely reported, but rarely from the composer's own mouth (it may be that he simply became less familiar with the music). "Michael Tippett was given to wild mis-statements," he had told Imogen Holst, admitting that he "always knew what Michael was feeling in his music, and it moved him," but "didn't think Michael always managed to convey what he was thinking".[50] Donald Mitchell claimed that in Britten's mind "there lurked a real scepticism about Michael's technique", and Robert Tear was sure that Britten "couldn't take Michael that seriously".[51] Tear was smarting from what he believed to be an out-and-out dismissal from Britten's world, having chosen to sing Dov in *The Knot Garden* over the offer of a role in *Owen Wingrave*. He was soon working once again at Aldeburgh, but the quarrel only exacerbated the situation. Alexander Goehr meanwhile thinks that "Britten always recognised the quality of Tippett somewhere. One can't imagine him enjoying many of the pieces, but nevertheless."[52] And, admittedly back in the 1940s, Britten had apparently said quietly to his librettist Ronald Duncan, in what Duncan thought was "genuine modesty", that "Michael's got some kind of depth I think I lack".[53]

All that survives is a final clutch of correspondence, sent over the years as Britten's health faded. In May 1973 he had had a heart valve replaced in hospital. Michael had written to him: "My dearest Ben, A tiny note to welcome you as you get back to your own home. As luck would have it your hospitalisation coincided precisely with the Bath Festival; or I would have seen you in London somehow. But now a letter only, with all my love and wishes, and longings, and what have you. Karl joins me of course in this. Home is home, and the air is fresh and good. Love to you both. Michael. No answer!"[54] That Christmas Michael had sent one of his rare festive greetings: "We've gotten lazy again about Christmas cards – but you be special. All love." And at Christmas the following year: "Blessings to you, dear Ben, and let no one bother you about me."[55]

On 10 January 1975 Britten wrote to Michael almost for the last time. He had been too ill to take part in a radio celebration of Michael's seventieth birthday, and told the producer: "Michael is a very old friend of mine and I am second to none in admiration of his works and striking personality."[56] To Michael he apologised for his absence on the airwaves. "You know though how much I treasure your friendship and your wonderful music."[57] On 24 September he wrote one final time: "Much love," the card concludes, "and please forgive us for typing – can't write properly now."[58] Just over a year later, on 4 December 1976, he died. Four days afterwards, Michael sent a condolence card to Peter Pears, who was a widower in all but legal status: "Dearest Peter. I loved Ben, as you know, though not as you did. There are many memories. He loved you in a manner that is rare. I suppose the music belongs to us all, but that love belongs to you. I don't mean this note to sound pretentious, please. Blessings. Michael. No reply is expected."[59] In this there is not only admiration and love, but a resigned envy of the lifelong bond that had united Britten and Pears. The latter lived on for another decade, during which time, at least among a younger generation, Michael's music only seemed to increase in popularity. With the pull of Britten removed, the two men maintained no great friendship. "Michael has always had the capacity to talk a lot of balls" was one of Pears's dismissals; Michael for his part found visiting Pears uncomfortable, thinking the house had become a mausoleum.[60]

He wrote one of Benjamin Britten's obituaries: "I want to say, here and now, that Britten has been for me the most purely musical person I have ever met and have ever known."[61]

The date seemed lucky: 7/7/77. The first night of the purportedly final opera by Michael Tippett, newly succeeded to the British compositional throne after Britten's death, was a major event in the musical world. During the sweltering summer of the previous year, a production of *The Midsummer Marriage* had been mounted by Welsh National Opera and this staging above all erased the final vestiges of suspicion. "How was it, one wonders," wrote a reviewer in the *Sunday Times*, "that we ever found this mixture misconceived, ill-digested, trendy? The difficulties have simply vanished."[62] Riding the wave of this success, the premiere of *The Ice Break* sold out, and come the first night there were queues for returns and vast coverage on television and in the newspapers. To coincide with the performances, an exhibition about Michael's life and career was mounted, entitled *A Man of Our Time*, funded by private donations of which 10 per cent, some £350 between them, came as personal gifts from Colin Davis and Peter Hall.[63]

Of all Michael's operas *The Ice Break* had the fewest second thoughts and the simplest gestation. Its finished plot, bar the alteration of a few names, was almost identical to his initial scenario. The curtain rises to the burble and hubbub of an airport, that strange, anonymous location of geographical and legal ambiguity in which he now spent so much of his life, despite having been in middle age before Heathrow was opened. Lev, a teacher, has been released from twenty years' prison and exile in what might have been a Soviet labour camp. His wife Nadia and son Yuri, who have emigrated to a country that might be America, await his arrival. Meanwhile Yuri's girlfriend, Gayle, has come to meet the "black champion", Olympion, to whom she and her friends are slavishly devoted, and with whom she flirts outrageously, in a misguided attempt to atone for white supremacy. Yuri, in jealousy, attacks Olympion. The single act of violence spirals out of control, and gang rivalries between blacks and whites explode into a fatal mob riot. The gangs, Michael specified, should be masked, rather than divided according to the skin colour of the singers.

It was a scenario that had emerged from his travels in America, and seemed to depict the USA and the USSR as two equally damaged societies, even as the American policy of détente was reaching its height. His ideas for the opera had begun to form in the late 1960s, as hippy idealism began to harden into anarchy, with protests in Paris and tanks in Prague. By the time The Ice Break reached the stage almost a decade later, the faith in flower power extolled by musicals such as Hair was already coloured by violence. During its composition Nixon resigned, relations with the Soviets became once again poor, and Aleksandr Solzhenitsyn was arrested and deported. Guided by his Russian producer and friend Anna Kallin, Michael had read what was available of Soviet dissident literature, and immersed himself in the work of the Acmeist poets (such as Anna Akhmatova and Osip Mandelstam), many of whom had suffered under Stalinist oppression. But The Ice Break had a larger reach than as merely a description of contemporary politics.

The usual interpretation of the "champion" Olympion is an athletic superhero followed by cheerleaders, but he is less Muhammad Ali and more Michael X, the self-styled "black revolutionary" and civil rights activist. The character of Gayle was named after Gale Benson, a British model whom Michael X and his followers had buried alive in Trinidad.[64] The revolutionary cults and communes set up in the name of freedom had ended in destruction, and the murders that followed in the wake of figures such as Michael X, the activist Malcolm X, or the cult leader Charles Manson rippled through the newspapers during *The Ice Break*'s gestation. (In 1975 Anthony Powell introduced to his panorama of the century, *A Dance to the Music of Time*, the dangerous figure of cult leader Scorp Murtlock.) The focus of Michael's opera, as the fallout of the 1960s hedonism became all too clear, was false gods, the damaging destruction of slavish devotion to trends and fashions, cliques and gangs. *The Ice Break* is, if nothing else, the most explicit rejection Michael ever made of the political beliefs that had fired his life some forty years before. His one-time dedication to Trotskyist groups and the efficacy of revolutionary violence is in stark contrast to the opera's bleak depiction of protest and political allegiance. His 1930s play *War Ramp* had approvingly depicted a soldier raising his weapon: "I've got to get my gun back somehow." In *The Ice Break*, a male chorus chants: "Every guy has a gun." Lev, the political prisoner, responds: "Violence is blind. Brutality takes over."

The opera's music is jangled with voodoo clarinets and percussion, out-of-control hoe-downs, Ku Klux Klan hymns, and gang chants. Violent riots are punctuated with volleys of gunfire. Body parts become percussion, and an orchestral line is scored for "knuckle, knee, or hard sticks". So disturbing was Walter Raines's choreography for the first production that there were "rumours that the chorus at Covent Garden initially refused to perform it".[65] The stage is eventually littered with bodies, which are carted off to the mortuary. Gayle and Olympion are shot dead. Yuri is grievously wounded. The Act Two curtain falls to a threnody of violin and cello, harp and electric guitar. Divorced from its stage action, a recording of the music can seem little more than a series of sound effects, but blooming amid the ferocity comes a yearning love duet for Olympion and his girlfriend, Hannah. She, a nurse, is given a lengthy soul-searching aria at the opera's centre as she attempts to make sense of the world in which she finds herself. By the end of the opera Yuri's mother has died, and he himself, shot in the riot, is in hospital, bound from head to foot in plaster, which is eventually cut away, and he is reborn like a bird from an egg, to exultant peals in the orchestra.

By now, Sally Groves remembers, "having a Tippett opera go through Schott was like a great ship being built on the Clyde. It took years and it took everybody's attention from time to time, and you'd be hammering at this end and somebody else would be hammering at that end. It was just an intense, intense time."[66] Peter Hall had been discussing the production with Michael for years, but by 1976, less than a year before opening night, he had pulled out, unable to combine the opera with his duties at the National Theatre. *The Ice Break* presented a challenge to his replacement. Michael had pushed even further the filmic cutting technique of *The Knot Garden* and called not only for instantaneous scene changes, but for a large chorus to whirl on and off stage in a matter of moments. The music owes little to the soundworld of the Broadway musical, but Michael had hoped for a staging that would arrive out of musical theatre. He had adored the imaginatively staged hits of the era such as *Jesus Christ Superstar* and *Godspell*, and despatched Colin Davis off to the latter to trawl (unsuccessfully) for singers.[67]

On a trip to New York, Michael had been impressed by the Kabuki-style production of Stephen Sondheim's musical about the Westernisation of Japan, *Pacific Overtures*. Its director, Hal Prince, was duly invited to a play-through of *The Ice Break*. "We never heard from him again," says Sally Groves, "he just ran in the opposite direction." John Tooley then approached the film director Ken Russell, "and he got quite excited about it". But the piano reduction, which Russell heard on tape, two pianists singing all the parts, was impenetrable. Tooley "got an immediate response, which said 'not on your life, I hate this music!'"[68] Time was now running so short that the Royal Opera House employed the tried-and-tested Sam Wanamaker, who had made such a success of *King Priam*. But he had filming commitments in Hollywood and was left with a startlingly short time to get *The Ice Break* up and running. He worked at speed with the renowned stage designer Ralph Koltai, seeking to solve the opera's challenges not with Kabuki simplicity, but with "a stage mechanism that could in an instant be transformed into another place and time".[69] The result was a set of steel-and-glass frames that trundled in and out, in the event noisily and slowly. Koltai was surprised by "just how low" the budget was, and displeased with the realisation of his ideas. Cast members describe the production as rather rushed. Josephine Barstow (singing Gayle, and killed off halfway through) can barely remember being in it. But for the American mezzo Beverly Vaughn, who created the role of Hannah, it was a formative experience:

> What impressed me the most about Michael Tippett was the commitment he had to people of colour. That surprised me at the time. And I did not feel uncomfortable with his writing. I could feel uncomfortable with Gershwin – a lot of us did *Porgy and Bess* – "Bess, you is my woman now" – the music is amazing, but did something inside of me feel "ouch"? Yeah. I did not feel that with Michael Tippett. I felt that some phrases [in the libretto] could sound a little dated, like my students now would say something I said sounded dated. But I don't remember one ounce of feeling that "eeek" that we people of colour can sometimes get, when it's not quite right. I couldn't believe it: it was a life-changing experience for me in every aspect, and it was a role where I didn't have to compromise my pride in being African-American. Rather it enhanced it. It beautified the role of an African-American young woman. Of all the characters, it was Hannah he allowed to develop. Come on! How could I *not* be happy?![70]

The critic Andrew Porter was a lone voice in describing the staging as "one of the most brilliant presentations of a difficult new opera I have seen". Most commented on the noise and ungainliness of the sets, and a radio broadcast of the premiere reveals a minute's pause between scenes, necessitating entirely interpolated chords from the brass section to give singers their notes.[71] The music's ninety-minute span was made slack by the Opera House's insistence on breaks between the acts; that the length of the two intervals outstripped the length of the opera caused a media ruckus (it was

soon nicknamed "The Coffee Break"). But the work itself, bar a
dissenting voice in the *Sunday Telegraph*, was an undoubted critical
success. "It is not every new opera that you want to hear again as
soon as possible"; "some of the greatest music in all Tippett"; "by
any count it is an important opera".

The libretto was "Tippett's finest, most cogent", deemed "fault-
less", of all his texts "the best".[72] But most critics noted Michael's
use of American slang, a number of them quoting, with varying levels of disparagement, lines such as "What's bugging you
man? Cool and jivey once, now touchy and tight." The line "you
mother-fucking bastard" (shouted in the opera's central act) did
not frequently emanate from an opera house's stage in the late
1970s. While maintaining that the opera needn't be set in America
at all, Michael had worked hard with Sam Wanamaker to ensure
accuracy. "I've had lots of help from America, with Sam most
helpful of all. He's changed at least twenty lines of the libretto
[. . .] we've had to get things right."[73] Many considered the slang's
employment misguided and inaccurate, an attempt to be trendy
that dated as soon as it got onto the stage. *Private Eye* would soon
coin the withering moniker, "Sir Michael Withit". Others thought
the slang's accuracy wasn't the point, merely a depiction of the
"inane posturings of youth", and Michael himself referred to it as
the "argot" of a clique. Sally Groves agrees: "It's a complete send-
up of all that hippie-hippie stuff."[74]

The most perplexing scene came towards the end of Act Three,
during which the chorus, off their heads on hallucinatory drugs,
are visited by a psychedelic messenger named "Astron". Early drafts
show that Michael conceived the part for a rock singer, and that the
scene was the very last to be completed, causing him endless trouble.[75] The finished score calls for a double voice, of counter-tenor
and mezzo-soprano, with added electronic distortion. Astron's message to the chorus is simple: "Take care for the Earth. God will take
care for himself." The response is instant adulation: "Our Saviour
Hero!" Astron's riposte is ironic, in pantomime falsetto: "Saviour?!
Hero?! Me!! You must be joking." Most thought the strange visitor
was a send-up, and the moment can veer dangerously close to Monty

Python ("He's not the Messiah, he's a very naughty boy!"). But the warning as to the perils of hero worship, put across with unnerving wit, is serious. In his willingness to disown saviour status, Astron may be said to be the bravest of the opera's characters. Plans to stage the moment with a hologram were soon deemed technically impossible, and a glitter of laser beams was used, redolent of nothing so much as a low-budget James Bond movie, and still clinging like a kitsch limpet to The Ice Break's reputation half a century on, despite lasers being mentioned in neither score nor libretto.[76]

Michael remained sure that the opera need not really be a portrayal of a specific time and place, and waited calmly for the slang to date sufficiently and for a director to harness the universal human story at the opera's heart, free from 1970s fashions and Cold War politics. An American production in 1979 had anti-Vietnam protestors flooding the auditorium. But that was the last staging of The Ice Break in Michael's lifetime.

DIARY:

Birmingham

Attending the first performance of *The Ice Break* in nearly forty years, I don't know whether I'm in the right place, walking through empty streets past corrugated-iron and graffitied garage doors. My one link to the original staging came when a friend of a friend rushed up to me at a concert with a plastic bag. Inside was a shoe, purchased at a charity auction, worn by the original Olympion. It is white and glittery, high-heeled, the epitome of 1970s fashion, and irreparably dated, like something out of *Mamma Mia*. Now, in April 2015, Graham Vick's Birmingham Opera Company is reviving the opera in an abandoned warehouse in the heart of Digbeth, just outside the city centre. Already the industrial wasteland sets the scene for an urban nightmare.

A few weeks earlier I attended one of the rehearsals in central Birmingham. The chorus is made up of locals, volunteers, schoolchildren. The music is to be taught to the chorus by ear. I sit in a circle of singers, feeling self-conscious, playing warm-up games and doing exercises. A clip of the opening is played on a tape. Nobody has heard of Tippett or of this opera. Nobody knows it is "difficult", or out of fashion. The ice-breaking motif plays. "It's like *Jaws*," somebody says. We begin learning some of the music of the riot: "Burn, baby! Burn!" The words are taken from the 1965 Watts riot in Los Angeles, and exploded into a shrapnel of complicatedly syncopated syllables: "B, b, b, b, b, burn". Within minutes, everyone has the motif from memory. The same with a complex, chromatic phrase from a later scene.

At the warehouse, for the performance, I can hear a great bubble of excitement from the makeshift changing rooms in the car park. Instead of producing *The Ice Break* as a timeless myth, or as a period piece, Graham Vick has set it in England, in April 2015. The space is vast, decked with the paraphernalia of an airport. Television screens show scrolling newsreels of frightening headlines, and an arrivals board lists flights delayed or cancelled. Large billboard advertisements glare from the walls, defaced or daubed with red paint. A sign, airport-yellow, proclaims: "Welcome to the United Kingdom". Immigration officers patrol the arena. It is just before the general election of 2015, and the refugee crisis and immigration are the main points of contention. Yuri and Gayle, loading their weapons at the end of the first act, take selfies with their guns, as if to share them on social media. Vick has cast the opera colour-blind, making notions of Russian and American identity irrelevant, and the colour of the gang to which any character might belong particularly superficial.

The audience stays on its feet through the un-intervalled ninety minutes, wandering through the large arena, shunted with some force from scene to scene. The orchestra is to the side. It is hard to tell who is punter and who performer. Intimate scenes are placed on large raised platforms, perilously inclined. The chorus suddenly streams through the warehouse, and through us, at high speed, their faces painted. Sometimes they get so close I can see their make-up melting under the lights.

What the staging instantly reveals is how much *The Ice Break* owes to Michael's theatrical endeavours in the 1930s: the time when he himself was advocating violent revolution, and belonged to a political group. Graham Vick seems to have revived the political pageant. *The Ice Break*'s warring gangs of Blacks and Whites recall T.S. Eliot's pageant-play *The Rock*, with its fight between Redshirts and Blackshirts, or *The Pageant of Labour*, which Michael conducted in the Crystal Palace, a venue not too dissimilar in scale to this gaping Digbeth warehouse. *The Pageant* set up a number of platforms in the huge glass building, and the action cut from stage to stage, self-consciously filmic. It's clear that *The Ice Break* works at its best only when the proscenium arch is completely removed, as if taking away a belt constricting the opera. Finally, so many of Michael's imaginings – a large chorus flooding a stage in just fifteen bars of music – have been solved. Where the opera's first production had to bring the scenes to the audience at lightning speed, here Graham Vick can bring the audience to the scenes. This promenade pageant-like staging seems to be written into the score.

The mob scenes, whether initiation ritual or gang warfare, are terrifying. Chilling skeins of gang snake their way through the audience, tights clamped tight to their faces, racist placards held aloft. Younger members of the mob have their masks forced on them. Policemen and border-control guards taunt prisoners; an elderly woman holds a nubile young man on a leash in some sadistic sexual role-play. Two young girls hang an older man on railings with his belt, taking selfies with the corpse. Close to the action, I find it nightmarish, feeling a culpably passive spectator rather than a silent witness. During the riot itself, nightmare turns to panic, as gunshots ricochet around the space. Young women in tracksuits weave in and out, carrying stolen electric equipment, flatscreen TVs and designer clothes, in direct emulation of the looting that accompanied riots in London after Mark Duggan was shot by the police in 2011.

At the arrival of Astron I feel that the character has once again stumped a production, and blasphemously wonder whether the scene might just be cut. Suddenly we seem back in the 1970s: tie-dyed costumes, tabs of LSD. The scene has become a rave, and Astron is hardly noticed: a man and a woman, dressed in angelic white, barely keeping their hands off each other, croon into a hand-held microphone with heavy distortion. It's hard to know what's going on. Maybe the scene will one day be solved; maybe it is unsolvable. As the revellers sing "Take care for the earth" sudden projections of fracking, of melting ice caps and birds clotted with oil, shoot around the walls.

We reach the end. *The Ice Break* is snapped off in its twenty-ninth scene, as if missing a thirtieth. Yuri is high atop his white platform. Vick has done away with the imagery of the plaster cast and instead the singer has been stripped fully naked, doused with water from either side, has embraced his father. Tableaux are scattered across the auditorium. Two men are married in a shower of confetti; placards held up against female genital mutilation; soldiers in camouflage. At the very centre, prisoners in orange jumpsuits kneel at knife-point in front of ISIS killers. Yuri himself seems to have become another champion: another Olympion, whose catchphrase he suddenly yells approvingly. Rebirth, it seems, cannot come without struggle and failure. The ice has frozen once again, at least for now. The wheel of rebirth and relapse, rise and fall, freeze and thaw, has been stilled at a moment of dangerous regression. *The Midsummer Marriage* ended with Yeats: "All things fall and are built again, and those that build them again are gay." At the end of *The*

Ice Break Lev sings, quoting Goethe: "Yet you will always be brought forth again, glorious image of God, and likewise be maimed, wounded afresh, from within or without." It's the Yeats turned inside out. All things are built again but fall. The final, chill, chords arrive: horn and bells, vibraphone, the unnatural buzz of the electric organ.

I trudge back to the Birmingham hotel. There is talk of "Tippett's triumphant failure", but the *Birmingham Post* finds the opera "a masterpiece", and "frighteningly contemporary". And, in the *Telegraph*: "*The Ice Break* emerges as nothing short of magnificent". Someone who had seen the first performance back in 1977 asks me how a work that seemed dated when it was new can today appear so frighteningly relevant. I return the next evening to see the opera, if opera it be, once again, and ache, as I never will again over the years of eventual writing, for Michael Tippett to be here, and to see this.

Sally Groves, who saw the piece through its composition, is standing next to me, brave and still behind dark glasses, just a few days after the death of her husband, Dennis Marks. He was in the early stages of writing a biography of Tippett, and as we walk together through these anonymous streets of railings and Portakabins and pylons, Sally wonders quietly whether I might take on the project.

PART SEVEN

NEW YEARS, LAST SONGS
1977–1998

"We shall not cease from exploration
And the end of all our exploring
Will be to arrive where we started
And know the place for the first time."

T.S. Eliot, "Little Gidding",
from *Four Quartets*

TWENTY-NINE

Breath

In his late twenties Michael Tippett was taken to the Pitt Rivers Museum in north Dorset. No more than a large white country house, the building served for overspill from the larger collection in Oxford, and inside was a screen on which a fast-motion black-and-white film showed a rabbit foetus developing over the course of fourteen hypnotising minutes, splitting with a wobble from one cell to two, from two to four, and finally to a seething cluster.[1] Michael had no head for dates or figures, but certain moments from his past could be put away for safe-keeping and used in his music when needed.

The Ice Break had tormented him. Writing it, thought Sally Groves, he had been "on very dangerous ground psychologically. He frightened himself."[2] Before the 1970s were over he would compose a triptych of pieces, each in one movement, that would lead his music into a world of lyricism that some thought he had left behind for good: a fourth symphony, which drew upon that film of the rabbit foetus he had seen so long ago; a fourth quartet; and a concerto for a trio of string soloists – violin, viola, and cello. To say that he was reintroducing lyricism to his work is to ignore that even in *The Ice Break* he had included some of his most expansive melodies. Nor can this final shift in his career be called the mellowing of old age, for it was to incorporate some of his most daring experiments. (The influence of television remained strong: the symphony and concerto contain strange and startlingly out-of-place interruptions that act as musical screen wipes, or as if one piece has briefly tuned into the frequency of another.) But he was embarking on what he knew would be a final act, and composing in the knowledge that each piece could be his last. After hearing a broadcast of *The Ice Break* he told Priaulx Rainier that, quite consciously, he was "in full retreat again – not back to opera [number] one maybe (wish that one could!) but toward something lyrical again. I only hope the symphony has done that already."[3]

The fourth symphony was his first piece begun from the happiness of a life openly shared with Bill Bowen, though lived alone in the womb of Nocketts. It was also his first premiere from an American orchestra. The commission had come as early as 1969, from the Chicago Symphony and its chief conductor Georg Solti, one of a clutch that also included Lutosławski's Symphony No. 3. Michael's own symphony was not begun until the first months of 1976, and he had finished, just before the premiere of *The Ice Break*, on 18 April 1977.[4] The orchestra's virtuosity was legendary, and Michael unleashed his imagination on the symphony like a flock of brightly plumed birds.

He had pondered fulfilling the commission with a setting of Robert Lowell's poem "For the Union Dead", which depicts historic Boston submerged by technology and concrete, and encompasses the American Civil War and civil rights movement. It is easy to see why Michael, so enthused by Charles Ives's evocation of the same landscape in the first of the *Three Places in New England*, might have been attracted to the poem. Perhaps pacifist scruples made him suspicious of Lowell's celebration of a right-minded commander in what the text deems a largely rightful war (or maybe he simply got wind of the fact that, back in 1975, Benjamin Britten had begun his cantata *Phaedra* using Lowell's translation of Racine, and backed off). So, another symphony it was to be, in which a line of Lowell's poem still resonates: "man's lovely, peculiar power to choose life and die". Michael considered the symphony's single movement a "birth-to-death" piece, as if exploring how a symphony might be a life, and a life a symphony. Absent from the earliest drafts is its most startling device, what the published score calls a "breathing effect" emanating from the depths of the players, a foetus in a womb, or a life on its deathbed, sound reduced to its essence, as if the orchestra itself had lungs. The sound of orgasmic heavy breathing on Serge Gainsbourg's "Je t'aime" had seen the song banned from the BBC in 1969; the same year Samuel Beckett premiered his thirty-five-second play Breath, consisting of exhalation and inhalation over a stage littered with rubbish. Breath was in the air. Beckett linked his play to the verse: "On entre, on crie, et c'est la vie. On crie, on sort, et c'est la mort."* The words could be a motto for the seven sections of Michael's symphony. Four sections combining the conventions of sonata and symphonic forms are interleaved with three development episodes, juxtaposing blocks of material in combinations of light and dark, energy and calm. The orchestra seems to breathe in and out in duet with the breath, rocking clarinets and violins marked as "heaving". At the centre of the symphony, the second development section is a hurtling climax of rasping unison orchestra, gasping for breath, asthmatic. As if remembering one tiny rabbit cell dividing into many, late in the piece Michael introduced a whirling fugal paraphrase of a fantasia by Orlando Gibbons. Towards the end the heavy brass chords that opened the symphony return, as does the breath, at once newborn and a death rattle. The orchestra fades into nothing and the piece stops breathing.

So, very nearly, did he. Earlier that year the Dallas Symphony Orchestra had encouraged audiences to vote for their favourite composer, and Michael won the poll, pushing Mahler into second place. Stopping off in Boston en route to Dallas to conduct the resulting concert, he suffered a sudden return of atrial fibrillation and ended up in intensive care. In London the newspapers began to ring round for obituary writers.[5] His recovery was speedy, but the brush with mortality, although he laughed it off, was a close one. Nevertheless, he was well enough to get to Chicago for the symphony's premiere, on 6 October 1977, which Georg Solti recalled working on "with the greatest joy and love", astonished

* "One enters, one cries, and that's life. One cries, one leaves, and that's death."

by how well the composer knew and lived inside his own music and "described with the clearest imagination how things should sound".[6] But Michael had only imprecise and hazy plans as to how the breathing effect might be achieved. At the premiere a wind machine was used. "A great work has been born", wrote the *Chicago Daily News*, but the breath had sounded less like breathing and rather more like a wind machine.[7] Subsequent attempts, with a player breathing into a microphone, were horribly reminiscent of obscene phone calls (cue chortles from the composer). Eventually tapes and floppy discs were prepared that allowed the breath to emanate from speakers placed at the heart of the orchestra, the sound introduced according to precise markings in the score; in 2018 new recordings were produced with a technical finesse impossible in Michael's lifetime.

After the symphony's premiere, he and Bill Bowen made a huge loop down through America for various performances that autumn, crossing over into Mexico, before shooting back to New York. Michael had been working intermittently on his fourth string quartet since the summer, but it had had a slow birth, its early stages interrupted by illness and travel and provoking "violent nervous attacks".[8] Much as he loved the genre, it had been over three decades since his last contribution to it, and the difference between quartets three and four can seem cavernous. At the Bath Festival he had met the players of the Lindsay Quartet, who became muses for his string writing. The score of Quartet No. 4 is one of intricate detail that drags the four instruments through the wringer, calling for lightning switches between bowing and pizzicato, the navigation of speedy and complex rhythms, and the production (in the finale) of notes bat-frequency high. Knocked sideways by a chance hearing in a television documentary of the slow movement from a Beethoven quartet, Michael could "no longer watch the screen, the emotion was so extreme". Soon the sound had flooded his own compositional plans: "Oh I must, I must before I die, find that sound in our own time!" But it is a sharp quotation from Beethoven's *Grosse Fuge* on which Michael's fourth quartet stubs its toe. The aimed-for lyricism arrives only at a high price, as if in reward for having traversed what Michael called the piece's "acid, ironic world of harmony".[9] The finale pitches extended passages of skittering semiquavers against "very tranquil" chords, no louder than breathing, and the piece melts into air, into thin air, the last bars nothing but some faint outline of music, a long way off. The reception of the premiere (in May 1979, eight months after it was finished) was not entirely happy, and Michael himself was "inclined to prefer quartet two and quartet three".[10]

In the middle of the quartet's composition had come one of his first truly extended breaks from music in half a century, when early in 1978 Michael embarked with Bill Bowen on a world tour, half professional, half holiday. They were not the most worldly of travellers and would set off without maps, bookings, or currency, but somehow got through, embarking on trips with a frequency that is evidence of Michael's craving for a release from the intense hot-house of his music studio. As if inheriting his father's fondness for foreign holidays and expensive hotels, he seemed to be recreating his pre-war childhood of glamorous travel, while compensating for the many years of his life spent locked in rural Surrey. They arrived in Singapore on 6 February, leaving for Bali two days later; then on to Perth, Sydney, and Adelaide (where *The Midsummer Marriage* was given its Australian premiere). By March they had travelled from Fiji to Hawaii, moving on 18 March to San Francisco, and, stopping off in Los Angeles, they were home by the spring.[11]

In Bali they had stayed first in Sanur, on the south-easternmost shore of the island, and then flown west across Indonesia to Yog-yakarta in Central Java. There, standing in the hotel, Michael heard, perhaps simply on a recording meant to provide lobby music for tourists, the traditional Indonesian gamelan ensemble, performing with a singer. Bill handed him a piece of card taken from inside a folded shirt from the laundry, and Michael took dictation from the melody. Gamelan music had been a feature of his first piano sonata, back in the late 1930s; hearing it *in situ* shunted it back into his mind. Once the fourth quartet was out of the way, Michael began his Triple Concerto late in 1978, its three protagonists (violin, viola, and cello) pitched against an orchestra infused with the timbres of the gamelan, the score calling for tuned gongs, an alto flute, bass oboe, and the melodies perfumed with percussion. The fourth symphony's unbroken span was a life cycle; the Triple Concerto's single movement depicts the progression from one day to the next. The London Symphony Orchestra had commissioned an orchestral piece, with the front-desk players to be featured, but it became clear, as the first section coughed the three virtuosic solo parts out into the light, that world-class players were needed. Claudio Abbado was booked to conduct; pulling out at the last moment, he was replaced by Colin Davis.[12] Finished on 30 November 1979, the Triple Concerto was premiered at the 1980 Proms, the first of nigh on a hundred performances across the world in the following year. Instantly clear was that Michael's slow shift into a new phase was complete. By the central section of the concerto, a long nocturne, the three solo instruments sing together in unison, their song clearly anchored in F major. The statement of renewed faith in tonality, however far from it Michael had travelled and continued to travel, was clear. "The fundamental difficulty of our time", he said not long afterwards, "is to be able to write the heart-easing tune which isn't a cliché." But he was sure that such a melody would have to be "placed against music that is hard-edged and possibly violent".[13] The finale of the Triple Concerto stalks on into a new day, while holding memories of what has gone before: the violin quotes briefly from the third act of *The Midsummer Marriage*, as if dreaming of the opera. Then strings and brass at full throttle. Then pulsing brass under a dusting of pizzicato. Then, seeming to come full circle, motifs from the opening section of the concerto return, but scrunched up, fighting for prominence, losing their battery life. The soloists try desperately to stay afloat. Gamelan performances peter out similarly. At the end, the players just put down their instruments . . . and stop.

Benjamin Britten was dead, William Walton writing little. Michael had no serious competition for the title of the country's leading composer. In 1979 he was made a Companion of Honour. Newspapers kept rediscovering him, rather overdoing the reports of confusion at his earlier premieres. His recordings were selling out in shops English and American, and his pieces were frequently programmed by orchestras across the world. As the country was dredged in snow and in strike over the long dark Winter of Discontent, the bodies unburied in the mortuaries and the rubbish uncollected in the streets, the need for the warmth and colour of Michael's music seemed only to increase.

Admiration could verge on adulation. "He has only to fart and the critics applaud," was Elisabeth Lutyens's bitter appraisal, clinging fast to her lifelong dislike (Michael's response was to write in support of her CBE nomination).[14] He once arrived off a plane in America to be greeted by fans, soon friends, Stephen Aechternacht and Victor Marshall, both wearing a T-shirt stating: "Turn on to Tippett". The slogan was quickly picked up by the press.

Michael was suspicious of the acclaim. "*The Ice Break* was too much of a success," he wrote to William Walton, in near-boastful self-deprecation. "Frightens me. I'm trying to get back to some 'everyday-ness', if you get me."[15] For some, though, the music confirmed that fame had not come without a price. The composer

David Matthews thinks that with acclaim came a refusal to improve scores, a removal of self-doubt, and Alexander Goehr agrees: "He was totally uncritical of himself."[16] Michael was certain, however. "The chorus of praise is something I don't like," he told Priaulx Rainier in 1980. "You must always say exactly what you feel – that is what I trust you for. [. . .] No piece one does is all good – nor are all pieces good that one does. I need to have inklings of what I might have done better."[17] Nevertheless it is true that, although performance had revealed to him fault-lines in his works (he admitted that he had miscalculated the scenic proportions of The Ice Break), he resolutely refused to return to compositions. Revisions were mainly done in his head during the years-long process of planning, which would see the structure of an entire piece mentally mapped out in full before a note was written down: "the music never comes first".[18] He was more willing than most to judge his scores objectively, and his increasing insistence that he merely wrote down the sounds he heard in his head, that he was music's vessel rather than its originator, seemed to lessen his responsibility for oddities as well as marvels. Composition was, furthermore, becoming an increasingly arduous task.

Always intensely myopic, from 1978 Michael had begun to suffer bilateral macular degeneration. He was left with a large hole in his left retina, while his right eye became milky beneath a large and inoperable cataract.[19] He had to rely on peripheral vision and a magnifying glass. Michael Tillett was still working as his amanuensis and noticed the mistakes beginning to creep into the manuscripts. The Ice Break was Michael's first opera to be written on specially prepared paper, with enlarged staves, and his piano was altered to accommodate a necessarily enormous music stand. "Several pages", Tillett described, "have no music at all," merely the instruction "as it was before, only a tone higher", and "many many notes are now ambiguously placed, partially on a line, partially in a space."[20] Examination of the dishevelled, nearly metre-high scores of this period reveals Michael's handwriting loosening and swelling, some notes as large as peas.

Such difficulties did little to alter Michael's dedication. His use of repeated musical blocks increases from this period onward, either as short cut or as strategy. Conversely, his orchestration and the annotation of his scores increase in detail and ambition, as if the failure of his eyes had sharpened his ears. He gave up on traditional Italian directions, spoke to his players in plain English, and sought to deepen and intensify his colours, giving the resonance of certain instruments a strange lacquer by combining them with others that are not intended to be heard so much as to intensify and polish the original sound. He continued to compose at the piano, but was now using the instrument only to "produce an outside sound to shut the rest of the outside world off", so that he could "hear accurately in my mind all the combined sounds of a large orchestra". This was, he said, "probably my only absolute gift – I can't tell you where I got it from, but I got it very sharply. I'm very very rarely mistaken."[21]

His inexorable loss of vision did not seem to alter his mood, and most found him as gleefully joyous as ever. Many perceived, as he began this last phase of life in partnership with Bill Bowen, a change in him that it is hard fully to get a handle on. Decades before, as he approached his fortieth birthday, Michael had written of himself: "As I get older, in many ways I get younger."[22] This still held true. Partly it was a physical alteration. "He started to look much more like his mum," remembers Karl Hawker's daughter Susan, who saw him intermittently. "It wasn't the Michael I knew. He was totally effete somehow, and feminine, which he'd never looked before."[23] He had cared little what he wore for comfort when at home, but now, at public appearances, he began to reject suits and dinner jackets in favour of brightly coloured or highly patterned clothes, and trainers or sandals above which his bony ankles would poke unsocked. To a grand reception at a British Embassy he would wear Hawaiian shorts, and in Brazil received a huge cheer having unwittingly chosen trainers in the colours of the local football team.[24] With fame and age arrived a further loosening of behavioural boundaries, a cheerily reckless disregard towards conventional attitudes. The novelist Alan Hollinghurst, standing in the foyer of the Royal Opera House for a revival of *King*

Priam, found someone behind him "running his hands firmly but flutteringly up and down from armpits to buttocks, somehow in a friendly and appreciative rather than creepy way". Thinking it was a friend, Hollinghurst turned to find Michael, whom he had never met. "I felt that it was playful and even flattering, though I quite see that someone else might not have done."[25] A frequent visitor to Nocketts was the composer David Haines, who became Michael's regular driver and an intimate friend:

> He was a grandfather figure, he was a father figure, he was a huge friend, and he was on the verge of being a lover. I loved him almost romantically. He had a number of other young men chasing him around, and he did try to get physical a few times, and I'd let it go a certain way but never really gave in. He would have liked more. I probably led him on a bit. If I was in the pool and nobody else was around I wouldn't bother to wear swimming trunks. Which pleased him. And why not?[26]

Spending more time in the company of young and often homosexual men, Michael may have imbibed tastes and mannerisms, as if a man whose sexual nature had had to remain secret for so long were now living an openly, even a flamboyantly, gay life with a vengeance. But few who knew him at this period found him camp; merely colourful. He wore nothing that, had he been an artist, would have looked out of place standing next to David Hockney at the Royal Academy's summer ball. But at classical-music concerts and the necessary rounds of first-night hobnobbing (at which, all but ignoring grandees, he tended to make a beeline for young enthusiasts), his "look" caused a stir. This was surely the intention, a brightly sly poke at convention and stuffiness. Few write-ups failed to appraise his clothes, and most found them evidence of at best eccentricity and at worst a desperate attempt to be down with the kids. Or, as one composer put it, "sheer old British battiness".[27] The commentary could wobble between eye-rolling affection and sharp mockery.

To those already inclined to mistrust Michael's injection of

popular culture into his later music, such appearances did little
to help his cause, and for some it was as if the late music were
itself becoming clothed in pink trainers and tie-dyed trousers. The
new millennium would have welcomed him more easily: tutting
descriptions of the "sad contrast" between early photos of Michael
in a suit and his later appearances read uncomfortably a few decades on.[28] "He was one of the few people in those days who dared
to do something like that," says Jill Gomez. "Now he'd be perfectly
normal."[29] The outfits, which were purchased with the help of
younger friends and colleagues, were in part nothing but clever
PR, a carefully cultivated image, and in this they were a success.
Soon Michael's public persona saw him become something of a
celebrity beyond the bounds of the music industry. He was, in
a way, the country's last celebrity classical composer. Partly this
was a result of his temperament, and he courted the publicity. But
classical-music broadcasts, rather than being neatly boxed in today's
highbrow containers of BBC Four or Sky Arts, could then reach
audiences of millions on the small number of available channels.
Channel 4 would happily devote an hour to analysis of some of
Michael's most challenging works.[30] Over the decades he found
himself featured more than once on the cover of the Radio Times, was
interviewed by the Big Issue, and appeared on Terry Wogan's chat
show alongside George Michael and Andrew Ridgeley of Wham!,
showing off his boomerang necklace from a recent trip to Australia, and topping off the ensemble with a cowboy hat. It was a
level of exposure unmatched by even the leading classical composers of the twenty-first century (the equivalent example today
would be for Harrison Birtwistle to be invited onto The Graham
Norton Show).

He had become the "grand old man of British music". Not that,
in his mid-seventies, he seemed old, grand, or markedly British.
His vowels could flatten into an American accent, and he would
refer to autumn as "fall".[31] Most suspected him of keeping a portrait in the attic, for over the years a man who had once seemed
strikingly youthful became almost eerily well preserved. His voice
grew lighter rather than gruffer, and he continued to walk for miles

each day. Few found him grand, as, conducting, he would lead uproarious rehearsals of the number "Burn down their houses!" (from *A Child of Our Time*) to the words "Pull down their trousers!", or laugh helplessly when a mezzo-soprano, in the same piece, accidentally supplanted the word "gods" with "sods". He seemed poised between self-mockery and self-congratulation, sending himself up with a casualness that could only have been risked by someone who took himself seriously. Students who wrote with admiration or queries would be startled to find him turning up in their college rooms, sitting for an hour talking about music and life without pause, and then departing.[32] School orchestras performing his pieces would write to him, receive no reply, and then see a rangy figure sitting, unannounced, at the back of the school hall. Members of choirs and orchestras mainly adored performing for him, although his conducting technique went from bad to worse as the score blurred beneath him, and his left hand was entirely taken up with keeping his place. "If there's any problem about visibility of beating please tell me," he would urge players. "I generally try for a clear downbeat, I don't always succeed in doing it – you must say if there's any problem." Even a crack team would dissolve under his beat: "You're not on the stick loves!" And then: "My fault! I always go wrong there, I'm doing it by heart, my fault, I'm sorry about all this . . ."[33]

Surely there was nobody else quite like him in the music world of the late twentieth century, his easy-going un-starchiness and wicked humour (he could tell eye-wateringly filthy jokes) all the more striking for combining so startlingly with his seven, and eventually his eight, decades. He was, in a word, fun. Television documentaries caught him cheating at croquet with the Lindsay Quartet and judging marmalade-making competitions. Interviewers, treating him to lunch at the Savoy or elsewhere, would note that he usually chose the most expensive thing on the menu. A single question would lead to a meandering monologue, punctuated with verbal ticks – "Come on!" "All right?" – and all delivered in a silvery staccato stream of nearly slurring rapidity, tricky to follow and (his biographer can vouch) hell to transcribe. Most were treated to a kind of misty eccentricity, and some saw through it: "Tippett's artless vagueness is somehow unconvincing: for all his whimsy you feel he knows exactly what he wants to say in his music, and you feel he knows he has said it."[34]

Against accusations of amateurism or decline he did little or nothing to defend himself. In private he slaved over compositional detail, and many marvelled at the precision of his ear. But in public he flatly refused to engage in conversation about the minutiae of his scores. In masterclasses, as in rehearsals, he prioritised sound and risk-taking over accuracy. "It doesn't have to be right you know!" he told Roger Norrington when hearing delightedly that a whole violin section would finally tackle the fiendish motif from *King Priam*. "OK, change the notes then!" was his response to Heather Harper as she navigated a tricky passage of the third symphony. To queries regarding certain notes he would reply, "The room is full of magic, darling," or "Where IS the gin?"[35] Partly these were the honest answers of somebody who had forgotten the notes he had put on paper fifty years before, partly they were a gentle reminder that music and composer must remain somehow separate. But, assuming they have survived the unconscious edits of memory and dislike, the responses come across as teasing intellectual escape routes which simultaneously tried to turn people's queries back upon themselves.

"Michael promoted this giggly image," thinks Sally Groves. "He became very *giggly*." Teasing humour can edge into cruelty, and with Michael's celebrity, she remembers, came the occasional jibe that went too far: "He could be quite hurtful." When bidding farewell to John Amis, he purportedly said: "It's nice to see you too." And added: "Occasionally."[36] Alexander Goehr, so close to Michael since childhood, openly admits he began to find some aspects of his character insufferable. "I went off him very much, both personally and musically. I stopped going [to see him] because there was a temperamental gap that I couldn't take any more." Self-professedly a pessimist, Goehr "couldn't bear Tippett's giggling optimism".[37] He shared a dislike of late Tippett, music and man, with colleagues at the University of Cambridge's Music Faculty, who did not pull their punches in essays and articles.[38] Many professed to preferring Michael's earlier pieces. Suspicions were raised all the louder so as to be heard over what was, for the most part, a chorus of praise. For some younger composers, not least the rebellious and genre-defying Steve Martland, Michael had become something of a hero, political, sexual, and musical.

The jackets and jokes were also a public armour against a swell of nerves. Like many who are charmingly gregarious, Michael appears to have been shy at all the publicity. He admitted that, waiting at the Albert Hall prior to a performance and the subsequent curtain call, "I got such nausea I had to be taken out."[39] Back at Nocketts, the thick plaster of public personality could fall away. Heightened joy, an almost hyperactively optimistic attitude, may be nothing but a fierce defence against a capacity for unhappiness, or simply an abject refusal, even an inability, to face the black dog. Stowed away beneath his cheerfulness lay the knowledge of hardship and endurance and grief. Michael was loyally tended by his house-keeper, Josey Sims, who was eventually joined by Heather Sweet. Visiting for five hours every day, cooking and keeping house, Josey for twenty-five years and Heather for almost as long, they saw more of Michael than anyone else. "I used to work Sundays," Josey remembers,

and he used to ring me up when he had a lot of visitors. "Oh love, it's such a mess." And I used to pop up, nine o'clock at night, some nights. He was a lovely man, really nice. Kind. Gentle. Lovely. I'd go up and he used to say, "Out here love" – you'd go to the pool, and he was floating – naked! He was different. Although he was a sir, there weren't no snobbery with him. I said to him one day, because he had a lot of posh visitors, "Don't you wish, Sir Michael, that I spoke a bit posher?" "Certainly not love. You are who you are, don't alter for anyone." And that's how he was, you know? Any workers come up, he was the same with the window cleaner as what he would with Yehudi Menuhin. And he never locked the door. One night he got home and there were a bloke sat on the settee asleep. He'd come in from a party down the road. And Tippett said, "Hello love. I'm off to bed. You go when you're ready."

"It was an adventure really," Heather agrees, "because we saw a different type of life to what we were used to. I shall never forget when my mum died, and he put his arm around me and he said, 'you're the matriarch now'. And he really meant it. What he said, he meant."[40] Soon both were accompanying him to concerts. "I got to be honest," Josey admits, "classical ain't my scene. But the ones we seen was lovely, and *A Child of Our Time*. At night, if a note come, he'd run down and write it down. In the morning you could hear the piano playing, and you'd open the door, and [if you interrupted him] he'd say 'Oh fuck it!'" Should one of them pass Michael during afternoon walks when he was deep in composition, their greetings would go ignored, their presence unregistered. And both had more private glimpses. "He did spend a lot of time on his own," Josey says now. "In the beginning he did, when he was much fitter like. I went up one morning and he was sat in the chair. Tears coming down his face. And I said, 'Whatever's the matter?' And he said, 'Oh, love. Don't get old.'"

As in his music, so in his life, which was beginning to curl back on itself. Interest was now such that books were being written, chiefly the major study by musicologist Ian Kemp (seemingly no relation to Isabel), who had worked at Schott. During his research Kemp began to lay Michael's past out before him, taking him to visit his childhood home and introducing him to a number of ghosts. Kemp tracked down a figure from the past: Wilfred Franks, object of Michael's first, most ardent, and most consuming love affair. The two men had not seen each other for forty years. In 1951 Wilfred, working as a sculptor for the Ford Motor Company, had married Daphne Rudd and started a family. In the early 1960s they had moved from London to Yorkshire, where Wilfred lectured for many years at Leeds Polytechnic. Eventually Michael was persuaded, when on holiday in Yorkshire with his oldest and still-dearest friend David Ayerst, to renew the acquaintance. David was a quietly scrutinising observer, as he had been when Michael, all those years ago, first drank in Wilfred on the station platform in Manchester: "The old magic was still there, but no longer assertive or possessive. In a chair by the window sat one of [Wilfred's] children with a Tippett score, which she was studying for her A level, on her knee. I shall not soon forget the sight of composer and student side by side while Wilf and I talked of the past [. . .]. It had been an awkward bridge to cross between past and present but the journey had been worthwhile."[41] Instantly clear was that Wilfred's political dedication remained undimmed, a fact which Michael, who had for so long rejected the practical interpretations of Marxism, found uncomfortable, especially on a second meeting a few years afterwards. He wrote to Wilfred in an attempt to clarify his feelings:

> We live too far apart for me to move gradually into some new present with you, across the fifty and more years' gap.
>
> At the memorable re-meeting I knew finally, through my body I guess, that the power of that past – the joys and the problems – love, sex, gender – which forced the break (violent on my side) was such that it would engender in me troubling and sterile illusions. [. . .] Then, at the second meeting, it was clear Marxism was still a vivid reality for you, but not for me. I love argument, but . . .
>
> If Bill and I come north again we might look in if it suited. If you and Daphne come south, the same, maybe. What I <u>would</u> like is for Daphne to ring Bill or me if you are suddenly at risk. And Bill would do the same if it matters.
>
> Love to you both. Mike.[42]

It was the old nickname by which Wilfred had known him.

THIRTY

Sound

Michael was withdrawing further into the cocoon of Nocketts. Approaching his eightieth birthday, and having undergone radiotherapy for a skin cancer in August 1980, he needed to prioritise his health. On Bill Bowen's extensive care and organisational assistance Michael became fiercely, even overwhelmingly, dependent, heading his official notepaper with Bill's address rather than his own: "I won't go on any big professional trip without him, and he gives up time for that."[1] Sally Groves has vivid memories of being in Salzburg with Michael when Bill was called away. "Michael wanted to try and ring Bill, and he couldn't get hold of him at the hotel. And he would just collapse in the road with a kind of desperation. It was terrifying."[2]

Celebrity had brought with it a full-time bureaucratic job, not least daily requests for charitable donations and petitions for signature. Michael put his name on the headed notepaper of a few boards and organisations, and continued to give money to the Peace Pledge Union. "Pacifists are the minutest minority of human beings now," he said sadly. "In a world armed to the teeth we have no power whatsoever. But we say just something: that there is another world."[3] Opening a peace exhibition in the courtyard of St Martin-in-the-Fields, he made a rare public statement, denouncing President Carter's support of the neutron bomb, "which would not damage cities but would kill human beings".[4] Mainly he tried to clear the diary, and remained fiercely protective of his privacy and his phone number, which he changed with almost paranoid frequency. In 1979, a "Tippett Office" had been set up, partly at Michael's own expense, first in a corner of Schott's, and then in independent premises, eventually run by Nicholas Wright, an art dealer friend of Bill's who took on a huge amount of promotion work behind the scenes. The new set-up resulted in various schemes of huge ambition and mixed success: a Tippett shop with a costly and short-lived outpost in New York, and (in the early 1990s) plans for an ongoing cultural roadshow called Typically Tippett, with Michael's music at the centre of a touring jamboree of concerts and talks. But these were abandoned in a pile of lawyers' letters and mounting debts. Relations between the disparate branches of Michael's professional life – Bill, the Office, Schott – could be poor, and Michael's friends sometimes admitted to feeling that too many gatekeepers had been employed. As he himself conceded: "It works marvellously for me. Perhaps sometimes tough on others."[5]

On trips to Mexico he had seen cities of Mayan ruins at Chichén Itzá and at Uxmal, seen the echoing pyramidal temples with acoustic resonances so extraordinary that the building seems to transmogrify a hand-clap into an imitation bird call. On the flights home, Michael passed the time relaying to Bill the entire structure and scenario of the echoing choral work that became The Mask of Time.[6] Eventually it would be a concert work, for choir, orchestra, and four soloists, but Michael resisted calling it an "oratorio". Its gestation can be said to have lasted nearly forty years, for he was clearly returning to the earliest incarnations of The Midsummer Marriage and King Priam, as masques inspired by the I Ching. His earliest titles for the new piece were The Masque and The Song of Changes; his earliest discussions with Bill pondered whether instrumental interludes "could be danced". By 1980 he had decided that the vocal numbers "would be so static, they seem to force one into the concert hall".[7] One of the major influences on the piece had been a television series called The Ascent of Man, a thirteen-part documentary shown on BBC2 in 1973 and presented by the scientist Jacob Bronowski. The series traced humanity's development from evolution and early human migration to the invention of tools, to scientific discovery, the Industrial

Revolution, the Holocaust, and the atomic bomb. *The Mask of Time*, a work of vast scale and ambition, was to trace a similar journey, using a piecemeal libretto that Michael fashioned from snatched memories of a lifetime's reading (copyright eventually proved a nightmare). The piece may best be thought of as a choral work in ten episodes, with Michael's mosaic technique now employed as if a camera were flicking from shot to shot, cutting from scene to scene, moment to moment, with the soloists sharing presenting duties. *The Mask of Time* is formed of fragments shored against the ruins of the century that, assembled, attempt some summation, some tentative exploration of the Dupanloup catechism, made famous by Gauguin. Where do we come from? What are we? Where are we going?

Michael began the text in January 1980: "It's alarming to think what has to be invented to bring it off." Work went quickly, aided by Bill Bowen, whom Michael openly acknowledged as his collaborator: "Bill and I have finished labouring at a libretto." By 13 March: "The big work has begun!"[8] It would take him three years. Throughout composition his eyesight deteriorated to the extent that, at the halfway point, it was decided he could no longer make his own clean ink copy to present to the publishers. Piles of manuscript paper were passed to the copyist Paul Broom and to Michael Tillett, who decoded them into legibility. Every single part was played through at the piano with Michael listening intently. "It was startling," Tillett remembered of one session, "before even the second bar had been played, to have the composer suddenly sit up with a cry of: 'That's not right!'"[9] Michael's working relationship with Tillett was now so intimate, and Tillett's ear so sharp and valuable, that the composer would calmly take comments from his assistant such as "seemed on paper incredibly puny", and promise to look again at the troublesome bars, although one downside of the new regime, not to mention the scale of *The Mask of Time*, was that each section was sent off for printing as soon as it was finished, making revisions along the way impossible.[10]

The Mask of Time begins with sound, great tidal waves of it. The chorus intones the word "sound" with mouths opening and closing, above a tolling of bells and a throb of brass. As Bill Bowen explains:

"For a composer the world is created when there is sound."[11] The first half then darts in and out of man's long evolution, just as the music seems to whizz through its own history, with quotations or half-quotations from Monteverdi and Dowland, Handel and Beethoven and Haydn, and, most frequently, from Michael's own work. The orchestra spins the world into view with a creation motif in the strings, spark and glitter in the percussion, woodwind dancing in the cosmos, fanfares of brass, a flock of violin-angels soaring through the sky. Soon a swarm of animal noises from the choir evokes a primordial jungle. It is the cruelties and nonsense of nature that are to the fore, mother insects devouring their offspring. Early man learns to hunt in order to survive, discovers agriculture, draws cave pictures. Atop a tall, echoing pyramid a human is sacrificed to the sun, which suddenly pulses and glares in blinding rays of brass and electric organ. Then Eden, or something like it, is introduced by a courtly duet between violin and viola, a sarabande for flute and harp, a foreboding quartet for unaccompanied soloists, half madrigal, half barbershop. The serpent is transmuted (via the I Ching) to a dragon; God to a ridiculous and aged "ancestor". The man and woman leave the pipe dream of paradise to the mournful madrigal of the chorus.

The second half of The Mask of Time begins with Shelley, a setting of his unfinished poem "The Triumph of Life", which is suddenly undercut by a dramatisation of the poet's death at sea, the tenor wrecked amid storms of brass quoting Michael's fourth symphony, doused with sea-sick and reeling violins and clinging to a creaking ground bass. Come the seventh section of The Mask, man is splitting the atom, with a drilling of double-tongued brass that descends into chaos, before the dropping of the bomb: brass, anvils, tam-tam, bass drum. Then, for the victims of war, a requiem. Michael had pondered setting Wilfred Owen, but eventually turned to two poems by Anna Akhmatova – Requiem and "Poem Without a Hero" – given to a keening solo soprano above a humming chorus accompanied by nothing but a single double-bass: "Goodbye I heard him whisper. You shall be my widow, Oh my dove, my star, my sister." The movement, a lake of mourning called "Hiroshima, Mon

Amour", was begun on 19 May 1982, with the Falklands War at
its height: that very day a helicopter pitched into the sea, killing
twenty-two British soldiers.[12] The last vocal number of *The Mask
of Time* is formed of three songs, zooming into small glimpses of
humanity. The Thracian women tear Orpheus's body to pieces and
throw his head into the river, but as it floats out to sea, it sings still.
A group of anti-Nazis in Japanese-occupied Peking gains hope from
hearing lectures on the I *Ching*. And, in a passage taken from Mary
Renault's novel *The Mask of Apollo*, a young actor stands in front of a
statue of Zeus and seems to hear it say: "O man, make peace with
your mortality, for this too is God."

In its evocation of the capacity for destruction inherent both in
man and in nature, *The Mask of Time* is a work of bitter honesty and
a strangely joyous stoicism. Horrors have been; horrors will be.
Paradise is an easily shattered illusion. Here, now, is the moment
to rejoice. The work had really been a gift, a love-token, for Bill
Bowen, and at its completion, on 16 December 1982, Michael
dedicated it to him. A section explicitly hymning the joys of love
and sex is absent from its wide and often bleak purview. But the
last movement may be said to contain within it an erotic yell, as a
surge of sound swells in the choir, embellished by the soloists with
frizzes of ululation. It was a dramatisation of Siegfried Sassoon's
poem:

Everyone suddenly burst out singing [. . .]
and the song was wordless; the singing will never be done.

And then, the score reads, "the sound is 'cut off' as though by the
closing of a door".

Michael had scaled a mountain range. Orchestras began to fight
over performances, and the premieres in America and in Britain
promised to be major events. The BBC arranged for a television
broadcast. Michael had a brief unwinding holiday in Morocco, and

attended the American premiere of *The Midsummer Marriage* (at San Francisco, in 1983), but slowing down was not an option. It was as if corking a flow of unstoppable invention risked a clot. He moved on to a long-promised guitar sonata for Julian Bream, eventually titled – filtering a Picasso painting through a poem by Wallace Stevens – *The Blue Guitar*. By the time it was premiered – in California, on 9 November 1983 – Michael had been awarded the highest honour his country could offer, having been made a member of the Order of Merit. His unlikely backer had been William Walton. "I unhesitatingly suggested you," Walton wrote to him, not long before his death. Michael forwarded Walton's card to Bill Bowen, his attitude towards honours summed up by the words he scrawled on the envelope: "Well, well!"[13]

In January 1984 Michael Tippett OM (he religiously crossed out the initials on his headed notepaper) went off for his second world tour, flying to Hong Kong and then on to Japan, where, bundled in furs against the cold, he laid flowers at the foot of the large curving cenotaph to the victims of Hiroshima, close to the Genbaku Dome, which had been the only structure left standing within four square miles. Bill Bowen stood behind him, watched him walk away "with his arm around our guide in a highly emotional state".[14] From Japan, Michael went to the Philippines and then to Australia, and he finished up in America, going from Los Angeles to Boston for the world premiere, led by Colin Davis on 5 April, of *The Mask of Time*.

In the short break between *The Mask*'s two halves, audience members were seen walking out. Critics deemed the music "prolix and amorphous", perceiving a "ponderousness of philosophy and humour", an "increasing dependence on ready-made devices".[15] Michael cared little. "Those that knew, knew," he told Colin Davis afterwards.[16] Come the British premiere, in the more resonant acoustic of the Albert Hall during that year's Proms, the reception was, mainly, euphoric. "One of the composer's most astonishingly assured accomplishments"; "a historic evening"; "what makes *The Mask of Time* such an overwhelmingly grand experience is the breadth of dramatic purpose, the breadth of vision".[17] The conductor was Andrew Davis (no relation to Colin). Decades before, he had been sitting in the Maida Vale studios for the 1963 broadcast of *The Midsummer Marriage*: "That was truly an epiphany for me. That piece has more beautiful music in it than any other piece I know, really." Taking over *The Mask of Time* was an arduous task: "Without a shadow of doubt the most difficult piece for chorus anyone has ever written. No question. Do I admire it? Absolutely."[18] After the Prom concert, *Newsnight* did vox-pop interviews with the audience. "I'm speechless," says one man, almost shaking. "That man is a dreamer of extraordinary dreams."[19] Following the television broadcast Paul McCartney sent Michael a fan letter.

Michael had got back to England in May 1984, and by December had composed, with an ease and delight rare for him, a fourth piano sonata. What started life as a handful of bagatelles soon morphed into his largest work for the keyboard yet, a five-movement, half-hour tribute to its first player Paul Crossley, whose demonstrations at Michael's piano of the various effects he could achieve with eight fingers, two thumbs, and three pedals set off spark after spark in the composer's imagination. Crossley was told on the phone: "You'll really need some fingers for the fourth movement." This duly arrived, a spiky jive of impossible speed, pausing temporarily for a two-part canon; the sonata finally finds peace with a theme and variations, the last spinning swirls of semiquavers into a "continuous flow of sound" that, far from being Michael's usual wrestle with "endings", simply wrote itself onto the page. Crossley gave the premiere in Los Angeles early the following year. Michael, he later said, had become "a sort of adoptive father to me".[20]

Amid all the activity came a number of snuffed candles, a period of four years within which the death of a great number of friends had to be borne. In 1983 his cousin Phyllis Kemp, whose volatile friendship he had patchily enjoyed since early childhood, had died after a long illness, in a hospital in East Berlin. Ruth Pennyman, benefactress of his work with the Boosbeck miners half a century ago, died that same year. In October the following year, Anna Kallin, radio producer and a dear friend – "my twin" Michael had lovingly called her – died, aged eighty-eight.[21] A year later came news of the death of Eric Walter White, friend, colleague, even a vicarious librettist. Last and perhaps hardest to bear would be the unexpected death, while on holiday in France in October 1986, of his beloved Priaulx Rainier.

From Karl Hawker Michael had now been separated for a decade. Karl had been itinerant, his mental health declining. Occasionally he tried to attend Michael's concerts, but his daughter Susan refused to go after a while: "It would be quite awkward, and Michael was not delighted." Both daughters attempted to keep in touch with Michael. But Sarah says she "felt I wasn't allowed to. Some kind of barrier came down. Some wall."[22] Karl had tried to live in Wales, moved to Cyprus, and eventually bought a flat in London. He stayed for a while with Sarah. "One night," she remembers, "he had been beaten up, he was in a terrible state. It was so awful – we were really worried, he was not doing well. And I think that he was very lonely." Karl started to hector not only Michael but colleagues such as Colin Davis, offering to paint for money, of which he was short. "He wanted Michael", Sarah says now, "to pay attention. And couldn't get him to pay attention." Susan admits: "I think he just felt that he had failed at absolutely everything, nothing in his life had worked for him. When he came back from Cyprus, he was virtually hallucinating, not just depressed. He came round to us in a really bad state, I offered him a cigarette, and he said, 'No, I can't have a cigarette, they're trying to poison them.'"

Early in 1984, while Michael was abroad, Karl had tried to kill himself, swallowing fifty paracetamol, but recovered. Soon afterwards he put all his belongings into a minivan that he owned, and set fire to it, saving only a coat and the picture of Michael that he had drawn. Then he took an overdose of temazepam. Sarah remembers: "The first time, he said the awful thing was trying to swallow all those pills, because it took him for ever. And the second time he managed it." Her sister Susan was away from home, and remembers the day, 30 May 1984. "We'd been staying with friends, and I tried to phone him. And I couldn't get through. We were sitting by the swimming pool, with the friend, and I just knew he was dead. I just knew it." Her husband went to Karl's flat.

Susan phoned Michael straight away. "I must have been quite

upset, obviously, and he just said to me, 'I'll phone you back when you're steadier.' And he never did. That's all he said. That's all he ever said to me about it." Michael did not attend Karl's funeral, and did not tell their mutual friend Ursula Vaughan Williams the news, which she found hard to forgive.[23] What innermost thoughts he had of this second lover lost to suicide, what self-recrimination he suffered, if any, are lost from view.

Susan: "I don't really hold either to blame, as it were. I think they both had difficulties in different ways." Sarah agrees: "I don't think there's any blame."

Michael spent the day of his eightieth birthday, 2 January 1985, in Houston, Texas. In London the Royal Opera House announced that they would mount not only a new production of *The Midsummer Marriage*, but revivals of Michael's other three operas, with Colin Davis at the helm. This plan was soon found to be financially unviable and hard to cast; only an inadequately rehearsed revival of *King Priam* ever came to fruition, and eventually toured to the Odeon of Herodes Atticus in Athens. More successful had been a Kent Opera production of *Priam*, directed by Nicholas Hytner and soon filmed: Michael adored Hytner's mixture of togas and trench coats with a passion, and Hytner calls *Priam* "the happiest opera production I ever did, and probably in many ways the best".[24]

Michael, peeved with the Opera House, sanctioned a new staging of *The Midsummer Marriage* by English National Opera. "This produced", remembers John Tooley, "a very angry exchange of letters between Michael and Colin Davis. I was hoping they would mend the fences."[25] They did, to a degree: a cordial correspondence was revived, and Davis continued to support and to conduct Michael's music a great deal. But neither he nor the Opera House, which had rejected Davis's nomination of Michael for the board, appears to have had a look-in when, to everyone's surprise, Michael began to mention that a fifth opera was percolating. Here, suddenly, was a tailpiece to be added to the four stage works that Michael had long insisted formed a complete set. The Tippett Office began to look for a commissioner. Michael's preference was for the opera to be premiered at the National Theatre, a venue that would proclaim a true amalgam of music and theatre, but was persuaded that the lack of orchestra pit was an insurmountable problem. Opera and television companies jostled for the job. Soon Glyndebourne Festival Opera, Houston Grand Opera, and the BBC snagged a third each of the commission, and between them met the fee over which the Tippett Office would brook no compromise: £100,000, nearly half a million today. Michael was already at work, almost entirely uninvolved with the bureaucratic wrangles over the premiere. The libretto, with its now characteristic mixture of street slang and metaphysics, was complete by Christmas 1985. The music began to flow early in 1986, and he prioritised it to such an extent that he had to turn down major commission offers from André Previn and from Yehudi Menuhin. "I am heartbroken," the latter wrote. "What about giving a violinist a role in your opera? That would be an innovation, don't you think? A semi-acting role on the stage in an opera – I have often wished for such a role."[26] It was not to be.

Had the committed companies seen the very earliest drafts of Michael's last opera, they might well have baulked. Under the working title first of The White Herons and then of You'd Better Believe It Baby,* the sketch scenario lists four students, Brer and Shimman, Mo and Zon, who are visited by other-worldly travellers. Together they end up in a polar dreamscape, amid igloos and giant pantomime pandas. A traffic warden emerges to complain that the flying saucer is illegally parked.[27] Most of this was scrapped, but the idea of time travel from other worlds remained in the eventual opera: New Year. During its composition Michael visited the Lovell telescope in Cheshire, and listened on headphones to the noise of a star

---

* "[T]he white heron | Shivers in a dumbfounded dream" (from Calvary by W.B. Yeats); "You better believe it, babe; 'cos in this madman's universe, well at least the dream's achieved" (from the theme song, by the rock band Meal Ticket, to the BBC play The Flipside of Dominick Hide). Another working title was The Lone Dreamer.

produced light-years away. The decades-long Space Race between America and the Soviets was starting to peter out. "For myself," he concluded,

> I can't accept the gods that have been presented to me. Any of them. But that doesn't free you – it still leaves you wrestling with the loneliness of the human being. Instead of having the lovely dream of paradise, we are alone. From looking at pictures of space, I get a feeling of immensity. And despite myself, I can't help wondering if somewhere there isn't a model of what we *could* be. I dreamed up a messenger – a space traveller, a pilgrim. Someone who brings us "news from nowhere" [to quote William Morris]. I named him Pelegrin.[28]

Michael Tippett, born in the age of gaslight and of Elgar, was embarking upon an opera that would be set in an urban jungle and feature the transformational effect on a dysfunctional ghetto of a spaceship containing three time travellers. The score was to include electronic elements and reference rap and reggae, and the action reflect the influence of popular television series. It was a move that seemed both paradoxical and inevitable; a final wrestling with Michael's own psychological journeys, his lifelong empathy with society's outcasts, and his belief in the power of dreams. He was looping back round to *The Midsummer Marriage* in his depiction of two worlds colliding: the real and the fantastic, the present and the future. The heroine, JoAnn, is a child psychologist trapped in a town riddled with gang violence. For fear of what she might find, she is unable to venture outside the safety of her small apartment (eventually the television film would strongly imply her to be a victim of child abuse). Meanwhile JoAnn's foster-brother, Donny, displaced and aimless, faces a life of institutionalisation. An outcast taunted by a revelling crowd, he is beaten half to death during the midnight festivities. At the suggestion of the pianist Paul Crossley, the opera was set on the day of the year that was, the world over, a sign of renewal, one of the few surviving universal rituals.

New Year is another metaphorical dramatisation of the journey to self-knowledge, the acknowledging of the light and the shadow. The heroines of The Midsummer Marriage had undergone their Mozartian trials of heavenly staircase and hellish underworld; JoAnn makes a strange transmutation of the classical journey into Hades and its waters of Lethe and Mnemosyne. She is ushered by the visitor, Pelegrin, into a magical dreamscape, where she can drink either from a fountain of blissful forgetfulness (whirlpools of semiquavers in violins and woodwind, droplets of percussion), or from a lake of painful remembrance (oboes blooming over harp and strings). She chooses the lake of remembrance.*

Influences on the opera were typically wide-ranging but came most of all from television. Caroline Ayerst shared evenings with Michael, remembering "us all sitting watching Dallas on TV; it wasn't sitting listening to Monitor or whatever the elite arts programmes were. He liked a bit of trash!"[29] The opera has a master of ceremonies called the Presenter who (although he appeared on stage in all productions) was conceived as an unseen voiceover. Each act begins with variations on a repeated theme, a jaunty twang led by saxophone and guitar, that almost becomes theme music. Michael even pondered concluding with what he imagined would be "end credits".[30] The BBC had had a hit in 1980 with a play called The Flipside of Dominick Hide about time travellers from the future. So taken with it had Michael been that his early drafts refer to a character called Dominick, and he retained many of the play's plot elements and its vocabulary of flying saucers and time slips. Just as influential was Blake's 7, a television series charting a political dissident who rebels against a totalitarian state ruling the universe some centuries into the future. The risk of such influences was the speedy dating of their technology and production values, which soon gained a cult status for their unintended humour. The libretto's mention

---

* Michael had prefaced the score of The Midsummer Marriage with a quotation from an Ancient Greek tablet, inscribed with an Orphic saying, that he had once seen in the British Museum: "I am the child of Earth and Starry Heaven." The tablet continues: "I am parched with thirst and I perish; but give me quickly refreshing water flowing forth from the lake of Memory."

of videos and cassettes bespeaks a world that has gone for ever. But Michael had not written a science-fiction opera. *New Year* was a fable, even a dark fairy tale, a modern myth for the technological age. His scenario was a metaphor for tentative healing and promise, for the transient but necessary dream of paradise, and for the need to stare into the heart of darkness and survive.

Saxophones (three) and electric guitars (two) are prominent in *New Year*, as is the extensive percussion section, in which Michael placed steel pans and brake drums (the circular hub which houses the brake on the wheel of a car). Plurality is to the fore, each character existing in different musical zones that barely communicate with each other and seem at odds: a fragmented music for a fragmented society, attuned to the sonic cacophony of the late twentieth century. It is a musically polylingual opera, and while the elastic melodies and billowing lyricism that Michael wove for JoAnn and Pelegrin now seemed his native tongue, with single syllables swagged like bright ribbon across dozens of notes, many doubted his accent in the passages of rap and dubstep that, with composer Steve Martland's guidance, he fashioned for Donny.[31] Spoken dialogue is more frequent than in any of Michael's other operas. The new-year setting allowed for a climactic chorus of "Auld Lang Syne", sent into rhythmic battle with a helter-skelter dance in the violins and, every thirteen quavers, the tolling midnight bell. Music to depict the landing and take-off of the spaceship, and to enhance the aural shimmer of the fountain and lake, Michael left to Bill Bowen, who had been deeply involved with the opera from the beginning and who, with the music engineer Mike Thorne, produced a pulsing electronic glow using a "synclavier", an early form of synthesiser or sampling system.

With its other-worldly elements and electronically enhanced soundscape, *New Year* would seem at first glance to sit alongside operas by Stockhausen or György Ligeti, and shares something of such composers' surreal and disturbing humour in its calls for peace and unity. But Michael's score leans closer to the world of the musical, while retaining many operatic conventions: arias, trios, and a huge quartet in the second act in which each character continuously tolls their resolution – "no way" – on a firm and bell-like E flat. He filled New Year with dance, would mention West Side Story in interview as frequently as Beethoven or Mozart, and had been especially inspired by the National Theatre's acclaimed production of Guys and Dolls in 1985. He could be found hymning the "sophistication" of Top of the Pops, and the Open University prepared a programme uniting his work with the musicals of Stephen Sondheim. Among his choices on Desert Island Discs a song by the Police rubbed shoulders with Ravel. In the early stages of composing New Year, Michael even made approaches to the Communards, a British pop duo soaring up the charts. Attracted perhaps by the openly homosexual content of their songs and by the soaring counter-tenor of the lead singer, Jimmy Somerville, he suggested a collaboration of some kind, to no avail.[32] New Year's montage of styles is most reminiscent of Leonard Bernstein's divisive "theatre piece" Mass, which incorporates dance, "street singers", rock band, recorded tape, and a Presenter-like "celebrant".

Michael had carved out three years to devote to the composition of New Year, and kept to his schedule pretty rigorously, until a sudden diagnosis, in early October 1987, of colorectal cancer. He remained calm, once again refusing to countenance a head-on collision with calamity. As Sally Groves remembers, "He was just not acknowledging it, in a sense, he was not going to give it house room, even though it was inside him. He said himself, 'I'm very old, this is going to grow very slowly, we're going to deal with it.' He would say when the scores were going to arrive, and they arrived – and that was true with New Year, even with his cancer. He was late but he wasn't that late and he just kept going and did it."[33] Michael speedily had an operation but was spared chemotherapy, and recovered quickly. David Ayerst and his wife moved temporarily to Nocketts to help care for him, and Heather and Josey rolled their sleeves up. Josey gets straight to the point: "I used to change that [temporary colostomy] bag every day, three times a day, and Heather used to burn it afterwards. We had a good combination because Heather could do the top, and I could do the bottom. I couldn't stand sick. Heather could sort that, and I could sort the bottom half!"[34] By November, less than a month after his diagnosis, Michael was back at work on New Year, and soon able to attend a three-week "Tippett and Debussy" festival in Manchester. The opera was finished on 19 December 1988, and the publicity machines whirred into action.

The great events of the century were now conveyed to Michael through the television screen at Nocketts, on which, in early June 1989, he watched a lone man wander among the Chinese tanks as they rolled into Tiananmen Square. In the autumn he flew to America for a tour that culminated in the premiere of New Year, in Houston, on 27 October. Footage of his trip shows him sturdy but small amid the skyscrapers and the glaring heat of the Texan fall. Carried down an airport escalator and away, he shuffles closer to Bill Bowen and puts one arm through his. But the film says nothing of the true nature of their relationship. As Michael had neared the end of New Year a clause had been added to a recent act of local government, stating that a local authority could not "intentionally promote homosexuality", nor "promote the teaching in any main-tained school of the acceptability of homosexuality as a pretended family relationship". The battle was far from over, and several charities and protest groups fought fiercely against "Section 28" and its promotion by Margaret Thatcher's government. Michael, in Bill Bowen's words, "never became a proselytising gay", and there is no glimpse of him standing in Stonewall rallies, nor any mention of homosexuality in his final works.[35] But he signed the petitions he was asked to, and allowed his Songs for Ariel to be performed at a benefit gala for gay charities, Before the Act. Alongside the actors Ian McKellen and Miriam Margolyes, he sponsored "the fifth European lesbian and gay festival of song" at the Hackney Empire, which supported the fight against Section 28. He would not live to see its repeal.

The fight was not only against the Thatcher government, but against a virulent disease and its often ignorant and frightened reception. Colin Lee, a music therapist working with a pianist facing death from AIDS, wrote how "Tippett as a composer, philosopher and humanitarian influenced my work as a music therapist and clinical improviser greatly at this time"; much of Lee's research was headed with quotations from Michael's work, which had helped Lee formulate his belief "that the inner world of music had no element of illness and so at its most essential level offered a release that was both liberating and spiritual".[36] On 20 October 1989, seven days before the premiere of *New Year*, the director of the London Sinfonietta, Michael Vyner, died of what his obituaries said was cancer. Vyner, who had worked at Schott and been Paul Crossley's partner, had died of complications from AIDS, aged forty-six. He had been a close friend of Michael's and was the dedicatee of the fourth piano sonata, but when a memorial concert was eventually arranged, Michael quietly refused to be involved, and did not attend Vyner's funeral (just as he had not gone to the funerals of Bronwen Wilson, Francesca Allinson, or Karl Hawker). As Crossley remembers: "There was something about funerals that bothered him, and I don't know what it was. I was incredibly upset. We had this huge memorial concert. People wrote pieces – Lutosławski, Birtwistle – and Michael wouldn't even come to the concert. He wouldn't come. As if there was something he couldn't face about it. And he knew I was upset by it."[37] Unlike his heroine, JoAnn, Michael would not drink from the lake of remembrance.

New Year had become something of a juggernaut, giving rise to Tippett festivals across America, and Michael could focus on little else. The production had a budget of half a million dollars, and the services of the innovative choreographer Bill T. Jones, who worked with the body language of hip-hop and street dance, had been secured for the dancing chorus. But the director, Peter Hall, was over-committed, and when he finally arrived in Texas was instantly at loggerheads with Krister St Hill, who was faced with the immense task of dancing and singing Donny. St Hill "adored" Michael on his brief visits to rehearsals, but thought Hall "had not prepared at all, and hardly knew what the opera was about", finding "the tension between director, choreographer, and conductor

[John DeMain] insane".[38] Andrew Davis, who was to conduct the British premiere, confirms: "Peter almost walked out. It was extremely fraught."[39] The pit turned out to be far too small for Michael's large orchestra, and the score had to be reduced, with percussionists playing in storage spaces beneath the seats. Michael had suggested to the designer, Alison Chitty, that she might set New Year partly in present-day Notting Hill, and the chorus was peopled with yuppies, bag ladies, punks. The ship transporting the sets to Texas from their English warehouse was nearly wrecked in Hurricane Hugo, but eventually JoAnn's small apartment and Pelegrin's spaceship found their way onto the stage of the Cullen Theater, in the form of two glass boxes on a complex hydraulic system that allowed them to rise and fall in a blaze of blue light. In the distance urban towers were spread out underneath a starry sky, and clouds of roses bloomed to form the paradise garden in which JoAnn (sung by Helen Field) dances with Pelegrin (Peter Kazaras). When the bells tolled midnight, real fireworks were let off. "The first complete run-through", remembers Krister St Hill, "turned out to be the opening night." Peter Hall noticed how the composer, in striped blazer, bow-tie, and pink trainers, "walked through all the Texan nobs apparently oblivious, though cannily picking up every absurdity". Michael was thrilled with what he saw on the stage, and wrote to Hall: "When the feared/unfeared moment came at curtain up on Friday, I realised I was seeing the most magical presentation at premiere of any theatre piece. A gift to me."[40]

The American critics disagreed, led by the New York Times, which thought that the opera "suffers seriously – I would say fatally – from the weakness of the libretto". The score was "an unconvincing concoction" that "fires off the mark in just about every way possible".[41] Over the course of the seven performances the vast auditorium was half empty seats and half perplexed Texan businessmen. Only a seventh of the tickets was sold.[42] British reviewers, flown over for the opening night, had likewise found the production disappointing, the musical performance unsure, and the libretto and scenario "a pretty baffling mixture of ideas", hampered especially by Donny's Caribbean-English patois. Ticket sales picked up at the Glyndebourne Festival the following summer, and Andrew Davis led a stronger performance with the original orchestration. Reviewers continued to think the opera a failure: "so naïve yet pretentious, so obscure yet blatant". But most found the score itself a success. "Some of the most lovely and inventive music he has ever written – an astonishing feat for a composer now in his mid-eighties. Equally amazing is his ability to capture the flavour of today's street life in contemporary sounds such as rap." "The originality of Tippett's instrumental ideas simply stuns the ear." "Tippett's musical vigour and inventiveness remain a marvel."[43] The production set off on tour in October 1990, and seems by then fully to have found its feet. Vernon Henry Junior, a backing vocalist from the Pet Shop Boys, was newly cast as the Presenter, singing close to the microphone with a disco croon, and making new sense for many of the most perplexing role.

On the surtitles for New Year Peter Hall had incorporated jokey catchphrases, apparently written by Michael, that most failed to find funny. Texans had bridled at Americanisms such as "Y'all have a nice night", and in Glyndebourne picnickers after the long supper interval laughed good-naturedly at "the picnic's over". One reviewer responded: "Alas, all too true."[44] New Year had been, at best, a noble failure. A planned recording fell through, and audience figures were low for the made-for-television film, shown on BBC2 in September 1991. Twenty years on, its boxy computer screens and sci-fi costumes seem artefacts from a bygone age. Michael turned eighty-five in January of the following year, and the reviews didn't seem to have damaged his reputation. BBC2 devoted an evening to him, and BBC Radio 3 played more than twelve hours of uninterrupted Tippett. He spent the day itself in the States. In the hotel room his phone rang: Christopher Fry, his friend from their teaching days at Hazelwood School, calling long-distance to send birthday greetings. "You know Kit," Michael told him, "I was very touched by your ringing me in America for my eighty-fifth !! birthday. It meant a lot."[45]

It was over sixty years since Michael had bought Christopher Fry a copy of H.G. Wells's Men Like Gods for his twenty-first birthday, thrilled by its depiction of a socialist utopia in a parallel universe. The lead character, Mr Barnstaple, longs to stay in utopia but can do this only "by returning into your own world". JoAnn, after her travels with Pelegrin, likewise returns to her native town, and leaves the opera to begin her work afresh with young victims of urban conflict. It had been many decades since Michael, embracing and questioning almost every creed available to a committed young adult in the years between the wars, had wholeheartedly believed in the possibility of building any kind of utopia: the political post-revolutionary utopia; the Christian utopia; or merely a utopia in A major. Such dreams, time and again, had cracked, been proven impossible by the century through which he had lived. But now? In June 1988, six months before completing New Year, Michael had watched a tribute concert for Nelson Mandela's seventieth birthday, broadcast live from Wembley Stadium. The headline act was the rock group Dire Straits, and the camera zoomed into the lead singer, Mark Knopfler, about to sing "Brothers in Arms". "This one is really for the gentleman in question this evening," says Knopfler. "Best birthday party we've ever been to. Thanks for having us." Then, without a change of tone: "One humanity, one justice."

Michael had found the last words of his opera, either as a tentative proffering of the world he had so long ago believed possible, or merely as a cheap slogan to which society could never live up. There is no grandiose gesture or wild chorus of hope. The words are given to the Presenter almost as a yell, of anger or of prophecy, the notes replicating with some accuracy Knopfler's laid-back rhythms and strange upward inflection on the word "humanity". Nineteen eighty-nine saw a revolutionary wave across Europe presage the eventual fall of the Soviet Union. By the time New Year reached Britain, Nelson Mandela had walked out of prison. And just thirteen days after the opera's world premiere Michael watched in amazement as the graffitied concrete of the Berlin Wall, which he had seen erected and through which he had often passed, tumbled and fell into dust amid cheering crowds.

THIRTY-ONE

The Lake

When Michael appeared on the Albert Hall stage after the first British performance of Byzantium, his setting of Yeats's poem, the audience could not fail to notice that, as he embraced Andrew Davis and kissed the soprano Faye Robinson, he was wearing a red shirt and a pair of trousers – one leg blue, one red – decorated with vividly colourful noughts and crosses.

Michael had planned a giant work for soprano and orchestra, a triptych with outer panels (using texts set by Charles Ives and by Henry Purcell) that eventually fell away, leaving only the Yeats.[1] During composition he had made a Yeatsian pilgrimage with the Ayersts to Ireland, where he sat on the poet's bed in Thoor Ballylee Castle, and saw his grave in County Sligo. The half-hour setting of the poem's five stanzas had taken him less than a year, and he had finished in December 1989, soon after returning to Wiltshire following the premiere of New Year. The piece does not so much set "Byzantium" as explode it and then set the shrapnel. Sally Groves believes it has "the most stunning beginning of almost anything you can think of": a trumpet fanfare above tuned gongs, before violins give way to a toppling percussion motif and a strange synthetic crackle from an electric keyboard emulating a marimba. The soprano part is acrobatic, aeronautic. Each line, each word, is broken down into its constituent parts or even syllables, which are then held up to the light and endlessly examined or repeated. The setting proffers a word-painting of a risky obviousness which is then snatched away: the word "dome" is stretched around a great cupola of notes, but not long afterwards the same soaring motif is used for the word "come", as if highlighting the half-rhyme but also the arbitrariness of musical illustration. Rather than a refutation of Michael's lifelong view that good poetry was destroyed by music, his grappling with the dense imagery of his beloved Yeats produced not a setting of "Byzantium" so much as a commentary on how "Byzantium" might be set. Yeats's final line becomes a wild keening strobe of echoes and chord clusters, the words themselves struck like instruments: ". . . that gong gong that gong gong tor tor tor mented sea, sea, that gong gong tor tor tor tor mented sea, sea, sea . . ."

The piece was premiered, on 11 April 1991, by Georg Solti, who was celebrating his final season with the Chicago Symphony Orchestra. The star soprano Jessye Norman was announced as the soloist, but for reasons unexplained, and just a week before the four performances (at Carnegie Hall in New York), she withdrew. Solti made no secret of his displeasure, and the gossip threatened to overwhelm the music itself. Faye Robinson – who had sung in the premiere of The Mask of Time and become a star turn in the third symphony – learned Byzantium in five days. The New York Times acclaimed its "wonderful welter of sound-evoking images", though Byzantium has since been called "the most utter failure ever achieved by a thoroughly respectworthy musician".[2]

Three months later, on 15 July, Michael finished a fifth, and final, string quartet, on which he had been working intermittently for over a year. It had had a "first glimmering" back in January 1990, was delayed for a three-month tour of America, Australia, and New Zealand, and begun in April.[3] Of all Michael's late pieces the most valedictory, the quartet is divided into two movements, combining the conventions of sonata form with layers and juxtapositions of different building blocks. Its epigraph is taken from a French folk-song: "Chantes, rossignol, chantes, toi qui as le coeur *gai*."* Michael's memory had taken him back to his Oxted cottage, where in nearby woods he would stand alone at night listening to the "peculiar, liquid tone" of the nightingale's song, "like someone sobbing from heartbreak".[4] The quartet, which never seeks accurately to transcribe birdsong, is poised on the brink of gaiety and heartbreak, turmoil and serenity. Michael had returned to Beethoven, his journey with his beloved musical father having followed the customary filial pattern: from imitation to argument, then rejection and, finally, reconciliation. His model was the slow movement of Beethoven's Quartet in A minor (the "holy song of thanksgiving"). Michael's second movement brings his players frequently together for a pattern of seven chords, a series of liquid drops transposed and varied. Ten days after completing the quartet, he phoned Michael Tillett and dictated down the line a new ending, the seven chords slowed, and reaching a warm, bright ray of the sunny A-major triad that had closed *The Midsummer Marriage* – but tipped into mystery and newness by the viola, which tightens the chord's inner elastic by pulling the third up into a fourth and adding the seventh-scrunch of a G sharp. It was a chord to close a career, but there was one more major piece to come. Peter Cropper of the Lindsay Quartet, which gave the premiere the following year, said that the experience of playing the piece to Tippett for the first time was "simply the greatest of my life". Michael, aged eighty-six, still had "the energy of a ten-year-old boy".[5]

Nevertheless, he was slowing down at least a little. He had continued to conduct and to record his own music, but became frustrated at the results when playing back the discs: "the old man trying to conduct the young man," he wrote woefully to Colin Davis.[6] Further professional engagements came with the publicity rounds of his autobiography, *Those Twentieth Century Blues*. The book provoked a furore, in that Michael and Bill parted company with the original publishers, Weidenfeld and Nicolson, who were concerned by the potentially libellous nature of certain gossipy sections about living

---

* "Sing, nightingale, sing, you who have a happy heart."

figures. Eventually Hutchinson issued a carefully edited version, and a copy found its way across the ocean to Douglas Newton, Michael's great love during the Second World War, who had been of such importance in the genesis of *The Midsummer Marriage*. Douglas, now one of the most eminent museum curators in New York, read the book avidly in his apartment on the Upper West Side. "It does strike me", he wrote to John Amis, "that there was always a sort of coarseness, I think the right word, about [Tippett's] attitudes to people that was a fundamental egotism disguised as the ruthlessness of genius." But his feelings for Michael, and for the book, in which he was only cursorily mentioned, were fond. "Some atmosphere of that peculiar time does come back, here and there. [. . .] One of the nice things that comes out of the book is that he's evidently happy, busy, famous, pleased with himself and discreetly rich. It's pleasant to know that virtue is sometimes rewarded."[7]

Douglas would survive Michael by three years. Retired from the Metropolitan Museum in New York, he outlived his second wife, drank a great deal, continued to write about the art he had spent much of his life studying, and spoke little if ever about his life with Michael Tippett and Francesca Allinson during the war. A series of strokes turned out to be the result of a fast-moving brain cancer, and on 18 September 2001, three days before his eighty-first birthday, he died in St Vincent's in downtown Manhattan, the primary admitting hospital for those injured in the attacks on the World Trade Center the week before, unaware of the dust and fumes still swirling in the street outside.

Douglas Newton had perceived Michael to be "happy, busy, famous, pleased with himself and discreetly rich", and was seemingly correct about four of his five inferences. Michael's financial difficulties, as he devoted his energies to one more major composition, were going from bad to worse. His income during the 1990s was by any standards high. He could earn $20,000 for fifteen minutes of music (such was the commission price for his brass arrangement of a section of *The Mask of Time*, called *Triumph*, one of a number of arrangements and paraphrases whose existence owes more to the fee than to creative inspiration). *Byzantium* had netted him $50,000 and *New Year* twice that sum. His royalties were considerable, as were his payments for lecture tours. His annual income now frequently exceeded £200,000, a figure twice as large in today's terms.[8] But his expenditure continued to exceed his earnings. Large tax bills and the interest clocking up on loans became a vicious spiral of debt. Music seemed to have eaten up all else. Invoices and tax statements were forwarded to others to deal with, unopened. Sally Groves is certain:

> He wasn't in control financially, he wasn't. I can remember him ringing me up and saying "Sally dear, the bailiffs are here and they want to take everything away." And I said, "Michael, I want you to put the man on to me," and I spoke to the bailiff and I said, "You are to go away, this man is an old man, you are to go away, we will deal with it." And I somehow persuaded Schott to pay off the bill.[9]

Josey Sims, who was trying to keep the household running, is blunt. "He was skint. We'd get in the bank. 'Sorry love. No money.' And I used to have to go outside, get in the phone box and ring Bill and say, 'Look Bill, there ain't no money again.' That were awful, that were embarrassing." Bill for his part remembers "the bank manager turning up just before lunch one day and saying, 'I'm sorry to bother you Sir Michael, but your account is a thousand pounds overdrawn.'"[10] Michael, at the still centre of the whirlpool, remained happy to live off the promise of further earnings. Unperturbed by the cries of woe from his accountants, he set off on another holiday.

Lakes had been studded through Michael's life and work, from family holidays in Italy when he was a teenager to the moment his second symphony sprang into life as he sat high above Lake Lugano listening to Vivaldi. In *New Year* he had placed a lake of remembrance, full of sorrow and joy. In Senegal, north-west Africa, a little way north-east of the capital, Dakar, there is a shallow pink lake called Lake Retba, separated from the Atlantic Ocean by a narrow line of sand-dunes. The lake contains an alga (*dunaliella salina*) that produces a red pigment able to absorb light. Catch the lake in bright sunlight and its waters can shine an eerie, dusty pink. Go on the wrong day and it turns a grudging terracotta. Workers dig up the salt deposited on the lake bed, diving into the pink water from canoes, and making white mounds on the lakeside. Michael travelled to Dakar in November 1990. With him went a young architect friend (met through Bill) called Graham Modlen, who had become a willing travel companion. "He wanted to see the world and see everyone," Modlen recalls. Michael was in good health, striding off on long walks, but the night before the trip to Lake Retba he had slipped and fallen in his bath, and Modlen had to haul him out. They drove to the lake the next morning, past an elephant carcass rotting on the side of the road, arriving in the midday light in time to see a sharp change of colour in the water. Modlen:

> It was a kind of earthy terracotta. Red-ish. The light was ahead of us and the reflections were in our faces, off the water. We could see the other shore, a flat horizon in the distance. I remember Michael talking about the twinkling light, and what effect it had on his mind, his imagination. And he was reflective then about his life, his age. And this cut-off from familiarity. He'd travelled – who knows where he hadn't been. But this landscape, I suspect, was sort of ethereally different. We were there an hour or so, not long. It was one of a number of places we went to. But it was this one he kept talking about, because of this strange effect on his retina, and then his imagination. It burned something in his retina.[11]

Michael had promised a ninetieth-birthday piece to Colin Davis, and even at the hotel in Senegal began to talk about translating the trip to the lake into music. "If I recall anything else," says Graham Modlen of their conversations, "it's this notion: this might be my last piece." The burning image glimmered and swirled for half a year before, once the fifth quartet was complete, a piece began to heave itself laboriously onto manuscript paper: not a sonic depiction of the lake, but an attempt to capture in music the dappled interplay between water and light and colour, and to chart a progression from dawn to dusk. On 19 August 1991 Michael wrote to Colin Davis in the language of Senegal: "*Enfin, ça commence. Les eaux de lac se tourbillonnent. Journées de travail, journées de vacance. Une année?*"* It took a fierce effort from all friends and supporters to get him through. The first chunk of *The Rose Lake* was finished in the spring of 1992, during a holiday on Tobago. Ten minutes of music had taken him eight months. By the time he reached the latter stages of the piece he was ailing badly and seems to have been unable to write at all. Several pages of the manuscript are missing and Michael Tillett laboriously took verbal dictation. The composer himself picked up the pen again in order to complete the piece, though he relied a great deal on the faintest shorthand which Tillett would carefully decode. "Can you please straighten this out for me," Michael would write in the score. "The seven notes should be . . ."[12] At some points there is nothing but rivulets of letters: C-D-F#, E-A-D . . .

He finished the piece on 22 April 1993, exhausted and depressed. During composition his brother Peter died, not long after the tentative renewal of a fraternal relationship that had long been distant (Peter's obituaries acclaimed one of the most distinguished naval historians of his generation). Six months later came the death of David Ayerst. Michael wrote his obituary in the *Guardian*. "He had a heart of gold, a gentle, mocking humour and a genuine love for people of all sorts, all ages. I shall miss him greatly."[13] It was a terrible blow. The two had shared annual holidays in their old age, David's linen suit and panama hat offset by Michael's bright shorts and sandals.

---

* "At last, it begins. The waters of the lake are swirling. Days of work, days of holiday. One year?"

Michael Tippett and David Ayerst on holiday, 1990

Wilfred Franks was up in Yorkshire. And Michael's old political sparring partner Alan Bush, now a widower in his nineties, lived quietly in Hertfordshire, slowly losing his memory, existing in the past, unable to comprehend even the collapse of the Soviet Union. He died in October 1995. "You cannot imagine what it's like when your entire generation has disappeared," Michael admitted to Paul Crossley. "Everybody's now gone."[14]

Waiting for *The Rose Lake* to reach a performance, Michael began to fade. Recurring skin cancers on his face necessitated frequent bouts of radiotherapy. When Bill and other visitors departed, and Josey and Heather left him to the television each evening, the house could seem large, and the countryside silent. Michael had made a close friend of his doctor, Nick Whyatt, to whom he dedicated *The Rose Lake*, and who remembers being rung up "at one o'clock in the morning, and he just wanted to talk, that's all". In Michael's medical report Whyatt had written "he is very lonely".[15]

There was one memorable public appearance, in London, on 15 May 1994. It was International Conscientious Objectors' Day, and the Peace Pledge Union, of which Michael was still president, had long wanted to commemorate objectors with a memorial of some kind. Eventually enough was raised to place a stone in Tavistock Square, and Michael, who half a century ago had been sent to prison as a conscientious objector, duly led the unveiling ceremony and pulled back a cloth from the large shard of grey volcanic slate that sits in the centre of the square, revealing the inlaid plaque:

TO ALL
THOSE WHO HAVE
ESTABLISHED AND
ARE MAINTAINING
THE RIGHT TO
REFUSE TO KILL

Their foresight and
courage give us hope

Today the stone is often strewn with white poppies. Close by is a statue of Mahatma Gandhi, and a cherry tree, planted in memory of the victims killed by the nuclear bombing of Japan. And now, hanging on nearby railings, is a plaque that remembers those killed in the bomb attack on the Route 30 bus as it drove through the square on 7 July 2005.

The premiere of *The Rose Lake* was scheduled for 19 February 1995, as part of a festival for Michael's ninetieth-birthday celebrations, during which, at an afternoon discussion, Colin Davis was heard to say, "Tippett is our greatest living composer, and that's that."[16] Every concert sold out. Michael's nerves took hold. "I well remember," says Sally Groves, "he was in abject terror, he was almost literally shitting himself in the first rehearsal. He just didn't know if he'd got it right."[17]

The Rose Lake speaks almost nothing of its compositional difficulties, which seem only to have increased Michael's ambition. He had once again used an extensive battery of percussion, and produced a series of cavorting leaps for an array of rototoms: drums tuned to a specific pitch by rotating the head. Less cumbersome and with a lighter sound than timpani, beloved of pop groups such as Pink Floyd, they had been patented just after Michael's seventieth birthday. Here he was, nearing ninety, laboriously learning how to write for them. He had used a small number for *Byzantium*, but *The Rose Lake* calls for three octaves, nearly forty individual drums, spread one to a note like a gigantic keyboard across the back of the stage. What Michael thought could be achieved by a single performer had eventually to be rearranged for two players who must sprint back and forth along the drums, mallets flashing. In early performances the drums were endlessly repositioned, and at one point it was very seriously suggested that the percussionists would find it easier on roller skates.

Michael had written with a new, possibly enforced, economy, opening up spaces in the orchestra that, like the alga in the lake, could take in light. Studded through *The Rose Lake* are five "Lake Songs", each one a variation reflecting and refracting motifs from the first, rising and then setting, with, floating at the centre, "The Lake in Full Song", its flocks of strings ducking and diving in ecstatic flight, lit by a midday glare of brass. The songs are inlaid into a characteristic backdrop mosaic of contrasting musical tiles, resulting in interludes that dart around the orchestra between the five pools of song. The songs are developmental, the interludes static; the songs have a tonal basis, the interludes are harmonically afloat. The piece teeters between forward and backward motion, between stability and progression. As T.S. Eliot had it, "at the still point, there the dance is, but neither arrest nor movement".

Michael, always keen to snap listeners out of their reverie, bookended *The Rose Lake* with an introduction and a coda. The piece does not rage against the dying of the light, but nor does it go gently. Its wispy coda, using material from the introduction, begins with trickles of harp that suddenly dissolve into woodwind chirrup. A final watery hiccup from the brass is marked in the score not with a bang but a "plop", as if Michael were signing off with his habitual "Well, well!" The premiere, the centrepiece of a festival called *Visions of Paradise*, went without a hitch, but in the silence following the final "plop", while Colin Davis's arm was still hanging in the air, two men shouted from the audience in unison, protesting against what they perceived to be the cacophony of contemporary music: "Visions of hell!" BBC technicians rushed to remove the protest from the broadcast, and the audience began to cheer and eventually to stand as the composer, arm-in-arm with Davis, was helped onto the stage of the Barbican concert hall. Even critics who had doubted Michael's recent pieces felt that *The Rose Lake*, advertised as a farewell, was a triumphant swansong.[18]

In interviews prior to the many subsequent performances he began to say that there was no more music in his brain. There was to be just a tiny punctuation mark to close his compositional life. He was persuaded by the controller of BBC Radio 3, Nicholas Kenyon, to contribute a three-minute miniature for the station's *Fairest Isle* season, celebrating the tercentenary of Purcell, whose reputation he had done much to secure. He returned to his most beloved Shakespeare, *The Tempest*, setting a speech of Caliban's: "Be not afear'd. The isle is full of noises, | Sounds, and sweet airs, that give delight and hurt not." A boogie-woogie from *The Knot Garden* slips into a Purcellian ground bass, and a patchwork of quotations from Michael's work, ghosts from his music, dances with the soloist.[19] That done, the manuscript paper was put away, the piano lid was closed, and the music stopped.

Nocketts was mortgaged to the hilt, the swimming pool had been wrecked by an electrical fire, and, isolated at the end of a drive that became impassable in cold weather, the building had become unsuitable for an ailing nonagenarian. Wiltshire was too far from friends and colleagues, not least Bill Bowen, now living in Battersea. In the autumn of 1995 Michael managed a two-month tour of America and Canada, but on his return it became clear that life alone was damaging both his physical and his mental health. On 9 April 1996, now ninety-one and almost blind, he said goodbye to Heather and to Josey for the last time: "He had a tear, we had a tear. Like I say, I never met a man like him to be honest."[20] He was moved into 13 Herons Place, a rented townhouse on a new-build estate in Isleworth, west London. The Thames flowed behind the house, the aeroplanes droned overhead. Nocketts was sold a month later, for £288,000, amid a scramble of packing and selling. There were more crime novels in Michael's relatively small library than there were scores. The Tippett Office continued, but Michael's day-to-day life now revolved around doctors' visits, haircuts, trips out to local cafés and restaurants, and shuffling walks along the towpath, watching the herons wading around Isleworth Ait, and the abandoned boats rusting in the dockyard.

Andrew Coster, a carer from a local agency, moved into the top floor of the house, eventually joined by his wife, Sunee. As Michael became less mobile, his bedroom had to be moved to the ground floor, where he sat by the window. A few trips abroad were managed, with much difficulty. Visitors came and went. Among them was Caroline Ayerst: "He'd got two very nice carers but in my memory he's always been a man who's got a view, a lovely view. He wouldn't have had the money to go to a rich old person's home. Isleworth wasn't a grand sort of place. I don't think you could *see* the river. So it wasn't . . . it wasn't a glorious end."[21]

There survives just one letter in Michael's hand sent from Herons Place. It is to Wilfred and Daphne Franks, its handwriting sprawling across the page, curly and childlike. It is Michael's last known letter:

Dear Wilf & Daphne. To ring you both, then talk only to Wilf, seems to me now, like a confused attempt, by me anyhow, to hold something from the past. Never works. So now, love to you <u>both</u> and good luck to all your next generation. For my part, however, I peer into the future.[22]

Still there were concerts to attend. *The Midsummer Marriage* became the first opera written since the Second World War to be given three new productions by Covent Garden. At the 1996 Proms, ninety-one-year-old Michael Tippett presented the Royal Philharmonic Society's gold medal to an eighty-seven-year-old Elliott Carter.

Just a few months later, in September, Michael had a stroke. It was reasonably severe, and left him partially paralysed, though mentally he remained sharp. Visitors over the next months were shocked at his appearance, for age and frailty had left him gaunt and shrivelled, and his face hung from his newly jutting cheekbones. Occasionally his frustration erupted, as Andrew Coster remembers: "When he was cross at you he went into his shell, he kind of cowered, and he still had that anger in him. And then everything, you could see, calmed down and he'd just look at you. 'Come here love.' 'Yes Michael?' 'Look. I'm terribly sorry, you know I didn't mean it.' I said: 'I know you didn't. And I understand. So don't worry. Rage at me however you like.' So it was like that."[23]

In May 1997 Michael watched Tony Blair (like himself, an old Fettesian) bring the Labour Party to a landslide victory. Blair had moved the party away from the socialism in which Michael had believed so fervently, but his election ended seventeen years of Tory rule and brought, as Bill Bowen remembered, "unbounded delight".[24] On 9 August Michael made it to the Albert Hall to watch Colin Davis and the National Youth Orchestra perform the *Ritual Dances*. Andrew Coster was in the box with him. "I had to hold him up. He couldn't stand obviously, and you've got the audience cheering. I had to hold him up. So he was waving. And it wouldn't stop. Incredible. Must have gone on for about five minutes."[25]

On 18 September John Amis, friend of half a century, who during the war had visited Michael in Wormwood Scrubs and swum naked with him in the Cornish sea, came to Isleworth:

The shock is indeed distressingly great. The old Michael has gone, leaving a wraith with sunken face and fairly useless limbs. [. . . He] still has his marbles – "I can still tick people off" (glint in the eye as of old). He messes his pap food but at lunch I find that there is one angle of profile where the Michael of old lurks but it is sad to find this bright-eyed Celt reduced to being a complete invalid. I didn't check his current account of memory but certainly his deposit account was sure. [. . .] He is hoping to go to Sweden for an enormous Tippett retrospective in November. As I talk to him I remember hearing about a certain African tribe that gives old people a good meal and then sinks them in bubbling consuming mud. Wouldn't it be a quick way of sparing this wonderful old genius any further indignity . . . and his heirs any further expense? Poor Michael asks me to come back but I'm not sure I have the heart to. There is no pathos apparent, no asking for pity, as indeed I guessed there would not be.[26]

The trip to Sweden for the retrospective – one of the biggest Tippett festivals ever mounted – was emphatically not a good idea for one so weak, but Michael set his heart upon going, insisting against common sense and the protestations of those around him. In the end he prevailed, and he flew to Stockholm, accompanied by the Costers, on 12 November. As soon as they arrived at the Nova Park Hotel in Huddinge, south-east of Stockholm, Michael became agitated, and flew into furies if he needed the loo or wanted a change of air. In the middle of the first night he woke Andrew Coster in distress and was rushed to hospital. Bill Bowen had travelled over separately, and joined them by the time the doctors had diagnosed pneumonia in both lungs and put Michael in intensive care. Andrew, Sunee, and Bill were sitting by his bed. Andrew remembers vividly:

Michael was fighting, fighting for his life. The main doctor held my hand and says, "I'm so sorry. He will go soon." So we was all just waiting for Michael to pass, really. I think we was all crying. So about ten or fifteen minutes after, about twenty minutes, I can't remember really, he came round. Miracle. He just come out of what he was in. Like "What's all the fuss about, what's the matter with you all standing round my bed?" kind of look.

Michael's unexpected recovery bought him an extra two months. In Stockholm he underwent several minor operations to his lungs, and spent a fortnight without eating, becoming dangerously frail. Andrew Davis was conducting the opening and closing concerts of the festival, and visited the hospital:

> It was deeply upsetting because it was like Michael wasn't there any more. It was like a sort of generic old man lying on the bed. There was nothing in the eyes any more. I can't tell you how distressing that was. Then that evening the Swedish Radio Orchestra did a performance of *A Child of Our Time* and when they got to the final ensemble I sat there weeping uncontrollably. Because there he was, in this hospital bed, just down the road.[26]

It became imperative to get Michael back to London, and on 24 November he returned via a specially chartered helicopter, staying for a period in Parkside Hospital, Wimbledon. The flight and the private medical treatment depleted his already battered resources, for he had neither health nor travel insurance. A tube was inserted into his windpipe to help him breathe, and it left him temporarily unable to speak. He then returned to the house in Isleworth. A hospital bed was installed in the living room, and there he lay, wired to an oxygen machine, tube-fed, as his body died on him inch by inch over these final weeks. Sally Groves was among his many visitors, and went for the last time on 21 December. "His face was very, very thin. Most beautiful, beautiful hands. The first time I went to see him he would sit upright in a chair. And we would talk. But he was terribly tired. There was a physical impediment. He talked very quietly. But he could talk. The second time I visited he was lying and couldn't get up. He was lying down. Close to death. You can feel it, can't you, death?"[28]

The bells rang in the new year. On 2 January 1998 Michael Tippett turned ninety-three, and insisted that champagne was poured into his feeding tube. That same day, and to his great delight, his great-great-niece was born.[29]

Thursday, 8 January started like any other day. In the afternoon, Andrew Coster returned from the local gym:

I opened the door, walked into the room. "Andrew" – Michael this is – "I can't breathe." He was struggling. I called straightaway the doctor. So we was just waiting for the doctor to come. So I'm just whispering in his ear, "Don't worry Michael. Everything's going to be fine. Everything's going to be fine. Don't worry." It was like he was struggling, but at peace. So the doctor came, a lady doctor. And the doctor just said, "This is the process of passing now." So we just had to wait basically, there was nothing more we could do. Couldn't use the [breathing] machine or anything. I think the doctor gave him . . . maybe morphine. We waited. And Michael was still kind of saying words, you know, you could hear words. So I went to Michael's face, because it was like he wanted to say something. So I went to his face and put my ear near his face. "What is it Michael? What is it?" He said, "Oh Andy." Andrew or Andy. I think it was Andy. So he said that twice. "Oh Andy, Oh Andy . . . ." And that was his last word. My name. Then he passed. We saw him pass. Saw his last breath. It was a big sigh. And that was it. His mouth was just . . . open.[30]

It was forty minutes past two in the afternoon. Bill Bowen had left instructions that in the not unexpected event of Michael's death, he was to be called immediately and nobody else was to be told. But on that day they couldn't get hold of him, and so Andrew and Sunee waited by the phone in limbo for some four hours, with Michael Tippett lying dead in the front room. It so happened that Bill was due to visit that evening and when he eventually arrived, Andrew caught him at the door to tell him the news. "He put his head down. He didn't go into the room at all, he didn't see Michael. So he didn't see the body at all. He went straight upstairs and he was like on this knowing-what-to-do procedure. But he was upset, because he was crying. We all were."

It was dark by this time. The news began to travel round the world. Andrew Coster went back into Michael's room: "I opened the French doors to let Michael's spirit out. You're free to go Michael, I said. Have a good journey."

DIARY:

London

Andrew Coster and his then wife Sunee lived with Michael in his Isleworth house for the last eighteen months of his life, as carers, nurses, confidantes, chauffeurs, cooks. Sunee has since returned to Thailand, and it has taken me a while to find a contact for Andrew. Welcomed into his living room, I find it hard to believe I'm there. He pauses the television – a Laurel and Hardy film, that remains frozen over the next two hours in *Another Fine Mess* that I find oddly transfixing. I ask Andrew only a few questions before he begins an exceptional monologue that he has plainly been waiting twenty years to deliver. It is no surprise to discover that he has since published a novel. The walls are adorned with his extraordinary paintings – mainly abstract, influenced by Jackson Pollock and, he tells me, by a Barbara Hepworth print that hung on the wall of Michael's house.

As Andrew relates Michael's various health crises, at times getting up to act out a special memory, I more than once find myself glancing at the Dicta-phone to check that its comforting little red light is blinking away happily, in a panic that I will lose a record of this conversation that has brought me closer to Michael Tippett than anything yet. At the first mention of the man he cared for two decades ago, Andrew's eyes are alight with nostalgia and rekindled affection.

I catch my breath after the interview draws to some sort of close, and Andrew gestures to a pile of bags and folders at the corner of the sofa. Like a magician gleefully pulling ever more rabbits out of his hat, he proceeds to present me with one of the most surprising Tippett archives I've yet encountered. There is no manuscript paper, no trove of hitherto undiscovered letters. Andrew and Sunee asked, amid the domestic scramble of sorting after Michael had died, whether they could keep a few bits of memorabilia. First come two brown leather purses, their contents strewn across the footstool in front of me. Bank cards: Lloyds Bank, Sir M. Tippett. AA breakdown insurance. A disabled parking sticker. Any number of parking tickets and (expensive) restaurant receipts, cards listing medical appointments, chiropodist appointments, haircuts. A great brick of a tape recorder that still works. Here are birthday cards, Christmas cards, travel itineraries, plane tickets, luggage tags, monogrammed handkerchiefs, and all the flotsam and jetsam accrued over two years of carting a distinguished composer across Europe, all the paraphernalia of getting a ninety-something-year-old man in failing health through the days. There are even X-Rays of Michael's chest, which Andrew holds up to the window, and I see the cirrus clouds of pneumonia streaked across the lungs, and the painfully thin torso. It feels almost indecent. Here is Michael Tippett – not in his own words or notes, nor in his role as Grand Old Man of British Music, but simply as an old, dying person. I want to feel haunted but instead am just disarmed by the defenceless grubbiness of these fragments. When Andrew produces a bright-red jacket of which I have seen photographs, stained at the neck, ripped at the arm, the atmosphere becomes uncanny. I realise that I have a strong temptation to smell the clothes, which I don't. Next come Faber-Castell pencils, sharpened over many years into stubs, evidently predating Andrew's time and used, he tells me, to put notes onto manuscript paper.

Andrew has carefully saved the best, the worst, thing until last. Suddenly he puts into my hand a dark-red container, about a foot high, with a screw-top. I know exactly what it is before I open the lid and look down to see a teaspoonful of grey dust at the bottom. Michael had always wanted his ashes to be scattered at his beloved Avebury, the henge monument of three stone circles, not far from Nocketts, that seemed like a set for *The Midsummer Marriage*. But Avebury forbids this, and Michael's will leaves the decision to others. In the event he was scattered in Richmond Park, underneath the "Malcolm Sargent" roses. Like Francesca Allinson, buried under the roots of her beloved trees all those decades before, he could help something grow. He would have giggled at the name – his old nemesis. For two months the gardeners left the patch of soil alone as a mark of respect. The walkways in Richmond Park have been changed since, and the roses aren't there any more.

But Andrew kept back a portion of the ashes. Inside the container is a piece of white card. "Southwest Middlesex Crematorium. The cremated remains of the late Sir Michael Kemp Tippett. Cremation Number 116887. Date: 15 January 1998." Strange and clichéd wisps of unsuitably religious phrases toll in my head. Once he had been conscientious objector number L15870. In Wormwood Scrubs he was prisoner number 5832. Now he is powder in red Tupperware. Cremation number 116887.

Playing back the recording later I am dismayed to hear nothing but my incoherent burbling. I have known Michael Tippett's childhood nickname, his favourite food (asparagus), his sexual tastes, his verbal ticks, his first love, the colour of his eyes, the contents of his dreams, his table manners, his bank statements, his earliest memories, his last words. But nothing prepares me for the curious, sad shyness of this strange introduction. Most of all I'm oddly gleeful at this amazing, unsettling souvenir of a life, and catch myself thinking, walking back to a Tube station through great mounds of dead leaves, whether any biographer before me has ever held their subject, quite literally, in the palm of an outstretched hand.

EPILOGUE

Just round the corner from the nursing home where Michael Tippett was born, John Amis, seventy-six years old, was in his London flat. "When [Bill] Bowen telephoned to say that Michael Tippett had died, I wept." Paul Crossley, on hearing the news, went to his piano and played through the first two piano sonatas. "What else could I do? My fingers expressed what I felt. But there was no reason to be sad. I loved it. He won't disappear."[1] For Bill's part: "I was fairly shattered. I don't remember it all in detail. The man was wonderful. He was a great mentor and in a sense it was a great love, because he was always ready to forgive. He accepted people for what they were. Always. He left me messages every day on my answerphone. The love never died. A mixture of love and deep respect. Because he had put his life into music."[2]

The funeral was at Hanworth Crematorium, on 15 January 1998. The Kreutzer Quartet played from Beethoven and from Tippett's String Quartet No. 3. The actor Alec McCowen (a friend of a friend) read from T.S. Eliot, Walt Whitman, and W.B. Yeats. Zoë Wanamaker, whose father had seen two Tippett operas into the world, recited Shakespeare, Auden, Blake, and ended with Siegfried Sassoon: "Everyone suddenly burst out singing [. . .] and the song was wordless; the singing will never be done."

Tippett's housekeepers, Josey and Heather, were in the congregation. "There weren't no mention of God," says Josey, which is what Tippett had stipulated. "It was nice," says Heather, "because they were just doing the service and a dove come right by the windows."[3] Wilfred Franks and his wife were invited. "We didn't go," his wife told a journalist. "Wilf didn't really want to." Asked why, Franks tried to explain. "Our relationship . . ." and then he broke off. "There is nothing more to say about Michael Tippett."[4] Franks spent the last years of his life living with family in Spain, and died in 2003, aged ninety-five. The last of their generation to go was Christopher Fry, who lived on, more or less forgotten by the theatrical world, and died in 2005, three years shy of his hundredth birthday. His last play was written to mark the millennium, and he called it *A Ringing of Bells*.

News of Tippett's death made the front pages. Television schedules were rearranged to pay tribute. In 1953 he had written to Priaulx Rainier: "We are in an age when only the very great genius can do what will live, and I'm certainly not that."[5] His obituaries disagreed, acclaiming "one of the greatest English composers since Elgar". The *Telegraph* thought him "assured of a place in the front rank", and the *Guardian* believed his music "destined to stay in the repertoire as long as classical music survives". "The final judgement is likely to be that few were greater."[6] On some aspects of his life they kept coy silence. Bill Bowen wrote to *The Times*: "Sir Michael Tippett would have hooted in derision at the final sentences of your otherwise admirable obituary. Instead of stating that he 'never married' and is 'survived by' (!) myself, why not say 'he was openly homosexual'? As his nearest and dearest for nearly three decades, I assure you that he always preferred honesty and candour to polite euphemisms."[7]

Tippett's centenary, in 2005, brought a large number of performances that, perhaps justifiably, led to accusations of overkill. BBC Radio 3 paid him the dubious tribute of setting up a debate on his music, with speakers for or against. Variations were written on a "theme of Michael Tippett"; his name was given to a school, a concert hall, and to a species of iris, deep purple, that grows in the greenhouses of Kew.

And that seemed to be it. His reputation fell so alarmingly that by the late 2000s, bar the continuing popularity of *A Child of Our Time*, it was as if Michael Tippett had been wiped from musical history. Dismissals of his work became more certain, just as opportunities to engage with it became scant. He disappeared from concert and opera seasons, and his music was broadcast rarely. Detractors felt vindicated: "Michael Tippett – a composer to forget", ran one headline. The numerous productions of his operas and their international success (in Australia, America, and Europe) were erased from the history books: "none of Tippett's operas caught on abroad or sold out at home", claims one account of his career. His comment that "nothing gets unjustly neglected" quickly took on a bitter dramatic irony. How was it that a composer who, in Ian Kemp's words, "contributed more to the English tradition than any other since Purcell" and was "one of the giants of the century" came to be so speedily forgotten?[8]

If only it were true, when it comes to the survival of a composer's music, that quality will out. But there are few whose immortality was less assured; few who suffered worse posthumous luck. A reputation is cemented above all else by money. Soon after Tippett's death it became apparent that his estate was in turmoil. The years of financial difficulty had taken their toll, exacerbated by the expense of a long stretch of ill health. Tippett's will named Bill Bowen as the chief beneficiary; there was a handful of legacies for close friends; and Amnesty International, Save the Children, and his beloved Peace Pledge Union were remembered to the tune of £25,000. The probate valuation of his estate was £156,718. But when the final sums were done, Tippett's debts amounted to £164,276.40. In exchange for the copyright of Tippett's pre-1957 compositions, which through a quirk in copyright law would have reverted to the composer's estate, Schott cleared the debt with a loan to be paid back out of royalties. The repayment took eight years. Only then did the Michael Tippett Foundation, the charitable trust Tippett had established in 1979, start to receive its share of his posthumous income. But this – as strictly stipulated by the terms of his will – may be used only to support young musicians and composers. Tippett died believing his music would survive without help, and, in a typical gesture of self-assured generosity, had cut off its financial lifeline. At the time of writing it is the case that not a penny of Tippett's royalties may be used to promote performance or study of his own music.[9]

The gap between the tributes at Tippett's death and the celebrations at his centenary was just seven years: a period so brief that it allowed no time for his achievements to settle. An estate needs torch bearers, but Tippett's great age saw him outlive the careers of many friends and colleagues who might have continued to support or perform his music. Bill Bowen missed the centenary year all but completely, recovering from a brain haemorrhage. Nicholas Wright, the manager of the Tippett Office – and, with Bowen, Tippett's co-executor – died in 2005. Tippett had severed all connections with any festival or town that might have been devoted to his music; his output can be difficult to perform and expensive to tour; he wrote relatively few short or occasional pieces that might fill a radio broadcast or be tucked into a concert programme; very little of his music lies within the abilities of most amateur groups; and he was obliged to sell a country house that could have been a mecca for fans and an archive to scholars. What seems remarkable is not that his star fell, but rather that his music managed to maintain even the slightest foothold in the new millennium that he had hoped to see.

Over the years of writing this book, Tippett has charmed and irritated, perplexed and thrilled me. I have lived his life more, it sometimes felt, than my own. His music was a constant, and I did not tire of it. I cannot listen to it objectively, and intense familiarity can smudge as easily as it can reveal. But I have written believing in the greatness of my subject, during a time when what once seemed his unquestionable importance was in danger of being forgotten. The reader will forgive me if, for these final pages, I let a burst of missionary enthusiasm take over.

"The value of his works up to but not necessarily including the second opera *King Priam* is uncontroversial", runs Tippett's entry

(2004) in the *Oxford Dictionary of National Biography*, also noting the "school of thought – articulated by the composer Robin Holloway and the musicologist Derrick Puffett among others – which sees the last three decades as a 'tragic decline'".[10] Tippett himself was happy to admit that not everything had been a success (of *The Ice Break*, for example: "I don't think it quite came off. It didn't do quite what I wanted").[11] But he maintained that his later music was among his best: "I hope I don't sound too pretentious, but there's been an increase of perhaps complexity, and depth certainly. You mature into a deeper sensibility, perhaps an old man's world." The third symphony he thought "deeper, richer, and with many more resonances in it" than the Concerto for Double String Orchestra.[12]

Tippett's music has often taken time to reveal all its secrets: unarguably, it is hard to play and tricky to grasp. The two decades since his death have not been long enough for the late works to settle themselves properly into his career. Much received opinion seems to have bedded in, meanwhile. Bright clothes do not a mystic make; "eccentric" is all too often a means of explaining a mode of living and thinking different to our own. But time seems to have branded Tippett something of a superannuated hippie: "the bonkers wizard of mysticism".[13] The title of his most famous essay collection, *Moving into Aquarius* (taken from a single paragraph in an essay on Schoenberg), has linked him yet further to new-age thinking of which, on close inspection, his work proves to be sharply critical. It is unusual, now, to read an appraisal of Tippett's career that does not mention the perceived failure of his last two operas and the weakness of his librettos. The case for the prosecution is extensive; the case for the defence rather shorter, although the composer and musicologist Malcolm Hayes has written that "the libretto of *The Ice Break* [. . .] deserves an unfashionable fanfare" and "is not the writing of someone whose literary skills are second-rate".[14] The voice of a character must not be confused with the voice of the composer: slang can say a great deal about those who choose to speak it. My own feeling is that if the librettos could somehow be considered in a vacuum free from the baggage of generally accepted disapprobation, audiences would find moments of clumsiness and impenetrability, but also of inspiration. I do not think that Tippett would disapprove of stagings that updated obsolete technology or outmoded vocabulary.

Meanwhile Tippett's political views, which made him for some a hero of humanitarianism, can still arouse disapproval and anger. The motives of conscientious objectors, especially to the Second World War, continue to be weighed in the balance, even as their cultural product endures. Alexander Goehr, himself an objector who accepted non-combatant duties, argues fiercely against Tippett's view that the gifted artist is exempt from even civilian war service: "I think of the poets whom [Tippett] set, who were killed in the war. And I think of Walter Leigh, who was a very gifted pupil of Hindemith's [killed in action in 1942]. I think of people who were killed on both sides, and I can't forgive Tippett for arguing that the reason why he shouldn't be in prison was because he had this artistic vision."[15]

Tippett has often been situated, as by the musicologist Philip Brett, within the "Britten era", whose "achievement" was that British classical music became "indelibly queer and left or conchie".[16] But neither politics nor sexuality was the motivating force for Tippett's creativity, which rarely reduces to self-portrait. It does an injustice to his imagination to assume he always composed in a code of autobiography, in need of cracking. The essence of his music is a compassionate universality, often at right angles to his own experience, as is never better proved by the sheer warmth and élan that triumphs in the music written from the depths of war and in the run-up to his prison sentence. Ian Kemp has much more persuasively banded him with Olivier Messiaen and Elliott Carter to form a trio of "important composers who seemed to stand back from the immediate pressures of the time".[17]

This is not to deny that Tippett lived deeply within his time, rather than on its edge; he was unusually attuned to its spirit, unusually reactive to its tumult. But his music was not embedded so concretely into its century that it cannot be removed. The title of his most famous work makes an easy pun for headlines and articles, but he should not be thought of as a man or a composer merely "of his time". He may be said to hold a mirror up to society, which is ephemeral, but also to humanity, which is constant. Frequently he risked being unfashionable so as to be bigger than fashion. Birmingham Opera Company's production of The Ice Break, it seemed to me, showed that the opera was not a depiction of 1970s society, but a dark fable that lent itself easily to reinvention. It was not – to invoke Derrick Puffett's phrase – Tippett's "retreat from mythology", but a reminder that myths can be urban as well as pastoral, and spring from a social context. "Relevance" may be over-emphasised as a criterion of quality, but the concerns of Tippett's music are ones of which we have desperate need in a world that seems more divided than ever. His was a timeless music, played in time.

In many ways Tippett was born too early, although he was aware of the good fortune of being born in England in 1905. It made him witness to two world wars, but he escaped, as so many composers of his generation did not, the sexual, political, or racial repressions that raged around the world during his ninety-three years. Imagining him for a moment transplanted to the twenty-first century, we might think of his watching on television as the planes flew into the Twin Towers, sitting in the Albert Hall as the spirituals from A Child of Our Time were included in a hastily reprogrammed memorial concert at that year's Proms, and thrilling to the eventual erection of the Freedom Tower on Ground Zero: "the rebuilding is finer than the building". Easy to imagine him marching in London against the Iraq War; easier still to imagine him becoming passionately sure that Britain should remain part of the European Union, but in fact he had approved of the Eurosceptic direction in which Tony Benn and others had led the Labour Party in the early 1980s.[18] What would he or his music have made of the social-media world and other technological advances? At the least, compositional software might have helped him in the years of his blindness. In the twenty years between his death and the publication of this book the Civil Partnership Act has been passed, same-sex marriage and same-sex adoption legalised. "He'd think it was wonderful," says Bill Bowen. "He belonged to the next century, almost."[19]

Much depends, in risking a value judgement, on where, in the mysterious alchemy of creation, in the transmission of music from soul to stave, the measuring tool is placed. Tippett struggled when writing down what he was hearing and imagining, the nearest parallel being not a painter who cannot draw but a writer who cannot spell. He was always punctilious about sound, often lackadaisical about notes, of which, it is often said of his music, there are too many (which could be likened to saying there is too much paint on a Jackson Pollock). His scores are awkwardly notated, frequently impractical, and contain mistakes and ambiguities. Some of the technical faults have been overstated, and to the many initial complaints of unplayability the riposte has been in triumphant further performances. He asks, even demands, of the listener a great deal. His music has been deemed embarrassing, and at the least it often requires audiences to collude with his own embarrassment threshold, always high. Art, for him, was not a place for politeness or caution.

In the awkwardnesses, in the disagreements, lies the element of who Tippett was as a composer. How could he have been other than fiercely divisive? Careers such as his do not, cannot, lead to unanimous or instant praise: for he refused, always, to compose within the bounds of his own technique. His skill and fluency as an orchestrator, and as a contrapuntalist, could be considerable, and many composers envied his ability to write straight into full score, or testified to his melodic gift, and to the accuracy and power of his ear and musicianship.[20] But, having mastered something, he moved on. To turn always to risk rather than comfort zone could be called self-sabotage, but it may be the cost of a ruthless commitment to invention and innovation. Tippett actively disdained his own facility, and would not be deceived by it into the production of music that was respectably competent. Instead he determinedly embraced the difficulties involved in widening his music's parameters: starting with an idea, and wrenching his technique up to meet it. A lack of fluency seemed to unleash, rather than constrict, his imagination; if nothing was initially possible, then nothing was impossible, either. He composed not because he could, but because he had to. The daring conclusion to draw is that he was not really a composer at all, but an extraordinary thinker who chose music out of several possible modes of expression, adding it to his roster of self-taught languages. Benjamin Britten apparently thought, with a slightly acidic perception, "that Tippett could have been just as distinguished if he had gone in for something other than music" and "wondered sometimes why he hadn't".[21] And Tippett himself admitted that the decision to compose "was almost a set of negatives", after other options, "education, politics, you name them", had dropped away. "And then one is left with this strange unknown."[22] That he therefore achieved what he did, gaining and never outliving the acclaim to which he had always looked forward with a seemingly unjustified certainty, must count as his triumph. The achievements are, I believe, threefold.

First, when on the staff at Morley College, and with the assistance of a powerful band of émigré musicians, he permanently altered and extended the musical repertoire enjoyed in this country, playing a major role in the restoration of composers such as Monteverdi and Purcell, conducting a number of historic British premieres, and reintroducing the counter-tenor voice to the world. His work with amateur and youth orchestras made a permanent contribution to generations of musicians.

Second, his five works for the theatre expanded the possibilities of staging, subject, and structure in British opera. While his last three may yet be deemed failed experiments in themselves, they must be seen, in their television-inspired transitions and their often game-changing first productions, as a vital bridge between the operas of Britten and of younger generations. The world of modern technology depicted in Nico Muhly's Two Boys; the contemporaneity of Jonathan Dove's Flight or Mark-Anthony Turnage's Anna Nicole and Greek; the homosexuality in operas based on Brokeback Mountain or Angels in America: all are topics that Tippett's operas were the first to include.

Third, Tippett produced music of, to use his phrase, "vitality ever-renewed" – over thirty-two hours of it. His was a creative urge that blazed steadily. There are some pieces that I listen to with more passion than others: at the bottom of the pile are the piano

concerto, the fourth quartet, *Songs for Dov*, and *New Year*, an opera
whose weaknesses it seems to me any Tippett advocate must come
to terms with (which is not to deny its many passages of wild
and wayward radiance). But I do not believe that Tippett suffered
a creative decline as he grew older. Of his last works *The Rose Lake*
and the fifth quartet seem, in their youth and in their leave-taking,
to encompass life. Tippett's especial wonder as a composer, and as
a thinker, lies for me in his opera *King Priam* and *The Vision of Saint
Augustine*; in the Concerto for Orchestra and Triple Concerto; and in
his last two symphonies and piano sonatas. In these he achieves an
articulation of thought in sound, melding an intellectual and moral
quest with an explosion of imagination and invention that seems to
remap British music: of his generation, he was the British composer who most successfully integrated his national inheritance with
the great experiments and developments of Europe and America.
Andrew Davis places him "up there with the greatest twentieth-
century composers on an international level".[23] It is Symphony No.
3, I think, that stands as Tippett's monument, his manifesto, and
his masterpiece.

Refusal to teach composition, join a faculty, or write a consistent
musical language has surely limited to some degree Tippett's own
presence in others' music. And the final proof of influence may
be rebellion. But his was a career that helped to shape the music
we hear today. Tippett admitted his debt to Britten; yet to be fully
explored is Britten's vital debt to Tippett. And while the two are
frequently banded together as much through geographical coincidence and force of habit than anything else, the pianist Graham
Johnson has said that "for a crucial period between 1943 and 1953,
Tippett's music was a major influence on Britten's work and vice
versa".[24] It may not be fanciful to consider Tippett "influencing"
Beethoven, in the sense of its being impossible to hear Beethov-
en's Ninth Symphony without hearing Tippett's third. Meanwhile
leading composers of the current generation, from Julian Anderson
to Michael Berkeley, James MacMillan to David Matthews, acknowledge Tippett's presence in their compositional DNA. The composer
George Benjamin writes:

My great friend Oliver Knussen used to say that the degree of exuberance in Tippett's music made it well-nigh irresistible. My own feelings are similar – and I have always admired both the energy and ardent lyricism of the earlier Romantic period as well as the more astringent though imposing tone of the modernist 1960s works. Such independence and strength of vision mark Tippett out as an outstanding figure in twentieth-century British music.[25]

But the influence of the greatest composers goes beyond the musical. If Tippett earns the word "visionary", it is not only in his depiction of transcendence and ecstasy, but in his dreams and aspirations for life on earth. His work is often banded into a tripartite division: an early period of counterpoint and lushly orchestrated melody; a middle period of fragmentation; and a late period of renewed lyricism. This will serve, but in many ways Tippett's output is a single epic of such neat structure that it appears planned from the outset, one of the most complete bodies of music ever composed. The late music seems to make sense of the early. Had he died or retired in mid-life his compositions would chart a slow erosion of hope. But his longevity permitted him a career in sonata form: an exposition of hope and optimism, a long development of bleakness and turmoil, and a recapitulation of joyousness tinged with the knowledge of all that has gone before. All things fall and are built again. His was a career that took a lifetime to conclude that hope and joy could emerge from the midst of terror, and that our need for visions of unity is not cancelled out by the inevitability of discord or the necessity of dialectic. In this conclusion lies his importance. This is not to confuse intention with achievement. It is Tippett's notes, in binding together light with shadow, Beethoven with blues, tradition with modernity, such that each is inconceivable without the other, which enact the unity-in-diversity of which he continued, with the peculiar naivety that exists within great courage, to believe humanity was capable. It is Tippett's music, the sound it makes, that both explodes and rebuilds joy and solace as it is played and listened to. In the final reckoning what should not be underestimated is the sheer enjoyment of hearing his music, of being guided through bleakness into consolation. "Do you think", he was asked in a television interview, "that if your music gave comfort, that would be worth it?" The answer was instantaneous and smiling. "Yes. Absolutely."[26]

Early in his life Tippett quoted T.S. Eliot approvingly to David Ayerst: "'the more perfect the artist, the more completely separate in him will be the man who suffers and the mind which creates'. I have come to realise that at last."[27] On these terms, a biography of Tippett may be deemed at worst distraction and at best a pleasure incidental to appreciation or understanding of his music. But he came to believe his life and music intertwined, each necessary to the other. And Eliot, later, seemed to retract his view that "the progress of the artist" is "a continual extinction of personality", claiming instead that the work of a great poet had to be "united by one significant, consistent, and developing personality".[28] No biographer could capture completely the personality threaded through Tippett's many twists and turns, his contradictions and consistencies, his boundless intellect. More will come, critical and praiseful, as he continues to make his steady and inexorable progress through the complex three-ply of relevance, datedness, and timelessness. His music will have to find a way of existing without him. It will take a while yet for old scores to be settled, for clear perspectives to be gained, for the clouds of controversy to part and reveal Michael Tippett, in all his shadow and light, finally whole. My hope is that, with his life narrated, his creations may more fully be understood, and so more easily fly free. Now, the music must speak for itself. The curtain rises.

Whether society has felt music valuable or needful I have gone on writing because I must. And I know that my true function within a society that embraces all of us, is to continue an age-old tradition, fundamental to our civilization, which goes back into pre-history and will go forward into the unknown future. This tradition is to create images from the depths of the imagination and to give them form whether visual, intellectual or musical. For it is only through images that the inner world communicates at all. Images of the past, shapes of the future. Images of vigour for a decadent period, images of calm for one too violent. Images of reconciliation for worlds torn by division. And in an age of mediocrity and shattered dreams, images of abounding, generous, exuberant beauty.

Michael Tippett
1905–1998

CAST LIST

MT = Michael Tippett

Allinson, (Enid) Francesca (1902–45): musician and writer who maintained a passionate friendship with MT in the 1930s and 1940s; author of *A Childhood* (Hogarth Press, 1938); committed suicide 6 April 1945; brothers Adrian (an artist) and Cyril also friends of MT.

Amis, John (1922–2013): arts administrator and broadcaster; friend and unofficial assistant to MT.

Auden, Wystan Hugh (1907–73): English-American poet, from whom MT twice rejected an invitation to collaborate.

Ayerst, David (1904–92): journalist, school inspector, teacher, and lifelong friend of MT; married (1936) Larema Fisher, to whose family MT became close.

Barker, George (1913–91): poet of the New Apocalyptics Movement with whom MT hoped to collaborate.

Barr, Margaret (1904–91): choreographer; founder of a school of dance-mime at Dartington Hall in Devon, for whose London performances MT wrote music.

Bergmann, Walter (1902–88): lawyer and musician who escaped Nazi Germany for England, where MT invited him to join the Music Department at Morley College; specialist in recorder and Early music.

Boult, Adrian (1889–1983): conductor; mentor to MT at Royal College of Music; conducted the troubled premiere of MT's Symphony No. 2.

Bowen, (William) Meirion "Bill" (1940–): musician and journalist; partner of and assistant to MT for four decades.

Britten, Benjamin (1913–76): composer; supporter of MT during the war and a lifelong friend.

Busch, William (1901–45): pacifist composer and friend of MT.

Bush, Alan (1900–95): composer, friend of MT; his committed communism led to their political disagreement.

Coster, Andrew (1960–): MT's carer from 1996, joined by his wife Sunee.

Crossley, Paul (1944–): pianist, friend of MT; first performer of third and fourth piano sonatas.

Davis, Colin (1927–2013): leading British conductor and major supporter of MT.

Despard, Charlotte (1844–1939): Anglo-Irish suffragist and founder of the Women's Freedom League; distant relation to MT's mother, Isabel, whom she much inspired.

Dienes, Paul (1882–1952): Hungarian mathematician and friend of MT, with whom he lived briefly in 1952.

Eliot, Thomas Stearns (1888–1965): Nobel Prize-winning poet; friend and mentor to MT.

Fisher, (Douglas) Bryan (1916–2004): brother-in-law of David Ayerst; conscientious objector; close friend and occasional lover of MT during the war.

Fisher, Shelagh (1909–2000): sister-in-law of David Ayerst to whom MT proposed marriage in 1936.

Forster, Edward Morgan (1879–1970): novelist; distant friend of MT.

Franks, Wilfred (1908–2003): British artist with whom MT pursued an intense love affair during the 1930s.

Fry, Christopher (1907–2005): poet and verse-dramatist, born Arthur Harris; close friend of MT's when both were on the staff of Hazelwood School, Oxted; wrote the text for *Dance, Clarion Air* and *Crown of the Year*.

Gardiner, Rolf (1902–71): English rural revivalist, co-founder of the Cleveland work camps; MT's involvement led to their disagreement.

Glock, William (1908–2000): music critic and early supporter of MT, to whom, with his wife Clement, he became close; eventually controller of music at the BBC (1960–73) and director of the Proms (1960–73).

Goehr, Alexander (1932–): composer to whom MT was a mentor and inspiration, both musically and politically, although the relationship cooled in MT's old age; son of Walter Goehr.

Goehr, Walter (1903–60): German conductor and one of MT's earliest advocates; conducted premiere of *A Child of Our Time*.

Götsch, Georg (1895–1956): leading figure in German Youth Movement; director of first Cleveland work camp, and of a music school in Frankfurt an der Oder, visited by MT in 1932.

Groves, Sally (1949–): publisher (eventually creative director) at Schott Music from 1974.

Haines, David (1956–): composer, trained at Bristol University; close friend of and often driver for MT.

Harber, Denzil Dean (1909–66): Trotskyist activist; leader of Youth Militant Group (or Bolshevik-Leninist Group), which MT joined in the 1930s.

Hartog, Howard (1913–90): music publisher at Schott; agent at Ingpen and Williams, which represented MT as a conductor; dedicatee of Symphony No. 3; married pianist Margaret Kitchin (who premiered Piano Sonata No. 2).

Hawker, Karl (1921–84): artist; conscientious objector; briefly MT's lover during the war; the relationship revived in 1958 and patchily continued until 1974; committed suicide in 1984.

Hawker, Susan (1947–) and **Sarah (1949–):** daughters of Karl Hawker and his wife, Anne.

Hepworth, Barbara (1903–75): sculptor; designer of *The Midsummer Marriage* and friend of MT.

Hopkins, Antony (1921–2014): composer and broadcaster; friend, with his first wife Alison Purves, of MT.

Hubback, Eva (1886–1949): feminist, economist, suffragist, and (from 1927) principal of Morley College, where she appointed MT as director of music in 1940.

Kallin, Anna Samoylovna "Niouta" (1896–1984): producer for BBC Third Programme; Oskar Kokoschka's mistress; lived in Chelsea with exiled Russian socialite Princess Salomea Nikolayevna Andronikova.

Kemp, Henry (1858–1944): MT's father; after studies at Oxford went into business with his father and faced criminal trial for his father's fraud; eventually owner of Beau-Site Hotel in Cannes, retiring off the proceeds and marrying in 1903; departed for Europe in 1919; returned, to Somerset, in 1931; moved to Exmouth early in the war where he died from injuries sustained in an air raid.

Kemp, Ian (1931–2011): publisher and musicologist; author of *Tippett: The Composer and His Music*, in the writing of which he became, with his wife the conductor Sian Edwards, MT's close friend.

Kemp, Isabel (1880–1969): MT's mother, a novelist, suffragist, and eventually painter.

Kemp, Peter (1904–92): MT's brother, a distinguished naval historian.

Kemp, Phyllis (1904–83): MT's cousin; her passionate Marxist politics led first to their closer union and eventually to a major row; fell out of contact from 1937 to 1948; moved to GDR; married Kunwar Muhammad Ashraf; professor at Humboldt University, Berlin; published a number of political articles and monographs.

Kennington, Eric (1888–1960): sculptor and official war artist in both world wars, with whom MT had a troubled relationship; MT felt much affection towards his son, Christopher (1925–2015).

Langford, Roy Mulholland (1900–58): actor, theatre manager, supposedly of White Russian descent; MT's lover from c.1924–1929; manager of theatres in Wimbledon and Hammersmith.

Layard, John (1891–1974): anthropologist and psychologist; MT's analyst and mentor.

Lewis, Ben and **Miriam**: tenants of MT's in Oxted, c.1938–44.

Machin, Arnold (1911–99): artist; imprisoned at Wormwood Scrubs as a conscientious objector.

Mark, Jeffrey (1898–1965): composer and economist; mature student at Royal College of Music during MT's tenure; dedicatee of Concerto for Double String Orchestra.

Maude, Evelyn (1891–1971): Oxted resident who became MT's "guardian angel".

Maynard, Edric (1917–47): conscientious objector in MT's circle; suffered from schizophrenia.

Minchinton, John (1928–90): conductor; occasional student of Herbert von Karajan and Pablo Casals; MT's assistant and sometime lover from c.1945; of much assistance in preparation of ink score of The Midsummer Marriage and subsequent works; premiered MT's Four Songs from the British Isles in 1958, in which year they parted acrimoniously; married Jessica Jenkins in 1974, continuing to conduct with, among others, the London Bach Group.

Modlen, Graham (1956–): architect; accompanied MT to Senegal in 1990, prior to the composition of The Rose Lake.

Morley, (Hugh) Oliver (1928–87): musically gifted son of mathematician and publisher Frank Morley; piano pupil of MT's 1935–39; made Associate, Royal College of Music and Fellow, Royal College of Organists; died unexpectedly in a National Autistic Society home in Gloucestershire.

Morris, Reginald Owen (1886–1948): professor at Royal College of Music; MT's most inspiring teacher.

Myant, Nick (1918–2015): pupil of David Ayerst at Blundell's School in Devon with whom MT had a close and loving friendship in the mid-1930s; eventually an internationally renowned expert in lipid research.

Newton, (Brean Leslie) Douglas "Den" (1920–2001): poet and museum curator, born in Malay States; began close friendship and eventually an affair with MT in 1939; conscientious objector working on various land schemes in Sussex and Cambridgeshire; potential collaborator for the opera that became The Midsummer Marriage; in 1946 married American writer Mary Lee Settle (1918–2005); moved to New York in 1956 and became revered curator of Oceanic Art, eventually chairman of the Department of Arts of Africa at Metropolitan Museum.

Parvin, Sidney: farmer on whose land was situated MT's first home in Oxted; brother (Edwin) Dudley the dedicatee of *Variations for Dudley*.

Pears, Peter (1910–86): tenor; partner and muse to Benjamin Britten, many of whose works he premiered; friend and supporter of MT; premiered *Boyhood's End*; *A Child of Our Time*; *The Heart's Assurance*; *Songs for Achilles*.

Pennyman, Ruth (1893–1983): landowner in Middlesbrough who, with her husband, Jim Pennyman, supported land schemes and work camps to help unemployed miners during the Great Depression; in which capacity she met MT, remaining a lifelong friend.

Rainier, (Ivy) Priaulx (1903–86): South African-born composer (of, inter alia, a violin concerto premiered by Yehudi Menuhin, a cello concerto premiered by Jacqueline du Pré, and vocal works for Peter Pears); grew close to MT after the war; member of Barbara Hepworth and Ben Nicholson's artists' colony in St Ives, Cornwall.

Russ, Aubrey (1891–1957): teacher; lawyer; friend of MT's after meeting at the Proms in the early 1920s; short-lived and ill-fated house-share with MT at Hazelwood School ended in scandal.

Sackville-West, Edward (1901–65): music critic and early promoter of MT's work; eventually a novelist.

Sargent, Malcolm (1895–1967): conductor; alumnus of Stamford School in Lincolnshire, where MT was also a pupil; MT's conducting teacher at the Royal College of Music; conducted first performance of Symphony No. 1, though remained sceptical about MT's compositions.

Sedgwick, Anthony (1919–43): pupil at Blundell's School in Devon to whom MT became close in the mid-1930s; drowned on convoy in the Mediterranean 1943.

Seiber, Mátyás (1905–60): Hungarian-born composer, employed by MT at Morley College.

Sellick, Phyllis (1911–2007): pianist; premiered *Fantasia on a Theme of Handel* and Piano Sonata No. 1; with her husband, pianist Cyril Smith (1909–74, a contemporary of MT's at the RCM), gave a concert at Wormwood Scrubs during MT's imprisonment.

Shaxson, Eric: stockbroker turned farmer; Oxted neighbour, with wife Dorothy, of MT, who taught their children at Hazelwood School; MT stayed at their home, Elmsted Farm in Midhurst, when his property was bombed in 1944.

Sims, Josey: MT's housekeeper at Nocketts.

Strecker, Wilhelm (1884–1958): director from 1920 of Schott Music, to which he invited MT to submit a portfolio of scores; son Hugo was a director of the London branch who, in agreeing to publish Piano Sonata No. 1, began MT's lifelong relationship with Schott.

Sweet, Heather: MT's housekeeper at Nocketts.

Sumsion, Herbert "John" (1899–1995): composer associated with Gloucester Cathedral and Three Choirs Festival; contemporary at Royal College of Music to MT, who fell in love with him.

Tillett, Michael (1922–2009): compositional assistant and amanuensis to MT for fifty years, producing vocal scores and helping MT through eventual blindness; director of music at Highgate School and Rugby School.

Tinkler, Frances (c.1869–1950): MT's piano teacher at Stamford School.

Tippett, George (1829–99): MT's paternal grandfather; initially a wealthy property tycoon, he went bankrupt and was imprisoned for fraud.

Tippett, Henry, Isabel, Peter – see Kemp (the family changed its name in the 1920s).

Turnbull, Fred: signalman at Oxted and Labour Party member; daughter Rose (b. 1923) developed an unreciprocated passion for MT.

Vaughan Williams, Ralph (1872–1958): composer; on the staff at Royal College of Music during MT's studies; supported MT during the war; his second wife Ursula Wood (1911–2007) became especially close to MT in widowhood.

Vyner, Michael (1943–1989): music publisher at Schott Music; musical director of London Sinfonietta.

White, Eric Walter (1905–85): arts writer and administrator; supporter and eventually friend of MT when working for CEMA and its successor, the Arts Council.

Wilson, Bronwen (1916–44): daughter of Ben and Miriam Lewis, with whom she shared MT's rental cottages in Oxted; married Jack Wilson, with whom she had two children, Ian (b. 1941) and Sheila (b. 1944); killed in a V-1 attack on the cottage, 8 August 1944.

Wogan, Judy (1888–c.1966): theatre owner and playwright; lover of Francesca Allinson; wrote text for *Miners*.

Wright, (James Stephen) Nicholas (1940–2005): Egyptologist and arts dealer; director of the Tippett Office.

LIST OF WORKS BY MICHAEL TIPPETT

The following is a complete list of the published works of Michael Tippett by date of completion, using the numbering system MT1–65. There follows a list of unpublished works, using the numbering system MTi–xxxiii. Each entry includes, where known or applicable: dates of composition; date of completion in square brackets; texts used; details of first performance. Only stand-alone arrangements by Tippett himself are included, as addenda to the original work (e.g. MT4a). Discrepancies with previous lists are explained within the main text.

MT1: String Quartet No. 1
1934–5 [23 September 1935]
rev. autumn 1943
Brosa Quartet; Mercury Theatre, London, 9 December 1935

MT2: Piano Sonata No. 1
1936–8 [1 July 1938]
rev. 1942, 1954
Phyllis Sellick; Queen Mary Hall, London, 11 November 1938

MT3: Concerto for Double String Orchestra
1938–9 [6 June 1939]
South London Orchestra and Marie Dare string quartet, cond. MT; Morley College, London, 21 April 1940

MT4: *A Child of Our Time*
1939–41 [c.April 1941]
Oratorio for soloists, chorus, and orchestra; text by the composer
Joan Cross, Margaret McArthur, Peter Pears, Roderick Lloyd, Morley College Choir, London Region Civil Defence Choir, London Philharmonic Orchestra, cond. Walter Goehr; Adelphi Theatre, London, 19 March 1944

MT4a: Five Negro Spirituals
[arr. 1957]

MT5: Fantasia on a Theme of Handel
1939/41 [11 November 1941]
For piano and orchestra
Phyllis Sellick, London Symphony
    Orchestra, cond. Walter Goehr;
    Wigmore Hall, London, 7
    March 1942

**MT6: Two Madrigals: The Source
    and The Windhover**
1941–2 [March 1942]
For unaccompanied choir, setting
    "The Source" by Edward
    Thomas; "The Windhover" by
    Gerard Manley Hopkins
Morley College Choir, cond.
    Walter Bergmann; Morley Col-
    lege, London, 17 July 1943

**MT7: String Quartet No. 2 in F
    sharp**
1942 [5 December 1942]
Zorian Quartet; Wigmore Hall,
    London, 27 March 1943

MT8: Boyhood's End
1943 [May 1943]
Cantata for tenor and piano, set-
    ting text from Far Away and Long
    Ago by W.H. Hudson
Peter Pears, Benjamin Britten;
    Morley College, London, 5 June
    1943

MT9: Fanfare No. 1 for brass
1943 [September 1943]
Band of the Northamptonshire
    Regiment; St Matthew's church,

Northampton, 21 September
1943

MT10: Plebs Angelica
1943–4 [January 1944]
Motet for double choir, setting a
    mediaeval Latin lyric
Fleet Street Choir, cond. T.B. Law-
    rence; Canterbury Cathedral, 16
    September 1944

MT11: The Weeping Babe
1944 [December 1944]
Motet for soprano solo and mixed
    choir, setting a poem by Edith
    Sitwell
BBC Singers, cond. Leslie Wood-
    gate; BBC studios, London, 24
    December 1944

MT12: Symphony No. 1
1944–5 [25 August 1945]
Liverpool Philharmonic Orchestra,
    cond. Malcolm Sargent; Phil-
    harmonic Hall, Liverpool, 10
    November 1945

**MT13: Preludio al Vespro di Monte-
    verdi for organ**
1946 [5 July 1946]
Geraint Jones; Central Hall, West-
    minster, 5 July 1946

MT14: String Quartet No. 3
1945–6 [September 1946]
Zorian Quartet; Wigmore Hall,
    London, 19 October 1946

**MT15: Little Music for String
    Orchestra**
1946 [c. October 1946]

Jacques Orchestra, cond. Reginald
  Jacques; Wigmore Hall,
  London, 9 November 1946

**MT16: Suite in D, for the Birthday of
Prince Charles**
1948 [c. November 1948]
BBC Symphony Orchestra, cond.
  Adrian Boult; BBC Third
  Programme, tx. 15 November
  1948 (pre-recorded)

MT17: The Heart's Assurance
1950–51 [April 1951]
Song cycle for high voice and
  piano, setting poems by Sidney
  Keyes and Alun Lewis
Peter Pears, Benjamin Britten;
  Wigmore Hall, London, 7 May
  1951

MT18: The Midsummer Marriage
1946–52 [11 October 1952]
Opera in three acts; text by the
  composer
Covent Garden Opera, cond. John
  Pritchard; soloists including
  Joan Sutherland (Jenifer) and
  Richard Lewis (Mark); scenery
  and costumes by Barbara Hep-
  worth; choreography by John
  Cranko; directed by Christopher
  West; Royal Opera House,
  London, 27 January 1955

MT18a: Ritual Dances
1949–50
Arrangement from Acts Two and
  Three of The Midsummer Marriage,
  for orchestra and optional
  chorus

Basel Kammerorchester, cond.
  Paul Sacher; Musiksaal, Basel,
  Switzerland, 13 February 1953

**MT19: Variations on an Elizabethan
Theme: A Lament**
1952–3
For string orchestra, part of the
  multi-composer Variations on an
  Elizabethan Theme
Aldeburgh Festival Orchestra,
  cond. Benjamin Britten; BBC
  Third Programme, tx. 16 June
  1953

MT20: Dance, Clarion Air
1953
Madrigal for five voices, setting
  words by Christopher Fry; part
  of the multi-composer A Garland
  for the Queen
Golden Age Singers and Cambridge University Madrigal
  Society, cond. Boris Ord; Royal
  Festival Hall, London, 1 June
  1953

MT21: Fanfare No. 2
1953 [c. May 1953]
Bournemouth Symphony
  Orchestra; Bournemouth, 15
  October 1953

MT22: Fanfare No. 3
1953 [June 1953]
RAF St Mawgan; St Ives church
  tower, Cornwall, 6 June 1953

**MT23: Fantasia Concertante on a
Theme of Corelli**
1952–3 [c. July 1953]

BBC Symphony Orchestra, cond.
MT; Usher Hall, Edinburgh, 29
August 1953

MT24: Divertimento on "Sellinger's Round"
1953–4 [July 1954]
For chamber orchestra
Collegium Musicum Zurich, cond.
Paul Sacher; Tonhalle, Zurich,
Switzerland, 5 November 1954

MT25: Four Inventions for descant and treble recorders
1954
Freda Dinn, Walter Bergmann;
Froebel Institute, London, 1
August 1954

MT26: Concerto for Piano and Orchestra
1953–5 [20 August 1955]
Louis Kentner, City of Birmingham
Symphony Orchestra, cond.
Rudolf Schwarz; Town Hall,
Birmingham, 30 October 1956

MT27: Sonata for Four Horns
1955 [12 December 1955]
Dennis Brain Wind Ensemble;
Wigmore Hall, London, 20
December 1955

MT28: Bonny at Morn
1956
Northumbrian folk-song set for
unison voices and recorders
Singers from international
Pestalozzi Children's Village;
Trogen, Switzerland, April
1956

MT29: Four Songs from the British Isles
1957 [c. July 1957]
For unaccompanied choir
London Bach Group, cond. John
Minchinton; Abbaye de Royau-
mont, Seine-et-Oise, France, 6
July 1958

MT30: Over the Sea to Skye
1957
For unaccompanied choir, discarded from MT29 for copyright
reasons
National Chamber Choir, cond.
Celso Antunes; National Gallery
of Ireland, 31 July 2003

MT31: Symphony No. 2
1955–7 [13 November 1957]
BBC Symphony Orchestra, cond.
Adrian Boult; Royal Festival
Hall, London, 5 February 1958

MT32: Crown of the Year
1958 [June 1958]
Cantata for chorus and instrumental ensemble, setting words by
Christopher Fry
Badminton School Choir and
ensemble, cond. MT; Badminton School, Bristol, 25 July
1958

MT33: Wadhurst
1958
Hymn tune setting John
Campbell's "Unto the Hills",
a paraphrase of Psalm 121;
written for the Salvation Army

MT34: Lullaby
1959
For six voices, setting a poem by
    W.B. Yeats
Deller Consort; Victoria and Albert
    Museum, London, 31 January
    1960

MT35: Music
1960
Unison song for voice(s) and
    piano; setting verses of a poem
    by John Keats
Combined choirs of the East
    Sussex and West Kent Choral
    Festival, cond. Trevor Harvey;
    Assembly Halls, Tunbridge
    Wells, 26 April 1960

MT36: Words for Music Perhaps
1960
Instrumental interludes, to be
    interleaved with recitations of
    poetry by W.B. Yeats
Bee Duffell, Sheila Manahan,
    Allan McCelland, instrumental
    ensemble, cond. MT; BBC Third
    Programme, tx. 8 June 1960

MT37: Songs for Achilles
1961
Three songs for tenor and guitar;
    text by the composer
Peter Pears, Julian Bream; Great
    Glemham House, Suffolk, 7
    July 1961

MT38: Magnificat and Nunc Dimittis
1961
For chorus and organ

St John's College Chapel Choir,
    cond. George Guest; St John's
    College Chapel, Cambridge, 13
    March 1962

MT39: King Priam
1958–61 [14 October 1961]
Opera in three acts; text by the
    composer
Covent Garden Opera, cond. John
    Pritchard; soloists including
    Forbes Robinson (King Priam);
    scenery and costumes by Sean
    Kenny; directed by Sam Wan-
    amaker; Coventry Theatre, 29
    May 1962

MT39a: Prelude, Recitative, and Aria
1964
Arrangement from Act Three of
    King Priam, for flute, oboe, and
    keyboard
Oriana Trio; BBC Third Pro-
    gramme, tx. 1 February 1964

MT40: Piano Sonata No. 2
1962 [March 1962]
Margaret Kitchin; Freemasons'
    Hall, Edinburgh, 3 September
    1962

**MT41: Incidental music for
Shakespeare's The Tempest**
1962 [16 May 1962]
Kerry Gardner (Ariel); ensemble
    dir. John Lambert; Old Vic
    Theatre, London, 29 May 1962

MT41a: Songs for Ariel
Three songs for voice and key-
    board or ensemble

Grayston Burgess, Virginia
  Pleasants; Fenton House,
  Hampstead, 21 September 1962

MT42: Praeludium for brass, bells, and percussion
1962 [August 1962]
BBC Symphony Orchestra, cond.
  Antal Doráti; Royal Festival
  Hall, London, 14 November
  1962

MT43: Concerto for Orchestra
1962–3 [June 1963]
London Symphony Orchestra,
  cond. Colin Davis; Usher Hall,
  Edinburgh, 28 August 1963

MT43a: Mosaic
1980
Arrangement of first movement,
  for wind band
National Symphony Orchestra
  of Washington, cond. Hugh
  Wolff; Wolf Trap Festival,
  Virginia, 29 June 1980

MT44: The Vision of Saint Augustine
1963–5 [10 April 1965]
For baritone solo, chorus, and
  orchestra
Dietrich Fischer-Dieskau, BBC
  Chorus and Symphony
  Orchestra, cond. MT; Royal Festival Hall, London, 19 January
  1966

MT45: Severn Bridge Variations: Variation 6
1966
For orchestra, part of the
multi-composer *Severn Bridge Var-*
  iations on the traditional Welsh
  melody "Braint"
BBC Training Orchestra, cond.
  Adrian Boult; Brangwyn Hall,
  Swansea, 11 January 1967

MT46: The Knot Garden
1965–9 [20 February 1969]
Opera in three acts; text by the
  composer
Covent Garden Opera, cond. Colin
  Davis; soloists including Joseph-
  ine Barstow (Denise) and Jill
  Gomez (Flora); set design by
  Timothy O'Brien; directed by
  Peter Hall; Royal Opera House,
  London, 2 December 1970

MT47: Songs for Dov
1969–70 [9 February 1970]
Three songs for tenor and
  orchestra, text by the composer
Gerald English, London Sinfonietta,
  cond. MT; University College,
  Cardiff, 12 October 1970

MT48: The Shires Suite
1965/69/70
For orchestra and chorus
Schola Cantorum of Oxford,
  Leicestershire Schools Sym-
  phony Orchestra, cond. MT;
  Cheltenham Town Hall, 8 July
  1970

MT49: In Memoriam Magistri
1971
For flute, clarinet, and string
  quartet

London Sinfonietta, cond. Elgar
Howarth; St John's, Smith
Square, London, 17 June 1972

MT50: Symphony No. 3
1970–72 [30 March 1972]
Heather Harper, London Sym-
phony Orchestra, cond. Colin
Davis; Royal Festival Hall,
London, 22 June 1972

MT51: Piano Sonata No. 3
1972–3 [1 March 1973]
Paul Crossley; Assembly Rooms,
Bath, 26 May 1973

MT52: *The Ice Break*
1973–6 [27 January 1976]
Opera in three acts, text by the
composer
Covent Garden Opera, cond. Colin
Davis; soloists including Heath-
er Harper (Nadia) and John
Shirley-Quirk (Lev); set design
by Ralph Koltai; directed by
Sam Wanamaker; Royal Opera
House, London, 7 July 1977

MT53: Symphony No. 4
1976–7 [18 April 1977]
Chicago Symphony Orchestra,
cond. Georg Solti; Orchestra
Hall, Chicago, 6 October 1977

MT54: String Quartet No. 4
1977–8 [26 September 1978]
Lindsay Quartet; Assembly Rooms,
Bath, 20 May 1979

**MT55: Triple Concerto
for violin, viola, and cello**
1978–9 [30 November 1979]
György Pauk, Nobuko Imai, Ralph
Kirshbaum, London Symphony
Orchestra, cond. Colin Davis;
Royal Albert Hall, London, 22
August 1980

MT56: *Wolf Trap Fanfare*
1980 [4 February 1980]
National Symphony Orchestra
of Washington, cond. Hugh
Wolff; Wolf Trap Festival,
Virginia, 29 June 1980

MT57: *The Mask of Time*
1980–2 [16 December 1982]
For soloists, chorus, and orchestra;
text written and compiled by
the composer
Faye Robinson, Yvonne Minton,
Robert Tear, John Cheek,
Tanglewood Festival Chorus,
Boston Symphony Orchestra,
cond. Colin Davis; Symphony
Hall, Boston, 5 April 1984

MT57a: *Triumph*
1992
A paraphrase on music from *The
Mask of Time*, for concert band
Ohio State Band and University
of Michigan State Band, cond.
Craig Kirchhoff; Ohio State
University, 24 February 1993

MT58: *The Blue Guitar*
1982–3
For solo guitar

Julian Bream; Ambassador Auditorium, Pasadena, California, 9
November 1983

MT59: Festal Brass with Blues
1983 [16 September 1983]
Fairey Engineering Band, cond.
Howard Williams; Hong Kong
Arts Festival, 6 February 1984

MT60: Piano Sonata No. 4
1983–4 [December 1984]
Paul Crossley; Japan America
Theatre, Los Angeles, 14
January 1985

MT61: New Year
1985–88 [19 December 1988]
Opera in three acts, text by the
composer
Houston Grand Opera, cond. John
de Main; soloists including
Helen Field (JoAnn); set design
by Alison Chitty; directed by
Peter Hall; Cullen Theater,
Wortham Theater Center, Houston, Texas, 27 October 1989

MT62: Byzantium
1989 [6 December 1989]
For soprano and orchestra, setting
the poem by W.B. Yeats
Faye Robinson, Chicago Sympho-
ny Orchestra, cond. Georg Solti;
Carnegie Hall, New York, 11
April 1991

MT63: String Quartet No. 5
1990–91 [15 July 1991]
Lindsay Quartet; Crucible Theatre,
Sheffield, 9 May 1992

MT64: The Rose Lake
1991–3 [22 April 1993]
A song without words for
orchestra
London Symphony Orchestra,
cond. Colin Davis; Barbican
Concert Hall, London, 19
February 1995

MT65: Caliban's Song
1995
For baritone and piano, setting
words from Shakespeare's The
Tempest
David Barrell, Iain Burnside, BBC
Radio 3 broadcast; 26 Novem-
ber 1995

**JUVENILIA AND UNPUBLISHED
WORKS**

* = no manuscript known to
survive

MTi: Hymn to Brahma
c.1923–4
High voice and piano, setting text
by Ralph Waldo Emerson

MTii: Blow, Bugle, Blow
c.1923–4
High voice and piano, setting text
by Alfred Tennyson

MTiii: Cradle Song
c.1923–4
Piano solo

MTiv: Piano Sonata in D minor
c.1923–4

MTv: *Woods in Winter*
c.1923–4
High voice and piano, setting
    text by Henry Wadsworth
    Longfellow

MTvi: *David Mourning Over Jonathan;
How Are the Mighty Fallen; Songs
of Bow** [Song of the Bow?]
c.1923–4

**MTvii: Suite for Strings in C
major***
1924
Royal College of Music, October
    1924

MTviii: *The Undying Fire*
c.1927
Unfinished cantata for baritone,
    chorus, and orchestra, setting
    text from H.G. Wells

MTix: *The Village Opera*
1927–8
Arrangement and realisation of
    Charles Johnson's three-act
    ballad opera *The Village Opera*
    (1729), for soloists and
    ensemble
Oxted and Limpsfield Players,
    cond. MT; Barn Theatre, Oxted,
    22 April 1928

MTx: Piano Sonata in C minor
c.1928–9
Cyril Smith; Barn Theatre, Oxted,
    15 December 1928 (first three
    of four movements)

MTxi: *Five Settings* **for violin,
cello, and piano**
1929
Incidental music for *Bolsters*, a
    mime play by Margaret Carter
Children's Theatre, Endell Street,
    London, 31 August 1929

MTxii: *Variations for Dudley*
1929
"Ten variations on a Swiss
    folk-song as harmonized by
    Beethoven"; written for or to
    be performed by Dudley Parvin

MTxiii: *Psalm in C*
1929, rev. 1931
For chorus, string quartet, and
    string orchestra, setting "The
    Gateway" by Christopher Fry
Oxted and Limpsfield Players; Barn
    Theatre, Oxted, 1929

MTxiv: Two Chorale Preludes
c.1929–30
For flute and clarinet
Evan and Pamela Maude; Oxted,
    c.1930

**MTxv: Overture and incidental
music for Don Juan***
c.1929–30
For a production of the play by
    James Elroy Flecker
Oxted and Limpsfield Players; Barn
    Theatre, Oxted, 28 February
    1930

**MTxvi: Sonata for Violin and
Piano***
c.1929–30

MTxvii: Concerto in D*
c.1929–30
For flutes, oboe, horns, and string
    quartet, and string orchestra [?]
Oxted and Limpsfield Orchestral
    Society; Barn Theatre, Oxted, 5
    April 1930

MTxviii: Three Songs
c.1929–30
Setting for high voice and piano
    of "Afternoon Tea", "Sea
    Love",* and "Arracombe
    Wood",* by Charlotte Mew
Eric Shaxson, Dora Milner; Barn
    Theatre, Oxted, 5 April 1930

MTxix: Jockey to the Fair
c.1929–30
Variations for piano solo
Leslie Orrie; Barn Theatre, Oxted,
    5 April 1930

MTxx: String Quartet in F minor
c.1929–30
John Morley, Helen Stewart,
    Maurice Hardy, Mary Gladden;
    Barn Theatre, Oxted, 5 April
    1930

**MTxxi: Piano Sonata in G-flat
    major***
1930

**MTxxii: Quartet No. 2 for
    Strings in F major**
c.1929–30, rev. October 1930

MTxxiii: Symphonic Movement
1930–31, unfinished

MTxxiv: String Trio in B flat
1932
Royal College of Music; 13 Janu-
    ary 1965

MTxxv: Symphony in B flat
1932
Orchestration of MTxxiv

MTxxvi: Symphony in B flat
1932–3 [16 November 1933],
    rev. 1934, 1938
(Retaining central movement of
    MTxxv)
South London Orchestra, cond.
    MT; Morley College, London, 4
    March 1934

MTxxvii: Robin Hood
1933–4
A folk-song opera, with dialogue
    by David Ayerst and lyrics by
    Ruth Pennyman
Miners' Hall, Boosbeck, North
    Yorkshire, 8 August 1934

MTxxvii-a: Song for Stella
c.1934
Arrangement for high voice and
    piano of song from Robin Hood

MTxxviii: Miners
1936
Music for dance-drama The Miners
    (dir. Margaret Barr), setting text
    by Judith Wogan
London, 1936

MTxxix: Dance of Two with Chorus*
1937
Music for dance-drama Dance of

Two with Chorus (dir. Margaret
Barr)
London, 1937

MTxxx: A Song of Liberty
1935–7 [1 May 1937]
Setting, for mixed choir and
    orchestra, of "A Song of Lib-
    erty" from The Marriage of Heaven
    and Hell by William Blake
South London Orchestra and "spe-
    cial choir", cond. MT; Morley
    College, London, 7 November
    1937

MTxxxi: The King's Hunt*
1937
Orchestration of a virginal piece
    by John Bull
South London Orchestra, cond.
    MT; Morley College, 7 Novem-
    ber 1937

MTxxxii: Robert of Sicily
1938
Children's opera for soloists,
    chorus, and ensemble, with
    script and lyrics by Christopher
    Fry
Royal Arsenal Co-operative
    Society mixed junior choirs;
    Co-operative Hall, Peckham,
    May 1938

MTxxxiii: Seven at One Stroke
Children's opera for soloists,
    chorus, and ensemble, with
    script and lyrics by Christopher
    Fry
Royal Arsenal Co-operative
    Society mixed junior choirs;
    Co-operative Hall, Peckham, 15
    April 1939

RECORDINGS

All a survey of Tippett recordings can do is bemoan the paucity of releases, make a plea for new interpretations, and invite the reader to type the name "Michael Tippett" into iTunes, YouTube, or Spotify, and explore. A good place to start would surely be two major compilations, available to download or to purchase on disc, which provide a useful overall survey:

> Tippett: *Orchestral and Chamber Works* (Piano Sonatas 1–3; String Quartets 1–3; *Fantasia Concertante*; Concerto for Double String Orchestra; Concerto for Orchestra; Triple Concerto; Symphonies 1–4; *Ritual Dances*; *Suite for the Birthday of Prince Charles*)
> [six CDs: Decca, 475 6750]

> Tippett: *Vocal Music* (*Boyhood's End*; *The Heart's Assurance*; *A Child of Our Time*; *Songs for Dov*; *Songs for Ariel*; *Songs for Achilles*; *Byzantium*; *The Knot Garden*, various songs)
> [four CDs: Decca, 475 717-2]

Only four of Tippett's five operas have been recorded (*New Year* is desperately awaited). The premieres of *The Midsummer Marriage* and *King Priam* are preserved on disc, although the sound quality of both leaves a lot to be desired. Otherwise, each opera is available only in a single, very good, studio version; each would benefit immeasurably from a fresh generation of interpreters. Much reveals itself in the cracks of comparison. The complexity and multi-layered nature of Tippett's compositions, best experienced live, are much better served by twenty-first-century technicians: the clarity of Martyn Brabbins's symphony cycle with the BBC Scottish Symphony Orchestra (Hyperion, CDA68203), or of the Heath Quartet's traversing of the five quartets (Wigmore Live, 0080/2), is streets ahead of recordings made in Tippett's lifetime.

A Child of Our Time is the most recorded of Tippett's work. My own selection would cherry-pick the soloists from a long out-of-print BBC disc (BBC Radio Classics 9130); the orchestral energy from Colin Davis's first release (Philips, 420 075-2); Richard Hickox's chorus (Chandos, 9276); and the authority of the version Tippett himself conducted at the end of his life (Naxos 8.557570).

Finally, a wave of the flag for two long-deleted recordings that can be obtained second-hand. Of all Tippett's compositions The Vision of Saint Augustine is the hardest to apprehend when not experienced live. The standard recording, still available, is conducted by Tippett himself (RCA Red Seal, 89498). But if the version conducted by David Atherton with the London Sinfonietta Chorus and Orchestra (BBC Radio Classics, 15656 91902) can be tracked down, the listener will find a performance that is superior in virtuosity, clarity, and balance. It seems to convey a different piece entirely. Likewise, Josephine Barstow's live performance of Symphony No. 3 (BBC Radio Classics, 15656 91402) has to be heard to be believed. Tippett attended the concert and accounted Barstow "glorious".

Of Priaulx Rainier's music little is available, though a search on Spotify or YouTube throws up a few digitally released gems, not least her string quartet; Quanta; and Peter Pears's performance of Cycle for Declamation. A blistering performance of Requiem, arguably her masterpiece, is available on disc (Redcliffe Recordings, RR 011).

April 2019

ACKNOWLEDGEMENTS

One of the greatest pleasures of researching and writing this book has been the friendships it gave rise to. I have relied upon the assistance of a great many people, and the care and effort with which so many have proffered help have been a marvel.

The passing-on of even the smallest pieces of information has frequently opened the door to mines of valuable material, and I am grateful indeed to the following for all their communication and assistance: Patrick Abrams; Gabriel Anderson; David Atherton; Dame Eileen Atkins; John Ayerst; Robert Barker; John Barlow; Humphry and Elizabeth Barnikel; Simon Barrow; Rupert Bawden; Charles Beauclerk; Sir George Benjamin; Hilary Benn; Michael Berkeley; John Biggs; Jonathan Black; Astra Blair; Joy Bounds; James Bowman; Martyn Brabbins; Maryjane Briant; John Bridcut; Peter Brook CH; Nicholas and Sarah Brown; Trevor Burrage; Humphrey Burton; Christina Butterfield; David Cairns; Patrick Carnegy; Donna Carr and the staff of Ormesby Hall; Jon Calver; Spencer Campbell; John Carnelley; Lily Chartreux; Malcolm Chase; Sally Clark; Jill Cochrane; Richard Coles; Joanne Coombs; John Copley; Anthony Coughlan; Maurice Davies; Paul Davies; Adrian Davis; Sue Davison; Mark Deller; Jonathan Del Mar; Zoltan, Bruce, and Jancis Dienes; Marcia Dixcy Jory; Kerry Downes; Jilly Edwards; Jenny Farrell; Lara Feigel; Nick Ferris; Helen Field; Duncan Fielden; Alexe Finlay; Catherine Fountain; Sarah Generes; Edmund Gordon; Samantha Grambow; Jane Greenwood; Jonathan Groves; David Haines; Maggi Hambling;

Charles Harrowell; Antony Harwood; Alison Hepburn; Martyn Hill; Alan Hollinghurst; Janet Hughes; Donald Hunt; Bruce Hunter; Joni Hurst; Alex Jarrett; Sonia, Cecily, and Fenella Jewers; Beverley and Tim Jollands; Morine Krissdottir; Lidia Kuhivchak; Winston Leese; Nicola LeFanu; Garry Lester; Stephan Lieske; the late Malcolm Mac-Donald; Kika Markham; Hannah Marshall; Jane Mathison; Belinda Matthews; Deborah May; Steve May; Richard Mayo; Jim McCue; Charlotte McDonaugh; David McDowell; Edward Mendelson; Michael Middeke; John Minford; Richard Morris; Margaret Mulvihill; Chris Myant; Justin Needle; Richard and Jane Neville; Larraine Nicholas; Rachel Nicholson; Paul Nieman; Clara Nissen; Timothy O'Brien; Brenda Ogdon; Rachel O'Higgins; Geoff Ogram; Peter Owens; Fred Parker; John Patrick; Stephen Pettitt; Andrew Plant; Anne Poulter; Stacey Prickett; Monica Prillaman; Ana Pumarejo; Jon Purcell; Alexandra Quinn; Bruce Reed; Karl Renner; Tim Reynish; Piers Ricketts; Alison Ridout; Faye Robinson; Dan Rootham; Mike Sage; Michael Sanders; Mischa and Ann Scorer; Nicholas Shaw; Andrew Shaxson; Katrina Sheppeard; Michael Sidnell; Sherry Simon; Claire Simpson; Denis Sims; Jeoffry and Maud Soden; Leonard and Jessica Soden; Nina Soufy; Penny Souster; Catherine Southon; Anne Spargo; Krister St Hill; Anne Stillman; Richard Sumsion; Gilbert Thompson; Mike Thorne; Ann Tonkin and Warren Langley; Sheila Townsend; Elizabeth and Francis Tregear; Pat Tuffin; Ian Venables; Graham Vick, Richard Willacy, and all at Birmingham Opera Company; Justin Vickers; George Walker; Robin Walker; Stephen Walsh; Aaron Watts; Iris and Nigel Weaver; James Wilkinson; Rex Woods; Avril Wright; Alan Wyburn-Powell; David Wykeham-George.

I am indebted to the existence and hospitality of a great many archives, the staff of which have either hosted me in person with knowledge and welcome, or made documents available digitally. Profound thanks to the following: Badminton School (Christobel Thomas); BBC Written Archives Centre (Samantha Blake); Blundell's School (Mike Sampson); Bodleian Library, University of Oxford (Alice Millea); Brighton College (Abigail Wharne); British Film Institute National Archive (Kathleen Dickson); British Library (Nicolas Bell, Andra Patterson, Richard Chesser, Chris Scobie); Britten-Pears

Foundation Library (Nicholas Clark, Sarah Bardwell, Lucy Walker); Cambridge University Library; Cumbria Archive Centre (Louise Smith); Dulwich College (Calista Lucy); Durham University Library, Archives and Special Collections (Michael Stansfield); Fettes College (Craig Marshall); Glyndebourne Opera (Julia Aries); Haileybury and Imperial Service College (Toby Parker); Hazelwood School (Nick Tappin); Henry Moore Foundation (Sophie Orpen); Houston Grand Opera (Brian Mitchell); Hull History Centre; Jesus College, Cambridge (Robin Darwall-Smith); King's College Cambridge Archive Centre (Peter Monteith); Kingston History Centre (Helen Swainger); Kingswood School (Zoë Parsons); Lady Margaret Hall, Oxford (Oliver Mahony); London Library (with the valuable support of its Carlyle Membership scheme); London Metropolitan Archive; London School of Economics Library (Anna Towlson); Machin Arts Foundation (Dominic Newton); Minet Library (Zoe Darani); Morley College (Elaine Andrews); Morris Library, South Illinois University (David R. Bond); The National Archives, Kew; National Co-operative Archive (Gillian Lonergan); Peace Pledge Union (Bill Hetherington); Pitt Rivers Museum, University of Oxford (Jeremy Coote); Royal Academy of Music Library (Ilse Woloszko); Royal College of Music Library (Mariarosaria Canzonieri); Royal Opera House Collections (Paul Beard); Rutgers University Libraries (Helene van Rossum); Schott Music; St Hilda's College, Oxford (Oliver Mahony); Stamford Endowed Schools (John Craddock); State Library of New South Wales (Bronwyn Leslie); Tate Gallery; Teesside Archives (Kimberley Starkie); University of California San Diego Library (Heather Smedberg, William Randall); University of Exeter, Special Collections (Angela Mandrioli, Caroline Walter); University of London, Senate House Library (Richard Temple); Victoria and Albert Museum, Department of Theatre and Performance; Warwick University, Modern Records Centre (Helen Ford); William Ready Division of Archives and Research Collections, McMaster University (Renu Barrett); William Walton Trust (Alessandra Vinciguerra).

Especial thanks to the Harry Ransom Center, University of Texas at Austin, for its award of a Research Fellowship in the Humanities, which offered vital encouragement and financial assistance, and allowed me to examine the Center's Tippett materials in person. I'm thankful to all the staff (especially Bridget Gayle Ground, Kate Hayes, Cristina Meisner, Kathryn Millan, and Richard Oram) for their welcome and help.

One of the great privileges of my research was to work in a number of private collections, and I am intensely grateful to the following for their meticulous preservation of material, and for so freely and generously making it available to me while answering the steady stream of my interminable questions. Their overwhelmingly kind hospitality allowed me the time and space in which to work and made research a true pleasure. Geoff and Marje Allen (Meirion Bowen collection); Caroline Ayerst (David Ayerst collection); Susan Barlow (Karl Hawker collection); Isla Baring (John Amis collection); Julia Busch (William Busch collection); Sian Edwards (Ian Kemp collection); Ardan Fisher (Bryan Fisher collection); Graham Hobbins (Shelagh Fisher collection); Kit and Jean Martin (Allinson collection); Susanna Morley Smithson and John Smithson (Oliver Morley collection); Alice and John Nissen (Evelyn Maude collection); Beatrix Taylor (Antony Hopkins collection); Gordon Waite (Nicholas Wright collection); Virginia-Lee Webb (Douglas Newton archive); Charmian and Derek Whitmell (Peter Kemp collection).

A number of Tippett's friends and colleagues kindly agreed to be interviewed, and the book has been enriched by the unstinting openness and honesty with which they shared their thoughts and memories, and the generosity with which they facilitated our conversations: Stephen Aechternacht; Caroline Ayerst; Susan Barlow; Dame Josephine Barstow; Meirion Bowen; John Constable; Andrew Coster; Paul Crossley; Sir Andrew Davis; Sian Edwards; Alexander Goehr; Jill Gomez; Sally Groves; David Haines; the late Raimund Herincx; Sir Nicholas Kenyon; David Matthews; Stella Maude; Graham Modlen; Sarah Phillips; Josey Sims; Heather Sweet; Sir John Tooley; Beverly Vaughn; Alison Watson; Charmian and Derek Whitmell; Nick and Anne Whyatt.

The extent of my debt to others' work is made clear by my Bibliography, but I would like especially to acknowledge the scholarship of the late Ian Kemp, and the support of his widow, Sian Edwards.

Sally Groves eased with humbling generosity my inheritance of this project from her late husband, Dennis Marks, to whose work and memory I pay tribute. I am immensely grateful to the Dennis Marks Trust for a generous grant towards the cost of printing and illustrations that not only enhanced the book beyond measure but offered blessing and encouragement to my continuation of Dennis's work. The research and expertise of Danyel Gilgan (on Wilfred Franks), Roger Savage (on Douglas Newton), and Helen Southworth (on Francesca Allinson) have been godsends, and I'm grateful to all three for sharing their work in progress and answering so many questions. The research into the Cleveland work camps by Malcolm Chase and Mark Whyman, who seized the opportunity to interview many involved, was a wonderful resource; Mark and Anne Whyman's hospitality went above and beyond the call of duty, and this book would be much impoverished without their kindness.

It is hard to imagine how Schott Music, especially Sam Rigby, Ian Mylett, Louisa Hungate, and Francesca McGeorge, could have been more encouraging and helpful (and I'm grateful to Sirikorn Green for her help in collating photographs). The Michael Tippett Foundation, not least its chairman Anthony Whitworth-Jones and secretary Gwyn Rhydderch, has given me unstinting advice and assistance. Geoff Allen and Keith Salway, trustees of the Tippett Will Trust, have provided the biographer's dreamed-for combination of help, encouragement, and freedom. Meirion Bowen has been a support from the beginning, and unfailingly munificent with his private collection of Tippett material. Simon Heilbron advised with scrupulous care on all legal aspects of the text. I thank my agent, Ian Drury of Sheil Land, and my commissioning editor, Alan Samson: in making this, my first book, a reality, they have changed the person I am on waking each morning. Simon Wright was the editor of one's dreams, wrestling my unwieldy manuscript into shape with sensitivity and scrupulousness, while patiently guiding me through the twists and turns of publication. I feel honoured by the care and attention paid by the whole team at Weidenfeld & Nicolson (Natalie Dawkins, Hannah Cox, and Elizabeth Allen), and Linden Lawson copy-edited with a near superhuman eye. The inventive and striking text design is by Clare Sivell; Simon Fox proofread meticulously; and my thanks to Marian Aird for her exemplary index.

The book and its writing were immeasurably improved by the indispensable wisdom, encouragement, and advice of Sally Groves, Jill Paton Walsh, Roger Savage, and Ruth Smith. I have been reliant on and blessed by their friendship. I send love and gratitude always to Yrja Thorsdottir and to Louise and Ian Soden. To them is owed the existence of this book, and much much else.

PERMISSIONS

Michael Tippett's unpublished work is © The Sir Michael Tippett Will Trust, and I am grateful to the trustees for permission to quote from letters, interviews, and other of Tippett's writings currently held in private collections.

Extracts from unpublished letters by T.S. Eliot are included by permission of Faber and Faber Ltd; and I gratefully acknowledge use of material from the Douglas Newton Archive, © 2001-present Virginia-Lee Webb Ph.D.

Material from private collections is included by the kind permission of Caroline Ayerst (estate of David Ayerst); Susan Barlow (estate of Karl Hawker); Sally Clark (Estate of Elizabeth Benn Shinkman); Kurosh Davis (estate of Colin Davis); Sian Edwards (estate of Ian Kemp); Ardan Fisher (estate of Bryan Fisher); Graham Hobbins (estate of Shelagh Fisher); Alice Nissen (estate of Evelyn Maude); Charmian and Derek Whitmell (estate of Peter Kemp). I am grateful to the following for their kind permission to reproduce images. *Plate sections*: Charmian and Derek Whitmell (images 1, 2, 3); Schott Music and the Tippett Will Trust (4, 18, 23, 38, 43, 44); Teesside Archives (5); Steve May (6); Malcolm Chase (7, 8); Helen Southworth (9); Alice Nissen (10, 20); Universal History Archive/ Contributor, via Getty Images (12); Nigel Henderson Estate, via Tate Archives (13); Susan Barlow (14, 16, 27); Erich Auerbach/ Stringer via Getty Images (15, 17); Caroline Ayerst (19, 25);

Ilse Cornwall-Ross (21); Rachel O'Higgins (22); Susanna Morley Smithson (24); Graham Hobbins (26); Alison Hepburn (28); BBC Written Archives (29); Mander and Mitchenson/University of Bristol, via ArenaPAL (30); Clive Barda, via ArenaPAL (31, 33); Mike Evans, via Bridgeman Images (32); Adam Fradgley and Exposure Photography (34); Guy Gravett/Glyndebourne Productions Ltd, via ArenaPAL (35); Baron/Stringer via Getty Images (36); Marjorie Allen (37); Graham Modlen (39, 45); Philip Griffin (40); Nicky Johnston (41); Tim Booth Photography (42); Maggi Hambling (46). Within text: Charmian and Derek Whitmell (pp. 15, 22, 26); Schott Music and the Tippett Will Trust (pp. 44, 61, 336); Fettes College (p. 66); Helen Southworth (p. 119); Caroline Ayerst (pp. 131, 589); Malcolm Chase (p. 146); Morley College (p. 254); Isla Baring (p. 265a); Beatrix Taylor (p. 265b); Cecil Beaton/Condé Nast, via Getty Images (p. 319); Kit and Jean Martin (p. 341); Susan Barlow (p. 455); Stephen Aechternacht (p. 553). While every effort has been made to trace or contact all copyright holders, the publishers would be pleased to rectify at the earliest opportunity any errors or omissions brought to their attention.

NOTES

The full and extremely extensive references for this book are available in the hardback edition and also on the author's website at: www.oliversoden.co.uk

In order to make the paperback a manageable and readable size, the author and publishers have decided not to include the notes. We hope readers will agree that, for most, the balance of convenience is best served by this policy.

BIBLIOGRAPHY OF WORKS
CITED AND CONSULTED

Diaries, letters, and editions are listed by author rather than by editor. Published scores and libretti are not listed; a complete catalogue of Michael Tippett's published works is available from Schott Music, London, KAT 69–99.

A. PUBLISHED WRITINGS BY MICHAEL TIPPETT

Individual essays and articles are cited to their most recent publication, with date of first publication or broadcast then given in square brackets.

Moving into Aquarius, 2nd edn (St Albans: Paladin Books, 1974)
  – "Contracting-in to Abundance", pp. 19–27 [1944]
  – "Poets in a Barren Age", pp. 148–56 [1972]
Music of the Angels, Essays and Sketchbooks of Michael Tippett, ed. Meirion Bowen (London: Ernst Eulenburg, 1980)
  – "International Workers' Music Olympiad", pp. 34–6 [1935]
The Operas of Michael Tippett, ed. Nicholas John (London: John Calder, 1985)
Selected Letters of Michael Tippett, ed. Thomas Schuttenhelm (London: Faber and Faber, 2005)
Those Twentieth Century Blues: An Autobiography (London: Hutchinson, 1991)
Tippett on Music, ed. Meirion Bowen (Oxford: Oxford University Press, 1995)
  – "Archetypes of Concert Music", pp. 89–108 [1995]

- "The Birth of an Opera", pp. 198–208 [1952]
- "Britten at Fifty", pp. 67–9 [1963]
- "Britten: First Encounters", pp. 66–7 [1980]
- "Britten: Obituary", pp. 70–72 [1976]
- "The Composer and Pacifism", pp. 282–6 [1944, rev. 1995]
- "A Composer's Point of View", pp. 3–6 [1948]
- "Dreaming on Things to Come", pp. 307–9 [1995]
- "Dreams of Power, Dreams of Love", pp. 220–27 [1995]
- "Holst", pp. 73–5 [1958]
- "*The Mask of Time*", pp. 245–55 [1982]
- "Schoenberg", pp. 25–46 [1952; 1965]
- "Shostakovich", pp. 78–82 [1980]
- "Sketch for a Modern Oratorio", pp. 117–77 [1939]
- "The Stage", pp. 269–74 [1995]
- "T.S. Eliot and *A Child of Our Time*", pp. 109–16 [1963]

"An Anchor of Gold", *Guardian*, 25 September 1992, p. 33

"The Composer's World", in *How Music Works*, ed. Spence and Swayne (1981), pp. 347–56

"COs ran an 'underground' paper in a London prison", *Peace News*, 29 June 1945, Peace Pledge Union archives

"Conclusion", in *A History of Song*, ed. Stevens (1960), pp. 461–5

"An Englishman Looks at Opera", *Opera News*, 2 January 1965, pp. 7–9

"A Magnetic Friendship: An Attraction of Opposites", in *Time Remembered*, ed. Stevenson (1981), p. 9

"Music in England, A Personal View", in *Twenty British Composers*, ed. Dickinson (1975), pp. 1–5 [1973]

"Seven at One Stroke", *Comradeship and the Wheatsheaf*, June 1939, p. 15

B. OTHER PUBLICATIONS

Interviews with Michael Tippett are listed by interviewer's name.

Aechternacht, Stephen, "Tippett in America/America in Tippett", *Composer*, 70 (Summer 1980), pp. 28–33

Allinson, Francesca, *A Childhood* (London: The Hogarth Press, 1938)

Amis, John, *Amiscellany: My Life, My Music* (London: Faber and Faber, 1985)

—— *My Music in London: 1945–2000* (London: Amiscellany Books, 2006)

Athill, Diana, *Alive, Alive Oh! And Other Things That Matter* (London: Granta, 2015)

Attfield, John, *With Light of Knowledge: A Hundred Years of Education in the Royal Arsenal Co-operative Society, 1877–1977* (London: Journeyman Press, 1981)

Auden, W.H., *Complete Works*, 6 vols, ed. Edward Mendelson (Princeton, NJ: Princeton University Press, 1997–2015)

Ayerst, David, *The Road to Now: The Early Life of David Ayerst* (1990); privately printed, Ayerst collection

—— "Young Michael Tippett: A Talk Given to The Burford Society" (1985); privately printed, Ayerst collection

Ayerst, John B., *Let Me Speak* (2015); privately printed, held by the author

Bacharach, A.L. (ed.), *British Music of Our Time* (Harmondsworth: Pelican, 1946)

Banfield, Stephen, *Gerald Finzi: An English Composer* (London: Faber and Faber, 1997)

Beaton, Cecil, *Photobiography* (London: Odhams Press, 1951)

Bellany, Peter, *Dorset Historic Towns Survey: Victorian and Edwardian Swanage* (Colliton Park: Dorset County Council, 2011)

Blishen, Edward, *A Cackhanded War* (London: Thames and Hudson, 1972)

Bornstein, Sam, and Richardson, Al, *Against the Stream: A History of the Trotskyist Movement in Britain, 1924–38* (London: Socialist Platform, 1986)

Bounds, Joy, *A Song of Their Own: The Fight for Votes for Women in Ipswich* (Stroud: The History Press, 2014)

Bowen, Meirion, *Michael Tippett*, 2nd edn (London: Robson Books, 1997)

Braddon, Russell, *Joan Sutherland* (London: Collins, 1962)

Brasch, Charles, *Indirections: A Memoir, 1909–1947* (Wellington, New Zealand: Oxford University Press, 1980)

Brett, Philip, *Music and Sexuality in Britten: Selected Essays*, ed. George E. Haggerty (Berkeley and Los Angeles, CA: University of California Press, 2006)

Britten, Benjamin, *Journeying Boy: The Diaries of the Young Benjamin Britten, 1928–1938*, ed. John Evans (London: Faber and Faber, 2009)

—— *Letters from a Life: The Selected Letters of Benjamin Britten, 1913–1976*, 6 vols, ed. Donald Mitchell, Philip Reed, and Mervyn Cooke (London: Faber and Faber, and Woodbridge: Boydell and Brewer, 1991–2012)

Brockway, Fenner (ed.), *The Flowery, 1942–44: The Scrubs "Conchie" Review* (London: Central Board for Conscientious Objectors, 1945)

Bullivant, Joanna, *Alan Bush, Modern Music and the Cold War* (Cambridge: Cambridge University Press, 2017)

Burton, Humphrey, Yehudi Menuhin: A Life (London: Faber and Faber, 2000)

Bush, Alan, and Ireland, John, The Correspondence of Alan Bush and John Ireland, 1927–1961, ed. Rachel O'Higgins (Aldershot: Ashgate, 2006)

Cairns, David, Responses: Musical Essays and Reviews (London: Secker and Warburg, 1973)

Camp, John, Holloway Prison: The Place and the People (Newton Abbott: David and Charles, 1974)

Carpenter, Humphrey, Benjamin Britten: A Biography (London: Faber and Faber, 1992)

—— The Envy of the World: Fifty Years of the BBC Third Programme and Radio 3 (London: Weidenfeld and Nicolson, 1996)

—— W.H. Auden: A Biography (London: George Allen and Unwin, 1981)

Chase, Malcolm, and Whyman, Mark, Heartbreak Hill: A Response to Unemployment in East Cleveland in the 1930s (North Yorkshire: Cleveland County Council, 1991)

Clare, Anthony, "In the Psychiatrist's Chair, with Michael Tippett", Listener, 14 August 1986, p. 10

Clarke, David, The Music and Thought of Michael Tippett: Modern Times and Metaphysics (Cambridge: Cambridge University Press, 2001)

—— (ed.), Tippett Studies (Cambridge: Cambridge University Press, 1999)

Colles, Henry, and Cruft, John, The Royal College of Music: A Centenary Record, 1883–1983 (London: Eyre and Spottiswoode, 1982)

Craft, Robert, Stravinsky: Chronicle of a Friendship, revised edn (Nashville, TN: Vanderbilt University Press, 1994, first published 1972)

Crawford, Elizabeth, The Women's Suffrage Movement: A Reference Guide 1866–1928 (London: Routledge, 2011)

Creaton, Heather (ed.), Sources for the History of London, 1939–45 (London: British Records Association, 1998)

Croall, Jonathan, Don't You Know There's a War On? The People's Voice, 1939–45 (London: Hutchinson, 1988)

Crutchley, Neil, Leicester Symphony Orchestra: The First Ninety Years (Leicester: Leicester Symphony Orchestra Publishing, 2013)

Davis, Colin, et al. (eds), A Man of Our Time (London: Schott, 1977)

Deed, B.L., A History of Stamford School (Cambridge: Cambridge University Press, 1954)

De-la-Noy, Michael, Eddy: The Life of Edward Sackville-West (London: The Bodley Head, 1988)

Del Mar, Jonathan, "Tippett: Symphony No. 2 in C, textual report"; privately printed, held by the author

Dickinson, Peter (ed.), *Lennox Berkeley and Friends: Writings, Letters and Interviews* (Woodbridge: The Boydell Press, 2012)

—— *Twenty British Composers* (London: J. and W. Chester, 1975)

Drummond, John, *Tainted by Experience: A Life in the Arts* (London: Faber and Faber, 2000)

Duncan, Ronald, *How To Make Enemies* (London: Hart Davis, 1968)

Eliot, T.S., *Christianity and Culture* (New York, NY: Harcourt, Brace and World, 1949)

—— *The Complete Prose of T.S. Eliot*, 6 vols, gen. ed. Ronald Schuchard (Baltimore, MA: Johns Hopkins University Press, and London: Faber and Faber, 2014–). Project MUSE.

—— *The Poems of T.S. Eliot*, 2 vols, ed. Christopher Ricks and Jim McCue (London: Faber and Faber, 2015)

Fisher, Bryan, *An Adventure in Living* (1998); privately printed, Fisher collection

Foreman, Lewis, "Forging a relationship and a role: Michael Tippett and the BBC, 1928–51", in *Michael Tippett: Music and Literature*, ed. Suzanne Robinson (2002), pp. 122–50

—— *From Parry to Britten: British Music in Letters 1900–1945* (London: B.T. Batsford, 1987)

Forster, E.M., *Journals and Diaries*, 3 vols, ed. Philip Gardner (London: Pickering and Chatto, 2011)

Fraser, Robert, *The Chameleon Poet: A Life of George Barker* (London: Jonathan Cape, 2001)

Gloag, Kenneth, and Jones, Nicholas (eds), *The Cambridge Companion to Michael Tippett* (Cambridge: Cambridge University Press, 2013)

Glock, William, *Notes in Advance: An Autobiography in Music* (Oxford: Oxford University Press, 1991)

Grant, Ted, *History of British Trotskyism* (London: Wellred Books, 2002)

Greene, Richard, *Edith Sitwell* (London: Virago, 2011)

Grogan, Christopher (ed.), *Imogen Holst: A Life in Music*, revised edn (Woodbridge: The Boydell Press, 2010)

Groves, Reginald, *The Balham Group: How British Trotskyism Began* (London: Pluto Press, 1974)

Hall, Fernau, *Modern English Ballet: An Interpretation* (London: Andrew Melrose, 1950)

Hall, Peter, *Making an Exhibition of Myself* (London: Sinclair Stevenson, 1993)

Hardwick, Michael and Mollie, *Alfred Deller: A Singularity of Voice* (London: Cassell, 1968)

Hare, William Rowan, "Memory of Michael Tippett", *Old Stamfordian Club Newsletter*, 19. Stamford Endowed Schools archives.

Harries, Meirion and Susie, *A Pilgrim Soul: The Life and Work of Elisabeth Lutyens* (London: Michael Joseph, 1989)

Hay, Ian (ed.), *The Fettes College Register, 1870–1922*, Fifth Edition (Edinburgh: Edinburgh University Press, 1923)

Hayes, Denis, *Challenge of Conscience: The Story of the Conscientious Objectors of 1939–1949* (London: George Allen and Unwin, 1949)

Headington, Christopher, *Peter Pears: A Biography* (London: Faber and Faber, 1992)

Hobbins, Shelagh Fisher, *Dear, I've Been Thinking*, 3 vols (1988); privately printed, Hobbins collection

Holloway, Mark, *Norman Douglas: A Biography* (London: Secker and Warburg, 1976)

Holloway, Robin, *On Music: Essays and Diversions, 1963–2003* (Brinkworth, Wilts.: Claridge Press, 2003)

Hopkins, Antony, *Beating Time* (London: Michael Joseph, 1982)

Hopkinson, Diana, *Family Inheritance: A Life of Eva Hubback* (London: Staples Press, 1954)

Houlbrook, Matt, *Queer London: Perils and Pleasures of the Sexual Metropolis, 1918–1957* (Chicago, IL: University of Chicago Press, 2005)

Hughes, Meirion, and Stradling, Robert, *The English Musical Renaissance 1840–1940: Constructing a National Music*, 2nd edn (Manchester: Manchester University Press, 2001)

Hurd, Michael, *Tippett* (London: Novello, 1978)

Jacobs, Arthur, *Henry J. Wood: Maker of the Proms* (London: Methuen, 1994)

Johnson, Graham, *Britten, Voice and Piano: Lectures on the Vocal Music of Benjamin Britten* (Aldershot: Ashgate, 2003)

Jung, Carl, *Analytical Psychology: Its Theory and Practice, The Tavistock Lectures* (London: Routledge and Kegan Paul, 1968)

——— *The Essential Jung: Selected Writings*, ed. Anthony Storr (London: Fontana Press, 1998)

Kemp, Ian (ed.), *Michael Tippett: A Symposium on his 60th Birthday* (London: Faber and Faber, 1965)

────── Tippett: The Composer and His Music (Oxford: Oxford University Press, 1987, first published 1984)

Kemp, Isabel; see Tippett, Isabel

Kemp, Peter, and Tippett, Michael, I Remember, I Remember, two drafts, c.1990; privately printed, Peter Kemp collection

Kennedy, Michael, Adrian Boult (London: Hamish Hamilton, 1987)

────── Portrait of Walton (Oxford: Oxford University Press, 1989)

Kildea, Paul, Benjamin Britten: A Life in the Twentieth Century (London: Penguin, 2013)

Kirsch, Jonathan, The Short, Strange Life of Herschel Grynszpan (New York, NY: Liveright, 2013)

Knight, Frida Stewart, Untitled Memoir (c.1990); privately printed, Whyman/Chase collection

Kokoschka, Oskar, Letters, 1905–1976, ed. Olda Kokoschka and Alfred Marnau, trans. Mary Whittall (London: Thames and Hudson, 1992)

Kramer, Ann, Conscientious Objectors of the Second World War: Refusing to Fight (Barnsley, South Yorkshire: Pen and Sword Books, 2013)

Lebrecht, Norman, Covent Garden: The Untold Story (London: Simon and Schuster, 2000)

Lee, Colin Andrew, Music at the Edge: The Music Therapy Experiences of a Musician with AIDS, 2nd edn (London: Routledge, 2005)

Lewis, Geraint (ed.), Michael Tippett O.M., A Celebration (Tunbridge Wells: Baton Press, 1985)

Linklater, Andro, An Unhusbanded Life: Charlotte Despard, Suffragette, Socialist and Sinn Feiner (London: Hutchinson, 1980)

Lloyd, Stephen, Constant Lambert: Beyond the Rio Grande (Woodbridge: Boydell and Brewer, 2014)

London, Louise, Whitehall and the Jews, 1933–1948 (Cambridge: Cambridge University Press, 2003)

MacClancy, Jeremy, "Layard, John Willoughby (1891–1974)", Oxford Dictionary of National Biography (Oxford: Oxford University Press, 2004); online edn, January 2019

Machin, Arnold, Artist of an Icon: The Memoirs of Arnold Machin (Kirstead, Norfolk: Frontier Publishing, 2002)

Mason O'Connor, Kristine, Joan Maynard: Passionate Socialist (London: Politico's, 2003)

Matthews, David, Michael Tippett, An Introductory Study (London: Faber and Faber, 1980)

McDowell, David, *Carrying On: Fettes College, War and the World, 1870–2010* (Leicester: Matador, 2012)

McKie, David, *Bright Particular Stars: A Gallery of Glorious British Eccentrics* (London: Atlantic Books, 2011)

McVeagh, Diana, *Gerald Finzi: His Life and Work* (Woodbridge: Boydell and Brewer, 2005)

Moody, A. David (ed.), *The Cambridge Companion to T.S. Eliot* (Cambridge: Cambridge University Press, 1994)

Morley, Sheridan, *The Authorised Biography of John Gielgud* (London: Hodder and Stoughton, 2001)

Mulvihill, Margaret, *Charlotte Despard: A Biography* (London: Pandora Press, 1989)

Needle, Justin, "Interview with Michael Tippett", *The Stamfordian*, Autumn 1983, pp. 37–41. Stamford Endowed Schools archives.

Newton, Douglas, "Michael Tippett", *Crescendo*, 14 (March 1948), pp. 5–6, 13

Nissen, Alice, *Gran – Memories of Evelyn Maude* (2012); privately printed, held by the author

Ollard, Richard, *A Man of Contradictions: A Life of A.L. Rowse* (London: Penguin, 1999)

Opie, June, *"Come and Listen to the Stars Singing": Priaulx Rainier – A Pictorial Biography* (Penzance: Alison Hodge, 1988)

Palmer, Andrew, *Encounters with British Composers* (Woodbridge: Boydell and Brewer, 2015)

Percival, John, *Theatre in My Blood: A Biography of John Cranko* (London: The Herbert Press, 1983)

Petherbridge, Edward, *Slim Chances* (Brighton: Indepenpress Publishing, 2011)

Philip, Robert, *A Keen Wind Blows: The Story of Fettes College* (London: James and James, 1998)

Pollack, Howard, *Aaron Copland: The Life and Work of an Uncommon Man* (London: Faber and Faber, 1999)

Ponsonby, Robert, *Musical Heroes: A Personal View of Music and the Musical World Over Sixty Years* (London: Giles de la Mare, 2009)

Powell, Neil, *Benjamin Britten: A Life for Music* (London: Hutchinson, 2013)

Prickett, Stacey, *Embodied Politics: Dance, Protest and Identities* (Binsted: Dance Books, 2013)

Puffett, Derrick, *Derrick Puffett on Music*, ed. Kathryn Bailey Puffett, 2nd edn (Abingdon: Routledge, 2016)

Pyatt, H. R. (ed.), *Fifty Years of Fettes: Memories of Old Fettesians, 1870–1920* (Edinburgh: T. and A. Constable, 1931)

Reed, Henry, *Hilda Tablet and Others* (London: BBC Books, 1971)

Reid, Charles, *Malcolm Sargent* (London: Hodder and Stoughton, 1968)

Richards, Denis, *Offspring of the Vic: A History of Morley College* (London: Routledge and Kegan Paul, 1958)

Richardson, John, *The Annals of London* (London: Cassell, 2000)

Robinson, Suzanne (ed.), *Michael Tippett: Music and Literature* (Aldershot: Ashgate, 2002)

Rumble, Jeffrey, *A Brockwell Boy* (London: Herne Hill Society, 2000)

Savage, Roger, *The Pre-History of "The Midsummer Marriage": Narratives and Speculations* (Abingdon: Routledge, 2019)

Schafer, Murray, *British Composers in Interview* (London: Faber and Faber, 1963)

Schuttenhelm, Thomas, *Michael Tippett's Fifth String Quartet: A Study in Vision and Revision* (Abingdon: Routledge, 2017)

——— *The Orchestral Music of Michael Tippett: Creative Development and the Compositional Process* (Cambridge: Cambridge University Press, 2013)

Settle, Mary Lee, *Learning to Fly* (New York, NY: W.W. Norton, 2007)

Sheppard, F.H.W. (ed.), *Survey of London: Volume 37, Northern Kensington* (London: London County Council, 1973)

Shinkman, Elizabeth Benn, *The Most Estimable Place and Time: Recollections of an English Childhood Before, During, and After World War I* (1990); privately printed, Benn collection

Sidnell, Michael, *Dances of Death: The Group Theatre of London in the Thirties* (London: Faber and Faber, 1984)

Slaughter, Barbara, "Interview with Wilfred Franks" (1999); British Library, MS Mus. 1814

Smyth, Ethel, *Memoirs*, ed. Ronald Crichton (Harmondsworth: Viking, 1987)

Soden, Oliver, "The Clarion Airs of Michael Tippett and Christopher Fry", *Musical Quarterly*, 97 (2014), pp. 616–60

——— "Tippett and Eliot", *Tempo*, 67 (October 2013), pp. 28–53

Southworth, Helen, *Fresca: A Life in the Making* (Eastbourne: Sussex Academic Press, 2017)

——— "Perfect Strangers? Virginia Woolf and Francesca Allinson", *Virginia Woolf Bulletin*, 39 (2012), pp. 16–23

Spence, Keith, and Swayne, Giles (eds), *How Music Works* (London: Macmillan, 1981)

Spender, Stephen, *Journals 1939–1983*, ed. John Goldsmith (London: Faber and Faber, 1985)

—— *The Temple* (London: Faber and Faber, 1988)

Stanford, Charles Villiers, *Musical Composition* (London: Macmillan, 1911)

Stanford, Derek, *Christopher Fry: An Appreciation* (London: Peter Nevill, 1951)

Stevens, Denis (ed.), *A History of Song* (London: Hutchinson, 1960)

Stevenson, Ronald (ed.), *Time Remembered: Alan Bush, an 80th Birthday Symposium* (Kidderminster: Bravura Publications, 1981)

Sutherland, Joan, *A Prima Donna's Progress* (London: Weidenfeld and Nicolson, 1997)

Theil, Gordon, *Michael Tippett, A Bio-Bibliography* (Westport, CT: Greenwood Press, 1989)

Thorpe, D.R., *Selwyn Lloyd* (London: Jonathan Cape, 1989)

Tillett, Michael, "Working for Tippett: Reminiscences" (1986); privately printed, British Library, MS Mus. 1765/3/2

Tippett, Isabel, "The Stuff that 'Eroes Are Made Of", *The Vote*, 19 August 1911, pp. 208–9

—— *The Waster* (London: John Long, 1912)

—— "Woman, Old or New?", *The Vote*, 31 August 1912, pp. 325–6; 7 September 1912, pp. 341–2

Tippett, Peter; see Kemp, Peter

Tooley, John, *In House* (London: Faber and Faber, 1999)

Trevelyan, Katharine, *Fool in Love* (London: Victor Gollancz, 1962)

Trotsky, Leon, *Writings, 1938–39*, ed. Naomi Allen and George Breitman (New York, NY: Pathfinder Press, 1974)

Upham, Martin, *The History of British Trotskyism to 1949*, Ph.D., University of Hull, 1980

Vaughan Williams, Ralph, *Letters, 1895–1958*, ed. Hugh Cobbe (Oxford: Oxford University Press, 2008)

Vaughan Williams, Ursula, *R.V.W.: A Biography of Ralph Vaughan Williams* (Oxford: Oxford University Press, 1964)

Vickers, Justin, "'The Ineffable Moments Will Be Harder Won': The Genesis, Creative Process and Early Performance History of Michael Tippett's *The Heart's Assurance*", D.Mus.A., University of Illinois, 2011

Von Sturmer, Caryll, *Margaret Barr: Epic Individual* (Dee Why, N.S.W.: L. von Sturmer, 1993)

Walton, William, *The Selected Letters of William Walton*, ed. Malcolm Hayes (London: Faber and Faber, 2002)

Warrack, Guy, *The Royal College of Music: The First 85 Years, 1883–1968*, 2 vols (London: Royal College of Music, 1977)

Wearing, J.P., *The London Stage 1920–1929: A Calendar of Productions, Performers, and Personnel*, 2nd edn (Lanham, MA: Rowman and Littlefield, 2014)

Wheen, Natalie, *Tippett's Time* (London: Channel 4 Television, 1995)

White, Eric Walter, *Tippett and His Operas* (London: Barrie and Jenkins, 1979)

Whitmell, Derek, *A Brief History of the Whitmell and Kemp Families*, 2018; privately printed, held by the author

Whittall, Arnold, *The Music of Britten and Tippett: Studies in Themes and Techniques*, 2nd edn (Cambridge: Cambridge University Press, 1990)

Whitton, Kenneth, *Dietrich Fischer-Dieskau: Mastersinger* (London: Oswald Wolff, 1981)

Whyman, Mark, *The Last Pennymans of Ormesby: The Lives of Jim and Ruth Pennyman*, 2 vols (North Yorkshire: Bargate Publications, 2008–9)

Woolf, Virginia, *Letters*, 6 vols, ed. Nigel Nicolson and Joanne Trautmann (London: The Hogarth Press, 1975–80)

C. MANUSCRIPT SOURCES

Documents are cited to their location at time of publication, but the British Library, to which much material will in due course be donated, should be the first port of call for future research.

BBC *Written Archives Centre, Reading*
    "Tippett, Sir Michael", RCONT 1 (and uncatalogued contracts, correspondence)
Bowen, Meirion, *private collection*
    Tippett, Michael, *War Ramp*
    —— correspondence with Meirion Bowen, Colin Davis, et al.
    —— papers relating to conscientious objection
    Tippett Office, papers and correspondence
British Library, *London*
    Tippett, Michael, music manuscripts, 1934–1977 (Add. MSS 61748-61804)
    —— music manuscripts, 1977–1983 (Add. MSS 63820-63840)
    —— music manuscripts, 1988–1991 (Add. MSS 71099-71103)

—— music manuscripts and notebooks, c.1923–1994 (Add. MSS 72001-72065)

—— early works (Add. MSS 72066-72071)

—— miscellaneous music manuscripts (MS. Mus 1757/1-3)

Tippett, Michael, letters to:

Amis, John (Add. MS 71178, ff. 151–89)

Bush, Alan (MS Mus. 449)

Crossley, Paul (MS Mus. 1757/5, ff. 6–16)

Davis, Colin (MS Mus. 1757/4, ff. 1–59)

Kemp, Ian (MS Mus. 1757/4, ff. 60–168)

Glock, William (MS Mus. 954, ff. 47–174)

Hartog, Howard (MS Mus. 1757/5, ff. 18–24)

Maude, Evelyn (MS Mus. 1757/5, ff. 25–32)

Newman, Ernest (MS Mus. 134, ff. 129–55)

Newton, (Brean Leslie) Douglas (MS Mus. 291-2)

Peacock, Carlos (MS Mus. 134, ff. 107–23)

Ponsonby, Robert (MS Mus. 1757/5, ff. 33–47)

Ruhm von Oppen, Beate (MS Mus. 1757/5, ff. 48–85)

Settle, Mary Lee (MS Mus. 292, ff. 179–84)

Tillett, Michael (MS Mus. 1765/2/1-3)

Vyner, Michael (Add. MS 70784, ff. 55–97, 99–107)

Allinson, (Enid) Francesca, Journal, 1937–41 (Add. MS 72052-3)

Bush, Alan, miscellaneous correspondence (MS Mus. 452-3)

Tillett, Michael, scores and papers relating to work as amanuensis to MT (MS Mus. 1765)

Britten-Pears Foundation Library, Aldeburgh, Suffolk

Tippett, Michael, letters to:

Britten, Benjamin, and Pears, Peter (uncatalogued)

Holst, Imogen (HOL/2/8/2)

Cambridge University Libraries

Tippett, Michael, letters to:

Barnes, George (King's College Library, GRB/1/1/1/42-3)

Forster, Edward Morgan (King's College Library, EMF/18/548)

Gardiner, Rolf, "Wilf" (Cambridge University Library, MS Gardiner/A/3/7)

Douglas Newton Archive, New York, NY

Allinson, Francesca, letters to Douglas Newton (box 3)

Harry Ransom Center, University of Texas at Austin

Tippett, Michael, personal library (706 vols, "Michael Tippett, former owner")

—— manuscript scores, drafts of opera libretto and synopses (Eric Walter White papers, 28.4-8)

Tippett, Michael, letters to:

    Duncan, Ronald (Ronald Duncan papers, 17.5)

    Sitwell, Edith (Edith Sitwell papers, 101.6)

    White, Eric Walter (Eric Walter White papers, 25.3, 25.7 and 28.7)

"Symphony of Youth" programme (Louis Golding papers, 3.5)

Hull History Centre

    Haston, Jock, papers: Bolshevik-Leninists [Youth Militant Group] minutes, bulletins, correspondence (GB 50 U DJH/2/A-C)

Kingston History Centre

    Tippett, Michael; Ayerst, David; Pennyman, Ruth, *Robin Hood* libretto, Beverley Press (KT149/4/14)

McMaster University Library, Ontario

    Tippett, Michael, letters to Sackville-West, Edward (RC0675)

Morris Library, South Illinois University, IL

    Tippett, Michael, letters to:

        Barker, George (1/1 MSS 162, box 1, folder 10)

        Morley, Frank (1/1 MSS 162, box 1, folder 10)

The National Archives, Kew

    Records of the Security Services: Communists and suspected communists: Phyllis Mary Kemp (KV 2/2032); and Alan Dudley Bush (KV 2/3520)

National Co-operative Archives, Manchester

    Royal Arsenal Co-operative Society committee minutes

    Comradeship and The Wheatsheaf; Co-operative News; Millgate Monthly

Peace Pledge Union Archives, London

    Michael Tippett file (uncatalogued)

Royal Academy of Music Archives, London

    Tippett, Michael, letters to Rainier, Praiulx (IPR/3/84)

Schott Archives, London

    Michael Tippett file (uncatalogued)

Tate Gallery Archives, London

    Tippett, Michael, letters to Hepworth, Barbara (TGA 200313/1)

Teesside Archives, North Yorkshire

    Tippett, Michael, letters to Pennyman, Ruth (uncatalogued)

Chase, Malcolm, interviews with Michael Tippett, David Ayerst, Marjorie Bradley, Wilfred Franks, and Marjorie Taylor, 1990 (cassettes, U/S/1516)

University of California, San Diego, Special Collections and Archives

Tippett, Michael, letters to Layard, John (John Willoughby Layard papers, MSS 84, box 16, folder 3)

Ayerst, David, letters to Layard, John (Layard papers, box 1, folder 11)

Hawker, Karl, letters to Layard, John (Layard papers, box 16, folder 3)

University of Exeter, Special Collections

Tippett, Michael, letters to Rowse, Alfred Leslie (EUL MS 113/3/1/T)

Victoria and Albert Museum Department of Theatre and Performance, London

Tippett, Michael, letters to:

Brook, Peter (THM/452/3/167)

Fry, Christopher (THM/319/9/288)

Fry, Christopher, script for *Seven at One Stroke* (GB (THM/319/1/14)

—— "Tribute to Michael Tippett" (THM/319/2/3) [c.1980]

Warwick University, Modern Records Centre, Coventry

Groves, Reginald, papers: correspondence with Ian Kemp, 1976 (MSS.172/M/1/18-22)

Harber, Denzil Dean, papers: Trotskyist movement, 1930s–1950 (MSS.151/1)

Maitland-Sara-Hallinan collection: Youth Militant, 1936–8

William Walton Trust Archives, Forio NA, Italy

Tippett, Michael, letters to Walton, William

Wright, Nicholas, private collection

Tippett, Michael, letters to (inter alia) Francesca Allinson, David Ayerst, Meirion Bowen, Anna Kallin, Nicholas Wright

Tippett Office, papers and correspondence

Also privately held collections of Cyril Allinson; (Enid) Francesca Allinson; John Amis; David Ayerst; William Busch; Jonathan Del Mar; T.S. Eliot; Karl Hawker; Antony Hopkins; Ian Kemp; Peter Kemp; David Matthews; Evelyn Maude.

D. RADIO AND TELEVISION BROADCASTS

Broadcasts are only listed if there is no published transcript.

A Plus 4 [MT interviewed by Mavis Nicholson], Channel 4, tx. 1985, dir. Bob Ando

Alan Bush: A Life, Channel 4, tx. 12 January 1986, dir. Anna Ambrose

Cultural Conchies, BBC Radio 3, tx. 17 November 2013, prod. Dennis Marks

Desert Island Discs [MT interviewed by Roy Plomley], BBC Radio 4, tx. 5 January 1985, prod. Derek Drescher

A Full Life [MT interviewed by Jill Cochrane], Television South, tx. 5 May 1985, prod. Richard Argent

The Levin Interviews: Michael Tippett, BBC2, tx. 7 June 1980, dir. Roy Chapman

Michael Tippett: A Birthday Celebration, BBC2, tx. 2 March 1975, prod. David Buckton

Monitor: Michael Tippett on Music in the Theatre, BBC TV, tx. 20 May 1962, ed. Huw Weldon

Music Now [MT interviewed by John Amis], BBC Radio 3, tx. 17 January 1975, prod. Denys Gueroult and Natalie Wheen

Omnibus: Ralph Vaughan Williams, BBC1, tx. 1 March 1970, dir. Stanley Williamson

Remaking the Dream, Channel 4, tx. 1988, dir. Spencer Campbell

Review: The Knot Garden, BBC2, tx. 4 December 1970, dir. Michael Macintyre

Reviving Robin, BBC Radio 3, tx. 28 November 2009, prod. Celia Quartermain

Sinfonietta II: Singing the uncertainties – Songs for Dov, Channel 4, tx. 1989, prod. Derek Bailey

Sir Michael Tippett [interviewed by John Warrack], BBC1, tx. 21 May 1969, dir. Denis Moriarty

Songs of Experience, BBC2, tx. 21 September 1991, dir. Mischa Scorer

South Bank Show: Sir Michael Tippett, ITV, tx. 24 June 1979, dir. Alan Benson

Tippett at Malvern, BBC2, tx. 23 November 1985, dir. Keith Cheetham

The World on its Dark Side, BBC2, tx. 8 May 1995, dir. Clive Flowers and Barrie Gavin

INTERVIEWS WITH OLIVER SODEN

Aechternacht, Stephen: Texas, 7 October 2017

Ayerst, Caroline: London, 15 April 2016

Barlow (née Hawker), Susan: London, 20 February 2017

Barstow, Dame Josephine: Lewes, West Sussex, 12 June 2016

Bowen, Meirion: London, 9 March 2018

Constable, John: London, 28 November 2017
Coster, Andrew: London, 8 November 2016
Crossley, Paul: London, 31 August 2017
Davis, Sir Andrew: video call, 1 May 2018
Edwards, Sian: Lewes, West Sussex, 6 January 2017
Goehr, Alexander: Cambridgeshire, 11 November 2016
Gomez, Jill: Cambridgeshire, 20 November 2017
Groves, Sally: London, 18 July 2016
Haines, David: video call, 9 August 2018
Herincx, Raimund: Bath, 31 August 2015
Kenyon, Sir Nicholas: London, 7 October 2016
Martin, Kit and Jean: Cambridgeshire, 28 May 2017
Matthews, David: London, 27 October 2016
Maude, Stella: Wells, 21 January 2017
Modlen, Graham: London, 3 November 2017
Phillips (née Hawker), Sarah: London, 15 April 2016
Sims, Josey: Calne, Wiltshire, 21 January 2017
Sweet, Heather: Calne, Wiltshire, 21 January 2017
Tooley, Sir John: Cambridgeshire, 11 November 2016
Vaughn, Beverly: video call, 14 August 2018
Watson (née Maude), Alison: Wookey, Somerset, 21 January 2017
Whitmell, Derek and Charmian: Oxfordshire, 12 February 2016
Whyatt, Nick and Anne: Lacock, Wiltshire, 27 January 2018

Changes in money value calculated by www.measuringworth.com
Much use has been made of www.findmypast.co.uk: England, Wales &
Scotland Census, 1851, 1861, 1871, 1881, 1891, 1901, 1911; England
& Wales Births, Marriages, Deaths, 1837–2008; Passenger Lists leaving
the UK, 1890–1960; England & Wales, Crime, Prisons and Punishment,
1770–1935

INDEX